Guide to
TCP/IP

D1469777

Laura A. Chappell
Ed Tittel

COURSE
TECHNOLOGY
™
THOMSON LEARNING

Australia • Canada • Mexico • Singapore • Spain • United Kingdom • United States

THOMSON
COURSE TECHNOLOGY

Guide to TCP/IP

by Laura A. Chappell and Ed Tittel

Contributing Author:
Mark Terwilliger

Managing Editor:
Stephen Solomon

Product Managers:
Laura Hildebrand, Kim Lindros

Technical Editors:
Tom Lancaster, Mark Mirrotto

Developmental Editor:
Betsy Newberry

Marketing Manager:
Toby Shelton

Reviewers:
Mark Mirrotto, Scott Haugdahl

Production Editor:
Aimee Poirier

Editorial Assistant:
Nick Lombardi

Cover Design:
Julie Malone

Text Designer:
GEX Publishing Services

Compositor:
GEX Publishing Services

BRIEF Contents

TABLE OF
Contents

CHAPTER ELEVEN
Monitoring and Managing Ip Networks   **475**

CHAPTER TWELVE
TCP/IP, NetBIOS, And WINS   **509**

CHAPTER THIRTEEN
Internet Protocol Version 6 (IPv6)   **555**

Preface

Welcome to the *Guide to TCP/IP*! TCP/IP stands for Transmission Control Protocol/Internet Protocol and defines the broad family of protocols and services that make the Internet possible as we know it today. In covering TCP/IP, this book offers you real-world examples, interactive examples, and many Hands-on Projects that reinforce key concepts and teach the use of important monitoring and management tools. This book also includes voluminous protocol traces or decodes that will help you understand what TCP/IP looks like, and how it behaves, on your networks.

This book offers in-depth coverage of all the salient models, protocols, services, and standards that govern TCP/IP, and that guide its behavior on modern networks. Throughout the book, we provide pointed questions to reinforce the concepts introduced in each chapter and to help prepare you to interact with TCP/IP in its native habitat—on most of the networks in use in the world today, that is. In addition to the review questions, we provide detailed Hands-on Projects that provide you firsthand experience in installing, configuring, using, and managing TCP/IP on a working network. Finally, to put a real-world slant on the concepts introduced in each chapter, we also include Case Projects that pose problems and require creative solutions that should prepare you for the kinds of situations and needs you'll face on a real, live network.

THE INTENDED AUDIENCE

This book is intended to serve the needs of individuals and information systems professionals who are interested in learning more about working with and on TCP/IP-based networks. These materials have been specifically designed to prepare individuals to take an active role in administering a network infrastructure that uses TCP/IP, either as its only protocol suite, or in concert with other protocol suites. Those students who work their way through this entire book should be well-equipped to recognize, analyze, and troubleshoot a broad range of TCP/IP-related networking problems or phenomena.

Chapter 1, "Introducing TCP/IP," states the broad outlines of TCP/IP's capabilities, and identifies its most important constituent elements—namely, the protocols and services that TCP/IP provides. In addition, it also explores the Open Systems Interconnection (OSI) reference model for networking, as standardized by the International Standards Organization (ISO) and compares and contrasts this standard model to the model around which TCP/IP is built. This chapter then covers the structure and origins of the standards documents known as Requests for Comment (RFCs) that describe and govern TCP/IP protocols, services, and practices. Finally, the chapter concludes with an overview of the key tool that will play a significant role throughout the remainder of the book—a special software utility called a protocol analyzer that captures, unpacks, and displays the contents of traffic on a network, including TCP/IP.

Chapter 2, "IP Addressing and Related Topics," covers the intricacies involved in managing unique IP addresses. Beginning with the anatomy of a numeric IP address, the chapter explores IP address classes, special cases such as broadcast and multicast addresses, and reviews the reasons why classless IP addressing exists. Here, you'll also find coverage of the binary mathematics involved in designing, recognizing, and calculating IP subnet masks, as you learn about subnetting and supernetting. This chapter concludes with a review of public and private IP addresses, network address translation services, and covers the ins and outs of obtaining and managing public IP addresses suitable for use on the Internet.

Chapter 3, "Data Link and Network Layer TCP/IP Protocols," covers the key TCP/IP protocols that operate at the Data Link and Network layers in the OSI reference model. In that context, it discusses data link protocols in general, examines IP frame types, and talks about hardware addresses in the IP environment, and the various protocols—particularly ARP and RARP—that support their use. The chapter covers TCP/IP's most important protocol at the Network layer, the Internet Protocol.

Chapter 4, "Internet Control Message Protocol (ICMP)," covers a key Network layer protocol for TCP/IP, whose job is to ferry status and error messages about IP traffic back to its senders, and to other "interested devices," such as routers or switches. Starting with a review of ICMP structures and functions, this chapter examines ICMP testing and troubleshooting methods, security issues, ICMP message types and code, and concludes with a thorough review of ICMP packet structures.

Chapter 5, "Transport Layer TCP/IP Protocols," covers two key protocols that operate at the Transport layer of the OSI reference model—the heavy-duty, robust, reliable Transmission Control Protocol (TCP), and the lighter-weight but faster User Datagram Protocol (UDP). TCP is examined in great detail with particular attention to its packet structures and functions, while UDP gets the brief coverage it deserves. The chapter concludes with a review of common UDP and TCP port addresses, and a discussion of common and appropriate uses for these two protocols.

Chapter 6, "Basic TCP/IP Services," jumps into the area of greatest interest to Internet users—the higher-level services and protocols that TCP/IP supports. Basic common TCP/IP services that include FTP, Telnet, SMTP, and HTTP, among numerous others, are explored and explained, and their message types and capabilities scrutinized. The chapter concludes with a broad discussion of how protocol analysis works for such higher-layer protocols (and the services they support) and how such traffic may be most effectively decoded.

Chapter 7, "Domain Name System (DNS)," tackles one of the Internet's most important infrastructure services—the Domain Name System that makes it possible for symbolic names like *microsoft.com* or *course.com* to be translated into equivalent numeric IP addresses. DNS is explored and explained, as are the name and address hierarchies and organizations that this service manages. DNS behavior is reviewed thoroughly, as are the common types of DNS servers in use. The chapter concludes with a discussion on troubleshooting DNS with exploration of some key DNS-related tools and utilities.

Chapter 8, "The Dynamic Host Configuration Protocol (DHCP)," covers the protocol and service used to manage and maintain IP addresses for client desktops and other network machines. It explains DHCP's origins and its ability to accommodate hosts that may not currently possess a valid IP address, and explores DHCP's address-handling characteristics and capabilities. DHCP's commands and options are reviewed, as are DHCP's modes of network operation. The chapter concludes with a discussion of DHCP troubleshooting, configuration, and inspection tools.

Chapter 9, "Securing TCP/IP Environments," covers problems, vulnerabilities, and issues that reflect TCP/IP's optimistic built-in security model in an increasingly pessimistic world (and Internet). Here, common points of attack on TCP/IP networks are enumerated, and the anatomy of typical attacks on IP-based networks is explored. The chapter concludes with a lengthy review of the many procedures, practices, routines, and fixes that must be applied to make TCP/IP networks as secure as possible. It also stresses the need for constant vigilance to maintain security on an ongoing basis.

Chapter 10, "Routing in the IP Environment," covers the concepts, terminology, and services associated with routing packets on an IP network, so that they may be delivered from their senders to their receivers. This chapter reviews common networking protocols, distinguishes between interior and exterior routing, and explains how to manage routing in a variety of common situations. It concludes with a discussion of troubleshooting tips and techniques, and a review of related tools and utilities.

Chapter 11, "Monitoring and Managing IP Networks," covers the key concepts and principles involved in network management, including the OSI network management model. It also explores the Simple Network Management Protocol (SNMP), a higher-layer TCP/IP management protocol used on many IP networks. It concludes with a discussion on troubleshooting SNMP consoles and services, and with a review of tools, utilities, and key files.

Chapter 12, "TCP/IP, NetBIOS, and WINS," reflects the somewhat Windows-centric nature of this text. NetBIOS is an upper-layer network protocol that's heavily used for file, print, and other services on Windows, IBM, and DECnet networks. This chapter explores the special relationship that NetBIOS enjoys with TCP/IP, and explains its role in recent and older versions of Windows operating systems. Along the way, it covers NetBIOS names, name resolution services, and how NetBIOS works using TCP/IP from the Transport layer on down. Finally, the chapter concludes with an exploration of the Windows Internet Name Service (WINS), a Windows-specific dynamic name resolution service that works for NetBIOS over TCP/IP in much the same way that DNS provides names to address resolution services for domain names and IP addresses.

Chapter 13, "Internet Protocol Version 6 (IPv6)," covers the newest, emerging version of TCP/IP known as IP version 6 (abbreviated IPv6 as in the name of this chapter). Here, you'll learn about the differences between IPv4 (the current version covered elsewhere in this book) and IPv6, and why IPv6 is both necessary and inevitable. You'll also explore IPv6's design, including its packet formats, changes to ICMP, what it does to upper-layer protocols and services, security improvement and implications, and about managing the IPv4-to-IPv6 transition. In short, this chapter should help networking professionals understand what IPv6 is, how it works, and what to do with it when it shows up on their networks.

The book also includes several appendices that are worthy of further investigation. **Appendix A** provides a list of all the important RFCs mentioned throughout the text. **Appendix B** provides a compendium of key IP resources available online. **Appendix C** is a reference to TCP/IP-related command-line utilities for Windows 2000. **Appendix D** provides a list of all the Windows 2000 Registry settings found in numerous tables in this book. **Appendix E** explains the files stored on the CD-ROM accompanying this book. **Appendix F** points you to important UDP and TCP port number information online. **Appendix G** points you to a comprehensive list of DHCP options.

FEATURES

To ensure a successful learning experience, this book includes the following pedagogical features:

- **Chapter Objectives:** Each chapter in this book begins with a detailed list of the concepts to be mastered within that chapter. This list provides you with a quick reference to the contents of that chapter, as well as a useful study aid.

- **Illustrations and Tables:** Numerous illustrations of server screens and components aid you in the visualization of common setup steps, theories, and concepts. In addition, many tables provide details and comparisons of both practical and theoretical information and can be used for a quick review of topics.

- **End-of-Chapter Material:** The end of each chapter includes the following features to reinforce the material covered in the chapter:

  - **Summary:** A bulleted list is provided which gives a brief but complete summary of the chapter

- **Key Terms List:** A list of all new terms and their definitions
- **Review Questions:** A list of review questions tests your knowledge of the most important concepts covered in the chapter

 Hands-on Projects: Hands-on projects help you to apply the knowledge gained in the chapter

 Case Study Projects: Case study projects take you through real-world scenarios

- **On the CD-ROM:** On the CD-ROM you will find a demo version of EtherPeek protocol analyzer software, NASK, Subnet Calculator, PacketScrubber and ProConvert (WildPackets, Inc.), NetScanTools Standard Edition trial version, NeoTrace Pro demo version (NeoWorx, Inc.), and sample protocol traces.

TEXT AND GRAPHIC CONVENTIONS

Wherever appropriate, additional information and exercises have been added to this book to help you better understand what is being discussed in the chapter. Icons throughout the text alert you to additional materials. The icons used in this textbook are as follows:

 The Note icon is used to present additional helpful material related to the subject being described.

 Each Hands-on Project in this book is preceded by the Hands-on icon and a description of the exercise that follows.

 Case Project icons mark the case project. These are more involved, scenario-based assignments. In this extensive case example, you are asked to implement independently what you have learned.

INSTRUCTOR'S MATERIALS

The following supplemental materials are available when this book is used in a classroom setting. All of the supplements available with this book are provided to the instructor on a single CD-ROM.

Electronic Instructor's Manual.   The Instructor's Manual that accompanies this textbook includes:

- Additional instructional material to assist in class preparation, including suggestions for classroom activities, discussion topics, and additional projects.
- Solutions to all end-of-chapter materials, including the Review Questions, Hands-on Projects, and Case Projects.

ExamView®   This textbook is accompanied by ExamView, a powerful testing software package that allows instructors to create and administer printed, computer (LAN-based), and Internet exams. ExamView includes hundreds of questions that correspond to the topics covered in this text, enabling students to generate detailed study guides that include page references for further review. The computer-based and Internet testing components allow students to take exams at their computers, and also save the instructor time by grading each exam automatically.

PowerPoint presentations.   This book comes with Microsoft PowerPoint slides for each chapter. These are included as a teaching aid for classroom presentation, to make available to students on the network for chapter review, or to be printed for classroom distribution. Instructors, please feel at liberty to add your own slides for additional topics you introduce to the class.

ACKNOWLEDGMENTS

The authors would like to thank Course Technology for this opportunity to write a usable TCP/IP textbook for the 21st century. We deeply appreciate their patience and indulgence, especially that of Stephen Solomon, our acquisitions editor, and Laura Hildebrand, our product manager, when we were bringing the many pieces of this book together. Thanks also to Betsy Newberry at CEP Inc., our developmental editor, whose great work turned these materials into the finely polished form they now take.

The authors would also like to thank the in-house team at LANWrights (*http://www. lanw.com*), who helped to bring this book to fruition, especially Kim Lindros, who did a wonderful job of managing the project on behalf of the authors and handling all the materials that flowed between us and Course Technology. Our thanks also to Dawn, Mary, and Karen for their occasional and much appreciated contributions to this manuscript, even if only to run stuff to FedEx at the last minute!

Ed Tittel: My profound thanks to Laura Chappell, for freeing up so much of her busy schedule to work on this book. Thanks also to Mark Terwilliger, for his contributions to Chapters 12 and 13, and to Tom Lancaster for his great, in-depth critiques, that became the focus of his equally great additions, emendations, and enhancements to our original work in Chapters 6, 9, 10, and 11. And I just have to thank Kim yet one more time, for managing a long, complex, and involved collection of materials with her usual no-nonsense attitude and aplomb. Finally, my thanks to Blackie, my perky, pesky 3-year-old black lab, who forced me away from the keyboard regularly enough to maintain a sense of perspective about all this stuff.

Laura Chappell: Special thanks to Ed Tittel for his enthusiasm and wonderful writing efforts on this book. Also very special and sincere thanks to Kim Lindros for her amazing ability to keep all the loose ends tied on this project. Thanks also to Mark Terwilliger and Tom Lancaster for their tremendous technical contributions to this title—this book could not have been completed in such a timely manner without your assistance. My great appreciation to Jill Poulsen of Protocol Analysis Institute and Brenda Krup from podbooks.com for their assistance in keeping other projects at bay as I focused on this title. Finally, my deepest thanks to my children, Scotty and Ginny, who make me laugh and enjoy life way beyond the packet-level.

Finally, the co-authors would like to thank each other for the camaraderie, hard work, and support that went into making this book.

Readers are encouraged to e-mail comments, questions, and suggestions regarding *Guide to TCP/IP* and the accompanying CD to the authors:

- Ed Tittel: etittel@lanw.com
- Laura Chappell: lchappell@packet-level.com

Read This Before You Begin

TO THE USER

This book is intended to be read in sequence, from beginning to end. Each chapter builds upon those that precede it to provide a solid understanding of TCP/IP concepts, protocols, services, and deployment practices. Readers are also encouraged to investigate the many pointers to online and printed sources of additional information that are cited throughout this book.

Some of the chapters in this book have additional materials that supplement the end-of-chapter projects. The CD included with this book contains the necessary supplemental files.

TO THE INSTRUCTOR

When setting up a classroom lab, make sure each workstation has Windows 2000 Server or Professional, Internet Explorer 5.0 or later, and a NIC in promiscuous mode. Students will install the EtherPeek for Windows demo, IP Subnet Calculator, and NetScanTools demo on these computers in the course of working through the book. In addition, students will need administrative rights on their workstations to perform many of the operations covered in the Hands-on Projects throughout the book. You might notice minor interface changes between the new EtherPeek demo software included on the CD and the EtherPeek figures included in the book. For a complete description of the changes, visit the Guide to TCP/IP Web page at *http://www.lanw.com/books/gd2tcpip.htm* (see p. xxii) or the *readme.doc* file on the CD.

VISIT OUR WORLD WIDE WEB SITE

Additional materials designed especially for you might be available for your course on the World Wide Web. Go to **http://www.course.com**. Search for this book title periodically on the Course Technology Web site for more details.

COPING WITH CHANGE ON THE WEB

Sooner or later, all the specifics we've shared with you about the Web-based resources we mention throughout the rest of this book will go stale or be replaced by newer information. In some cases, the URLs you find here may lead you to their replacements; in other cases, the URLs will lead nowhere, leaving you with the dreaded 404 error message, "File not found."

When that happens, please don't give up! We created a handy online document titled "Guide to TCP/IP," which lists all of the URLs mentioned in this book. Visit the page at *http://www.lanw.com/books/gd2tcpip.htm*. We will review and update these links regularly, but should you encounter a broken link in the interim, please send e-mail to tcpipupdates@lanw.com, and we'll fix it as soon as possible.

In addition, there's always a way to find what you want on the Web, if you're willing to invest some time and energy. To begin with, most large or complex Web sites—and Microsoft's qualifies on both counts—offer a search engine. As long as you can get to the site itself, you can use this tool to help you find what you need.

Finally, don't be afraid to use general search tools such as *http://www.search.com*, *http://www.altavista.digital.com*, or *http://www.excite.com* to find related information. Although certain standards bodies may offer the most precise and specific information about their standards online, there are plenty of third-party sources of information, training, and assistance in this area that do not have to follow the party line like a standards group typically does. The bottom line is: if you can't find something where the book says it lives, start looking around. It's got to be around there, somewhere!

LAB REQUIREMENTS

Following are the hardware and software requirements to perform the end-of-chapter projects:

- Pentium II 400 MHz CPU or higher
- 128 MB of RAM
- 4 GB hard disk with at least 1 GB of storage available
- CD-ROM drive
- Network interface card in promiscuous mode connected to a LAN
- Windows 2000 Server, Windows 2000 Professional, or Windows XP system with updated Internet Explorer 5.0 or later
- Windows 2000 Server system Service Pack 2 (or the most current SP that's been available for more than 30 days)
- Access to a Windows 2000 Professional or Windows 2000 Server system with TCP/IP installed and configured. An IP address must be defined either statically or via DHCP.
- Internet access

1

INTRODUCING TCP/IP

After reading this chapter and completing the exercises you will be able to:

♦ Understand TCP/IP's origins, history, and design goals

♦ Understand the Open Systems Interconnection network reference model, often used to characterize network protocols and services, and how it relates to TCP/IP's own internal networking model

♦ Define the terms involved and explain how TCP/IP protocols, sockets, and ports are identified

♦ Explain the process by which TCP/IP standards and other documents, called Requests for Comments (RFCs), are created, debated, and formalized (where appropriate)

♦ Understand and apply the basic practices and principles that underlie network protocol analysis

This chapter introduces the background and history of the collection of networking **protocols** known as **TCP/IP**, which is an abbreviation for **Transmission Control Protocol/Internet Protocol**. Two of the most important protocols in the overall collection known as TCP/IP are the **Transmission Control Protocol (TCP)**, which handles reliable delivery for messages of arbitrary size, and the **Internet Protocol (IP)**, which manages the **routing** of network transmissions from sender to receiver, among other capabilities.

In addition, this chapter also covers TCP/IP's networking model, its various ways of identifying specific protocols and services, how TCP/IP standards are defined and managed, and which elements of the TCP/IP collection are most noteworthy. The chapter concludes with an overview of the art and science of protocol analysis, which uses special tools to gather data directly from a network itself, characterize a network's traffic and behavior, and examine the details inside the data that's moving across a network at any given point in time.

WHAT IS TCP/IP?

The large collection of networking protocols and services called TCP/IP denotes far more than the combination of the two key protocols that gives this collection its name. Nevertheless, these protocols deserve an initial introduction: Transmission Control Protocol, or TCP, handles reliable delivery for messages of arbitrary size, and defines a robust delivery mechanism for all kinds of data across a network; the Internet Protocol, or IP, manages the routing of network transmissions from sender to receiver, along with issues related to network and computer addresses, and much more. Together, these two protocols ferry the vast bulk of data that moves across the Internet, even though they represent only a tiny fraction of the total collection that is TCP/IP.

To gain a better appreciation for the importance of TCP/IP, consider this: anyone who uses the Internet must also use TCP/IP because it's no exaggeration to say that the Internet runs on TCP/IP. TCP/IP's roots run deep and long, as computing technologies go—all the way back to 1969, in fact. A working understanding of where TCP/IP comes from, and what motivated its original design, can enhance one's understanding of this essential collection of protocols (often called a **protocol suite**). For that reason, you will explore this protocol suite's roots and design goals in the following section.

THE ORIGINS AND HISTORY OF TCP/IP

In 1969, an obscure arm of the United States Department of Defense (DoD), known as the **Advanced Research Projects Agency (ARPA)**, funded an academic research project for a special type of long-haul network, called a **packet-switched network**. In a packet-switched network, individual chunks of data (called **packets**) can take any usable path between the sender and receiver. The sender and receiver are identified by unique network addresses, but do not require all packets to follow the same path in transit (though they often do). The network built as a result of this project is known as the **ARPANET**.

TCP/IP's Design Goals

The design of the ARPANET and protocols that evolved to support it were based on the following government needs:

- A desire to withstand a potential nuclear strike. This explains the need for packet switching, in which routes from sender to receiver can vary as needed, as long as a valid route exists. It also explains why robust and reliable delivery was a concern, in a world in which things might blow up at any time!

- A desire to permit different kinds of computer systems to easily communicate with one another. Because proprietary networking was the order of the day, and the government owned many different kinds of incompatible networks and systems, it was necessary that the technology permit dissimilar systems to exchange data.

- A need to interconnect systems across long distances. The late 1960s was an era of "big iron," in which large, expensive individual systems with terminals dominated the computer landscape. In that day and age, interconnecting multiple systems meant interconnecting far-flung locations. Thus, the original ARPANET linked systems at the Stanford Research Institute (SRI), the University of Utah in Salt Lake City, and two campuses in the University of California system at Los Angeles and San Bernadino.

These design goals may not seem terribly important in the early 21st century. That's because the threat of nuclear holocaust has largely subsided, and networking is taken for granted. Likewise, high-bandwidth, long-distance data communications is a big business. Some would argue, however, that the Internet is responsible for at least the latter two of those three conditions holding true!

A TCP/IP Chronology

TCP/IP didn't really appear on the scene until the 1970s and early 1980s. By this time, early networking researchers realized that data had to be moved across different kinds of networks, as well as among multiple locations. This was especially necessary to permit local area networks, such as **Ethernet**, to use long-haul networks, such as the ARPANET, to move data from one local network to another. Although work on TCP/IP began in 1973, it wasn't until 1978 that **Internet Protocol version 4** (also known as **IPv4**, the very same version used today on most TCP/IP networks) came into existence.

The original Internet (notice the initial capital letter) helped establish a model for a network composed of other networks. Thus, the term internetwork (notice the lack of an initial capital letter) refers to a single logical network composed of multiple physical networks, which may all be at a single physical location, or spread among multiple physical locations. We distinguish the *Internet* as a proper name for the world-wide collection of publicly accessible networks that use TCP/IP, from *internetworks*, which are anywhere in the world, and may or may not be part of the Internet (and may not necessarily use TCP/IP, even though the majority of internetworks worldwide do).

In 1983, the Defense Communications Agency (DCA, now known as the **Defense Information Systems Agency**, or **DISA**) took over operation of the ARPANET from DARPA (Defense Advanced Research Projects Agency, a.k.a. ARPA). This allowed more widespread use of the Internet, as more colleges and universities, government agencies, defense facilities, and government contractors began to rely on the Internet to exchange data, e-mail, and other kinds of information. In the same year, the DoD instituted its requirement that all computers on the Internet switch to TCP/IP from a hodgepodge of earlier, mostly experimental protocols that were used on the ARPANET since its inception. In fact, some people argue that the Internet and TCP/IP were born at more or less the same instant. By no coincidence whatsoever, 1983 also marks the year that the Berkeley Software Distribution version of UNIX, known as 4.2BSD, incorporated support for TCP/IP in the operating system. There are also those who argue that this step—which exposed computer professionals at colleges and universities around the world to TCP/IP—helps explain how the birth and proliferation of Internet protocols and technologies became the colossus it is today.

At roughly the same time—we're still in 1983—the all-military MILNET was split off from the ARPANET. This divided the infrastructure of the Internet into a military-only side, and a more public, freewheeling side that included all nonmilitary participants. Initial development of name server technology at the University of Wisconsin in 1983, which allowed users to locate and identify network addresses anywhere on the Internet (this remains a hallmark of its operation to this day), capped off a record year in the official Internet story.

From here, the Internet and TCP/IP enjoyed a series of events and firsts that ultimately resulted in the global Internet as we know it today. Here are some additional highlights of that history:

- *1986*: The **National Science Foundation (NSF)** launches a long-haul, high-speed network, known as **NSFNET**, that creates a network backbone running at 56 Kbps (or a little faster than the supposed top speed for modern modems today). NSF also imposed a set of policies, known as the **Acceptable Use Policies (AUPs)**, that governed how the Internet was supposed to be used, and set the tone for how users continue to interact on the Internet to this day.

- *1987*: Number of hosts on the Internet breaks 10,000.

- *1989*: Number of hosts on the Internet breaks 100,000.

  NSFNET backbone upgraded to T1 speeds, at 1.544 megabits per second (Mbps).

- *1990*: McGill University releases the **Archie** protocol and service, based on TCP/IP, which permit users on the Internet to search text-based document archives of all kinds from any location.

  ARPANET ceases doing business under that name, and commercial, academic, government, and communications company operations begin supporting the Internet as a cooperative venture.

  Work begins in earnest on the **Hypertext Transfer Protocol (HTTP)** and the notion of the Worldwide Web is born at **Centre European Researche Nucleaire (CERN)** in Geneva, Switzerland.

- *1991*: The **Commercial Internet Exchange (CIX)**, a consortium of Internet operators, system providers, and other commercial operations with Internet interests, is formed. Some view this as the birth of the "modern Internet" because this is when commerce first became "legal" on the Internet.

1

Thinking Machines Corporation releases the **Wide Area Information Service (WAIS)**, a TCP/IP-based protocol and service. It allows online searches of multimegabyte databases across the Internet.

University of Minnesota releases **Gopher**, a TCP/IP-based protocol that not only allows searching of text-based archives and other data types online, but also links all such archives together into a single virtual information universe known as "Gopherspace."

- *1992*: The Internet Society (ISOC) is chartered.

  Number of hosts on the Internet breaks one million.

  NSFNET backbone upgraded to T3 speeds, at 44.736 Mbps.

  CERN releases HTTP and Web server technology to the public ("birth of the Web").

- *1993*: The **Internet Network Information Center (InterNIC)** is chartered to manage **domain** names.

  The first-ever, high-powered graphical browser, Mosaic, emerges from the **National Center for Supercomputing Applications (NCSA)**. This starts the Web revolution.

  The U.S. White House goes online at *whitehouse.gov*.

- *1994*: U.S. Senate and House of Representatives establish information servers on the Internet.

  Online junk mail and shopping malls begin to proliferate.

- *1995*: Netscape launches Netscape Navigator and begins the commercialization of the Web.

  Number of hosts on the Internet breaks five million.

- *1996*: Microsoft launches Internet Explorer Web browser, even though Netscape dominates the Web browser marketplace.

Today, few aspects of commerce, communications, and information access do not touch the Internet or are not touched by the Internet. Living without e-mail, the Web, and online e-commerce has rapidly become both unthinkable and intolerable. As we move further into the 21st century, new services and new protocols continue to show up on the Internet, but TCP/IP keeps going strong!

For more information about the fascinating history of the Internet, visit the ISOC's "Internet History" Web page at *http://www.isoc.org/internet/history/*.

Who "Owns" TCP/IP?

Given that its roots are everywhere, and that its reach is unlimited, the ownership and control of TCP/IP is puzzling. As it happens, even though TCP/IP and protocols fall under the purview of some specific standards-making bodies, which we'll discuss later,

TCP/IP falls squarely into the public domain because it's been funded with public monies since its inception. Thus, both everybody and nobody own TCP/IP, per se.

Meet the Standards Groups that Manage TCP/IP

The standards groups that are involved with TCP/IP are as follows:

- *Internet Society (ISOC)*: The **Internet Society (ISOC)** is the parent organization for all the various Internet boards and task forces. It is a nonprofit, nongovernmental, international, professional membership organization. It is funded through individual membership dues, corporate contributions, and occasional support from several governments. Visit its home page at *http://www.isoc.org.*

- *Internet Architecture Board (IAB):* The **Internet Architecture Board (IAB)**, a.k.a. Internet Activities Board, is the parent organization for the standards-making and research groups that handle current and future Internet technologies, protocols, and research. The IAB also provides oversight for the architecture for all Internet protocols and procedures, and editorial oversight for the documents known as **Requests for Comments (RFCs)**, wherein Internet standards are stated, and so forth. Visit the IAB home page for more information at *http://www.iab.org.*

- *Internet Engineering Task Force (IETF)*: The **Internet Engineering Task Force (IETF)** is the group responsible for drafting, testing, proposing, and maintaining official Internet standards through the agencies of multiple working groups under its purview. The IETF and the IAB use a process accurately described as "rough consensus" to create Internet standards. This means that all participants in the standards-making process must more or less agree before a standard can be proposed, drafted, or approved. Sometimes that consensus can be pretty rough indeed! For more information about the IETF, visit *http://www.ietf.org.*

- *Internet Research Task Force (IRTF)*: The **Internet Research Task Force (IRTF)** is responsible for the more forward-looking activities of the ISOC, and handles research and development work for topics too far-out or impractical for immediate implementation, but which may (or may not) have a role to play on the Internet some day. Visit its home page at *http://www.irtf.org.*

- *Internet Societal Discussion Forum (ISDF):* The **Internet Societal Discussion Forum (ISDF)** is a discussion forum that explores how the Internet can be a force for social development and change. This forum's purpose is to discover how the Internet can be available and usable for all people everywhere, regardless of social and economic circumstances. Visit its homepage at *http:// www.isoc.org/members/discuss/isdf.shtml.*

- *Internet Corporation for Assigned Names and Numbers (ICANN)*: The **Internet Corporation for Assigned Names and Numbers (ICANN)** is ultimately responsible for managing all Internet domain names, network addresses, and protocol parameters and behaviors. In practice, ICANN oversees registration and management of addresses and domain names, but delegates customer interaction, money collection, database maintenance, and so forth, to commercial authorities. Visit ICANN's home page at *http://www.icann.org*. Also, there's a list of accredited and accreditation-qualified name registrars on the ICANN site at *http://www.icann.org/registrars/accredited-list.html*.

Of all these organizations, the most important one for TCP/IP is the IETF because it is responsible for creating and managing RFCs, wherein the rules and formats for all related protocols and services must be described.

TCP/IP STANDARDS AND RFCs

Although RFC sounds like a pretty tentative name for a document, the impact of RFCs on TCP/IP is nothing less than overwhelming and complete. Although RFCs must go through a multi-step process of proposals, drafts, test implementations, and so forth before they can become official standards, they provide the documentation necessary to understand, implement, and use TCP/IP protocols and services on the Internet.

Within the collection of RFCs, older versions of RFCs are sometimes (or often) replaced by newer, more up-to-date versions. Each RFC is identified by a number, and "new numbers" fall at present in the 3300s range. When two or more RFCs cover the same topic, they usually also share the same title. In that case, the RFC with the highest number is considered to be the current version, and all older, lower-numbered versions are said to be obsolete.

One special RFC is titled "Internet Official Protocol Standards." At this writing, the current version of that RFC is numbered 2700. If you visit your favorite Internet search engine (for example, Yahoo, Altavista, Excite, or AskJeeves), you can find many locations for Internet RFCs online. We recommend using the search string "RFC 2700" to find RFC 2700, or "RFC 2026" to find RFC 2026. (It can be important to put the entire string in quotation marks, depending on how your search engine works.) We like the site at Ohio State University, where the index for all RFCs is available at *http://www.cis.ohio-state.edu/Services/rfc/index.html*. (Choose the Index link, then search for a particular RFC, or choose the Keyword Search link and enter the RFC number of your choice.)

RFC 2026 is another important document. It describes how an RFC is created, and what processes it must go through to become an official standard, adopted by the IETF. It also describes how to participate in that process.

A potential Standard RFC begins its life when a process or protocol is developed, defined, and reviewed, and then tested and reviewed further by the Internet community. After that RFC is revised, tested further, proven to work, and shown to be compatible with other Internet standards, it may then be adopted as an official **Standard** RFC by the IETF. It is then published as a Standard RFC and assigned a number.

Actually, an RFC passes through numerous specific steps in becoming a standard, and acquires specific status designations along that path. These are fully defined in RFC 2026. For example, a potential Standard RFC goes through three phases on its way to becoming a standard. It starts as a **Proposed Standard**; moves up to a **Draft Standard**; and, if formally adopted, becomes an **Internet Standard**, or a Standard RFC. Eventually, such an RFC can also be designated as a **Retired Standard**, or a **Historic Standard**, when replaced by a newer RFC.

Best Current Practice (BCP) is another important category for RFCs. A BCP does not define a protocol or technical specifications; rather, a BCP defines a philosophy, or a particular approach, to a network design or implementation that is recommended as tried and true, or that enjoys certain desirable characteristics worthy of consideration when building or maintaining a TCP/IP network. BCPs are not standards, per se, but because they present highly recommended design, implementation, and maintenance practices, they are well worth reading and applying where appropriate.

OSI NETWORK REFERENCE MODEL OVERVIEW

Before we explore more details about TCP/IP protocols and services, let's explore a model of how networks operate in general. This will help you better understand what protocols are for, and what roles they play on modern networks. This model is a **network reference model**, but is formally known as the **International Standards Organization Open Systems Interconnection** network reference model, sometimes called the **ISO/OSI network reference model**.

Governed by ISO standard 7498, the ISO/OSI network reference model, or reference model (also referred to as the seven-layer model), was developed as part of an international standards initiative in the 1980s that was supposed to usher in a new and improved suite of protocols specifically designed to replace TCP/IP. But while the OSI protocols were never widely adopted outside Europe, the reference model has become a standard way to talk about networking, and explain how networks operate. In spite of the effort to complete the OSI protocols and services, which took nearly 10 years and cost many billions of dollars to design and implement, TCP/IP remained the open standard protocol suite of choice, and remains so to this day.

Models Break Networking into Layers

The reference model's value lies in its ability to break a big technical problem—namely, how to handle networking all the way from hardware to the high-level software involved in making networks work—into a series of interconnected and interrelated sub-problems, and then solve each sub-problem individually. Computer scientists call this approach **divide and conquer**.

A divide and conquer approach permits concerns related to networking hardware to be completely separated from those related to networking software. In fact, it even permits networking software to be further subdivided into multiple **layers**, each of which represents a separate kind or class of networking activity (read more about this in the section titled "The ISO/OSI Network Reference Model"). Thus, constructing a series of independent but interconnected layers of hardware and software that work together to enable one computer to communicate with another across a network can solve the larger problem of networking.

In fact, a layered approach to networking is a very good thing. That's because the kind of expertise that makes it possible for an electrical engineer to specify how a network medium must behave, and what kinds of physical interfaces are necessary to attach to such a networking medium, is quite different from the kinds of expertise that software engineers must possess. In fact, software engineers must not only write drivers for network interfaces, they must also implement the various networking protocols that operate at various layers in the reference model (or in another layered model for whatever networking protocols may be in use).

Before we dive into the details of the reference model, and describe its layers, you should understand and appreciate these key points about networking:

- The big problem of networking is easier to solve when broken into a series of smaller problems.

- Layers operate more or less independently of one another, thereby enabling modular design and implementation of specific hardware and software components to implement specific network functions.

- Because individual layers encapsulate specific, largely independent functions, changes to one layer need not affect other layers.

- Individual layers work together on pairs of computers, so that sending layers perform operations on one layer that are in some sense "reversed" or "undone" by the operations performed at the same layer on the receiver. Because such layers work in concert across the network, they are called **peer layers**.

- Different expertise is needed to implement the solutions necessary for the networking functions or tasks handled at each layer.

- The layers in a network implementation work together to create a general solution to the general problem known as networking.

- Network protocols usually map into one or more layers of the reference model.

- TCP/IP itself is designed around a layered model for networking.

In fact, this abstract reference model for networking is also expressed in somewhat different terms as part of TCP/IP's very definition. But the key insight that makes divide and conquer such a powerful tool for implementing networks has been part and parcel of TCP/IP's design from its earliest beginnings. This very abstraction is one of the reasons why TCP/IP is so good at allowing different computers, operating systems, and even types of networking hardware to communicate with one another.

The ISO/OSI Network Reference Model

The reference model described in OSI Standard 7498 breaks network communication into seven layers, as follows (named from the top down, as illustrated in Figure 1-1):

- Application layer
- Presentation layer
- Session layer
- Transport layer
- Network layer
- Data Link layer
- Physical layer

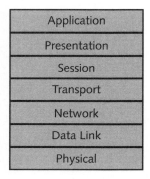

Figure 1-1   ISO/OSI network reference model layers

The roles that each of these model layers plays are explained later in this chapter. In the next section, you will learn how layers in the reference model behave, in a more general way.

How Protocol Layers Behave

Within the context of the reference model, layers exist to encapsulate or isolate specific types of functionality to allow the divide and conquer approach to be applied to networking. In general, layers in the reference model exist to provide services to the layer above (where applicable), and to deliver data to (for outbound traffic) or accept data from (for inbound traffic) the layer below.

In general, for each layer in a model that is implemented in code (you learn why this is important when we discuss how the layered model for TCP/IP differs from the reference model in the section titled "The TCP/IP Networking Model"), the software handles packages of data that are sometimes called **protocol data units (PDUs)**. PDUs are often generically described as packets (for packages of data), irrespective of the layer in the model addressed.

PDUs typically include "envelope information" in the form of specific headers and trailers. In this case, a header represents a layer-specific label for whatever PDU it precedes. Likewise, a trailer (which may be optional for some layers and some specific protocols) may include error-detection and error-correction information, explicit "end of data" flags, or other data designed to clearly indicate the end of a PDU.

The reference model, as shown in Figure 1-1, looks something like a layer cake as it presents a stack of named layers from which the model is built. Because this stack-like structure so accurately depicts how many networking protocol suites are implemented—including TCP/IP—it is common to talk about the components of hardware and software that map into this model as a **protocol stack** when implemented on a specific computer. Thus, on a Windows computer, the **network interface card (NIC)**, the driver that permits the operating system to "talk" to the NIC, and the various software components that make up TCP/IP's other layers, may be called a protocol stack, or more accurately, the TCP/IP protocol stack for that machine.

In the following sections, we examine the seven layers of the reference model in more detail, starting at the bottom of the stack.

Physical Layer

The **Physical layer** includes the physical transmission medium (cables or wireless media) that any network must use to send and receive the signals that constitute the physical expression of networked communications. The details of such signaling, along with the physical and electrical characteristics of the interfaces to the network medium, are specified in the Physical layer. The Physical layer's job is to activate, maintain, and deactivate network connections. Senders initiate a connection to transmit data across the network medium, and receivers respond to attempts to establish connections, ultimately to accept incoming transmissions from the network medium.

A simplistic view of the Physical layer is that it concerns itself with the networking hardware and the connections that permit that hardware to access some networking medium. In addition, this layer also coordinates the sending and receiving of signals across the networking medium, and determines what kinds of cables, connectors, and network interfaces must be used to access a specific area on a network.

The Physical layer manages communications with the network medium going down the protocol stack, and handles conversion of outgoing data from the bits that computers use into the signals that networks use. For incoming messages, the Physical layer reverses this process and converts incoming signals from the networking medium into the bit patterns that must be sent to the computer through the network interface.

PDUs at the Physical layer consist of specific serial patterns of signals that correspond to bit patterns for frames at the Data Link layer.

Data Link Layer

The **Data Link layer** is situated between the Physical layer and the Network layer in the reference model. Its job is to enable reliable transmission of data through the Physical layer at the sending end, and to check such reliability upon reception at the receiving end. The Data Link layer also manages **point-to-point transmission** across the networking medium, from one computer to another on a single logical or physical **cable segment**. It recognizes individual devices on the local medium through a special address that uniquely identifies each individual interface. Because the Data Link layer manages point-to-point communications between interfaces, it also handles **local area network (LAN)** connections between the machines to which those interfaces are attached.

In the course of managing connections between machines, the Data Link layer also handles sequencing of data from sender to receiver, as patterns of bits must be mapped into corresponding patterns of signals for transmission from sender to receiver, and the process reversed on the receiving end. To that end, the Data Link layer can also control the pace at which data is transmitted from sender to receiver—a process called **media flow control** that responds to local congestion conditions and helps keep the network medium from becoming swamped by local traffic. Finally, the Data Link layer requests data transfers to occur when outgoing PDUs are ready to be transmitted, and also handles accepting and constructing incoming PDUs for incoming data.

PDUs at the Data Link layer must fit into specific bit patterns that map into the carrying capacity of the network medium in terms of format, structure, and maximum data size. Data Link layer PDUs are called **frames** or **data frames**.

Network Layer

The **Network layer** is where notions of network location are addressed, and where the intricacies involved in directing a PDU from sender to receiver are handled. Thus, the Network layer handles the logical addresses associated with individual machines on a network, which permits the Domain Name System to correlate human-readable names for such machines with unique, machine-readable numeric addresses. The Network layer also uses that **addressing** information to determine how to send a PDU from a sender to a receiver when the source and destination for traffic do not reside on the same physical segment on a network.

The Network layer also embodies the notion of multiple simultaneous connections between different IP addresses, so that numerous applications can maintain network connections at the same time. The Network layer is able to identify which network connection belongs to an individual process or application on a computer, and direct traffic not only to the proper receiver from its sender, but also deliver the incoming data to a specific process or application on the receiving machine. This explains how you can have a Web browser session open on your machine at the same time you're reading e-mail, and this is what permits incoming e-mail messages to be delivered to your e-mail client, and incoming Web pages to be delivered to your Web browser, without mixing up the two data streams involved.

In fact, the Network layer is even flexible enough to recognize and use multiple routes between a sender and a receiver, while ongoing communications are underway. The technique that's used to forward or relay individual PDUs from a sender to a receiver using one or multiple routes is called packet switching, and that's why the Network layer handles forwarding and relaying on a per-PDU basis. In fact, the Network layer is also sensitive to delays associated with routes, and can manage how much traffic is sent across them, while it is forwarding data from a sender to a receiver. This process is called **congestion control**, and helps networks avoid being overrun when high levels of activity occur from time to time.

Given this terminology, we hope it's obvious that the PDU associated with the Network layer is called a packet.

Transport Layer

The **Transport layer**'s name is highly evocative of its function: this layer's job is to ensure reliable end-to-end transmission of PDUs from sender to receiver. To enable this function to occur, the Transport layer often includes end-to-end error-detection and error-recovery data. Such data is usually packaged as a part of the trailers for Transport layer PDUs, where special values called **checksums** are calculated before and after data delivery, then compared to check whether error-free delivery occurred. If the checksum as sent agrees with the checksum as calculated locally, it is assumed that error-free delivery occurred; if not, some protocols at the Transport layer are smart enough to request retransmission of PDUs when errors are detected.

Finally, because the amount of data that may be sent from sender to receiver is arbitrary in size, but the containers for such data that can transport it from end to end have a fixed maximum size (called the **MTU**, for **maximum transmission unit**), the Transport layer also handles the activities known as segmentation and reassembly. Simply put, **segmentation** involves cutting up a big message into a numbered sequence of chunks, called segments, in which each chunk represents the maximum data payload that the network media can carry between sender and receiver. In equally simple terms, **reassembly** describes the process whereby the chunks as sent are put back into their original order and used to re-create the data in the form it took before it was segmented for transmission.

The Transport layer is equipped to request retransmission of all erroneous or missing PDUs when reassembly is underway, so that it can guarantee reliable delivery of data from sender to receiver. As the foregoing discussion suggests, the PDUs used at the Transport layer are called **segments**, or **data segments**.

Session Layer

The **Session layer** is where ongoing communications between a sender and a receiver, somewhat like a telephone conversation, are set up, maintained, and then terminated, or torn down, as needed. Thus, the Session layer defines mechanisms to permit senders and receivers to request that a conversation start or stop, and to keep a conversation going even when traffic may not otherwise flow between the two parties involved.

In addition, the Session layer includes mechanisms to maintain reliable ongoing conversations, called **checkpoints**. Checkpoints define the last point up to which successful communications are known to have occurred, and define the last known point to which a conversation must be rolled back for missing or damaged elements to be replayed to recover from the effects of missing or damaged data. Likewise, the Session layer defines a variety of mechanisms whereby conversations that fall out of synchronization are resynchronized.

The Session layer's primary job is to support communications between two networked parties, in which a sequence of messages or PDUs is typically exchanged. A good example of this type of interaction occurs when a user logs on to a database (the set-up phase), enters a bunch of queries (the data exchange phase), and then logs off when finished (the tear-down phase).

Session PDUs come in a variety of types (the OSI protocol suite recognizes more than 30 distinct PDUs) so PDUs at this level are generically known as Session PDUs, or SPDUs.

Presentation Layer

The **Presentation layer** manages the way data is presented to the network (on its way down the protocol stack), and to a specific machine/application combination (on its way up the protocol stack). In other words, the Presentation layer handles transforming data from generic, network-oriented forms of expression to more specific, platform-oriented forms of expression, and vice versa. This facility is what permits such radically different types of computers—which may differently represent numbers and characters—to communicate with each other across a network.

By convention, a special computer facility is said to reside at the Presentation layer. This facility is sometimes called a redirector (in Microsoft terms), or a network shell (in Novell NetWare and UNIX terms). Either way, this facility's job is to distinguish requests for network resources from local ones, and to redirect such requests to the appropriate local or remote subsystem. This permits computers to use a single subsystem to access resources, whether they reside on the local machine, or across the network on a remote machine, without having to discriminate by the type of resource involved. It makes it much easier for developers to build applications that can access local or remote resources at will. Likewise, it also makes it easier for users to access such resources because they can simply request the resources they need, and let the redirector worry about how to satisfy their requests.

The Presentation layer can also supply special data-handling functions for applications, including protocol conversions (when applications use protocols distinct from those used for networked communications, as may be the case for e-commerce, database, or other transaction-oriented services), data encryption (for outgoing messages), decryption (for incoming ones), data compression (for outgoing messages), or expansion (for incoming ones). For this kind of service, whatever the Presentation layer does on the sending side, the Presentation layer must undo on the receiving side, so that both sides of the connection share similar views of the data at some point.

As with the Session layer, Presentation PDUs come in a variety of types, and are generically called Presentation PDUs.

Application Layer

Although the temptation is always strong to equate the **Application layer** with whatever application is requesting network services (and there's always an application involved when network access is requested), the Application layer defines an interface that applications can use to request network services, rather than referring directly to applications themselves. Thus, the Application layer basically defines the kinds of services that applications can request from the network, and stipulates the forms that data must take when accepting messages from, or delivering messages to, such applications.

In the most direct way, the Application layer defines a set of access controls over the network, in the sense that it determines what kinds of things applications can ask the network to carry or deliver, and what kind of activities the network can support. This is where things, such as permissions to access specific files or services, or determining which users are allowed to perform what kinds of actions to specific data elements, are enforced.

As with the two preceding layers, Application PDUs are generically called Application PDUs.

THE TCP/IP NETWORKING MODEL

Because TCP/IP's architecture was designed long before the OSI reference model was finalized in the 1980s, it should come as no surprise that the design model that describes TCP/IP differs somewhat from the OSI reference model. Figure 1-2 shows the layers identified for the native TCP/IP model, and maps its layers to those of the reference model. These layers are quite similar, but not identical, to the layers in the OSI reference model. That's because some functions associated with the Session layer and the Presentation layer for the OSI reference model appear in the TCP/IP Application layer, while some aspects of the Session layer from the OSI reference model appear in the TCP/IP Transport layer as well.

By and large, the Transport model for both layers maps together quite well, as does the Network layer from the OSI reference model and the Internet layer from the TCP/IP model. Just as the TCP/IP Application layer more or less maps to the three Application, Presentation, and Session layers in the OSI reference model, the TCP/IP Network Access layer also maps to both the Data Link and the Physical layers in the OSI reference model.

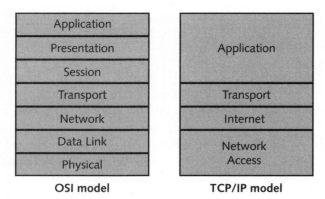

Figure 1-2   OSI reference model and TCP/IP networking model layers

TCP/IP Network Access Layer

The TCP/IP Network Access layer is sometimes called the Network Interface layer. Either way, it's the layer wherein LAN technologies, such as Ethernet, token ring, and wireless media and devices, come into play. It's also the layer in which WAN and connection-management protocols, such as **Serial Line Internet Protocol (SLIP)**, **Point-to-Point Protocol (PPP)**, and **X.25**, come into play. Diverging somewhat from PDU terminology for the OSI reference model, PDUs at this layer are called datagrams, though they may also generically be called packets.

At the Network Access layer, the **Institute for Electrical and Electronic Engineers (IEEE)** standards for networking apply. These include the **IEEE 802** family of standards, which features the following components of interest, among others:

- *802.1 Internetworking*: a general description of how internetworking (exchanging data from one physical network to another) works for the entire 802 family

- *802.2 Logical Link Control*: a general description of how logical links between two devices on the same physical network may be established and managed

- *802.2 Media Access Control*: a general description of how media interfaces are identified and accessed on a network, including a scheme to create unique MAC layer addresses for all media interfaces

- *802.3 CSMA/CD*: **CSMA/CD** stands for **Carrier Sense Multiple Access with Collision Detection** and refers to how the networking technology more commonly called Ethernet operates and behaves. This family also includes Gigabit Ethernet (802.3*z*), along with 10 Mbps and 100 Mbps varieties, despite the name for 802.12 as "High-Speed Networking."

- *802.5 Token Ring*: a general description of how the networking technology developed at IBM, known as token ring, operates and behaves

For more information about the IEEE 802 family of standards, visit the IEEE's Web site at *http://www.ieee.org*, and then search on "802".

TCP/IP Network Access Layer Protocols

The most important TCP/IP Network Access layer protocols include SLIP and PPP. SLIP is an older, more simple-minded serial line protocol that supports only TCP/IP-based communications. It is described in RFC 1055, and it originated on UNIX systems (on which it is still in use to some extent today, especially on older systems). SLIP includes no built-in security capabilities, or data delivery enhancements, and is only seldom used anymore for establishing network connections across serial lines (such as telephone lines or other on-demand connection types) to the Internet or to private TCP/IP networks.

PPP is a more modern serial line protocol, which is widely used for Internet and private TCP/IP network connections. PPP is protocol neutral, and may be used to simultaneously ferry a range of protocols across a single serial line connection. The Windows implementation of PPP supports all the major Windows protocols—namely, TCP/IP, **Internetwork Packet Exchange Sequenced Packet Exchange (IPX/SPX)**, and **NetBIDS Enhanced User Interface (NetBEUI)**, along with tunneling protocols, such as **Point-to-Point Tunneling Protocol (PPTP)**, and other **Virtual Private Network (VPN)** protocols—across a single connection. Other implementations add support for numerous other protocols—including **AppleTalk** and **Systems Network Architecture (SNA)**—to this mix. PPP is the serial line protocol of choice nowadays primarily because it supports a variety of security options that include encryption of login information, or encryption of all traffic across the serial link, and a much richer mix of protocols and services than SLIP can support. PPP is described in RFC 1661.

TCP/IP Internet Layer Functions

The TCP/IP Internet layer protocols handle routing between machines across multiple networks, and also manage network names and addresses to facilitate such behavior. To be more specific, the Internet layer handles three primary tasks for TCP/IP:

1. *MTU fragmentation*: When a route carries data from one type of network to another, the largest chunk of data that the network can carry, an MTU, can vary. When data moves from a medium that supports a larger MTU to a medium that supports a smaller MTU, that data must be chunked up into smaller pieces to match the smaller of the two MTUs involved. This need only be a one-way transformation (since smaller packets need not be combined into bigger ones when the relationship goes the other way), but it must be performed while the data is in transit.

2. *Addressing*: This defines the mechanism whereby all network interfaces on a TCP/IP network must be associated with specific, unique bit patterns that identify each interface individually, and also identify which network (or even network locale) that interface belongs to.

3. *Routing*: This defines the mechanism that forwards packets from sender to receiver, in which numerous intermediate relays may be involved in achieving delivery from sender to receiver. This function not only includes the processes involved in successful delivery, but also includes methods to track delivery performance and report on errors when delivery fails, or is otherwise hampered.

Thus, the Internet layer handles moving data from sender to receiver. It also repackages data into smaller containers when required, and handles issues of identifying where sender and receiver are located, and how to get from "here" to "there" on a network.

Internet Layer Protocols

The primary protocols that function at the TCP/IP Internet layer include the following:

- *Internet Protocol (IP)*: Internet Protocol (IP) routes packets from sender to receiver.

- *Internet Control Message Protocol (ICMP)*: **Internet Control Message Protocol (ICMP)** manages IP-based routing and network behavior.

- *Packet Internetwork Groper (PING)*: **Packet Internetwork Groper (PING)** checks accessibility and round-trip time between a specific sender and receiver pair of IP addresses.

- *Address Resolution Protocol (ARP)*: **Address Resolution Protocol (ARP)** converts between numeric IP network addresses and **Media Access Control (MAC) addresses** on a specific cable segment (always used for the final step of packet delivery).

- *Reverse ARP (RARP)*: **Reverse Address Resolution Protocol (RARP)** converts a MAC layer address into a numeric IP address.

- *Bootstrap Protocol (BOOTP)*: **Bootstrap Protocol (BOOTP)** is the precursor to the **Dynamic Host Configuration Protocol (DHCP)** which manages network allocation of IP addresses and other IP configuration data. BOOTP permits network devices to obtain boot and configuration data across the network, instead of from a local drive.

- *Routing Information Protocol (RIP)*: **Routing Information Protocol (RIP)** defines the original and most basic routing protocol for local routing regions within local internetworks.

- *Open Shortest Path First (OSPF)*: **Open Shortest Path First (OSPF)** defines a widely used, link-state routing protocol for local or interior routing regions within local internetworks.

- *Border Gateway Protocol (BGP)*: **Border Gateway Protocol (BGP)** defines a widely used routing protocol that connects to common Internet backbones, or other routing domains within the Internet where multiple parties jointly share responsibility for managing traffic.

By the time you finish this book, you will know quite a bit more about all of these protocols, and a fair amount more about several other related protocols as well. For now, you need to understand the relationship between their names, acronyms, and basic functions, and that all of these are networking protocols that function at Layers 2 and 3 (ARP and RARP), and 3 (all the others mentioned above) of the OSI reference model.

TCP/IP Transport Layer Functions

Devices that operate on the Internet are generically identified as **hosts**, so the TCP/IP Transport layer is also sometimes called the host-to-host layer because this layer involves moving data from one host to another. The basic functions that Transport layer protocols provide include reliable delivery of data from sender to receiver, plus the necessary fragmentation of outgoing messages prior to transmission, and their reassembly prior to delivery to the Application layer for further processing. Thus, the OSI reference model and the TCP/IP model map more or less to one another.

TCP/IP Transport Layer Protocols

There are two TCP/IP Transport layer protocols: the Transmission Control Protocol (TCP) and the **User Datagram Protocol (UDP)**. These two transport protocols come in two flavors: connection-oriented and connectionless, whereby TCP is **connection-oriented**, and UDP is **connectionless**. Here, the distinction rests on TCP's practices of negotiating and maintaining a connection between sender and receiver prior to sending data, obtaining a positive acknowledgment for data that is successfully transmitted, and obtaining a request for retransmission of missing or erroneous data. UDP simply transmits data in what's called a "best-effort delivery," and does no follow-up checking on its receipt.

Because TCP makes a connection and explicitly checks its work, it's called connection-oriented; because UDP makes no such checks, it's called connectionless. This makes TCP much more reliable, but also slower and more cumbersome, than UDP. But it also allows TCP to provide guaranteed delivery services at the protocol level, which UDP does not offer.

TCP/IP Application Layer

The TCP/IP Application layer is also known as the **Process layer** because this is where the protocol stack interfaces with applications or processes on a host machine. The user interfaces to a process or application are defined here. The common overlap between TCP/IP protocols and services occurs here as well. For example, **File Transfer Protocol (FTP)**, **Telnet**, etc. represent specific TCP/IP-based protocols, and also define services for file transfer, terminal emulation, etc.). Most of the higher-level TCP/IP-based services we discuss later in this course operate at the TCP/IP Application layer.

The best-known TCP/IP-based services use TCP as transports, rather than UDP. But some services **(Network File System**, **NFS)** often use UDP for transport. No matter what transport is used, higher-level services all depend on IP for their networking protocol (that's why there are separate protocols at the Network or Internet layer to provide special-purpose network services, such as ICMP, ARP, and RARP).

TCP/IP services depend on two elements to operate:

1. In UNIX terminology, a special "listener process," called a **daemon**, operates on a server to handle incoming user requests for specific services. On Windows NT, a process called INETINFO.EXE appears in the Task Manager's Processes tab whenever the Web server, IIS, or FTP server is running (on a UNIX host, the FTP service is associated with a process named *ftpd*, and Internet services run under a process named *inetd*).

2. Each TCP/IP service has an associated **port address** that uses a 16-bit number to identify a specific process or service. Addresses in the range from 0 to 1024 are often called **well-known port addresses** and associate a specific port address with a specific service. For example, FTP's well-known port address is port 21. We cover this topic in more detail later in this chapter.

Any daemon or listener process essentially hangs around, listening for attempts to connect on the well-known port address (or addresses) associated with its services. A well-known port address can often be changed as a configuration option, which is why you sometimes see Web **Uniform Resource Locators**, or **URLs**, that specify a different port address at the end of the domain name portion of the string. Thus, a URL might appear as *http://www.lanw.com:8080/staff/etbio.htm* to indicate that an alternate port address of 8080 should be used to establish the connection, rather than the default standard port address of 80.

When a connection request arrives, the listener process checks to see if the request should be allowed to proceed. If so, it creates another temporary process (on UNIX), or spawns a separate execution thread (on Windows NT or 2000) to handle that particular request. This temporary process or thread lasts only long enough to service that user request, and uses temporary port addresses in the range from 1025 through 65,535 to handle it. (Sometimes services use four port addresses so both parties can send and receive data at the same time.) As soon as a process or thread is created to handle some specific request, the listener process or daemon returns to its job of listening for additional requests for service.

TCP/IP PROTOCOLS, SERVICES, SOCKETS, AND PORTS

Think back for a moment to the discussion of TCP/IP chronology that appears earlier in this chapter. You may recall that TCP/IP's inclusion in the version of UNIX known as **4.2BSD** was a milestone in its history. We explained that this inclusion exposed the worldwide research and academic communities to the joys and sorrows of working with TCP/IP.

Actually, there's a lot more to the relationship between UNIX and TCP/IP than its successful introduction may suggest. For a good while after this relationship formed, the connection between UNIX and TCP/IP was strong and useful. Thus, not only did the introduction of TCP/IP into UNIX greatly enhance that operating system's networking abilities, the techniques that were used to describe and configure TCP/IP protocols and services within the UNIX environment have also become customary for TCP/IP at large, even when UNIX may not be the operating system. In fact, the terminology describes how data conveyed by TCP/IP to a specific network host is handled once it is delivered to its destination.

On any given computer running TCP/IP, numerous applications may be running at the same time. On many desktops, for example, it's typical for users to have an e-mail program, a Web browser, and an FTP client all open and running at the same time. Within the TCP/IP environment, a mechanism is required to permit multiple applications to be distinguished from one another, and the transport protocols (TCP or UDP) to handle multiple outgoing streams of data (from distinct applications) before they are passed to IP for addressing and delivery instructions. It's necessary to reverse this process for incoming data. The incoming stream of Transport layer PDUs must be inspected and separated, and the resulting messages delivered to the appropriate requesting application.

Combining the various sources of outgoing data into a single output data stream is called **multiplexing**; breaking up an incoming data stream so that separate portions may be delivered to the correct applications is called **demultiplexing**. This activity is typically handled at the Transport layer, where outgoing messages are also broken into chunks sized for the networks over which they'll travel, and where incoming messages are reassembled in correct order from a stream of incoming chunks.

To help make this job easier, TCP/IP uses **protocol numbers** to identify distinct protocols, and those protocols use **port numbers** to identify specific Application layer protocols and services. Because this technique originated in the UNIX environment through a series of configuration files, this explains how the techniques used in all TCP/IP implementations came to exist.

Numerous port numbers are reserved to identify well-known protocols. **Well-known protocols** (also called **well-known services** in some contexts) assign a series of numbers to represent a sizable collection of TCP/IP-based network services, such as file transfer (FTP), terminal emulation (Telnet), and e-mail (**SMTP**, **POP3**, and **IMAP**). Well-known and preassigned protocol numbers and port numbers are documented in the Assigned Numbers RFC. UNIX machines define these values in two text files: protocol numbers are defined in /etc/protocols, and port numbers are defined in /etc/services.

TCP/IP Protocol Numbers

In an IP **datagram** header, the protocol number appears as its 10th byte. (Chapter 3 discusses IP datagrams in detail.) This 8-bit value indicates which Transport layer protocol should accept delivery of incoming data. A complete list of protocol numbers for TCP/IP can be found at *http://www.iana.org*; we reproduce the first 20 entries in Table 1-1.

Table 1-1   TCP/IP Protocol Numbers

Number	Acronym	Protocol Name
0	IP	Internet Protocol
1	ICMP	Internet Control Message
2	IGMP	Internet Group Management
3	GGP	Gateway-to-Gateway Protocol
4	IP	IP in IP (**encapsulation**)
5	ST	Stream
6	TCP	Transmission Control Protocol
7	UCL	User Control List
8	EGP	Exterior Gateway Protocol
9	IGP	any private interior gateway
10	BBN-RCC-MON	BBN RCC Monitoring
11	NVP-II	Network Voice Protocol
12	PUP	Peripheral Update Protocol
13	ARGUS	ARGUS protocol
14	EMCON	Emergency Condition
15	XNET	Cross Net Debugger
16	CHAOS	Chaos protocol
17	UDP	User Datagram Protocol
18	MUX	Multiplexing
19	DCN-MEAS	DCN Measurement Subsystems
20	HMP	Host Monitoring Protocol

On a UNIX system, the contents of the text file /etc/protocols need not contain every entry in the Assigned Numbers RFC. To work properly, /etc/protocols must identify which protocols are installed and used on a particular UNIX machine. For that reason, we do not include the entire list of protocol numbers in this chapter. To look up the numbers associated with the protocols you're using on your system, please visit *http://www.iana.org* and look for information about protocol numbers. (*Hint:*You can use the Find command in your Web browser to look up protocols by acronym or full name.)

TCP/IP Port Numbers

After IP passes incoming data to TCP or UDP at the Transport layer, the protocol must perform its duties, then pass that data to its intended **application process** (whatever program is running that should accept that data on the user's behalf). TCP/IP application processes are sometimes called **network services** and are identified by port numbers. The **source port number** identifies the process that sent the data, and the **destination port number** identifies the process that is to receive that data. Both of these values are represented by 2-byte (16-bit) values in the first header word of every TCP segment or UDP packet. Because port numbers are 16-bit values, they may fall anywhere in the range from 0 to 65,535 when expressed in decimal form.

Speaking historically, port numbers below 256 were reserved for well-known services, such as Telnet and FTP, and numbers from 256 to 1024 were reserved for UNIX-specific services. These days, all port addresses below 1024 represent well-known services, and there are many so-called **registered ports** associated with specific application services in the range from 1024 through 65,535. Here again, perusal of *http://www.iana.org* is the quickest way to understand what's what in this sizable address space.

TCP/IP Sockets

Well-known or registered ports represent preassigned port numbers that have specific associations to particular network services. This simplifies the client/server connection process because both sender and receiver agree by convention that particular services are associated with particular port addresses. In addition to such agreed-upon port numbers, there is another type of port number known as a dynamically allocated port number. These numbers are not preassigned; rather, they are used, as needed, to provide a temporary connection between a sender and a receiver for a limited exchange of data. This permits each system to maintain numerous open connections, and to assign each connection its own unique, dynamically allocated port address. These port addresses fall in the range of addresses over 1024, in which any port number not currently in use represents fair game for such temporary use.

After a client or server uses a well-known port address to establish communications, the connection established (called a **session**) is invariably handed to a temporary pair of socket addresses that provides the sending and receiving port addresses for further communications between sender and receiver. The combination of a particular IP address (for the host machine on which the process is running) and a **dynamically assigned port address** (where the connection is maintained) is called a **socket address** (or **socket**). Because IP addresses and dynamically assigned port numbers are both guaranteed to be unique, each socket address is also guaranteed to be unique across the entire Internet!

DATA ENCAPSULATION IN TCP/IP

At each layer in the TCP/IP protocol stack—the Network Access, Internet, Transport, and Application layers (where TCP/IP's many application protocols and services, each represented by one or more **well-known port numbers**, operate)—outgoing data is packaged and identified for delivery to the layer underneath. Incoming data, on the other hand, has its encapsulating information from the underlying layer stripped off before it's delivered to its upper-layer partner.

Thus, each PDU has its own particular opening component called a **header** (or **packet header**) that identifies the protocol in use, the sender and intended recipient, and other information. Likewise, many PDUs also include a characteristic closing component called a **trailer** (or **packet trailer**) that provides data integrity checks for the data portion of the PDU, known as the **payload**. The enclosure of a payload between a header and an (optional) trailer is what defines the mechanism known as encapsulation, where data from an upper layer gets manipulated and then enclosed with a header (and, possibly, a trailer) before being passed to the layer below, or across the networking medium for delivery elsewhere.

Studying the actual contents of any communications on the network medium—or "across the wire" as it's sometimes called—requires that you understand typical header and trailer structures, and can reassemble data moving across the network up the protocol stack into something that approximates its original form. In a nutshell, that work represents the task known as protocol analysis, which is the topic of discussion for the remainder of this chapter.

ABOUT PROTOCOL ANALYSIS

Protocol analysis (also referred to as **network analysis**) is the process of tapping into the network communications system, capturing packets that cross the network, gathering network statistics, and **decoding** the packets into readable form. In essence, a protocol analyzer *eavesdrops* on network communications. Many protocol analyzers can also transmit packets—a useful task for testing a network or device. You perform protocol analysis using a software or hardware/software product that is loaded on a desktop or portable computer.

EtherPeek for Windows (WildPackets, Inc.) and Sniffer Network Analyzer (Network Associates) are two very popular Windows-based protocol analyzers. A demo version of the EtherPeek program is included on the CD that accompanies this book.

Useful Roles for Protocol Analysis

Protocol analyzers are often used to troubleshoot network communications. Typically, analyzers are placed on the network and configured to capture the problematic communication sequence. By reading the packets that cross the cabling system, you can identify faults and errors in the process.

For example, if a Web client cannot connect to a specific Web server, a protocol analyzer can be used to capture the communication. Reviewing this communication reveals the processes used by the client to resolve the IP address of the Web server, locate the hardware address of a local router, and submit the connection request to the Web server.

Protocol analyzers are also used to test networks. Testing can be performed in a passive manner by listening to unusual communications, or in an active manner by transmitting packets onto the network. For example, if a firewall is configured to block a specific type of traffic from entering the local network, a protocol analyzer can listen to the traffic from the firewall to determine if unacceptable traffic is forwarded. Alternately, an analyzer can

1

be configured to transmit test packets to the firewall in order to determine if certain unacceptable traffic will be forwarded by that firewall.

Protocol analyzers can also be used to gather trends on network performance. Most analyzers have the ability to track short- and long-term trends on network traffic. These trends may include, but are not limited to, network utilization, packets-per-second rate, packet size distribution, and protocols in use. The administrator can use this information to track subtle changes on the network over time. For example, a network reconfigured to support DHCP-based addressing experiences greater broadcasts due to the DHCP discovery process. For more information on DHCP, refer to Chapter 8, "The Dynamic Host Configuration Protocol (DHCP)."

In this book, we use a protocol analyzer as a teaching tool. We examine various packet structures and communication sequences used in TCP/IP networking. Several analyzer demo programs are included on the CD that accompanies this book. For information on the contents of the accompanying CD, refer to Appendix E, "About the CD."

Analyzers are available for a variety of platforms including Windows 95, Windows 98, Windows NT, Windows 2000, UNIX, Linux, and Macintosh. For a list of popular protocol analyzer solutions, refer to the document *Protocol Analyzer Vendors* on the CD that accompanies this book.

Protocol Analyzer Elements

Figure 1-3 depicts the basic elements of a protocol analyzer. Different analyzers offer a variety of features and functions, but the following elements are the basic set seen on most analyzer solutions today.

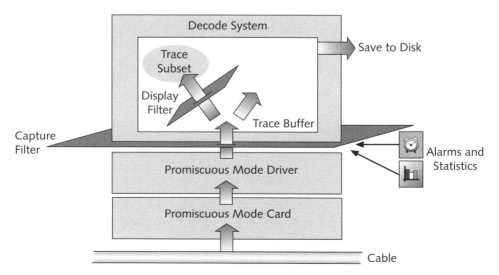

Figure 1-3 Network analyzer elements

The basic elements are:

- Promiscuous mode card and driver
- Packet filters
- Trace buffer
- Decodes
- Alarms
- Statistics

Promiscuous Mode Card and Driver

As shown in Figure 1-3, packets enter the analyzer system from the network where the analyzer is connected using a network interface card. The network interface card and driver used on the analyzer must support **promiscuous mode operation**. A card that runs in promiscuous mode can capture **broadcast packets**, **multicast packets**, and **unicast packets** sent to other devices, as well as error packets. For example, an analyzer running with a promiscuous mode card and driver can see **Ethernet collision fragments**, **oversized packets**, **undersized packets** (a.k.a. **runts**), and packets that end on an illegal boundary.

These latter types of data reflect transmission errors, and are normally ignored by network interface cards when they're not operating in promiscuous mode. An Ethernet collision fragment represents the garbled traffic that appears on a network when two packets transmitted at more or less the same time run into one another, producing a random hash of signals. Collisions increase in frequency as traffic volumes go up, and it's important to be able to gather statistics about occurrence. Oversized packets exceed the MTU for the type of network in use, and generally indicate some kind of problem with a network interface card, or its driver software. Undersized packets, also known as runts, do not meet requirements for minimum packet sizes, and also indicate potential hardware or driver problems. Packets that end on an illegal boundary do not close properly, and may have been truncated, or affected by hardware or driver problems as well. (See the IEEE 802.3 specifications at *http://www.ieee.org* for more information.)

Many over-the-counter network cards and drivers run in promiscuous mode and are recommended by analyzer manufacturers. In the case of the EtherPeek for Windows demo software included on the CD that accompanies this book, EtherPeek can show errors only when it is used with the special Digital driver supplied with the full version of EtherPeek and a compatible NIC.

The list of compatible network interface cards for EtherPeek for Windows is available from the WildPackets Web site at *http://www.wildpackets.com/support/hardware/etherpeek_win#later*.

 Since this textbook is not focused on data link errors, you do not need to install the EtherPeek driver. You should, however, ensure that you are using a compatible NIC.

Packet Filters

Figure 1-3 shows packets flowing through a **packet filter** that defines the type of packets the analyzer wants to capture. For example, if you are interested in the type of **broadcasts** that are crossing a network, you can set up a filter that allows only broadcast packets to flow into the analyzer. When filters are applied to incoming packets, they are often referred to as **capture filters**, or **pre-filters**.

You can also apply filters to a set of packets *after* it has been captured. This enables you to create subsets of interesting packets that are easier to view than the entire set. For example, if you set up a filter to capture broadcast packets and you do indeed capture 1000 broadcasts, you can apply a second filter (a display filter) based on a specific source address to create a subset of broadcast packets. This may reduce the amount of packets you need to view to a reasonable amount.

Filters can be based on a variety of packet characteristics including, but not limited to:

- Source data link address
- Destination data link address
- Source IP address
- Destination IP address
- Application or process

In Project 1-5 at the end of this chapter, you will create a filter to capture IP-based packets on your network.

Trace Buffer

The packets flow into the analyzer's **trace buffer**, a holding area for packets copied off the network. Typically, this is an area of memory set aside on the analyzer, although some analyzers allow you to configure a "direct to disk" save option. The packets in the trace buffer can be viewed immediately after they are captured, or saved for viewing at a later time.

Many analyzers have a default trace buffer size of 4 MB. This is typically an adequate size for most analysis tasks. Consider how many 64-byte packets can fit into a 4 MB trace buffer.

The EtherPeek for Windows demo software included in this book is limited to a maximum of 250 packets in the trace buffer.

Decodes

Decodes are applied to the packets that are captured into the trace buffer. These decodes enable you to see the packets in a readable format with the packet fields and values interpreted for you. Decodes are packet translation tools.

For example, decodes can separate all the fields of an IP header within a packet, defining the source and destination IP addresses, and the purpose of the packet. Figure 1-4 illustrates the difference between an undecoded view (the lower window) and a decoded view (the upper window).

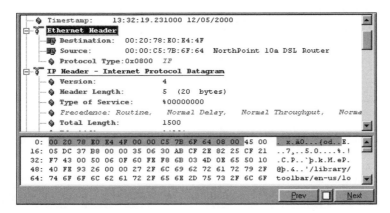

Figure 1-4   Decoded packet (upper window) and undecoded packet (lower window)

Alarms

Many analyzers have a set of configurable **alarms** that indicates unusual network events or errors. The following lists some typical alarms that are included with most analyzer products:

- Excessive broadcasts
- Utilization threshold exceeded
- Request denied
- Server down

Statistics

Many analyzers also display **statistics** on network performance, such as the current packet-per-second rate, or network utilization rates. Network administrators use these statistics to identify gradual changes in network operations, or sudden spikes in network patterns. Figure 1-5 displays an EtherPeek for Windows pie chart that represents the packet size distribution on a network. It is only one example of the network statistics available on an analyzer.

Each analyzer has a different set of capabilities. These elements listed are common elements found in most analyzer solutions. Refer to the analyzer manufacturer Web sites listed in the document *Protocol Analyzer Vendors* on the CD that accompanies this book for more information on analyzer elements.

1

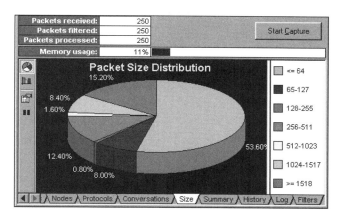

Figure 1-5   Packet Size Distribution pie chart in EtherPeek for Windows

Placing a Protocol Analyzer on a Network

A protocol analyzer can only capture packets that it can see on the network. In some cases, you can place the analyzer on a network close to the device of interest. In other cases, you must reconfigure network devices to ensure the analyzer can capture packets.

On a network that is connected with hubs, you can place the analyzer anywhere on the network. All traffic is forwarded out of all ports on a hubbed network.

On a network that is connected with switches, an analyzer only sees multicast packets, broadcast packets, packets specifically directed to the analyzer device, and the initial packets sent to addresses that do not have ports identified yet (typical during the network startup time). There are basically three options for analyzing switched networks:

- Hubbing out
- Port redirection
- Remote Monitoring (RMON)

Hubbing Out

By placing a hub between a device of interest (such as a server) and the switch, and connecting the analyzer to the hub, you can view all traffic to and from the server.

If you are analyzing a full-duplex communication, you need an additional full-duplex splitter, often referred to as a "tap." This tap effectively duplicates all RX (receive) and TX (transmit) communications down a single RX channel into the analyzer. The Century Taps are an example of full-duplex tap products that can be used with an analyzer. Refer to *http://www.finisar.com/virtual/virtual.php?virtual_id=52* for more information.

Port Redirection

Many switches can be configured to redirect (actually, to copy) the packets traveling through one port to another port. By placing your analyzer on the destination port, you can listen in on all the conversations that cross the network through the port of interest. Switch manufacturers refer to this process as port spanning or port mirroring.

Remote Monitoring (RMON)

RMON uses **Simple Network Management Protocol (SNMP)** to collect traffic data at a remote switch and send the data to a management device. The management device, in turn, decodes the traffic data and can even display entire packet decodes.

Figure 1-6 illustrates the three standard methods for analyzing a switched network.

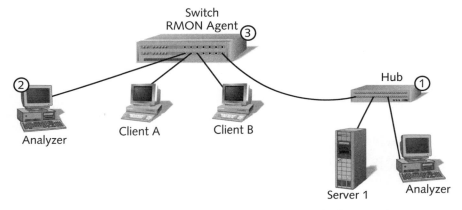

Figure 1-6 Three basic methods of analyzing a switched network

In Figure 1-6, method 1 depicts an analyzer that is hubbed out, method 2 depicts an analyzer capturing packets from a redirected port, and method 3 depicts an RMON Agent loaded on the switch.

For more information on switching technology, refer to *The Switch Book: The Complete Guide to LAN Switching Technology*, by Rich Seifert (John Wiley & Sons; 1st Edition, June 27, 2000; ISBN: 0471345865).

CHAPTER SUMMARY

◻ TCP/IP was designed with the following goals in mind: (1) to support multiple, packet-switched pathways through the network so that transmissions can survive all conceivable failures; (2) to permit dissimilar computer systems to easily exchange data; (3) to offer robust, reliable delivery services for both short- and long-haul communications; and (4) to provide comprehensive network access with global scope. Although it's been revised and changed since its initial implementation, TCP/IP's ongoing success derives in no small part from meeting those goals.

❏ Initial implementations of TCP/IP were funded under the auspices of the Advanced Research Projects Agency (ARPA), a research and development arm of the U.S. Department of Defense (DoD). Until the late 1980s, the ARPANET—which evolved into what we know today as the Internet—remained largely in government hands, supported by government funding. But the DoD's requirement that all communications on ARPANET use TCP/IP, and the more or less simultaneous inclusion of TCP/IP in 4.2BSD UNIX in 1983, helped make TCP/IP and the Internet as nearly synonymous as we think of them today.

❏ Even though the U.S. government no longer has much involvement in the TCP/IP community (other than as yet another interested party), TCP/IP remains in the public domain as an open and collaborative set of standards and best practices. The documents that govern TCP/IP standards and practices are called RFCs, and the process of their creation, development, and approval involves representatives from government, industry, research, and academia. The standards creation and management processes fall within the IETF, and final approval of Internet Standards rests in its parent organization, the IAB. Although the process of creating such standards is rightfully called "rough consensus," this process works well enough to define literally hundreds of protocols and services used every day on the Internet.

❏ As Standard RFCs go through the approval process, they begin life as Proposed Standard documents. After discussion and debate, and demonstration that two or more separate reference implementations can successfully interoperate, RFCs can become Draft Standards. After further discussion and revisions, and approval from the parent working group within the IETF, the Draft is turned over to the IAB for final approval. When the Draft is approved, it becomes a Standard RFC (sometimes called an "Internet Standard").

❏ Another popular type of RFC is an informational (non-standard) RFC called a Best Current Practice, or BCP. Although these documents do not have the force of a Standard RFC, they do provide useful information that represents best approaches to designing, configuring, implementing, or maintaining TCP/IP-based networks and related services. For those reasons, BCPs are highly regarded, and can be useful tools for network administrators seeking to make the most out of their TCP/IP networks.

❏ In general, networking is a big, complex problem that is most easily solved if broken up into a series of smaller, less complex, and interrelated problems. The ISO/OSI network reference model breaks networking into seven distinct layers that allow issues related to hardware, media, and signaling to be separated from issues related to software and services. Likewise, this model permits activities in software to be distinguished on the basis of machine-to-machine communications, handling information delivery from any sender to any receiver, moving large amounts of data across the network, and handling various issues related to ongoing communications, data formats, and application interfaces for network access. TCP/IP uses an older, simpler, four-layer model that lumps the latter three issues into a single application/services layer, but is otherwise very much like the ISO/OSI reference model.

❑ TCP/IP uses a variety of encapsulation techniques at its various layers to label the type of data contained in the contents, or payloads, of its PDUs. TCP/IP also uses numbering techniques to identify well-known protocols at the lower layers (protocol numbers), and to support ready access to well-known applications and services at upper layers (well-known ports). When a client makes a request to a server that requires an ongoing exchange of information, a listening process on the server creates a temporary connection that combines a computer's numeric IP address with a specific port address for the process involved (called a socket address). This ensures that the right process on the right computer may be accessed on both sending and receiving machines.

❑ Protocol analysis is a process whereby a network interface is used to inspect all traffic moving across a segment of network medium. Protocol analyzers are software programs that can manage this task, and can capture not only "healthy" (properly formed) traffic, but also erroneous or ill-formed traffic. This lets protocol analyzers characterize network traffic on a descriptive basis (the protocols used, the active station addresses, the conversations, and the parties involved), and on a statistical basis (percentage of errors, percentage of traffic per protocol, peak loads, low loads, average loads, and so forth). Much of the remaining text depends on putting the topical and theoretical discussions about TCP/IP protocols together with the traces and decodes (formatted contents of packets) to see how theory and practice fit together.

KEY TERMS

4.2BSD — The version of the Berkeley Software Distribution (BSD) of UNIX that was the first to include a TCP/IP implementation.

Acceptable Use Policy (AUP) — A formal policy document that dictates what kinds of online behavior or system use is acceptable to the overall user community.

Address Resolution Protocol (ARP) — This Network layer protocol translates numeric IP addresses into the equivalent MAC layer addresses necessary to transfer frames from one machine to another on the same cable segment or subnet.

addressing — A method of assigning a unique symbolic name or numerical identifier to an individual network interface on a network segment, to make every such interface uniquely identifiable (and addressable).

Advanced Research Projects Agency (ARPA) — An agency within the U.S. Department of Defense that funded forward-thinking research in computing technology.

alarm — Notification of events or errors on the network.

AppleTalk — The native protocol suite for Apple Macintosh computers.

Application layer — The uppermost layer of the ISO/OSI network reference model (and the TCP/IP model) where the interface between the protocol suite and actual applications resides.

application process — A system process that represents a specific type of network application or service.

Archie — A TCP/IP-based archive protocol based on databases of anonymous FTP directories around the Internet, where users can search for content based on filenames and associated titles.

ARPANET — An experimental network, funded by ARPA, designed to test the feasibility of a platform-neutral, long-distance, robust and reliable internetwork that provided the foundation for what we know today as the Internet.

Best Current Practice (BCP) — A specific type of Internet RFC document that outlines the best ways to design, implement, or maintain TCP/IP-based networks.

Bootstrap Protocol (BOOTP) — A Layer 3 or TCP/IP Internet layer protocol designed to permit diskless workstations to obtain network access and an operating system image across the network as they begin booting.

Border Gateway Protocol (BGP) — A widely used routing protocol that connects to common Internet backbones (for example, Internet Service Providers), or other routing domains within the Internet where multiple parties jointly share responsibility for managing traffic.

broadcast — A specific type of network transmission (and address) that is meant to be noticed and read by all recipients on any cable segment where that transmission appears; a way of reaching all addresses on any network.

broadcast packet — A type of network transmission intended for delivery to all devices on the network. The Ethernet broadcast address is 0xFF-FF-FF-FF-FF-FF.

cable segment — Any single collection of network media and attached devices that fits on a single piece of network cable, or within a single network device, such as a hub, or in a virtual equivalent, such as a local area network emulation environment on a switch.

capture filter — A method used to identify specific packets that should be captured into a trace buffer based on some packet characteristic, such as source or destination address.

Carrier Sense Multiple Access with Collision Detection (CSMA/CD) — The formal name for the contention management approach that Ethernet uses, CSMA basically means "listen before attempting to send" (to make sure no later message tramples on an earlier one), and "listen while sending" (to make sure that messages sent at roughly the same time don't collide with one another).

Centre European Researche Nucleaire (CERN) — The European Organization for Nuclear Research, where Tim Berners-Lee invented the protocols and services that defined the World Wide Web between 1989 and 1991.

checkpoint — A point in time at which all system state and information is captured and saved so that subsequent failure in systems or communications can resume at that point in time, with no further loss of data or information.

checksum — A special mathematical value that represents the contents of a message so precisely that any change in the contents will cause a change in the checksum; calculated before and after network transmission of data, then compared—if transmitted and calculated checksums agree, the assumption is that the data arrived unaltered.

Commercial Internet Exchange (CIX) — An early consortium of commercial Internet users that pioneered the extension of Internet use to e-commerce and business communications.

congestion control — A TCP mechanism, also available from other protocols, that permits network hosts to exchange information about their ability to handle traffic volumes, and thereby cause senders to decrease or increase the frequency and size of their upcoming communications.

connectionless — A type of networking protocol that makes no attempt to cause network senders and receivers to exchange information about their availability or ability to communicate with one another; also known as "best-effort delivery."

connection-oriented — A type of networking protocol that relies on explicit communications and negotiations between sender and receiver to manage delivery of data between the two parties.

daemon — Taken from Clerk Maxwell's famous physics idea, a daemon is a computer process whose job is to "listen" for connection attempts for one or more specific network services, and to hand off all valid attempts to temporary connections known as sockets attempts.

data frame — The basic PDU at the Data Link layer, a frame represents what will be transmitted or received as a pattern of bits on a network interface.

datagram — The basic protocol data unit at the TCP/IP Network Access layer. Used by connectionless protocols at the Transport layer, a datagram simply adds a header to the PDU, supplied from whatever Application layer protocol or service uses a connectionless protocol, such as UDP; hence, UDP is also known as a datagram service.

Data Link layer — Layer 2 of the ISO/OSI network reference model, the Data Link layer is responsible for enabling reliable transmission of data through the Physical layer at the sending end, and for checking such reliability upon reception at the receiving end.

data segment — The basic PDU for TCP at the Transport layer. *See also* segment.

decode — The interpreted value of a PDU, or a field within a PDU, performed by a protocol analyzer or similar software package.

decoding — The process of interpreting the fields and contents of a packet, and presenting the packet in a readable format.

Defense Information Systems Agency (DISA) — The agency within the DoD that took over operation of the Internet when ARPA surrendered its control in 1983.

demultiplexing — The process of breaking up a single stream of incoming packets on a computer, and directing its components to the various active TCP/IP processes based on socket addresses in the TCP or UDP headers.

destination port number — The port address for an incoming TCP/IP communication that identifies the target application or service process involved.

display filters — Filters that are applied to the packets that reside in a trace buffer for the purpose of viewing only the packets of interest.

divide and conquer — A computer design approach that consists of decomposing a big, hairy problem into a series of smaller, less-complex and interrelated problems, each of which can be solved more or less independently of the others.

domain — The name of a first-level entry in the domain name hierarchy, such as *ibm.com*, *lanw.com*, or *podbooks.com*.

Draft Standard — A Standard RFC that has gone through the draft process, been approved, and for which two reference implementations must be shown to work together before it can move on to Internet Standard status.

dynamically assigned port address — A temporary TCP or UDP port number allocated to permit a client and server to exchange data with each other only as long as their connection remains active.

Dynamic Host Configuration Protocol (DHCP) — A TCP/IP-based network service and Application layer protocol that supports leasing and delivery of TCP/IP addresses and related configuration information to clients that would otherwise require static assignment of such information. For that reason, DHCP is a profound convenience for network users and administrators both.

encapsulation — The enclosure of data from an upper-layer protocol between a header and an (optional) trailer for the current layer, to identify sender and receiver, and possibly, to include data integrity check information.

Ethernet — A network access protocol based on carrier sense, multiple access, and collision detection.

Ethernet collision fragments — The garbled traffic on a network produced when two packets transmitted at about the same time collide, resulting in a hodgepodge of signals.

File Transfer Protocol (FTP) — A TCP/IP Application layer service and protocol designed to facilitate transfer of files between a client and a server across a network.

frame — The basic PDU at the Data Link layer of the ISO/OSI reference model.

Groper — A TCP/IP Application layer protocol and service that provides access to various types of indexed text and other types of data online, which predates the Web, and presents its contents as a hierarchically structured list of files.

header — That portion of a PDU that precedes the actual content for the PDU, and usually identifies sender and receiver, protocols in use, and other information necessary to establish context for senders and receivers.

Historic Standard — An Internet RFC that was superseded by a newer, more current version.

host — TCP/IP terminology for any computer that possesses one or more valid TCP/IP addresses (and hence, is reachable on a TCP/IP-based network). A host can also be a computer that offers TCP/IP services to clients.

Hypertext Transfer Protocol (HTTP) — The TCP/IP Application layer protocol and service that supports access to the World Wide Web.

IEEE 802 — A project undertaken by the IEEE in 1980 that covers Physical and Data Link layers for networking technologies in general (802.1 and 802.2), plus specific networking technologies, such as Ethernet (802.3) and token ring (802.5), among others.

Institute for Electrical and Electronic Engineers (IEEE) — An international organization that sets standards for all kinds of electrical and electronic equipment, including network interfaces and communications technologies.

International Standards Organization (ISO) — An international standards organization based in Geneva, Switzerland that sets standards for information technology and networking equipment, protocols, and communications technologies.

International Standards Organization Open Systems Interconnection — *See* International Standards Organization *and* Open Systems Interconnection.

Internet Architecture Board (IAB) — The organization within the Internet Society that governs the actions of both the IETF and the IRTF, and has final approval authority for Internet Standards.

Internet Control Message Protocol (ICMP) — A Layer 3 (Internetwork layer) TCP/IP protocol used to exchange information about network traffic conditions, congestion, and reachability of specific network addresses.

Internet Corporation for Assigned Names and Numbers (ICANN) — The organization within the Internet Society that is responsible for proper assignment of all domain names and numeric IP addresses for the global Internet; works in tandem with private companies called name registrars to manage domain names, and with ISPs to manage assignment of numeric IP addresses.

Internet Engineering Task Force (IETF) — The organization within the Internet Society that's responsible for all currently used Internet standards, protocols, and services; and for managing the development and maintenance of Internet Requests for Comment (RFCs).

Internet Message Access Protocol (IMAP) — A TCP/IP-based messaging protocol that allows users to maintain customized message stores on an e-mail server, yet access and manage their e-mail messages on any workstation.

Internet Network Information Center (InterNIC) — A quasi-governmental agency that was responsible for assigned names and numbers on the Internet (this responsibility now falls on ICANN).

Internet Protocol (IP) — The primary Network layer protocol in the TCP/IP protocol suite, IP manages routing and delivery of most real data on TCP/IP-based networks.

1

Internet Protocol version 4 (IPv4) — The current version of IP that's in broadest public use at present (a new version IPv6 is currently under development and partly specified, but not yet widely deployed).

Internet Research Task Force (IRTF) — The forward-looking research and development arm of the Internet Society, the IRTF reports into the IAB for direction and governance.

Internet Societal Task Force (ISTF) — The arm of the Internet Society charged with evaluating the societal impact of Internet access, and with making sure that underprivileged or underserved communities can benefit from Internet access as much as possible.

Internet Society (ISOC) — The parent organization under which the rest of the Internet governing bodies fall, ISOC is a user-oriented, public-access organization that solicits end-user participation and input to help set future Internet policy and direction.

Internet Standard — A RFC document that specifies the rules, structure, and behavior of a current Internet protocol or service.

Internetwork Packet Exchange/Sequenced Packet Exchange (IPX/SPX) — The protocol suite associated with earlier implementations of Novell's NetWare network operating system; TCP/IP has largely supplanted IPX/SPX on most modern networks.

ISO/OSI network reference model — The official name for the seven-layer network reference model often used to describe how networks operate and behave.

layer — A single component or facet in a networking model that handles one particular aspect of network access or communications.

local area network (LAN) — A single network cable segment, subnet, or logical network community that represents a collection of machines that can communicate with one another more or less directly (using MAC addresses).

maximum transmission unit (MTU) — The biggest single chunk of data that can be transferred across any particular type of network medium (1518 bytes is the MTU for conventional Ethernet, for example).

Media Access Control (MAC) address — A special type of network address, handled by a sublayer of the Data Link layer, that's normally preassigned on a per-interface basis to uniquely identify each such interface on any network cable segment (or virtual facsimile). ICANN controls assignment of vendor IDs and interface numbers to make sure all such addresses are guaranteed to be unique. When IP frames are transferred from one interface to another, the MAC layer addresses for the sender and receiver are used to effect the transfer.

media flow control — The management of data transmission rates between two devices across a local network medium that guarantees the receiver can accept and process input before it arrives from the sender.

multicast packet — A packet sent to a group of devices, such as a group of routers.

multiplexing — The process whereby multiple individual data streams from Application layer processes are joined together for transmission by a specific TCP/IP transport protocol through the IP protocol.

National Center for Supercomputing Applications (NCSA) — An arm of the University of Illinois at Champaign-Urbana, where supercomputer research is undertaken, and where the first graphical Web browser, Mosaic, was developed and released in 1994.

National Science Foundation (NSF) — A U.S. government agency charged with oversight and support for government-funded scientific research and development. *See also* NSFNET.

NetBIOS Enhanced User Interface (NetBEUI) — An implementation of NetBIOS protocols and services undertaken by IBM, 3Com, and Microsoft in the 1980s, still used for basic networking in a variety of Microsoft, IBM, and other operating systems.

network analysis — The same as protocol analysis, but a less intimidating term.

Network Basic Input/Output System (NetBIOS) — A high-level set of network protocols and services, developed by Sytek Corporation for IBM in the mid-1980s, that is still widely used in IBM, Microsoft, and other network operating systems.

Network File System (NFS) — A TCP/IP-based, network-distributed file system that permits users to incorporate files and directories on machines across a network to be treated as an extension of their local desktop file systems.

network interface card (NIC) — A hardware device used to permit a computer to attach to and communicate with a local area network.

Network layer — The Network layer operates at Layer 3 of the ISO/OSI network reference model; it handles the logical addresses associated with individual machines on a network by correlating human-readable names for such machines with unique, machine-readable numeric addresses. It also uses addressing information to determine how to send a PDU from a sender to a receiver when the source and destination do not reside on the same physical network segment.

network reference model — *See* ISO/OSI network reference model.

network services — A generic TCP/IP term for a protocol/service combination that operates at the Application layer in the TCP/IP network model.

NSFNET — A public network operated by the National Science Foundation in the 1980s to support the Internet backbone.

Open Shortest Path First (OSPF) Protocol — A sophisticated Layer 3 or TCP/IP Internet layer routing protocol that uses link-state information to construct routing topologies for local internetworks, and provides load-balancing capabilities. (See Chapter 10 for a complete explanation of this routing protocol.)

Open Systems Interconnection (OSI) — The name of an open-standard internetworking initiative undertaken in the 1980s, primarily in Europe, and originally intended to supersede TCP/IP. Technical and political problems prevented this anticipated outcome from materializing, but the ISO/OSI reference model remains an enduring legacy of this effort.

1

oversized packets — Packets that exceed the MTU for the network, and usually point to a problem with a NIC or its driver software.

packet — A generic term for a PDU at just about any layer in a networking model, this term is most properly applied to PDUs at Layer 3, or the TCP/IP Internet layer.

packet filter — A specific collection of inclusion or exclusion rules to be applied to a stream of network packets that determines what is captured (and what is ignored) from the original input stream.

packet header — *See* header.

Packet Internetwork Groper (PING) — A TCP/IP Internet layer protocol that's used to determine reachability of a remote host, and to measure round-trip travel time when sending data from a sender to a receiver.

packet-switched network — A network in which data packets may take any usable path between sender and receiver, where sender and receiver are identified by unique network addresses, and there's no requirement that all packets follow the same path in transit (though they often do).

packet trailer — *See* trailer.

payload — That portion of a PDU that contains information intended for delivery to an application or to a higher-layer protocol (depending on where in the stack the PDU is situated).

peer layer — Analogous layers in the protocol stacks on a sender and a receiver, the receiving layer usually reverses whatever operations the sending layer performs (which is what makes those layers peers).

Physical layer — Layer 1 in the ISO/OSI network reference model, the Physical layer is where connections, communications, and interfaces—hardware and signaling requirements—are handled.

Point-to-Point Protocol (PPP) — A Layer 2 or TCP/IP Network Interface layer protocol that permits a client and a server to establish a communications link that can accommodate a variety of higher-layer protocols, including IP, AppleTalk, SNA, IPX/SPX, NetBEUI, and many others; today's most widely used serial line protocol for making Internet connections.

point-to-point transmission — A type of network communication where pairs of devices establish a communications link to exchange data with one another; the most common type of connection used when communicating with an Internet Service Provider.

Point-to-Point Tunneling Protocol (PPTP) — A Layer 2 or TCP/IP Network Interface layer protocol that permits a client and a server to establish a secure, encrypted communications link that can accommodate just about any kind of PPP traffic.

port address — *See* port number.

port number — A 16-bit number that identifies either a well-known application service, or a dynamically assigned port number for a transitory sender-receiver exchange of data through TCP or UDP.

Post Office Protocol version 3 (POP3) — A TCP/IP Application layer protocol that supports client downloads of incoming e-mail addresses from an e-mail server to e-mail client software. When using POP3, clients normally manage e-mail messages on their desktop machines.

pre-filter — A type of data filter applied to a raw input stream in a protocol analyzer that selects only packets that meet its criteria for capture and retention; since this filter is applied before data is captured, it's called a pre-filter.

Presentation layer — Layer 6 of the ISO/OSI reference model, the Presentation layer is where generic network data formats are translated into platform-specific data formats for incoming data, and vice versa for outgoing data. This is also the layer where optional encryption or compression services may be applied (or reversed).

Process layer — A synonym for the TCP/IP Application layer, where high-level protocols and services, such as FTP and Telnet, operate.

promiscuous mode operation — Network interface card and driver operation used to capture broadcast packets, multicast packets, packets sent to other devices, as well as error packets.

Proposed Standard — An intermediate level for standards-track RFCs, where a Draft Standard goes through initial review, and has two or more reference implementations built to demonstrate interoperability between implementations.

protocol — A precise set of standards that governs communications between computers on a network. Many protocols function in one or more layers of the OSI reference model.

protocol analysis — The process of capturing packets off the network for the purpose of gathering communication statistics, observing trends, and examining communication sequences.

protocol data unit (PDU) — At any layer in a networking model, a PDU represents the package for data at that layer, including a header and a payload, and in some cases, a trailer.

protocol number — An 8-bit numeric identifier associated with some specific TCP/IP protocol.

protocol stack — A specific implementation of a protocol suite on a computer, including a network interface, necessary drivers, and whatever protocol and service implementations are necessary to enable the computer to use a specific protocol suite to communicate across the network.

protocol suite — A named family of networking protocols, such as TCP/IP, IPX/SPX, or NetBEUI, where each such family enables computers to communicate across a network.

reassembly — The process applied at the Transport layer where messages segmented into multiple chunks for transmission across the network are put back together in the proper order for delivery to an application on the receiving end. The IP Fragment Offset field (discussed in Chapter 3) is used to identify the order of the fragments for reassembly.

registered port — A TCP or UDP port number in the range from 1024 to 65,535 and associated with a specific Application layer protocol or service. IANA maintains a registered port number list at *http://www.iana.org*.

Remote Monitoring (RMON) — A TCP/IP Application layer protocol designed to support remote monitoring and management of networking devices, such as hubs, servers, and routers.

Request for Comment (RFC) — An IETF standards document that specifies or describes best practices, provides information about the Internet, or specifies an Internet protocol or service.

Retired Standard — An RFC that has reached Standard designation, but that is no longer current, and has been replaced by a newer RFC.

Reverse Address Resolution Protocol (RARP) — A Layer 2 or TCP/IP Network Access protocol that translates numeric IP addresses into MAC layer addresses (usually to verify that the identity claimed by a sender matches its real identity). This protocol was superceded by DHCP.

routing — The process whereby a packet makes its way from a sender to a receiver based on known path (or routes) from the sending network to the receiving network.

Routing Information Protocol (RIP) — A simple, vector-based TCP/IP networking protocol used to determine a single pathway between a sender and a receiver on a local internetwork.

runts — *See* undersized packets.

segment — The name of the PDU for the TCP protocol in a TCP/IP environment.

segmentation — The process whereby TCP takes a large message that exceeds an underlying network medium's MTU, and breaks it up into a numbered sequence of chunks that are less than or equal to the MTU in size.

Serial Line Internet Protocol (SLIP) — An IP-only serial line protocol still used to access some UNIX systems. SLIP was once the primary serial protocol used to connect point-to-point, via a modem or other access device, from a user machine or a local network to another local network, service provider, or user machine. SLIP supports only TCP/IP protocols and offers only basic delimitation services. That's why it's no longer widely used for Internet connections.

session — A temporary, but ongoing exchange of messages between a sender and a receiver on a network; also, the name of the ISO/OSI reference model layer that manages such message exchanges.

Session layer — Layer 5 in the ISO/OSI reference model, the Session layer handles setup, maintenance, and tear-down of ongoing exchanges of messages between pairs of hosts on a network.

Simple Mail Transfer Protocol (SMTP) — A TCP/IP Application layer protocol that handles transmission of e-mail messages from clients to servers, and message routing from a source server to a destination server.

Simple Network Management Protocol (SNMP) — A TCP/IP Application layer protocol that provides basic network device registration and management capabilities.

socket — *See* socket address.

socket address — A numeric TCP/IP address that concatenates a network host's numeric IP address (first four bytes) with the port address for some specific process or service on that host (last two bytes) to uniquely identify that process across the entire Internet.

source port number — The port address for the sender of a TCP or UDP PDU.

Standard — An RFC that is officially approved as a specification for a particular protocol or service is called an Internet Standard, or a Standard RFC.

statistics — Short- or long-term historical information regarding network communications and performance, as captured by a protocol analyzer or other, similar software.

Systems Network Architecture (SNA) — The name of a protocol suite developed by IBM for use in its proprietary mainframe- and minicomputer-based networking environments.

Telnet — A TCP/IP Application layer protocol and service that permits a client on one network host to interact with another network host as if the machine were a terminal attached to the other machine.

trace buffer — An area of memory or hard disk space set aside for the storage of packets captured off the network by a protocol analyzer.

trailer — An optional, concluding portion of a PDU that usually contains some kind of data integrity check information for the preceding content of that PDU.

Transmission Control Protocol (TCP) — A robust, reliable, connection-oriented protocol that operates at the Transport layer in both the TCP/IP and ISO/OSI reference models, and that gives TCP/IP part of its name.

Transmission Control Protocol/Internet Protocol (TCP/IP) — The name of the standard protocols and services in use on the Internet, denoted by the names of two of its key constituent protocols: the Transmission Control Protocol, or TCP, and the Internet Protocol, or IP.

Transport layer — Layer 4 of the ISO/OSI network reference model and the third layer of the TCP/IP network model, the Transport layer handles delivery of data from sender to receiver.

undersized packets — Packets that are below minimum packet size requirements, and point to potential hardware or driver problems.

unicast packet — A packet sent to a single device on the network.

Uniform Resource Locator (URL) — Web terminology for the address that specifies the protocol (http://), location (domain name), directory (/directory-name/), and filename (example.html) to request a Web browser to access the resource.

User Datagram Protocol (UDP) — A connectionless, best-effort transport protocol in the TCP/IP protocol suite, UDP operates as an alternative to TCP.

Virtual Private Network (VPN) — A network connection (containing one or more packaged protocols) between a specific sender and receiver, in which the information sent is often encrypted. A VPN uses public networks—such as the Internet—to deliver secure, private information from a sender to a receiver.

well-known port address — *See* well-known port number.

well-known port number — A 16-bit number that identifies a preassigned value associated with some well-known Internet protocol or service that operates at the TCP/IP Application layer. Most well-known port numbers fall in the range from 0 to 1024, but IANA (see *http://www.iana.org*) also documents registered port numbers above that range that behave likewise.

well-known protocol — An 8-bit number that appears in the header of an IP packet and identifies the protocol in use, as per IANA (see *http://www.iana.org*).

well-known service — A synonym for a recognizable TCP/IP protocol or service, these assignments are documented at the IANA site (*http://www.iana.org*).

Wide Area Information Service (WAIS) — A TCP/IP Application layer protocol and service designed to provide search access to a variety of document formats, including text, word-processing, database, and other specific file formats.

X.25 — A popular standard for packet-switched data networks originally defined by the International Telephony Union (ITU), and widely used for data communications networks outside North America.

REVIEW QUESTIONS

1. Which of the following items represent design goals that motivated the development of TCP/IP? (Choose all that apply.)

   a. robust network architecture

   b. reliable delivery mechanisms

   c. permit dissimilar systems to exchange data

   d. support for long-haul connections

   e. high performance

2. What is the name of the version of IP that is most widely used today?

   a. IPv1

   b. IPv2

   c. IPv4

   d. IPv6

3. Which of the following milestone events for TCP/IP occurred in 1983? (Choose all that apply.)

   a. NSF launches the NSFNET.

   b. The Department of Defense mandates TCP/IP as the "official ARPANET protocol."

   c. TCP/IP appears in the 4.2BSD UNIX distribution.

   d. Initial development of name server technology occurs.

4. Which of the following organizations develops and maintains RFCs?

   a. ISOC

   b. IAB

   c. IRTF

   d. IETF

5. Which of the following organizations manages Internet domain names and network addresses?

   a. ICANN

   b. IETF

   c. IRTF

   d. ISOC

6. What is the title of RFC 2700?

   a. Index of Official Protocols

   b. Index of Internet Official Protocols

   c. Internet Official Protocol Standards

   d. The Internet Standards Process

7. Which of the following steps must a Standard RFC go through to become an official standard? (Choose all that apply, and list them in the correct order of occurrence.)

   a. Draft Standard

   b. Historic Standard

   c. Proposed Standard

   d. Retired Standard

   e. Standard (sometimes called "Internet Standard")

8. A Best Current Practice (BCP) RFC is a special form of Standard RFC. True or false?

   a. True

   b. False

9. List the seven layers of the ISO/OSI network reference model in ascending order, starting with Layer 1.

   a. Application

   b. Data Link

   c. Network

   d. Physical

   e. Presentation

   f. Session

   g. Transport

1

10. Which of the following statements represent benefits of a layered approach to networking? (Choose all that apply.)

    a. takes a big problem and breaks it into a series of smaller interrelated problems

    b. allows individual layers to be insulated from one another

    c. permits expertise to be applied from different disciplines for different layers

    d. permits hardware issues to be kept separate from software issues

11. Which terms represent parts of a PDU that are always present in any PDU? (Choose all that apply.)

    a. header

    b. payload

    c. checksum

    d. trailer

12. Which of the following components operate at the Physical layer? (Choose all that apply.)

    a. network interface cards (NICs)

    b. segmentation and reassembly

    c. connectors

    d. cables

13. What is the common name for PDUs at the Data Link layer?

    a. frames

    b. packets

    c. segments

    d. Data Link PDUs

14. What functions does the Session layer provide?

    a. segmentation and reassembly

    b. session setup, maintenance, and tear-down

    c. checkpoint controls

    d. data format conversions

15. Which of the following TCP/IP network model layers maps most nearly to single layers in the ISO/OSI network reference model?

    a. TCP/IP Network Access layer

    b. TCP/IP Internet layer

    c. TCP/IP Transport layer

    d. TCP/IP Application layer

16. Which of the following two TCP/IP protocols operate at the TCP/IP Transport layer?

    a. ARP

    b. PPP

    c. TCP

    d. UDP

    e. XNET

17. In UNIX terminology, a listener process that operates on a server to handle incoming requests for services is called a _____.

    a. listener

    b. monitor

    c. daemon

    d. service

18. The process of combining multiple outgoing protocol streams at the Transport and Networks layers in TCP/IP is called _____.

    a. folding

    b. multiplexing

    c. unfolding

    d. demultiplexing

19. On any system, only those protocol numbers for protocols that are actually in use must be defined on that system. True or false?

    a. True

    b. False

20. The purpose of a TCP/IP port number is to identify which aspect of a system's operation for incoming and outgoing protocol data?

    a. Network layer protocol in use

    b. Transport layer protocol in use

    c. sending or receiving application process

    d. none of the above

21. Which of the following terms is a synonym for a dynamically assigned port address, used to service a temporary TCP/IP connection for data exchange?

    a. protocol number

    b. well-known port address

    c. registered port address

    d. socket address

22. Which of the following activities may occur during the protocol analysis process? (Choose all that apply.)

    a. yapping into network communications

    b. capturing packets "off the wire"

    c. gathering statistics

    d. decoding packets into readable form

    e. retransmitting captured packets for testing

23. Why is promiscuous mode operation important for protocol analysis?

    a. It isn't.

    b. It allows the protocol analyzer to capture and inspect all traffic on the network medium, including errors and malformed packets.

    c. It bypasses normal packet-level security on a network.

    d. It enables the protocol analyzer to gather statistics.

24. A packet filter that's applied to incoming data in a protocol analyzer may be called a _____. (Choose all that apply.)

    a. capture filter

    b. data filter

    c. pre-filter

    d. post-filter

25. Which of the following features are typical for most protocol analyzers? (Choose all that apply.)

    a. Packet filters may be applied to incoming data before capture, or to stored data after capture.

    b. Decodes may be applied to packets in the trace buffer.

    c. Alarms may be set to flag unusual network events or conditions.

    d. They display various statistical reports and graphs based on traffic analysis.

    e. They include built-in trend analysis and capacity-planning tools.

HANDS-ON PROJECTS

Project 1-1

The following Hands-on Projects assume that you are working in a Windows 2000 environment.

To manually install the EtherPeek for Windows demo software:

Before installing the software, ensure that you meet all the system requirements as listed in the *Installation.txt* file contained in the *\Analyzers\Ether* directory on the CD that accompanies this book.

1. Insert the CD-ROM included with this book in your CD-ROM drive.
2. Double-click the **My Computer** icon.
3. Double-click the **CD-ROM** drive icon.
4. Double-click the **Ether** folder icon.
5. Double-click the **epwdemo.exe** file.
6. After the WinZip Self-Extractor window appears, click **Setup**. The InstallShield Wizard runs.
7. Click **Next** on the Welcome screen.
8. In the installation Notes screen, read the pre-installation notes and click **Next**.
9. The User Information screen appears. Enter your name and company name, and then click **Next**.
10. The Choose Destination Location screen appears. Click **Next** to accept the default application destination (C:\Program Files\WildPackets\EtherPeek Demo).
11. If a previous version of the EtherPeek for Windows demo was installed, an uninstall window appears. Click **Yes** to uninstall any previous versions of the EtherPeek for Windows demo, and then click **OK** when you are notified that the Uninstall process was successfully completed.
12. In the Start Copying Files screen, click **Back** if you need to change any settings. If not, click **Next**.
13. In the Setup Complete screen, you are prompted to view the *readme.txt* file or start the EtherPeek demo. Clear both check boxes, and click **Finish**. The EtherPeek for Windows demo software is installed.

Project 1-2

To start the EtherPeek for Windows demo program:

1. Click **Start**, point to **Programs**, and then click **WildPackets EtherPeek Demo**. The list of EtherPeek demo limitations appears. Click **OK**.

2. If the Select Adapter window appears, click the adapter installed in your system. Click **OK**.

3. Leave the EthernetPeek Demo window open if you are continuing on to Hands-on Project 1-3.

Project 1-3

To capture basic packets:

1. Follow the steps in Project 1-2 to launch the EtherPeek for Windows demo program if it is not already open.

2. Click the **Capture** menu, and click **Start Capture**.

3. The Capture Options window appears. Click **OK** to accept the default buffer size of 1024 kilobytes.

4. The Capture window appears. The Capture window number increments each time you start a new capture process. Click the **Start Capture** button in the Capture window. If no traffic shows up in the Capture window, follow Steps 5 through 9 to generate some packets from your workstation. The Capture window is only active for 30 seconds in the demo. If you do not complete Steps 5 through 9 within 30 seconds, close the Capture window, and follow Steps 1 through 4 again.

5. Click **Start**, point to **Programs**, point to **Accessories**, and then click **Command Prompt**. A Command Prompt window opens.

6. Type **ftp server1**, and then press **Enter**. Assuming you do not have an FTP server named server1, your request fails.

7. Type **quit**, and press **Enter** to exit the FTP program.

8. Type **exit**, and press **Enter** to close the Command Prompt window.

9. The demo automatically stops capturing after 30 seconds. If the demo is still capturing, click the **Stop Capture** button to stop the capture process. Otherwise, click **OK** in the capture stopped notification message box.

10. Proceed immediately to the next project.

Project 1-4

This project assumes you followed the steps in Hands-on Project 1-3, and the EtherPeek for Windows demo program is open.

To explore basic packets and statistics:

1. The Capture window now displays the basic information about the packets you captured. Click the **down scroll arrow** to view the entire list of packets (if they

scroll out of view). Click and drag the Capture window handles so you can view more packets, if desired.

2. Click the **Nodes** tab at the bottom of the Capture window to view the list of devices for which the EtherPeek analyzer captured packets. Do you recognize your IP addresses? Do you see any broadcast address?

3. Click the **Protocols** tab at the bottom of the Capture window to view the protocols identified by EtherPeek.

4. Click the **Conversations** tab at the bottom of the Capture window to view the conversations identified by EtherPeek. Highlight the lines that contain the value *Ethernet Broadcast* in the Net Node 2 column. View the associated values in the Net Node 1 field to identify the MAC addresses of the workstations that sent those broadcast packets to the network.

5. Click the **Size** tab at the bottom of the Capture window to view the packet size distribution of the packets in the trace buffer. Packet sizes are listed in bytes. Which packet size is most common in your trace buffer?

6. Click the **Summary** tab at the bottom of the Capture window to view the summary of information about the trace buffer contents. Scroll through the summary to identify the type of communications seen in the trace buffer.

7. Click the **History** tab at the bottom of the Capture window to view the Utilization graph created by EtherPeek for the time you captured data.

8. Click the **Log** tab at the bottom of the Capture window to view the EtherPeek Capture Log.

9. Close the Capture window by clicking the **Close** button in the upper-right corner. You'll focus on the Filter tab in the next project.

Project 1-5

To create a basic filter for IP traffic:

1. Follow the steps in Project 1-2 to start the EtherPeek for Windows demo program if it is not already open.

2. Click **Capture**, and then click **Start Capture** from the menu bar.

3. The Capture Options window appears. Click **OK** to accept the default buffer size of 1024 kilobytes.

4. The Capture window appears. Click the **Filters** tab to view available pre-built filters included with the EtherPeek product.

The EtherPeek for Windows demo software allows only five captures during each launch. If you receive an error message indicating that the software will not open another Capture window, simply close the EtherPeek program, and reopen it.

1

5. Click the **Broadcast** check box. This sets a filter for all packets sent to the broadcast Ethernet address (0xFF-FF-FF-FF-FF-FF).

6. Click the **Start Capture** button to begin capturing broadcast packets.

7. Click the **Packets** tab at the bottom of the Capture window to view the packets captured in this process. Examine the types of broadcasts identified in the Protocol column. When the *Capture has been stopped* message appears, click **OK**.

   If no broadcast packets appear in the Packets window, follow Steps 8 through 11 to generate traffic from the Command Prompt window.

8. Click **Start**, point to **Programs**, point to **Accessories**, and then click **Command Prompt**. A Command Prompt window opens.

9. Type **ftp server1**, and then press **Enter**. Assuming you do not have an FTP server named server1, your request fails.

10. Type **quit,** and press **Enter** to exit the FTP program.

11. Type **exit**, and press **Enter** to close the Command Prompt window. If you proceed immediately to the next project, skip Step 1.

Project 1-6

To examine a complete packet decode:

1. Follow the steps in Project 1-3 or Project 1-5 to capture some packets using the EtherPeek for Windows demo program.

2. Click the **Packets** tab at the bottom of the Capture window to view the list of packets captured by EtherPeek.

3. Double-click any packet in the Capture window to open the packet decode window. Resize the top portion of the window (the full decode portion) and the bottom portion of the window (the hexadecimal window), as necessary.

4. Click the **Ethernet Header** label in the upper portion of the decode window. Note that the corresponding area in the undecoded packet is highlighted in the lower portion of the decode window.

5. Scroll through the full decode portion to examine the entire contents of the packet fully decoded.

6. When finished, close the EtherPeek for Windows demo program.

CASE PROJECTS

1. You are asked to visit a small law firm to help troubleshoot some network connectivity problems. The law firm's network consists of 11 workstations connected by a single 24-port hub. A senior partner describes the problem as "consistent," and explains that every morning there is a five-minute delay to connect to the main server on the network. The senior partner indicates that every user on the network has the same problems. Of course, you brought your protocol analyzer. Where should you tap into this network?

2. Your company just bought a new subsidiary based in Des Moines, IA. While your local operation already uses TCP/IP for local networking and Internet access, the new subsidiary uses Novell NetWare 4.0 with IPX/SPX protocols for local access, and the IPX-to-IP gateway to access the Internet. What kinds of arguments might you use to persuade your colleagues in Des Moines to switch their network to TCP/IP?

3. Describe a method you can use to determine which IP protocols are in use on your network so you can define the minimum possible protocol list for your UNIX machines.

4. Explain why excessive occurrences of errors can be bad for a network. Likewise, explain why excessive broadcast traffic may have negative consequences.

CHAPTER

2

IP ADDRESSING AND RELATED TOPICS

After reading this chapter and completing the exercises you will be able to:

♦ Understand IP addressing, anatomy and structures, and addresses from a computer's point of view

♦ Recognize and describe the various IP address classes from A to E, and explain how they're composed and used

♦ Understand the nature of IP address limitations, and how techniques like Classless Inter-Domain Routing and Network Address Translation ease those limitations

♦ Define the terms *subnet* and *supernet*, and apply your knowledge of how subnets and supernets work to solve specific network design problems

♦ Understand how public and private Internet addresses are assigned, how to obtain them, and how to use them properly

♦ Recognize the importance and value of an IP addressing scheme

This chapter covers the structure and function of IP (Internet Protocol) addresses—those arcane four-number sequences that look like 24.29.72.3, but which uniquely identify all network interfaces that use TCP/IP on the entire Internet. As you come to understand and appreciate IP addresses, you will learn how they are constructed, the classes into which they may (or may not) be relegated, and what roles these addresses play as traffic finds its way around a network. In fact, you will learn to identify how many devices can be attached to a network based on the structure of its IP address, and how to manipulate this structure to subdivide or aggregate addresses to meet specific connectivity needs.

IP Addressing Basics

Although human beings prefer **symbolic names**—for instance, we think it's easier to remember a string, such as *www.course.com,* than a **numeric address**, such as 199.95.72.8—computers are the opposite. They deal with **network addresses** in the form of bit patterns that translate into decimal numbers. Thus, what we express as 199.95.72.8 in decimal notation, a computer "sees" as: 11000111010111101001000000001000.

This helps to explain why IP uses a three-part addressing scheme, as follows:

- *Symbolic:* This consists of names that take a particular form, such as *support.dell.com,* or *mercury.kherson.ua.* As it happens, these names are called **domain names**. To be valid, any domain name must correspond to at least one unique **numeric IP address**. But domain names only point to numeric addresses; they are not the same as such addresses. Nevertheless, domain names are very important because they are what most people remember and use to identify specific hosts on the Internet (and on their own networks). You'll learn a lot more about domain names in Chapter 7 of this book, as you learn about the **Domain Name System (DNS)** and the related protocols and services that make it possible to translate symbolic domain names and numeric IP addresses.

- *Logical numeric:* This consists of a set of four numbers, separated by periods, as in 172.16.1.10. Each of these four numbers must be smaller than 256 in decimal to be represented in eight binary digits, or bits. This puts the range for each number between zero and 255, which are the lowest and highest values that can be represented in an 8-bit string. You're probably used to referring to such 8-bit numbers as *bytes,* but the TCP/IP community likes to call them **octets** (which means the same thing). Most of what we talk about in this chapter concentrates on how to read, understand, classify, use, and manipulate logical numeric addresses.

  It's also important to understand that numeric IP addresses (which is how most people refer to those four-number dotted strings) are logical network addresses. Each numeric IP address functions at the Network layer of the ISO/OSI network reference model (or the Internet layer of the TCP/IP network model, if you prefer) to assign a unique set of numbers to each and every network interface on a network (and across the entire Internet, in fact, for all machines visible on that network). To describe this form of IP address, numeric IP addresses use what is formally called **dotted decimal notation** (four numbers separated by periods, or dots).

- *Physical numeric:* This consists of a 6-byte numeric address, burned into firmware (on a chip) by network interface manufacturers. The first three bytes (known as the **organizationally unique identifier**, or **OUI**) identify the manufacturer of whatever interface is in use; the final three bytes provide another unique numeric identifier that causes any interface on a network to have a unique **physical numeric address**.

2

The physical numeric address functions at a sublayer of the Data Link layer in the OSI network reference model, called the **Media Access Control (MAC) layer**. For that reason, it's also known as a MAC layer address (or MAC address). Although there's more to it than this explanation suggests, it is the job of the Logical Link Control (LLC) sublayer in the Data Link layer software (usually at the driver level) to enable the network interface to establish a point-to-point connection with another network interface on the same physical cable segment. ARP (Address Resolution Protocol) is used to permit computers to translate numeric IP addresses to MAC layer addresses, and RARP (Reverse ARP) is used to translate MAC layer addresses to numeric IP addresses.

For the remainder of this chapter though, you'll concentrate on numeric IP addresses. But it's important to remember that IP addresses have links to domain names to make it possible for users to identify and access resources on a network. It's also important to recognize that when actual network communication occurs, IP addresses are translated into MAC layer addresses so that a specific network interface is identified as the sender, and another specific network interface is identified as the receiver, for all such communications.

In keeping with the layered nature of network models, it makes sense to associate the MAC layer address with the Data Link layer (or the TCP/IP Network Access layer, if you prefer to think in terms of that model), and to associate IP addresses with the Network layer (or the TCP/IP Internet layer). At the Data Link layer, one network interface arranges a transfer of frames from itself to another network interface, so all communications occur on the same physical or local network.

As data moves through intermediate hosts between the original sender and the ultimate receiver, it does so between pairs of machines, where each pair resides on the same physical network. Obviously, most of these machines must be attached to multiple physical networks so that what enters that machine on one interface can leave it on another interface, thereby moving from one physical network to another. This basically represents a series of interface-to-interface connections that move the data from MAC address to MAC address at the Data Link layer.

At the Network layer, the original sender's address is represented in the IP source address field in the IP packet header, and the ultimate recipient's address is represented in the IP destination address field in the same IP packet header. Even though MAC layer addresses change all the time, as a frame moves from interface to interface, the IP source and destination address information is preserved. The IP destination address value, in fact, is what drives the sometimes-long series of intermediate transfers, or **hops**, which occur as data makes its way across a network from sender to receiver.

ANATOMY OF AN IP ADDRESS

Numeric IP addresses use dotted decimal notation when expressed in decimal numbers, and take the form n.n.n.n, in which *n* is guaranteed to be between zero and 255 for each and every value. Remember, each number is an 8-bit number that is called an octet in standard IP terminology. For any domain name to resolve to a network address, be it on the public Internet, or somewhere on a private intranet, that domain name must correspond to at least one numeric IP address.

The numeric values in dotted decimal representations of numeric IP addresses are usually decimal values, but may occasionally appear in hexadecimal (base 16) or binary (base 2) notation. When working with dotted decimal IP addresses, you must be certain you know what form of notation is in use. Binary representations are easy to recognize because each element in the string is represented by eight binary digits (including leading zeroes, just for consistency's sake). But it's possible to confuse decimal and hexadecimal, so be sure you know which one you're working with before you perform any calculations.

Duplication of numeric IP addresses is not allowed because that would lead to confusion. In fact, which network interface "really" owns an IP address when duplication occurs is such a troublesome issue that the convention is to drop all interfaces that share a single address from the network. Thus, if you ever configure a machine with an IP address and it isn't able to access the network, you might reasonably speculate that IP address duplication occurred. If you notice that another machine becomes unavailable at around the same time, or someone else complains about that phenomenon, then you can be sure that address duplication occurred!

Also, there is a notion of "neighborhood" when it comes to interpreting numeric IP addresses. Proximity between two numeric IP addresses (especially if the difference is only in the rightmost one or two octets) can sometimes indicate that the machines to which those addresses correspond reside close enough together to be on the same general network, if not on the same physical cable segment. (More on this appears later in the section titled "Of IP Networks, Subnets, and Masks," in which we discuss subnets.)

IP ADDRESS CLASSES

You already know that IP addresses take the form n.n.n.n. Initially, these addresses were further subdivided into five classes, from Class A to Class E. For the first three classes of addresses, divide the octets as follows to understand how they behave:

```
Class A    n    h.h.h
Class B    n.n    h.h
Class C    n.n.n    h
```

In this nomenclature, *n* refers to a portion of the network address used to identify networks by number, and *h* refers to a portion of the network address used to identify hosts by number. If more than one octet is part of the network or **host portion** of the address, then the

2

bits are simply concatenated to determine the numeric address (subject to some limitations, which we explain shortly). For example, 10.12.120.2 is a valid Class A address. The **network portion** of that address is 10, whereas the host portion is 12.120.2, treated as a three-octet number. When seeking evidence of proximity in IP addresses, please consider that "neighborliness" is inherently a networking phenomenon so it's related to proximity within the network portion of an IP address, not within the host portion of the network address.

Address Classes D and E are for special uses. Class D addresses are used for multicast communications, in which a single address may be associated with more than one network host machine. This is useful only when information is broadcast to more than one recipient at a time so it should come as no surprise that video and teleconferencing applications, for example, use **multicast addresses**.

But multicast addresses also come in handy when a class of devices, such as routers, must be updated with the same information on a regular basis. (That's why, as you'll learn in Chapter 10 when we discuss routing, some routing protocols use a multicast address to propagate routing table updates.) Although you may see Class D addresses on your networks from time to time, you will only see Class E addresses if your network is conducting IP-related development work or experiments. That's because Class E addresses are reserved entirely for experimental use.

More About Class A Addresses

Expressed in binary form (ones and zeroes only), Class A addresses always take the form:

```
0bbbbbbb.bbbbbbbb.bbbbbbbb.bbbbbbbb
```

The leading digit is always zero, and all other digits (marked with a *b* in the preceding example) can be either ones or zeroes. Note that this scheme reduces the total number of networks possible by the most significant bit. Thus, even though you can represent 255 as an 8-bit number, the requirement that a zero appears in the first position limits the number of networks that can be addressed as Class A networks to 128 (or the numbers from 00000000 to 01111111, in which zero counts as a number and the highest legal value is 127).

 We include periods to separate octets in the binary forms of addresses in this chapter. This is intended purely as a visual aid—the actual machine-readable address does not contain periods.

On any IP network, addresses consisting of all zeroes and all ones are reserved for special uses, so of those 128 possible network addresses, only those from 00000001 to 01111110 (or 1 to 126, in decimal terms) are considered usable. Furthermore, the address for network 10 (00001010) is reserved for private network use (as stipulated in RFC 1918). Also, by convention, the address 127.n.n.n is reserved for **loopback** testing (or checking the integrity and usability of a TCP/IP protocol stack installed on any computer—read more on this in Chapter 3). Thus, there are a maximum of 124 Class A networks that are addressable on the public Internet.

Because the remaining three octets in a Class A address are available to hosts, this means that there are 3 * 8, or 24, bits worth of address space available within each Class A network. You calculate the number of addresses by raising two to the number of bits in the address (or 2^{24} in exponential notation), then subtracting two from that number. That's because all zeroes and all ones are reserved, and not normally used for host addresses, just as they are reserved for special network addresses. This number calculates to 16,777,214.

Class A address information is summarized in Table 2-1.

Table 2-1   Class A Address Facts and Figures

Maximum networks	2^7 - 2	126
Maximum usable networks	2^7 - 4	124
Hosts per network	2^{24} - 2	16,777,214
Private IP address	10.0.0.0	1
Address range	1.0.0.0	126.0.0.0

More About Class B Addresses

Class B addresses always take the form:

```
10bbbbbb.bbbbbbbb.bbbbbbbb.bbbbbbbb
```

The leading two digits are 10, and the remaining digits (marked with a *b*) can be either ones or zeroes. Note that this scheme reduces the total number of networks possible by the two most significant bits. Because of the way that Class B addresses are laid out (the first two octets define the network number, and the second two octets define the host number), this leaves 14 bits worth of usable address space in the network portion of such addresses. Thus, the maximum number of usable network addresses is 2^{14} - 2 (you always have to subtract two for the all zeroes and all ones addresses), which calculates to 16,382. Furthermore, RFC 1918 stipulates that 16 Class B addresses, from 172.16.0.0 to 172.31.255.255, are reserved for private use. This means that the maximum number of **public IP addresses** for Class B is 16,382 - 16, or 16,366.

Because the remaining two octets in a Class B address are available to hosts, this means that there are 2 * 8, or 16, bits worth of address space available within each Class B network. You calculate the number of addresses by raising two to the number of bits in the address (or 2^{16} in exponential notation), then subtracting two from that number. That's because all zeroes and all ones normally may not be used as host addresses as they are reserved in network addresses as well. This number calculates to 65,534.

Table 2-2 summarizes Class B address information.

Table 2-2   Class B Address Facts and Figures

Maximum networks	2^{14} - 2	16,382
Maximum usable networks	2^{14} - 18	16,366
Hosts per network	2^{14} - 2	65,534
Private IP address	172.16.0.0 to 172.31.255.255	16
Address range	128.0.0.0	191.255.0.0

More About Class C Addresses

Class C addresses always take the form:

```
110bbbbb.bbbbbbbb.bbbbbbbb.bbbbbbbb
```

The leading three digits are 110, and the remaining digits (marked with a *b*) can be either ones or zeroes. Note that this scheme reduces the total number of networks possible by the most significant three bits. Because of the way that Class C addresses are laid out (the first three octets define the network number, and the last octet defines the host number), this leaves 21 bits worth of usable address space in the network portion of such addresses. Thus, the maximum number of usable network addresses is 2^{21} - 2 (you always have to subtract two for the all zeroes and all ones addresses), which calculates to 2,097,150. RFC 1918 stipulates that 256 Class C addresses, from 192.168.0.0 to 192.168.255.255, are reserved for private use. This means that the maximum number of public IP addresses for Class C is 2,097,150 - 256, or 2,096,894.

Because only the remaining octet in a Class C address is available to hosts, this means that there are eight bits worth of address space available for hosts to use within each Class C network address. You calculate the number of addresses by raising two to the number of bits in the address (or 2^8 in exponential notation), then subtracting two from that number. That's because all zeroes and all ones are reserved, and normally not usable as host addresses, just as they are with network addresses. This number calculates to 254.

Class C address information is summarized in Table 2-3.

Table 2-3   Class C Address Facts and Figures

Maximum network	2^{21} - 2	2,097,150
Maximum usable networks	2^{21} - 258	2,096,894
Hosts per network	2^8 - 2	254
Private IP address	192.168.0.0 to 192.168.255.255	256
Address range	192.0.1.0	223.255.255.255

Not to unduly confuse matters, but RFC 1878 (finalized in December 1995) allows the all zeroes and all ones addresses to be used for hosts. You might say it returns those reserved addresses to the address pool, and this works as long as all routers in the network use a modern routing protocol, such as RIPv2, OSPF, and so forth. Your authors decided to leave those addresses out of address space calculations because this approach represents the safest way to allocate address space, without risking the use of what might sometimes be an illegal address. When it comes to configuring your own networks and calculating usable address space, check your router documentation and contact your **Internet Service Provider (ISP)** to find out if these addresses are usable.

More About Address Classes D and E

Hopefully, it is intuitively obvious that Classes D and E pick up where C leaves off. That is, Class D addresses always take the form:

1110bbbb.bbbbbbbb.bbbbbbbb.bbbbbbbb

Class E addresses always take the form:

11110bbb.bbbbbbbb.bbbbbbbb.bbbbbbbb

Remember, Class D is used for multicast addresses so that multiple users can "share" a single IP address (in direct violation of the rules for Classes A through C) and receive the same broadcast across a network from a single transmission. Conservation of bandwidth explains why multicast addresses are important for streaming data, like video or teleconferencing, or for information that is of interest to multiple consumers, like routing table updates. The address range for Class D addresses runs from 224.0.0.0 to 239.255.255.255.

Class E addresses are used only for experimental purposes. The address range for Class E addresses runs from 240.0.0.0 to 247.255.255.255. Unless you're working in a research and development environment, it's unlikely that you'll ever encounter such an address on any networks you use.

NETWORK, BROADCAST, MULTICAST, AND OTHER SPECIAL IP ADDRESSES

Normally, when an IP packet moves from its sender to its receiver, the network portion of the address directs that traffic from the sender's network to the receiver's network. The only time the host portion of the address comes into play is when the sender and receiver both reside on the same physical network or subnet. Although frames may be traveling from network to network for the majority of machine-to-machine transfers, most of these transfers occur only to move the packet ever closer to the destination network. On a local network, although all kinds of traffic may be whizzing by, individual hosts normally read only incoming traffic that is addressed to them, or that must be read for other reasons (such as a multicast addressed to a service active on that host).

As we explained how to calculate the number of available addresses in a range of IP numeric values, we repeatedly mentioned the idea that you must deduct two addresses from the total number that may be calculated by the number of bits in the address. That's because any IP address that contains all zeroes in the host portion, such as 10.0.0.0 for the private IP Class A address, denotes the address for the network itself. The important thing to recognize is that a network address cannot identify a particular host on a network simply because it identifies the entire network itself.

You'll recall that we said two addresses are reserved from each numeric IP address range. In addition to the network address, the "other address" that cannot be used to identify a particular host on any network is the address that contains all ones in the host portion, such as 10.255.255.255 (or 00001010.11111111.11111111.11111111 in binary, in which you can see that the last three octets—the host portion of this network address—consist entirely of ones) for the Class A 10.0.0.0 network.

This special address is called the **broadcast address** because it represents a network address that all hosts on a network must read. Although broadcasts still have some valid uses on modern networks, they originated in an era when networks were small and of limited scope, in which a sort of "all hands on deck" message represented a convenient way to ask for services when a specific server could not be explicitly identified. Under some circumstances—as when a DCHP client issues a DHCP Offer message (covered in detail in Chapter 8 of this book)—broadcasts still occur on modern TCP/IP networks, but broadcast traffic is seldom forwarded from one physical network to another these days, and remains a purely local form of network traffic in most cases.

Broadcast Packet Structures

IP broadcast packets have two destination address fields—one Data Link layer destination address field, and one destination network address field. Figure 2-1 depicts an Ethernet packet that contains the destination data-link address 0xFF-FF-FF-FF-FF-FF (the broadcast address—represented by the hexadecimal value flag, 0x, at the beginning of the string) and the decimal destination IP address 255.255.255.255. This packet is a Dynamic Host Configuration Protocol (DHCP) broadcast packet. Chapter 8 covers DHCP in detail.

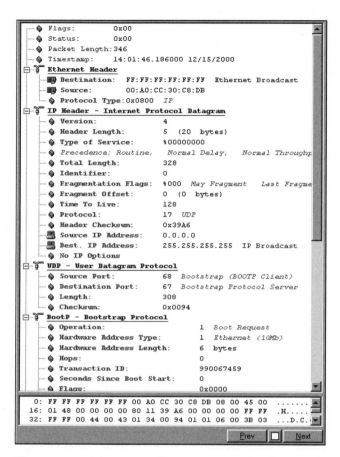

Figure 2-1   Ethernet packet containing the destination data-link address of
0xFF-FF-FF-FF-FF-FF and the destination IP address of 0x255.255.255.255

Multicast Packet and Address Structures

When a host uses a service that employs a multicast address (such as the 224.0.0.9 address used for RIPv2 router updates), it registers itself to "listen" on that address, as well as on its own unique host address (and the broadcast address). That host must also inform its **IP gateway** (the router or other device that will forward traffic to the host's physical network) that it is registering for this service so that device will forward such multicast traffic to that network (otherwise, it will never appear there).

Registration informs the network interface card to pass packets sent to that address to the IP stack so that their contents can be read, and tells the IP gateway to forward such traffic onto the physical network, where the listening network interface resides. Without such explicit registration (part and parcel of subscribing to the related service), this traffic will be ignored, or unavailable. The Internet Corporation for Assigned Names and Numbers

(ICANN) allocates multicast addresses on a controlled basis. Formerly, addresses were under the auspices of **IANA**, the **Internet Assigned Numbers Authority**.

Multicast packets are quite interesting because the Data Link layer destination address is based on the Network layer multicast address. Figure 2-2 depicts a multicast Open Shortest Path First (OSPF) packet. The destination data-link address is 0x01-00-5E-00-00-05. The destination Network layer address is 224.0.0.5.

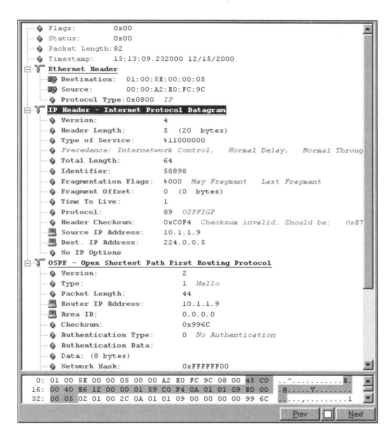

Figure 2-2   Multicast OSPF packet

As mentioned earlier in this section, multicast addresses are assigned by ICANN. In Figure 2-2, the destination network address 224.0.0.5 is assigned to multicast all OSPF routers.

The Data Link layer address 0x01-00-5E-00-00-05 is obtained with the following calculation:

1. Replace the first byte with the corresponding 3-byte OUI. In this case, 224 is replaced with 0x00-00-5E (assigned to IANA).

2. Change the first byte to an odd value (from 0x00 to 0x01).

3. Replace the second through fourth bytes with their decimal equivalents.

Figure 2-3 depicts these steps.

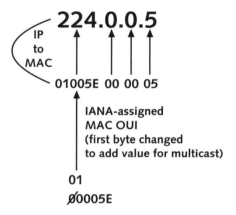

Figure 2-3   Data Link layer address conversion

 You may sometimes hear about an anycast address, another special IP address. Because this type of IP address is specific to IPv6, we discuss it in Chapter 13, which covers this new version of IP. For now, it suffices to say that packets sent to an anycast address go to the nearest interface with that address. Anycast is not used in IPv4.

THE VANISHING IP ADDRESS SPACE

Originally, when IP addresses were assigned for public use, they were assigned on a per-network basis. This helps explain why there are virtually no unassigned Class A or Class B network addresses left. Likewise, the available number of Class C addresses is pretty low as well; less than 15% of all Class Cs remain unassigned at present. With the ever-increasing demand for public IP addresses for Internet access, it should come as no surprise that, as early as the mid-1990s, experts began to predict that the Internet would "run out" of available IP addresses.

Recently, however, the causes for concern have abated somewhat. Here's why:

- The technocrats at the IETF introduced a new way to carve up the IP address space—**Classless Inter-Domain Routing**. **CIDR**, pronounced "cider" or "sidder," permits existing addresses to be combined into larger routing domains with more host addresses than simple addition of the normal number of host addresses for each domain would supply. This technique is the one that ISPs favor, and helps explain how an apparently shrinking address space has been able to accommodate a lot more users in the past few years. An entire section on CIDR titled "Classless Inter-Domain Routing (CIDR)" appears later in this chapter.

- A brisk trade in existing IP network addresses sprung up during the same time. These days, the "going rate" for a Class C network address is at least $10,000, and a Class B can fetch as much as $250,000. Some of the few private companies that own Class A addresses were acquired, or publicly traded, on the strength of an asset that is theoretically worth as much as $64 million! Many companies and individuals rent, rather than own, IP addresses from their ISPs today. As you might guess, this discovery of value in the IP address space helped spur additional technical and business innovations to extract more value from IP address assets.

- RFC 1918 reserves three ranges of IP addresses for private use—a single Class A (10.0.0.0–10.255.255.255), 16 Class Bs (172.16.0.0–172.31.255.255), and 256 Class Cs (192.168.0.0–192.168.255.255). By definition, these addresses are not routed across the Internet because they may be freely used by anyone. No single organization can "own" these addresses; therefore, these addresses may not be used on the public Internet either because they are not guaranteed to be unique.

  When used in tandem with a technology called **Network Address Translation** (a.k.a. **NAT**), **private IP addresses** can help lift the "cap" on public IP addresses. That's because a single public IP address on the "Internet side" of a **firewall** or **proxy server** can "front" for an arbitrary number of private IP addresses on the "private side" of the same firewall or proxy server. In other words, NAT lets networks use private IP addresses internally, and maps them to a single public IP address externally. This gives companies lots of addressing flexibility (they can even use a Class A address internally, if they choose), and helps reduce the number of public IP addresses they must own or use.

By combining all the tactics and technologies described in the preceding list, the current IP address space was stretched a good deal further than many experts imagined. Although there is still some legitimate concern about running out of IP addresses voiced from time to time, the panic factor abated substantially.

One of the design goals that drives the next generation of IP (known as IPv6; the current generation is known as IPv4) is to increase the address space from 32 bits to 128 bits. Experts say this provides enough address space to give every square foot of the earth's surface its own unique IP address. Given the increasing presence of all kinds of devices on networks, and the growing tendency to add Internet access to cell phones and TV sets, this may be a very good thing! In the next sections of the chapter, you will change gears from learning about types of IP addresses and their uses, to explore the techniques and mathematics whereby numeric IP addresses may be understood and manipulated. Roll up your sleeves, and get out your pencils!

Understanding Basic Binary Arithmetic

Working with IP addresses, especially for subnetting and supernetting—which you will tackle in the section titled "IP Subnets and Supernets" later in this chapter—is much simpler if you understand the basics of binary arithmetic. For the purposes of this text, you must master four different kinds of binary calculations:

1. Converting binary to decimal
2. Converting decimal to binary
3. Understanding how setting increasing numbers of high-order bits to 1 in 8-bit binary numbers corresponds to specific decimal numbers
4. Understanding how setting increasing low-order bits to 1 in 8-bit binary numbers corresponds to specific decimal numbers

Before we tackle each of these subjects, there's another apparent anomaly that you must understand before binary counting makes sense. This is best illustrated with a sample question: "How many numbers are there between zero and three (or 00 to 11, in binary)?" Calculate the answer by subtracting the lower number from the higher number, and then adding one. Thus 3 - 0 = 3 + 1 = 4. This may be demonstrated by enumerating the binary digits from zero to three as follows (numbers in parentheses will be decimal equivalents): 00 (0), 01 (1), 10 (2), 11 (3). Four numbers appear in that list, so our formula holds true! Another apparent anomaly is that any number raised to the zero power is always equal to one. (You'll use that fact when converting exponential notation to binary numbers.)

Converting Decimal to Binary

This is extremely easy, if you don't mind thinking mathematically. If you find this approach too challenging, we suggest an alternate approach. The following approach has the advantage of working for any number, no matter how large or small. Simply divide the number by two, write the remainder (which must be 0 or 1), then write the dividend, and repeat until the dividend is zero.

Let's convert the decimal number 125 to binary, as an example:

```
125 divided by 2 equals 62, remainder 1
 62 divided by 2 equals 31, remainder 0
 31 divided by 2 equals 15, remainder 1
 15 divided by 2 equals  7, remainder 1
  7 divided by 2 equals  3, remainder 1
  3 divided by 2 equals  1, remainder 1
  1 divided by 2 equals  0, remainder 1
```

To produce the binary number that corresponds to 125, you write the digits starting with the last remainder value, and work your way up: 1111101. Now, let's check the work involved. The exponential expansion of 1111101 is $1*2^6 + 1*2^5 + 1*2^4 + 1*2^3 + 1*2^2 + 0*2^1 + 1*2^0$ (1111101).

The alternate approach to convert the number depends on what mathematicians like to call a "step function." This particular approach depends on knowing the decimal values for various powers of two, and then applying steps similar to the first approach, except that each number must be positioned between the nearest power of two that's greater than or equal to the number in question, and less than or equal to the number in question. Here's an example:

```
125 is less than 128 (2⁷) and more than 64 (2⁶)
125 minus 64 is 61
61 is less than 64 (2⁶) and more than 32 (2⁵)
61 minus 32 is 29
29 is less than 32 (2⁵) and more than 16 (2⁴)
29 minus 16 is 13
13 is less than 16 (2⁴) and more than 8 (2³)
13 minus 8 is 5
5 is less than 8 (2³) and more than 4 (2²)
5 minus 4 is 1
```

Note that although there's an entry for 2^6, 2^5, 2^4, 2^3, 2^2, and 2^0, there is no entry for 2^1, so it shows up as 0 when converted to binary (any number you subtract from a previous result produces a one for the corresponding power of two; a missing number produces a zero). One is always one, even in binary. Thus, $125 = 1*2^6 + 1*2^5 + 1*2^4 + 1*2^3 + 1*2^2 + 0*2^1 + 1*2^0$. Read the multipliers from left to right to convert to binary, and you end up with 1111101.

You should practice on some numbers of your own to make sure you understand one method or another. (Expect to see related problems in the Review Questions at the end of this chapter.)

Converting Binary to Decimal

This is extremely easy, if you know your powers of two. Follow these steps, using 11011011 as the example number:

1. Count the total number of digits in the number (11011011 has eight digits).

2. Subtract one from the total (8 - 1 = 7). That is the power of two to associate with the highest exponent for two in the exponential notation for that number.

3. Convert to exponential notation, using all the digits as multipliers.

   11011011, therefore, converts to:

   $$11011011 = 1*2^7+1*2^6+0*2^5+1*2^4+1*2^3+0*2^2+1*2^1+1*2^0$$
   $$= 128+64+0+16+8+0+2+1 = 219$$

Practice this on some numbers of your own to make sure you understand the method.

High-order Bit Patterns

Sometimes, we block off bits in 8-bit numbers from the top down. (These are called the most significant bits because they represent the highest numeric values.) In an 8-bit number, there's little or no value in blocking less than two bits, or more than six bits, so the bit patterns you care about most appear in the second through the sixth positions in this list of possibilities:

Binary	Decimal
10000000	128
11000000	192
11100000	224
11110000	240
11111000	248
11111100	252
11111110	254
11111111	255

If you simply memorize these correspondences, then you'll be well-equipped to deal with subnet masking problems, as you'll see in the section titled "IP Subnets and Supernets" later in this chapter.

Low-order Bit Patterns

Here, we stand the previous example on its head, and start counting up through the bit positions in 8-bit numbers from right to left, adding ones as we increment. Note that each of these numbers is the same as two raised to the power of the number of bits showing, minus one. If you memorize the values of the powers of two from one through eight, you can calculate this table in your head in a flash!

```
Binary            Decimal         Exponent
00000001             1            2¹ - 1
00000011             3            2² - 1
00000111             7            2³ - 1
00001111            15            2⁴ - 1
00011111            31            2⁵ - 1
00111111            63            2⁶ - 1
01111111           127            2⁷ - 1
11111111           255            2⁸ - 1
```

Memorizing these numbers, or learning how to calculate them, will prepare you to deal with supernet masking problems, as you'll see in the section titled "IP Subnets and Supernets" later in this chapter. As with subnet masks, you seldom deal with supernet masks of more than four to six bits, but these numbers are easy enough to calculate on demand, and you should learn how to do so.

OF IP NETWORKS, SUBNETS, AND MASKS

If two network interfaces are on the same physical network, they can communicate directly with one another at the MAC layer. But how does the software "know" that this is the case when communications are initiated between two machines? The key to this puzzle lies in a special bit pattern called a subnet mask (which must be defined for any network interface that uses TCP/IP).

In fact, each of the three primary IP address classes—namely A, B, and C—also has an associated default subnet mask. An examination of these values tells so much of the story involved with subnet masking that you should be able to understand the concept simply by comparing the layout of those address classes with their corresponding subnet masks.

But first, let's provide a definition: a **subnet mask** is a special bit pattern that "blocks off" the network portion of an IP address with an all-ones pattern. Thus, the default masks for Classes A, B, and C should be fairly obvious:

```
Class         Layout          Default Mask
Class A     n     h.h.h       255.0.0.0
Class B     n.n     h.h       255.255.0.0
Class C     n.n.n     h       255.255.255.0
```

(Note: *n* signifies network; *h* signifies host portion of address.)

From a completely simplistic viewpoint, every time an *n* occurs in the address layout, symbolizing the entire network portion of that address, a 255 replaces that value in the default subnet mask. The mathematics that explain this process, knowing that a subnet mask replaces the network portion of the address with the all-ones bit pattern, comes from recognizing that the value 255 corresponds to the bit pattern 11111111. Thus, each 255 masks off one of the octets that makes up the network portion of the address.

IP Subnets and Supernets

The reason why concepts like subnets and supernets are important for TCP/IP networks is because each of these ideas refers to a single "local neighborhood" on such a network, seen from a routing perspective. When network addresses are further subdivided beyond their defaults for whatever class an address belongs to, what is involved is "stealing bits" from the host portion of the address, and using those stolen bits to create multiple routing regions within the context of a single network address.

Thus, a subnet mask that is larger than the default mask for the address in use divides a single network IP address into multiple subnetworks. So, for a Class B address, in which the default subnet mask is 255.255.0.0, a subnet mask of 255.255.192.0 indicates that it's stealing two bits from the host portion to use for subnet identification (because 192 decimal is 11000000 in binary, and shows that the upper two bits are used for the network portion). One way to describe this kind of network address layout is that there are eight bits of the network prefix and two additional bits of subnetting. Here, the **network prefix** identifies the number of bits in the IP address, counting from the left that represents the actual network address itself, and the additional two bits of subnetting represent the bits that were borrowed from the host portion of that IP address to extend the network portion. The entire network address, including the network prefix and the subnetting bits, is called the **extended network prefix**.

With a 2-bit subnet mask, you can identify a total of four possible subnets because each of the possible patterns that the two subnet bits can form—00, 01, 10, and 11—can identify a potential subnetwork. But, as with network and host addresses, the total number of usable subnet addresses is reduced by two because the all zeroes (00 in this case) and all ones (11 in this case) are reserved for other purposes. This activity of stealing bits from the host portion to further subdivide the network portion of an address is called subnetting a network address, or **subnetting**.

From a routing perspective, subnetting allows network administrators to match subnetworks to actual routing regions on their networks so that machines on the same physical network can communicate using MAC layer addresses. Other pairs of machines that wish to communicate, but do not reside on the same physical network, belong to different subnetworks. (Their numeric IP addresses differ somewhere in the subnetwork portion of those addresses.) This is where the real sense of numerical neighborhoods that we talked about earlier in this chapter comes into play.

When a computer on one subnet wishes to communicate with a computer on another subnet, traffic must be forwarded from the sender to a nearby IP gateway to send the message on its way from one subnet to another. An IP gateway is a device that interconnects multiple IP networks or subnets. It is often called a "router" because it usually stores "reachability" information about many networks, chooses the best (shortest, fastest, or least expensive) path or "route" for each packet it receives, and then sends the packet on its way.

Here again, subnetting means stealing bits from the host portion of the address, and using those bits to divide a single network address into multiple subdivisions called subnets. **Supernetting**, on the other hand, takes the opposite approach: by combining contiguous network addresses, it steals bits from the network portion and uses them to create a single, larger contiguous address space for host addresses. In the sections that follow, you will have the opportunity to investigate some examples that help cement these concepts. For more information on subnetting, please consult RFC 1878 "Variable Length Subnet Table for IPv4." (Among many other places, you can access it at *http://andrew2.andrew.cmu.edu/rfc/rfc1878.html.*)

Calculating Subnet Masks

There are several varieties of subnet masks that you can design for a network, depending on how you want to implement an address segmentation scheme. The simplest form of subnet masking uses a technique called **constant-length subnet masking (CLSM)**, in which each subnet includes the same number of stations and represents a simple division of the address space made available by subnetting into multiple equal segments. Another form of subnet masking uses a technique called **variable-length subnet masking (VLSM)** and permits a single address to be subdivided into multiple subnets, in which subnets need not all be the same size.

When it comes to designing a subnet masking scheme, if all segments must support roughly the same number of devices, give or take 20%, CLSM makes the most sense. But if one or two segments require larger numbers of users, while other segments require a lesser number, VLSM will let you make more effective use of your address space. (The only way to use CLSM in such a case would be to design for the biggest segments, which would waste lots of addresses on those segments with smaller populations.) In a VLSM addressing scheme, different subnets may have different extended network prefixes, reflecting their differing layouts and capacities. Of course, the binary nature of subnetting means that all subnets must still fit into the same kinds of structures described for CLSM. It's just that in VLSM, some of the individual higher-level subnet address spaces can be further subdivided into smaller sub-spaces, if that's desirable. For an extended discussion of subnetting schemes and design approaches, please read 3Com's excellent white paper titled "Understanding IP Addressing: Everything You Ever Wanted to Know," by Chuck Semeria, at *http://www.3com.com/nsc/501302.html.*

Designing a Constant-Length Subnet Mask   To design a CLSM subnet mask, in which each portion of the network has the same number of addresses, follow these steps:

1. Decide how many subnets are needed.

2. Because the number of subnets needed must be represented by a bit pattern, add two to the number of subnets needed (one for the network address, the other for the broadcast address), then jump to the nearest higher power of two. If the result of the sum is an even power of two, you can use it directly.

3. Reserve bits of the host portion's address from the top down.

4. Be sure that there are enough host addresses left over on each subnet to be usable.

5. Always use the formula 2^b - 2 to calculate the number of usable subnets from a mask, in which b is the number of bits in the subnet mask, and two is subtracted to account for the network (all zeroes) and broadcast (all ones) addresses that every IP network and subnetwork require.

Here's an example to help you put this method to work:

1. ABC Inc. wants 12 subnets for its Class C address 200.10.10.0. No subnet needs more than 10 host addresses.

2. Add two (for network and broadcast addresses) to 12 to get 14. The nearest power of two is 16, which equals 2^4. This means a 4-bit subnet mask is required.

3. Reserving four bits from the top down creates a subnet mask with the pattern 11110000. The decimal value for this number is 128+64+32+16, or 240. This extends the default subnet mask for the Class C address from 255.255.255.0 to 255.255.255.240. (This is because we're "stealing" four bits from the host portion of the address.)

4. To calculate the number of host addresses for each subnet, reverse the logic from the subnet mask. In English, this means that every bit used for the subnet mask cannot be used for host addresses. Count the number of zeroes left over in the subnet mask to determine the number of bits left over for the host addresses. In this case, that number is four.

5. The same formula that's used to calculate the number of subnets works to calculate the number of hosts, in which b becomes the number of bits in the host address—namely 2^b - 2, or 2^4 - 2, which equals 14.

Remember, the whole purpose of this exercise is to compare the number of hosts needed for each subnet to the number you just calculated. In other words, if you need more than 14 hosts per subnet, this subnet mask does not produce the desired results. But because only 10 hosts are needed per subnet, as stated in the requirements for ABC Inc., this design works as required.

As a quick summary, here's what you just did: Based on the requirements for 12 subnets in a Class C address, in which no individual subnet needs more than 10 host addresses, you calculated that a 4-bit subnet mask is required. Because the corresponding bit pattern, 11110000, equates to 240 in decimal, the default subnet mask for Class C, 255.255.255.0, must be changed to steal those four bits from the host portion of the address, so the actual subnet mask becomes 255.255.255.240.

Because the remaining four bits for the host portion allow up to 14 host addresses per subnet, and the requirements call for no more than 10 addresses per subnet, the design works as intended. But always remember this last step, check your work—renumbering IP networks is a messy, tedious business and you don't want to be forced to do this over!

Another Constant-Length Subnet Mask Example Let's pick a more ambitious design this time, which shows how subnet masks or host addresses can extend across multiple octets.

1. XYZ Corporation, a large multinational company with hundreds of offices worldwide, wants 300 subnets for its Class B address 178.16.10.0. No subnet needs more than 100 host addresses.

2. Add two (for network and broadcast addresses) to 300 to get 302. The nearest power of two is 512, which equals 2^9. This means a 9-bit subnet mask is required.

3. Reserving nine bits from the top down creates a subnet mask with the pattern 11111111 10000000. Because this subnet mask extends across two octets, the subnet must be calculated separately for each octet. For the first host portion octet, the value is 255 because all the bits are set to ones. For the second octet, the first bit (which equals 2^7) is the only one set to a 1; this translates to a decimal value of 128. This extends the default subnet mask for the Class B address from 255.255.0.0 to 255.255.255.128 (because we're "stealing" nine bits from the host portion of the address, this produces an extended network prefix of /25).

4. To calculate the number of host addresses for each subnet, reverse the logic from the subnet mask. This means that every bit used for the subnet mask cannot be used for host addresses. Count the number of zeroes left over in the subnet mask to determine the number of bits left over for the host address.

5. In this case, that number is seven. The same formula that's used to calculate the number of subnets works to calculate the number of hosts, in which b becomes the number of bits in the host address—namely $2^b - 2$, or $2^7 - 2$, which equals $128 - 2$, or 126.

Remember, the whole purpose of this exercise is to compare the number of hosts needed for each subnet to the number you just calculated. In other words, if you need more than 126 hosts per subnet, this subnet mask does not produce the required results. But because only 100 hosts are needed per subnet, as stated in the requirements for XYZ Corporation, this design works as intended.

Designing a Variable-Length Subnet Mask Designing and configuring variable-length subnet masks is more time-consuming and difficult, but makes much better use of available address space. A simple example will explain how this might be the case. Let's assume that Plotchnik University (PU) has a Class B address, and it needs 135 subnets to support all of the various campuses, offices, and operations. Because 135 is between 128 and 256, a CLSM subnet mask requires eight bits so that the default subnet mask for Class B—namely 255.255.0.0—becomes 255.255.255.0 for PU, providing support for the necessary number of subnets. So far, so good.

But let's suppose that over half the subnets at PU require support for 30 devices or less. That means all of those networks that could work with a 5-bit subnet mask must waste an extra three bits of space (or up to 224 unused addresses per subnet)! As you can probably guess, VLSM was devised to cover this contingency. Instead of following the method from the preceding section on CSLM, you must:

- Analyze the requirements for individual subnets.

- Aggregate those requirements by their relationships to the nearest power of two that is at least two greater (remember the all-zeroes and all-ones networks require representation) than the number of such subnets required.

- Use the subnets that require the largest number of devices to decide the minimum size of the subnet mask. (Remember, the smaller the subnet mask, the lower the number of subnets it supports, but the higher the number of host addresses left over.)

- Aggregate subnets that require smaller numbers of hosts within address spaces defined by the largest subdivisions (those defined in the previous step).

- Define a VLSM scheme that provides the necessary number of subnets of each size to fit its intended use best by aggregating subnets large and small to create the most efficient network traffic patterns. In other words, neighboring subnets with the same extended network prefix should be placed in the same "container" defined by a higher-level network prefix, if possible. Assume your design calls for several subnets with three bits of subnetting, and you have needs for 30 subnets with five bits of subnetting. This means that three 3-bit prefix containers will be required because each can only offer 14 unique 5-bit sub-subnets, as it were. If you place those 5-bit subnets together within the addresses that fall into any single 3-bit subnet range and are most likely to exchange data with each other, this results in the most efficient routing behavior possible.

Thus, VLSM makes it possible to create routing hierarchies and limit traffic on the backbone by making sure that smaller subnet address spaces can access the resources they need as efficiently as possible. One way to do this is to make sure that the servers such subnets access most frequently are attached directly to that subnet, or that they're in the same 3-bit subnet address space as the original subnets, even if that 3-bit subnet space was subdivided into fourteen 5-bit containers.

Calculating Supernets

Supernets "steal" bits from the network portion of an IP address to "lend" those bits to the host part. As part of how they work, supernets permit multiple IP network addresses to be combined and make them function together as if they represent a single logical network. This greatly improves performance for communications inside the local network because it eliminates the need for internal routing. Incidentally, this also permits more hosts to be addressed on a supernet than in the combination of multiple addresses. Here's why:

1. Combining eight Class C addresses steals three bits from the network portion of the address and adds them to the host portion of the address.

2. Thus, rather than supporting only eight bits for the host address portion, the supernet now supports 11 bits (8 + 3) for host addresses. The resulting subnet mask looks like this: 255.255.248.0 (rather than the default 255.255.255.0). There are two ways to calculate a supernet mask. Recognizing that you're stealing three bits from the right side of the third octet, you should also recognize that the resulting bitmask for that octet becomes 11111000, which calculates to 248. The other way to calculate this value is to recognize that the largest number that can be represented in three binary bits is 111, which calculates to $2^3 - 1$, or seven, in decimal. If you subtract that number from 255, you get 248, the same answer, more quickly than with the other formula. Because both methods work, use whichever one is easiest for you.

3. The number of usable hosts for this supernet, using the old familiar $2^b - 2$ formula, is $2^{11} - 2$, which calculates to 2046.

4. Each individual Class C address can only address 254 ($2^8 - 2$) hosts. Eight times 254 is 2032. Because 2046 - 2032 = 12, supernetting eight Class C addresses yields access to some additional hosts, when compared to using each Class C address separately.

It's actually far more important that supernetting allows an entire group of hosts to be reached through a single router address, and for those hosts to communicate directly with each other, rather than requiring routing among all the hosts in that address pool.

It is hoped that this helps illustrate why supernetting is a useful tool for ISPs that can combine multiple Class C addresses to serve larger populations than might seem possible. In fact, the combination of supernetting with VLSM gives ISPs the ability to slice and dice address spaces with surprising efficiency and facility.

CLASSLESS INTER-DOMAIN ROUTING (CIDR)

CIDR gets its name from the notion that it ignores the traditional A, B, and C class designations for IP addresses, and can therefore set the network-host ID boundary wherever it wants to, in a way that simplifies routing across the resulting IP address spaces. One way to think of this principle is to imagine that a CIDR address sets the boundaries between the network and host portions of an IP address more or less arbitrarily, constrained only by the IP address space that an ISP, organization, or company might need to manage. When multiple IP addresses are available, best use of CIDR results if those addresses are contiguous (so they can be managed in one or more logical blocks that operate at specific bit boundaries between the host and network portions of the address). Using CIDR also requires that routers be informed that they're dealing with CIDR addresses.

The CIDR specification is documented in RFCs 1517, 1518, and 1519. Basically, CIDR allows IP addresses from Class A, B, or C to be combined and treated as a larger address space, or subdivided arbitrarily, as needed. Although CIDR can sometimes be used to combine multiple Class C addresses, it can also be used to subdivide Class A, B, or C addresses (especially when VLSM techniques are applied) to make the most efficient use of whatever address space is available. Most experts agree that CIDR's most positive impact on the Internet is the reduction in the number of individual Class C addresses that must be recognized (many are now aggregated and function with smaller subnet masks, thereby involving fewer entries in top-level routing tables).

When configuring a router to handle a CIDR address, the routing table entry takes the form *address, count,* in which *address* is the starting address for a range of IP addresses, and *count* is the number of addresses combined to create a larger address space.

Creating a CIDR address is subject to the following limitations:

- All the addresses in the CIDR address must be contiguous. Use of the standard network prefix notation for addresses, however, also makes it tidy and efficient to carve up any kind of address, as needed. When multiple addresses are aggregated, this requires that all such addresses be in numerical order so that the boundary between the network and the host portion of the address can move to reflect such aggregation.

- When address aggregation occurs, CIDR address blocks work best when they come in sets that are greater than one, and equal to some lower-order bit pattern that corresponds to all ones—namely in groups of 3, 7, 15, 31, and so on. That's because this makes it possible to steal the corresponding number of bits (two, three, four, five, and so on) from the network portion of the CIDR address block, and use them to extend the host portion instead.

- CIDR addresses are commonly applied to Class C addresses (which are small, and relatively more plentiful). But for organizations that wish to subdivide existing Class A or Class B addresses, CIDR also works very well.

- To use a CIDR address on any network, all routers in the routing domain must "understand" CIDR notation. This is typically not a problem for most routers that are newer than eight years old because most router vendors began to support CIDR addresses when the current version of the RFC was approved in September 1993.

The prefix notation mentioned earlier in the chapter, as it relates to Class A (/8), Class B (/16), and Class C (/24) addresses, really comes into its own when you see CIDR addresses that use this notation. Thus, if you see a network address of 192.168.5.0 /27, you immediately know two things: that you're dealing with a Class C address, and that this address was subnetted with three additional bits worth of network space so the corresponding subnet mask must be 255.255.255.224. This notation is both compact and efficient, and explicitly denotes whatever subnet or supernet scheme may be in use for the IP network(s) in use.

PUBLIC VERSUS PRIVATE IP ADDRESSES

In the section titled "IP Address Classes" earlier in this chapter, you learned that RFC 1918 designates specific addresses, or address ranges, within the Class A, B, and C address space for use as private IP addresses. This means that any organization that wishes to can use these private IP addresses within its own networking domains without obtaining prior permission or incurring any expense.

The private IP address ranges may be expressed in the form of IP network addresses, as shown in Table 2-4.

Table 2-4 Private IP Address Information

Class	Address (range)	Networks	Total Private Hosts
Class A	10.0.0.0	1	16,777,214
Class B	172.16.0.0–172.31.0.0	16	1,048,544
Class C	192.168.0.0–192.168.255.0	256	65,024

When selecting the kinds of private IP addresses to use, you want to trade your needs for the number of hosts per network, against your willingness to subnet larger address classes (usually Class B), or to supernet smaller address classes (usually Class C). On our networks, we tend to use the Class B addresses and subnet them in the third octet, leaving the fourth octet for host addresses. (For our small networks, a maximum of 254 hosts per subnet hasn't proved problematic.) If you decide to use private IP addresses on your networks, you must review your networking requirements for the number of subnets and the number of hosts per subnet, and choose accordingly.

You already know one of the disadvantages of using private IP addresses—such addresses may not be routed across the public Internet. Thus, it's important to recognize that if you want to connect your computers to the Internet, and also use private IP addresses within your own local networks, you must add some extra software to whatever device sits at the boundary between the private side of your networks and the public side of the Internet, to make that connection workable. This sometimes depends on translating one or more private IP addresses into a public IP address for outgoing traffic, and reversing that translation for incoming traffic. Another technique, known as address masquerading, or address substitution, may be performed by boundary devices that include proxy server capabilities, to replace private IP addresses with one or more public IP addresses as outbound traffic exits the server, and to replace such public addresses with their proper private equivalents as incoming traffic passes through the server.

Private IP addresses have one other noteworthy limitation. Some IP services require what's called a secure **end-to-end connection**—IP traffic must be able to move in encrypted form between the sender and receiver without intermediate translation. Thus, if either party to such a connection uses a public IP address, both parties must use a public IP address because the address for the "private end" of the connection cannot be routed across the Internet. Secure protocols like IP Security (IPSec) make this a requirement, as do some virtual private networking technologies. So, if you want to use such services on your network, you may not be able to use private IP addresses.

Ultimately though, private IP addresses have great value for many organizations simply because the vast majority of machines on TCP/IP networks are client workstations. Because these client machines seldom, if ever, advertise services accessible to a broad audience (or to the Internet at large), there is no real down side to using private IP addresses for such machines. Most clients simply want to read e-mail, access the Web and other Internet services, and use local networked resources. None of these requirements mandates using a public IP address, nor forbids the use of a private IP address. Thus, the introduction of private IP addresses has greatly eased most organizations' needs for public IP addresses.

That said, public IP addresses remain important for identifying all servers or services that must be accessible to the Internet. This is, in part, a reflection of the behavior of the DNS that manages translations between symbolic domain names like *www.course.com,* and numeric IP addresses like 199.95.72.8. Because human beings prefer to think in terms of such symbolic names, and computers can use only the equivalent numeric IP addresses to access such public hosts, the way changes to the mapping between names and addresses are handled is important to the stability and usability of the Internet itself.

You will learn much more about these details in Chapter 7. For now, be aware that it takes a relatively long time—up to 72 hours in some cases—for name-to-address changes to DNS to take complete effect across the Internet. It's very important that publicly accessible servers not only use public IP addresses (how else would they be publicly accessible), but also that those addresses change as infrequently as possible to keep the many copies of the translation information scattered widely across the Internet as correct as possible.

In more practical terms, this means that most organizations need public IP addresses only for two classes of equipment:

- Devices that permit organizations to attach networks to the Internet. These include the external interfaces on boundary devices of all kinds, such as routers, proxy servers, and firewalls, that help maintain the perimeter between the "outside" and "inside" on networks.

- Servers that are designed to be accessible to the Internet. These include public Web servers, e-mail servers, FTP servers, news servers, and whatever other kind of TCP/IP Application layer services an organization may want to expose on the public Internet.

Interestingly, even though the number of such devices (or, more appropriately, the number of such network interfaces because each network interface on a boundary device or server must have its own unique IP address) is not small, it pales when compared to the number of clients or purely internal devices and servers on most organization networks. Exact estimates are hard to find, but it's not unreasonable to place the number somewhere in the hundreds to thousands in one neighborhood. (For every public IP address that's required, there can be as many as 100 to 1000 private IP addresses in use as well.)

Managing Access to IP Address Information

Although use of private IP addresses mandates NAT or a similar address substitution or masquerade capability, some organizations elect to use address substitution or masquerade even when they use perfectly valid public IP addresses on their internal networks. That's because allowing clients inside the network boundary to interact with the network without some form of address "hiding" could reveal the address structure of that internal network to knowledgeable outsiders who may try to use that information to break through organizational boundaries—from the public Internet into an organizational networking environment—and attack that network for a variety of reasons (none of them good).

That's why it's considered good IP security to use a proxy server, or some similar kind of service, that interposes itself between traffic inside the boundary and traffic outside the boundary. When outbound traffic passes through the proxy from the internal network, the proxy service replaces internal network addresses with one or more different addresses so that the traffic that actually travels over the public Internet does not reveal the address structure of the internal network to outsiders.

Likewise, proxy servers can provide what is sometimes called **reverse proxying**. This permits the proxy server to front for servers inside the boundary by advertising only the proxy server's address to the outside world, and then forwarding only legitimate requests for service to internal servers for further processing. Here again, outsiders see only the address that the proxy server advertises on the internal server's behalf, and remain unaware of the invisible middleman, in most cases.

Thus, one of the most important services that a proxy server provides is to manage what source addresses appear in outbound packets that pass through it. This prevents details about the internal network's actual addresses from leaking to outsiders, who might otherwise use address scanning utilities to see exactly which addresses in any given address range are in use. Given what you know about how subnetting and supernetting work, this information, in turn, could allow outsiders to determine what kinds of subnet masks are in use, and how an internal network is laid out. By blocking this information, savvy IP network administrators limit potential opportunities for break-ins or other attacks.

OBTAINING PUBLIC IP ADDRESSES

Unless you work for an organization that has possessed its own public IP addresses since the 1980s (or acquired such addresses through merger or acquisition), it's highly likely that whatever public IP addresses your organization uses were issued by the very same ISP who provides your organization with Internet access. This is one of the details that makes the decision to change from one ISP to another so challenging. Because all devices accessible to the Internet must have public IP addresses, changing providers often means going through a tedious exercise called **IP renumbering**. When this happens, you must switch the addresses on every machine that uses an address from the old ISP to another unique address you obtain from the new ISP.

Historically, IANA managed all IP-related addresses, protocol numbers, and well-known port addresses, and also assigned MAC layer addresses for use in network interfaces. Today, ICANN manages this task, and you must contact them to apply for an IP address range from the few remaining public Class C addresses. Although IANA is no longer operating as the governing body for this activity, you can still find a lot of useful information about IP addresses and numbers at *http://www.iana.org*; likewise, you can find such information at *http://www.icann.org*.

Given the scarcity of public IP addresses at present, only ISPs, or other organizations with extremely compelling reasons to request such addresses, are likely to be granted a public IP address by ICANN. In the vast majority of cases, you must negotiate with an ISP to obtain an address range, along with whatever other Internet access services you may require.

IP ADDRESSING SCHEMES

To the uninitiated, it may appear that all these IP addresses are randomly assigned, or perhaps generated automatically by some computer somewhere. However, a great deal of thought has gone into the strategy for allocating IP addresses around the world. In this section, we discuss the need for IP addressing schemes, and how to create and document one.

The Network Space

There are a number of critical factors that typically constrain IP addressing schemes, and we look at these in two groups. The first group of constraints determines the number and size of networks. These are:

- Number of physical locations
- Number of network devices at each location
- Amount of broadcast traffic at each location
- Availability of IP addresses
- Delay caused by routing from one network to another

Although it's possible to bridge from one physical location to another across a WAN connection, in practice, it is only done with protocols that aren't capable of routing at all, such as SNA or NetBEUI. Routing (instead of bridging) is primarily done to prevent unnecessary broadcasts from clogging expensive WAN circuits. This tells us that the minimum number of IP networks needed is one for every location in a company, plus one for each WAN link.

Next, because IP addresses are scarce, we want our networks to be as small as possible, but they should have at least enough usable addresses (remember, usable addresses = [total number of addresses in the network] - 2) to give one address to each device, and allow adequate room for growth.

Last, recall that an IP network is a broadcast domain. This means that when one host on the network sends a broadcast, every other host on that network must receive and process it. So the speed of your network links and your hosts' processors, and the number and nature of protocols in use, all combine to constrain the practical size of your network.

Generally speaking, the more broadcasts you have, the fewer hosts you should have per network. And, the more protocols you have, the fewer hosts you should have per network.

In most routers, the Layer 3 routing decisions are typically made by software, so it's relatively slow when compared to similar decisions made at Layer 2 by switches. This is because switches make their decisions with specialized hardware known as **Application Specific Integrated Circuits (ASICs)**. A relatively new device known as a **layer-3 switch** simply implements the layer-3 logic from the software into its own ASICs. The result is much faster routing. In practice, layer-3 switching allows you to partition a large network into many smaller subnets with almost no loss of performance.

The second group that helps us determine how to choose which IP addresses go where are design objectives:

- Minimize the size of the routing tables
- Minimize the time required for the network to "converge"
- Maximize flexibility and facilitate management and troubleshooting

The time it takes to route from one network to another is affected by the size of the routing table: the larger the table, the more time it takes to search through it. However, at this point, we already defined the number of networks necessary, so how do we reduce the number of routes in the routing table? The answer is called **route aggregation**, or **summary addresses**.

A critical concept to understand here is that there is not a one-to-one relationship between networks and routes to networks. If a router receives a route to 10.1.1.0/25 and 10.1.1.128/25, it can advertise a route to 10.1.1.0/24 to its upstream neighbors, instead of the two /25 routes.

Another advantage to summarization is that if the 10.1.1.128/25 network gets disconnected, routers that have a route to 10.1.1.128/25 will have to remove it, but routers that only have summary routes will not know that a change has occurred.

The point of all this is simply to number your networks so they can be easily summarized, which will minimize the number of routes in your routing tables, and also allow your routing tables to be more stable, which allows processor time to be spent passing packets instead of fiddling with the routing table.

The Host Space

Now that you understand some of the factors involved in numbering the networks, let's take a brief look at assigning IP addresses to hosts.

The advantages of a well-thought-out host naming strategy are a more flexible environment, and one that is easier to support. For example, you have 500 branch offices around the world, each with a /24 network, and each uses a numbering convention such as the following:

IP Address	Description
10.x.x.0	Network address
10.x.x.1 to 10.x.x.14	Switches and managed hubs
10.x.x.17	DHCP and DNS server
10.x.x.18	File and print server
10.x.x.19 to 10.x.x.30	Application servers
10.x.x.33 to 10.x.x.62	Printers
10.x.x.65 to 10.x.x.246	DHCP clients
10.x.x.247 to 10.x.x.253	Miscellaneous and static clients
10.x.x.254	Default gateway address
10.x.x.255	Broadcast address

You can easily identify devices by their IP addresses, regardless of which office they're in. Even more important, and less obvious, is that these address groups should be done in binary, not decimal. This means that you want to keep your groups inside binary boundaries. The reason is that, in the future, you may want to implement layer-3 switching to reduce the broadcast traffic, and if the devices fit in a binary boundary, you won't have to readdress them. In this example, servers can be identified by 10.x.x.16/28, even though the servers themselves are configured with a 255.255.255.0 subnet mask. If you started them at .10 and went to .20, it might make more sense in decimal, but in reality, it will only lead to confusion. Another reason this is a good idea is that one day, you will want to classify your traffic to apply **Quality of Service** (QoS) or policies of some sort. You could apply a rule that says traffic to and from 10.x.x.32/27 (printers) gets a lower priority than other traffic. If the printers weren't in a binary boundary, some of them would be excluded from the rule, or some other devices could be mistakenly included. Another very common application is firewall rules. You might want to say that all traffic from 10.x.x.0/26 (network equipment, servers, and printers) to the Internet is denied. This could prevent the servers from becoming launchpads for hackers to attack other networks, while still allowing our DHCP clients access through the firewall.

As you can see, a well-planned IP addressing scheme not only dramatically improves the performance of your network, but also makes maintenance and support tasks much simpler, and allows a lot of flexibility.

CHAPTER SUMMARY

❒ IP addresses provide the foundation for identifying individual network interfaces (and therefore computers or other devices as well) on TCP/IP networks. Understanding address structures, restrictions, and behavior is essential to designing TCP/IP networks and appreciating how existing TCP/IP networks are organized.

❒ IP addresses come in five classes named A through E. Classes A through C use the IPv4 32-bit address to establish different break points between the network and host portions of such network addresses. Class A uses a single octet for the network address, and three octets for the host address; Class B uses two octets each for network and host portions; and Class C uses three octets for the network portion and one octet for the host portion. Thus, only a few (124) Class A networks exist, but each can support more than 16,000,000 hosts; numerous (over 16,000) Class B networks exist, and each can support around 65,000 hosts; finally, approximately 2,000,000 Class C networks exist, each with only 254 hosts per network.

❒ Understanding binary arithmetic is essential to knowing how to deal with IP addresses, particularly when working with subnet masks. Knowing how to convert from decimal to binary, and vice versa, helps you understand how the concept of stealing bits from the host portion of an IP address permits a network to be subdivided into logical subnetworks, or subnets. Likewise, it helps you understand how stealing bits from the network portion of multiple contiguous IP addresses increases the number of addressable hosts.

❒ To help ease address scarcity, the IETF created a form of classless addressing called Classless Inter-Domain Routing (CIDR) that permits the network-host boundary to fall away from octet boundaries. CIDR is best used to aggregate multiple Class C addresses to decrease the number of networks, while increasing the total number of addressable hosts. This technique is called supernetting.

❒ Likewise, to make best use of IP network addresses, a technique called subnetting permits additional bits to be taken from the host portion of a network. Recognizing the following bit patterns (decimal values follow in parentheses) helps when calculating or examining subnet masks: 11000000 (192), 11100000 (224), 11110000 (240), 11111000 (248), and 11111100 (252).

❐ Several techniques exist to hide internal network IP addresses from outside view, including address masquerading and address substitution. These techniques replace the actual internal network address from the source field in the IP header with a different value that reveals nothing about the actual address structure of the originating network. Either Network Address Translation software, or a proxy server, usually handles this kind of task.

❐ Within the Class A, B, and C IP address ranges, the IETF has reserved private IP addresses or address ranges. Any organization may use these private IP addresses without charge and without obtaining prior permission, but private IP addresses may not be routed across the public Internet. Another important job for Network Address Translation software, in fact, is to map a range of private IP addresses to a single public IP address to permit computers that use private IP addresses to obtain Internet access.

❐ When it comes to obtaining public IP addresses, the Internet Corporation for Assigned Names and Numbers (ICANN; previously the Internet Assigned Numbers Authority, or IANA, handled this task) is the ultimate authority. Today, unassigned public IP addresses are extremely scarce, and therefore unlikely to be allocated to most ordinary organizations. In fact, most IP address assignments come from ISPs that subdivide already assigned Class A, B, or C addresses to assign public IP addresses to their customers.

Key Terms

anycast address — A new type of address in IPv6, an anycast address is an ordinary address that can be assigned to more than one host or interface. Packets pointed to an anycast address are delivered to the holder of that address nearest to the sender in terms of routing distance. An anycast address does not apply to IPv4.

Application Specific Integrated Circuit (ASIC) — A special-purpose form of integrated circuit. An ASIC provides a way to implement specific programming logic directly into chip form, thereby also providing the fastest possible execution of such programming logic when processing data. ASICs are what make it possible for high-speed, high-volume routers to perform complex address recognition and management functions that can keep up with data volumes and time-sensitive processing needs.

broadcast address — The all-ones address for a network or subnet, this address provides a way to send the same information to all interfaces on a network.

Classless Inter-Domain Routing (CIDR) — A form of subnet masking that does away with placing network and host address portions precisely on octet boundaries, but instead uses the /n prefix notation, in which n indicates the number of bits in the network portion of whatever address is presented.

constant-length subnet masking (CLSM) — An IP subnetting scheme in which all subnets use the same size subnet mask, which therefore divides the subnetted address space into a fixed number of equal-size subnets.

2

domain name — A symbolic name for a TCP/IP network resource; the Domain Name System (DNS) translates such names into numeric IP addresses so that outbound traffic may be addressed properly.

Domain Name System (DNS) — The TCP/IP Application layer protocol and service that manages an Internet-wide distributed database of symbolic domain names and numeric IP addresses so that users can ask for resources by name, and get those names translated into the correct numeric IP addresses.

dotted decimal notation — The name for the format used to denote numeric IP addresses, such as 172.16.1.7, wherein four numbers are separated by periods (dots).

end-to-end connection — A network connection in which the original sending and receiving IP addresses may not be altered, and where a communications connection extends all the way from sender to receiver while that connection remains active.

extended network prefix — The portion of an IP address that represents the sum of the network portion of the address, plus the number of bits used for subnetting that network address. A Class B address with a 3-bit subnetting scheme would have an extended network prefix of /19, 16 bits for the default network portion, plus three bits for the subnetting portion of that address, with a corresponding subnet mask of 255.255.224.0.

firewall — A network boundary device that sits between the public and private sides of a network, and provides a variety of screening and inspection services to ensure that only safe, authorized traffic flows from outside to inside (used in the sense of a barrier designed specifically to block the spread of fire in houses or cars).

hop — A single transfer of data from one network to another, through some kind of networking device. Router-to-router transfers are often called hops. The number of hops often provides a rough metric of the distance between a sender's network and a receiver's network. The number of routers that a packet must cross, or the number of routers that a packet crosses, represents the hop count from the source network to the target network.

host portion — The rightmost bits in an IP address, allocated to identify hosts on a supernetwork, network, or subnetwork.

Internet Assigned Numbers Authority (IANA) — The arm of the ISOC originally responsible for registering domain names and allocating public IP addresses. This job is now the responsibility of ICANN.

Internet Service Provider (ISP) — An organization that provides Internet access to individuals or organizations as a primary line of business. Currently, ISPs are the source for public IP addresses for most organizations seeking Internet access.

IP gateway — TCP/IP terminology for a router that provides access to resources outside the local subnet network address. (A default gateway is the name given to the TCP/IP configuration entry for clients that identifies the router they must use to send data outside their local subnet areas.)

IP renumbering — The process of replacing one set of numeric IP addresses with another set of numeric IP addresses because of a change in ISPs, or an address reassignment.

layer-3 switch — A type of networking device that combines hub, router, and network management functions within a single box. Layer-3 switches make it possible to create and manage multiple virtual subnets in a single device, while offering extremely high bandwidth to individual connections between pairs of devices attached to that device.

loopback — An address that points directly back to the sender. In IPv4, the Class A domain 127.0.0.0 (or 127.0.0.1 for a specific machine address) is reserved for loopback. In IPv6, there is a single loopback address, written "::1" (all zeroes, except for that last bit, which is one). By passing traffic down through the ICP/IP stack, then back up again, the loopback address can be used to test a computer's TCP/IP software.

Media Access Control (MAC) layer — A sublayer of the Data Link layer. This layer is part of the Media Access Control definition, in which network access methods, such as Ethernet and token ring, apply.

multicast address — One of a block of addresses reserved for use in sending the same message to multiple interfaces or nodes. Members of a community of interest subscribe to a multicast address in order to receive router updates, streaming data (video, audio, teleconferencing), and so on. In IPv4, the Class D block of addresses is reserved for multicast. In IPv6, all multicast addresses begin with 0xFF. ICANN, with the help of IANA, manages all such address adjustments.

network address — That portion of an IP address that consists of the network prefix for that address; an extended network prefix also includes any subnetting bits. All bits that belong to the extended network prefix show up as ones in the corresponding subnet mask for that network.

Network Address Translation (NAT) — A special type of networking software that manages network connections on behalf of multiple clients on an internal network, and translates the source address for all outbound traffic from the original source to the address of the outbound network interface. NAT software also manages forwarding replies to all outgoing traffic back to its original sender. NAT software is often used to allow clients using private IP addresses to access the Internet.

network portion — The leftmost octets or bits in a numeric IP address, the network portion of an IP address identifies the network and subnet portions of that address. The value assigned to the prefix number identifies the number of bits in the network portion of any IP address. (For example, 10.0.0.0/8 indicates that the first eight bits of the address are the network portion for the public Class A IP address.)

network prefix — That portion of an IP address that corresponds to the network portion of the address; for example, the network prefix for a Class B address is /16 (meaning that the first 16 bits represent the network portion of the address, and 255.255.0.0 is the corresponding default subnet mask).

numeric address — *See* numeric IP address.

numeric IP address — An IP address expressed in dotted decimal or binary notation.

octet — TCP/IP terminology for an 8-bit number; numeric IPv4 addresses consist of four octets.

2

organizationally unique identifier (OUI) — A unique identifier assigned by IANA or ICANN that's used as the first three bytes of a NIC's MAC layer address to identify its maker or manufacturer.

physical numeric address — Another term for MAC layer address (or MAC address).

private IP address — Any of a series of Class A, B, and C IP addresses reserved by IANA for private use, documented in RFC 1918, intended for uncontrolled private use in organizations. Private IP addresses may not be routed across the Internet because there is no guarantee that any such address is unique.

proxy server — A special type of network boundary service that interposes itself between internal network addresses and external network addresses. For internal clients, a proxy server makes a connection to external resources on the client's behalf and provides address masquerading. For external clients, a proxy server presents internal resources to the public Internet as if they are present on the proxy server itself.

public IP address — Any TCP/IP address allocated for the exclusive use of some particular organization, either by IANA or ICANN, or by an ISP to one of its clients.

Quality of Service (QoS) — A specific level of service guarantee associated with Application layer protocols in which time-sensitivity requirements for data (such as voice or video) require that delays be controlled within definite guidelines to deliver viewable or audible data streams.

reverse proxying — The technique whereby a proxy server presents an internal network resource (for example, a Web, e-mail, or FTP server) as if it were present on the proxy server itself so that external clients can access internal network resources without seeing internal network IP address structures.

route aggregation — A form of IP address analysis that permits routers to indicate general interest in a particular network prefix that represents the "common portion" of a series of IP network addresses, as a way of reducing the number of individual routing table entries that routers must manage.

subnet mask — A special bit pattern that masks off the network portion of an IP address with all ones.

subnetting — The operation of using bits borrowed from the host portion of an IP address to extend and subdivide the address space that falls beneath the network portion of a range of IP addresses.

summary address — A form of specialized IP network address that identifies the "common portion" of a series of IP network addresses used when route aggregation is in effect. This approach speeds routing behavior and decreases the number of entries necessary for routing tables.

supernetting — The technique of stealing bits from the network portion of an IP address and lending those bits to the host part, creating a larger address space for host addresses.

symbolic name — A human-readable name for an Internet resource, such as *www.course.com* or *msnnews.microsoft.com*. Also, a name used to represent a device instead of an address. For example, the name *serv1* could be a symbolic name for a device that uses the IP address 10.2.10.2.

variable–length subnet masking (VLSM) — A subnetting scheme for IP addresses that permits containers of various sizes to be defined for a network prefix. The largest subnet defines the maximum container size, and any individual container in that address space may be further subdivided into multiple, smaller sub-containers (sometimes called sub-subnets).

REVIEW QUESTIONS

1. The following type of address is used to identify the sender and receiver in an IP packet header:

   a. domain name

   b. symbolic name

   c. numeric IP address

   d. return address

2. The 8–bit numbers that denote various portions of an IP address are called:

   a. bytes

   b. dotted decimals

   c. octets

   d. bit strings

3. Which of the following terms is a synonym for a physical numeric address?

   a. hardware address

   b. MAC layer address

   c. PROM address

   d. RIPL address

4. Which of the following protocols translates from a numeric IP address to a physical numeric address?

   a. ICMP

   b. IP

   c. ARP

   d. RARP

5. Which of the following types of IP addresses includes the most host addresses?

   a. Class A

   b. Class B

   c. Class C

   d. Class D

   e. Class E

2

6. Which of the following types of IP addresses includes the most network addresses?

   a. Class A

   b. Class B

   c. Class C

   d. Class D

   e. Class E

7. Which of the following types of IP addresses is used for multicast services?

   a. Class A

   b. Class B

   c. Class C

   d. Class D

   e. Class E

8. A Class A network address of 12.0.0.0 is written as 12.0.0.0/8 in prefix notation. True or false?

   a. True

   b. False

9. Which of the following formulas describes the number of networks in an IP address?

   a. two raised to the number of bits in the network portion of the address

   b. two raised to the number of bits in the host portion of the address, minus two

   c. two raised to the number of bits in the network portion of the address, minus two

   d. 256 minus the number of bits in the host portion of the address

10. Which of the following formulas describes the number of hosts in an IP address?

   a. two raised to the number of bits in the host portion of the address

   b. two raised to the number of bits in the host portion of the address, minus two

   c. two raised to the number of bits in the network portion of the address, minus two

   d. 256 minus the number of bits in the network portion of the address

11. Which of the following subnet masks is the default for a Class B IP address?

   a. 255.0.0.0

   b. 255.255.0.0

   c. 255.255.255.0

   d. 255.255.255.255

12. Which of the following IP addresses is not a private IP address?

    a. 10.16.24.24

    b. 172.16.5.7

    c. 192.168.36.74

    d. 224.0.0.9

13. A default gateway is:

    a. any IP router

    b. an IP router attached to the Internet

    c. an IP configuration element that names the router/gateway for a particular subnet

    d. an IP configuration element that names the boundary router to the Internet

14. The broadcast address for the Class B network 172.16.0.0 is:

    a. 172.16.0.1

    b. 172.16.0.255

    c. 172.16.255.0

    d. 172.16.255.255

15. Which of the following tools or techniques helped to alleviate IP address scarcity? (Choose all that apply.)

    a. CIDR

    b. subnetting

    c. NAT

    d. increased use of private IP addresses

16. Which RFC covers Classless Inter-Domain Routing (CIDR)?

    a. 1519

    b. 1878

    c. 1918

    d. 2700

17. What is the decimal value of 11110000 (a 4-bit subnet mask)?

    a. 192

    b. 224

    c. 240

    d. 248

18. How many subnets does the 11110000 subnet mask produce?

    a. 2

    b. 6

    c. 14

    d. 30

2

19. How many hosts are available per subnet on a Class B network with a subnet mask of 255.255.248.0?

    a. 1022

    b. 2046

    c. 4096

    d. 8190

20. How many contiguous Class C addresses are required to extend the host address by four bits?

    a. 3

    b. 7

    c. 15

    d. 31

21. How many host addresses are there for an address with a /21 prefix (21 bits for the network address)?

    a. 254

    b. 510

    c. 1022

    d. 2046

22. Select all valid limitations to which private IP addresses are subject. (Choose all that apply.)

    a. may not be routed on the Internet

    b. may not be used without permission from ICANN or an ISP

    c. will not work with NAT software

    d. may not work with protocols that require secure end-to-end connections

23. What kinds of devices absolutely require public IP addresses? (Choose all that apply.)

    a. any device attached directly to the Internet

    b. any server whose services should be available to the Internet

    c. every client on an internal network

    d. every server on an internal network

24. Which of the following services perform address hiding? (Choose all that apply.)

    a. e-mail

    b. FTP

    c. NAT

    d. proxy

25. What does IP renumbering involve?

    a. assigning new IP addresses to all boundary devices

    b. assigning new IP addresses to all routers

    c. assigning new IP addresses to all servers and routers

    d. assigning new IP addresses to all network interfaces

HANDS-ON PROJECTS

Project 2-1

In this project, you define a range of network and host addresses that can be used on a sub-netted Class B network. The network number assigned to you is 191.15.0.0. You define a network addressing system that supports 24 networks by subnetting the given address. This project uses the IP Subnet Calculator on the CD that accompanies this book.

To manually install the IP Subnet Calculator:

1. Insert the CD that accompanies this book in your CD-ROM drive.

2. Open **Windows Explorer**, double-click the **CD-ROM** icon, scroll down to the **Subnet** folder, double-click it to open it, and then double-click the **IPCALC.EXE** file.

3. Click the WinZip **Setup** button.

4. Click **Next** in the Welcome! screen.

5. Click the **I Agree** button in the WildPackets IP Subnet Calculator 3.2.1 Installation window.

6. Click **Next** to accept the default installation path (unless your instructor gives you an alternate path).

7. Click **Next** to install the program.

8. Click **Next** after viewing the installation readme text.

9. Click **Finish** to complete the installation.

To use the IP Subnet Calculator:

1. Open the IP Subnet Calculator (click **Start**, point to **Programs**, and then click **WildPackets IP Subnet Calculator**).

2. Enter the address **191.15.0.0** in the IP Address field.

3. Click the **Subnet Info** tab.

4. Click the down arrow next to the **Max Subnets** field.

5. Your network must support 24 subnets. Choose the number **30** from the drop-down list. Note the Subnet Mask field automatically changes to identify the network mask required to support 30 subnets.

6. Click the **Subnets/Hosts** tab to view the list of possible subnetworks and the host ID range.

7. When you are finished with this project, close the IP Subnet Calculator program.

Project 2-2

You will need a computer with Internet access and a Web browser to complete this project.

To visit the Ralph Becker "IP Address Subnetting Tutorial" Web site:

1. Open your Web browser (click **Start**, point to **Programs**, and click **Internet Explorer**; or see your instructor if you use a different browser).

2. Enter the following URL in the Address text box:

   http://www.ralphb.net/IPSubnet/index.html

3. Step through the tutorial, which provides more information and additional examples of IP subnetting.

4. Close the Web browser, unless you plan to proceed immediately to the next project.

Project 2-3

You will need a computer with Internet access and a Web browser to complete this project. You will access the 3Com Web site to look for information about IP addressing. Feel free to spend some time browsing this Web site after you complete the steps.

To find IP addressing information at the 3Com Web site:

Access and read the 3Com white paper "Understanding IP Addressing" to further cement the information covered in this chapter of the book.

1. Open your Web browser (click **Start**, point to **Programs**, and click **Internet Explorer**; or see your instructor if you use a different browser).

2. Enter the following URL in the Address text box:

   http://www.3com.com

3. **Click** the country link of your choice.

4. Type **Understanding IP Addressing** in the Search field, and then click the **Search** button.

5. **Click** the **3Com Press Box Technical Papers** hyperlink. The Technical Papers list appears.

6. Scroll down the list to locate the document titled "Understanding IP Addressing: Everything You Ever Wanted To Know," dated April 26, 1996, by Chuck Semeria. Click the hyperlink **Understanding IP Addressing** to access this document and read the article.

7. Close the Web browser, unless you plan to proceed immediately to the next project.

Project 2-4

You will need a computer with Internet access and a Web browser to complete this project. You access the IETF Web site to look for information about RFC 1878. Feel free to spend some time browsing this Web site after you complete the steps.

To examine RFC 1878:

1. Open your Web browser (click **Start**, point to **Programs**, and click **Internet Explorer**; or see your instructor if you use a different browser).

2. Enter the following URL in the Address text box:

   http://www.ietf.org

3. Click the **RFC Pages** hyperlink.

4. Enter **1878** in the IETF repository retrieval RFC number field, and then click **go**.

   Identify the Class B network address that supports 32 subnets for IP address 191.15.0.0. How many bits are defined for the subnet portion of the address?

5. Close the Web browser.

Project 2-5

To design a subnet structure:

For a Class B network address, you are asked to design a subnet structure to meet stated requirements. Feel free to use pencil and paper, or the IP Subnet Calculator introduced in Hands-on Project 2-1, to solve this problem.

1. For the Class B network address 172.16.0.0, XYZ Corporation wants 60 subnets, each with a minimum of 1000 host addresses.

2. Is this request mathematically possible? If not, explain why. If so, answer the following additional questions:

   a. Calculate the required subnet mask that meets these specifications. What subnet mask is required?

   b. What is the maximum number of subnets that this design allows?

   c. How many workstations will each subnet accommodate?

   d. What is the network address, the range of host addresses, and the broadcast address for the first usable subnet that this design permits?

Project 2-6

To design a supernet structure:

You are asked to design a supernet structure to meet stated requirements for four contiguous Class C network addresses, 192.168.8.0 through 192.168.11.255. Feel free to use pencil and paper, or the IP Subnet Calculator introduced in Hands-on Project 2-1, to solve this problem.

1. Design the largest possible supernet, given the range of Class C addresses from 192.168.8.0 through 192.168.11.255.

2. Calculate the required supernet mask that meets these specifications.

3. What is the maximum number of IP network addresses that can be combined from this address range?

4. How many hosts will the supernet accommodate?

CASE PROJECTS

1. You are asked to design a network for a medium-size company. The company decides to use the 10.0.0.0 private IP address. The network will span six buildings with a router in each building to join the networks. Currently, the company has approximately 1000 workstations in the following locations:

   - Building 1   200 workstations

   - Building 2   125 workstations

   - Building 3   135 workstations

   - Building 4   122 workstations

   - Building 5   312 workstations

   - Building 6   105 workstations

   Design a simple addressing solution that leaves ample room for growth and is easy to administer. Explain what happens to your design if the number of hosts per network jumps to over 1024 per building.

2. ABC Incorporated wants to implement a TCP/IP network for its only site. It has 180 employees and two buildings, and requires Internet access for an e-mail server, a single Web server, a single FTP server, and two routers, each with a single high-speed Internet interface. If the company wants to hold ISP costs to an absolute minimum, what kinds of IP addresses should they primarily use? What is the smallest block of public IP addresses that ABC Incorporated can purchase to cover its needs? (*Hint*: IP address blocks come in groups equal to $2^b - 1$, in which *b* is the number of bits in the total address block.)

3. What kinds of applications might prevent ABC Incorporated from using private IP addresses on its internal networks for end users? If ABC must use public IP addresses, what size block must it purchase to accommodate all users and public points of presence? What difference does it make, if any, to your answer if Building A houses 110 employees and all but one of the public Internet interfaces, and Building B houses 70 workers and a single public Internet interface?

4. XYZ Corporation, a widget distributor based in Geneva, Switzerland, recently finished a round of mergers and acquisitions in the United States. As a result, XYZ wants to consolidate its acquired networks into one cohesive, finely tuned network that conforms to corporate standards. The new office locations are shown in Figure 2-4, along with the number of users at each site.

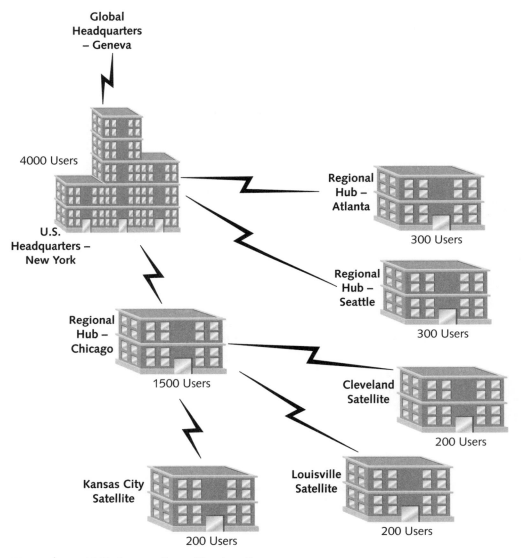

Figure 2-4   XYZ Corporation office locations

In addition to the new offices, each regional hub supports eight branch sales offices, each with 10 and 20 users, but no servers or network-attached printers. The New York (NY) campus consists of three buildings with equal numbers of users in each. Because most of the network traffic in NY is Telnet access to the mainframe, the NY LAN administrators want one IP network for each building. The Graphics and Media Departments are located in Chicago, and users on this campus have complained about network performance for years. Their campus consists of two eight-story buildings with a maximum of 100 people per floor, and each floor has its own file and print servers. XYZ approved the purchase of layer-3 switches to be implemented next quarter.

Headquarters in Geneva allocated the 10.12.0.0/18 range of addresses for all offices in the United States. Your executive team in NY informed you that they expect to grow by at least 20% in the next two years, and want you to allocate IP addresses to each location to meet the company's needs now and in the future. You do not have to provide the host addressing conventions, but you should provide the summary address that will be passed from each location upstream toward headquarters. Also, you should conserve as much address space as possible for future regional hubs.

3

DATA LINK AND NETWORK LAYER TCP/IP PROTOCOLS

After reading this chapter and completing the exercises you will be able to:

♦ Understand the role that data link protocols, such as SLIP and PPP, play for TCP/IP

♦ Distinguish among various Ethernet and token ring frame types

♦ Understand how hardware addresses work in a TCP/IP environment, and the services that ARP and RARP provide for such networks

♦ Appreciate the overwhelming importance of the Internet Protocol (IP), and how IP packets behave on TCP/IP networks

♦ Understand the structures and functions of an IP header

♦ Appreciate the function of the Maximum Transfer Unit (MTU) for any physical medium, and why fragmentation is sometimes required at the Network layer

This chapter covers key TCP/IP protocols that operate at the Data Link and Network layers of the OSI reference model. Here, you learn about the various kinds of data link protocols that make it possible to connect to the Internet using an analog telephone line and a modem, X.25, or an always-on digital technology, such as T1, a cable modem, or a Digital Subscriber Line (DSL). You also learn how IP frames may be identified by type for Ethernet or token ring, and how special protocols make it possible to translate between MAC layer hardware addresses and numeric IP addresses, and vice versa. Finally, you explore the capabilities of the Internet Protocol (IP), upon which so much of TCP/IP's networking capabilities depend. In particular, you learn how IP packets are organized internally, and how they're handled as they move across a TCP/IP–based network from sender to receiver.

DATA LINK PROTOCOLS

The Data Link layer performs several key jobs with the two most important being:

- Managing access to whatever networking medium is in use, called Media Access Control (usually abbreviated as MAC)

- Creating temporary point-to-point links between a pair of MAC layer addresses to enable data transfer, called Logical Link Control (usually abbreviated as LLC)

That's why the IEEE subdivided the Data Link layer into a MAC sublayer and an LLC sublayer when it designed the 802 family of network specifications, and why data link protocols play a key role in enabling the transfer of data from a particular sender to a particular receiver under some circumstances. This is called a **point-to-point** data transfer because it involves shipping data from a specific MAC layer address that represents the point of transmission to another specific MAC layer address that represents the point of reception on a single network segment, or TCP/IP subnet.

Interestingly enough, this same point-to-point technique also works for data transfer across wide area network (WAN) links—such as analog telephone lines, digital connections, or X.25—which is why certain TCP/IP data link protocols may sometimes be called **WAN protocols**. The **data encapsulation** techniques used to enclose packet payloads for transmission across WAN links differ from those used for LAN connections, and involve specialized protocols that operate at the Data Link layer. These specific protocols are:

- Serial Line Internet Protocol (SLIP)

- Point-to-Point Protocol (PPP)

- Special handling for X.25, frame relay, and Asynchronous Transfer Mode (ATM) connections

The rest of this chapter covers these protocols. The key to understanding the material is to recognize that both SLIP and PPP support a straightforward point-to-point connection between two parties, or nodes, on a link. These kinds of two-party connections include **analog phone lines**, **Digital Subscriber Line (DSL)** connections, and **T-carriers**, such as **T1**, **T3**, **E1**, or **E3**. Because all parties on this kind of link are known to each other (and identities are established as the link is negotiated), point-to-point links do not include or require explicit Data Link layer addresses. Other kinds of WAN links support IP network segments, in which there may be more than two nodes active, that therefore require explicit addresses at the Data Link layer. That's why special handling is necessary for X.25, frame relay, and Asynchronous Transfer Mode (ATM) WAN links, which use packet or **circuit-switching** technologies, and must explicitly address sender and receiver at the Data Link layer.

Cable modems are another popular Internet access technology that permits cable television companies to use existing broadband cable infrastructures to provide two-way Internet access to customers. Although they operate at WAN distances (over two miles for some cable segments), such systems use standard Ethernet II frames and behave more or less like Ethernet LANs.

3

Generally speaking, WAN encapsulation of frames at the Data Link layer involves one or more of the following services (they vary according to the requirements of the type of link used):

- *Addressing*: For WAN links in which more than two nodes are involved in possible connections, a unique destination address is required.

- *Bit-level integrity check*: With a **bit-level integrity check**, checksums calculated before and after transmission, when compared, indicate if the message changed as it was received. Such checks occur at each step in the transmission path (for each sender and receiver) when packet-switching networks are used and forwarding occurs.

- *Delimitation*: Data link frames require specific end-of-frame markers, and each frame's header and trailer must be distinct from its payload. With the **delimitation** service, **delimiters** mark these information boundaries.

- *Protocol identification (PID)*: When WAN links support multiple protocols, some method to identify individual protocols in the payload is required. A **protocol identification (PID)** in the header (discussed in the section titled "Point-to-Point Protocol (PPP)" later in this chapter) supplies this information.

The Serial Line Internet Protocol (SLIP)

SLIP is the original point-to-point protocol for TCP/IP traffic, still used for connecting to some ISPs today (mostly for access to older UNIX hosts). SLIP is also sometimes used to manage communications or networking equipment through a dial-up serial port connection. SLIP is a simple packet-framing protocol described in RFC 1055. Because it supports only TCP/IP (meaning no protocol ID is required), and is used only in point-to-point links (meaning no addressing is needed), frame delimitation is the only service that SLIP delivers (it skips the bit-level integrity check entirely).

SLIP uses a special END character (0xC0) that is placed at the beginning and end of each IP datagram to delimit the payload. Thus, two END characters separate two IP datagrams: one END character at the end of the first datagram, the next at the beginning of the next datagram. To avoid confusing legitimate END characters used as delimiters with 0xC0 sequences that may occur in a datagram's payload, SLIP replaces that sequence with its own ESC character (0xDB), followed by 0xDC whenever it occurs. (Note that the SLIP ESC character is not the same as the **American Standard Code for Information Interchange (ASCII)** ESC character; the hex DB-DC sequence is usually denoted 0xDB-DC.)

If the SLIP ESC character occurs in a frame's payload, 0xDB-DD replaces it. On the receiving end, 0xDB-DC is translated back into 0xC0, and 0xDB-DD is translated back into 0xDB, to avoid mistaken replacements. The upshot is that this technique supports SLIP delimiters without changing SLIP frame payloads.

As specified in RFC 1055, the maximum size of a SLIP IP datagram is 1006 bytes. This MTU was dictated by the characteristics of UNIX drivers in use when the RFC was created. Most systems continue to set the upper bound for SLIP datagrams at 1006 bytes, but Windows 2000 permits MTUs of 1500 bytes for SLIP datagrams to avoid **fragmentation** when a SLIP connection links two Ethernet segments. (You will learn more about fragmentation and reassembly of datagrams in the section titled "Fragmentation and Reassembly" later in this chapter.)

As datagram protocols go, SLIP is quite primitive. RFC 1144 was developed to permit IP and TCP headers to be compressed when sent across a SLIP link. (Because source and destination addresses are learned when the connection is set up, there's no need to repeat this information in every header that uses the link.) This version of SLIP is called **compressed SLIP (C-SLIP)**. Although Windows 2000 dial-up connections can use SLIP or C-SLIP to attach to a remote host, Routing and Remote Access does not support inbound SLIP or C-SLIP connections. Neither of these point-to-point protocols is used very much anymore.

Point-to-Point Protocol (PPP)

PPP is a general-purpose, point-to-point protocol that overcomes SLIP's deficiencies, and provides WAN data link encapsulation services similar to those available for LAN encapsulations. Thus, PPP provides not only frame delimitation, but also protocol identification and bit-level integrity check services. (Remember, addressing is not necessary on a point-to-point link, in which only two parties are involved in communications.)

RFC 1661 provides the detailed specifications for PPP, and includes the following characteristics:

- Encapsulation methods that support simultaneous use of multiple protocols across the same link. (In fact, PPP supports a broad range of protocols, including TCP/IP, NetBEUI, IPX/SPX, AppleTalk, SNA, DECNet, and many others.)

- A special **Link Control Protocol (LCP)** used to negotiate the characteristics of any point-to-point link established using PPP.

- A collection of negotiation protocols used to establish the Network layer properties of protocols carried over the point-to-point link, called **Network Control Protocols (NCPs)**. RFCs 1332 and 1877 describe an NCP for IP, known as the **Internet Protocol Control Protocol (IPCP)**, used to negotiate an IP address for the sending party, addresses for DNS servers, and (optional) use of the Van Jacobsen TCP compression protocol, where possible.

PPP encapsulation and framing techniques are based on the ISO **High-level Data Link Control (HDLC)** protocol, which is in turn based on IBM's work on the **Synchronous Data Link Control (SDLC)** protocol used as part of its Systems Network Architecture (SNA) protocols. It's not necessary to fully understand either HDLC or SDLC to understand PPP, except to note that its predecessors are both well known, well understood, and widely implemented protocols (which allows PPP to leverage those implementations). HDLC-like framing for PPP frames is fully described in RFC 1662.

Although PPP framing supports addressing and link control information derived from HDLC, most PPP implementations use an abbreviated form that skips this unnecessary information. Instead, LCP handles address and control field information during PPP link setup, and otherwise dispenses with this information. Thus, the fields in the PPP header and trailer include the following values:

- *Flag*: The Flag is a single-byte delimiter field set to 0x7E (binary value: 01111110) to indicate the boundary between the end of one PPP frame and the beginning of another PPP frame. Unlike SLIP, only a single Flag value appears between frames.

- *Protocol identifier*: The protocol identifier is a 2-byte field that identifies the upper-layer protocol ferried by the PPP frame.

- *Frame Check Sequence (FCS)*: The **Frame Check Sequence (FCS) field** is a 2-byte field that provides bit-level integrity checks for data as sent. (It's recomputed upon receipt, then compared to the sent value; if the two values agree, the assumption is that the data was transmitted successfully; if they disagree, the payload is discarded.)

As with SLIP, PPP must supply a method to replace Flag values should they occur in a frame's payload. Replacement methods differ, however, depending on what kind of connection is in use. For synchronous links, such as analog phone lines, in which characters are sent in as individual bytes, a character replacement approach like that used for SLIP is used for PPP. These substitution methods are covered in RFCs 1661 and 1662.

When PPP is used with synchronous technologies, such as T1, **Integrated Services Digital Network (ISDN)**, DSL, or **Synchronous Optical Network (SONET)** links, a faster, more efficient technique of bit substitution is used, rather than the wholesale character replacement used with asynchronous links. Here, any sequences of six 1 bits in a row (remember, the binary value of the Flag character is 01111110) can be escaped by inserting an extra zero after the fifth 1 bit in a row (and stripped out upon receipt). This supports much more efficient (and faster) encoding of potentially illegal values for such link types, and helps explain why PPP is the most popular of all point-to-point protocols used with TCP/IP. Another reason for PPP's popularity is its support for a multilink PPP implementation that allows multiple data channels of the same bandwidth to be aggregated to handle a single data stream between a single sender and a single receiver. (Two modem lines or two ISDN channels can easily be combined to double the bandwidth between pairs of devices for very little overhead cost.)

PPP supports a default MTU of 1500 bytes, which makes it ideal for interconnecting Ethernet-based networks (or peers). LCP can, however, negotiate higher or lower MTUs between PPP peers, depending on what kinds of networks they're attached to (token ring networks use higher MTUs, but other older networks, such as ARCnet, use lower MTUs).

Special Handling for PPP Links

When any particular switched technologies, such as X.25, frame relay, or ATM, are used to link together PPP peers, additional control and addressing information must be included in PPP headers to manage the connection. This type of connection confers a considerable advantage when errors can be detected and handled at the Data Link layer. That's because recognizing and reacting to errors at this layer takes only milliseconds, whereas handling them at the Transport layer can take an appreciable fraction of a second, and at the Application layer, entire seconds!

For switched technologies, bidirectional connections, called virtual circuits, must normally be negotiated (or are otherwise available, as when permanent virtual circuits may have already been established) between a pair of peers that wishes to exchange data. The following RFCs describe encapsulation of PPP datagrams for these technologies:

- *X.25*: RFC 1356

  X.25 is a standard set of protocols defined in the 1970s by the International Telecommunications Union (ITU), and designed to send datagrams across a public packet-switched data network using noisy, narrow-bandwidth, copper telephone lines. Originally designed to link dumb terminals to mainframes, X.25 became popular in Europe and elsewhere in the world where national telephone monopolies made it difficult to create international data links using only telephone modems. (X.25 provides a reasonable and workable alternative.) Although X.25 isn't required for smart protocol suites like TCP/IP, it's widely available, works well, and remains a popular technology for international WAN links. In a nutshell, that's why PPP supports X.25.

- *Frame relay*: RFC 2427

  Unlike X.25, **frame relay** assumes that digital-quality transmission lines are available for creating WAN links; thus, frame relay includes none of the error-detection and error-correction capabilities that improve X.25's reliability, but that also limit its overall bandwidth and efficiency. Frame relay doesn't attempt to correct transmission errors; it simply discards any corrupted frames it detects, relying on upper-layer protocols to coordinate any required retransmission of data. Frame relay is a popular WAN link technology because it can be metered by actual usage, and its costs are not sensitive to distance (unlike phone lines or X.25 connections). Frame relay's support for virtual circuits also allows its users to create many logical point-to-point and multi-point connections through a single physical interface. This explains why PPP connections using frame relay are popular for medium to large organizations that can afford its costs.

■ *ATM*: RFCs 1557 and 1626

Asynchronous Transfer Mode, or **ATM**, is a high-speed, long-haul broadband cell-switched networking technology that offers astonishing and ever-increasing bandwidth. ATM lets virtual circuits be established between communication peers, but relies on higher-layer protocols (for example, TCP) to provide reliable communications. ATM segments all traffic into 48-byte sequences with a 5-byte header to create a 53-byte ATM frame called a cell. ATM's use of fixed-length transmission units permits it to run at extremely high speeds with maximum efficiency. Today, ATM connections at rates up to an astonishing 13.37 Gbps are available using SONET, and ATM readily accommodates data, fax, voice, and video traffic as a single aggregated data stream. This explains why PPP connections using ATM are so important on the Internet backbone, where major telecommunications carriers ferry the biggest aggregated streams of TCP/IP traffic.

FRAME TYPES

At the Data Link layer, protocol data units are called frames; in TCP/IP terminology, these PDUs may also be called IP datagrams, which can be encapsulated in a variety of frame types. In this section, we examine TCP/IP communications on the most common types of local area networks in use today—Ethernet and **token ring**.

Ethernet Frame Types

The **Ethernet II frame type** is the **de facto standard** frame type used for IP datagram transmissions over Ethernet networks. Thus, Ethernet II frames receive the most coverage in this chapter and in this book. The Ethernet II frame has a **protocol identification field** (the Type field) that contains the value 0x0800 to identify the encapsulated protocol as IP.

Before an IP datagram is transmitted onto the cable, the **data link driver** puts the leading frame onto the datagram. The driver also ensures that the frame meets the minimum frame size specification. The minimum Ethernet frame size is 64 bytes. The maximum Ethernet frame size is 1518 bytes. If a frame does not meet the minimum frame size of 64 bytes, the driver must **pad** the Data field.

The Ethernet NIC performs a **Cyclical Redundancy Check (CRC)** procedure on the contents of the frame, and places a value at the end of the frame in the Frame Check Sequence field. Finally, the NIC sends the frame, led by a **preamble**, which is a leading bit pattern used by the receiver to correctly interpret the bits as ones and zeroes.

For more information on Ethernet technology, visit Charles Spurgeon's Web site at *http://www.ethermanage.com/ethernet/ethernet.html*. To order the IEEE 802.3 CSMA/CD specification, visit *http://shop.ieee.org/store/* (type **802.3 specification** in the search text box, and then click **Go**). To view common questions regarding the IEEE 802.3 standard, visit the IEEE 802.3 Interpretations page at *http://grouper.ieee.org/groups/802/3/interp/*.

There are three Ethernet frame types that TCP/IP can use:

- Ethernet II
- Ethernet 802.2 Logical Link Control (LLC)
- Ethernet 802.2 Sub-Network Access Protocol (SNAP)

Ethernet II Frame Structure

Figure 3-1 depicts the format of an Ethernet II frame.

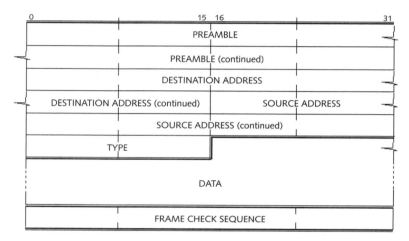

Figure 3-1   Ethernet II frame structure

The Ethernet II frame type consists of the following values, fields, and structure:

- Preamble
- Destination Address field
- Source Address field
- Type field
- Data field
- Frame Check Sequence field

Preamble   The preamble is eight bytes long and consists of alternating ones and zeroes. As its name indicates, this special string of bits precedes the actual Ethernet frame itself, and is not counted as part of the overall frame length. The final byte ends in a pattern of 10101011, indicating the start of the Destination Address field. This field provides the necessary timing used by the receiver to interpret the ones and zeroes in a frame, and builds in the time necessary for Ethernet circuitry to recognize and begin to read incoming data.

Destination Address Field   The Destination Address field is six bytes long and indicates the **data link address** (also referred to as the **hardware address** or MAC address) of the destination IP host. The destination address may be broadcast, multicast, or unicast. Address Resolution Protocol (ARP) is used to obtain the hardware address of the destination IP host (if the destination is local), or the next-hop router (if the destination is remote). ARP is covered in the "Address Resolution Protocol" section later in this chapter.

3

Source Address Field   The Source Address field is six bytes long and indicates the sender's hardware address. This field can only contain a unicast address—it cannot contain a broadcast or multicast address.

Type Field   The Type field is two bytes long and identifies the protocol that is using this frame type. Table 3-1 illustrates some of the assigned type numbers maintained by IANA, available online at *http://www.iana.org.*

Table 3-1   Assigned Protocol Types (by Number)

Type	Protocol
0x0800	IPv4
0x0806	Address Resolution Protocol
0x809B	AppleTalk
0x8137	Novell Internetwork Frame Exchange (IPX)
0x6004	DEC LAT

Data Field   The Data field can be between 46 and 1500 bytes.

Frame Check Sequence Field   The Frame Check Sequence field is four bytes long and includes the result of the CRC calculation.

 For additional information on TCP/IP networking over the Ethernet medium, download and review RFC 894, "A Standard for the Transmission of IP Datagrams over Ethernet Networks."

Upon receipt of an Ethernet II frame, an IP host checks the validity of the contents by performing a CRC check on its contents, and comparing the result to the value contained in the Frame Check Sequence field.

After confirming that the destination address is intended for the recipient (or the broadcast address, or an accepted multicast address), the receiving NIC strips off the Frame Check Sequence field and hands the frame to the Data Link layer.

At the Data Link layer, the frame is examined to determine the actual destination address (broadcast, multicast, or unicast). At this point, the protocol identification field (the Type field in the Ethernet II frame structure, for example) is examined.

The remaining data link frame structure is then stripped off so the frame can be handed up to the appropriate Network layer (IP in this case).

In this section, we concentrate on the Ethernet II frame structure, which is the most popular frame structure used on Ethernet TCP/IP networks. The Ethernet II frame type is the default frame type for TCP/IP on Windows 2000 on Ethernet networking. The IEEE 802.2 specification also defines a method for TCP/IP to run over the **IEEE 802.3** frame structure. We cover the IEEE 802.2 LLC frame structure in the next section, even though IP is not typically seen over this frame type.

Ethernet 802.2 LLC Frame Structure

Figure 3-2 depicts the format of an Ethernet 802.2 **Logical Link Control (LLC)** frame. Although similar to the Ethernet II frame structure, the Ethernet 802.2 LLC frame type uses a SAP field instead of a Type field to identify the protocol that is using the frame. The value 0x06 is assigned to IP.

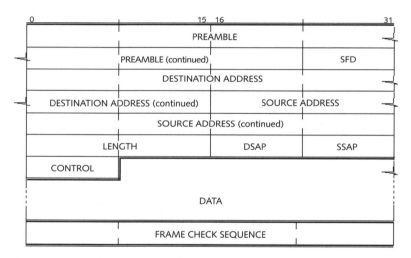

Figure 3-2   Ethernet 802.2 frame structure

The Ethernet 802.2 LLC frame type consists of the following fields:

- Preamble
- Start Frame Delimiter (SFD) field
- Destination Address field
- Source Address field
- Length field
- Destination Service Access Point (DSAP) field
- Source Service Access Point (SSAP) field

- Control field
- Data field
- Frame Check Sequence (FCS) field

In the next section, we highlight only the fields that are unique to the 802.2 LLC frame structure.

Preamble   The preamble is seven bytes long and consists of alternating ones and zeroes. Unlike the Ethernet II frame structure, this preamble does not end in consecutive ones. The Start Frame Delimiter field is used to mark the beginning of the Destination Address field.

Start Frame Delimiter (SFD) Field   The 1-byte SFD field consists of the pattern 10101011 and indicates the start of the Destination Address field. As you may notice, the 802.2 preamble and Start Frame Delimiter field are equivalent to the Ethernet II frame's preamble.

Length Field   The 2-byte Length field indicates the number of bytes in the data portion of the frame. The possible values are between 0x002E (46 decimal) and 0x05DC (1500 decimal). This frame does not use a Type field in this location—it uses a **Service Access Point (SAP)** field to indicate the upcoming protocol.

Destination Service Access Point (DSAP) Field   This 1-byte field indicates the destination protocol. Table 3-2 lists some of the assigned SAP numbers (defined by the IEEE).

Table 3-2   Assigned SAP Numbers

Number	Destination Protocol
0	Null LSAP
2	Indiv LLC Sublayer Mgt
3	Group LLC Sublayer Mgt
4	SNA Path Control
6	DOD IP
14	PROWAY-LAN
78	EIA-RS 511
94	ISI IP
142	PROWAY-LAN
170	SNAP
254	ISO CLNS IS 8473
255	Global DSAP

Source Service Access Point (SSAP) Field   This 1-byte field indicates the source protocol (typically the same as the destination protocol).

Control Field This 1-byte field indicates whether this frame is **unnumbered format** (connectionless) or **informational/supervisory format** (for connection-oriented and management purposes).

Next, we examine the Ethernet SNAP frame structure.

Ethernet SNAP Frame Structure

RFC 1042, "A Standard for the Transmission of IP Datagrams over IEEE 802 Networks," specifies how IP traffic should be encapsulated in 802.2 LLC frames that include the **Sub-Network Access Protocol (SNAP)** portion. Although Windows 2000 defaults to transmitting IP and ARP communications over the Ethernet II frame type, you can edit the Registry to support transmission of IP and ARP over the Ethernet 802.2 SNAP frame structure by adding the ArpUseEtherSNAP **Registry setting**, as listed in Table 3-3.

Table 3-3 ArpUseEtherSNAP Registry Setting

Registry Information	Details
Location	HKEY_LOCAL_MACHINE\SYSTEM\CurrentControlSet\ Services\Tcpip\Parameters
Data type	REG_DWORD
Valid range	0–1
Default value	0
Present by default	No

The Registry entry ArpUseEtherSNAP must be set to 1 to enable use of the Ethernet 802.2 SNAP frame format for IP and ARP traffic over Ethernet. When the Ethernet 802.2 SNAP entry is disabled, the Windows 2000 host can still receive Ethernet 802.2 SNAP frame structures from another IP host, but the Windows 2000 host replies using the Ethernet II frame type. This functionality requires the original transmitting host to automatically switch to the Ethernet II frame type to support subsequent communications between the two hosts.

Figure 3-3 depicts the format of an Ethernet SNAP frame. Although similar to the Ethernet 802.2 frame structure, the Ethernet SNAP frame uses an Ether Type field instead of a SAP field to identify the protocol that is using the frame. The Ether Type field values are the same as the Ethernet Type field values used in the Ethernet II frames covered earlier in this section. However, SNAP frames may be distinguished by their use of 0xAA, AA, and 03 within the DSAP, SSAP, and Control fields, respectively.

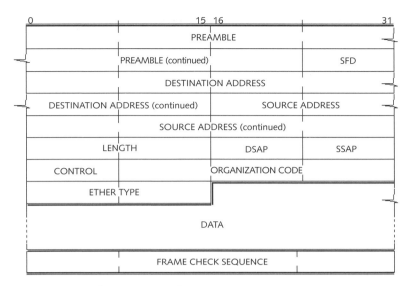

Figure 3-3 Ethernet SNAP frame structure

The Ethernet SNAP frame type consists of the following fields:

- Preamble
- Start Frame Delimiter (SFD) field
- Destination Address field
- Source Address field
- Length field
- Destination Service Access Point (DSAP) field
- Source Service Access Point (SSAP) field
- Control field
- Organization Code field
- Ether Type field
- Data field
- Frame Check Sequence (FCS) field

In this section, we highlight only the fields that are unique to the Ethernet SNAP frame structure.

Organization Code Field This 3-byte field identifies the organization that assigned the Ethernet type number used in the Ether Type field that follows.

Ether Type Field The 2-byte Ether Type field indicates the network protocol that is using this Ethernet SNAP frame format. This field contains the value 0x0800 for all IP communications, and the value 0x0806 for ARP communications.

In all other chapters of this book, we use the Ethernet II frame structures in the examples and the configurations.

Token Ring Frame Types

The **IEEE 802.5** standard defines token ring networking. Token ring networks rely on a **physical star design**, although they use a **logical ring transmission path**, as shown in Figure 3-4.

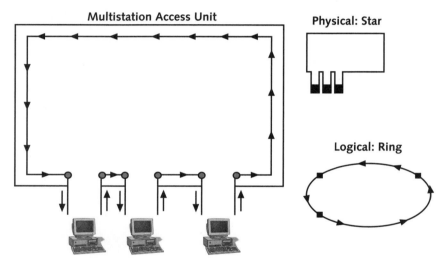

Figure 3-4   Token ring networks are physically stars, but logically rings

On a token ring network, each token ring workstation acts as a **repeater**—repeating each packet received back onto the network. If the frame was destined for the receiving token ring workstation, the station makes a copy of the frame as it repeats the frame back onto the network.

In the same manner that Ethernet NICs perform an error-checking routine on the contents of transmitted packets, token ring frames also include a Frame Check Sequence field.

Cisco has some excellent documentation on token ring technology. View its site at *http://www.cisco.com*.

There are two variations of token ring frames: **Token Ring 802.2 LLC frames** and **Token Ring SNAP frames**.

Token Ring 802.2 LLC Frame Format

As shown in Figure 3-5, the standard Token Ring 802.2 LLC frames include the same LLC fields used by the Ethernet 802.2 LLC frame.

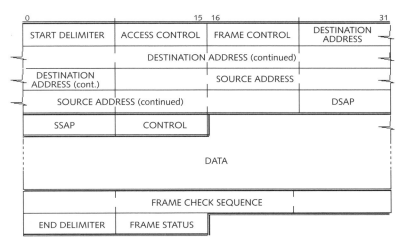

Figure 3-5   Token Ring 802.2 LLC frame structure

This frame type consists of the following fields:

- Start Delimiter field
- Access Control field
- Frame Control field
- Destination Address field
- Source Address field
- Destination Service Access Point (DSAP) field =(LLC 802.2)
- Source Service Access Point (SSAP) field (LLC 802.2)
- Control field (LLC 802.2)
- Data field
- Frame Check Sequence field
- End Delimiter field
- Frame Status field

Start Delimiter Field   The 1-byte Start Delimiter field is used to designate the beginning of a token ring frame.

Access Control Field   The 1-byte Access Control field indicates whether the upcoming fields constitute a **token** or a frame, the priority of the token or frame, and if the frame or token already circled the ring once.

Frame Control Field   This 1-byte field indicates whether the frame contains token ring management information or data.

Destination Address Field   This 6-byte field indicates the destination hardware address. This field can contain unicast, multicast, or broadcast addresses. Please note also that token ring and Ethernet read MAC addresses in opposite order: Ethernet reads the value bytewise from right to left, whereas token ring reads the value bytewise from left to right.

Source Address Field   This 6-byte field indicates the source hardware address. This field must contain a unicast address.

Destination Service Access Point (DSAP) Field (LLC 802.2)   This 1-byte field is the start of the LLC section, and indicates the destination protocol. Like the Ethernet 802.2 LLC frame structure, the Token Ring 802.2 LLC frame has DSAP, SSAP, and Control fields. Refer back to the Ethernet 802.2 frame information for a sample of assigned SAP values.

Source Service Access Point (SSAP) Field (LLC 802.2)   This 1-byte field indicates the source protocol in use. This field value is typically the same as the destination SAP protocol.

Control Field (LLC 802.2)   This 1-byte field indicates whether this frame is unnumbered (connectionless) or supervisory/informational (for connection-oriented and management purposes).

Data Field   This field can be between zero and 18,000 bytes long and contains the TCP/IP data.

Frame Check Sequence Field   The Frame Check Sequence field is four bytes long and includes the result of the CRC calculation used to error check the packet.

End Delimiter Field   This 1-byte field indicates the end of the token ring frame (except for the Frame Status field).

Frame Status Field   This 1-byte field is used to indicate if the frame's destination address was recognized, and if the frame was copied.

Next, we examine the Token Ring SNAP frame structure.

Token Ring SNAP Frame Format

The Token Ring SNAP frame format expands the standard 802.2 LLC layer by adding an Organization Code field and an Ether Type field. That's right—even though this is a token ring frame, the SNAP format can use an Ether Type field value. This field contains the value 0x0800 for all IP communications, and 0x0806 for ARP communications. See Figure 3-6.

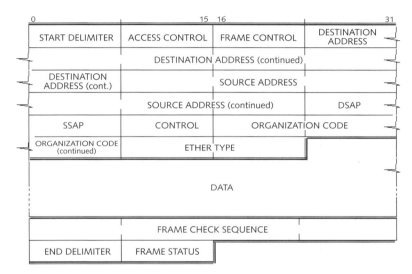

Figure 3-6   Token Ring SNAP frame structure

The Token Ring SNAP frame consists of the following fields:

- Start Delimiter field
- Access Control field
- Frame Control field
- Destination Address field
- Source Address field
- Destination Service Access Point (DSAP) field (LLC 802.2)
- Source Service Access Point (SSAP) field (LLC 802.2)
- Control field (LLC 802.2)
- Organization Code field
- Ether Type field
- Data field

- Frame Check Sequence field
- End Delimiter field
- Frame Status field

In this section, we detail only the fields that are unique to the Token Ring SNAP frame format.

Organization Code Field   This 3-byte field identifies the organization that assigned the Ethernet type number used in the Ether Type field that follows.

Ether Type Field   The 2-byte Ether Type field indicates the network protocol that is using this Ethernet SNAP frame format. This field contains the value 0x0800 for all IP communications, and the value 0x0800 for all ARP communications.

 James Messer (of Network Associates) wrote an excellent FAQ (Frequently Asked Questions) document on token ring. Read it online at *http://www.networkuptime.com/faqs/token-ring/index.html*. Access the IEEE 802.5 specification ordering information online at *http://shop.ieee.org/ store/* (type **802.3 specification** in the search text box, and then click **Go**).

HARDWARE ADDRESSES IN THE IP ENVIRONMENT

IP addresses are used to identify individual IP hosts on a TCP/IP internetwork. A hardware address is required to get the packet from one IP host to another IP host on a single network.

For example, to get from one IP host to another IP host that is located on the other side of a router, the source needs to know the IP address of the destination IP host. The source must perform some manner of hardware address resolution to learn the hardware address of the router so it can build a data link header (such as an Ethernet header) to get the packet to the local router. When the packet is received at the router, the router must go through the same hardware address resolution process to determine the next local hardware address for the packet.

TCP/IP networking uses ARP to determine the hardware address of the local target for the packet. IP hosts maintain an **ARP cache**—a table of hardware addresses learned through the ARP process—in memory. An IP host refers to the ARP cache first, before issuing an ARP request onto the network. If the desired hardware address is not found in cache, the IP host broadcasts an ARP request.

 ARP is defined in RFC 826.

Figure 3-7 depicts the basic functionality of ARP. In this graphic, we can see the source IP host, 10.1.0.1, uses ARP to obtain the hardware address of the local target.

3

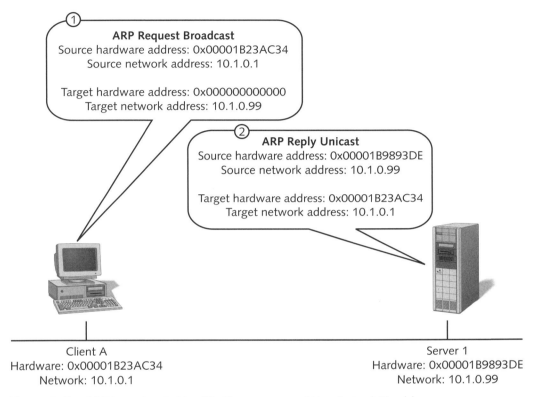

ARP Request Broadcast
Source hardware address: 0x00001B23AC34
Source network address: 10.1.0.1

Target hardware address: 0x000000000000
Target network address: 10.1.0.99

ARP Reply Unicast
Source hardware address: 0x00001B9893DE
Source network address: 10.1.0.99

Target hardware address: 0x00001B23AC34
Target network address: 10.1.0.1

Client A
Hardware: 0x00001B23AC34
Network: 10.1.0.1

Server 1
Hardware: 0x00001B9893DE
Network: 10.1.0.99

Figure 3-7   ARP broadcasts identify the source and the desired IP address

ARP is used only to find the hardware address of local IP hosts. If the IP destination is remote (on another network), the IP host must refer to its **routing tables** to determine the proper router for the packet. This is referred to as the **route resolution process**.

ARP is not routable—it does not have a Network layer component in the packet structure, as shown in Figure 3-8.

As simplistic as ARP is, it is often the protocol that signals problems with network addressing or configuration, as you will learn in the "If Remote, Which Router?" section later in this chapter.

ARP can also be used to test for a **duplicate IP address** on the network. Before an IP host begins to communicate on an IP network, it should perform a duplicate IP address test. During the duplicate address test process, an IP host sends an ARP request for its own IP address (referred to as a gratuitous ARP), as shown in Figure 3-9. The host cannot initialize its TCP/IP stack if another host replies to the duplicate IP address test—a reply indicates that the IP address is already in use.

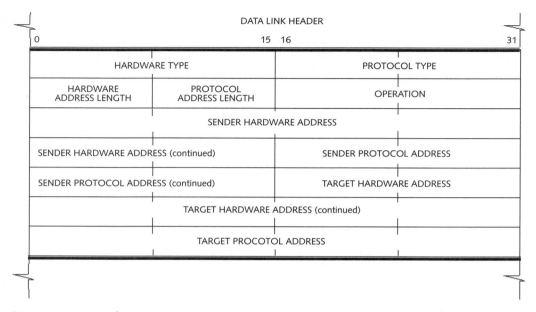

Figure 3-8   ARP frame structure

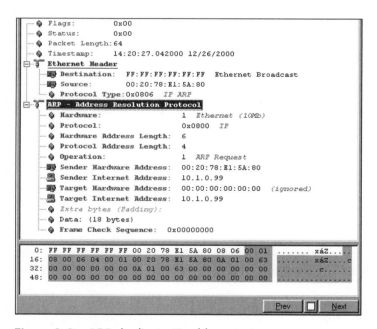

Figure 3-9   ARP duplicate IP address test

Viewing the packets in a simple ARP transaction should further clarify ARP usage.

ARP Packet Fields and Functions

By default, Windows 2000 uses the Ethernet II frame type for all ARP traffic. There are two basic ARP packets—the ARP request packet and the ARP reply packet. Both packets use the same format, as you can see in Figures 3-10 and 3-11.

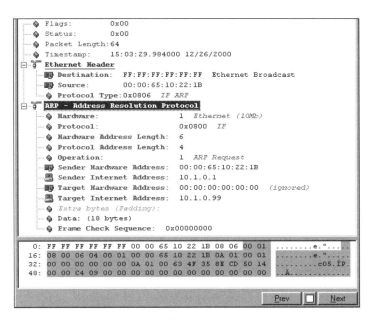

Figure 3-10 ARP request for IP host 10.1.0.99

The most confusing part of ARP is the interpretation of the sender and target address information. When an ARP broadcast is being sent from a host (Host A in this example), the sending host—Host A—puts the hardware and IP address in the Sender Address fields.

The Target Internet Address field includes the IP address of the desired IP host. The Target Hardware Address field is set to all zeroes to indicate that the information is not known, as shown in Figure 3-10.

The ARP specification dictates that the Target Hardware Address field can be set to a value other than all zeroes. In some implementations of ARP, the source sets the destination address to all ones, which may confuse some routers, causing them to broadcast the ARP packet onto all connected networks. This type of problem is easy to spot with a network analyzer, and is documented in Microsoft Knowledge Base article Q199773 (available online at *http://support.microsoft.com/support/kb/articles/Q199/7/73.ASP*).

Figure 3-11 shows the ARP reply packet. In this reply, the target and sender information is reversed to show that the ARP responder is now the sender. The original station performing the lookup is now the destination.

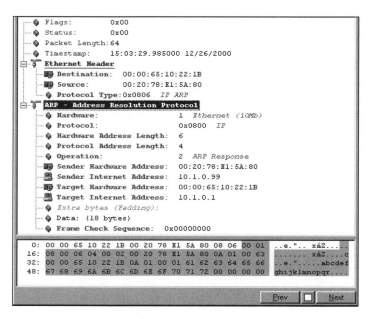

Figure 3-11   ARP reply packet is a unicast packet

Interestingly, the IP host that replies updates its own ARP cache to include the IP address and hardware address of the IP host that was looking for it. This is a logical step because most likely there will be a two-way conversation between the IP hosts, so the responding IP host eventually needs the requesting IP host's address.

Hardware Type Field

This field defines the hardware or data link type in use, is also used to determine the hardware address length, which makes the Length of Hardware Address field redundant.

Table 3-4 is a partial list of assigned hardware type numbers derived from the online list at *http://www.iana.org*.

Protocol Type Field

This field defines the protocol address type in use, and uses the standard protocol ID values that are also used in the Ethernet II frame structures. These protocol types are defined at *http://www.iana.org/assignments/ethernet-numbers*.

Table 3-4   Hardware Type Numbers

Number	Hardware Type
1	Ethernet
6	IEEE 802 Networks
7	ARCnet
11	LocalTalk
14	SMDS
15	Frame Relay
17	HDLC
19	Asynchronous Transmission Mode
20	Serial Line
21	Asynchronous Transmission Mode

This field uses the same values assigned to the Ethernet Type field. At this time, IP is the only protocol that uses ARP for address resolution. This field also determines the length of the protocol address, making the Length of Protocol Address field redundant.

Length of Hardware Address Field

This field defines the length (in bytes) of the hardware addresses used in this packet. This field is redundant because the Hardware Type field also determines the length value.

Length of Protocol Address Field

This field indicates the length (in bytes) of the protocol (network) addresses used in this packet. This field is redundant because the Protocol Type field also determines this value.

Opcode Field

This field defines whether this ARP packet is a request or reply packet, and defines the type of address resolution taking place. Table 3-5 lists the ARP and Reverse ARP (RARP) operation codes.

Table 3-5   ARP and RARP Operation Codes

Code Value	Packet Type
1	ARP request
2	ARP reply
3	RARP request
4	RARP reply

RARP is a process that enables an IP host to learn a network address from a data link address. RARP is defined in RFC 903 and covered later in the "Reverse ARP (RARP)" section of this chapter.

Sender's Hardware Address Field

This field indicates the hardware address of the IP host that sends this request or reply.

Sender's Protocol Address Field

This field indicates the protocol, or network, address of the IP host that sends this request or reply.

Target Hardware Address Field

This field indicates the desired target's hardware address, if known. In ARP requests, this field is typically filled with all zeroes. In ARP replies, this field should contain one of the following:

- The hardware address of the desired IP host if the sender and destination share a common data link
- The hardware address of the next router in the path to the destination if they don't share a common data link. This is known as the **next-hop router** to that IP host, in which that device will be the first of one or more routers that will convey the data from sender to receiver. Each network, or router-to-router transition, is counted as a hop.

Target Protocol Address Field

This field indicates the desired target's protocol, or network, address.

ARP Cache

ARP information (hardware addresses and their associated IP addresses) is kept in an ARP cache in memory on most operating systems, including Linux, BSD UNIX, Windows 95, Windows 98, Windows NT, and Windows 2000. These operating systems also have tools for viewing ARP cache entries, manually adding or deleting entries in the ARP cache, and loading table entries from a configuration file. On Windows-based systems, the command *arp -a* is used to view the table contents, as shown in Figure 3-12.

```
C:\WINDOWS\arp -a

Interface: 10.1.0.1 on Interface 0x2000003
  Internet Address      Physical Address      Type
    10.1.0.2            00-00-1b-09-f3-d6    dynamic
    10.1.0.99           00-20-78-e1-5a-80    dynamic
```

Figure 3-12   Type arp -a to read the local host's ARP table

Windows-based systems also have a utility you can use to view your IP and hardware addresses. You can use the Windows utility **WINIPCFG** on Windows 95 systems. You can use the command-line utility **IPCONFIG** on Windows 98 and Windows 2000 systems. Figure 3-13 shows the result of running the IPCONFIG utility on a Windows 2000 device.

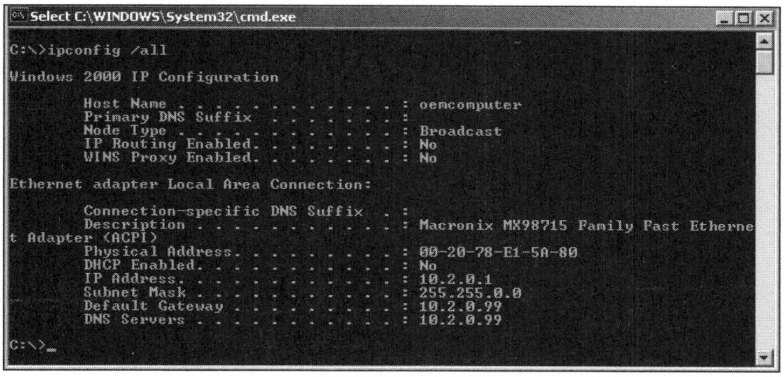

Figure 3-13   IPCONFIG utility indicates the device's IP and hardware addresses

As you can see in Figure 3-13, the IPCONFIG utility displays the adapter address (physical address) 00-20-78-E1-5A-80, the IP address 10.2.0.1, and the subnet mask 255.255.0.0. The IPCONFIG utility also indicates that the **default gateway** is 10.2.0.99.

On a Windows 2000 system, ARP cache entries are kept in memory for 120 seconds (two minutes); this varies from a more common default of 300 seconds (five minutes) on most other kinds of networking equipment. IP hosts must consult these tables before transmitting ARP broadcasts. If an entry exists in the ARP cache entries, the IP host uses the existing entry instead of transmitting an ARP request on the network.

You can change the entry lifetime in the ARP cache using the ArpCacheLife Registry setting, as listed in Table 3-6.

Table 3-6   ArpCacheLife Registry Setting

Registry Information	Details
Location	HKEY_LOCAL_MACHINE\SYSTEM\CurrentControlSet\ Services\Tcpip\Parameters
Data type	REG_DWORD
Valid range	0–0xFFFFFFFF
Default value	120
Present by default	No

Windows 2000 retains ARP cache entries longer than 120 seconds if they were referenced while in the cache. The ArpCacheMinReferencedLife Registry entry is used to extend the referenced ARP entry past the default 600 seconds (10 minutes).

Proxy ARP

Proxy ARP is a method that allows an IP host to use a simplified subnetting design. Proxy ARP also enables a router to "ARP" in response to an IP host's ARP broadcasts. Figure 3-14 shows a proxy ARP configuration that consists of one network that is divided by a router, but maintains a single network address on both sides. The IP host 10.1.0.1 was configured with a subnet mask of 255.0.0.0. This IP host believes that the destination 10.2.77.33 is on the same network—network 10.0.0.0. Because the source host believes that the destination host is on the same network, the source host knows that it can ARP for its hardware address.

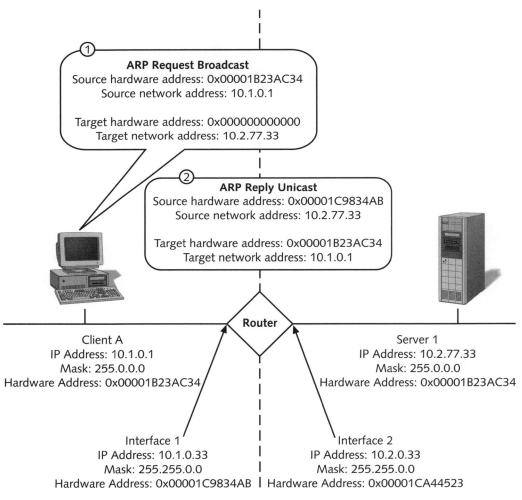

Figure 3-14 ARP proxy network design

But the destination is not on the same network. The destination host, 10.2.77.33, is on a separate network, but a connecting router was configured to support proxy ARP. When 10.1.0.1 sends an ARP looking for the hardware address 10.2.77.33, the proxy ARP router does not forward the broadcast; instead, it replies to the ARP request, and supplies the router's hardware address on Interface 1 (the interface that is on the same network as the requesting IP host).

You should be aware that proxy ARP is not a common configuration.

Reverse ARP (RARP)

Reverse ARP is, as its name implies, the reverse of ARP. RARP is used to obtain an IP address for an associated data link address. RARP was initially defined to enable **diskless workstations** to find their own IP addresses. RARP hosts would broadcast a RARP request and include their own hardware addresses, but leave the source IP addresses blank (all zeroes). A RARP server on the local network would answer the request, supplying the RARP host with its IP address by filling in the target IP address in the reply packet.

BOOTP, and eventually DHCP, replaced RARP. Both BOOTP and DHCP offer a more robust, flexible method of assigning IP addresses.

RARP is documented in RFC 903.

NETWORK LAYER PROTOCOLS

The primary function of Network layer protocols is to move datagrams through an internetwork connected by routers. Network layer communications are end-to-end communications that define the originator as the source Network layer address, and the target as the destination Network layer address. When packets are sent to network routers, these routers examine the destination network address to determine which direction to forward the packets, if possible.

Internet Protocol is the Network layer protocol used in the TCP/IP suite. Currently, IP version 4 (IPv4) is widely implemented. **Internet Protocol version 6** (IPv6) is undergoing some initial implementations. IPv6 is covered in Chapter 13.

The functionality and fields of IPv4 communications are documented in RFC 791, "Internet Protocol." The next section focuses only on IPv4.

ABOUT INTERNET PROTOCOL (IP)

In this section, we examine how an IP datagram is formed, how an IP host learns whether the destination is local or remote, how packets are fragmented and reassembled, as well as the details of IP packet structures. This section also defines basic IP routing processes used to get an IP datagram through an internetwork.

Sending IP Datagrams

IP offers connectionless service with end-to-end Network layer addressing. The best way to illustrate how an IP datagram is formed and sent is by example. In Figure 3-15, we have one host (10.1.0.1) communicating with another IP host (10.2.0.2) that is located on the other side of a router.

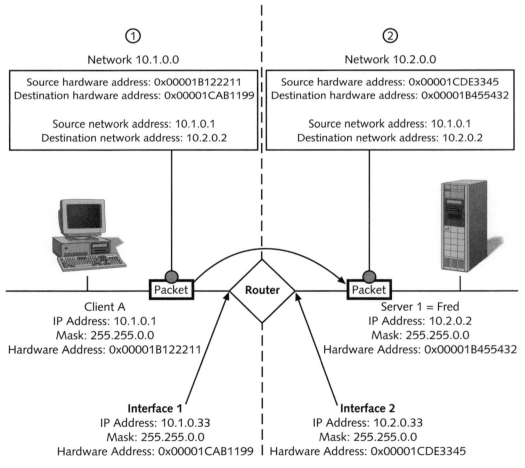

Figure 3-15   Data link header is stripped off and reapplied by the IP router as the packet
is forwarded

Building an IP datagram packet to send on the wire has certain requirements. We must know the:

- IP addresses of the source and destination
- Hardware address of the source and next-hop router

An IP host can use a manually entered destination IP address or the DNS to obtain a destination's IP address. For example, if you type *telnet 10.2.0.2*, your system knows the destination IP address. If you use the command *telnet fred*, however, your system needs to resolve the name *fred* to an IP address. This is called the **name resolution process**. Chapter 7 covers DNS in detail.

As mentioned earlier in this chapter, before launching the ARP process, the IP host must know whether the destination is local or remote. Should the IP host be sending the packet directly to the desired destination, or should it send the packet to a local router? This is called the route resolution process.

Once the route resolution process is completed, the IP host can begin the ARP process to locate the desired destination hardware address.

Route Resolution Process

The route resolution process enables an IP host to determine if the desired destination is local or remote. If the destination is remote, this process enables the IP host to determine the next-hop router.

Local or Remote Destination?

Upon determination of the IP address of the desired destination, the IP host compares the network portion of the destination address to its own local network address.

In our example, Fred's IP address is 10.2.0.2. The local IP host (Client A) has the IP address 10.1.0.1, with the subnet mask 255.255.0.0. Consider the following process:

1. The source IP address is 10.1.0.1.
2. The source IP mask is 255.255.0.0.
3. The local network number is 10.1.0.0.
4. Fred's IP address is 10.2.0.2.
5. Fred's network is 10.2.0.0.
6. Because Fred's network address differs from the local network address, Fred is remote from the source.
7. The source must go through a router to reach Fred.
8. The source needs the hardware address of the router.

9. The source examines its routing tables.

10. The source transmits an ARP for the router's hardware address.

If Remote, Which Router?

Now that the local IP host knows that the destination is remote, the IP host must determine the hardware address of the appropriate router for the packet. Remember that hardware addresses are used only to get packets from one IP host on a network to another IP host on the same network. The router receives a packet addressed to its hardware address, strips off the data link header, examines the Network layer header to determine how to route the packet, and then reapplies a data link header to move the packet along on the next network.

The IP host looks in its local routing tables to determine if it has a host entry or network router entry for the target. A host entry matches the entire four bytes of the destination address, and indicates the local router that can forward packets to the desired destination. A network entry indicates that a route to the destination network is known, but a route to the individual host is not known. This is typically sufficient because the router closest to the destination is responsible for getting the packet to the destination host.

If neither a host entry nor network entry is listed, the IP host checks for a default gateway entry.

The default gateway offers a path of *blind faith*—because the IP host does not have a route to the destination, it sends the packet to the default gateway, and just hopes the default gateway can figure out what to do with the packet. Default gateways typically do one of the following:

- Forward the packet (if they have a route to the destination)
- Send an ICMP reply, called an ICMP redirect, that points to another local router that has the best route to the destination
- Send an ICMP reply indicating that it's unclear where to send the packet— the destination is unreachable

If the destination is remote, and a source knows a next-hop router or default gateway that can forward the packet, the source must use ARP to resolve the hardware address of the next-hop router or default gateway. Naturally, the source checks its ARP cache first. If the information does not exist in cache, the source sends an ARP broadcast to get the hardware address of the next-hop router.

If IP hosts cannot communicate with each other, you can use a protocol analyzer to determine what went wrong. Perhaps one of the following faults occurred:

- The IP host can ARP only for IP hosts that are local—perhaps the actual destination is remote (check the source subnet mask and the destination's IP address).

- Perhaps the destination is local, but not replying to the ARP because it is not completely functional (a duplicate IP address was detected, or the destination is simply down).

- Maybe the IP address the source received from a name resolution process, such as DNS, is incorrect. No IP host is using the desired IP address.

It is not uncommon for problems to occur in the route resolution process. In Figure 3-16, we see that the subnet mask placed on the source host is 255.0.0.0. When we place this mask on the destination IP address 10.2.12.4, it implies that the destination is local to the source (on the same network—network 10.0.0.0). The source begins to ARP for the hardware address that is associated with 10.2.12.4.

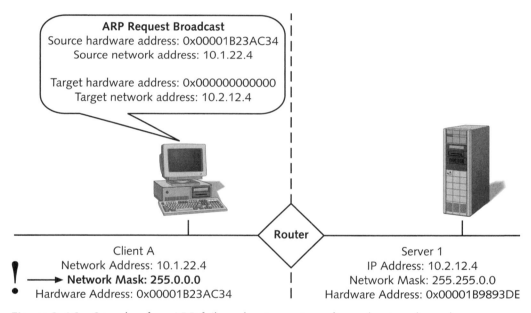

Figure 3-16   Sample of an ARP failure due to a misconfigured network mask

Will 10.2.12.4 answer? No. Routers do not forward ARP broadcasts, and no one else on the source's network is set up to reply on behalf of that IP host.

When you look at communications at the packet level, you can find the definitive answers to these questions—unlike *blind* troubleshooting, where you simply guess at the solution until one works out.

Now that we followed an IP packet through an internetwork, it is time to examine the following unique characteristics of IP communications:

- Lifetime of an IP datagram

- Fragmentation and reassembly

- Service delivery options
- IP header fields and functions

LIFETIME OF AN IP DATAGRAM

All IP packets have a predefined lifetime indicated in each packet's **Time to Live (TTL)** field. This ensures that packets cannot indefinitely circle a **looped internetwork**. Although routing protocols attempt to prevent loops, and the best routes are chosen when forwarding packets, there may be times when a link is reconfigured or temporarily shut down. In this case, the network may have a temporary loop.

The recommended starting TTL value is 64. The default TTL in Windows 2000 is 128. The TTL value is formally defined as a number of seconds. In actual practice, however, the TTL value is implemented as a hop count. Each time a packet is forwarded by a router, the router must decrement the TTL field by one. Switches and hubs do not decrement the TTL value—they do not look at the Network layer of the packet.

If a packet with TTL=1 arrives at a router, the router must discard the packet because it cannot decrement the TTL to zero and forward the packet.

If a packet with TTL=1 arrives at a host, what should the host do? Process the packet, of course. The hosts do not need to decrement the TTL value upon receipt.

 Chapter 4, "Internet Control Message Protocol (ICMP)," explains how one troubleshooting utility, **TRACEROUTE**, uses the TTL value and the timeout process to trace the end-to-end path through an internetwork.

In Windows 2000, you can set the default TTL for a host using the DefaultTTL Registry setting, as listed in Table 3-7.

Table 3-7   DefaultTTL Registry Setting

Registry Information	Details
Location	HKEY_LOCAL_MACHINE\SYSTEM\CurrentControlSet\Services\Tcpip\Parameters
Data type	REG_DWORD
Valid range	1–255
Default value	128
Present by default	No

FRAGMENTATION AND REASSEMBLY

IP fragmentation enables a larger packet (for example, a token ring 4096-byte packet) to be automatically fragmented by a router into smaller packets to cross a link that supports a smaller MTU, such as an Ethernet link. Once fragmented, however, no reassembly occurs until those fragments arrive at the destination, where they will be reassembled at the Transport layer.

When a packet is fragmented, all fragments are given the same TTL value. If they take different paths through a network, they may end up at the destination with varying TTL values. When the first **fragment** arrives at the destination, however, the destination host begins counting down from the TTL value of that packet. All fragments must arrive before that timer expires, or the fragment set is considered incomplete and unusable. The destination sends an ICMP reply to the source stating that the packet's lifetime has expired.

Fragments are reassembled at the destination host. For example, if a router must fragment a 4096 packet to forward the packet onto an Ethernet network that only supports a 1518 MTU, the router must perform the following tasks to properly fragment the packet:

- The router places the original packet's IP header Identification field value in all three fragments.

- The router decrements the TTL value by one, and places the new TTL value in each fragment.

- The router calculates the relative location of the fragmented data, and includes that value in the **Fragment Offset field** of each fragment.

- The router sends each fragment off as a separate packet with a separate data link header and checksum calculation.

Figures 3-17 through 3-19 show the first, middle, and last fragments of a fragment set. In Figure 3-18, the Fragment Offset value of 1480 indicates that it is not the first fragment of the set. It's not the last fragment in the set either, as denoted by the More Fragments bit setting.

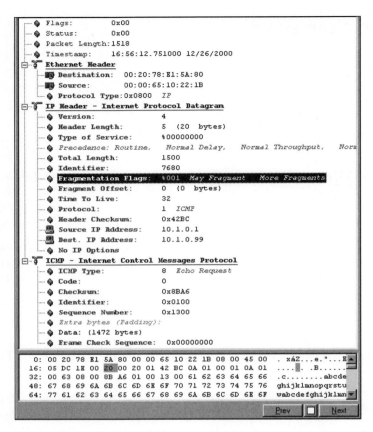

Figure 3-17   First packet of a fragment set (More to Come bit is set to 1 and the offset is 0)

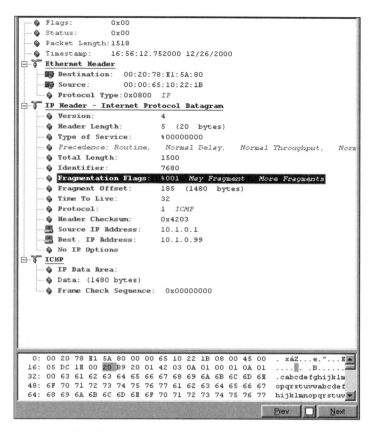

Figure 3-18   Second packet of a fragment set (More to Come bit is set to 1 and the offet is 185 [1480 bytes])

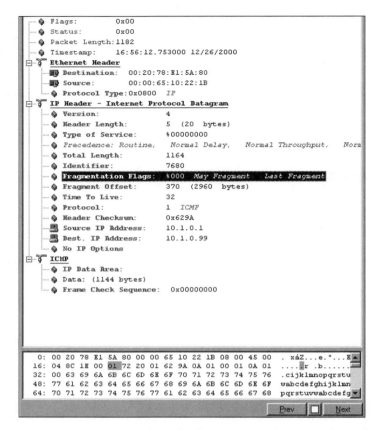

Figure 3-19   Last packet of a fragment set (More to Come bit is set to 0 and the offset is 370 [2960 bytes])

 This trace was obtained by forcing an IP host to fragment a large ICMP echo packet by using the following command: ping –l 4096 10.0.0.1.

When the fragments arrive at the destination IP host, they are put back in order based on the Fragment Offset value contained in the IP header.

Fragmentation has some ugly characteristics that make it undesirable traffic on a network. First, the fragmentation procedure takes processing time at the router or IP host that is fragmenting the packet. Second, all fragments must arrive before the expiration of the first-received fragment's TTL timer. If one of the fragments does not arrive in time, the receiver sends an ICMP message type 11 (Time Exceeded) with a code 22 (Fragmentation Reassembly Time Exceeded). In this case, the IP host that sent the packet re-sends another single packet (fragmented again). On a network that is low on available bandwidth, the **fragment retransmission process** causes more traffic on the wire.

SERVICE DELIVERY OPTIONS

IP supports a method for defining **packet priority** and **route priority**. The **Type of Service (TOS)** field in the IP header (detailed in the "Type of Service (TOS)" section later in this chapter) is separated into two distinct fields:

- Precedence
- Type of Service

Precedence

A router uses **precedence** to determine what packet to send when several packets are queued for transmission from a single-output interface. Some applications can be configured to support a higher precedence to receive high-priority treatment.

There are eight levels of precedence. Level 0 is set for routine traffic that has no priority. Levels 1 through 5 are for prioritized traffic with a higher value, indicating a higher priority. Precedence Levels 6 and 7 are reserved for network and internetwork control packets.

One example of precedence use is **Voice over IP (VoIP)**. The precedence for VoIP traffic may be set to five to support VoIP real-time functionality.

Type of Service (TOS)

Routers use TOS to select a routing path when there are **multiple paths** available.

TOS functionality requires that the routing protocol understands and maintains varying views of the network based on the type of service possible. For example, a router must recognize that a satellite link is high delay because of the distance to the satellite. OSPF and **Border Gateway Protocol (BGP)** are two examples of routing protocols that support multiple types of services.

There are six possible types of services, as listed in Table 3-8.

Table 3-8   Type of Service Values

Binary	Decimal	Type of Service
0000	0	Default (no specific route defined)
0001	1	Minimize Monetary Cost
0010	2	Maximize Reliability
0100	4	Maximize Throughput
1000	8	Minimize Delay
1111	15	Maximize Security

Only one of the TOS bits can be set at a time.

In Windows 2000, you can set the default TOS for a host using the DefaultTOS Registry setting, as listed in Table 3-9.

Table 3-9 DefaultTOS Registry Setting

Registry Information	Details
Location	HKEY_LOCAL_MACHINE\SYSTEM\CurrentControlSet\ Services\Tcpip\Parameters
Data type	REG_DWORD
Valid range	0–255
Default value	0
Present by default	No

The Registry entry is set in decimal for the entire TOS field. For example, to configure a host to use routine precedence and maximum reliability, you would set the DefaultTOS to four (00000100).

RFC 1349 defines the use of IP TOS and suggests uses of the TOS functionality, as listed in Table 3-10.

Table 3-10 Type of Service Functionality

Protocol	TOS Value	Functionality
TELNET	1000	Minimize Delay
FTP Control	1000	Minimize Delay
FTP Data	0100	Maximize Throughput
TFTP	1000	Minimize Delay
SMTP Command phase	1000	Minimize Delay
SMTP Data phase	0100	Maximize Throughput
DNS UDP Query	1000	Minimize Delay
DNS TCP Query	0000	Routine
DNS Zone Transfer	0100	Maximize Throughput
NNTP	0001	Minimize Monetary Cost
ICMP Errors	0000	Routine
ICMP Requests	0000	Routine
ICMP Responses	0000	Routine
Any IGP	0010	Maximize Reliability
EGP	0000	Routine
SNMP	0010	Maximize Reliability
BOOTP	0000	Routine

IP HEADER FIELDS AND FUNCTIONS

Figure 3-20 depicts the entire IP header structure. This section details the header fields and their functions. For more details on each field, refer to RFC 791.

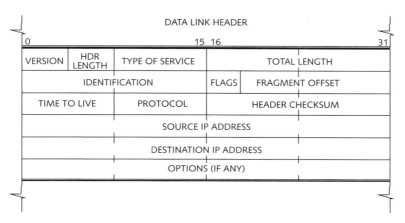

Figure 3-20   IP header structure

Version Field

The first field in the IP header is the Version field. We are currently at version 4.

Header Length Field

This field is also referred to as the Internet Header Length (IHL) field. This field denotes the length of the IP header only. This is necessary because the IP header can support options, and therefore may vary in length.

This field value is provided in multiples of four bytes. For example, the actual decimal decode is five. The analyzers multiply that value by four bytes to come up with the true IP Header Length value of 20 bytes. Because the options are rarely used, the size of the IP header is typically 20 bytes.

Type of Service Field

As mentioned earlier, the TOS field actually has two components: precedence and Type of Service. Precedence is defined in the first three bits, and may be used by routers to prioritize traffic that goes through **router queues**. Type of Service is defined in the next four bits, and should be used by routers to follow a specified path type. The last bit of the entire TOS field is reserved and set at zero. The sections within the Type of Service field are shown in Figure 3-21.

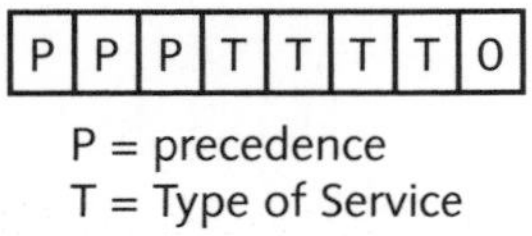

P	P	P	T	T	T	T	0

P = precedence
T = Type of Service

Figure 3-21   TOS field includes precedence and TOS bits

Table 3-11 lists the possible settings in the precedence bits.

Table 3-11   Precedence Bits Settings

Binary	Decimal	Purpose
111	7	Network Control
110	6	Internetwork Control
101	5	CRITIC/ECP
100	4	Flash Override
011	3	Flash
010	2	Immediate
001	1	Priority
000	0	Routine

When you convert these binary values to decimal, the bits have the decimal values listed in Table 3-12.

Table 3-12   Decimal Values Based on Bit Position

Bit	Decimal Value
Bit 2	4
Bit 1	2
Bit 0	1

For example, the binary value 111 is decimal value 7 (4 + 2 + 1).

Table 3-13 lists the possible settings in the Type of Service bits.

Table 3-13   Type of Service Bit Settings

Binary	Purpose
0000	Default (no specific route defined)
0001	Minimize Monetary Cost
0010	Maximize Reliability
0100	Maximize Throughput
1000	Minimize Delay
1111	Maximize Security

For example, a packet with the binary value 00010000 in the TOS field requires routine service (000) through the lowest delay path (1000).

Some analyzers only show the four basic service types (Default, Delay, Throughput, and Reliability).

RFC 2474, "Definition of Differentiated Service Field (DS Field) in the IPv4 and IPv6 Headers," recommends a complete redefinition of the TOS field values and functions.

Most likely you will find this field set at 00000000 (default).

Total Length Field

This field defines the length of the IP header and any valid data (does not include any data link padding). In the example shown in Figure 3-22, the total length is 213 bytes. The IP header is the first 20 bytes, indicating that the remaining packet length is 193 bytes.

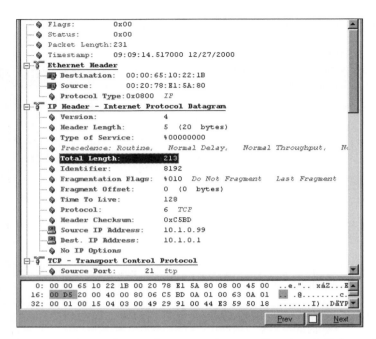

Figure 3-22   Subtract the IP Header Length value (20) from the Total Length value (213) to determine the amount of data that follows the IP header

Identification Field

Each individual packet is given a unique ID value when it is sent. If the packet must be fragmented to fit on a network that supports a smaller packet size, the same ID number is placed in each fragment. This helps identify fragments that are part of the same set of data.

Flags Field

The Flags field is actually three bits long; the bit value assignments are shown in Table 3–14.

Table 3-14   Flags Field Values

Location	Field Definition	Value/Interpretations
Bit 0	Reserved	Set to 0
Bit 1	Don't Fragment Bit	0=may fragment; 1=don't fragment
Bit 2	More Fragments Bit	0=last fragment; 1=more to come

Typically, fragmentation is allowed. However, an application may, for some reason, decide not to allow fragmentation. If so, it sets the Don't Fragment bit to one.

If fragmentation is allowed, and a packet must be fragmented to cross a network that supports a smaller MTU, the Don't Fragment bit is set to zero. When the packet is split into multiple fragments (three fragments, for example) the first and second fragments have the More Fragments bit set to one. The last fragment has the More Fragments bit set to zero to indicate that it is the final fragment in the set.

Is fragmentation a good thing? Sometimes. Of course, if you have mixed media types (Ethernet and token ring, for example), you may need fragmentation to get that 4096-byte token ring packet through the 1518-byte Ethernet network by splitting it up into multiple packets. Fragmentation does take time and extra overhead however.

Fragment Offset Field

If the packet is a fragment, this field shows where to place this packet's data when the fragments are reassembled into a single packet (at the destination IP host).

This field gives the offset in 8-byte values. For example, the first fragment may have an offset of zero and contain 1400 bytes of data (not including any headers). The second fragment would have an offset value of 175 ($175 \times 8 = 1400$).

This field is only in use if the packet is a fragment.

Time to Live (TTL) Field

This field denotes the remaining lifetime (defined as seconds, but implemented as hops through routers) of the packet. Typical starting TTL values are 32, 64, and 128.

Protocol Field

Headers should have some field that defines what is coming up next. For example, in a TCP/IP packet, an Ethernet header should have a protocol identification field (the Type or Ether Type field) to indicate what IP is coming up next. The IP header, likewise, has a Protocol field to indicate what is coming up next. The common values in the Protocol field are listed in Table 3-15.

Table 3-15   Common Protocol Field Values

Number	Description
1	Internet Control Message Protocol (ICMP)
2	Internet Group Management Protocol (IGMP)
6	Transmission Control Protocol (TCP)
8	Exterior Gateway Protocol (EGP)
9	Any private interior gateway, such as Cisco's IGRP
17	User Datagram Protocol (UDP)
45	Inter-Domain Routing Protocol (IDRP)
88	Cisco EIGRP
89	Open Shortest Path First (OSPF)

The values 134–254 are unassigned, and 255 is reserved by IANA. To obtain the most current list of Protocol field values, visit *http://www.iana.org/assignments/protocol-numbers*.

Header Checksum Field

The IP Header Checksum field provides error detection on the contents of the IP header only—it does not cover other contents of the packet, nor does it include the Checksum field itself in the calculation.

This is an **error-detection mechanism** in addition to the data link error-detection mechanism (such as the Ethernet CRC). This additional checking mechanism is required for packets that pass through routers. For example, when an Ethernet packet arrives at a router, the router performs the data link CRC to ensure that the packet was not corrupted along the way. After the packet passes the CRC check and is considered good, the router strips off the data link header, leaving behind an unencapsulated Network layer packet. If the packet does not have any error-detection process in place, a faulty router can alter the data and then apply a new data link header (with a new CRC on the invalid packet) and send the packet on. This Network layer error-checking mechanism is required to check router packet corruption.

Source Address Field

This is the IP address of the IP host that sent the packet. In some cases, such as during the DHCP boot up process, the IP host may not know its IP address, so it may use 0.0.0.0 in this field.

This field cannot contain a multicast or broadcast address.

Destination Address Field

This field can include a unicast, multicast, or broadcast address. This is the final destination of the packet.

Options Fields

The IP header can be extended by several options (although these options are not often used). If the header is extended with options, those options must end on a 4-byte boundary because the Internet Header Length (IHL) field defines the header length in 4-byte boundaries.

Table 3-16 lists only a partial set of options. For the complete list, refer to *http://www.iana.org*.

Table 3-16 Options Field Values

Number	Name
0	End of Options List
3	Loose Source Route
4	Time Stamp
7	Record Route
9	Strict Source Route

As you might guess, the IP header options exist primarily to provide additional IP routing controls (or to record the route that individual packets take between sender and receiver). As such, they can be useful when testing or debugging code or specific connections, but are seldom used otherwise.

CHAPTER SUMMARY

❑ Because they manage access to the networking medium, data link protocols also manage the transfer of datagrams across the network. Normally, this means negotiating a connection between two communications partners, and transferring data between them. Such transfers are called point-to-point because they move from one interface to another on the same network segment or connection.

❑ When WAN protocols, such as SLIP or PPP, come into play, it's possible to use analog phone lines, digital technologies that include ISDN, DSL, or T-carrier connections, or switched technologies, such as X.25, frame relay, or ATM, to establish links that can carry IP and other datagrams from a sender to a receiver. At the Data Link layer, this means that protocols must deliver services, such as delimitation, bit-level integrity checks, addressing (for packet-switched connections), and protocol identification (for links that carry multiple types of protocols over a single connection).

❑ Ethernet II frames are the most common frame type on LANs, but a variety of other frame types exist that carry TCP/IP over Ethernet or token ring networks. Other Ethernet frame types that can carry TCP/IP include Ethernet 802.2 LLC frames and Ethernet 802.2 SNAP frames; token ring frame types include Token Ring 802.2 LLC frames and Token Ring SNAP frames.

❑ Understanding frame layouts is crucial for proper handling of their contents, regardless of the type of frame in use. Such frame types typically include start markers or delimiters (sometimes called preambles), destination and source MAC layer addresses, a Type field that identifies the protocol in the frame's payload, and the payload itself, which contains the actual data inside the frame. Most TCP/IP frames end with a trailer that stores a Frame Check Sequence field used to provide a bit-level integrity check for the frame's contents. By recalculating a special value called a Cyclical Redundancy Check (CRC), and comparing it to the value stored in the FCS field, the NIC can accept the frame for further processing, or silently discard it when a discrepancy occurs.

❏ At the lowest level of detail, it's important to understand the differences in field layouts and meanings when comparing various frame types for any particular network medium. You should understand the differences between Ethernet II frames, Ethernet 802.2 LLC frames, and Ethernet SNAP frames, and the differences between Token Ring 802.2 LLC frames and Token Ring SNAP frames.

❏ Because hardware or MAC layer addresses are so important when identifying individual hosts on any TCP/IP network segment, it's imperative to understand how TCP/IP manages the translation between MAC layer addresses and numeric IP addresses. For TCP/IP, the Address Resolution Protocol (ARP) provides this all-important role and helps create and manage the contents of tables of such translations on all hosts called the ARP cache. Because ARP can check the validity of the address assigned to any machine by performing an ARP request for a machine's own address, ARP can also detect IP address duplication when it occurs on a single network segment.

❏ Understanding ARP packet fields greatly helps to illuminate the address resolution process, particularly the use of the "all-zeroes" address in the Target Hardware Address field to indicate that a value is needed. ARP also includes information about hardware type, protocol type, length of hardware address (varies with the type of hardware), length of protocol address, and an Opcode field that identifies what kind of ARP or RARP packet is under scrutiny.

❏ A more advanced mechanism called proxy ARP permits a router to interconnect multiple network segments and make them behave like a single network segment. Because this means that hardware addresses are required from all segments that act like a single network segment, proxy ARP's job is to forward ARP requests from one actual network segment to another, when required; to enable hardware address resolution; and then to deliver corresponding replies to their original senders. Also, when a router configured for proxy ARP receives an ARP broadcast, it responds with its own address. When it receives the subsequent data packet, it forwards this along, according to its routing tables.

❏ Network layer protocols make their way into the Data Link layer through a process known as data encapsulation. Building IP datagrams, therefore, depends on understanding how to map the contents of an IP packet into a datagram that carries an IP packet as its payload. This process requires obtaining a numeric IP address for the destination (and may involve initial access to name resolution services such as DNS), and then using ARP (or the ARP cache) to map the destination address to a hardware address. (It is possible to use the hardware address of a known router or a default gateway instead, which can then begin the routing process from the sending network to the receiving network.)

❏ When a frame must travel from one network segment to another, a process to resolve its route must occur. Local destinations can be reached with a single transfer at the Data Link layer, but remote destinations require forwarding and multiple hops to get from sender to receiver. Thus, it's important to understand the role of local routing tables that describe all known local routes on a network, and the role of the default gateway that handles outbound traffic when exact routes are not known.

3

Here, ICMP comes into play to help manage best routing behaviors, and report when destinations may be unreachable.

❑ Other important characteristics of IP datagrams include: Time to Live (TTL) values, which prevent stale frames from persisting indefinitely on a network; fragmentation of incoming frames when the next link on a route uses a smaller MTU than the incoming link (reassembly of fragments always occurs when frames ultimately arrive at the destination host); and service delivery options to control packet and route priorities (seldom used, but worth understanding).

❑ The chapter concludes with a summary overview of all fields in an entire IP header. It brings together all the topics discussed in earlier sections, and permits inspection of entire IP datagram headers to map out their contents. Ultimately, this provides the map by which it is possible to examine and decode the addressing and handling instructions associated with any IP datagram.

KEY TERMS

American Standard Code for Information Interchange (ASCII) — The most widely used method for encoding character (keyboard) data into a collection of 8-bit digital patterns for input, storage, and display on a computer.

analog phone lines — Conventional voice-grade phone lines may be used with standard telephone modems (modulator/demodulator devices) that convert digital data into analog signals for transmission over such lines, and reconvert analog signals back into digital data on the receiving end of a point-to-point connection.

ARP cache — A temporary table in memory that consists of recent ARP entries. Entries in the ARP cache are discarded after two minutes on Windows 2000 systems.

Asynchronous Transfer Mode (ATM) — A variable-speed, long-haul broadband networking technology that supports extreme bandwidth in its fastest versions. ATM lets virtual circuits be established between communication peers, and relies on higher-layer protocols (for example, TCP) to provide reliable communications. ATM segments all traffic into 48-byte sequences with a 5-byte header to create a 53-byte ATM frame called a cell. ATM's use of fixed-length transmission units permits it to run at extremely high speeds with maximum efficiency.

bit-level integrity check — A special mathematical calculation performed on the payload of a packet (a datagram at the Data Link layer) before the datagram is transmitted, whose value may be stored in a datagram's trailer. The calculation is performed again on the receiving end and compared to the transmitted value; if the two values agree, the reception is assumed to be error-free; if the two values disagree, the datagram is usually silently discarded (no error message).

Border Gateway Protocol (BGP) — An inter-domain routing protocol that replaces Exterior Gateway Protocol (EGP) and is defined in RFC 1163. BGP exchanges reachability information with other BGP routers.

cable modem — A communication device designed to send and receive networking signals, mainly for Internet access, over two data channels on a broadband CATV network. Although cable TV lines can support bandwidth up to 27 Mbps, the more common rate for cable modem users is 1.5 Mbps (the local provider's data rate).

circuit switching — A method of communications wherein a temporary or permanent connection between a sender and a receiver, called a circuit, is created within a communications carrier's switching systems. Because temporary circuits come and go constantly, circuits are switched around all the time, hence the term.

compressed SLIP (C-SLIP) — A special form of SLIP that does away with source and destination address information as data is transmitted across the link. (This information is negotiated between point-to-point communication peers as the link is established, and need not be sent with every frame; omitting this data improves communication efficiency.)

Cyclical Redundancy Check (CRC) — A special 16- or 32-bit equation performed on the contents of a packet. The result of the CRC equation is placed in the Frame Check Sequence field at the end of a frame. A CRC is performed by NICs on all outgoing and incoming packets.

data encapsulation — The technique whereby higher-level protocol data is enclosed within the payload of a lower-layer protocol unit, and labeled with a header (and possibly, a trailer) so that the protocol data unit may be safely transmitted from a sender to a receiver. At the Data Link layer, this means providing necessary delimitation, addressing, bit-level integrity check, and protocol identification services in the header and trailer.

data link address — The address of the local machine based on the hardware address. The data link address is also referred to as the MAC address.

data link driver — The software that enables the NIC to communicate with a local operating system. The data link driver places the frame (except the CRC) around the IP datagram and ensures packets are of proper length before handing the frame to the NIC. On incoming frames, the data link driver examines the protocol identification field and passes the packet to the appropriate protocol stack.

de facto standard — A standard that is adopted by the majority, but not by a governing body, such as the IEEE.

default gateway — The name given to the router IP address through which a machine attached to a local network must pass outbound traffic to reach beyond the local network, thereby making that address the "gateway" to the world of IP addresses outside the local subnet. Also, a gateway of last resort, where packets are sent when no host route entry or network entry exists in the local host's route table.

delimitation — The use of special marker bit strings or characters, called delimiters, that distinguish the payload of a PDU from its header and trailer, and that may also mark the beginning (and possibly the end) of a PDU itself, as transmitted.

delimiter — A special bit string or character that marks some boundary in a PDU, be it at the beginning or end of a PDU, or at the boundary between the header and the payload, or the payload and the trailer.

3

Digital Subscriber Line (DSL) — The generic name for a family of always-on digital lines normally provided by local telephone companies or exchange carriers to link homes or businesses to communications carriers, normally for Internet access. DSL is subject to distance limitations of 17,500 feet from the interface equipment where the DSL line connects to a (usually optical) carrier link and the customer premises.

diskless workstation — A workstation that does not contain a hard drive or floppy disk drive from which to boot or read host configuration information.

duplicate IP address — An IP address that is already assigned to another IP host. IP hosts must perform a duplicate IP address test upon boot up to ensure the address is not already assigned to another IP host. If the address is already in use, the local host's IP stack cannot be initialized.

E1 — A standard European digital communications service used to carry thirty 64-Kbps digital voice or data channels, along with two 64-Kbps control channels, for a total bandwidth of 2.048 Mbps of service. E1 is widely used outside North America as a replacement for T1 service.

E3 — A standard European digital communications service used to carry 16 E1 channels for a total bandwidth of 34.368 Mbps of service. E3 is widely used outside North America as a replacement for T3 service.

error-detection mechanism — A method for detecting corrupted packets. The CRC process is an error-detection mechanism. The IP header checksum is another method of error detection.

Ethernet II frame type — The de facto standard frame type for TCP/IP communications.

fragment — In terms of IP networking, a fragment is a piece of a larger set of data that must be divided to cross a network that supports a smaller MTU than the original packet size.

Fragment Offset field — The field that defines where a fragment should be placed when the entire data set is reassembled.

fragment retransmission process — The process of retransmitting the original unfragmented packet due to transmission error, or fragment packet loss.

fragmentation — The process of dividing a packet into multiple smaller packets to cross a link that supports a smaller MTU than the link where the packet originated.

Frame Check Sequence (FCS) field — The type of bit-level integrity check used in the trailer of PPP datagrams; the specific algorithm for the FCS is documented in RFC 1661. The FCS field contains a CRC value. All Ethernet and token ring frames have an FCS field.

frame relay — Assumes that digital-quality transmission lines support its WAN links; thus, frame relay includes none of the error-detection and error-correction capabilities that improve X.25's reliability, but that also limit its overall bandwidth and efficiency. Frame relay doesn't attempt to correct transmission errors; it simply discards any corrupted frames it detects, relying on upper-layer protocols to coordinate any required retransmission of data. Frame relay is a popular WAN link technology because it can be metered by actual usage, and its costs are not sensitive to distance (unlike phone lines or X.25 connections).

This explains why PPP connections using frame relay are popular for medium to large organizations that can afford frame relay costs.

hardware address — The address of the NIC. This address is typically used as the data link address.

High-level Data Link Control (HDLC) — A synchronous communication protocol.

IEEE 802.3 — The IEEE-defined standard for a carrier sense, multiple access method with collision detection.

IEEE 802.5 — The IEEE-defined standard for token-passing ring Media Access Control method.

informational/supervisory format — A connection-oriented format that can be used by LLC packets.

Integrated Services Digital Network (ISDN) — An early dial-up digital link technology developed for use on standard telephone lines in the 1980s. Basic rate (BRI) ISDN offers two 64-Kbps voice or data channels and a 16-Kbps data/control channel to consumers for a total bandwidth of 144 Kbps. Primary rate (PRI) ISDN is a heavier-duty version that offers twenty-three 64-Kbps voice or data channels and a single 64-Kbps control/data channel for an aggregate of 1.544 Mbps (identical to T1's bandwidth). PRI is available to businesses and communications carriers. Because ISDN is at least as expensive as faster technologies such as cable modem and DSL for consumers, its usage in the first world is declining rapidly.

Internet Protocol Control Protocol (IPCP) — A special TCP/IP Network Control Protocol used to establish and manage IP links at the Network layer.

Internet Protocol version 6 (Ipv6) — The successor to the IPv4 protocol. IPv6 is currently specified, but not yet in full deployment.

IPCONFIG — A command-line utility used to identify the local host's data link address and IP address.

Link Control Protocol (LCP) — A special connection negotiation protocol that PPP uses to establish point-to-point links between peers for ongoing communications.

Logical Link Control (LLC) — The data link specification for protocol identification as defined by the IEEE 802.2 specification. The LLC layer resides directly above the Media Access Control layer.

logical ring transmission path — The transmission path used by token ring networks, where packets are repeated back onto a ring and pass in a logical, sequential order from one ring station to the next.

looped internetwork — A sub-optimal condition in an internetwork that results in a packet crossing a network segment more than once. Routing protocols attempt to prevent loops, but when they occur, they forward the packet until its TTL reaches zero.

multiple paths — More than one path to a destination. Meshed and topologically complex networks, such as the Internet, often contain multiple paths. Multiple paths provide redundancy for fault tolerance, and greater bandwidth use.

name resolution process — The process of obtaining an IP address based on a symbolic name. DNS is a name resolution process.

Network Control Protocol (NCP) — Any of a family of TCP/IP Network layer protocols used to establish and manage protocol links made at the Network layer (TCP/IP's Internet layer).

next-hop router — The local router that is used to route a packet to the next network along its path.

packet priority — A TOS priority that defines the order in which packets should be processed through a router queue.

pad — Bytes placed at the end of the Ethernet Data field to meet the minimum field length requirement of 46 bytes. These bytes have no meaning and are discarded by the incoming data link driver when the packet is processed.

physical star design — The physical layout of a token ring network, where all devices on the network are connected via cable back to a central device, such as a switch or a hub. Logically, however, token ring is a true ring based on the packet transmission path.

point-to-point — A type of Data Link layer connection, in which a link is established between exactly two communications partners so that the link extends from one partner (the sender) to the other (the receiver).

preamble — The initial sequence of values that precedes all Ethernet packets. Placed on the front of the frame by the outgoing NIC and removed by the incoming NIC, the preamble is used as a timing mechanism that enables receiving IP hosts to properly recognize and interpret bits as ones or zeroes.

precedence — A definition of priority for an IP packet. Routers may process higher-priority packets before lower-priority packets when a router queue is congested.

protocol identification (PID) — A datagram service necessitated when any single protocol carries multiple protocols across a single connection (as PPP can do at the Data Link layer); PIDs permit individual datagram payloads to be identified by the type of protocol they contain.

protocol identification field — A field that is included in most headers to identify the upcoming protocol. The PID of Ethernet headers is the Type field. The PID of IP headers is the Protocol field.

proxy ARP — The process of replying to ARP requests for IP hosts on another network. A proxy ARP network configuration effectively hides subnetting from the individual IP hosts.

Registry setting — A configuration that controls the way in which Windows devices operate. There are numerous settings that define how Windows 2000 operates in a TCP/IP environment.

repeater — A device that repeats bits regardless of their meaning, and without interpretation. A hub repeats bits received in one port out all other ports. A token ring station repeats bits received on the incoming receive pair out the transmit pair.

route priority — A TOS priority that defines the network to route packets. The router must support and track multiple network types to make the appropriate forwarding decision based on the TOS defined in the IP header.

route resolution process — The process that a host undergoes to determine whether a desired destination is local or remote and, if remote, which next-hop router to use.

router queues — A router buffering system used to hold packets when the router is congested.

routing tables — Local host tables maintained in memory. The routing tables are referenced before forwarding packets to remote destinations in order to find the most appropriate next-hop router for the packet.

Service Access Point (SAP) — A protocol identification field that is defined in the 802.2 LLC header that follows the MAC header.

Sub-Network Access Protocol (SNAP) — A variation of the 802.2 LLC layer that uses Ethernet type numbers to identify the upcoming protocol.

Synchronous Data Link Control (SDLC) — A synchronous communication protocol.

Synchronous Optical Network (SONET) — A family of fiber-optic digital transmission services that offers data rates from 51.84 Mbps to 13.27 Gbps. SONET was created specifically to provide the flexibility necessary to transport many different kinds of digital signals together, including voice, video, multimedia, and data traffic, and to permit equipment from different vendors to interoperate. SONET provides the infrastructure for high-rate ATM services that in turn support the Internet backbone, and the backbones for most large-scale communications carriers (such as WorldCom and AT&T).

T1 — A digital signaling link, whose name stands for trunk level 1, used as a standard for digital signaling in North America. T1 links offer aggregate bandwidth of 1.544 Mbps, and can support up to 24 voice-grade digital channels of 64 Kbps each, or may be split between voice and data.

T3 — A digital signaling link, whose name stands for trunk level 3, used as a standard for digital signaling in North America. T3 links offer aggregate bandwidth of 28 T1s, or 44.736 Mbps. T3 runs on coax or fiber-optic cable, or via microwave transmission, and is becoming a standard link for small- and mid-scale ISPs.

T-carrier — The generic telephony term for trunk carrier connections that offer digital services to communications customers directly from the communications carrier itself (usually a local or long-distance phone or communications company). It is possible, however, to run trunk lines all the way from one location to another, but such lines will always transit the carrier's premises at one or more points in such a connection.

Time to Live (TTL) — An indication of the remaining distance that a packet can travel. Although defined in terms of seconds, the TTL value is implemented as a number of hops that a packet can travel before being discarded by a router.

token — A special sequence of fields that indicates a token ring device has the right to transmit a frame of data onto the network media.

token ring — A token-passing ring Media Access Control protocol. The IEEE 802.5 specifications define the MAC and functional processes of token ring networking.

Token Ring 802.2 LLC frame — A token ring frame that includes the 802.2 LLC layer, which includes a protocol identification field (the Service Access Point field).

Token Ring SNAP frame — A token ring frame that includes the SNAP header, a variation on the 802.2 LLC header. The Token Ring SNAP frame uses an Ether Type value to identify the upcoming protocol.

TRACEROUTE — A utility that uses multiple PING commands to establish the identity and the round-trip times for all hosts between a sender and a receiver.

Type of Service (TOS) — A process used to define a type of path that a packet should take through the network. TOS options include the greatest throughput, lowest delay, and most reliability.

unnumbered format — A format of 802.2 LLC packet that is connectionless.

Voice over IP (VoIP) — A network method that bypasses the traditional public switched telephone system and uses IP (for example, the Internet or an intranet) to support voice communication.

WAN protocol — A type of data link protocol designed to transport data over large distances, typically with features that allow carriers to meter usage and bill subscribers. Examples include analog telephone lines, ISDN, T-carrier links, frame relay, or ATM between pairs of communications partners.

WINIPCFG — A Windows-based utility used to identify the local host's data link address and IP address.

X.25 — A standard set of protocols defined in the 1970s by the International Telecommunications Union (ITU), designed to send datagrams across a public packet-switched data network using noisy, narrow-bandwidth, copper telephone lines. Remains popular outside North America, where obtaining other forms of end-to-end WAN links can be difficult.

REVIEW QUESTIONS

1. SLIP supports which of the following WAN encapsulation services? (Choose all that apply.)

   a. addressing

   b. bit-level integrity check

   c. delimitation

   d. protocol identification

2. When used over an asynchronous connection like an analog telephone link, PPP supports which of the following WAN encapsulation services? (Choose all that apply.)

   a. addressing

   b. bit-level integrity check

   c. delimitation

   d. protocol identification

3. For which of the following link types must PPP provide addressing as part of its WAN encapsulation services? (Choose all that apply.)

   a. analog telephone link

   b. T-carrier link

   c. X.25 connection

   d. ATM connection

4. Which of the following protocols does PPP support, but not SLIP? (Choose all that apply.)

   a. TCP/IP

   b. IPX/SPX

   c. NetBEUI

   d. AppleTalk

5. Windows 2000 can make outbound SLIP connections, but can accept only inbound PPP connections. True or false?

   a. True

   b. False

6. PPP encapsulation techniques are based on IBM's SDLC, which is based on ISO HDLC. True or false?

   a. True

   b. False

7. Which of the following network technologies offers the highest bandwidth to PPP?

   a. ISDN

   b. DSL

   c. cable modem

   d. SONET

8. Which of the following Ethernet frame types is the de facto standard frame type?

   a. Ethernet I

   b. Ethernet II

   c. Ethernet 802.2 LLC

   d. Ethernet 802.2 SNAP

9. What is the first step that an IP host performs when it receives an Ethernet II frame?

   a. Check the hardware address to see if it should be read further.

   b. Check the validity of the FCS value.

   c. Strip off the FCS field and hand the packet to the Data Link layer.

   d. Examine the payload to determine the actual destination address.

10. In an Ethernet 802.2 LLC frame, what field replaces the Type field?

    a. Etype

    b. SAP

    c. Control field

    d. Data field

11. What designator in the Service Access Point fields in an Ethernet SNAP frame structure identifies the frame type?

    a. 0

    b. 6

    c. 170

    d. 255

12. What happens when a Windows 2000 host receives Ethernet 802.2 SNAP frame structures, if the Ethernet 802.2 SNAP entry is disabled in that machine's Registry?

    a. The receiving machine ignores all Ethernet 802.2 SNAP frames.

    b. The receiving machine receives the SNAP frame and replies using the same frame type.

    c. The receiving machine receives the SNAP frame but replies using the default Ethernet II frame type.

    d. The receiving machine receives the SNAP frame and automatically switches to the SNAP frame type.

13. Token ring networks use a physical ring design with a logical star transmission path. True or false?

    a. True

    b. False

14. The Token Ring SNAP frame format supports an Ether Type field value. True or false?

    a. True

    b. False

15. Which of the following statements best describes the role of the ARP cache?

    a. a special area of memory on routers where already-resolved IP hardware address translations are stored

    b. a special area of memory on IP hosts where already-resolved IP hardware address translations are stored

    c. a special file where already-resolved IP hardware addresses are stored as a computer is powered down, then read as it is powered back up

    d. a special file where symbolic name to IP address translations are stored

16. An IP host always broadcasts an ARP request first, before checking to see if the necessary value is stored in its ARP cache. True or false?

    a. True

    b. False

17. When looking for a destination address for a datagram ultimately bound for a remote network, an IP host must check which structure to obtain the necessary information?

    a. ARP cache

    b. routing tables

    c. a source route request

    d. proxy ARP to get the hardware address for the destination machine

18. ARP can perform duplicate IP address checks. True or false?

    a. True

    b. False

19. What happens when an IP host sends a reply to an IP host that requested its hardware address?

    a. Nothing, other than sending the reply.

    b. The sending host responds with an ARP request to the original requesting host.

    c. The sending host uses the contents of its reply to the requesting host to add an entry for the requesting host to its ARP cache.

    d. The sending host uses the contents of its reply to update the entry for the requesting host in its ARP cache.

20. Which of the following protocols have made RARP largely unnecessary on modern TCP/IP networks? (Choose all that apply.)

    a. ARP

    b. BOOTP

    c. DHCP

    d. DNS

HANDS-ON PROJECTS

Project 3-1

The following Hands-on Projects assume that you are working in a Windows 2000 environment, and that you have installed the EtherPeek for Windows demo software (included on the accompanying CD).

To view your local ARP cache:

1. Click **Start**, point to **Programs**, point to **Accessories**, and click **Command Prompt**. A Command Prompt window appears.

2. Enter **arp –a** to view your ARP cache. Write any entries that appear in your ARP cache.

3. At the command prompt, type **ping *ip_address***, replacing *ip_address* with the IP address of another IP host in the classroom. Do not use the IP address of an IP host that already appears in your ARP cache. Be certain you receive a ping reply. If your ping is unsuccessful, try pinging another IP host.

4. Enter **arp –a** to view your ARP cache again. Write the new entry that appears in your ARP cache.

   You should see the IP address and hardware address of the IP host you just pinged. You can now go to that system and examine the ARP cache to verify that your own IP address and hardware address were added to that system's ARP cache.

5. Close the Command Prompt window.

Project 3-2

To read your local route table:

1. Click **Start**, point to **Programs**, point to **Accessories**, and click **Command Prompt**.

2. At the command prompt, type **route print**, and then press **Enter**. Your local routing table appears. The table may look similar to Figure 3-23.

```
C:\WINDOWS\Desktop>route print

Active Routes:

    Network Address          Netmask  Gateway Address       Interface  Metric
          0.0.0.0          0.0.0.0        10.1.0.99        10.1.0.1       1
        127.0.0.0        255.0.0.0        127.0.0.1        127.0.0.1       1
         10.1.0.1  255.255.255.255        127.0.0.1        127.0.0.1       1
    10.1.255.255  255.255.255.255         10.1.0.1         10.1.0.1       1
        224.0.0.0        224.0.0.0         10.1.0.1         10.1.0.1       1
  255.255.255.255  255.255.255.255         10.1.0.1          0.0.0.0       1

C:\WINDOWS\Desktop>
```

Figure 3-23   Viewing a host's local routing tables

3. Close the Command Prompt window.

The process of manually adding routes to the local route table is covered in Chapter 10.

Project 3-3

To open a saved trace file and examine an ARP packet decode:

You must copy the trace files from the CD that accompanies this book to your hard disk for use in the Hands-on Projects. To do so, insert the CD into your CD-ROM drive. In Windows Explorer, open the zip file in the Trace folder and save the contents to your hard disk. A folder named **Course Technology\ 18654-2** is created that contains folders and trace files.

1. Click **Start**, point to **Programs**, and then click **WildPackets EtherPeek Demo** to start the analyzer program.
2. Click **OK** to close the EtherPeek demo information window.
3. Click **File**, **Open**.
4. Insert the CD that accompanies this book into your CD-ROM drive. Open the **18654–2\Ch3** folder on your hard disk.
5. Select the trace file **arp.pkt**. Click **Open**. The packet summary window appears and displays the seven packets in this trace file.
6. Double-click the first packet in the trace file to open the packet decode window. Carefully examine this ARP packet. Answer the following questions about Packet #1 in this trace:
   a. What is the IP address of the source that sent this packet?
   b. What IP address is this IP host trying to resolve?
   c. What is the purpose of this packet?
7. Close the decode window of Packet #1. Leave the EtherPeek demo program open, and proceed immediately to Hands-on Project 3-4.

Project 3-4

To filter out all ARP traffic in the trace file:

1. Follow Hands-on Project 3-3 to open the **arp.pkt** trace file (if not already open).
2. This trace file includes some ARP, ICMP, and NetBIOS traffic. To highlight only the ARP packets (requests and replies), click the **Protocols** tab at the bottom of the trace file window. The Protocols window appears. If the window cannot display all the protocol entries, click the down scroll arrow until you can see the ARP protocol and the Req and Rsp rows.
3. Right-click the **ARP** row to open the protocols menu, as shown in Figure 3-24.

3

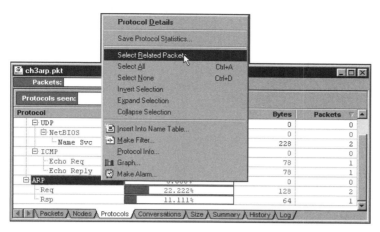

Figure 3-24   Filtering on all ARP traffic

4. Click **Select Related Packets**, and then click **By Protocol** in the resulting shortcut menu. EtherPeek displays the Selection Results window and indicates the number of packets that are related to the ARP selection, as shown in Figure 3-25.

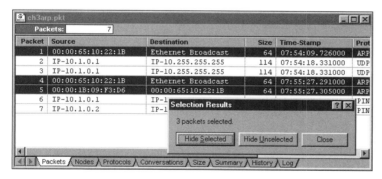

Figure 3-25   All ARPs in the trace buffer are highlighted

5. Click **Hide Unselected**. You should now have a trace summary window that displays only three ARP packets—Packets #1, #4, and #5. What is the purpose of Packets #4 and #5?

6. If the capture stopped notification dialog box appears, click **OK**. Close the trace summary window, and proceed immediately to Hands-on Project 3-5.

Project 3-5

To view and analyze IP traffic:

1. Follow Hands-on Project 3-3 to start the EtherPeek for Windows demo program (if not already open), and access the **18654–2\Ch3** folder on your hard disk.

2. Click the file **ftp.pkt**. Click **Open** to open the packet summary window. This trace depicts a simple FTP login process. The FTP host is 10.1.0.1. The FTP server is 10.1.0.99.

3. Because we can see the host 10.1.0.1 ARP for the destination 10.1.0.99, we can assume the two IP hosts are on the same network. Double-click **Packet #3** and answer the following questions:

   a. What frame type does this IP packet use?

   b. What is the length of the IP header?

   c. What is the remaining lifetime of this packet?

   d. How much data (in bytes) follows the IP header?

   e. Can this packet be fragmented if necessary?

   f. What protocol follows the IP header?

   g. What TOS is this application requesting?

4. Close the decode window for Packet #3.

5. Double-click **Packet #20** and answer the following questions:

   a. What frame type does this IP packet use?

   b. What is the length of the IP header?

   c. What is the remaining lifetime of this packet?

   d. How much data (in bytes) follows the IP header?

   e. Can this packet be fragmented if necessary?

   f. What protocol follows the IP header?

   g. Does this packet come from an FTP client or the FTP server?

6. Close the decode window for Packet #20. Close the **ftp.pkt** trace file. Proceed immediately to Hands-on Project 3-6.

Project 3-6

To identify connectivity problems depicted by ARP traffic patterns:

1. In this project, you view the trace file taken when a user (IP address 10.1.0.1) complains that he/she cannot FTP to an FTP server at 10.2.23.11. Follow Project 3-3 to start the EtherPeek for Windows demo program (if not already open), and access the **18645-2\Ch3** folder on your hard disk.

2. Click the file **problem1.pkt**. Click **Open** to open the packet summary window. Answer the following questions about this communication:

   a. Can the FTP host 10.1.0.1 communicate on the network?

   b. Can the host 10.1.0.1 FTP successfully to another destination?

3. Examine Packets #38 through #41. Why can't the host 10.1.0.1 perform file transfer to 10.2.23.11?

4. Close the **problem1.pkt** trace file. Proceed immediately to Hands-on Project 3-7.

Project 3-7

To examine fragmented IP packets:

1. In this example, one host (10.1.0.1) is sending a fragmented ping to 10.1.0.99. Follow Project 3-3 to start the EtherPeek for Windows demo program (if not already open), and access the **18654-2\Ch3** folder on your hard disk.

2. Click the file **fragments.pkt**. Click **Open** to open the packet summary window.

3. Double-click **Packet #3** to open the first packet in the fragment set. Click the **Prev** and **Next** buttons to move through the packets and answer the following questions:

   a. What is the maximum amount of data that can be placed after the Ethernet header in this packet?

   b. Do all the fragments of this set use the same Identification field value?

   c. What are the Fragment Offset values listed in each fragmented packet of the first fragment set (the ping request)?

   d. When the final packet is reassembled, how large is the data portion after the IP header?

4. Close the EtherPeek for Windows demo program.

CASE PROJECTS

1. You work in the headquarters of a large pharmaceutical company based in Atlanta, GA. A technician in your Portland, OR office sent you a trace file for review. The technician states that she captured the communications from an IP host that cannot connect to anyone on the other side of the local router. The problematic IP host can communicate with all the local systems without any problems What process might be problematic here? What should you look for in the trace file?

2. Your company recently acquired a small business and moved its computing operation to your main campus. It uses a 16 MB token ring network that supports a maximum packet size of 17 KB. Throughout the rest of the campus, your company uses 100 B Ethernet that supports a maximum packet size of 1518 B. How does mixed media affect your IP traffic? What should you look for in your network trace files when you evaluate performance of your internetwork?

3. You're interested in determining how far packets traveled before reaching your company's gateway to the Internet. What field should you look at to determine the distance from the source? Can you make a definitive statement about the distance traveled based on this field?

4. Explain the difference between IP precedence and Type of Service functionality. Give examples of how you might use both characteristics on your network.

4

INTERNET CONTROL MESSAGE PROTOCOL (ICMP)

After reading this chapter and completing the exercises you will be able to:

♦ Understand ICMP's routing and delivery error-reporting services

♦ Explain ICMP's role in the Path MTU process, and when it applies

♦ Understand how ICMP's Echo and Echo Reply packets support the PING and TRACEROUTE functions

♦ Explain how the ICMP Destination Unreachable message documents routing or delivery errors

♦ Understand how the ICMP Source Quench message helps compensate for various forms of network congestion

♦ Explain the proper function of the ICMP Redirect process, and the layout of ICMP Redirect messages

♦ Understand how router discovery uses both ICMP Router Advertisement and ICMP Router Solicitation messages, and how these messages behave

♦ Explain how other types of ICMP messages, including ICMP Time Exceeded and ICMP Parameter Problem, provide additional delivery failure information

---

Although IP is certainly the best-known Network layer protocol in the TCP/IP family, it's by no means the only such protocol. This chapter covers **Internet Control Message Protocol (ICMP)**, an important error- and information-handling TCP/IP protocol that also operates at the Network layer. Starting with an overview of the various roles it can play, this chapter describes ICMP's capabilities, packet layouts, and field formats, and explains how ICMP helps support various forms of error reporting, Path Maximum Transfer Unit (MTU) Discovery, reachability analysis, **route tracing**, and other routing-related functions.

ABOUT THE INTERNET CONTROL MESSAGE PROTOCOL

ICMP is an important Network layer protocol because it provides information about network activity and routing behavior that IP itself cannot convey.

When it comes to diagnosing and repairing problems with TCP/IP connectivity, you must know where to obtain information about how packets move from their sources to their destinations on an IP internetwork. For any network node to communicate and exchange data with another network node, some way of forwarding packets from the sender to receiver must exist. This concept is called **reachability**.

Normally, usable forwarding paths are discovered in the contents of local IP routing tables that reside on the various hosts between sender and receiver. Discovery of such paths also takes advantage of the default gateway's role as the router that passes traffic outside a local network when an explicit external routing path is not known. (Chapter 5 provides additional information about routing.)

ICMP provides a way to return information to senders, in the form of specific kinds of ICMP messages, about routes traveled (including reachability information) as packets get forwarded, and a possible way to return error information to a sender when routing or reachability problems prevent delivery of an IP datagram. This capability nicely complements IP's datagram delivery services because ICMP provides what IP itself cannot—routing, reachability, delivery error reports, and control information. Thus, if IP represents a swarm of commuters on the highway from point A to point B, ICMP represents commuters with cell phones in the stream of traffic, reporting which exits are blocked, and which portions of the highway are congested.

ICMP's ability to report errors, congestion, or other network conditions does nothing to enhance IP's best-effort delivery approach. In fact, ICMP messages themselves are nothing more than specially formatted IP datagrams, subject to the same conditions as other IP packets in the general network traffic. And, even though ICMP can report on errors or **network congestion** (which occurs when network traffic starts to exceed handling capacities), it's up to the IP host that receives incoming ICMP messages to act on the content of those messages. What ICMP has to say, and what hosts may choose to do about it, supplies the bulk of this chapter's content.

Overview of ICMP and RFC 792

Request For Comment (RFC) 792, titled "Internet Control Message Protocol," provides the basic specification for all valid ICMP messages, and defines the kinds of information and services that ICMP can deliver. This RFC also makes the following points about the relationship between IP and ICMP, to help you better understand the relationship between these two Network layer TCP/IP protocols:

- ICMP provides a mechanism for gateways (routers) or destination hosts to communicate with source hosts.

- ICMP messages take the form of specially formatted IP datagrams, with specific associated message types and codes. This chapter explores and explains the types and codes associated with ICMP messages.

- ICMP is a required element in some implementations of TCP/IP, most notably those TCP/IP protocol stacks judged suitable for sale to the U.S. government, and ICMP is usually present to provide an essential part of IP's support fabric.

- ICMP reports errors only about processing of non-ICMP IP datagrams. To prevent an endless loop of messages about error messages, ICMP conveys no messages about itself, and provides information only about the first fragment in any sequence of fragmented datagrams.

Although RFC 792 was published in 1981, it defines the primary functions of and blueprints for ICMP messages to this day. In a more demonstrative and expository way, the many sections in this chapter that explore and explain ICMP messages derive directly from this document. For more information, consult RFC 950, which explains how ICMP messages may be used to permit hosts to discover their network addresses and subnet masks on demand.

ICMP's Vital Roles on IP Networks

As mentioned earlier, ICMP's job is to provide a variety of information about IP routing behavior, reachability, routes between specific pairs of hosts, delivery errors, and so forth. Each type of capability lends itself to specific applications, many of which are quite useful for network monitoring and troubleshooting. These are documented in Table 4-1, which lists ICMP message types, and provides a brief explanation of how they may be used.

Table 4-1   ICMP Message Types and Their Uses or Significance

ICMP Message Type	Use or Significance
ICMP Echo/Echo Reply	Supports functionality for reachability utilities like PING and TRACERT; essential when installing, configuring, and troubleshooting IP networks
ICMP Destination Unreachable	Documents when routing or delivery errors prevent IP datagrams from reaching their destinations; code values are extremely important. Also used for Path MTU Discovery between pairs of hosts
ICMP Source Quench	Permits a receiving host or intermediate gateway to instruct a sending host to adjust (lower) its sending rate to ease congestion problems
ICMP Redirect	Permits a gateway (router) on a non-optimal route between sender and receiver to redirect traffic to a more optimal path
ICMP Router Discovery	Permits hosts to request information about local routers, and routers to advertise their existence on an IP network

Table 4-1   ICMP Message Types and Their Uses or Significance (continued)

ICMP Message Type	Use or Significance
ICMP Time Exceeded	Indicates that an IP datagram's TTL, or a fragmented IP datagram's reassembly timer, has expired; can indicate either a too-short TTL, or the presence of a routing loop in a network (which must be removed)
ICMP Parameter Problem	Indicates some error occurred while processing the IP header of an incoming datagram, causing that datagram to be discarded; catchall for ambiguous or miscellaneous errors, it indicates further investigation is required

Table 4-1 provides only brief explanations of these functions, but they provide a foundation upon which much serious TCP/IP network and router troubleshooting can rest. These ICMP message types, and their applications, will be explored in greater depth throughout the rest of this chapter.

TESTING AND TROUBLESHOOTING SEQUENCES FOR ICMP

ICMP's most common uses are testing and troubleshooting. Two of the most well-known utilities, PING and TRACEROUTE, rely on ICMP to perform **connectivity tests** and **path discovery**.

Connectivity Testing with PING

Although many people may be familiar with the PING utility, they may not be aware that PING is actually an **ICMP Echo process**. The process is quite simple, actually. An **ICMP Echo Request packet** consists of an Ethernet header, IP header, ICMP header, and some undefined data. This packet is sent to the target host, which echoes back that data, as shown in Figure 4-1.

The ICMP echo request is a connectionless process with no guarantee of delivery—it is truly a best-effort process.

Most PING utilities send a series of several echo requests to the target in order to obtain an **average response time**. These response times are displayed in **milliseconds** (thousandths of a second), as shown in Figure 4-2, but should not be considered evidence of the typical round-trip latency time between devices. These times should be considered a snapshot of the current **round-trip time**. They do not take into account that some routers give ICMP traffic a lower priority than true routing traffic, causing a slower round-trip latency time to appear during a PING test.

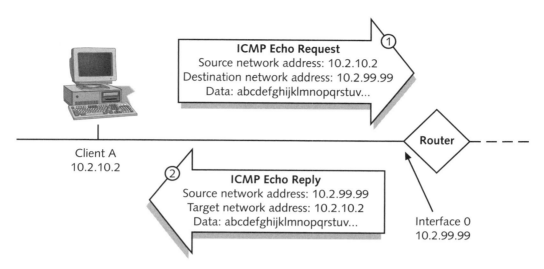

Figure 4-1   PING utility uses ICMP echo requests and replies

The PING utility included with Windows 2000 sends a series of four ICMP echo requests with a one-second ICMP Echo Reply Timeout value. The echo requests consist of 32 bytes of data (an alphabetical pattern) in a **fragmentable** IP packet. The Windows 2000 PING utility supports IP addresses and names, and uses traditional name resolution processes to resolve symbolic names to IP addresses, whenever possible. Figure 4-2 shows the results of a PING operation.

```
C:\WINDOWS>ping 10.3.99.99

Pinging 10.3.99.99 with 32 bytes of data:

Reply from 10.3.99.99: bytes=32 time=5ms TTL=255
Reply from 10.3.99.99: bytes=32 time=5ms TTL=255
Reply from 10.3.99.99: bytes=32 time=5ms TTL=255
Reply from 10.3.99.99: bytes=32 time=5ms TTL=255

Ping statistics for 10.3.99.99:
    Packets: Sent = 4, Received = 4, Lost = 0 (0% loss),
Approximate round trip times in milli-seconds:
    Minimum = 5ms, Maximum =  5ms, Average =  5ms
```

Figure 4-2   PING utility provides feedback on success and round-trip times

Chapter 7 provides additional information on name resolution.

Routers typically do not respond to ICMP echo requests sent to a multicast or broadcast address. Most host TCP/IP stacks do not allow you to ping the broadcast address either.

The **command-line parameters** used with PING can affect the appearance and functionality of these ICMP Echo packets. The following lists a few of the parameters available with the PING utility that is included with Windows 2000:

- –l *size*, where *size* is the number of data bytes to send
- –f, which sets the Don't Fragment bit
- –i *TTL*, where *TTL* sets the value of the TTL field in the IP header
- –v *TOS*, where *TOS* sets the TOS field value in the IP header
- –w *timeout*, where *timeout* sets the number of milliseconds to wait for a reply

Appendix C, "Command-Line IP Utilities," provides a complete list of supported PING parameters.

Path Discovery with TRACEROUTE

The **TRACEROUTE** utility identifies a **path** from the sender to the target host using ICMP echo requests and some manipulation of the TTL value in the IP header. TRACEROUTE results provide a list of routers along a path, as well as the round-trip latency time to each router. Some implementations of TRACEROUTE also attempt to resolve the names of the routers along a path.

The following describes the steps TRACEROUTE uses to identify the path from the local host (Host A) to a remote host (Host B) across an internetwork, as shown in Figure 4-3.

1. Host A sends an ICMP Echo Request packet to Host B's IP address with a TTL value of one.

2. Router 1 cannot decrement the TTL value to zero and forward the packet, so Router 1 discards the packet and sends an ICMP Time Exceeded-TTL Exceeded in Transit message back to Host A. Router 1 sets the TTL value of this ICMP Time Exceeded message to a default value, such as 128.

3. Host A notes the IP address of the responding router (Router 1).

4. Host A sends an ICMP Echo Request packet to Host B's IP address with a TTL value of two.

5. Router 1 decrements the ICMP Echo Request packet's TTL value to one and forwards the packet to the next-hop router (Router 2).

6. Router 2 cannot decrement the TTL value to zero and forward the packet, so Router 2 discards the packet and sends an ICMP Time Exceeded-TTL Exceeded in Transit message back to Host A. Router 2 sets the TTL value of this ICMP Time Exceeded message to a default value, such as 128.

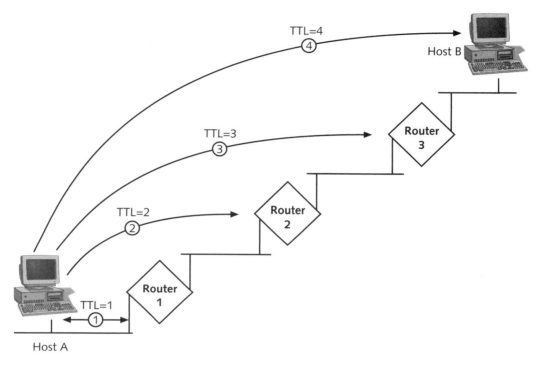

Figure 4-3   TRACEROUTE alters the TTL value to find routers along a path

7. Host A notes the IP address of the second router (hop) along the path.

8. Host A sends an ICMP Echo Request packet to Host B's IP address with a TTL value of three.

9. Router 1 decrements the ICMP Echo Request packet's TTL value to two and forwards the packet to the next-hop router (Router 2).

10. Router 2 decrements the ICMP Echo Request packet's TTL value to one and forwards the packet to the next-hop router (Router 3).

11. Router 3 cannot decrement the TTL value to zero and forward the packet, so Router 3 discards the packet and sends an ICMP Time Exceeded-TTL Exceeded in Transit message back to Host A. Router 3 sets the TTL value of this ICMP Time Exceeded message to a default value, such as 128.

12. Host A notes the IP address of the third router (hop) along the path.

13. Host A sends an ICMP Echo Request packet to Host B's IP address with a TTL value of four.

14. Router 1 decrements the ICMP Echo Request packet's TTL value to three and forwards the packet to the next-hop router (Router 2).

15. Router 2 decrements the ICMP Echo Request packet's TTL value to two and forwards the packet to the next-hop router (Router 3).

16. Router 3 decrements the ICMP Echo Request packet's TTL value to one and forwards the packet to the final destination (Host B).

17. Host B sends an ICMP Echo Reply packet.

18. Host A notes the round-trip time for the ICMP echo test to Host B.

The command-line parameters that **TRACERT** (the Windows version of TRACE-ROUTE) uses can affect the appearance and functionality of this process. The following lists a few of the parameters available with the TRACERT utility that is included with Windows 2000:

- -d, which instructs TRACERT to *not* perform a DNS reverse query on the routers

- -h *max_hops*, where *max_hops* defines the maximum TTL value to use

- -w *timeout*, where *timeout* indicates how long to wait for a reply before displaying an asterisk (*)

For a complete list of supported TRACERT parameters, refer to Appendix C.

Path Discovery with PATHPING

New to Windows 2000, the **PATHPING** utility is a command-line utility that uses ICMP echo packets to test router and link latency, as well as packet loss. For more information on PATHPING, refer to Appendix C.

Path MTU Discovery with ICMP

RFC 1191, **Path MTU Discovery**, defines a method for discovering a **Path MTU (PMTU)** using ICMP. In Chapter 3, we focused on how a router can fragment an IP packet destined for a network with a smaller MTU. We also indicated that fragmentation does not make optimal use of bandwidth due to the high **overhead** from the multiple headers required to get one chunk of data across the network. PMTU Discovery enables a source to learn the currently supported MTU across an entire path, without supporting fragmentation.

Using PMTU, a host always sets the Don't Fragment bit in the IP header to one (indicating that the packet *cannot* be fragmented by a router along the path). If a packet is too large to be routed on a network, the receiving router discards the packet and sends an ICMP Destination Unreachable: Fragmentation Needed and Don't Fragment was Set message back to the source. PMTU-capable routers also include the MTU of the **restricting link** (a link that does not support forwarding based on the current packet format and configuration) in the ICMP reply.

Upon receipt of the Fragmentation Needed and Don't Fragment was Set ICMP reply that indicates the restricting link's MTU size, the PMTU host must either reduce the MTU size of the message accordingly and retransmit the data, or remove the Don't Fragment flag in the IP header and retransmit the packet using the original size. Reducing the size based on the restricting link's MTU size ensures the packet crosses the router that previously discarded it.

During this process, a PMTU host may receive a Fragmentation Needed and Don't Fragment was Set ICMP response from one router, decrease its MTU size, and retransmit only to have another Fragmentation Needed and Don't Fragment was Set ICMP packet sent from another router further along the path. The process of PMTU continues until the **end-to-end minimum MTU size** is discovered. This process also continues to recheck itself after the PMTU is discovered. For example, consider the network depicted in Figure 4-4. Host A and Host B can both use the same MTU—18,000 bytes. Their communications use Path #1— packets greater than 1518 bytes must be fragmented.

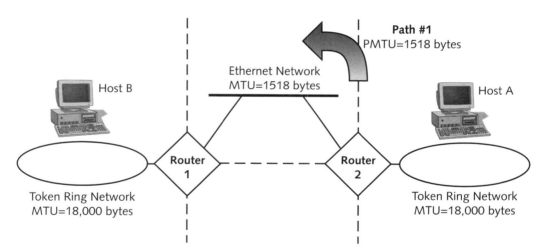

Figure 4-4   PMTU Discovery automatically determines the PMTU of a path to eliminate fragments

Let's examine step by step the PMTU process shown in Figure 4-4:

1. Host A sends a 4096-byte packet to Host B. The packet is sent to Router 2 (Host A's default **gateway**).

2. Router 2 knows this 4096-byte packet cannot be sent on the Ethernet network. Router 2 discards the packet and sends Host A a Fragmentation Needed and Don't Fragment was Set ICMP packet that indicates that 1500 is the MTU of the next link.

3. Host A re-sends the packet using a maximum MTU size of 1518.

4. Router 2 strips off the token ring header and applies an Ethernet header before forwarding the packet across the Ethernet network.

The PMTU specification defined in RFC 1191 requires the PMTU host to periodically try a larger MTU to see if the **allowable data size** has increased. For example, consider Figure 4-5, in which we implement a redundant token ring link between Router 1 and Router 2.

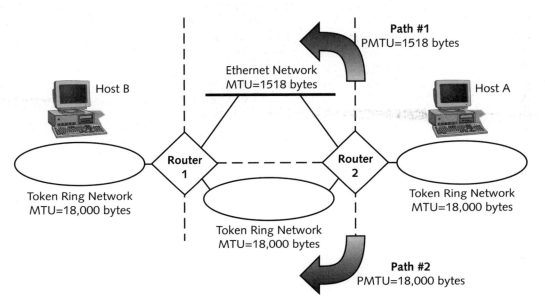

Figure 4-5   Periodic testing of larger MTU sizes ensures eventual discovery of a larger MTU path

If Router 2 uses a routing protocol that recognizes the **throughput difference** between a 10-Mbps Ethernet network and a 16-Mpbs token ring network, Router 2 should use Path #2 when forwarding packets. This path change is transparent to the PMTU client (Host A). This is why the specification recommends that the PMTU host try sending a packet larger than the current PMTU no sooner than five minutes after the PMTU was decreased due to receipt of a Fragmentation Needed and Don't Fragment was Set ICMP packet. The specification also dictates that **backwards compatibility** be provided to routers that cannot include the MTU value in the ICMP Fragmentation Needed and Don't Fragment was Set ICMP packet, by gradually decreasing the PMTU size until no more Fragmentation Needed and Don't Fragment was Set ICMP packets are sent back by the router.

You can set two PMTU parameters in Windows 2000—EnablePMTUDiscovery and EnablePMTUBHDetect. The EnablePMTUDiscovery Registry setting enables or disables PMTU Discovery on the Windows host. (See Table 4-2.)

Table 4-2 EnablePMTUDiscovery Registry Setting

Registry Information	Details
Location	HKEY_LOCAL_MACHINE\SYSTEM\CurrentControlSet\Services\Tcpip\Parameters
Data type	REG_DWORD
Valid range	0 or 1
Default value	1
Present by default	No

PMTU Discovery is enabled by default. Setting the EnablePMTUDiscovery value to zero disables this process.

The EnablePMTUBHDetect Registry setting defines whether the Windows 2000 host should detect **black hole routers**. A black hole router **silently discards** packets without indicating the cause, thereby thwarting any **auto-recovery** or **auto-reconfiguration** attempts. Many administrators disable ICMP responding for security reasons. (Refer to Chapter 9 for more details on security issues relating to ICMP.) For example, if a router does not support PMTU, and is configured so it will not send ICMP **Destination Unreachable packets**, the PMTU host may send a large packet that never gets routed. Without some feedback from the router, the host cannot determine that PMTU was the problem. The host would simply retransmit the packet until a timeout or **retry counter** expires, and the communication would be unsuccessful. If the EnablePMTUBHDetect setting is enabled, the PMTU host retries the large MTU a few times and, if no response is received, the PMTU host automatically sets the PMTU to 576 bytes.

See Table 4-3 for information about the EnablePMTUBHDetect Registry setting.

Table 4-3 EnablePMTUBHDetect Registry Setting

Registry Information	Details
Location	HKEY_LOCAL_MACHINE\SYSTEM\CurrentControlSet\Services\Tcpip\Parameters
Data type	REG_DWORD
Valid range	0 or 1
Default value	0
Present by default	No

The EnablePMTUBHDetect setting is disabled by default.

Routing Sequences for ICMP

Whereas routing protocols, such as Routing Information Protocol (RIP) and Open Shortest Path First (OSPF), provide route information to routers on a network, ICMP can provide some routing information to hosts. Routers can use ICMP to provide a default gateway setting to a host (if the host requests assistance). Routers can also send ICMP messages, called ICMP Redirect messages, to **redirect** a host to another router that is believed to have a more **optimal route**. This is further discussed in the section titled "Redirection" later in this chapter.

Section 4.3 of RFC 1812, "Requirements for IP Version 4 Routers," lists how IP routers should handle **ICMP error messages** and **ICMP query messages**.

Router Discovery

IP hosts typically learn about routes through manual configuration of the default gateway parameter and redirection messages (covered in the section titled "Redirection" later in this chapter). When a host boots up without a default gateway setting, that host may issue an **ICMP Router Solicitation** packet to locate a local router. Windows 98 and Windows 2000 hosts automatically send ICMP Router Solicitation packets when they boot up without a default gateway setting. This is, as you learn later in this section, a configurable parameter. This process is referred to as ICMP Router Solicitation and **ICMP Router Discovery**. IP hosts send ICMP Router Solicitations and routers reply with ICMP Router Advertisements.

By default, the ICMP Router Solicitation packet is sent to the all-routers IP multicast address 224.0.0.2. Although RFC 1812 dictates that IP routers "must support the router part of the ICMP Router Discovery protocol on all connected networks on which the router supports either IP multicast or IP broadcast addressing," many do not. If a router does not support the router portion of ICMP Router Discovery, the host's Router Solicitation requests go unanswered.

In the case of an IP host that resides on a network that supports multiple IP routers, the IP host may receive multiple replies—one reply from each locally connected IP router. Typically, the hosts accept and use the first reply received as the default gateway. Figure 4-6 depicts a network that consists of multiple routers, and a host that is missing the default gateway setting. In this scenario, Host A, 10.2.10.2, sends an IP multicast to locate a local router to use as a default gateway. Because Router 1 supports the router portion of ICMP Router Discovery, it replies with its own IP address. Host A adds Router 1's IP address to its routing tables.

In Figure 4-6, only one router—the local router—replies. Router 2 is not on the same network as Host A, and the IP multicast is not forwarded by Router 1. Host B is already configured with a default gateway—it does not need to perform ICMP Router Solicitation.

Windows 2000 hosts can be reconfigured so they will not use ICMP Router Solicitation by editing the PerformRouterDiscovery Registry setting, as listed in Table 4-4.

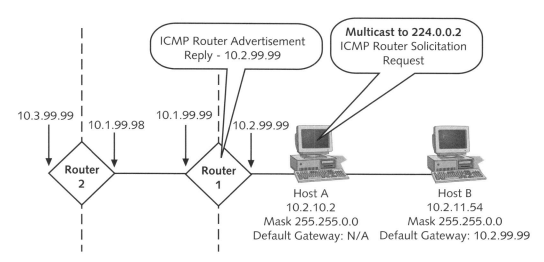

Figure 4-6   Hosts can discover local routers using the Router Discovery process

Table 4-4   PerformRouterDiscovery Registry Setting

Registry Information	Details
Location	HKEY_LOCAL_MACHINE\SYSTEM\CurrentControlSet\Services\Tcpip\Parameters\Interfaces\<*interface*>
Data type	REG_DWORD
Valid range	0 or 1
Default value	1
Present by default	Yes

Changing the PerformRouterDiscovery value to zero disables the ICMP Router Discovery process.

On Windows 2000 hosts, the SolicitationAddressBCast Registry setting can be configured to use a subnet broadcast (such as 10.2.255.255 during the Router Discovery process) instead of the all-routers multicast address. See Table 4-5 for information about the SolicitationAddressBCast Registry setting.

Table 4-5   SolicitationAddressBCast Registry Setting

Registry Information	Details
Location	HKEY_LOCAL_MACHINE\SYSTEM\CurrentControlSet\Services\Tcpip\Parameters\Interfaces\<*interface*>
Data type	REG_DWORD
Valid range	0 or 1
Default value	0
Present by default	No

Changing the SolicitationAddressBCast value to one enables the Windows 2000 host to use the IP subnet broadcast to perform ICMP Router Solicitation.

Router Advertising

As mentioned previously, IP hosts typically learn about routes through the manually configured default gateway setting and the process of redirection (covered next). Alternately, some routers can be configured to send periodic ICMP Router Advertisement packets. These periodic ICMP Router Advertisements do not mean that ICMP is a routing protocol. They simply allow hosts to passively learn about **available routes**.

Routers can periodically send these ICMP Router Advertisements in response to ICMP Router Solicitation packets. If configured to do so, routers periodically send **unsolicited** ICMP Router Advertisements to the all-hosts multicast address 224.0.0.1. These advertisements typically include the IP address of the router that sent the ICMP Router Advertisement packet. The router also includes a Lifetime value to indicate how long the receiving host should keep the route entry. The default Lifetime value for route entries is 30 minutes. After 30 minutes passes, the **expired route entry** is removed from the route tables, and the host may issue a new ICMP Router Solicitation packet, or wait and passively listen for an ICMP Router Advertisement packet.

The default **advertising rate** is between seven to 10 minutes.

ICMP Router Advertising is covered in greater detail in RFC 1256, "ICMP Router Discovery Messages."

Redirection

ICMP can be used to point a host to a better router if required. For example, in Figure 4-7, 10.2.99.99 is the default gateway setting for Host A (10.2.10.2/16). This host wants to communicate with Host B at IP address 10.3.71.7.

Host A's route resolution process goes through the following six steps:

1. Host A places its own network mask (255.255.0.0) on the destination address 10.3.71.7 to determine that Host B is on another network.

2. Host A examines its routing tables to locate a **host route entry** for 10.3.71.7. No such entry exists.

3. Host A examines its routing tables to locate a **network route entry** for 10.3.0.0. No such entry exists.

4. Host A examines its routing tables to locate a default gateway entry. Host A's default gateway setting is 10.2.99.99.

5. Host A examines its ARP cache to locate an entry for 10.2.99.99's hardware address. Host A finds the hardware address 0x00107B8143E3 associated with 10.2.99.99's IP address.

6. Host A builds a packet addressed to the IP address 10.3.71.7, and sends this packet to the default gateway's hardware address.

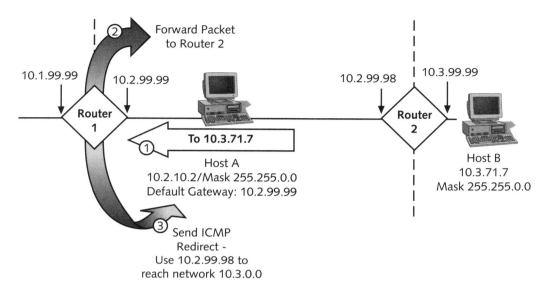

Figure 4-7   Routers send ICMP Redirects to hosts to indicate an optimal path off the local network

When Router 1 receives the packet, it performs the required error-checking tasks, strips off the datalink header, and ensures the packet TTL is greater than one. Once this process is successfully completed, Router 1 checks its routing tables to determine how to forward the packet. At this time, Router 1 notes that it does not contain the best route to the destination—10.2.99.98 offers the optimal route to get a packet from network 10.2.0.0 to network 10.3.0.0. Router 1 sends an ICMP Redirect packet to Host A. The ICMP Redirect packet indicates that 10.2.99.98 is the optimal router address to use when trying to reach network 10.3.0.0. Host A now re-sends the packet; this time, however, it addresses the packet to 10.2.99.98's hardware address.

The redirection process only serves IP hosts; it does not serve IP routers. In other words, if one router forwards a packet to another router that does not offer an optimal path, no ICMP Redirect packet is sent back to the first router to notify it of a better path. The packet is simply forwarded. We rely on robust routing protocols that use **metrics** to determine the best path. Chapter 10 provides additional information on IP routing protocols.

Security Issues for ICMP

Because ICMP provides information about network configurations and connectivity status, you can use it to learn how a network is designed and configured. You can also use ICMP as part of a **reconnaissance process** to learn about active network addresses and active processes. These reconnaissance processes often precede a network break-in. Because ICMP can be used as an information-gathering tool, some companies limit the amount of ICMP traffic that flows through their networks.

When **hackers** decide to infiltrate a network, they typically start with a list of the IP hosts on the network (unless the target is a single known system). An IP **host probe** process is one method of obtaining a list of the active hosts on a network. The IP host probe is performed by sending a PING packet (ICMP Echo Request packet) to each host within a range, and noting the responses. Who replied? The devices that reply are considered valid targets to the hacker. Typically, the next step in the hack is a **port probe**. Chapter 9 covers port probing in greater detail.

Once hackers know the addresses of the active devices on the network, they can target their next reconnaissance process, the port probe, to those devices. Because many systems do not reply to pings sent to the broadcast address, typical IP host probes are sent unicast to each possible address. This type of probe process is typically done through a script rather than manually. Many hacker sites, such as *http://www.atstake.com/research/tools/index*, include tools that can easily be instructed to scan specific IP address ranges.

Now that you understand the various uses and abuses that ICMP supports, it's time to dig deeper into the layout that ICMP messages follow, and the various message types that ICMP supports. These topics provide the subject matter for the rest of this chapter.

ICMP PACKET FIELDS AND FUNCTIONS

The value one in the IP header Protocol field denotes that an ICMP header follows the IP header (see Figure 4-8). The ICMP header consists of two portions—the constant portion and the variable portion. In this section, we cover each portion of the header structure, the functions of the various ICMP packet types, and provide examples of ICMP query and error messages found on the network.

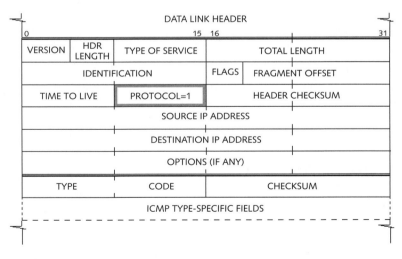

Figure 4-8   Protocol field value "1" indicates that ICMP follows the IP header

Constant ICMP Fields

ICMP packets contain only three required fields after the IP header: Type, Code, and Checksum. In some ICMP packets, however, there are additional fields that provide information or details on the message. For example, an ICMP Redirect packet needs to include the address of the gateway for the packet redirect. Upon receipt of this packet, a host should add a dynamic route entry to its routing tables, and begin using the new routing information immediately. Figure 4-8 shows the constant fields of the ICMP header.

4

 Refer to RFCs 792, 1191, and 1256 for further details on the ICMP frame structures listed in this section.

Type Field

The Type field lists types of ICMP messages that can be sent on the network. The following list is based on IANA documentation. To obtain the most current version of this list, access *http://www.iana.org*.

Table 4-6 lists the ICMP Type numbers assigned.

Table 4-6   ICMP Type Numbers

Type	Name	References
0	Echo Reply	RFC 792
1	Unassigned	
2	Unassigned	
3	Destination Unreachable	RFC 792
4	Source Quench	RFC 792
5	Redirect	RFC 792
6	Alternate Host Address	JBP
7	Unassigned	
8	Echo	RFC 792
9	Router Advertisement	RFC 1256
10	Router Solicitation	RFC 1256
11	Time Exceeded	RFC 792
12	Parameter Problem	RFC 792
13	Timestamp	RFC 792
14	Timestamp Reply	RFC 792
15	Information Request	RFC 792
16	Information Reply	RFC 792
17	Address Mask Request	RFC 950
18	Address Mask Reply	RFC 950

Table 4-6 ICMP Type Numbers (continued)

Type	Name	References
19	Reserved (for Security)	Solo
20–29	Reserved (for Robustness Experiment)	ZSu
30	Traceroute	RFC 1393
31	Datagram Conversion Error	RFC 1475
32	Mobile Host Redirect	David Johnson
33	IPv6 Where-Are-You	Bill Simpson
34	IPv6 I-Am-Here	Bill Simpson
35	Mobile Registration Request	Bill Simpson
36	Mobile Registration Reply	Bill Simpson
37	Domain Name Request	Bill Simpson
38	Domain Name Reply	Bill Simpson
39	SKIP	Markson
40	Photuris	Bill Simpson
41–255	Reserved	JBP

Not all of these ICMP packet types are currently in use. Some are in development, or are only used on an experimental basis.

The initials *JBP* identify Jon B. Postel. Jon Postel was one of the founders of the Internet Protocol suite. With a long beard and an intensely brilliant mind, he helped shape the communications system of the Internet and millions of private networks until his untimely death in October 1998. You can learn more about this luminary at *http://www.postel.org/remembrances*.

Code Field

Many of these ICMP packet types have a Code field. Table 4-7 lists the codes that can be used with Destination Unreachable ICMP packets.

Table 4-7 Type 3: Destination Unreachable Codes

Code	Definition
0	Net Unreachable
1	Host Unreachable
2	Protocol Unreachable
3	Port Unreachable
4	Fragmentation Needed and Don't Fragment was Set
5	Source Route Failed

Table 4-7   Type 3: Destination Unreachable Codes (continued)

Code	Definition
6	Destination Network Unknown
7	Destination Host Unknown
8	Source Host Isolated
9	Communication with Destination Network is Administratively Prohibited
10	Communication with Destination Host is Administratively Prohibited
11	Destination Network Unreachable for Type of Service
12	Destination Host Unreachable for Type of Service
13	Communication Administratively Prohibited
14	Host Precedence Violation
15	Precedence Cutoff in Effect

Table 4–8 lists the codes that can be used with ICMP Redirect packets.

Table 4-8   Type 5: Redirect Codes

Code	Definition
0	Redirect Datagram for the Network (or subnet)
1	Redirect Datagram for the Host
2	Redirect Datagram for the Type of Service and Network
3	Redirect Datagram for the Type of Service and Host

Table 4–9 lists the code that can be used with ICMP Alternate Host Address packets.

Table 4-9   Type 6: Alternate Host Address Code

Code	Definition
0	Alternate Address for Host

Table 4–10 lists the codes that can be used with ICMP Time Exceeded packets.

Table 4-10   Type 11: Time Exceeded Codes

Code	Definition
0	Time to Live Exceeded in Transit
1	Fragment Reassembly Time Exceeded

4

Table 4-11 lists the codes that can be used with ICMP Parameter Problem packets.

Table 4-11   Type 12: Parameter Problem Codes

Code	Definition
0	Pointer Indicates the Error
1	Missing a Required Option
2	Bad Length

Table 4-12 lists the codes that can be used with ICMP Photuris packets.

Table 4-12   Type 40: Photuris Codes

Code	Definition
0	Reserved
1	Unknown Security Parameters Index
2	Valid Security Parameters, but Authentication Failed
3	Valid Security Parameters, but Decryption Failed

Checksum Field

The Checksum field provides error detection for the ICMP header only. The fields that follow the Checksum field vary depending on the particular ICMP message that is sent. In the next section, we examine the most common ICMP packet types, interpretation of their codes, and their complete ICMP structures.

The Varying ICMP Structures and Functions

Several ICMP packets, such as an ICMP Redirect, must send specific information in the ICMP portion of the packet. These packets support additional fields as defined in this section.

Types 0 and 8: Echo Reply and Echo Packets

ICMP Type 8 is used for Echo Request packets; ICMP Type 0 is used for Echo Reply packets. The Code field is always set to zero on these packets. Both ICMP packets use the same structure, as shown in Figure 4-9.

RFC 792 indicates that the Identifier and Sequence fields are used to aid in matching echo messages with echo replies. As an example, RFC 792 states that the "identifier might be used like a port in TCP or UDP to identify a session, and the sequence number might be incremented on each echo request sent. The echoer returns these same values in the echo reply."

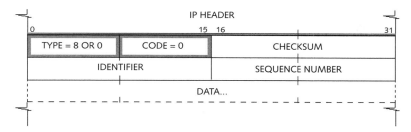

Figure 4-9   ICMP Echo Request and Echo Reply packet structure

Windows 2000 PING packets contain the following characteristics:

- The Identifier field is set to 256 decimal (or 0×100).

- On the first echo sent, the Sequence Number field value is set to a multiple of 256 decimal (0×100). In each subsequent echo, this field is incremented by 256 decimal (0×100).

- The data field contains the value "abcdefghijklmnopqrstuvwabcdefghi."

Figure 4-10 shows the decode of an Echo Request packet from 10.2.10.2 to 10.2.99.99. Figure 4-11 shows the response.

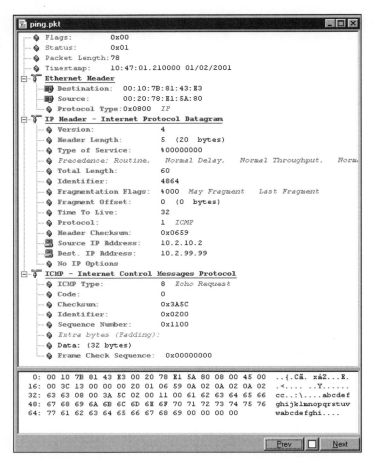

Figure 4-10 ICMP Echo Request packet from 10.2.10.2

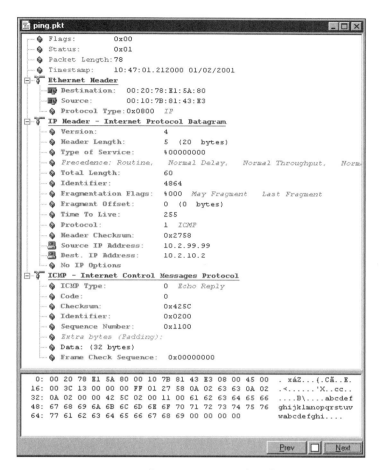

Figure 4-11   ICMP Echo Response packet from 10.2.99.99

As you note in Figures 4-10 and 4-11, the Identifier and Sequence Number fields match on the request and reply. The data contained in the ICMP packet also matches.

Type 3: Destination Unreachable Packets

Network troubleshooters often closely track ICMP Destination Unreachable packets. As you learn in this section, some versions of these packets can indicate a configuration or service fault somewhere on the network. ICMP Destination Unreachable packets use the structure shown in Figure 4-12.

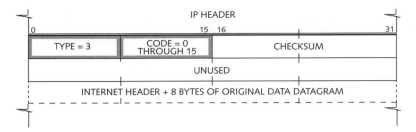

Figure 4-12   ICMP Destination Unreachable packet structure

As shown in Figure 4–12, the host that sends the Destination Unreachable packet must return the IP header and eight bytes of the original datagram that triggered this response. For example, as shown in Figure 4–13, if an IP host sends a DNS query to a host that does not support DNS, the ICMP Destination Unreachable reply contains the IP header and the first eight bytes of data that was in the original DNS query. By looking at the ICMP packet alone, we can tell exactly what triggered the ICMP reply, who sent the original problem packet, and the source and destination port numbers contained in the original packet (because these numbers are contained within eight bytes following the IP header).

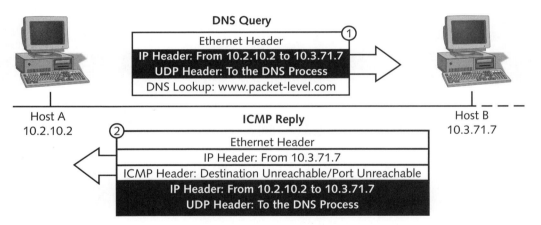

Figure 4-13   Many ICMP packet types include a portion of the triggering packet inside the ICMP reply

It may be confusing to see two IP headers in a single packet when you examine these ICMP packets. Remember to read the packet from start to finish to identify the IP header that is being used to get the datagram through the network (the first IP header in the packet), and the IP header that is simply being sent to help identify the problem (the second IP header).

Although RFC 792 only requires the eight bytes that follow the IP header to be sent in an ICMP reply, it is acceptable and even desirable for as much data as possible to be returned.

As depicted in Figure 4–12, a total of 16 possible codes are currently assigned to the ICMP Destination Unreachable Type number. Not all of these codes are commonly used, but the RFC allows for them in case they are needed. In this section, we define each code individually.

Code 0: Net Unreachable   Code 0 packets can be sent by routers to indicate that the router knows about the network number used in the incoming packet, but believes it is not *up* at this time—perhaps it is too far away to reach. In theory, this is a wonderfully defined code; however, how would the router know which portion of the IP address is the network portion, and which part is the host portion? Networks are now heavily sub-netted and no standard definitive boundaries exist due to the deployment of variable-length subnet masks and Classless Inter-Domain Routing (CIDR). If a router cannot forward a packet because it does not contain an entry for the destination, it will most likely send a Code 1: Host Unreachable packet to the originator.

Code 1: Host Unreachable   A router sends this reply to indicate that the router could not locate the destination host. Currently, this reply is also sent when the destination network is unknown. Figure 4–14 shows a decoded Host Unreachable message. By looking at the ICMP header reply and the second IP header in this packet (with the Identifier value 9984), we can see the cause for this error message. It appears that a device 10.2.10.2 sent an ICMP Echo Request packet to a nonexistent host 10.4.88.88.

We minimized the Ethernet and IP headers in Figure 4-14 to view more of the ICMP reply structure.

Figure 4-14   ICMP packet indicates that the target host, 10.4.88.88, cannot be found

Code 2: Protocol Unreachable A host or router can send this error message to indicate that the protocol defined in the IP header cannot be processed. For example, if an **Internet Group Management Protocol (IGMP)** packet is sent to a host using a TCP/IP stack that does not support or understand IGMP, the host issues this Protocol Unreachable field. This reply is specifically associated with the values contained in the IP header's Protocol field.

Code 3: Port Unreachable A host or router can send this reply to indicate that the sender does not support the process or application you are trying to reach. For example, if a host sends a NetBIOS Name Service packet (port 137) to a host that does not support NetBIOS Name Service, the ICMP reply would be structured like the packet shown in Figure 4-15.

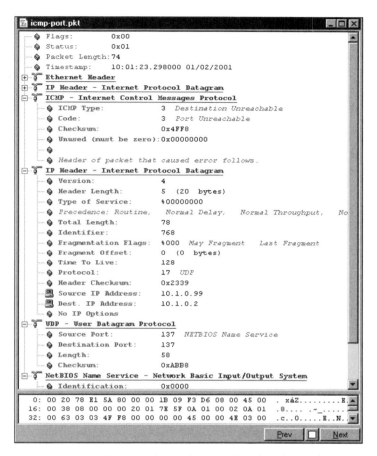

4

Figure 4-15   ICMP packet indicates that the destination port, 137, is not supported on
the target

Code 4: Fragmentation Needed and Don't Fragment Was Set   There are two ver-
sions of this ICMP reply—the standard version that simply states the packet had the
Don't Fragment bit set when it reached a router that needed to fragment it, and the
PMTU version that includes information about the restricting link.

As shown in Figure 4-16, routers that support PMTU Discovery place the MTU of the
restricting link into the 4-byte area previously marked "unused" by RFC 792.

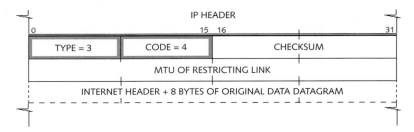

Figure 4-16   ICMP Destination Unreachable structure used for PMTU Discovery

Code 5: Source Route Failed   A router sends this ICMP reply to indicate that the router cannot use the strict or loose source routing path specified in the original packet. If the original packet defined strict source routing, perhaps the router does not have access to the next router indicated in the strict route path list. If the original packet defined loose source routing, perhaps the router has no next-hop router that can forward the packet.

Code 6: Destination Network Unknown   This ICMP packet is obsolete. Routers send the Code 1: Host Unreachable message when they do not know about and cannot forward packets to the desired network.

Code 7: Destination Host Unknown   A router sends this ICMP packet to indicate that it cannot reach a directly connected link, such as a point-to-point link.

Code 8: Source Host Isolated   This ICMP packet is obsolete. Previously, routers sent this packet to indicate that a host was isolated and its packets could not be routed.

Code 9: Communication with Destination Network Is Administratively Prohibited   A router sends this ICMP packet to indicate that the router was configured to block access to the desired destination network. Because these communications may be blocked for security reasons, most routers do not generate these ICMP messages.

Code 10: Communication with Destination Host Is Administratively Prohibited A router sends this ICMP message to indicate that the desired host cannot be reached because the router was configured to block access to the desired destination host. Again, for security reasons, many routers won't generate this message.

Code 11: Destination Network Unreachable for Type of Service   A router sends this ICMP message to indicate that the Type of Service (TOS) requested in an incoming IP header, or the default TOS (0), is not available through this router for the desired network. Only routers that support TOS can send this type of ICMP message.

Code 12: Destination Host Unreachable for Type of Service A router sends this ICMP message to indicate that the TOS requested in an incoming IP header is not available through this router for that specific host. Only routers that support TOS can send this type of ICMP message.

Code 13: Communication Administratively Prohibited A router sends this ICMP message to indicate that the router cannot forward a packet because packet filtering prohibits such activity. Because packet filtering is usually applied for security reasons, many routers do not send this reply to help maintain secrecy regarding their filtering configurations.

Code 14: Host Precedence Violation A router sends this ICMP message to indicate that the Precedence value defined in the sender's original IP header is not allowed for the source or destination host, network, or port. This also results in the discard of the offending packet.

Code 15: Precedence Cutoff in Effect A router sends this ICMP message to indicate that a network administrator imposed a minimum level of precedence to obtain service from a router, and a lower-precedence packet was received. Such packets are discarded and may also result in transmission of this particular ICMP message.

Type 4: Source Quench

A router or host may use Source Quench as a way to indicate that it is becoming congested or overloaded. For example, if a router is overloaded and begins to drop packets, it may send a Source Quench message to hosts to request that they slow or stop sending data to that router. This reduces the amount of incoming traffic, thereby giving the router or host time to recover from overload conditions.

When a Windows 2000 host receives a Source Quench message, it checks whether the ICMP Source Quench message indicates trouble with TCP communications. If so, the Windows 2000 host treats the Source Quench message as a lost TCP segment. By default, most current routers do not issue Source Quench messages because they can further congest a problematic link.

Chapter 5 provides more details on TCP congestion control.

ICMP Source Quench packets use the structure shown in Figure 4-17.

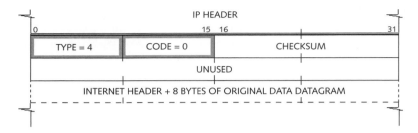

Figure 4-17   ICMP Source Quench packet structure

Type 5: Redirect

Routers send ICMP Redirect messages to hosts to indicate that a preferable route exists. ICMP Redirect packets use the structure shown in Figure 4-18. The ICMP Redirect packet has a 4-byte field for the preferred gateway's address.

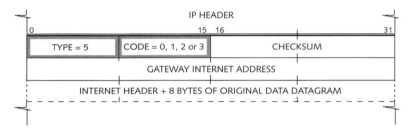

Figure 4-18   ICMP Redirect packet structure

Ideally, clients should update their routing tables to indicate the optimal path to be used for subsequent communications.

Code 0: Redirect Datagram for the Network (or Subnet)   A router can send this ICMP message to indicate that there is a better way to get to the desired network. Because routers cannot determine which portion of a destination address is the network portion, and which portion is the host portion, they use Code 1 in the ICMP Redirect replies.

Code 1: Redirect Datagram for the Host   A router can send this ICMP message to indicate that there is a better way to get to the desired host. This is the most common ICMP Redirect message seen on networks. Figure 4-19 depicts a decoded ICMP Redirect packet. In this packet, we can see the router 10.2.99.99 (source IP address in the IP header) is informing host 10.2.10.2 (destination IP address in the IP header) that the best route to the desired host is 10.2.99.98. Figure 4-7 shows the network design that corresponds to this ICMP Redirect process.

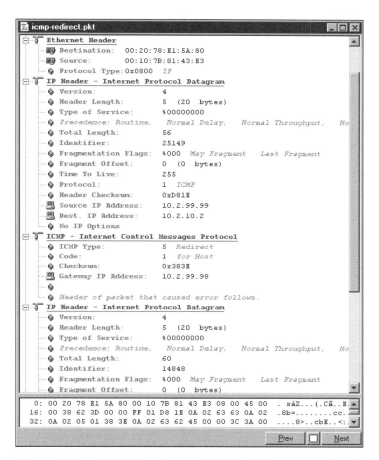

Figure 4-19   Default gateway 10.2.99.99 does not offer the best route

Code 2: Redirect Datagram for the Type of Service and Network   A router can send this ICMP message to indicate that there is a better way to get to the desired network using the desired TOS. Again, because routers cannot determine which portion of a destination address is the network portion, and which portion is the host portion, they use Code 3 in ICMP Redirect replies for TOS issues.

Code 3: Redirect Datagram for the Type of Service and Host   A router can send this ICMP message to indicate that there is a better way to get to the destination host using the TOS requested.

Types 9 and 10: Router Advertisement and Router Solicitation

As mentioned in the "Router Discovery" section earlier in this chapter, hosts send Router Solicitation packets and routers respond with Router Advertisement packets. ICMP Router Solicitation packets use the structure shown in Figure 4-20.

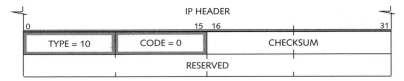

Figure 4-20   ICMP Router Solicitation packet structure

This Solicitation packet structure is very simple. It does not need to contain any information other than the ICMP Type and Code number. As mentioned in the "Router Discovery" section of this chapter, these packets are addressed to the all-router multicast address 224.0.0.2 by default. In some cases, hosts may be configured to send these packets to the broadcast address (in case the local routers do not process multicast packets).

ICMP Router Advertisement packets use the structure shown in Figure 4-21.

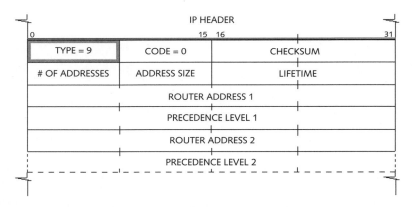

Figure 4-21   ICMP Router Advertisement packet structure

The ICMP Router Advertisement packets include the following fields after the ICMP Checksum field:

- *# of Addresses*: The number of router addresses advertised in this packet

- *Address Size*: The number of 4-byte increments used to define each router address advertised. Because this version includes a 4-byte Precedence field, as well as a 4-byte IP Address field, the Address Size value is two (2 × 4 bytes).

- *Lifetime*: The maximum number of seconds that this router information may be considered valid

- *Router Address 1*: Sending router's local IP address

- *Precedence Level 1*: Preference value of each router address advertised. Higher values indicate greater preferences. A higher precedence level may be configured at a router (if the router supports the option) to ensure that one router is more likely to become the default gateway for local hosts.

Type 11: Time Exceeded

Routers (Time to Live Exceeded in Transit) or hosts (Fragmentation Reassembly Time Exceeded) can send these ICMP packets. ICMP Time Exceeded packets use the structure shown in Figure 4-22.

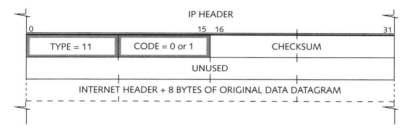

Figure 4-22   ICMP Time Exceeded packet structure

Code 0: Time to Live Exceeded in Transit A router sends these ICMP messages to indicate that a packet arrived with a TTL value of one. Routers cannot decrement the TTL value to zero and forward it, so they must discard the packet and send this ICMP message.

Code 1: Fragment Reassembly Time Exceeded Hosts send these ICMP messages when they do not receive all fragment parts before the expiration (in seconds of holding time) of the TTL value of the first fragment received.

 When a router is acting as a host and assembling packets, it may issue a Code 1: Fragment Reassembly Time Exceeded message.

When the first packet of a fragment set arrives at the destination, the TTL value is interpreted as "seconds of lifetime remaining." A timer begins counting down in seconds. If all fragments of the set do not arrive before the timer expires, the entire fragment set is considered invalid. The receiver sends this message back to the originator of the fragment set, causing the original packet to be re-sent.

Type 12: Parameter Problem

These errors indicate problems not covered by the other ICMP error messages. ICMP Parameter Problem packets use the structure shown in Figure 4-23.

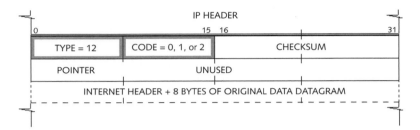

Figure 4-23   ICMP Parameter Problem packet structure

Code 0: Pointer Indicates the Error This ICMP error includes a Pointer field that indicates where in the returned IP header and datagram the error occurred.

Code 1: Missing a Required Option This ICMP error message indicates that the sender expected some additional information in the Option field of the original packet.

Code 2: Bad Length This ICMP error message indicates that the original packet structure had an invalid length.

Types 13 and 14: Timestamp and Timestamp Reply

This ICMP message was defined as a method for one IP host to obtain the current time. The value returned is the number in milliseconds since midnight, **Universal Time (UT)**, formerly referred to as **Greenwich Mean Time (GMT)**. Both ICMP Timestamp and Timestamp Reply packets use the same structure, as shown in Figure 4-24.

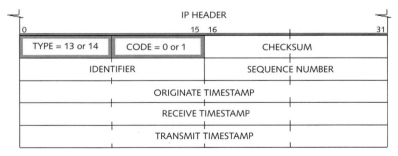

Figure 4-24   ICMP Timestamp and Timestamp Reply packet structure

The timestamp requestor enters the current send time in the Originate Timestamp field. The receiver enters its current time value in the Receive Timestamp field as the packet is processed. The receiver next places the current timestamp in the Transmit Timestamp field at the moment it sends the packet back to the requestor.

Other protocols, such as **Network Time Protocol (NTP)**, provide a more robust and functional **time synchronization** method.

Types 15 and 16: Information Request and Information Reply

This ICMP message provides a way for a host to find out what network it is on. Both ICMP Information Request and Information Reply packets use the same structure, as shown in Figure 4-25.

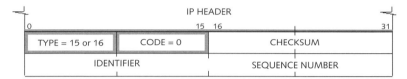

Figure 4-25   ICMP Information Request and Information Reply packet structure

To use this feature, a host sends an Information Request packet and leaves the source and destination IP address fields set to zero. The destination hardware address is broadcast. Routers reply using the Information Reply packet. The IP header in the replies contains the network address, thereby enabling hosts to learn their network addresses.

Types 17 and 18: Address Mask Request and Address Mask Reply

The ICMP Address Mask Request and Address Mask Reply processes are intended to provide diskless hosts with a method to determine their network mask information. Both ICMP Address Mask Request and Address Mask Reply packets use the same structure, as shown in Figure 4-26.

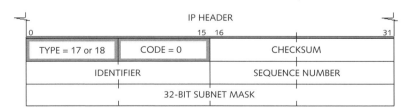

Figure 4-26   ICMP Address Mask Request and Address Mask Reply packet structure

Type 30: Traceroute

This is an interesting ICMP packet type. It is documented in RFC 1393, but not currently in use because it requires some added functionality in the IP routers it traverses, and it also adds a new option to IP. Basically, the Traceroute process requires a host to send a single IP packet with the new Traceroute option (the IP Traceroute Option packet) to a destination. The destination sends an IP Traceroute Option Reply packet. When forwarding these packets, routers along the path are automatically triggered to send an ICMP Traceroute Return packet to the host that initiated the Traceroute process. This ICMP Traceroute packet contains information taken from the IP Traceroute Option Outbound and Return packets as they passed the local router.

The ICMP Traceroute packets use the structure shown in Figure 4-27.

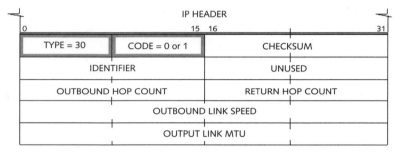

Figure 4-27 ICMP Traceroute packet structure

The Outbound Hop Count field indicates the hop count seen on the outbound IP Traceroute Option packet as it arrived at the router. The Return Hop Count field contains the hop count value seen in the return IP Traceroute Option packet when it arrived at the local router. The Output Link Speed indicates the speed of the link over which the IP Traceroute packet is next sent. This field is defined in bytes per second, not bits per second. The Output Link MTU indicates the MTU size of the link over which the IP Traceroute Option Outbound/Return packet is sent next.

By taking full advantage of ICMP's various capabilities, it's possible to examine how IP is working, and how it gets from "here" to "there" on a network. But, because it's also possible to put ICMP to work for more nefarious ends, you may find that security measures prevent its use for PING or TRACERT when entering some networks. You have to accept this as a consequence of network administrators' cautious approach to revealing information about their networks to outsiders. Nevertheless, you may find ICMP and its various services to be invaluable in managing your own networks, and in troubleshooting reachability problems when they occur.

CHAPTER SUMMARY

- ICMP provides vital feedback about IP routing and delivery problems. ICMP also provides important IP diagnostic and control capabilities that include reachability analysis, congestion management, route optimization, and timeout error reports.

- Although ICMP messages fall within various well-documented types, and behave as a separate protocol at the TCP/IP Network layer, ICMP is really part and parcel of IP itself, and its support is required in any standards-compliant IP implementation. RFC 792 describes ICMP, but numerous other RFCs (such as 950, 1191, and 1812) describe additional details about how ICMP should behave, and how its messages should be generated and handled.

- Two vital TCP/IP diagnostic utilities, known as PING and TRACEROUTE (invoked as TRACERT in the Windows environment), use ICMP to measure round-trip times between a sending and receiving host, and to perform path discovery for a sending host and all intermediate hosts or routers between sender and receiver.

- ICMP also supports Path MTU (PMTU) Discovery between a sender and a receiver, which helps to optimize performance of data delivery between pairs or hosts by avoiding fragmentation en route. This occurs by establishing the smallest MTU required for the path between sender and receiver, and then transmitting all datagrams of that size or smaller from the sending host.

- Route and routing error information from ICMP derives from numerous types of ICMP messages. These include the ICMP Router Solicitation (which hosts use to locate routers) and ICMP Router Advertisement messages (which routers use to advertise their presence and capabilities), as well as the various codes for the ICMP Destination Unreachable message, which documents many possible causes for delivery failures.

- ICMP also supports route optimization through its ICMP Redirect message type, but this capability is normally restricted only to trusted sources of information because of potential security problems that uncontrolled acceptance of such messages can cause.

- Although ICMP has great positive value as a diagnostic and reporting tool, those same capabilities can be turned to nefarious purposes as well, which makes security issues for ICMP important. When hackers investigate networks, ICMP host probes often represent early stages of attack.

- Understanding the meaning and significance of the ICMP Type and Code fields are essential to recognizing individual ICMP messages and what they are trying to communicate. ICMP message structures and functions can vary, depending on the information that any such message seeks to convey.

Key Terms

advertising rate — The rate at which a service (typically a routing service) is announced on a network. An example of an advertising rate is the 10-minute advertising rate for ICMP Router Advertisement packets.

allowable data size — The amount of data that can be transferred across a link; the MTU.

auto-reconfiguration — The process of automatically changing the configuration of a device. For example, when a PMTU host receives an ICMP Destination Unreachable: Fragmentation Needed and Don't Fragment was Set ICMP packet, that host can reconfigure the outgoing MTU size to match the size dictated by the restricting link.

auto-recovery — The process of automatically recovering from a fault. For example, the process of black hole detection enables a host to auto-recover from a communication failure caused by a router that does not forward packets and does not send any messages indicating that an error occurred.

available routes — The known functional routes on an internetwork. Available routes are not necessarily the optimal routes. On IP networks, routers periodically advertise available routes.

average response time — The median time required to reply to a query. The history of network average response times is used to provide a measurement for comparison of current network responses.

backwards compatibility — A feature that enables a device, process, or protocol to operate with earlier versions of software or hardware that do not support all the latest, up-to-date or advanced features. For example, a PMTU host can automatically and incrementally reduce the MTU size it uses until it learns the supported PMTU size.

black hole router — A router that cannot forward packets for some reason (such as an unsupported PMTU size), and does not inform the source of the communication fault. IP hosts typically require additional capabilities to detect and recover from communications that fail due to black hole routers.

command-line parameter — Options added to a command issued at a prompt (not in a windowed environment). For example, in the command *arp -a*, the *-a* is the parameter for the command *arp*.

connectivity tests — Tests to determine the reachability of a device. IP PING and TRACEROUTE are two utilities that can be used for connectivity testing.

Destination Unreachable packets — ICMP packets that indicate a failure to reach a destination due to a fragmentation problem, parameter problem, or other problem.

end-to-end minimum MTU size — The smallest data size that can be sent from one host to another host on an internetwork. Packets may be fragmented to reach the end-to-end minimum MTU size, or the PMTU process can be used to determine the minimum size.

expired route entry — A route entry that is considered "too old" and won't be used to forward data through an internetwork. Expired route entries may be held in a routing table for a short time in anticipation that the route will become valid again as another device advertises it.

fragmentable — Able to be fragmented. A packet must have the May Fragment bit set in order to allow an IP packet to be fragmented if necessary.

gateway — In the TCP/IP environment, the term "gateway" is used to refer to a Network layer forwarding device typically known as a router. The default gateway is the router a host sends a packet to when the host has no specific route to a destination.

Greenwich Mean Time (GMT) — The mean solar time of the meridian of Greenwich used as the prime basis of standard time throughout the world. Greenwich, England, is where east meets west at the Greenwich Meridian (0° Longitude). Also referred to as *Universal Time (UT)*.

hacker — A person who uses computer and communications knowledge to exploit information or functionality of a device.

host probe — A reconnaissance process used to determine which hosts are active on an IP network. Typically, the PING process is used to perform a host probe.

host route entry — A route table entry that matches all four bytes of the desired destination. Network route table entries only match the network bits of the desired address.

ICMP Echo process — An ICMP process whereby a host sends an Echo packet to another host on an internetwork. If the destination host is active and able, it echoes back the data that is contained in the ICMP Echo packet.

ICMP Echo Request packet — A packet that is sent to a device to test connectivity. If the receiving device is functional and can reply, it should echo back the data that is contained in the data portion of the Echo Request packet.

ICMP error messages — Error messages sent using the ICMP protocol. Destination Unreachable, Time Exceeded, and Parameter Problem are examples of ICMP error messages.

ICMP query message — ICMP messages that contain requests for configuration or other information. ICMP Echo, Router Solicitation, and Address Mask Request are examples of ICMP query messages.

ICMP Router Discovery — A process in which hosts send ICMP Router Solicitation messages to the all-router multicast address (224.0.0.2). Local routers that support the ICMP Router Discovery process reply with an ICMP Router Advertisement unicast to the host. The advertisement contains the router's address and a Lifetime value for the router's information.

ICMP Router Solicitation — The process that a host can perform to learn of local routers. ICMP Router Solicitation messages are sent to the all-routers multicast address of 224.0.0.2.

Internet Control Message Protocol (ICMP) — A key protocol in the TCP/IP protocol suite that provides error messages and the ability to query other devices. IP PING and TRACEROUTE utilities use ICMP.

4

Internet Group Management Protocol (IGMP) — A protocol that supports the formation of multicast groups. Hosts use IGMP to join and leave multicast groups. Routers track IGMP memberships and only forward multicasts on a link that has active members of that multicast group.

metrics — Measurements that may be based on distance (hop count), time (seconds), or other values.

millisecond — One-thousandth of a second.

network congestion — A condition that occurs when the delivery time for packets (also known as network latency) increases beyond normal limits. Congestion can result from several causes, including problems with network links, overloaded hosts or routers, or unusually heavy network usage levels. Packet loss is identified as a characteristic of network congestion.

network route entry — A route table entry that provides a next-hop router for a specific network.

Network Time Protocol (NTP) — A time synchronization protocol defined in RFC 1305. NTP provides the mechanisms to synchronize and coordinate time distribution in a large, diverse Internet operating at varying speeds.

optimal route — The best route possible. Typically, routing protocols are used to exchange routing metric information to determine the best route possible. The optimal route is defined as either the route that is quickest, most reliable, most secure, or considered *best* by some other measurement. When TOS is not used, the optimal route is either the closest (based on hop count) or the highest throughput route.

overhead — The non-data bits or bytes required to move data from one location to another. The datalink header is the overhead required to move an IP packet from one device to another across a network. The IP header is additional overhead required to move a packet through an internetwork. Ideally, bandwidth, throughput, and processing power should be devoted to moving high amounts of data bytes— not high amounts of overhead bytes.

path — The route that a packet can take through an internetwork.

path discovery — The process of learning possible routes through a network.

Path MTU (PMTU) — The MTU size that is supported through an entire path; the lowest common denominator MTU through a path. The Path MTU is learned through the PMTU Discovery process.

Path MTU Discovery — The process of learning the MTU that is supported through an entire path. ICMP is used for PMTU Discovery.

PATHPING — A Windows 2000 utility used to test router and path latency, as well as connectivity.

port probe — A reconnaissance process used to learn which processes are active on a host device. Typically, port probes use scripted programs to send out sequential queries to obtain all active port information.

reachability — The ability to find at least one transmission path between a pair of hosts so that they can exchange datagrams across an internetwork.

reconnaissance process — The process of learning various characteristics about a network or host. Typically, reconnaissance probes precede network attacks.

redirect — Point out another path. Using ICMP, a router can redirect a host to another, more optimal router.

restricting link — A link that does not support forwarding based on the current packet format and configuration. PMTU is used to identify restricting links so hosts can re-send packets using an acceptable MTU size.

retry counter — A counter that tracks the number of retransmissions on the network. The most common retry counter found in TCP/IP networking is the TCP retry counter. If a communication cannot be completed successfully before the retry counter expires, the transmission is considered a failure.

round-trip time — The amount of time required to get from one host to another host and back. The round-trip time includes the transmission time from the first point to the second point, the processing time at the second point, and the return transmission time to the first point.

route tracing — A technique for documenting which hosts and routers a datagram traverses in its path from the sender to the receiver (the TRACEROUTE or TRACERT commands use PING in a systematic way to provide this information).

silent discard — The process of discarding a packet without notification to any other device that such a discarding process occurred. For example, a black hole router silently discards packets that it cannot forward.

throughput difference — The comparative difference in throughput between two paths. Throughput, is measured in Kbps or Mbps.

time synchronization — The process of obtaining the exact same time on multiple hosts. Network Time Protocol (NTP) is a time synchronization protocol.

TRACEROUTE — *See* TRACERT.

TRACERT — The name of the Windows command that uses multiple PING commands to establish the identity and round-trip times for all hosts between a sender and a receiver.

Universal Time (UT) — *See* Greenwich Mean Time (GMT); sometimes also called Universal Coordinating Time (UCT), or Zulu Time.

unsolicited — Unrequested. Unsolicited replies are typically advertisements that occur on a periodic basis. For example, ICMP Router Advertisements typically occur on a seven- to 10-minute basis.

REVIEW QUESTIONS

1. ICMP is a distinct Network layer TCP/IP protocol that has nothing in common with IP. True or false?
   a. True
   b. False

2. What is the name of the concept that indicates that a path exists between two TCP/IP hosts on an internetwork?
   a. path discovery
   b. PMTU
   c. reachability
   d. route tracing

3. Which of the following services does ICMP add to basic IP datagram delivery services? (Choose all that apply.)
   a. improved reliability for datagram delivery
   b. reachability analysis support
   c. path discovery services
   d. delivery error reporting
   e. network congestion management
   f. network utilization metrics

4. It's up to the IP host that receives incoming ICMP messages to act on the content of those messages. True or false?
   a. True
   b. False

5. Which of the following RFCs describes ICMP?
   a. 792
   b. 950
   c. 1191
   d. 1812

6. Which of the following RFCs prescribes certain kinds of ICMP behavior or capability? (Choose all that apply.)
   a. 950
   b. 1001
   c. 1191
   d. 1812
   e. 1918

7. ICMP only reports errors about IP datagrams. Errors about error messages are not reported. True or false?

   a. True

   b. False

8. Which of the following ICMP message types relates to reachability analysis?

   a. Destination Unreachable

   b. Echo/Echo Reply

   c. Redirect

   d. Source Quench

9. Which of the following ICMP message types reports delivery errors?

   a. Destination Unreachable

   b. Echo/Echo Reply

   c. Redirect

   d. Source Quench

10. Which of the following ICMP message types relates to congestion control?

   a. Destination Unreachable

   b. Echo/Echo Reply

   c. Redirect

   d. Source Quench

11. Which of the following ICMP message types relates to route optimization?

   a. Destination Unreachable

   b. Echo/Echo Reply

   c. Redirect

   d. Source Quench

12. Which of the following Windows command-line utilities performs connectivity or reachability tests?

   a. PING

   b. TRACERT

   c. TRACEROUTE

   d. IPCONFIG

13. Which of the following Windows command-line utilities performs path discovery tests?

   a. PING

   b. TRACERT

   c. TRACEROUTE

   d. IPCONFIG

14. Which of the following command-line parameters for the PING command governs the Time to Live value?

    a. f

    b. i

    c. l

    d. w

15. Which of the following command-line parameters for the PING command governs the Reply Timeout value?

    a. f

    b. i

    c. l

    d. w

16. Which of the following path discovery command-line parameters turns off reverse DNS lookups?

    a. –a

    b. –d

    c. –h

    d. –w

17. What additional functionality does PATHPING provide?

    a. reports on all visited hosts and routers between a sender and a receiver

    b. resolves all possible IP addresses into symbolic names for visited nodes

    c. uses the ICMP Traceroute message type

    d. tests router and link latency

18. Which of the following statements best defines the intent of the PMTU process?

    a. determines the largest possible MTU in the path between sender and receiver

    b. determines the smallest possible MTU in the path between sender and receiver

    c. instructs the sender what MTU to use to avoid further fragmentation en route

    d. justifies the inclusion of the Don't Fragment flag in ICMP messages

19. Which of the following statements best describes a black hole router?

    a. a router that discards all incoming traffic

    b. a router that does not support PMTU, but is configured to send Destination Unreachable messages

    c. a router that does not support PMTU, and is configured not to send Destination Unreachable messages

    d. a router that does not support PMTU

20. What IP router functions does RFC 1812 include? (Choose all that apply.)

    a. how to avoid creating black hole routers

    b. how to handle ICMP error messages

    c. how to handle ICMP query messages

    d. how to report router delivery errors

21. Which of the following accurately represents the default advertising rate for unsolicited ICMP Router Advertisements?

    a. every 30 seconds

    b. every 60 seconds

    c. two to five minutes

    d. seven to 10 minutes

22. The ICMP redirection process serves only IP routers, not IP hosts. True or false?

    a. True

    b. False

23. What type of scan occurs when a series of PING requests for a range of IP addresses is performed?

    a. port scan

    b. protocol scan

    c. host probe

    d. network mapping

24. Which of the following ICMP Type numbers identifies Echo and Echo Reply messages? (Choose all that apply.)

    a. 0

    b. 1

    c. 3

    d. 8

    e. 30

25. Which of the following ICMP Type numbers relates to Router Advertisement and Solicitation messages? (Choose all that apply.)

    a. 8

    b. 9

    c. 10

    d. 11

    e. 12

HANDS-ON PROJECTS

Project 4-1

The following Hands-on Projects assume that you are working in a Windows 2000 environment, and that you installed the EtherPeek for Windows demo software (included on the accompanying CD).

To ping another device on the network:

1. Click **Start**, point to **Programs**, point to **Accessories**, and then click **Command Prompt**. The Command Prompt window opens.

2. Enter **ping** to view the available command-line parameters. Keep the Command Prompt window open while you follow the next steps to launch the EtherPeek demo program.

3. Click **Start**, point to **Programs**, and then click **WildPackets EtherPeek Demo**.

4. The list of EtherPeek demo limitations appears. Click **OK**.

5. The Select Adapter window may appear. Click the adapter installed on your system. Click **OK** to close the Adapter Selection window.

6. Click **Capture** on the menu bar, and then click **Start Capture**.

7. The Capture Options window appears. Click **OK** to accept the default buffer size of 1024 kilobytes. The Capture window appears. The Capture window number increments each time you launch a new capture process.

8. Click the **Start Capture** button in the Capture window.

9. Click the **Command Prompt** button on the taskbar, or use **Alt+Tab** to make the Command Prompt window active.

10. Type **ping** *ip_address*, where *ip_address* is the address of another device on the network. You should have some packets in your EtherPeek trace buffer.

11. Do *not* close the Command Prompt window. Click the **EtherPeek Demo** button on the taskbar, or use **Alt+Tab** to make the EtherPeek window active.

12. If the demo is still capturing, click the **Stop Capture** button. (If the program automatically stopped capturing, click **OK** in the resulting message box.)

13. Scroll through the packets you captured in your trace buffer. You should see several ICMP Echo Requests and ICMP Echo Reply packets. Because no filter was applied before running this capture, you may have other students' traffic in your buffer as well as your own. In the next project, you will build a filter that enables you to capture only your own traffic.

14. Close the Capture window in the EtherPeek demo, leave the EtherPeek demo and Command Prompt windows open, and proceed immediately to the next project.

Project 4-2

This project assumes you are continuing from Hands-on Project 4-1.

To build a filter for your own traffic:

1. Click the **Start or Stop Capture** button ![icon] on the EtherPeek toolbar.
2. The Capture Options window appears. Click **OK** to accept the default buffer size of 1024 kilobytes. The Capture window appears.
3. Click the **Filters** tab at the bottom of the Capture window.
4. Click the **Insert** button ![icon]. The Edit Filter window appears.
5. Type **My IP Address** in the Filter text box.
6. Click the check box labeled **Address filter**.
7. Click the down arrow next to the Type box (next to the Address 1 box). The list of possible addresses is shown. Click **IP**.
8. Enter your IP address in the Address 1 box. Because we are interested in any traffic that is flowing to and from your station, leave the *Any address* option selected in the Address 2 section. Your Edit Filter window should look similar to Figure 4-28.

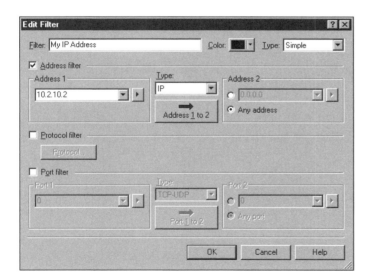

Figure 4-28   Building your IP Address filter

9. Click **OK**. The Edit Filter window closes. You see the filter list again.
10. Scroll down to find the **My IP Address** filter. By default, your new filter is listed in black text.
11. Click the check box next to the **My IP Address** filter. This filter is saved with the EtherPeek demo software when you close the application.
12. Click the **Packets** tab.

13. Now that you selected a filter on your own traffic only, repeat steps 8 through 13 of Hands-on Project 4-1.

14. Close the Command Prompt window and proceed immediately to the next project.

Project 4-3

This project assumes that you are continuing from Hands-on Project 4-2.

To determine and test the allowable MTU on your network:

1. On a sheet of paper, write your network's maximum packet size (including headers). For example, Ethernet networks support 1518 bytes.

2. Write the overhead of the Data Link layer header and trailer.

3. Write the overhead of the IP header.

4. Write the overhead of an ICMP header in an Echo Request packet.

5. Subtract the values written for Steps 2, 3, and 4 from Step 1. Write your result. This is your network MTU. Test your MTU by performing Steps 6 through 8.

6. Click **Start**, **Programs**, **Accessories**, **Command Prompt**. The Command Prompt window appears.

7. Enter **ping –f –l** *mtu ip_address*, where *mtu* is the number of the result from Step 5, and *ip_address* is the address of another host on your network. The –f parameter is used to indicate that this packet should not be fragmented. The –l mtu parameter is used to define the size of the Data field that this echo packet supports. Was your ping successful? If you calculated your MTU properly, your ping should successfully receive replies.

8. Now, increase the MTU to see the reaction. Add two to the MTU value you obtained in Step 5. Repeat Step 7 entering the command **ping –f –l** *mtu+2 ip_address*, where *mtu+2* is two digits higher than the MTU value determined in Step 5. Was your ping successful? Write the Windows message you received when performing this task.

9. Close the Command Prompt window and the EtherPeek demo program.

Project 4-4

To interpret the difference between two ICMP Echo packets:

1. Start the EtherPeek demo according to the instructions in Project 4-1.

2. Click **File**, **Open**, and select the trace file **ping.pkt** contained in the **18654-2\Ch4** folder on your hard disk.

3. Double-click **Packet #1**. This is an ICMP Echo Request packet. Review the ICMP portion of the packet. Answer the following questions about this packet:

   a. What is the ICMP Identifier number in Packet #1?

   b. What is the ICMP Sequence Number in Packet #1?

   c. What is the ICMP Checksum value of Packet #1?

4. Click the **Decode Next** button to view Packet #2 and answer the following questions.

   a. What is the ICMP Identifier number in Packet #2?

   b. What is the ICMP Sequence Number in Packet #3?

   c. What is the ICMP Checksum value of Packet #4?

5. The Identifier and Sequence Numbers are the same in both packets. Why is the ICMP Checksum value different in each packet?

6. Close the EtherPeek demo program, unless you proceed immediately to the next project. In that case, skip Step 1 in Hands-on Project 4-5.

Project 4-5

To identify the cause of an ICMP error message:

1. Start the EtherPeek demo program according to the instructions in Hands-on Project 4-1.

2. Click **File**, **Open**, and select the trace file **icmplab.pkt** contained in the **18654-2\Ch4** folder on your hard disk.

3. Examine Packets #1 and #2 in this trace. Answer the following questions:

   a. What type of ICMP packet was sent?

   b. What ICMP Code number was used?

   c. What is the purpose of this ICMP packet?

   d. What is the IP address of the host that caused this ICMP packet to be sent?

   e. Why was this packet sent?

4. Close the EtherPeek demo program.

Project 4-6

This Hands-on Project assumes that you have Internet access.

To trace the route to another device on the Internet:

1. Click **Start**, point to **Programs**, point to **Accessories**, and then click **Command Prompt**. The Command Prompt window opens.

2. Enter **tracert** to view the available command-line parameters. Keep the Command Prompt window open while you follow the next steps to launch the EtherPeek demo program.

3. Click **Start**, point to **Programs**, and then click **WildPackets EtherPeek Demo**.

4. The list of EtherPeek demo limitations appears. Click **OK**.

5. The Select Adapter window may appear. Click the adapter installed in your system. Click **OK** to close the Adapter Selection window.

6. Click **Capture** on the menu bar, and then click **Start Capture**.

7. The Capture Options window appears. Click **OK** to accept the default buffer size of 1024 kilobytes. The Capture window appears. The Capture window number increments each time you start a new capture process.

8. Click the **Filters** tab and select the **My IP Address** filter (created in Hands-on Project 4-2).

9. Click **Start Capture** in the Capture window.

10. Click the **Command Prompt** button on the taskbar, or use **Alt+Tab** to make the Command Prompt window active.

11. Type **tracert** *ip_address*, where *ip_address* is the address supplied by your instructor for this project, and then press **Enter**.

12. Once your route tracing session completes successfully, close the Command Prompt window. Make the **EtherPeek Demo** window active.

13. If the demo is still capturing, click the **Stop Capture** button. (If the program automatically stopped capturing, click **OK** in the resulting message box.) Click the **Packets** tab. Scroll through the packets you captured in your trace buffer. Answer the following questions about your TRACEROUTE process:

    a. What was the starting TTL value?

    b. How many routers did you cross to reach your destination?

    c. Did all the routers along the path answer?

    d. How many packets did this route tracing process require?

CASE PROJECTS

1. You reconfigured a network using brand new routers. You are not certain if you configured the most appropriate default gateway settings for your hosts. How can you use an analyzer to determine if your default gateway settings are appropriate?

2. You are asked to check your company's configurations to determine if any filters should be built to stop certain ICMP traffic. Your supervisor asks for a list of ICMP traffic that is of concern, and the reasons why such packets could be a problem. Build a list for your supervisor. Include at least five ICMP packets, and list why they would be a problem on the network.

3. You moved to San Diego to work with a large sports apparel company. Its network grew through various corporate acquisitions—it is truly a mix of media, speeds, computers, and applications. You are not sure if this network's hosts and routers support PMTU Discovery to reduce fragments on the network. Write a brief plan defining how you can test this network for PMTU support.

4. Throughout the RFCs, you notice the initials JBP and the name Jon B. Postel. Access IANA's Web site (*http://www.iana.org*) and search for information on Jon Postel. Write a single paragraph defining Jon Postel's effect on the development of IP and other related Internet protocols.

5

TRANSPORT LAYER TCP/IP PROTOCOLS

After reading this chapter and completing the exercises you will be able to:

♦ Understand the concepts involved in connectionless and connection-oriented transport protocols, including the function of port numbers

♦ Explain why connectionless protocols require less overhead and offer faster performance than connection-oriented protocols

♦ Understand the key features and functions of the User Datagram Protocol (UDP)

♦ Explain the mechanisms that drive segmentation, reassembly, and retransmission for the Transmission Control Protocol (TCP)

♦ Explain how TCP connections are managed through setup, maintenance, and teardown phases

♦ Identify key UDP and TCP port addresses

♦ Understand both customary and appropriate uses and application services that involve either UDP or TCP transport protocols

As TCP/IP's Network layer protocols provide network address, routing, and delivery functions, TCP/IP's Transport layer protocols provide the mechanisms necessary to move messages of arbitrary size from sender to receiver across a network. Although the Transmission Control Protocol (TCP) that helps give the overall protocol stack its name is arguably more important than the only other TCP/IP transport protocol—the User Datagram Protocol (UDP)—both of these protocols perform vital roles in enabling the transfer of arbitrary data across a network. As you make your way through this chapter, you'll come to understand the vital notions involved in connectionless versus connection–oriented transport mechanisms, and the concomitant impact these mechanisms have on complexity, robustness, reliability, and overhead.

Basically, a transport protocol provides a way to deliver messages from a sender to a receiver across a network. More sophisticated transport protocols take outgoing messages of arbitrary size and break them into chunks small enough to fit inside an IP packet that can travel across whatever network medium may be in use. Additional elaborations on this theme require establishing a connection between the sender and receiver. When the bandwidth available to a connection exceeds what a single higher-layer service wants to consume, Transport layer protocols can interleave multiple packets from different messages within that connection—a technique known as multiplexing—to use available bandwidth more effectively. These elaborations require connection-oriented transport services, covered later in this chapter. We begin the chapter with the simplest of all transport protocol types—connectionless protocols.

Understanding Connectionless Transport Protocols

Connectionless protocols provide the simplest kind of transport services because they simply package messages, taken as is from the TCP/IP Application layer, into datagrams. Basically, a datagram slaps a header onto the higher-layer data and passes it to the IP layer, where that datagram is fitted with an IP header and packetized, after which it may be transmitted across the network. This method is called **best-effort delivery** because it comes with no built-in delivery checks or retransmission characteristics that improve reliability above and beyond what's inherent in protocols and network technology beneath a connectionless Transport layer protocol, such as UDP.

The reason that a datagram service like UDP is so simple and straightforward is that it depends on whatever higher-layer protocol that uses it for transport to handle the kinds of sophisticated functions that a connection-oriented protocol like TCP provides. This turns out to be a smart design decision on modern networks because the overhead of providing the various delivery guarantees and reliability mechanisms that TCP provides comes at a cost. More capability means more overhead because of the information that must be gathered, exchanged, and managed to provide that capability.

This means that UDP runs up to 40% faster than TCP, under some conditions, because it does next to nothing! In practice, this usually means all datagrams in a UDP sequence match the MTU for the medium at the transmitting machine in size, except for the last datagram, which needs to be only as long as the final leftover payload and header information require. That's because the Application layer protocol does the necessary slicing and dicing before it hands off to UDP, even though segmentation is normally considered a Transport layer function. Likewise, the Application layer protocol simplifies the services it requires from UDP by handling its own reassembly and error management on the other end of the delivery cycle.

It's also typical for connectionless protocols to handle the following kinds of tasks:

- *Message checksum*: Although connectionless protocols don't track transmission behavior or completeness of delivery (that's what best-effort delivery means), they can optionally include a checksum for each datagram. This makes it easy for the transport protocol to report to a higher-layer protocol whether the packet made it to the destination in the same form as when it left the sender, without having to handle the potentially gory details involved. (You'll learn a lot about those in the section titled "Transmission Control Protocol (TCP)" later in this chapter).

- *Higher-layer protocol identification*: Generally speaking, all TCP/IP transport protocols use two port address fields in their headers to identify specific Application layer protocols, or specific processes on the sending and receiving hosts, so they can exchange messages at that higher layer. This is the mechanism that identifies an Application layer protocol through the well-known port addresses associated with most higher-layer TCP/IP protocols and services. This mechanism also permits application processes that use those protocols or services to exchange data to identify each other uniquely while ongoing (or even multiple streams of) communication between a sender and a receiver may be underway. Thus, even though a connectionless protocol has no internal methods for creating, managing, and terminating connections, it does provide a mechanism for such activities to occur at the Application layer. You'll learn considerably more about port addresses and their various uses throughout the course of this chapter.

5

USER DATAGRAM PROTOCOL (UDP)

Since UDP is the only connectionless TCP/IP protocol at the Transport layer, it should come as no surprise that all of the characteristics ascribed to connectionless TCP/IP protocols in the preceding section apply directly and completely to UDP itself. Thus, it's entirely appropriate to provide the following detailed description for UDP (which is based on the content of RFC 768, wherein UDP is completely described):

- *No reliability mechanisms*: Datagrams are not sequenced and are not acknowledged. Most applications or services that use UDP supply their own reliability mechanisms, or track timeout values for datagrams, and retransmit when a datagram's timeout counter expires.

- *No delivery guarantees*: Datagrams are sent without any promise of delivery so, again, the Application layer must provide tracking and retransmission mechanisms.

- *No connection handling*: Each datagram is an independent message that the sender transmits without UDP providing any way to establish, manage, or close a connection between sender and receiver.

- *Identifies Application layer protocol conveyed*: As noted previously, the UDP header includes fields that identify port addresses, also known as port numbers, for sending and receiving Application layer services or processes.

- *Checksum for entire message carried in UDP header*: As packaged, each UDP header may optionally include a checksum value that can be recalculated upon delivery, and compared to the value as sent. However, it's up to the Application layer service or protocol to act on this information—UDP does nothing more than provide this data, and does not require that a checksum be calculated, per se.

- *No buffering services*: UDP doesn't manage where incoming data resides in memory before delivery, or where outgoing data resides before transmission. All memory management for *data in motion* must be handled at the Application layer for services that use UDP; it sees strictly one datagram at a time.

- *No segmentation*: UDP provides no services to break up arbitrarily large messages into discrete, labeled chunks for transmission, or to reassemble sequences of labeled chunks upon reception. UDP only sends and receives datagrams; the Application layer protocol or service must handle segmentation and reassembly, when required.

Notice that UDP is as much defined by what it does not provide (all the missing characteristics listed are typical for TCP rather than UDP), as by what it does provide (basically, a checksum mechanism and identification of port addresses for sender and receiver for higher-layer uses).

UDP Header Fields and Functions

When the Protocol field of an IP header contains the value 17 (0x11), the UDP header follows the IP header. The UDP header is short and simple—only eight bytes long. The UDP header's main function is to define the process or application that is using the IP and UDP Network and Transport layers. Figure 5-1 shows the layout of the UDP header.

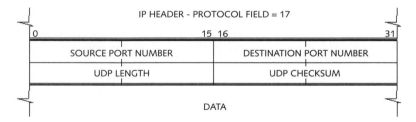

Figure 5-1   UDP header is only eight bytes long

UDP is defined in RFC 768. The UDP header contains only four fields:

- Source Port Number field

- Destination Port Number field

- UDP Length field

- UDP Checksum field

In the next sections, we examine the field values and functions of the UDP header.

Source Port Number Field

The Source Port Number field defines the application or process that sends the packet using the UDP transport. In some cases, a temporary port number is used.

Port numbers are defined in three ranges: well-known port numbers, registered port numbers, and **dynamic port numbers**.

Well-Known Port Numbers (0 through 1023) Well-known port numbers are assigned to the key or **core services** that systems offer. Well-known port numbers are between 0 and 1023. Until 1992, the well-known port number range was between 1 and 255.

Registered Port Numbers (1024 through 49151) Registered port numbers are assigned to industry applications and processes, for example, 1433 is assigned to the Microsoft SQL Server process. Some TCP/IP systems use between 1024 and 5000 for temporary port numbers, although IANA includes that range as part of their dynamic port numbers range.

Dynamic Port Numbers (49152 through 65535) Dynamic ports (also referred to as **ephemeral ports**) are used as **temporary ports** for specific communications. IANA defines a range of numbers, the dynamic port numbers range, for identification of dynamic ports. Some of the more common well-known port numbers are listed in Table 5-1.

Table 5-1   Common Well-Known Port Numbers

UDP Port Number	Application or Process
67	Bootstrap Protocol Server (also DHCP Server)
68	Bootstrap Protocol Client (also DHCP Client)
161	Simple Network Management Protocol (SNMP)
162	Simple Network Management Protocol (SNMP) Trap
520	Routing Information Protocol (RIP)

In most cases, an application or process can use the same number, whether it is running over UDP or TCP, because the UDP and TCP port numbers assigned are the same. In some rare cases, however, the UDP and TCP port numbers assigned do not support the same service—UDP port 520 is a perfect example. The UDP port number 520 is assigned to Router Information Protocol (RIP). The TCP port number 520 is assigned to the Extended File Name Server (EFS) process. Refer to *http://www.iana.org* for the complete list of assigned port numbers, and a definition of the three types of port numbers found in UDP and TCP headers.

As you can see from the contents of Table 5-1, UDP comes into play when reliability is not an issue, either because the sending host may not have sufficient "intelligence" to provide or understand reliability mechanisms (as is the case with DHCP), or where regular management or routing polling or advertisement means that constant communication offsets reliability requirements through sheer repetition. In other circumstances, either the data carried or the services provided are sufficiently important—or one-time transmission is highly desirable—and increased needs for reliability or delivery guarantees come into play. That's when connection-oriented transport (discussed later in this chapter) is needed.

Destination Port Number Field

This field value defines the destination application or process that uses the IP and TCP headers. In some instances, the source and destination port numbers are the same for client and server processes. In other instances, you may find a separate and unique number for the client and server process (as in the case of DHCP). Still another variation is to allow the client to use dynamic port numbers for its side of the communications, and well-known port numbers, or registered port numbers, for the server side of the communications.

Length Field

The Length field defines the length of the packet from the UDP header to the end of **valid data** (not including any data link padding, if padding is required). This field provides a redundant measurement because this information can be determined using the IP header value, and the knowledge that the UDP header is eight bytes long. For example, consider the packet shown in Figure 5-2.

Following is the interpretation of the Length fields shown in Figure 5-2:

- IP Header Length = 5 (denoted in 4-byte increments). The IP header is 20 bytes long.

- IP Total Length = 52. The data after the IP header is 32 bytes (subtract the 20-byte IP header).

- UDP Length = 32. The data after the IP header (including the UDP header) is 32 bytes, which we just learned from the Total Length field in the IP header. Subtract the 8-byte UDP header, and you know that there must be 24 bytes of data following the UDP header itself.

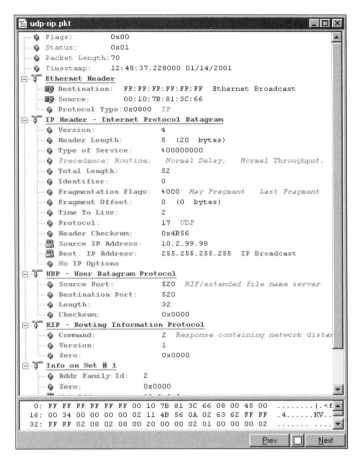

```
udp-rip.pkt                                            _ □ ✕
   ◆ Flags:        0x00                                        ▲
   ◆ Status:       0x01
   ◆ Packet Length:70
   ◆ Timestamp:    12:48:37.228000 01/14/2001
⊟ ⅋ Ethernet Header
   ▦ Destination:  FF:FF:FF:FF:FF:FF  Ethernet Broadcast
   ▦ Source:       00:10:7B:81:3C:66
   ◆ Protocol Type:0x0800  IP
⊟ ⅋ IP Header - Internet Protocol Datagram
   ◆ Version:         4
   ◆ Header Length:      5  (20  bytes)
   ◆ Type of Service:    %00000000
   ◆ Precedence: Routine,   Normal Delay,   Normal Throughput,
   ◆ Total Length:      52
   ◆ Identifier:        0
   ◆ Fragmentation Flags:  %000  May Fragment   Last Fragment
   ◆ Fragment Offset:    0  (0  bytes)
   ◆ Time To Live:      2
   ◆ Protocol:        17  UDP
   ◆ Header Checksum:    0x4B56
   ▣ Source IP Address:  10.2.99.98
   ▣ Dest. IP Address:   255.255.255.255  IP Broadcast
   ◆ No IP Options
⊟ ⅋ UDP - User Datagram Protocol
   ◆ Source Port:      520  RIP/extended file name server
   ◆ Destination Port:   520
   ◆ Length:         32
   ◆ Checksum:        0x0000
⊟ ⅋ RIP - Routing Information Protocol
   ◆ Command:        2  Response containing network distan
   ◆ Version:         1
   ◆ Zero:          0x0000
⊟ ⅋ Info on Net # 1
   ◆ Addr Family Id:    2
   ◆ Zero:          0x0000                                     ▼
─────────────────────────────────────────────────────────
 0: FF FF FF FF FF FF 00 10 7B 81 3C 66 08 00 45 00  ........{.<f ▲
16: 00 34 00 00 00 00 02 11 4B 56 0A 02 63 62 FF FF  .4......KV..
32: FF FF 02 08 02 08 00 20 00 00 02 01 00 00 00 02  ........ .... ▼
                                      ┌──────┬─┬──────┐
                                      │ Prev │□│ Next │
                                      └──────┴─┴──────┘
```

Figure 5-2   UDP is used to carry connectionless services, such as RIP

Checksum Field

The UDP Checksum field is optional—in the case of Figure 5-2, the sender generated no checksum. If a checksum is used, the checksum calculation is performed on the contents of the entire datagram—namely the UDP header (except the UDP Checksum field itself), the datagram payload, and a **pseudo-header** that is derived from the IP header. The UDP pseudo-header is not actually contained in the packet—the UDP pseudo-header is used only to calculate the UDP header checksum, and associate the UDP header with the IP header. This pseudo-header consists of the IP header Source Address field, the Destination Address field, an unused field (set to zero), the Protocol field, and the UDP Length field. Figure 5-3 shows the UDP pseudo-header.

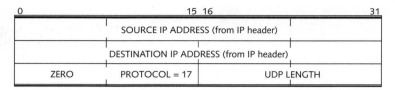

Figure 5-3   UDP pseudo-header

UDP Port Numbers and Processes

Both UDP and TCP use port numbers to define the source and destination processes or applications. As mentioned in the "Destination Port Field" section earlier in this chapter, the source and destination port numbers are not necessarily the same within a conversation. A host may open a dynamic source port number to send a DNS query. Upon receipt of the DNS query packet, a host examines the IP header to identify the Transport layer protocol in use. Next, the receiving host examines the Destination Port Number field to determine how to handle the incoming packet.

Figure 5-4 shows how packets are demultiplexed, based on the type number, protocol number, and port number.

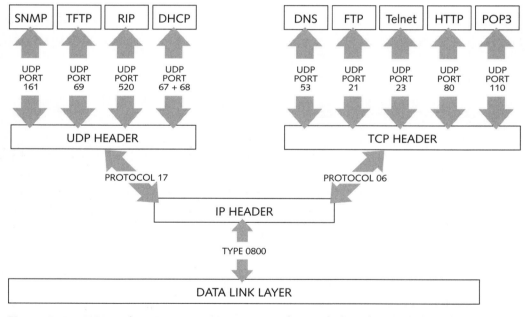

Figure 5-4   TCP and UDP communications are forwarded to the appropriate Application layer protocol based on the destination port number

By default, Windows 2000 supports a maximum port number of 5000. The file called SYSTEM in the SystemRoot\system32\drivers\etc folder contains the list of port numbers supported.

You can increase the supported maximum user port number by adding the MaxUserPort Registry entry, as shown in Table 5-2.

Table 5-2 MaxUserPort Registry Setting

Registry Information	Details
Location	HKEY_LOCAL_MACHINE\SYSTEM\CurrentControlSet\ Services\Tcpip\Parameters
Data type	REG_DWORD
Valid range	5000–65534
Default value	5000
Present by default	No

UDP's fundamental simplicity is clearly reflected in the relatively small number of UDP-related Registry values and settings in Windows NT and Windows 2000. As you will see at the conclusion of the next section, TCP's complexity likewise leads to a greater number of related settings and controls.

UNDERSTANDING CONNECTION-ORIENTED PROTOCOLS

Connection-oriented protocols create a **logical connection** directly between two peers on an internetwork. Connection-oriented protocols track the transfer of data, and ensure it arrives successfully through **acknowledgments** and **sequence number tracking**. An acknowledgment is a **positive response**, indicating a set of data arrived. Connection-oriented peers use sequence number tracking to identify the amount of data transferred, and any **out-of-order packets**. Connection-oriented protocols have a **timeout mechanism** that indicates when a host waited too long for a communication, and such communication should be assumed lost. Connection-oriented protocols also have a **retry mechanism** that enables them to recover lost data by retransmitting it a specified number of times.

TCP is a connection-oriented protocol. Applications that rely on data reaching its destination use TCP instead of UDP.

TRANSMISSION CONTROL PROTOCOL (TCP)

TCP offers connection-oriented services with sequencing, **error recovery**, and a **sliding window** mechanism. Because of TCP's **end-to-end reliability** and flexibility, TCP is the preferred transport method for applications that transfer large quantities of data and require reliable delivery services.

TCP hosts create a **virtual connection** with each other using a **handshake process**. During the handshake process, hosts exchange a sequence number that is used to track data as it transfers from one host to another.

TCP transfers data as a continuous stream of bytes, with no knowledge of the underlying **messages** or message boundaries that might be contained in that **byte stream**. Upon receipt, the upper-layer application interprets the byte stream to read the messages contained therein.

The maximum TCP segment size is 65,495 bytes. This number is reached by subtracting 20 bytes for an IP header, and another 20 bytes for the TCP header from the Total Length Size field value. Figure 5-5 depicts how data is segmented and prefaced by a series of headers, including a TCP header, an IP header, and the Ethernet header.

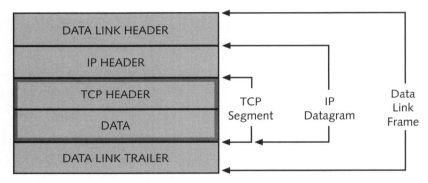

Figure 5-5   Enclosed information in packets is referred to by different names, depending on the protocol layer

In this section, we cover the primary functions and features of TCP communications:

- TCP startup connection process (TCP handshake)
- TCP keep-alive process
- TCP connection termination process
- TCP sequence and acknowledgment process
- TCP error-detection and error-recovery process
- TCP congestion control process
- TCP sliding window process
- TCP header fields and functions

TCP Startup Connection Process (TCP Handshake)

TCP offers a connection-oriented transport that begins with a handshake between two hosts. One host initiates the handshake to another host to: (a) ensure the destination host is available, (b) ensure the destination host is listening on the destination port number, and (c) inform the destination host of the initiator's sequence number so the two sides can track data as it is transferred.

The TCP handshake uses a three-step process between two hosts, as depicted in Figure 5-6.

5

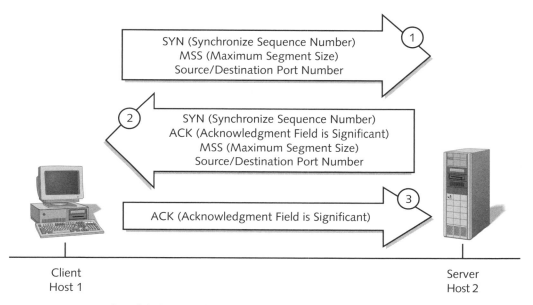

Figure 5-6   TCP handshake is a three-packet process

1. Host 1 sends a TCP packet to Host 2. This packet does not contain any data; it contains only Host 1's starting sequence, the desired destination port number, and an indication of the **Maximum Segment Size (MSS)** that can fit in each TCP packet.

2. Host 2 responds with its starting sequence number and an indication of the maximum segment size. The Acknowledgment bit is set in this reply. This acknowledges receipt of the first packet of the handshake.

3. Host 1 acknowledges receipt of Host 2's sequence number and segment size information. This third packet completes the handshake process.

For details on the sequence numbers and how they increment, refer to the section titled "TCP Sequence and Acknowledgment Process" later in this chapter. Next, we look inside the packets to get a feel for what a TCP header contains during the connection establishment phase.

Handshake Packet #1

Figure 5-7 shows the TCP header of Packet #1 of the handshake.

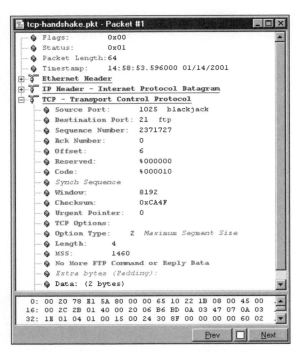

Figure 5-7   First packet in a TCP handshake

In the initial packet, the sender, Host 1, inserts a self-assigned initial sequence number in the TCP header Sequence Number field (2371727). This number is used to track the sequence of data sent to Host 2, and ensure packets are not missing. This packet has one flag set—SYN (for Synchronize sequence number)—to indicate that this packet is used to synchronize the sequence numbers between hosts.

The Acknowledgment (Ack) Number field contains the next expected sequence number from the other side of the communication. Because this is the first packet in the handshake, however, Host 1 does not know what sequence number Host 2 will use. The 4-byte Acknowledgment Number field is left at zero in the first packet of the handshake process.

The Offset field defines the length of the TCP header. (It is typically 24 bytes during the first two packets of the handshake, but 20 bytes for regular data exchange). In Figure 5-7, the Offset value is six (24 bytes).

In this packet, you notice that Host 1 defined an MSS of 1460 bytes. This value is appropriate for an Ethernet packet, and can be calculated as follows:

```
1460    Data after TCP header
  20    Typical TCP header size
  20    Typical IP header size
  18    Typical Ethernet header size (including 4-byte CRC)
1518    Maximum Ethernet packet size
```

The TCP header also defines the desired process or application for this connection—port 21, File Transfer Protocol (FTP).

Handshake Packet #2

Figure 5-8 shows the TCP header of Packet #2 of the handshake process.

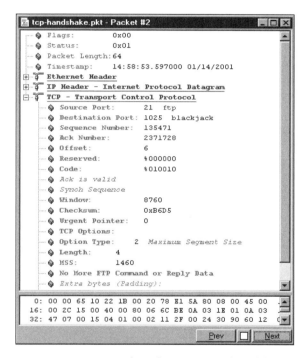

Figure 5-8   Second packet in a TCP handshake

Host 2 defined its starting sequence number as 135471. The Acknowledgment Number field value is 2371728. This is the next sequence number that Host 2 expects to receive from Host 1. This packet has two flags set—SYN and ACK (acknowledging receipt of Host 1's first packet). This packet also indicates that the MSS is 1460 bytes from this host as well.

Handshake Packet #3

Figure 5-9 shows the TCP header of Packet #3 of the handshake.

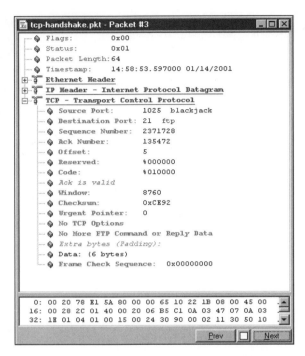

Figure 5-9   Third packet in a TCP handshake

Host 1's sequence number is now 2371728. The Acknowledgment Number field value is now set to 135472. This indicates that the next expected sequence number from Host 2 is 135472. The final packet in the handshake process has the ACK flag set to indicate receipt of Host 2's sequence number information.

There are two Registry settings that can be used to control TCP connection establishment. The first, the TcpMaxConnectRetransmissions Registry setting, is defined in Table 5-3.

Table 5-3   TcpMaxConnectRetransmissions Registry Setting

Registry Information	Details
Location	HKEY_LOCAL_MACHINE\SYSTEM\CurrentControlSet\ Services\Tcpip\Parameters
Data type	REG_DWORD
Valid range	0–255
Default value	2
Present by default	No

The TcpMaxConnectRetransmissions Registry setting defines the number of SYN **retries** sent when attempting to establish a TCP connection. The second setting, the TcpNumConnections Registry setting, is defined in Table 5-4.

Table 5-4   TcpNumConnections Registry Setting

Registry Information	Details
Location	HKEY_LOCAL_MACHINE\SYSTEM\CurrentControlSet\ Services\Tcpip\Parameters
Data type	REG_DWORD
Valid range	0–0xFFFFFE
Default value	0xFFFFFE (16,777,214) connections
Present by default	No

The TcpNumConnections setting defines the number of TCP connections that can be open at one time.

TCP Half-Open Connections

TCP half-open connections occur when the handshake process does not end successfully with a final ACK. The **half-open connection** communication sequence occurs in the following order:

```
SYN >>>>>
<<<<< ACK SYN
<<<<< ACK SYN
<<<<< ACK SYN
```

In this case, Host 1 sends the first handshake packet, the SYN packet, to Host 2. Host 2 replies with an ACK SYN packet. Host 1 should finish the handshake by sending the third packet, the ACK packet, but it does not. Perhaps Host 1 lost network connectivity or locked up. This connection is considered half-open. It is taking up resources on Host 2—we do not know the status of Host 1.

One **Denial of Service (DoS)** attack—the SYN attack—uses this **two-way handshake** with the incrementing source port to overload the destination. If you see excessive connection establishment routines back-to-back, you should be suspicious of the cause. Chapter 9 provides details on how to protect a network against the SYN attack.

TCP Keep-Alive Process

Once the TCP connection is established, a **keep-alive process** can maintain the connection when there is no data sent across the wire. The Application layer may perform keep-alive processes, such as the NetWare **watchdog process**, that maintains a connection between a NetWare host and server. If the application cannot maintain a connection, the keep-alive process may become the responsibility of TCP. If implemented, only the server process initiates TCP keep-alives.

TCP keep-alives are disabled by default on Windows 2000, although an application may enable TCP keep-alives, if desired by the programmer. Windows 2000 has two keep-alive Registry settings. The KeepAliveTime setting defines how long to wait before sending the first TCP keep-alive packet. The KeepAliveInterval setting defines the delay between keep-alive retransmissions when no acknowledgments are received.

You can change the setting of the KeepAliveTime Registry entry, as shown in Table 5-5.

Table 5-5   KeepAliveTime Registry Setting

Registry Information	Details
Location	HKEY_LOCAL_MACHINE\SYSTEM\CurrentControlSet\Services\Tcpip\Parameters
Data type	REG_DWORD
Valid range	0–0xFFFFFFFF
Default value	0x6DDD00 (7,200,000) milliseconds
Present by default	No

You can alter the KeepAliveInterval time by setting its Registry entry, as shown in Table 5-6.

Table 5-6   KeepAliveInterval Registry Setting

Registry Information	Details
Location	HKEY_LOCAL_MACHINE\SYSTEM\CurrentControlSet\Services\Tcpip\Parameters
Data type	REG_DWORD
Valid range	0–0xFFFFFFFF
Default value	0x3E8 (1000) milliseconds
Present by default	No

 The number of retries is defined by the TcpMaxDataRetransmissions Registry setting (covered in the section titled "TCP Error-Detection and Error-Recovery Process" later in this chapter).

TCP Connection Termination

The TCP connection termination process requires four packets. As shown in Figure 5-10, the first TCP peer, Host 1, sends a TCP packet with no data. This packet has the FIN and ACK flags set in the packet. The second peer, Host 2, sends an ACK in response. Host 2 now sends a TCP packet with no data and the FIN and ACK flags set. Finally, Host 1 returns an ACK response.

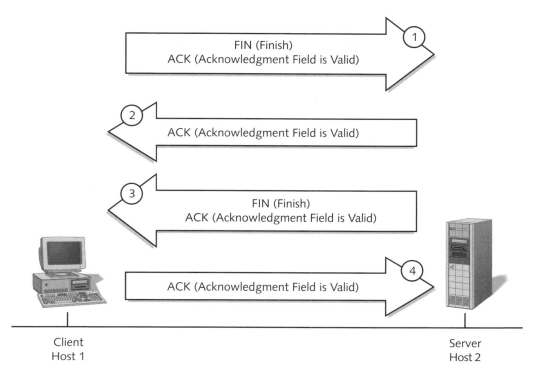

Figure 5-10   TCP connection termination process uses four packets

TCP Connection States

TCP communications go through a series of connection states, as listed in Table 5-7.

Table 5-7   TCP Connection States

Connection State	Description
CLOSED	There is no TCP connection.
LISTEN	The host is listening and ready to accept a connection on a port.
SYN SENT	The host sent a SYN packet.
SYN RECD	The host received a SYN packet and sent a SYN-ACK response.
ESTABLISHED	The three-way handshake completed successfully (regardless of which host initiated it). Data can be transferred (providing there is an acceptable window size available).
FIN-WAIT-1	The first FIN-ACK packet to close a connection was sent.
FIN-WAIT-2	The host sent a FIN-ACK packet and received an ACK response.
CLOSE WAIT	The host received a FIN-ACK and sent a FIN-ACK.

Table 5-7   TCP Connection States (continued)

Connection State	Description
LAST ACK	The host sent an ACK, in response to the FIN-ACK that it received.
CLOSING	A FIN-ACK packet was received, but the ACK value does not match the FIN-ACK sent. This indicates that both sides are attempting to close the connection at the same time.
TIME WAIT	Both sides sent FIN-ACKs and ACKs. The connection is closed, but the hosts must wait at least four minutes before reusing any of the connection parameters.

You can control the **Time Wait delay**, which is the amount of time that a TCP host waits before reusing parameters. The default Time Wait delay is four minutes, as recommended by RFC 793.

To control the Time Wait delay, set the TcpTimedWaitDelay Registry value, as shown in Table 5-8.

Table 5-8   TcpTimeWaitDelay Registry Setting

Registry Information	Details
Location	HKEY_LOCAL_MACHINE\SYSTEM\CurrentControlSet\ Services\Tcpip\Parameters
Data type	REG_DWORD
Valid range	30–300
Default value	0xF0 (240)
Present by default	No

In the next section, we examine how data is tracked to ensure reliable delivery.

TCP Sequence and Acknowledgment Process

The sequence and acknowledgment process guarantees that packets are ordered properly and protects against missing segments. During the handshake process, each side of the connection selects its own starting sequence number. They increment this sequence number by the amount of data included in each packet.

For example, Figure 5-11 shows the summary of a file transfer process. The arrows link the acknowledgments with the data set they are acknowledging. The first packet is an acknowledgment for data received earlier. (The data scrolled off the window.)

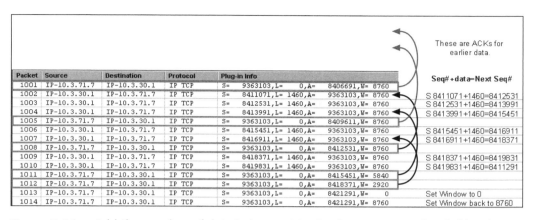

These are ACKs for earlier data.

Packet	Source	Destination	Protocol	Plug-in Info				Seq#+data=Next Seq#
1001	IP-10.3.71.7	IP-10.3.30.1	IP TCP	S=	9363103,L=	0,A=	8406691,W= 8760	
1002	IP-10.3.30.1	IP-10.3.71.7	IP TCP	S=	8411071,L= 1460,A=		9363103,W= 8760	S 8411071+1460=8412531
1003	IP-10.3.30.1	IP-10.3.71.7	IP TCP	S=	8412531,L= 1460,A=		9363103,W= 8760	S 8412531+1460=8413991
1004	IP-10.3.30.1	IP-10.3.71.7	IP TCP	S=	8413991,L= 1460,A=		9363103,W= 8760	S 8413991+1460=8415451
1005	IP-10.3.71.7	IP-10.3.30.1	IP TCP	S=	9363103,L=	0,A=	8409611,W= 8760	
1006	IP-10.3.30.1	IP-10.3.71.7	IP TCP	S=	8415451,L= 1460,A=		9363103,W= 8760	S 8415451+1460=8416911
1007	IP-10.3.30.1	IP-10.3.71.7	IP TCP	S=	8416911,L= 1460,A=		9363103,W= 8760	S 8416911+1460=8418371
1008	IP-10.3.71.7	IP-10.3.30.1	IP TCP	S=	9363103,L=	0,A=	8412531,W= 8760	
1009	IP-10.3.71.7	IP-10.3.30.1	IP TCP	S=	8418371,L= 1460,A=		9363103,W= 8760	S 8418371+1460=8419831
1010	IP-10.3.30.1	IP-10.3.71.7	IP TCP	S=	8419831,L= 1460,A=		9363103,W= 8760	S 8419831+1460=8411291
1011	IP-10.3.71.7	IP-10.3.30.1	IP TCP	S=	9363103,L=	0,A=	8415451,W= 5840	
1012	IP-10.3.71.7	IP-10.3.30.1	IP TCP	S=	9363103,L=	0,A=	8418371,W= 2920	
1013	IP-10.3.71.7	IP-10.3.30.1	IP TCP	S=	9363103,L=	0,A=	8421291,W= 0	Set Window to 0
1014	IP-10.3.71.7	IP-10.3.30.1	IP TCP	S=	9363103,L=	0,A=	8421291,W= 8760	Set Window back to 8760

Figure 5-11   Add the number of data bytes sent to the Sequence Number field to learn the next sequence number used

Packets #1002, #1003, and #1004 contain data (1460 bytes in each packet). Packet #1008's Acknowledgment Number field value indicates that it is acknowledging all data received up to Packet #1002 (up to byte 8412531). Packet #1011 acknowledges data up to byte 8415451 (Packet #1004).

Interestingly, in this trace file, we see the host send an ACK noting that the window size (the receiver's available buffer space) is now set to zero. It almost immediately transmits another ACK, setting the window size back to 8760 for this file transfer.

When you analyze the sequence and acknowledgment process, keep this equation in mind:

```
Sequence Number In + Bytes of Data Received =
Acknowledgment Number Out
```

Figure 5-12 depicts a simple sequenced communication. (Remember, the Acknowledgment Number field contains the value of the next sequence number expected from the other side.)

The Acknowledgment Number field only increments when data is received. Because the data flow can change directions (Host 1 sends data to Host 2, and then Host 2 sends data back to Host 1), the Sequence Number field on one side may increment for a while, and then stop incrementing as the Sequence Number field on the other side of the communication begins to increment.

Figure 5-12 starts with Host 1 sending data, and then reverses when Host 2 has data to send. This is typical of two-way communications.

During the TCP startup and **teardown sequences**, the Sequence Number and Acknowledgment Number fields increment by one, even though no valid data is sent or received. This can be confusing because you just learned that the Sequence Number field only increments when data is sent.

Host 1:   ⟶

Sequence number 1 with 9 bytes of data
Acknowledgment Number field = 100

Host 2:   ⟵

Sequence number 100 with no data (ACK)
Acknowledgment Number field = 10 (in 1 + 9 bytes of data)

Host 1:   ⟶

Sequence number 10 with 5 bytes of data
Acknowledgment Number field = 100

Host 2:   ⟵

Sequence number 100 with no data (ACK)
Acknowledgment Number field = 15 (in 10 + 5 bytes of data)

Host 2:   ⟵

Sequence number 100 with 20 bytes of data*
Acknowledgment Number field = 15

Host 1:   ⟶

Sequence number 15 with no data (ACK)
Acknowledgment Number field = 120 (in 100 + 20 bytes of data)

* Host 2 is now sending data to Host 1.

Figure 5-12   Simple sequenced communication

TCP Error-Detection and Error-Recovery Process

There are many reasons why communication sequences fail. A sender's data packet may be involved in a collision. The acknowledgment may never make it back because there are problems with the routers along the path. Whatever the reason for communication errors, TCP was designed with an error-recovery process to detect and recover from these errors.

The first error-detection and error-recovery mechanism is the **retransmission timer**. The value specified by this timer is referred to as the **retransmission timeout (RTO)**. Every time data is sent, the retransmission timer starts. When replies are received, the retransmission timer stops. The host measures the round-trip time (RTT). This RTT and an average deviance from the RTT are used to determine the RTO setting.

When the retransmission timer expires, the sender retransmits the first unacknowledged TCP data segment first. The sender then doubles the RTO value. The RTO value doubles each time the sender retransmits the TCP data segment. This process continues until the sender reaches its retransmission limit.

In Windows 2000, the maximum retransmission count is set in the TcpMaxData-Retransmissions Registry setting, as shown in Table 5-9.

Table 5-9   TcpMaxDataRetransmissions Registry Setting

Registry Information	Details
Location	HKEY_LOCAL_MACHINE\SYSTEM\CurrentControlSet\ Services\Tcpip\Parameters
Data type	REG_DWORD
Valid range	0–0xFFFFFFFF
Default value	5
Present by default	No

Based on the TCP retransmit process, the retransmission operation occurs in the following increments:

- 1st retransmit: RTO seconds
- 2nd retransmit: 2 × RTO seconds
- 3rd retransmit: 4 × RTO seconds
- 4th retransmit: 8 × RTO seconds
- 5th retransmit: 16 × RTO seconds

Figure 5-13 provides an example of the retransmit timer and process in action. In this example, the host, 10.3.30.1, sends Packet #102, but never receives an Acknowledgment packet. The Acknowledgment packet would contain the Acknowledgment Number field value 5405497. This trace shows the retransmission process getting exponentially longer between retransmissions.

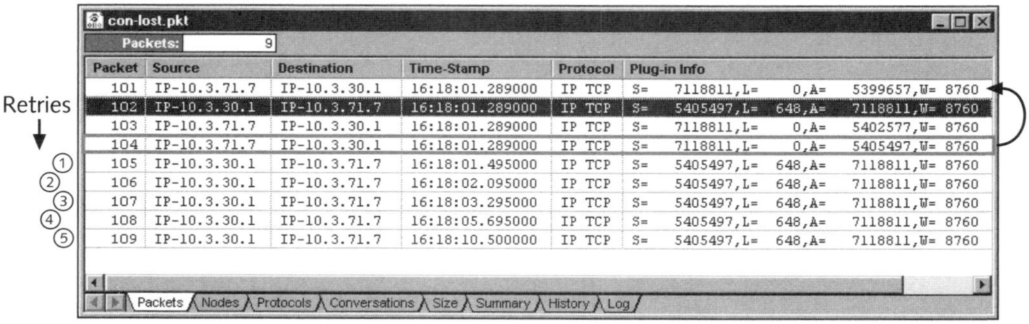

Figure 5-13   Server sends several TCP packets at exponentially longer interval times

Note that the retransmissions do not fall on exact exponential boundaries—this is not unusual. Sometimes the process does not occur on an exact boundary; other times the analyzer processing time affects the timestamps.

In Windows 2000, the TcpInitialRTT Registry setting defines the initial RTO, as shown in Table 5-10.

Table 5-10   TcpInitialRTT Registry Setting

Registry Information	Details
Location	HKEY_LOCAL_MACHINE\SYSTEM\CurrentControlSet\ Services\Tcpip\Parameters
Data type	REG_DWORD
Valid range	0–0xFFFF (seconds)
Default value	3 (seconds)
Present by default	No

This TcpInitialRTT value is used for the timeout of the handshake packets, and the initial data segments sent over a new connection. As successive segments are sent, the RTO value is adjusted from this TcpInitialRTT value to a value represented by the current RTT (with a deviance factor).

TCP Congestion Control

Congestion is the overloading of the network or a receiver. Overloading of the network occurs when there is too much data on the network medium. Adding more data ensures overload and causes packet loss. Overloading a receiver occurs when the number of data bytes is greater than the **advertised window** (defined in the Window field in the receiver's TCP header). The **current window** is always the lesser of what the network and receiver can handle.

Figure 5-14 depicts the elements of the network and receiver congestion. The network congestion is easy to understand—this is simply what the network can handle. The receiver window size, however, is more difficult to identify. The receiver window size is defined by the receiver's available buffer space. When TCP data is received, it is placed in this **TCP buffer area**. The Application layer protocol retrieves the data from the buffer at its own rate.

TCP has four defined congestion control mechanisms to ensure the most efficient use of **bandwidth**, and quick error and congestion recovery. TCP supports **windowing**—the process of sending numerous data packets in sequence without waiting for an intervening acknowledgment. The size of the window is based on the amount of traffic the network can handle (the congestion window), and the receiver's available buffer space (the receiver's advertised window). The four mechanisms, defined in detail in RFC 2581, are:

- Slow Start
- Congestion Avoidance
- Fast Retransmit
- Fast Recovery

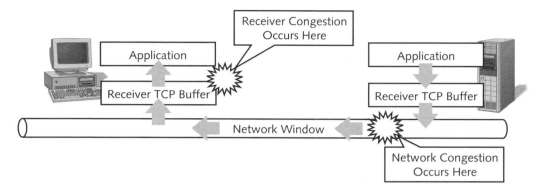

Figure 5-14   Network window and receiver window determine the current congestion window size

In the next section, we examine each of these mechanisms in detail.

Slow Start

When a TCP host starts up, the size of the congestion window is not known. The initial value of the window being used is twice the sender's MSS setting. For example, if a host's MSS size is 1460, the initial window the host uses is 2920 bytes. The MSS increases this window for every ACK received that acknowledges new data.

Congestion Avoidance

Once the window size has increased using the **Slow Start algorithm**, if an error occurs (a timeout), the window size is divided in half. Next, the **Congestion Avoidance algorithm** is used to increase the window size in a linear manner.

Fast Retransmit/Fast Recovery

When an out-of-order data segment is received, the receiver should immediately send **duplicate ACKs**. These duplicate ACKs both indicate which sequence number was expected. The Fast Recovery process dictates that when a host receives three duplicate ACKs, it must immediately start retransmitting the **lost segments**, without waiting for the retransmission timer to expire.

The window size gradually increases, as defined in RFC 2581. The maximum receive window size can be set using the GlobalMaxTcpWindowSize setting, as shown in Table 5-11.

Table 5-11   GlobalMaxTcpWindowSize Registry Setting

Registry Information	Details
Location	HKEY_LOCAL_MACHINE\SYSTEM\CurrentControlSet\ Services\Tcpip\Parameters
Data type	REG_DWORD
Valid range	0–0x3FFFFFFF (bytes)
Default value	0x4000 (16,384 bytes)
Present by default	No

The maximum receive window size for an interface can be set using the Tcp-WindowSize setting, as shown in Table 5-12. This setting, if existent, overrides the GlobalMaxTcpWindowSize Registry setting for the interface on which it is configured.

Table 5-12   TcpWindowSize Registry Setting

Registry Information	Details
Location	HKEY_LOCAL_MACHINE\SYSTEM\CurrentControlSet\ Services\Tcpip\Parameters\Interface*Interfacename*
Data type	REG_DWORD
Valid range	0–0x3FFFFFFF (bytes)
Default value	0xFFFF (the lesser of 17,520 for Ethernet, 65,535 bytes for other networks, or GlobalMaxTcpWindowSize; see file Regentry.chm for other exceptions)
Present by default	No

The Regentry.chm file, included in the Windows 2000 Resource Kit, is the ultimate resource for Windows 2000 Registry information.

TCP Sliding Window

TCP supports a sliding window mechanism—if you look at the data that is sent, and you move a window over it, the left side of the window is the data that was acknowledged. The right side defines the boundary of data that can be sent, based on the receiver's advertised window. Figure 5-15 illustrates this more clearly.

As you can see in Figure 5-15, the data set A+B was sent and acknowledged. The current window sent data set C+D+E+F, and the sender is waiting for an acknowledgement. The window now moves to the right to send the next data set, G+H+I+J. The window continues to slide to the right as acknowledgements are received.

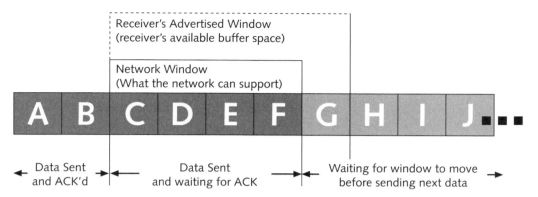

Figure 5-15   Window slides based on acknowledgements received

There are some interesting exceptions to the standard windowing operation. For example, the **Nagle algorithm** (named after John Nagle, author of RFC 896) defines that when small data segments are being sent, but not acknowledged, no other small segments can be sent. This small data is seen in interactive applications such as Telnet.

Another interesting aspect of TCP windowing is the **Silly Window Syndrome (SWS)**. SWS is caused when enough data is sent to a TCP host to fill its receive buffer, thereby putting the receiver in a **zero-window state**. The receiver advertises a window size of zero until the Application layer protocol retrieves data from the receiver buffer. In an SWS situation, the Application layer protocol only retrieves one byte from the buffer. This causes the host to advertise a window of one. Upon receipt of this window information, the sender transmits a single byte of information. The new window size is certainly the most inefficient method of data transfer. Receivers can avoid SWS by not advertising a new window size until they have at least as much buffer space as the MSS value. Senders can avoid this problem by not sending data until the advertised window is at least the size of the MSS value.

TCP Header Fields and Functions

Now we examine the TCP header structure shown in Figure 5-16. You should recognize some characteristics of the TCP header, such as the Source and Destination Port Number fields. Let's examine the other aspects of the TCP header structure.

Source Port Number Field

See UDP Source Port Number field definition.

Destination Port Number Field

See UDP Destination Port Number field definition.

5

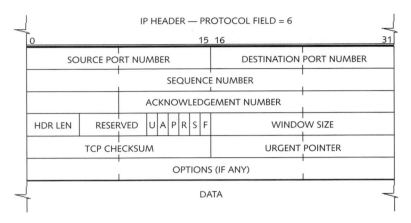

Figure 5-16   TCP header is at least 20 bytes long

Sequence Number Field

This field contains a number that uniquely identifies the TCP segment. This sequence number provides an identifier that enables TCP receivers to identify when parts of a communication stream are missing. The sequence number increments by the number of data bytes contained in the packet. For example, in Figure 5-17, the current TCP sequence number is 1720360319, and the packet contains 42 bytes of data (subtract the 20-byte IP header length and the 20-byte TCP header length from the Total Length field value of 82, as seen in the IP header).

Each TCP host self-assigns its own sequence number. The process of incrementing this sequence number is covered further under the section titled "TCP Sequence and Acknowledgement Process" later in this chapter.

Acknowledgement Number Field

The Acknowledgement Number field indicates the next expected sequence number from the other side of the communications. For example, in Figure 5-17, the sender states the next TCP expected sequence number from the other host is 248606632.

Data Offset (Field)

This defines the length of the TCP header in 4-byte increments. A value of five in this field indicates that the TCP header is 20 bytes long. We need this field because the TCP header length can vary, depending on the TCP header options used. Although the UDP Option field is rarely used, the TCP Option field is almost always used during the TCP connection setup to establish the maximum amount of data that can be placed after a TCP header.

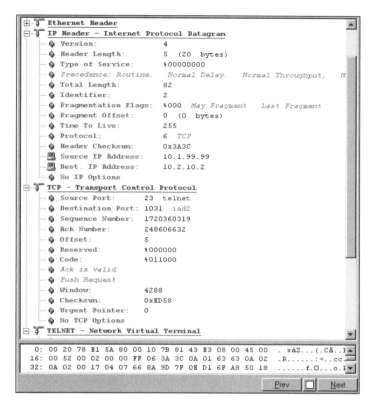

Figure 5-17   Decoded TCP header

Flags Field

Table 5-13 describes the flags used in the TCP header.

Table 5-13   TCP Flag Settings

Flag Setting	Description
URG (Urgent)	Indicates Urgent Pointer field should be examined. If this flag is set, the Urgent Pointer field tells the receiver where it should start reading bytes contained in the data portion of the packet.
ACK (Acknowledgement)	The Acknowledgement Number field is relevant. The acknowledgement number indicates the next expected sequence number from the other TCP peer.
PSH (Push)	Bypasses buffering and passes data straight to upper layer. This is used for time-critical or single-stroke applications. Upon receipt of a packet with the Push flag set, the receiver must not buffer the data—it must pass directly up to the Application layer protocol.

Table 5-13   TCP Flag Settings (continued)

Flag Setting	Description
(Reset)	Closes the connection. This is used to shut down the connection entirely. This flag is also used to refuse a connection (for whatever reason).
SYN (Synchronize)	Synchronizes sequence numbers—handshake process. This flag is used during the handshake process to indicate that the sender is notifying the TCP peer of its Sequence Number field value.
FIN (Finish)	The transaction is finished. This flag is used to indicate that the host completed a transaction. The FIN flag itself does not explicitly close the connection. If, however, both peers send TCP FIN packets and respond with appropriate ACKs, the connection will be closed.

Window Field

This field indicates the size of the TCP receiver buffer in bytes. For example, in Figure 5-17, the sender indicates that it can receive a stream of data up to 4288 bytes in length. A window size of zero indicates that a sender should stop transmitting—the receiver's TCP buffer is full.

Checksum Field

This TCP checksum is a bit strange, just like the UDP checksum. The checksum is performed on the contents of the TCP header and data (not including data link padding), as well as a pseudo-header derived from the IP header. The TCP pseudo-header is similar to the UDP header—it is only used for the checksum calculation; it is not an actual header itself. The TCP pseudo-header consists of three fields taken from the IP header—the IP Source Address field value, the IP Destination Address field value, and the Protocol field value. The TCP pseudo-header also includes the value of the TCP Length field.

You can get more information about the TCP pseudo-header from RFC 793.

Urgent Pointer Field

This field is only relevant if the URG pointer is set. If the URG pointer is set, the receiver must examine this field to see where to look/read first in the packet. RFC 1122 interprets the Urgent Pointer field value differently than RFC 793. Windows 2000 can be configured to interpret the Urgent Pointer field according to RFC 1122, if desired. See Table 5-14 for TcpUseRFC1122UrgentPointer Registry setting information.

Table 5-14   TcpUseRFC1122UrgentPointer Registry Setting

Registry Information	Details
Location	HKEY_LOCAL_MACHINE\SYSTEM\CurrentControlSet\ Services\Tcpip\Parameters
Data type	REG_DWORD
Valid range	0–1
Default value	0
Present by default	No

By default, Windows 2000 hosts are configured to use the Urgent Pointer field interpretation defined in RFC 793.

TCP Options Field(s)

This Options field is… well, optional. One option you will certainly see in use is the MSS option—it is used in the first two packets of the three-way handshake process. The purpose of this option is to define what segment size the hosts supports. The hosts use the lowest common denominator between the two MSS values.

Some of the TCP options are listed in Table 5-15.

Table 5-15   TCP Options

Option	Definition	Reference
2	Maximum Segment Size – Defines the maximum amount of data that the sender can place after the TCP header.	RFC 793
3	Window Scale – Expands the TCP window size value to a 32-bit value, while using the 16-bit field.	RFC 1323
4	Selective ACK (SACK) Permitted – States that the sender can use **Selective Acknowledgments** to ACK-specific packets, within a set of data segments.	RFC 2018
5	SACK – Used within the SACK packet.	RFC 2018
8	Timestamp Option – Specifically sets the RTO value and overrides any calculated RTO defined.	RFC 1323

The complete "TCP Option Numbers" list can be found online at *http://www.iana.org/ assignments/tcp-parameters*. Here again, the complexity and broad capability of TCP means that this list of options is neither short nor terribly straightforward. It is only occasionally necessary to venture into other TCP options beyond those documented in the concluding section of this chapter.

COMMON AND APPROPRIATE USES FOR TCP AND UDP

Given that TCP is robust and reliable, and UDP is not, why would any Application layer protocol or service choose UDP for transport when TCP is readily available? The short answer to that question is overhead. Because TCP is robust and reliable, it carries a lot of baggage, including additional header fields, and explicit meta-messages in the form of TCP messages that convey information about the connection, rather than data to be passed across that connection.

For some lightweight services, such as Microsoft Messenger Service (which you can run from the command line using the net send command, and which pops up a message on the target screen or screens), TCP is overkill, and UDP is used instead. For other applications that may be invoked during boot up, or when a computer has only limited network capability (perhaps it can only broadcast), UDP provides an obvious vehicle to transport boot requests for BOOTP, and address requests for DHCP.

Likewise, for applications, such as RIP, that rely on regular updates of routing tables, and track timeout values as part of ordinary behavior, the extra reliability of TCP isn't necessary, and UDP is used instead. Finally, some application developers decided to create their own specific reliability and delivery mechanisms, such as those used in NFS, to guarantee delivery of files across a network, rather than relying on the general-purpose mechanisms in TCP. In most of these cases, avoiding unneeded complexity, or improving overall performance, drives the selection of UDP.

On the other hand, TCP was designed in an era when 300-bps communication was considered fast, and when noisy lines or intermittent communications problems made long-haul, reliable transmission of data inherently risky without access to a robust, reliable transport service. For purely local area network use, TCP is probably overkill in all cases. But as soon as the Internet comes into play, where anything goes, and often does (both wrong and right), TCP's reliability and robustness still have great value. That explains why most information delivery services designed for use on the Internet tend to use TCP transports rather than UDP, simply because they allow application developers to concentrate on providing a service, rather than handling reliability and delivery issues. For example, NFS was originally designed (and is still primarily used) as a local area file access method. That design decision favored UDP because it offered faster performance; FTP, which offers similar file access mechanisms over the Internet, uses TCP to ensure reliable delivery between any two points on the globe.

Historically, TCP is a more important transport than UDP, and is still used for the majority of TCP/IP Application layer protocols and services. But it is no longer as important as it once was because long-haul and local area networks have significantly increased speed, capacity, and reliability since TCP/IP first appeared on the scene. Although TCP remains popular as a transport, it's important to remember that it's always faster (but not necessarily easier) to manage robustness and reliability at the hardware level rather than the software level. With the availability of cell-oriented transmission technologies, such as ATM and SONET, there are those who might argue that TCP's days are numbered because these lower-layer transmission technologies could make TCP's capabilities unnecessary. But as long as the Internet infrastructure remains the hodgepodge of transmission technologies that it is today, TCP will continue to play a vital role in ensuring correct and complete delivery of important data.

CHAPTER SUMMARY

- Transport protocols come in two types: connectionless, which are lightweight, unreliable, and provide only best-effort delivery services; and connection-oriented, which provide robust, reliable end-to-end delivery services, including explicit acknowledgement, segmentation and reassembly of arbitrary-sized messages, connection negotiation and management mechanisms, and retransmission of missing or erroneous segments. Because connectionless protocols are lightweight, they outperform connection-oriented protocols due to lower internal message overhead, and no need for control and management message traffic (acknowledgements, retransmissions, congestion control, and so on).

- The User Datagram Protocol, UDP, is the connectionless protocol associated with the TCP/IP protocol suite. It is commonly associated with Application layer protocols and services, such as BOOTP, DHCP, SNMP, NFS, and RIP, that either provide their own reliability mechanisms, or do without such mechanisms.

- In keeping with its simple capabilities, the UDP header is short and simple, consisting primarily of a protocol identifier in the IP header, an optional checksum value, and source and destination port addresses for the Application layer protocols or processes on the sending and receiving ends of a transmission.

- The Transmission Control Protocol, TCP, is the heavyweight, connection-oriented protocol that helps name the TCP/IP protocol suite. It remains associated with the majority of TCP/IP Application layer protocols, especially those, such as Telnet, FTP, and SMTP, where reliable data delivery is desirable.

- In keeping with its more diverse, more robust capabilities, the TCP header is longer and more complex, including a variety of flags, values, and message types used to deliver acknowledgements, manage traffic flow, request retransmissions, and negotiate connections between hosts.

- Appropriate (and historical) uses for UDP concentrate on Application layer services that manage their own reliability and connections, such as NFS, and on *chatty* protocols and services, such as DHCP, SNMP, or RIP that rely on simple controls and fail-safes, and broadcast or periodic transmissions to handle potential reliability, deliverability, or reachability problems.

- Appropriate (and historical) uses for TCP concentrate on providing reliable delivery of user services such as terminal emulation (Telnet and remote utilities), file transfer (FTP), e-mail (SMTP), and news (NNTP), where potentially important data must be delivered whole and intact, or not at all (and flagged with an error message).

KEY TERMS

acknowledgement — Notification of successful receipt of data. The ACK flag is set in acknowledgement packets.

advertised window — The amount of data that a receiver states it can handle in its TCP buffer space. The actual window size is based on the lower value of the number of bytes that the network can handle and the advertised window. An advertised window of zero indicates that the receiver has no available TCP buffer space. To avoid Silly Window Syndrome, the sender must not send any more data until the receiver advertises a window size of at least the size of the MSS.

bandwidth — A measurement of the amount of information that can cross a network. For example, Ethernet has 10-Mbps bandwidth available.

best-effort delivery — A simple network transport mechanism that relies on the underlying Network, Data Link, and Physical layer facilities available to handle delivery of PDUs from sender to receiver, without adding additional robustness or reliability features; UDP uses best-effort delivery.

byte stream — A continuous stream of data that contains no boundaries.

congestion — A condition of overload on a network or at a receiver. When the network is congested, senders cannot continue to send TCP packets. To avoid congesting a receiver, the receiver advertises a window size of zero.

Congestion Avoidance algorithm — A defined method to avoid overloading a network. This mechanism is used to slowly and incrementally increase the window size of communications.

connectionless protocol — A protocol that simply sends datagrams without establishing, managing, or otherwise handling a connection between sender and receiver; UDP is a connectionless transport protocol.

core services — Primary and key services used in TCP/IP networking. FTP, DNS, and DHCP are considered core services. These services are assigned the well-known port numbers between 0 and 1023.

current window — The actual window size being used at the time. A sender determines the current window size by using the receiver's advertised window and the network congestion window (what the network can handle).

Denial of Service (DoS) — An attack that causes a system to refuse services because it is busy handling attack requests. For example, repeated two-way handshakes may be caused by a TCP SYN attack. Chapter 9 provides additional information on TCP/IP security.

duplicate ACKs — A set of identical acknowledgements that is sent back-to-back to a TCP sender to indicate that out-of-order packets were received. Upon receipt of these duplicate ACKs, the sender retransmits the data without waiting for the retransmission timer to expire.

dynamic port number — A temporary port number used just for one communication process. These port numbers are cleared after the connection is closed and a four-minute wait time.

end-to-end reliability — A characteristic offered by connection-oriented services to guarantee that data arrives successfully at the desired destination.

ephemeral port — *See* temporary port.

error recovery — The procedure for retransmitting missing or damaged data. Two examples of error recovery are the immediate drop in the current window size, and immediate retransmission of data—before the retransmission timer expires.

half-open connections — A TCP connection that is not completed with a final acknowledgement. These half-open connections may be an indication of a TCP SYN attack.

handshake process — The process of setting up a virtual connection between TCP peers. The handshake process consists of three packets used to set up the starting sequence number that each TCP peer will use for communications. The TCP peers also exchange the receiver window size and an MSS value during this process.

keep-alive process — The procedure of maintaining an idle connection. TCP connections can be kept alive through TCP keep-alive packets if configured to do so. If the Application layer protocol offers a keep-alive process, the TCP layer should not perform the keep-alive process.

logical connection — A virtual connection between hosts, sometimes referred to as a circuit. The TCP handshake is used to set up a logical connection between TCP peers.

lost segment — A section of TCP data that does not arrive at the destination. Upon detection of a lost segment, a TCP sender must decrease the congestion window to one-half of the previous window size. Lost segments are assumed to be caused by network congestion.

Maximum Segment Size (MSS) — The maximum amount of data that can fit in a TCP packet after the TCP header. Each TCP peer shares the MSS during the handshake process.

messages — Data that has distinct boundaries and command information within the packet.

Nagle algorithm — A method stating that when small packets are sent, but not acknowledged, no further packets shall be sent. The Nagle algorithm is relevant on a network that supports numerous small packets due to support of interactive applications, such as Telnet.

out-of-order packets — Packets that do not arrive in the order defined by the sequence number. When a TCP host receives out-of-order packets, that host sends duplicate ACKs that indicate the packets arrived out of order.

positive response — An affirmative acknowledgment that data was received. TCP headers with the ACK flag set indicate that the Acknowledgment Number field is valid, and provide the next-expected sequence number from the TCP peer.

pseudo-header — A false header structure used to calculate a checksum. The UDP and TCP checksums are based on the pseudo-header values.

retransmission timeout (RTO) — The time value that determines when a TCP host retransmits a packet after it was lost. The RTO value is exponentially increased after an apparent connection loss.

retransmission timer — The timer that maintains the RTO value.

retries — The number of times a TCP peer re-sends data when no acknowledgement is received.

retry mechanism — A method for detecting communication problems and re-sending data across the network.

Selective Acknowledgment — Also referred to as SACK, this method defines how a TCP peer can identify specific segments that were successfully received. This functionality is defined in RFC 2018.

sequence number tracking — The process of following the current sequence number sent by a TCP peer, and sending an acknowledgement value to indicate the next-expected sequence number.

Silly Window Syndrome (SWS) — A TCP windowing problem caused by an application removing only small amounts of data from a full TCP receive buffer, thereby causing a TCP peer to advertise a very small window. To address this problem, TCP hosts wait until the window size reaches the MSS value.

sliding window — A set of data that is sent along a sliding timeline. As transmitted data is acknowledged, the window moves over to send more data to the TCP peer.

Slow Start algorithm — A method for sending data in exponentially increasing increments, starting typically at twice the MSS value. The Slow Start algorithm is used to learn the network's maximum window size.

TCP buffer area — A queuing area used to hold incoming and outgoing TCP packets. If a TCP packet has the Push flag set, the packet should not be held in either the incoming or outgoing TCP buffer area.

teardown sequence — The process of closing a TCP connection.

temporary port — A port that is used for the duration of the connection. The port numbers assigned to temporary ports are also called dynamic port numbers or ephemeral port numbers.

Time Wait delay — An amount of time that a TCP host must not use connection parameters after closing down that connection.

timeout mechanism — A method for determining when to stop re-sending data across packets. The timeout mechanism consists of a retry timer and a maximum number of retries.

two-way handshake — A two-packet handshake that is not fully completed. This process is indicative of the TCP SYN attack.

valid data — Data that follows the headers, but does not consist of any padding or extraneous data.

virtual connection — A logical connection between two TCP peers. The virtual connection requires end-to-end connectivity.

watchdog process — A process used by NetWare servers to determine whether the NetWare clients are still active and maintaining the connection between the two devices.

windowing — The process of acknowledging multiple packets with a single acknowledgement.

zero-window state — A situation when a TCP peer advertises a window value of zero. A TCP host cannot continue sending to a TCP peer that advertises a window of zero.

REVIEW QUESTIONS

1. Which of the following abbreviations identifies the TCP/IP transport protocols? (Choose all that apply.)

    a. IP

    b. TCP

    c. UDP

    d. FTP

2. Whereas UDP is a _____ protocol, TCP is a _____ protocol.

    a. transport

    b. network

    c. connectionless

    d. connection-oriented

3. Select all of the following services that are characteristic of a connection-oriented protocol. (Choose all that apply.)

    a. connection handling

    b. delivery guarantees

    c. segmentation and reassembly

    d. message-level checksum in header

    e. explicit transmission acknowledgement

4. A connection-oriented protocol creates more overhead than a connectionless protocol. True or false?

    a. True

    b. False

5. Connectionless protocols usually run slower than connection-oriented protocols. True or false?

    a. True

    b. False

6. For connectionless protocols, the Application layer protocol or service must provide messages that do not exceed a datagram's MTU. True or false?

    a. True

    b. False

5

7. Which of the following services does UDP provide? (Choose all that apply.)

a. segmentation

b. optional header checksum

c. identifies source and destination port addresses

d. explicit transmission acknowledgement

e. reassembly

8. How many bytes are in a UDP header?

a. 4

b. 8

c. 16

d. 32

9. What range of addresses traditionally defines a well-known port address?

a. 0–1023

b. 1–512

c. 10–4097

d. 0–65535

10. What range of addresses corresponds to the registered port numbers?

a. 0–1023

b. 1024–65535

c. 1024–47999

d. 1024–49151

11. What range of addresses corresponds to the dynamic port numbers?

a. 0–1023

b. 1024–49151

c. 49152–65535

d. 49152–64000

12. Identical UDP and TCP port numbers always map to the same TCP/IP protocol or service. True or false?

a. True

b. False

13. An acknowledgement is tantamount to a positive response, indicating that a set of data arrived at its destination. True or false?

a. True

b. False

14. What are the mechanisms that TCP uses to track the transfer of data and its successful delivery? (Choose all that apply.)

    a. logical connection between peers

    b. acknowledgements

    c. sequence numbers

    d. retry mechanism

15. What characteristic makes TCP preferable for reliable delivery requirements?

    a. sequencing

    b. error recovery

    c. end-to-end reliability

    d. handshake process

16. The name of the TCP process used to maintain an active connection between peers is called:

    a. TCP startup connection

    b. TCP connection termination

    c. keep-alive

    d. congestion control

17. How many steps occur in the TCP handshake process?

    a. two

    b. three

    c. four

    d. none of the above

18. Which of the following statements best defines a half-open connection?

    a. The handshake process does not end with a final SYN.

    b. The handshake process does not end with a final ACK.

    c. The handshake process does not end with a final FIN.

    d. The handshake process does not end, period.

19. TCP keep-alives are enabled by default on Windows 2000. True or false?

    a. True

    b. False

20. What is the proper response to a TCP connection termination?

    a. Host 1 sends a TCP packet with no data, with FIN and ACK flags set.

    b. Host 2 sends a TCP packet with no data, with FIN and ACK flags set.

    c. Host 2 sends an ACK to respond, followed by a TCP packet with no data and FIN and ACK flags set.

    d. Host 1 returns an ACK response.

21. TCP acknowledgements include sequence numbers to indicate what was received. True or false?

    a. True

    b. False

22. Which of the following mechanisms is part of TCP's error-detection and error-recovery capabilities?

    a. sequencing and reassembly

    b. retransmission timer

    c. explicit acknowledgement

    d. congestion control

23. The current TCP window size is always the greater of what the network and the receiver can handle at any given moment. True or false?

    a. True

    b. False

24. Where is TCP data stored when it is received?

    a. on the receiver's network interface card

    b. inside the TCP window

    c. in the TCP buffer area

    d. inside the network window

25. What is the initial size of the TCP congestion window?

    a. twice the maximum receive buffer size

    b. twice the Maximum Transfer Unit size

    c. twice the sender's MSS

    d. twice the receiver's MSS

26. What sequence of events signals the TCP Fast Recovery process?

    a. duplicate ACKs

    b. three sets of duplicate ACKs

    c. duplicate FINs

    d. three duplicate FINs

27. What two statements define the edges of the TCP sliding window mechanism? (Choose both correct answers.)

    a. acknowledged data plus the receiver's window size

    b. all data that was received

    c. all data pending transmission

    d. all data that was acknowledged

28. Which of the following values is a valid TCP Flag setting? (Choose all that apply.)

   a. SYN

   b. ACK

   c. NUL

   d. FIN

   e. PSH

29. Which two RFCs differ in their treatment of the TCP Urgent Pointer, URG?

   a. 1001

   b. 793

   c. 1918

   d. 1122

30. If the Trivial File Transfer Protocol (TFTP) is described as a lightweight, unreliable file transport mechanism, which TCP transport is it most likely to use?

   a. UDP

   b. TCP

5

HANDS-ON PROJECTS

Project 5-1

The following Hands-on Projects assume that you are working in a Windows 2000 environment, and that you installed the EtherPeek for Windows demo software.

To examine the UDP header structure:

1. Follow the instructions in Project 1-2 to launch the EtherPeek for Windows demo program.

2. Click **File, Open**.

3. Open the **18654-2\Ch5** folder on your hard disk.

4. Select the trace file **dns-moviefone.pkt**. Click **Open**. The packet summary window appears and displays the 14 packets in this trace file.

5. The Protocol column indicates that the first two packets are UDP-based and the subsequent packets are TCP-based. Double-click the **first packet** in the dns-moviefone.pkt trace file. Answer the following questions about Packet #1:

   a. What field in this packet indicates that this is a UDP-based communication?

   b. What type of source port is used in this communication?

   c. What is the Application layer protocol supported by this packet?

d. What is the length of the UDP header?

e. How many bytes of data are contained in this packet?

5. Click the **Close** button to close the Packet #1 decode window. Do not close the trace file. You'll use it to complete Project 5-2.

Project 5-2

To examine the TCP handshake process:

1. Follow the instructions in Project 5-1 to open the **dns–moviefone.pkt** file, if it is not already open.

2. Packets #3, #4, and #5 represent the TCP handshake process. Double-click **Packet #3** to open the packet decode window. Answer the following questions about Packet #3:

    a. What field in this packet indicates that this is a TCP-based communication?

    b. What type of source port is used in this communication?

    c. What Application layer protocol is the source host trying to connect to?

    d. What is the length of the TCP header?

    e. What is the purpose of Option 1 used in the TCP header? (Refer to RFC 793.)

    f. What is the sequence number used by the source?

    g. Why is the Acknowledgement Number field value set at zero?

3. View Packet #4 by clicking the **Decode Next** button at the bottom of the decode window. Answer the following questions about Packet #4:

    a. What is the sequence number used by the sender of Packet #4?

    b. Do both sides of this communication use the same MSS?

4. View Packet #5 by clicking the **Decode Next** button at the bottom of the decode window. Answer the following questions about Packet #5:

    a. Did this handshake complete properly?

    b. What is the length of this TCP header?

    c. Are any TCP options defined in this packet?

    d. What window size is this sender advertising?

5. Click the **Close** button to close the Packet #5 decode window. Do not close the trace file. You'll use it to complete Project 5-3.

Project 5-3

To examine the TCP sequence and acknowledgement process:

1. Follow the instructions in Project 5-1 to open the **dns-moviefone.pkt** file, if it is not already open.

2. Answer the following questions about the TCP communications shown in this trace file. Use the Decode Next and Decode Prev buttons, or double-click a packet in the Capture window, to open the desired packets.

   a. What window size is advertised in most of the TCP communications?

   b. Are there any out-of-order packets in the TCP communications?

   c. This trace file does not show the entire communication sequence that occurred between these two devices. What sequence number would 192.168.0.89 use after packet 14?

3. Click the **Close** button to close the packet decode window, and then click the **Close** button to close the packet window.

Project 5-4

To examine the TCP header structure:

1. With the EtherPeek demo program open, click **File**, **Open**, and open the **transfer.pkt** file located in the **18654-2\Ch5** folder on your hard disk. There are 94 packets in this trace file.

2. Answer the following questions based on the contents of the packets in this trace file:

   a. What well-known port number(s) is(are) used in this communication?

   b. How many handshake processes occur between these devices? List the packets that contain handshake sequences, and the ports referenced during each of the handshake sequences.

   c. Does either host ever advertise a window size of zero?

   d. Which packet provides the acknowledgment for the data sent in Packet #84?

   e. Are there any out-of-order packets in this communication?

   f. What is the minimum window size seen in this communication?

3. Click the **Close** button to close the EtherPeek for Windows demo program.

CASE PROJECTS

1. You are hired to inventory a company's network. You must document all the network devices, their addresses (hardware and network), and the applications that run on the network. Describe how you can use EtherPeek to obtain a listing of the network applications.

2. You work for a large software development company. The company is hiring new programmers and engineers at a phenomenal pace. Your team is in charge of developing a new application called the "commode diode system." What steps should you take to ensure you are not using a registered port number? How can you ensure that no one uses the same port number your application uses?

3. Your boss asks you to inventory all the software running on the network. You've been running the full version of EtherPeek on your network for several weeks now. You've built a long list of all the source and destination port numbers seen on your network. As you examine this list, you find that there are more than 100 port numbers that are not listed on the IANA port list. There are also about 20 port numbers that belong to applications you know are not running on your network. What happened? Why are your research results so far off base?

4. You work for a large banking firm headquartered in New York. Your internetwork consists of more than 100 primary servers and about 3000 clients scattered along the East Coast of the United States. Over the past month, you have been looking at the performance statistics of the network and the critical devices. Today, you are examining the file transfer traffic to and from one of your main servers. You notice that the window size is very small in all the file transfers to and from this device. What could be the reason? How can you investigate further?

5. You work as a network technician for an Internet-based wholesaler of pharmaceutical supplies. Your network consists of 20 Web servers that host your company's e-commerce system. Several of your e-commerce servers are suddenly receiving duplicate ACKs from the server that maintains your worldwide shipping rates. Is this a problem worth investigating? If so, what will you look for?

6. Your company publishes children's books. Your authors use FTP to submit their materials electronically to one of your internal servers. Today, one of your authors calls stating that he cannot connect to your server. He is not technically oriented and doesn't know why he can't connect—he doesn't care either. He won't be able to make the deadline if he can't transfer the materials electronically. What should you look for when analyzing the traffic from this author to your FTP server?

CHAPTER 6

BASIC TCP/IP SERVICES

After reading this chapter and completing the exercises you will be able to:

♦ Understand how TCP/IP Application layer protocols and services work

♦ Explain the capabilities, message types, and request/reply architectures for a variety of basic TCP/IP services, including FTP, Telnet, SMTP, and HTTP

♦ Understand the operations of other basic TCP/IP services, including Echo, Quote of the Day, Chargen, Whois, TFTP, Finger, Remote Procedure Call (RPC), NetBIOS services over TCP/IP (also known as NBT), and SNMP

♦ Explain how to decode packets that contain Application layer protocols, and how to relate message types or other similar information to the kinds of requests and replies moving between a client and a server (or between hosts in general)

The importance of the underlying protocols at TCP/IP's Network and Transport layers cannot be overstated, but the capabilities that the TCP/IP Application layer protocols and services provide are equally important. In fact, TCP/IP couldn't really do anything for end users without these capabilities. Because the Application layer protocols are invariably associated with some kind of service—for example, the File Transfer Protocol (FTP) is associated with remote file transfer and related file access services—the terms "protocol" and "service" tend to be used interchangeably when it comes to TCP/IP Application layer components.

In fact, there are literally hundreds of TCP/IP Application layer protocols, each with an attendant service, documented in the vast library of RFCs. We cannot possibly explore all of them in this chapter (or in this book either, for that matter) so we cover the basic elements—what some might even call "traditional TCP/IP services" because they are such an essential part of the environment that TCP/IP defines. We devote other chapters, or parts of chapters, in this book to key TCP/IP protocols and services that help support the overall TCP/IP infrastructure. In this chapter, you will learn about the basic kinds of services for accessing e-mail, files, other computers, and so forth, which TCP/IP delivers so well.

How Upper-layer IP Protocols Work and Behave

The fundamental behavior of TCP/IP Application layer protocols depends on the existence of a variety of well-understood conventions and behaviors, as follows:

- Specifications for the message structures that the protocol or service supports
- Definition of a well-known port address (or addresses) on which servers listen for service requests
- Availability of appropriate software components that implement the various roles that hosts can play in requesting or providing such services

The conventions are intentionally quite abstract because of the various roles that hosts can play in this process. The types of messages that generally occur within TCP/IP Application layer services are called **request/reply messages**. Generally, clients request services using **request messages**, and servers reply to such messages using **reply messages**. For this reason, Application layer services are often said to adhere to a request/reply architecture.

When the role of the client, or requester, of such services generally differs dramatically from the role of the server, or provider, of such services, the Application layer service may be said to adhere to a **client/server** architecture. The HTTP protocol that underlies the World Wide Web is a good example of this kind of architecture, where Web browsers take the client role, and specialized Web server software takes the server role, and those two roles (and the functions they provide) are generally divided so that the client requests services from the server, and the server replies to such requests.

Sometimes, however, the division between client and server is not so distinct, and roles may change. There are numerous TCP/IP Application layer services (the popular music exchange service, Gnutella, is a good example) in which any client can also be a server, and vice versa. These kinds of services are generally called **peer-to-peer services** because all hosts can take either role with each other. Nevertheless, these services still make use of request and reply messages to ferry requests for service and their related replies across the network between pairs of hosts, employing whatever Application layer protocol may be in use.

Interestingly, there are many TCP/IP Application layer services in which two kinds of traffic occur. One type of traffic may be characterized as client/server traffic, in that it consists of request messages from clients, with corresponding replies from servers. This general category encompasses traditional IP services, such as e-mail, FTP, Telnet, and so forth, where clients can be any end-user machine, and servers are usually big, powerful computers (that may or may not be PCs) that act purely as servers. But it's also possible for one desktop machine to request services from another desktop machine, as in the file- and print-sharing services found in modern Windows implementations. In fact, this kind of service allows clients and servers to fluidly change roles, so that one PC might be a client to another PC in one case, but the roles might reverse in another situation. Thus, client/server does not always involve a PC making requests from a dedicated server somewhere on a network.

Another type of traffic may be characterized as **server–to–server traffic**, in which server-specific information is replicated from one server to another. This either creates additional copies of important data so that loss of a single server will not result in the loss of that server's data, or allows multiple servers to handle requests for the same data so that the processing load can be distributed across as many servers as have copies of that data. For obvious reasons, this latter technique is called **load balancing**. Sophisticated TCP/IP infrastructure support services like the Domain Name System (DNS) employ **replication** to provide redundancy protection against server failure, and to improve performance through load balancing. Likewise, specialized hardware and software permit multiple Web servers to manage copies of the same Web sites so that large user populations can access the same data, yet still enjoy reasonable response times.

When servers exchange data with one another, this process is usually called replication. Replication can occur between pairs of servers in one of two ways. If the server that is to receive the copy initiates the data transfer, it's referred to as a **pull** operation because the receiver essentially pulls the data from the sender. If the sender initiates the transfer, it's called a **push** operation because the sender essentially pushes the data to the receiver. Some services rely exclusively on either push or pull; others permit servers to be configured to push or pull, as needed. Other services allow for **push–pull** replication, where maximum reliability is obtained by allowing senders to initiate transfers after data sets change, and receivers to periodically initiate transfers to ensure that data sets stay relatively consistent across multiple copies.

The fundamental importance of request/reply message architectures to TCP/IP Application layer services should now be apparent. They provide the foundation upon which all such services rest. Likewise, the various roles that TCP/IP hosts employing such services can play—namely clients, servers, and peers—should also be well understood. Finally, the notion that server-to-server traffic is important to ensure data availability and improve performance is the key to push, pull, or push–pull transfers between pairs of servers. In the sections that follow, you'll take a more detailed look at some of the most basic and widely used Application layer services on TCP/IP networks today, and examine the specifics of their requests and replies, and so forth.

6

UNDERSTANDING FTP

FTP offers a method for transferring files over a connection-oriented transport, or TCP. FTP is documented in RFC 959.

FTP Elements

The key components of an FTP communication include the user interface (UI), protocol interpreter (PI), FTP commands, data transfer process (DTP), files transferred, TCP-based **command connection**, and TCP-based **data transfer connection**. Figure 6-1 depicts the basic elements and their relationships to each other.

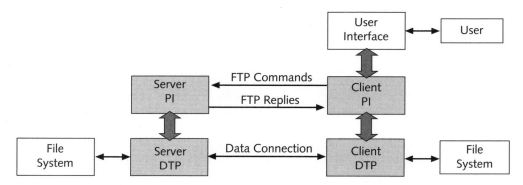

Figure 6-1   FTP communications use separate connections for commands and data

FTP User Interface (UI)

The UI offers the visual front end to the user. For example, the Windows FTP.EXE file offers an MS-DOS-based UI with only a prompt to guide you though the FTP process. Third-party products, such as Ipswitch's WS_FTP Pro product, offer an FTP client application with a graphical, **intuitive interface**.

 For more information on WS_FTP, visit *http://www.ipswitch.com*.

Protocol Interpreter (PI)

The PI interprets the user's commands, initiates the control connection from the user's dynamic port to the server's FTP port (which uses well-known port number 21), initiates the FTP commands (listed in the "FTP Commands" section in this chapter), and monitors the data transfer process.

For example, Table 6-1 lists the commands that the user enters, and the FTP command that the PI builds from those user commands.

Table 6-1   FTP PI Interpretation

User Command	FTP Command
CD mystuff	CWD mystuff
GET resume.doc	RETR resume.doc
PUT timecard.doc	STOR timecard.doc
DIR	NLST

FTP Commands

FTP uses a series of commands that follows directly after the TCP header. These commands are received and processed by the receiving PI. The basic FTP commands are listed in Table 6-2. Additional FTP commands are listed in RFC 959.

Table 6-2   FTP Commands

Command	Description
USER *username*	User Identifies the user accessing the file system. Typically, this is the first command sent after the underlying connection is established (the TCP handshake completes successfully).
PASS *password*	Password Sends the user's password (this information passes across the wire unencrypted by default)
CWD *pathname*	Change Working Directory Changes the current directory
QUIT	Quit Terminates the command connection
PORT *h1,h2,h3,h4,p1,p2* (*h* indicates the host's IP address bytes; *p* indicates the port number)	Port Sets up a data connection port number
PASV	Passive Asks the server to listen on a non-default data port and wait for the client to establish a new connection on that port number
TYPE *code*	Type Indicates the data representation type to be used in transfer (for example, ASCII, EBCDIC, and Image [binary] are three possible data types)
RETR *pathname/filename*	Retrieve Gets a file from the server DTP
STOR *pathname/filename*	Store Sends a file to the server DTP

Table 6-2 FTP Commands (continued)

Command	Description
DELE *pathname/filename*	Delete Deletes a file
RMD *pathname*	Remove Directory Deletes a directory on the FTP server
MKD *pathname*	Make Directory Creates a directory on the FTP server
PWD	Print Working Directory Displays the current directory path that the client accesses
NLST [*pathname/filename*]	Name List Obtains the directory list from the server
HELP	Help Shows the command list supported by the server

File System

The file system at either end of an FTP communication may consist of various file formats, such as ASCII, **Extended Binary Coded Decimal Interchange Code (EBCDIC)**, and binary.

Data Transfer Process (DTP)

DTP is the process of actually moving the data across the data connection only—when the RFC is followed strictly, data is not moved using the command connection. The DTP runs over a TCP connection made between the FTP client and FTP server after the FTP command connection is made.

TCP-based Command Connection

The command connection runs over TCP and is created automatically when an FTP connection is established in response to an open command from the FTP client, using server FTP port number 21. The client uses a dynamic port number to handle the other end of a command connection. This command connection must remain open while any data transfer is in progress, and provides a separate pathway for command information to be exchanged in parallel with the data transfer connection.

TCP-based Data Transfer Connection

The data transfer connection also runs over TCP. By default, this data transfer connection is created by the server. If the user issues the PASV command (and the server accepts it), the client can create the data transfer connection.

The Transport—TCP

FTP relies on TCP to establish the underlying connection, track the order of packets, define and adjust the data transfer window according to the rules of congestion control and avoidance, and recover from data loss.

Sample FTP Communications

FTP is an Application layer protocol that relies on TCP. The FTP commands immediately follow the FTP header, as shown in Figure 6-2.

Figure 6-2   FTP commands and data follow directly after the TCP header

The best way to understand how FTP works on the network is to view an FTP communication a single packet at a time. Table 6-3 defines the packet-by-packet sequences that occur in an FTP file transfer operation, in which *S* is the FTP server and *C* is the FTP client.

Table 6-3   FTP Communication Sequences

Process	Packet Sequences
Establish FTP command connection (three-way TCP handshake) Server port 21 Client port 1054	C > S TCP SYN S > C TCP SYN ACK C > S TCP ACK

Display Welcome screen The ACKs are not shown in this summary.	S > C FTP Reply 220
	         Service ready for new user
	         Server Welcome screen
	         (may require several packets)
	C > S FTP USER *username*
	S > C FTP Reply 331
	         User name okay, need password
	C > S FTP PASS *password*
	S > C FTP Reply 230 User logged in, proceed
	C > S FTP PORT *IP address, port number*
	S > C FTP Reply 200 Command okay
	C > S FTP NLST

Establish FTP data connection (three-way TCP handshake) Server port 1042 Client port 1055	C > S TCP SYN S > C TCP SYN ACK C > S TCP ACK

Get the directory list using data connection	S > C FTP Reply 150 Directory list follows
	         (multiple packets to send directory list)
	S > C FTP Reply 226 Listing Complete
	         Request to close data connection
	         (uses command connection)

Close data connection Server port 1042 Client port 1055	C > S TCP FIN S > C ACK C > S TCP FIN S > C ACK
Change to eGames directory	C > S FTP CWD eGames S > C Requested file action complete C > S FTP PORT *IP address, port number* S > C FTP Reply 200 Command okay C > S FTP NLST
Establish FTP data connection (three-way TCP handshake) Server port 1043 Client port 1056	C > S TCP SYN S > C TCP SYN ACK C > S TCP ACK

Get the directory list using the new data connection	S > C FTP Reply 150 Directory list follows
	         (multiple packets to send directory list)
	S > C FTP Reply 226 Listing Complete
	         Request to close data connection
	         (uses command connection)

Table 6-3 FTP Communication Sequences (continued)

Process	Packet Sequences	
Close data connection Server port 1043 Client port 1056	C > S S > C C > S S > C	TCP FIN ACK TCP FIN ACK
Request new data connection and file	C > S S > C C > S	FTP PORT *IP address, port number* FTP Reply 200 Command okay FTP RETR *filename*
Establish FTP data connection (three-way TCP handshake) Server port 1044 Client port 1057	C > S S > C C > S	TCP SYN TCP SYN ACK TCP ACK
Server sends file to client	S > C S > C	150 File follows ok (multiple packets to send file) FTP Reply 226 Transfer Complete Request to close data connection (uses command connection)
Close data connection Server port 1044 Client port 1057	C > S S > C C > S S > C	TCP FIN ACK TCP FIN ACK
Close command connection	C > S S > C	Quit Server closing command connection
Close data connection Server port 21 Client port 1054	C > S S > C C > S S > C	TCP FIN ACK TCP FIN ACK

6

For the complete list of FTP protocol commands, refer to RFC 959, or to your favorite implementation's Help files. (For the built-in Windows version of command-line FTP, try entering *ftp help* on the command line to see a list of commands, or *ftp help <command>* to get help on any specific FTP command by name.) If however, you use a graphical implementation of FTP (such as WS_FTP Pro, or a similar product), be aware that the buttons or graphical controls you use to control FTP activities will probably not use standard FTP command syntax, even though that is what the software sends to the server behind the scenes.

In the next section, we examine the popular Telnet service, used to permit a user on one computer to enter commands remotely on another computer, as if he or she was logged on to that machine locally.

UNDERSTANDING TELNET

Telnet offers a **bidirectional** byte-oriented communication. Originally designed to offer a communications method for **terminal access**, Telnet commonly uses well-known port 23 on the server side (although some administrators change the port number for security reasons), and a dynamic port number on the client side. Telnet is documented in RFCs 854 (Telnet) and 855 (Telnet Options).

Telnet Elements

Telnet hosts exchange information about options that they support as they establish a connection with another host. This remote host is referred to as a Network Virtual Terminal (NVT), or a virtual, generic host. These options use the DO, DON'T, WILL, WON'T structure to define what features they support. All Telnet communications use the server port number 23 to exchange the option information and Telnet data, as shown in Figure 6-3.

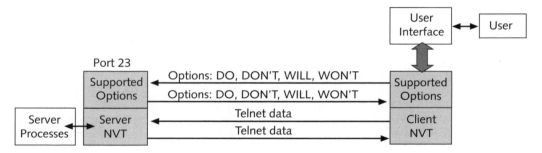

Figure 6-3   Telnet uses DO, DON'T, WILL, and WON'T to negotiate supported options

NVT

Each side of a Telnet communication is referred to as an NVT—the client NVT typically initiates the Telnet connection, whereas the server NVT offers some services to the client. In the traditional sense, the NVT is considered a printer-keyboard device that receives bytes from the other host and prints the information. It sends data entered via the keyboard to the other host.

DO, DON'T, WILL, WON'T Structure

During the initial Telnet connection establishment process, the hosts propose and accept or deny the use of specific parameters in the communications. The following structures are used for this negotiation process:

- 253 (0xFD)   DO
- 254 (0xFE)   DON'T
- 251 (0xFB)   WILL
- 252 (0xFC)   WON'T

These operators are the most widely used structures. A host sends one of these operators, such as DO or WILL, and follows it with an option code. The option is accepted when the other host responds with a DO or WILL. Returning a DON'T or WON'T indicates that a host does not accept an option.

Options

Options are parameters or conventions used for the Telnet connection. For example, the Echo option is used to define whether a Telnet host echoes back data characters it receives over the Telnet connection. The Telnet Echo option is covered in detail in RFC 857.

Table 6-4 shows a partial list of the options registered for Telnet. Refer to *http://www.iana.org* for a complete list of Telnet options.

Table 6-4   Telnet Options List

Option	Name	References
0	Binary Transmission	RFC 856
1	Echo	RFC 857
2	Reconnection	NIC 50005
3	Suppress Go Ahead	RFC 858
4	Approx Message Size Negotiation	ETHERNET
5	Status	RFC 859
6	Timing Mark	RFC 860
7	Remote Controlled Trans and Echo	RFC 726
8	Output Line Width	NIC 50005
9	Output Page Size	NIC 50005
10	Output Carriage-Return Disposition	RFC 652
11	Output Horizontal Tab Stops	RFC 653
12	Output Horizontal Tab Disposition	RFC 654
13	Output Formfeed Disposition	RFC 655
14	Output Vertical Tabstops	RFC 656
15	Output Vertical Tab Disposition	RFC 657
16	Output Linefeed Disposition	RFC 658
17	Extended ASCII	RFC 698
18	Logout	RFC 727
19	Byte Macro	RFC 735

Table 6-4   Telnet Options List *(continued)*

Option	Name	References
20	Data Entry Terminal	RFC 1043, RFC 732
21	SUPDUP	RFC 736, RFC 734
22	SUPDUP Output	RFC 749
23	Send Location	RFC 779
24	Terminal Type	RFC 1091
25	End of Record	RFC 885
26	TACACS User Identification	RFC 927
27	Output Marking	RFC 933
28	Terminal Location Number	RFC 946
29	Telnet 3270 Regime	RFC 1041
30	X.3 PAD	RFC 1053
31	Negotiate About Window Size	RFC 1073
32	Terminal Speed	RFC 1079
33	Remote Flow Control	RFC 1372
34	Linemode	RFC 1184
35	X Display Location	RFC 1096
36	Environment Option	RFC 1408
37	Authentication Option	RFC 2941
38	Encryption Option	RFC 2946

Some options require that additional information be exchanged between hosts. For example, when an option requires a parameter, the simple DO, DON'T, WILL, and WON'T functions are not sufficient. To support additional information exchange, both hosts must agree to discuss the parameters, and then use the command SB to begin **subnegotiation**.

Sample Telnet Communications

Telnet information immediately follows the TCP header, as shown in Figure 6-4.

In Figure 6-4, you can see the host suggesting four options:

- Echo
- Suppress Go Ahead
- Terminal Type
- Negotiate About Window Size

Table 6-5 (see p. 266) lists the various steps involved in a Telnet operation used to configure a Cisco router, in which *C* denotes the client system that initiates the Telnet connection, and *R* denotes the router that the client configures.

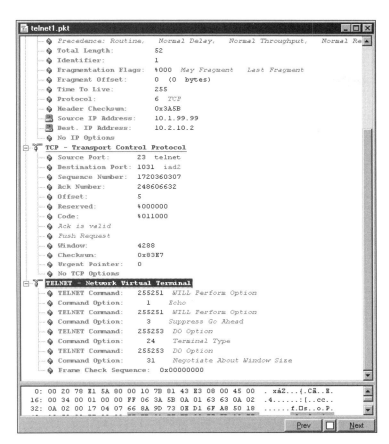

Figure 6-4 Telnet data and options follow immediately after the TCP header

For more information on Telnet, see RFC 854. Here again, you can easily investigate the client side of Telnet on a Windows system by typing *telnet /?* at the command line.

Telnet remains an important and widely used TCP/IP service to this day, despite its ancient origins. Note that secure implementations of Telnet, often called **Stelnet** (for **Secure Telnet**), are becoming increasingly available. These implementations use the **Secure Sockets Layer (SSL)** interface to encrypt traffic between a Telnet client and a Telnet server, and thereby avoid exposing account names and passwords on the network, which otherwise pass as clear text (and may therefore be easily sniffed by a protocol analyzer such as EtherPeek). If you, or your organization, need to use Telnet across any public or insecure links, we strongly suggest that you use a secure implementation, if at all possible. (As we write this chapter, unfortunately, there are no secure Telnet implementations available for Windows 2000 or Windows XP. However, the passage of time should remedy this situation.)

Table 6-5   Telnet Communication Sequences

Process	Packet Sequences	
Establish Telnet connection (three-way TCP handshake) Router port 23 Client port 1031	C > R R > C C > R	TCP SYN TCP SYN ACK TCP ACK
Negotiate options The ACKs are not shown in this summary.	R > C	Telnet options list - WILL Echo - WILL Suppress Go Ahead - DO Terminal Type - DO Negotiate About Window Size Request password
	C > R	Telnet options client supports - DO Echo - DO Suppress Go Ahead - WILL Terminal Type - WON'T Negotiate About Window Size
	R > C	Subnegotiation: Terminal Type
	C > R	Subnegotiation: Terminal Type—ANSI
	R > C	Telnet options - DON'T Negotiate About Window Size
	C > R	Telnet options - WON'T Negotiate About Window Size
	C > R	Telnet Data Password sent via multiple packets with return ACKS
	R > C	Screen prompts from router

UNDERSTANDING SMTP

Simple Mail Transfer Protocol (SMTP) is the most widely used protocol for sending electronic mail (e-mail) on the Internet. SMTP sends and receives e-mail messages through the use of a Sender-SMTP process and a Receiver-SMTP process that perform e-mail transmission and receipt services. The basic architecture of SMTP communications is shown in Figure 6-5.

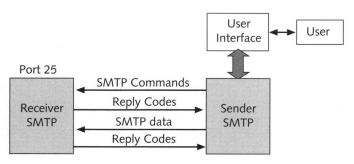

Figure 6-5   Sender-SMTP and Receiver-SMTP processes transfer e-mail over TCP

SMTP Elements

The Sender-SMTP and Receiver-SMTP processes are client or server applications that support SMTP functionality. Typically the Sender-SMTP transmits a request to initialize an SMTP connection on the Receiver-SMTP server port 25. Once the underlying TCP connection is established, the Receiver-SMTP responds with a numerical code 220, indicating that the server is ready to accept SMTP commands and information. The client then issues a HELO or EHLO command (depending on if the client is using standard SMTP or the SMTP extensions, as specified in RFC 1869 on Mail Service Extensions).

Sender-SMTP and Receiver-SMTP

The Sender-SMTP and Receiver-SMTP are processes that support the SMTP commands listed in RFC 821 (SMTP) and RFC 1869 (Mail Service Extensions). The Sender-SMTP sends mail commands and mail messages. The Receiver-SMTP sends reply codes, indicating the response to the codes and mail messages sent.

SMTP Commands

Although an initial set of SMTP commands was included in RFC 821, this list was expanded by IANA. Table 6-6 provides a list of the SMTP commands registered through IANA.

Table 6-6   SMTP Commands

Keywords	Description	Reference
HELO	Initiates an SMTP session	RFC 821
EHLO	Initiates an SMTP session from a Sender-SMTP that supports SMTP mail service extensions	RFC 1869
MAIL	Initiates mail transfer; identifies Sender-SMTP e-mail address	RFC 821
RCPT	Identifies the mail recipient	RFC 821
DATA	Initiates mail data transfer	RFC 821
VRFY	Verifies recipient exists	RFC 821
RSET	Aborts current mail transaction	RFC 821
NOOP	Used to test connection with server	RFC 821
QUIT	Close SMTP communication	RFC 821
SEND	Send to user's terminal	RFC 821
SOML	(Send Or MaiL) Send to user terminal or mail	RFC 821
SAML	(Send And MaiL) Send to user terminal and mail	RFC 821
EXPN	Expand the mailing list	RFC 821
HELP	Supply helpful information	RFC 821
TURN	Turn around the operation	RFC 821

Table 6-6   SMTP Commands (continued)

Keywords	Description	Reference
8BITMIME	Use 8-bit data	RFC 1652
SIZE	Message size declaration	RFC 1870
VERB	Verbose	Eric Allman
ONEX	One message transaction only	Eric Allman
CHUNKING	Chunking	RFC 1830
BINARYMIME	Binary MIME	RFC 1830
CHECKPOINT	Checkpoint/restart	RFC 1845
PIPELINING	Command pipelining	RFC 2197
DSN	Delivery Status Notification	RFC 1891
ETRN	Extended Turn	RFC 1985
ENHANCED-STATUSCODES	Enhanced Status Codes	RFC 2034
STARTTLS	Start TLS	RFC 2487

SMTP Reply Codes

The Receiver–SMTP sends status replies that include a numeric reply code. Table 6–7 lists the supported reply codes for SMTP.

Table 6-7   SMTP Reply Codes

SMTP Reply Code	Description
211	System status or system help reply
214	Help message
220	*<domain>* Service ready
221	*<domain>* Service closing transmission channel
250	Requested action ok and completed
251	User not local; will forward to *<forward-path>*
354	Start mail input; end with <CRLF>.<CRLF>
421	*<domain>* Service not available, closing connection
450	Mailbox unavailable, requested mail action not taken
451	Local error in processing, action aborted
452	Insufficient system storage, action not taken
500	Syntax error, command unrecognized
501	Syntax error in parameters or arguments
502	Command not implemented
503	Bad sequence of commands
504	Command parameter not implemented

Table 6-7   SMTP Reply Codes (continued)

SMTP Reply Code	Description
550	Mailbox unavailable, action not taken
551	User not local; please try <forward-path>
552	Exceeded storage allocation, action aborted
553	Mailbox name not allowed, action not taken

Sample SMTP Communications

SMTP commands and reply codes immediately follow the TCP header, as shown in Figure 6-6.

Figure 6-6   EHLO command indicates sender supports SMTP extensions

In Table 6-8, we examine the various steps involved in sending e-mail using SMTP. In this communication, *S* represents the SMTP server and *C* represents the SMTP client sending e-mail.

Table 6-8 SMTP Communication Sequences

Process	Packet Sequences	
Establish SMTP TCP connection (three-way TCP handshake) Server port 25 Client port 1047	C > S S > C C > S	TCP SYN TCP SYN ACK TCP ACK
Establish initial SMTP communication	S > C C > S S > C	SMTP 220: ESMTP server ready (date/time) SMTP EHLO Command SMTP 250: Hello (client IP address) SMTP 250: 8BITMIME SMTP 250: SIZE
Send mail to the SMTP server	C > S S > C C > S S > C C > S S > C C > S S > C	SMTP MAIL Command (includes source e-mail address) SMTP 250: Sender ok SMTP RCPT Command (include recipient e-mail address) SMTP 250: Recipient ok SMTP DATA Command SMTP 354: Start mail input Client sends e-mail message SMTP 250: Message accepted
Close the SMTP and TCP connection	C > S C > S S > C C > S	SMTP QUIT Command TCP FIN SMTP 221: Closing connection and ACK Reset (indicates client already closed the listening port 1047)

SMTP is documented in RFC 821. It's much harder to explain how to invoke or use SMTP than other TCP/IP Application layer services we discuss here because it occurs behind the scenes in some e-mail clients and some server-to-server mail transfers on the Internet. The majority of e-mail clients today use SMTP to send outgoing mail through some nearby SMTP server, which assumes the task of storing (if the addressee belongs to the same domain) or forwarding (if the addressee belongs to a different domain) such messages. That's why many e-mail and messaging systems, including SMTP, are also known as **store and forward** systems.

In the next section, you will learn about the Hypertext Transfer Protocol, which provides the underpinnings for the World Wide Web. There are many who believe that this protocol, coupled with its widespread use within browsers, is responsible for the phenomenal popularity and ubiquity of the Internet itself.

UNDERSTANDING HTTP

The Hypertext Transfer Protocol (HTTP) is an application-level protocol that provides distributed information from various **hypermedia** systems. HTTP has been in use on the Web since 1990. Currently, HTTP v1.0 (documented in RFC 1945) is widely implemented, but HTTP v1.1 is a Proposed Standard (documented in RFC 2616).

HTTP uses a request/response model, in which HTTP clients send a request to the server and expect a reply packet that contains a status code. Requests include a **Uniform Resource Identifier (URI)** that identifies the desired Web resource. By default, HTTP communications use port 80. In this section, we define the basic elements that are common to HTTP versions 1.0 and 1.1.

6

HTTP Elements

HTTP clients send HTTP requests that contain a method, or command, that indicates what the client wants. The requests also contain a URI indicating the desired resource. HTTP servers respond with a numeric code (the status code) and data (if appropriate). Figure 6-7 indicates how these elements work together to transfer HTTP data.

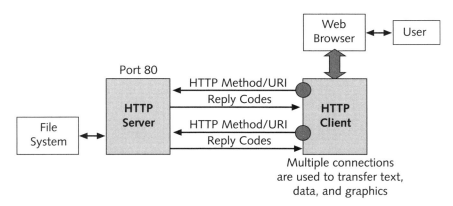

Figure 6-7   HTTP communications use commands, methods, and reply codes to support the exchange of data

Uniform Resource Identifiers

A URI, also referred to as a Web address, is a combination of a Uniform Resource Locator (URL) and a **Uniform Resource Name (URN)**. In accordance with RFC 1945, "Uniform Resource Identifiers are simply formatted strings which identify—via name, location, or any other characteristic—a resource."

HTTP Methods

HTTP methods are commands that the HTTP client issues to the HTTP server. HTTP v1.0 only defined three methods—HTTP v1.1 expanded the list, as shown in Table 6-9.

Table 6-9   HTTP v1.0 and 1.1 Methods

Method	Description
GET	Retrieves the information identified by the URI contained in the request
HEAD	Retrieves the meta information related to the desired URI
POST	Sends data to the HTTP server (the data should be placed as a new subordinate of the resource identified by the URI in the request)
OPTIONS	Determines the options and/or requirements associated with a resource or the capabilities of a server
PUT	Sends data to the HTTP server (the data should be stored in the URI indicated in the POST request)
DELETE	Deletes the resource defined by the URI in the DELETE request
TRACE	Invokes a remote, Application layer loopback of the request message, allowing the client to see what the server receives from the client
CONNECT	Used to connect to a proxy device and tunnel through to the ultimate endpoint (for example, SSL tunneling)

Status Codes

The HTTP server sends status codes to indicate success or failure of the request. The HTTP status codes defined in HTTP v1.1 are listed in Table 6–10.

Table 6-10   HTTP v1.1 Status Codes

Status Code	Definition
1xx	Informational
100	Continue
101	Switching Protocols
2xx	Successful
200	OK
201	Created
202	Accepted
203	Non-Authoritative Information
204	No Content
205	Reset Content
206	Partial Content
3xx	Redirection 3xx

Table 6-10   HTTP v1.1 Status Codes (continued)

Status Code	Definition
300	Multiple Choices
301	Moved Permanently
302	Found
303	See Other
304	Not Modified
305	Use Proxy
306	(Unused)
307	Temporary Redirect
4xx	Client Error 4xx
400	Bad Request
401	Unauthorized
402	Payment Required
403	Forbidden
404	Not Found
405	Method Not Allowed
406	Not Acceptable
407	Proxy Authentication Required
408	Request Timeout
409	Conflict
410	Gone
411	Length Required
412	Precondition Failed
413	Request Entity Too Large
414	Request—URI Too Long
415	Unsupported Media Type
416	Requested Range Not Satisfiable
417	Expectation Failed
5xx	Server Errors
500	Internal Server Error
501	Not Implemented
502	Bad Gateway
503	Service Unavailable
504	Gateway Timeout
505	HTTP Version Not Supported

6

Sample HTTP Communications

HTTP commands and status codes immediately follow the TCP header, as shown in Figure 6–8.

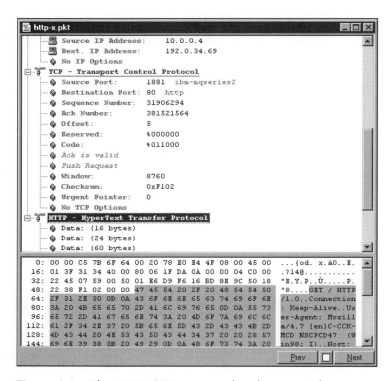

Figure 6-8   The HTTP GET command and status codes

In Table 6–11, we examine the various steps involved in browsing a Web site (*http://www.iana.org*) using HTTP. In this communication, *S* represents the HTTP server and *C* represents the HTTP client.

Table 6-11   HTTP Communication Sequences

Process	Packet Sequences	
Establish TCP connection (three-way TCP handshake) Server port 80 Client port 1881	C > S	TCP SYN
	S > C	TCP SYN ACK
	C > S	TCP ACK

Table 6-11 HTTP Communication Sequences (continued)

Process	Packet Sequences	
Get Web page **Send client attributes** **Server attributes**	C > S	HTTP Get Request (URL: www.iana.org) Provide Connection, User-Agent, Host, Accept, Accept-Encoding, Accept-Language and Accept-Charset
	S > C	HTTP Get Reply; Code 200 Provide Time, Server Type, Last Modified Date/Time, Etag, Accept-Ranges, Content-Length, Keep-Alive, Content-Type Start Web page download Continue this connec- tion to get the Web page while the client opens additional connections to get the graphic images.
Establish 2nd TCP connection (three-way TCP handshake) Server port 80 Client port 1882	C > S S > C C > S	TCP SYN TCP SYN ACK TCP ACK
Get first graphic page **Send client attributes** **Server attributes**	C > S	HTTP Get iana1.jpg Provide same client information as well as referrer (the page that listed the graphic file that the client wants to get)
	S > C	HTTP Get Reply; Code 200 Provide same attribute information Start sending *iana1.jpg* Continue this connection to get the graphic while the client opens another connection to get the next graphic image. Close the connection when the graphic downloads successfully.
Establish 3rd TCP connection (three-way TCP handshake) Server port 80 Client port 1883	C > S S > C C > S	TCP SYN TCP SYN ACK TCP ACK
Get first graphic page **Send client attributes** **Server attributes**	C > S	HTTP Get blueball.gif Provide same client information as well as referrer (the page that listed the graphic file that the client wants to get)
	S > C	HTTP Get Reply; Code 200 Provide same attribute information Start sending *blueball.gif* Continue this connection to get the graphic until the entire image downloads to the client. Close the connection when the graphic downloads successfully.

The communications shown in Table 6–11 continue along the same general lines—open a TCP connection, send a GET request for a graphic, receive a file, and finally, close the connection when the graphic file downloads—as each user browses the Web, moving from page to page, downloading its constituent parts with each move.

There's another flavor of HTTP that's worth mentioning in this context, which we do not cover in detail in this book: the HTTPS protocol represents a secure implementation of HTTP that incorporates use of SSL, or a secure shell (SSH) interface of some kind, to encrypt traffic moving between a secure client and a secure server. This mode of operation is typical for commercial transactions of all kinds on the Web, for everything from placing credit card orders, to reviewing confidential financial records, making stock trades, fund transfers, or other activities that involve the transfer of sensitive information. TCP port 443 is assigned to the HTTP protocol that uses TCP with Transport layer security over SSL. UDP port 443 is assigned to the HTTP protocol that uses UDP with Transport layer security over SSL to support secure Web communications.

In the sections that follow, we cover numerous basic TCP/IP services, but in much less detail than the preceding services. Here, our goal is to simply describe their capabilities, rather than examine their request/reply messages, options, and other operational or behavioral minutiae.

OTHER COMMON IP-BASED SERVICES

The complete TCP/IP protocol suite includes a variety of applications that enhance the capability of the basic TCP/IP protocol stack. These applications include the following, among many others:

- Echo (TCP and UDP)
- Quote of the Day (QOD)
- Character Generator (Chargen)
- Whois
- Trivial File Transfer Protocol (TFTP)
- Finger
- Remote Procedure Call (RPC)
- Simple Network Management Protocol (SNMP)

We do not have sufficient space in this book to subject these other basic services to the same level of scrutiny or detail that we provided for FTP, Telnet, HTTP, and SMTP. We do, however, describe these services and outline their basic functions; please consult the referenced RFCs if you are interested in more details about their message formats, options, and structures.

Echo

Echo is a TCP or UDP service that *echoes* all characters received on the port that it listens to back to the sender. Because some routers are configured to refuse incoming ICMP Echo Requests, you can use a UDP or TCP Echo to determine whether a router is active or not. Echo is also commonly used for debugging networked applications to make sure they are correctly emitting output (as judged by what the receiver returns in reply to an Echo Request).

UDP port 7 is assigned to the UDP Echo process. TCP port 7 is assigned to the TCP Echo process. Both TCP and UDP Echo services are documented in RFC 862.

Quote of the Day (QOD)

Quote of the Day (QOD) is a service that simply sends a short message in reply to any request packet. Originally designed as a debugging tool to solicit random input simply and easily without having to generate significant input, QOD has become a popular way for system administrators to deliver pithy sayings to users when they log on to a TCP/IP host.

UDP port 17 is assigned to the UDP Quote of the Day process, and TCP port 17 to the TCP Quote of the Day process. Both TCP and UDP Quote of the Day services are documented in RFC 865.

Character Generator (Chargen)

The **Character Generator (Chargen)** service outputs a continuing sequence of characters in response to a client request to this service. It is often used as a debugging tool to test how a system behaves when the client abruptly terminates ongoing TCP or UDP communication. This is called a "rude abort" in the governing RFC. Basically, this service responds by sending a long or continuous stream of characters in response to a client request, as a way of checking TCP or UDP communications.

TCP port 19 is assigned to the TCP Chargen process, UDP port 19 to the UDP Chargen process. Both UDP and TCP Character Generator services are documented in RFC 864.

Windows 2000 and Simple TCP/IP Utilities

Windows 2000 includes a set of TCP/IP utilities called Simple TCP/IP Services that includes Chargen, Daytime, Discard, Echo, and Quote of the Day client and server utilities. (**Daytime** reports the date and time when requested; **Discard** simply instructs the receiver of whatever packet is sent to silently discard that traffic.) However, these utilities are not installed by default when the operating system is installed. To install these utilities and test some of the services we discuss here, follow this sequence of instructions:

1. Click **Start**, point to **Settings**, and then click **Network and Dial-up Connections**. In the Network and Dial-up Connections window, select **Optional Networking Components** from the **Advanced** menu.

2. Highlight the **Networking Services** entry in the Components pane, then click the **Details** button. The Networking Services window opens.

3. Click the check box to the left of the **Simple TCP/IP Services** entry in the Subcomponents of Networking Services pane, then the **OK** button, and then click **Next**.

4. You are prompted to insert the Windows 2000 CD that corresponds to the version of software you're using (Professional, Server, and so forth). Insert the CD, and the rest of the installation should complete automatically.

After installation is completed, you will be able to use these utilities, but only if at least one other machine has them installed as well (one machine must act as a server to your client, unless you direct these commands at your own machine).

Whois

Whois is a TCP-based query/response server that provides basic directory services for some Internet users. The whois command looks up domain names, indicates where they're registered, and identifies primary and secondary DNS servers for the DNS database in which the entry resides. As you experiment with this command, you'll learn that many domain names are not registered in the databases that the Whois utility searches, even though you may be able to ping the same domain name successfully (which means the domain name is resolved successfully to a numeric IP address). This limited utility makes Whois less useful than it was in earlier days of the Internet, when it could tell you something about nearly every host in use.

Whois was originally described in RFC 812, which has been superseded by RFC 954. For Whois, UDP processes use UDP port 43, and TCP processes use TCP port 43.

TFTP

Trivial File Transfer Protocol (TFTP) was designed as a simple peer-to-peer protocol for lightweight file transfer between two IP hosts. Basically, TFTP was designed to make it easy for users to transfer files from one system to another wherever they are logged on. Thus, if you establish a Telnet session with another host, and realize you forgot to transfer a file to the host you're logged on to remotely, you can use TFTP from the Telnet command line to grab a file from your local host, and transfer it to the remote host within the context of your current Telnet session. For that reason, we sometimes call TFTP the "whoops! I forgot…" service.

On the other hand, TFTP has more important roles to play. It's often used to load executable images to diskless workstations that can't obtain files or images from a local hard drive. Likewise, TFTP provides a faster, more lightweight service to download configuration files, patches, fixes, or updates to networking hardware of all kinds (such as routers, switches, and other devices that generally lack disk drives). Finally, TFTP's design permits the UDP protocol to be used in broadcast fashion so it can simultaneously service multiple clients. (Because FTP uses TCP, it requires a three-way handshake between the client and each server, and it must send separate packets to each client; TFTP's use of UDP permits it to broadcast a single set of packets that all recipients on a single subnet can read.)

TFTP is documented in RFC 1350. UDP port 69 is assigned to the UDP Trivial File Transfer service, TCP port 69 to the TCP Trivial File Transfer service. Windows 2000 provides access to TFTP from the standard command line. Enter *tftp /?* to view online Help instructions.

Finger

The **Finger** User Information Protocol provides a mechanism for obtaining information about TCP/IP hosts or users. Because the Finger service has enabled several well-documented points of system attack, this service is seldom enabled for external access on well-managed Internet hosts. If you're logged on to a host and want to find information about another user on that same host, the finger command usually works, but is no longer usable for remote host or user lookup. (Most attempts to use Finger result in a "connection refused" error message because system administrators routinely close the TCP and UDP ports associated with Finger to the outside world.)

Finger is documented in RFC 1288. The UDP Finger process uses UDP port 79; the TCP Finger process uses TCP port 79. The finger command works from the Windows command line, but its universal shutdown limits its value and use.

Remote Procedure Call (RPC)

Remote Procedure Call (RPC) defines a programming mechanism originally developed at Sun Microsystems for programmers to easily develop so-called distributed applications (a procedure within a process on one computer that communicates or invokes another procedure running within a different process on the same computer, or on some other computer on the network). RPC technology, which is still used fairly widely, enables software developers to build custom networked applications using a standard TCP/IP Application layer communications service that works either with TCP or UDP transports.

Of course, any services built with RPC must manage their own communications because they can rely only on the ability to access and exchange data with other RPC processes through this interface. Thus, developers who use RPC to permit processes to communicate remotely must create and manage their own authentication, session management, and error-handling codes, along with the custom or special-purpose service they seek to provide.

The RPC service is documented in RFC 1257, as originally defined at Sun Microsystems. The RPC service over TCP uses TCP port 111; over UDP the RPC service uses UDP port 111.

6

Simple Network Management Protocol (SNMP)

The first word in the name Simple Network Management Protocol (SNMP) understates the capability and complexity of the actual SNMP service. SNMP has been the subject of more than 60 RFCs, implying that it is not terribly simple; over 25 books in print on the subject of SNMP should confirm this hypothesis. Because we can't go into much detail on this service here, suffice it to say that SNMP was created to permit remote monitoring and management of devices and hosts for which SNMP agents were created. An agent's job, in this context, is to report on specific events about which it was instructed to communicate, and to respond to requests for information from other SNMP software components (sometimes called remote monitoring [RMON] agents—or more generically, management consoles) that occasionally poll SNMP-managed hosts or devices for current status and behavior statistics.

The key RFCs for SNMP are 1442–1450 and 1903–1910, with numerous others also applicable for certain situations. For normal SNMP traffic, the associated UDP and TCP port number is 161; for specific SNMP event reporting (**SNMP trap**, in SNMP terminology), the UDP and TCP port number is 162.

NetBIOS Over TCP/IP

All versions of Windows prior to Windows 2000 depend on an Application layer protocol called the Network Basic Input/Output System (NetBIOS). This protocol was originally developed by Sytek Corporation for IBM in the early 1980s to make networked applications easy to implement on PCs. Even though nobody outside the IBM, Microsoft, and DECnet communities would consider **NetBIOS over TCP/IP** (often abbreviated as **NetBT** or **NBT**) to be a basic TCP/IP service, it has been a must-have until recently for Windows and related platforms. In fact, as long as Windows 3.x, 9x, or NT systems remain in use on a network, NBT must be available if some other protocol, such as IPX or NetBEUI, is not available to handle NetBIOS information in order for older Windows clients to behave properly and fully interact in a Microsoft network environment.

That's because basic name resolution services, the browser service (that sits behind Network Neighborhood on older Windows systems), domain replications services, and other messaging and networking infrastructure services too numerous to mention here all depend on NetBIOS to work. If TCP/IP is the only protocol in use on a network—as is common on many modern networks—NetBIOS over TCP/IP is mandatory if any version of Windows older than Windows 2000 is to fully participate on that network. Table 6-12 shows the TCP and UDP port numbers associated with NBT services in the Windows environment; RFCs 1001 and 1002 describe how NBT works. (Microsoft has since enhanced these services for its own benefit, so consult a Microsoft technical reference, such as TechNet, to obtain the most complete view of how NBT works in the Microsoft network environment.)

Table 6-12   NetBIOS Over TCP/IP Protocols and Port Addresses

Abbreviation	Port/Protocol	Full Name	Notes
Naming svc	135/TCP	Locator Service	Host identification system commonly used by NBT
Naming svc	135/UDP	Locator Service	Host identification system commonly used by NBT
Profile naming	136/TCP	Profile Naming System	Host and user profile system commonly used by NBT
Profile naming	136/UDP	Profile Naming System	Host and user profile system commonly used by NBT
netbios-ns	137/TCP	NetBIOS Name Service	Used to advertise NBT name services, handle name service requests
netbios-ns	137/UDP	NetBIOS Name Service	Used to advertise NBT name services, handle name service requests
netbios-dgm	138/TCP	NetBIOS Datagram Service	Used as a lightweight message transport for NetBIOS messages and other packets
netbios-dgm	138/UDP	NetBIOS Datagram Service	Used as a lightweight message transport for NetBIOS messages and other packets
netbios-ssn	139/TCP	NetBIOS Session Service	Provides session setup, maintenance, and teardown for NetBIOS-based applications
netbios-ssn	139/UDP	NetBIOS Session Service	Provides session setup, maintenance, and teardown for NetBIOS-based applications

6

A working understanding of NetBIOS naming and related services is essential to a proper understanding of how TCP/IP and NetBIOS interoperate on Windows networks. For that reason, we cover this topic more completely later in this book.

DECODING UPPER-LAYER PROTOCOLS

Through Application layer decodes, analyzers offer a vision into the contents of application communications. These decodes are essential to effective application analysis and troubleshooting. Analyzers decode the Application layer fields based on the specifications or documented field locations and values of those applications.

Figure 6-9 shows a decoded packet with the **data offset values** displayed. These offsets can be displayed by clicking the **Show Offsets** button on the toolbar.

Figure 6-9   EtherPeek demo configured to show offsets of each field in a packet

As you can see in Figure 6-9, EtherPeek indicates that the Number of Answers field resides at offsets 48 and 49 of the packet. The field is two bytes long and contains the value 0x0002, as shown in the highlighted bytes in the hex window (below the decode window). Using these offsets, we can build special filters to identify any other packets that match specific values in specific fields. For example, we built a filter (see Figure 6-10) that looks for the value 0x0002 at offset 48 (decimal) of a packet. If you apply this filter to all DNS traffic, you catch all DNS replies that contain two answers in the packet.

Learning how to decode TCP/IP Application layer traffic largely depends on two separate but simultaneous forms of analysis:

- Understanding the specific service's request/reply messages, and learning how to recognize related headers and payload information

- Learning to assemble multiple lower-layer packets to reconstitute Application layer messages when payloads exceed the MTU for a single packet (performing necessary reassembly to put longer higher-layer messages together from their lower-layer constituent elements)

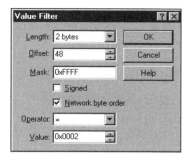

Figure 6-10 Filtering on DNS traffic based on the offset and value of the Source Port field

6

Fortunately, many of the protocol analyzers available in today's marketplace—including the program we use in this text, WildPackets EtherPeek—can do much of this work for you, as long as the software supports the particular TCP/IP service whose packets you want to decode. But, understanding the messages you're likely to encounter and knowing how to interpret related flags, options, and message types remain the key to successfully decoding Application layer traffic of just about any kind! Those are the skills that you should take away from this chapter.

CHAPTER SUMMARY

- ❏ The foundation upon which all TCP/IP Application layer services rest is a request/reply message architecture, in which clients send requests, and servers issue corresponding replies. When the client and server roles are clearly distinct and separate, such services may be called client/server services; when a client can also act as a server, and vice versa, such services may be called peer-to-peer services. Among its hundreds of Application layer services, the TCP/IP protocol suite includes many instances of both kinds.

- ❏ Certain client/server Application layer services also involve server-to-server traffic, in which multiple servers cooperate to share common data. The sharing process is called replication and may occur as a push operation, in which the sending server initiates data transfer, or as a pull operation, in which the receiving server initiates data transfer. Some TCP/IP Application layer services even use push-pull replication, so that a server whose data was changed can immediately push its data to replication partners after the change is completed, but other servers can also request replication at regular intervals to make sure their copies of data are as current as possible.

- ❏ FTP is a file transfer service that permits a local host to connect to a remote host, navigate and manage files on the remote system, and transfer files to and from that remote host. Although FTP is an old TCP/IP service, it remains useful today.

- ❏ Telnet provides a method to log on and access the command line on a remote computer using TCP/IP, a technique known as terminal emulation (because it makes the local host behave as if it were a terminal attached to the remote host). Because Telnet provides a convenient way to operate on a remote host across a network, it too remains useful to this day. Security problems with Telnet (especially moving account and password information as clear text) prompted development and widespread adoption of Secure Telnet implementations in many organizations.

❑ HTTP provides the underpinnings for the leading service and protocol used on today's Internet—namely the World Wide Web. HTTP's rich collection of message types, and its ability to invoke other protocols (including e-mail, news, and FTP) makes it a powerful tool for general remote data access. Its hyperlinking abilities make it easy for users to move rapidly through huge information spaces, and explain why the Web is so compelling and appealing to most Internet users.

❑ SMTP provides store and forward services for e-mail messages, and manages how e-mail is routed from its sender to its designated receiver(s). SMTP makes global e-mail possible on today's Internet, and continues to deliver one of the most useful and valuable networking services around.

❑ Other common TCP/IP Application layer services include Echo (which echoes the data delivered to a receiver back to the sender), Chargen (which generates arbitrary sequences of characters to test outgoing communications), QOD (which generates a short string, usually a joke or epigram that changes on a daily basis), TFTP, Finger, Remote Procedure Call (RPC), NetBIOS over TCP/IP (also known as NBT), and SNMP.

❑ Understanding how to decode Application layer protocols means learning how to identify and interpret request and reply messages related to such protocols, and how to reassemble related payloads, when necessary. Fortunately, many modern protocol analyzers (for example, EtherPeek) are able to assist with this task.

KEY TERMS

bidirectional — Two-way. Traffic that is bidirectional goes both ways. In the case of HTTP communications, data flows from the server to the client, and requests flow from the client to the server.

Character Generator (Chargen) — A basic TCP/IP service that uses TCP and UDP port 19. In response to any request message, a Chargen server generates an arbitrary stream of characters to test reply-handling capabilities.

client/server — A type of relationship between two computer hosts in which one host takes on the role of requesting services (the client) and the other the role of responding to service requests (the server)—these roles are seldom, if ever, reversed.

command connection — A connection that carries only commands and their associated replies. No data crosses a command connection.

data offset value — A numerical count that indicates the number of bits or bytes within a field, or the payload in which specific information of interest begins; works as a "start indicator" for specific data items or elements in packets.

data transfer connection — A connection that carries only data. This type of connection is typically established after a command connection is set up. The data connection does not carry commands.

Daytime — A basic TCP/IP service that responds to any service request with the date and time as known to the host that handles the incoming service request.

Discard — A basic TCP/IP service that silently discards all incoming traffic; generally used to test a requester's ability to emit outgoing communications.

Echo — A UDP- or TCP-based connection-testing protocol. These Echo communications simply send packets to the Echo socket to receive an Echo Reply. This type of Echo process is used as an alternative to the ICMP Echo process.

Extended Binary Coded Decimal Interchange Code (EBCDIC) — Developed by IBM back in the punch card days, EBCDIC is an 8-bit character set. Today, EBCDIC may still be used to access some IBM mainframes; however, ASCII is a more popular character set.

Finger — Short for Finger User Information Protocol, Finger provides information about individual users or hosts on the Internet; a once-popular service, Finger traffic is seldom permitted from outside a host's local area network because of past security exploits using Finger.

hypermedia — An extension to hypertext that includes the ability to link to graphics, sound, and video elements, as well as text elements.

intuitive interface — An interface that is self-explanatory, requiring little or no training to navigate.

load balancing — A method of distributing the processing load for service requests by directing individual requests for service to multiple machines in a way that causes the numbers of such requests per machine to be as nearly equal (or balanced) as possible.

NetBIOS over TCP/IP (NetBT or NBT) — A set of request/reply messages defined to enable the Application layer API, known as the Network Basic Input/Output System (NetBIOS), originally developed at Sytek for IBM in the early 1980s to work with TCP/IP transport and network protocols. NBT is required for older versions of Windows (those released prior to Windows 2000) on TCP/IP-only networks to support basic Microsoft network messaging and services.

peer-to-peer services — An Application layer service in which the roles of client and server are fluid so that a host that is a client to a server for one request/reply stream could potentially be the server to the other host acting instead as a client for another request/reply stream.

pull — A method of replicating server data in which the receiver initiates the transfer, thereby pulling that data from its original source.

push — A method of replicating server data in which the sender initiates the transfer, thereby pushing that data to the receiver.

push-pull — A method for replicating data in which the sender initiates data transfer when server data changes, but where receivers also initiate periodic data transfer to maintain ongoing database consistency.

6

Quote of the Day (QOD) — A basic TCP/IP service that delivers a short stream of text (usually a joke or an epigram) in response to a request for service.

Remote Procedure Call (RPC) — A programming interface developed at Sun Microsystems, later standardized as an RFC, that permits a procedure running within a process on one host to use TCP/IP transport and network protocols to invoke and communicate with another procedure in some other process (on the same host or a remote host). RPC was created to make it easier for application developers to create networked applications, and it is still widely used today.

replication — A technique for controlled copying of data from one repository to another, usually with the idea of improving that data's robustness (if one server goes down, the other server(s) where a copy resides can continue to function) and availability (if multiple servers can handle the same data, the processing load involved can be distributed, or balanced, across all such servers, thereby improving response time to user requests).

reply message — An Application layer service packet sent from one host to another that responds to the other host's request for service.

request message — An Application layer service packet sent from one host to another that requests the target host to provide some service.

request/reply message — The collection of messages that an Application layer protocol supports; all such messages define the capabilities of the overall service that the protocol provides.

Secure Sockets Layer (SSL) — A standard programming interface that encrypts outgoing data before passing it to the Transport layer, and that decrypts incoming data before passing it to the Application layer. SSL provides a handy way to improve the security of networked communications.

Secure Telnet (Stelnet) — A special implementation of Telnet that uses SSL, or a secure shell, to encrypt outgoing traffic, and decrypt incoming traffic, to prevent such traffic from being snooped en route between sender and receiver.

server-to-server traffic — Traffic between servers that provide an identical service, usually to replicate and synchronize copies of the same data across multiple servers. For critical services like DNS, this kind of traffic helps ensure data robustness and availability.

SNMP trap — A way for an SNMP agent running on a remote device or host to signal an alarm (an indicator that some error or other untoward event occurred) or alert (an indicator that some threshold value has been exceeded) to a remote management agent for further processing.

store and forward — A technique whereby e-mail messages are delivered to a particular server, messages slated for delivery to local clients are stored, and messages slated for delivery to remote clients are forwarded to another e-mail server for routing to their ultimate destination.

subnegotiation — A secondary process of negotiation that allows for the exchange of parameter information. Telnet uses subnegotiation when the standard set of options and the DO, DON'T, WILL, WON'T system is inadequate.

terminal access — An unintelligent terminal in which all the data, storage, program processing, and so forth, is handled by the remote host. Thus, only text to be displayed on the terminal and keyboard responses sent from the terminal cross the network.

Trivial File Transfer Protocol (TFTP) — A basic TCP/IP Application layer service that supports lightweight file transfer from a local host to a remote host (especially in the context of a local user who's logged on to the remote host).

Uniform Resource Identifier (URI) — A generic term for all types of names and addresses that refer to objects on the Web. An URL is one kind of URI.

Uniform Resource Name (URN) — A URI with a commitment to persistence and availability. URIs are documented in RFC 2141.

Whois — A client utility used to access a remote server database of domain or IP address registries. Because many domain names are not registered in the databases that Whois searches, this utility is not very useful.

6

REVIEW QUESTIONS

1. What kind of message architecture supports all TCP/IP Application layer protocols and services?

   a. client/server

   b. peer-to-peer

   c. request/reply

   d. push-pull

2. When the TCP/IP host that initiates contact with another TCP/IP host nearly always makes requests, and the contacted host invariably responds to those requests, what kind of relationship exists between those hosts for that service?

   a. client/server

   b. peer-to-peer

   c. request/reply

   d. push-pull

3. When a TCP/IP host can initiate contact with another TCP/IP host to make a request for service, but the other host can turn around and do the same thing, what kind of relationship exists between those hosts for that service?

   a. client/server

   b. peer-to-peer

   c. request/reply

   d. push-pull

4. When two servers want to exchange data, and the sending host originates the transfer of data to the receiver, what is this kind of transfer operation called?

   a. pull

   b. push

   c. push–pull

   d. store and forward

5. When two servers can exchange data, and the sender initiates transfer to the receiver once data changes occur, but the receiver periodically initiates transfers, what is this kind of transfer called?

   a. pull

   b. push

   c. push–pull

   d. store and forward

6. Which two advantages are derived immediately when replicating data across multiple servers?

   a. backup and recovery

   b. availability

   c. redundancy

   d. robustness

7. Which form of FTP client operates as a popular, standalone software application?

   a. command-line FTP program

   b. embedded FTP code

   c. Web-based FTP access

   d. graphical FTP program

8. Which software component on an FTP server handles incoming user commands?

   a. command interpreter

   b. protocol interpreter (PI)

   c. runtime library

   d. user interface

9. Which of the following ongoing connections does FTP maintain during an active session? (Choose all that apply.)

   a. session connection

   b. client connection

   c. command connection

   d. server connection

   e. data connection

10. Telnet supports only unidirectional, byte-oriented communications. True or false?

    a. True

    b. False

11. Telnet passes account names and passwords in clear text from the local host to the remote host. True or false?

    a. True

    b. False

12. Which of the following statements best describes the Sender-SMTP?

    a. sends reply codes, including responses to codes and mail messages sent

    b. forwards e-mail messages from one server to another

    c. sends mail commands and mail messages

    d. tracks delivery and reception of all mail messages sent

13. Which of the following statements best describes the Receiver-SMTP?

    a. sends responses to all mail messages received

    b. sends reply codes, including responses to codes and mail messages received

    c. forwards e-mail messages from one server to another

    d. sends mail commands and mail messages

14. A store and forward e-mail system stores all inbound messages destined for local clients, and forwards all inbound messages destined for clients on other e-mail servers. True or false?

    a. True

    b. False

15. The generic name used to identify a Web resource is a(n):

    a. Uniform Resource Locator (URL)

    b. Uniform Resource Name (URN)

    c. Uniform Resource Identifier (URI)

    d. Universal Naming Convention (UNC)

16. The abbreviation for the secure implementation of HTTP is called:

    a. SHTTP

    b. HTTPS

    c. SSL

    d. SSH

17. Which of the following basic TCP/IP services responds to a service request with an arbitrary stream of characters?

    a. Finger

    b. Echo

    c. Chargen

    d. QOD

    e. Whois

18. Which of the following basic TCP/IP services can provide information about registered domain names?

    a. Finger

    b. Echo

    c. Chargen

    d. QOD

    e. Whois

19. Which of the following basic TCP/IP utilities is not included in the Simple TCP/IP Utilities in Windows NT and Windows 2000?

    a. Echo

    b. Chargen

    c. QOD

    d. Whois

20. Why is Finger so seldom available to users on most Internet servers?

    a. It's no longer needed.

    b. It's no longer popular.

    c. It proved to be vulnerable to security exploits.

    d. The term has an unpleasant connotation under some circumstances.

21. RPC provides a standard mechanism to create custom distributed applications over TCP/IP. True or false?

    a. True

    b. False

22. An SNMP agent must be present on a host or device for it to report to a remote management console. True or false?

    a. True

    b. False

23. NetBIOS over TCP/IP is required on any networks that include versions of Windows older than Windows 2000, no matter what protocols are in use. True or false?

    a. True

    b. False

24. Which of the following Windows services uses NBT on a TCP/IP-only Microsoft network? (Choose all that apply.)

    a. browser service

    b. domain replication services

    c. FTP services

    d. Web access

25. Which of the following statements best explains the importance of data offset values when decoding Application layer protocols?

    a. Those values pinpoint the location of key fields, such as Application layer header information.

    b. Those values allow the contents of the payload to be inspected at will.

    c. Those values determine where key fields start and stop.

    d. Those values determine how the Application layer payload should be interpreted.

6

HANDS-ON PROJECTS

Project 6-1

The following Hands-on Projects assume that you are working in a Windows 2000 environment, and that you installed the EtherPeek demo program, as described in Project 1-1.

To install the NetScanTools 4.12 trial software:

Before installing the software, ensure you meet all system requirements listed in the *readme.txt* file contained in the *NetScanToolsDemo* folder on the CD accompanying this book.

1. Insert the CD-ROM included with this book in your CD-ROM drive.

2. Double-click the **My Computer** icon.

3. Double-click the **CD-ROM** drive icon.

4. Navigate to the **NetScanToolsDemo** folder.

5. Double-click **NST412.EXE**.

6. The NetScanTools 4.12 Welcome window appears. Click **Next** to continue the installation.

7. After reviewing the Northwest Performance Software, Inc. Software License Agreement, click **Yes**.

8. The Choose Destination Location window appears. Click **Next** to accept the default application destination (C:\Program Files\nwps\NetScanTools\Program).

9. By default, the installation backs up all replaced files. You are prompted to select a directory for your backup files. The default directory is C:\Program Files\nwps\ NetScanTools\Program\BACKUP. Click **Next** to accept the default directory.

10. The Select Program Manager Group dialog box appears. Click **Next** to accept the default Program Manager Group (NetScanTools 4.1).

11. The Start Installation screen appears. Click **Next** to begin the installation.

12. After the files are copied, the Installation Complete dialog box appears. By default, NetScanTools 4.12 is configured to run after you accept this screen. Clear the check box so the demo does not automatically run after the installation. Click **Finish** to close this window.

13. If the evaluation reminder dialog box appears, click **OK**.

14. Continue to Hands-on Project 6-2.

Project 6-2

To launch the NetScanTools 4.12 trial software:

1. Click **Start**, point to **Programs**, point to **NetScanTools 4.1**, and then click **NetScanTools**.

2. The Reminder window appears. Click **OK**.

3. The Tip of the Day window appears. Click **Close**.

4. The Welcome window appears. Click **Continue**.

5. Continue to Hands-on Project 6-3.

Project 6-3

For this Hands-on Project, your instructor provides a target domain name.

To view and analyze Whois communications:

1. The NetScanTools 4.12 trial program should already be running. If not, refer to Hands-on Project 6-2 to start the program.

2. To start the EtherPeek demo program, click **Start**, point to **Programs**, and then click **WildPackets EtherPeek Demo**.

3. Click **OK** to close the EtherPeek Demo information window.

4. If the Select Adapter window appears, select your network adapter, and click **OK**.

5. Click **Capture** on the menu bar, and then click **Start Capture**.

6. The Capture Options window appears. Click **OK** to accept the default buffer size of 1024 kilobytes. The Capture window appears. The Capture window number increments each time you start a new capture process.

7. Click the **Filters** tab, and then select the **My IP Address** filter (created in Hands-on Project 4-2).

8. In a moment, you will capture the packets of a Whois communication, one at a time. Remember that the EtherPeek demo only captures 250 packets, or runs for 30 seconds, whichever comes first. This is the reason for using a filter on your own traffic. Most likely, you must capture each communication in separate capture processes. Click the **Start Capture** button.

9. Press **Alt+Tab** as many times as necessary to return to the NetScanTools demo.

10. Click the **Whois** tab. Enter the domain name provided by your instructor in the Enter Query field. Click the **Query** button.

11. When the Whois query is complete, click **Stop**.

12. Press **Alt+Tab** as many times as necessary to return to the EtherPeek demo.

13. Click the **Stop Capture** button. Click the Packets tab. Review the packets saved in your demo. Answer the following questions about your captured packets:

    a. What port number does the Whois process use?

    b. Is this process TCP-based or UDP-based?

    c. When was this Whois database last updated?

14. Close the EtherPeek demo program, unless you proceed immediately to the next project.

15. Press **Alt+Tab** to return to the NetScanTools trial program. Click the **Exit** button to close the program.

Project 6-4

To view and analyze an FTP connection:

Your instructor will supply you with an FTP server IP address, user name, and password to use in this project.

1. Click **Start**, point to **Programs**, point to **Accessories**, and then click **Command Prompt**. A Command Prompt window appears. You will execute FTP commands from this window after you start the EtherPeek demo to capture your packets.

2. If the EtherPeek demo is not running, click **Start**, point to **Programs**, and then click **WildPackets EtherPeek Demo** to start the analyzer program.

3. Click **OK** to close the EtherPeek Demo information window.

4. Click **Capture** on the menu bar, and then click **Start Capture**.

5. The Capture Options window appears. Click **OK** to accept the default buffer size of 1024 kilobytes. The Capture window appears. The Capture window number increments each time you start a new capture process.

6. Click the **Filters** tab, and select the **My IP Address** filter (created in Hands-on Project 4-2).

7. In a moment, you will capture the packets of an FTP session. Remember that the EtherPeek demo only captures 250 packets, or runs for 30 seconds, whichever comes first. This is the reason for using a filter on your own traffic. Be certain you can complete Steps 7 through 12 within 30 seconds. If you don't, close the Capture window and follow Steps 4 through 12 again. Click the **Start Capture** button.

6

8. Press **Alt+Tab** as many times as necessary to return to the Command Prompt window.

9. Note the IP address of the FTP server that your instructor supplied. At the command prompt, type **ftp *ip_address*** (where *ip_address* is the FTP server address provided by your instructor). Ensure you can connect to the FTP server before proceeding. If you have any connection problems, recheck the IP address, or consult with your instructor.

10. When prompted, enter your user name and password supplied by the instructor.

11. Type **dir**, and press **Enter**. The directory list appears.

12. Type **quit**, and press **Enter**, and then type **exit**, and press **Enter**. The Command Prompt window closes.

13. If the EtherPeek window is not active, press **Alt+Tab** until it is the active window. Click the **Stop Capture** button if the capture is still running. Again, the EtherPeek demo only captures packets for 30 seconds. The capture process may have automatically stopped. If so, click **OK** in the capture stopped notification dialog box. Next, you examine the FTP communications to answer a series of questions.

14. Click the **Packets** tab. Scroll through the FTP communications. Double-click the packets of interest and use the **Decode Prev** and **Decode Next** buttons to answer these questions about your FTP session:

    a. What FTP commands did your FTP client session issue during this exercise?

    b. How many connections did your FTP client open with the FTP server to log on and transfer the directory list?

    c. Were your user name and password visible in the trace file?

15. Close the EtherPeek demo program.

Project 6-5

To view and analyze an HTTP session:

This Hands-on Project assumes that you are using either Microsoft Internet Explorer or Netscape Navigator to access the Internet, and that you have a working Internet connection. Your instructor will let you know what Web site to access in this project.

1. Start your Internet browser.

2. Click **Start**, point to **Programs**, and then click **WildPackets EtherPeek Demo** to start the analyzer program.

3. Click **OK** to close the EtherPeek Demo information window.

4. Click **Capture** on the menu bar, and then click **Start Capture**.

5. The Capture Options window appears. Click **OK** to accept the default buffer size of 1024 kilobytes. The Capture window appears. The Capture window number increments each time you start a new capture process.

6. Click the **Filters** tab, and select the **My IP Address** filter (created in Hands-on Project 4-2).

7. In a moment, you will capture the first packets of an HTTP session. Remember, the EtherPeek demo only captures 250 packets, or runs for 30 seconds, whichever comes first. This is the reason for using a filter on your own traffic. The Web site you access will probably require more than 250 packets to access and download the home page images. Click the **Start Capture** button.

8. Press **Alt+Tab** as many times as necessary to return to the browser window. Enter the URL of the Web site your instructor provides. After the home page loads completely, press **Alt+Tab** as many times as necessary to return to the EtherPeek Capture window. Click the **Stop Capture** button if the capture is still running. Again, the EtherPeek demo only captures packets for 30 seconds. The capture process may have automatically stopped. If so, click **OK** in the capture stopped notification dialog box. Next, you examine the HTTP communications to answer a series of questions.

9. Click the **Packets** table. Scroll through the HTTP communications. Double-click the packets of interest and use the **Decode Prev** and **Decode Next** buttons to answer these questions about your HTTP session:

   a. What HTTP version does your client support?

   b. What HTTP version does the server support?

   c. Can you identify the operating system and any other attributes of the HTTP server?

   d. Can you identify any of the graphic elements that are downloaded when you access this page?

   e. How many connections did your HTTP process require?

10. Close the Internet browser.

11. Close the EtherPeek demo program.

CASE PROJECTS

1. You are a network administrator at a large law firm in San Francisco. Your network users are starting to call with complaints that they cannot connect to your HTTP server. The HTTP server sits on the other side of a firewall that blocks all ICMP Echo packets. What processes could be used to test connectivity to the HTTP server?

2. You're an entrepreneur who designed the ultimate network tool! Now you're ready to launch your Web site. What tool can you use to determine if your domain name is used?

3. You work the night shift at a software development company, and manage six Web servers that host the company's commerce solution for medical and dental supplies. You notice that traffic across the network dropped significantly below the typical nighttime levels. You suspect there may be a problem with the HTTP servers. Define the type of packet filters that you might build to capture traffic destined to your six critical Web servers.

7

DOMAIN NAME SYSTEM (DNS)

After reading this chapter and completing the exercises you will be able to:

♦ Understand the types of services that DNS provides

♦ Explain the structure and layout of the domain name hierarchy and the DNS namespace

♦ Understand how DNS servers handle name resolution requests, including the role of nearby and root servers in the resolution process, and the difference between recursive and iterative name resolution requests

♦ Explain how DNS queries and responses work, and how they handle name resolution, DNS record lookups, zone data transfers, and reverse DNS queries

♦ Understand the types of roles that DNS servers can play on a network, including the root servers, primary and secondary DNS servers for a particular zone, and caching-only DNS servers

♦ Employ basic name resolution utilities to test DNS server configurations, and inspect the contents of key DNS records on such servers

If there's one TCP/IP Application layer service that provides the glue that ties together the entire Internet, it's the Domain Name System (DNS). That's because DNS provides the essential ability to convert symbolic domain names, such as *microsoft.com* or *course.com,* into corresponding numeric IP addresses, such as 207.46.230.229 and 195.95.72.8, respectively. Without that translation service, we humans would have to remember numeric IP addresses for all our Internet destinations. DNS also supports other services, such as e-mail, by translating addresses of the form *etittel@lanw.com* into the IP addresses for the proper server that can handle such traffic. Without DNS, you can safely speculate that the Internet would not be nearly as successful.

That said, DNS is itself something of a technological tour de force. The combination of all DNS databases everywhere represents the entire mapping of all valid domain names to corresponding valid IP addresses, and these databases are located all over the Internet (and the physical globe as well). Each individual database runs independently and, in some senses, can be said to own, as well as control, the data it contains. Despite its widely distributed and decentralized structure, DNS works very well, and provides a robust, reliable, and stable foundation upon which Internet addressing depends. By the time you finish reading this chapter, you should have a much keener appreciation of what a phenomenal accomplishment DNS represents.

DNS History and Background

The impetus for DNS came early in the Internet's development. That's because early methods for resolving symbolic names, such as *microsoft.com* and *course.com,* to numeric IP addresses relied completely on static text files, called **HOSTS**, which contained a list of every known host name, possible aliases, and a corresponding numeric IP address. This approach was simple to implement and worked on a small scale, but by 1982, the ARPANET (the Internet's government-sponsored predecessor) had enough hosts to make it increasingly difficult to maintain all the HOSTS files needed to permit users to translate any and all domain names to their corresponding IP addresses, and vice versa.

Once the number of known hosts (and domain names) grew into the thousands, maintaining and distributing a current, static HOSTS file for the whole Internet turned into a nasty, difficult problem. System administrators began to balk at the requirement to perform daily downloads of increasingly large files, and the environment began growing and changing faster than static methods could handle gracefully.

Thus, Paul Mockapetris created the original RFCs for DNS in response to this situation—namely RFCs 882 and 883—and in 1984, built the first reference implementation of DNS, which he named JEEVES. Kevin Dunlap wrote another implementation of DNS, called **BIND (Berkeley Internet Name Domain)**, for BSD UNIX version 4.3 in 1988. Since then, BIND has become the most popular DNS implementation in use, and it's available for most flavors of UNIX, as well as Windows 2000.

From its very beginnings, DNS was designed as a distributed database of information about domain names and addresses. Individual portions of such databases are sometimes called **database segments**, meaning they include only a portion of the overall namespace that DNS can access for its clients. In fact, DNS combines the following virtues:

- *It allows local control over domain name database segments.* This meets the need of servers to maintain control over the domain names and related IP addresses that fall under their purview. DNS allows control over distinct portions of the global database for the Internet as a whole so that those with administrative responsibility can manage their domain names and addresses without outside interference.

- *Data from all database segments is available everywhere.* Because any host on the Internet can communicate with any other host on the Internet, name-to-address translations must be available for all hosts as well. DNS makes it possible to find valid domain names anywhere on the Internet, and obtain the IP addresses to which those names correspond, among other services. This function is really what makes today's Internet possible.

■ *Database information is robust and highly available.* DNS is a key service on the Internet. Without name resolution, remote hosts can be difficult or impossible to access (as anyone who's encountered an occasional problem with DNS can attest). Thus, it is essential that DNS be both **robust** (resilient in the face of errors and failures) and highly **available** (quick to respond to requests for service). By incorporating support for replication, which permits multiple copies of the same data to be maintained on separate servers, thereby avoiding the loss of access to data that a single copy would allow, DNS is designed to be highly robust. By **caching** DNS data from one or more database segments on one or more DNS servers, DNS also provides a mechanism whereby it can attempt to satisfy name resolution requests locally before attempting them remotely, thereby greatly improving the speed of such name resolution.

Although DNS was designed over 15 years ago, and has been subject to various enhancements and improvements, it still represents one of the most effective uses of **distributed database technology** in the world today. It may seem complex on first exposure, but its basic functions and capabilities are remarkably simple, especially considering the volume of data involved, and its constant, reliable operation.

DNS Database Structure

The structure of the DNS database mirrors the structure of the domain namespace itself. This can best be understood as a **tree structure** (actually, it's an inverted tree because the **root** is usually drawn at the top of such a figure). The directory of your hard disk, which has a disk drive letter as its root, and various levels of folders and subfolders "branching off" that root, has the same kind of structure.

In the domain namespace, all domains meet at the root, which is identified by a single period (.). Beneath the root, you find the top-level or primary domains. In the United States, these top-level domains usually take the form of the following three-letter codes:

■ *.com*: Used primarily for commercial organizations

■ *.edu*: Used for educational institutions, such as schools, colleges, and universities

■ *.gov*: Used for the U.S. federal government

■ *.mil*: Used for the U.S. military

■ *.net*: Used primarily for service providers and online organizations

■ *.org*: Used primarily for nonprofit organizations, associations, and professional societies

You also see domain names that end in two- or three-letter country codes, as specified in ISO Standard 3166. In this system, *.us* represents the United States, *.ca* for Canada, *.fr* for France, *.de* for Germany (Deutschland), and so forth. For a complete list of such codes, consult the listing at *ftp://ftp.ripe.net/iso3166-countrycodes.txt*.

Organizational domain hierarchies are beneath the top-level domain names. For small companies, such as your authors' companies—LANWrights, Inc. and the Protocol Analysis Institute, LLC—this might consist of single domain names, such as *lanw.com* or *podbooks.com*. For large organizations, such as IBM, you might see domain names with four or more components, each separated by a period, as in *houns54.clearlake.ibm.com*. The tree diagram for this IBM domain name is depicted in Figure 7-1.

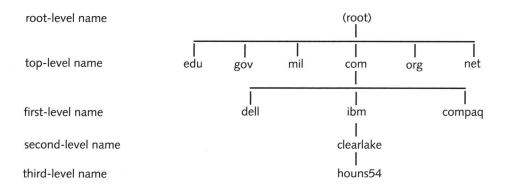

Figure 7-1   Tree diagram of the IBM domain name *houns54.clearlake.ibm.com*

The entire domain space for the Internet thus fits beneath the root. Fifteen root name servers act as the top of the DNS hierarchy worldwide. They provide the ultimate source for all name lookups that can't be resolved through other means, as you'll learn later in this chapter.

Note that domain names start at the bottom of the tree and work their way up, and each name is followed by a period to delimit one part of the name from another. Thus, the tree above translates into *houns54.clearlake.ibm.com*. Notice the final period at the end of that name. When you examine record data in DNS database files, you should understand that this final period (which refers to the root of the DNS hierarchy, rather than the end of an utterance of some kind) is important when constructing **fully qualified domain names (FQDNs)**. In fact, an FQDN consists of all elements of a domain name, in which each is followed by a period, and the final period stands for the root of the DNS hierarchy itself.

One more essential ingredient is required for DNS to work—there must be at least one valid IP address to go along with each unique domain name. Maintaining that name-to-address correspondence remains DNS' most important function to this day.

A DNS Overview

Each location in the DNS namespace corresponds to some node in the graphical tree that depicts its structure, as shown in the extremely focused snapshot of a tree in Figure 7-1. In fact, each node in that tree forms the root of a new subtree in the overall hierarchy, in which each such subtree represents a database segment (also known as a domain) in the overall domain namespace.

DNS' great power and flexibility rest on its ability to arbitrarily partition the tree and create containers for database information, wherever needed. In fact, domains (such as *ibm.com*) can be broken into **subdomains** (such as *clearlake.ibm.com*), as needed. This permits local control over database segments; in essence, it's a form of **delegation of authority**. And, while a domain requires registration (for a fee) with a central authority, local administrators can create subdomains easily, at no charge.

By pushing custodianship of database segments far enough down into the domain hierarchy, local administrative groups can take responsibility for all the names and addresses that they must manage. The problem of managing a huge, complex namespace (the total Internet) becomes more controllable by breaking it up into containers for specific sets of DNS servers, addresses, users, and machines that are small enough for one or two network administrators to manage.

At a fundamental level, then, it is also important to recognize that any valid domain name ultimately resides within some specific DNS database, in which a specific server has control over that entry. This concept is explained in greater detail in the next section, wherein you learn more about the kinds of records that can exist in a DNS database.

DNS Database Records

Data associated with domain names, address records, and other specific data of interest to the Domain Name System is stored on a DNS server in special database records called **resource records (RRs)**. Resource records are divided into classes, of which only the Internet class is of interest to most users. (There are special classes that work only at MIT, and another special-purpose class that's no longer used.)

Within the Internet class, records belong to a named taxonomy of record types, as documented in pages 13 through 21 of RFC 1035. Many such record types are in use. The nine most commonly used RR types are listed in alphabetical order and explained below:

- *Address (A) record*: An **address (A) record** stores domain name-to-IP address translation data.

- *Canonical name (CNAME) record*: A **canonical name (CNAME) record** is used to create aliases.

- *Host information (HINFO) record*: A **host information (HINFO) record** stores descriptive information about a specific Internet host.

- *Mail exchange (MX) record*: A **mail exchange (MX) record** is used to route SMTP-based e-mail on the Internet, and identify the IP address for a domain's master e-mail server.

- *Name server (NS) record*: A **name server (NS) record** is used to identify all DNS servers in a domain.

- *Pointer (PTR) record*: A **pointer (PTR) record** stores IP address-to-domain name translation data, and supports the operation known as a **reverse DNS lookup**.

- *Start of Authority (SOA) record*: A **Start of Authority (SOA) record** identifies the name server that is authoritative for a specific **DNS database segment**; in other words, it identifies the master DNS server for a specific domain or subdomain.

- *Text (TXT) record*: A **text (TXT) record** may be used to add arbitrary text information to a DNS database, usually for documentation.

- *Well-known services (WKS) record*: A **well-known services (WKS) record** lists the IP-based services, such as Telnet, FTP, HTTP, and so forth, which an Internet host can supply.

In the sections that follow, you'll learn more about these individual record types and how they're used, including snapshots from some actual DNS database files. As is the case with so many other UNIX-derived data files, DNS database files consist entirely of text-only (ASCII) data, and are therefore easy to inspect using the text editor of your choice.

Delegating DNS Authority

As a company the size of IBM, or an organization the size of the U.S. Air Force, might readily agree, some domains are simply too big and too complex to reside in a single database container. That's the primary reason why DNS permits the database record for the **primary DNS server** for *ibm.com* to delegate authority for various subdomains to DNS servers lower in the domain namespace. You can think of this as a digital form of passing responsibility further down the hierarchy, without distorting either the metaphor or the actual behavior of DNS.

Actually, such delegation of authority translates into assignment of authority for subdomains to different domain name servers, usually at various locations within an organization's overall scope and geographical layout. Once such authority is delegated, the database for the *ibm.com* name server includes NS records that point to name servers that are authoritative for specific subdomains. In addition, the *ibm.com* server's database might contain certain database records for addresses that do not fall into any specific subdomains. These could include certain addresses and other information at corporate headquarters, or field staff information for those who lack a permanent site affiliation. This structure is quite flexible, and can be adapted to nearly any kind of company organization or geographical layout.

The organization of the global DNS database is designed to make it quick and easy for name servers to point to other name servers when such name servers are not authoritative for specific subdomains. Thus, much of what's involved in navigating the domain namespace that DNS servers manage collectively consists of following records that point to specific, authoritative name servers for specific subdomains. This is what permits name servers to forward proper DNS records when name resolution requests originate at the root of the DNS hierarchy.

Types of DNS Servers

There are three kinds of DNS servers that you may encounter in any given DNS subdomain. These are as follows:

- *Primary DNS server, a.k.a. master server.* The primary master name DNS server (or **master server**) is where the primary DNS database files for the domain(s) or subdomain(s) for which that server is authoritative reside. This file is an ASCII snapshot of the DNS database that the server loads into memory while it runs. This database segment is called a **zone**; therefore, this file is sometimes called a **zone file** or a **zone data file**. The **primary master** is distinguished from other name servers for a domain by its ability to always read its data from a zone file on disk when the DNS service starts up. The designation of primary master is also an important configuration item when setting up a DNS server of any kind. For any DNS zone, there can be only one primary master name server.

- *Secondary DNS server, a.k.a. slave server.* A **secondary DNS server** (also called a **secondary master** or **slave server**) gets its data for the zone from the master server for that zone. In most DNS implementations, a secondary can read its data from a local file, but always checks to see if its on-disk version is as current as the version on the primary server. It does so by checking a specific field in its SOA record, and comparing it to a corresponding value in the master server's database. Where differences are noted, the secondary can update its database from the primary domain name server. It's important to understand that the zone data on a secondary always originates from a primary server. However, most DNS implementations include ways to limit updates only to data that has changed on the primary (which must then be copied to the secondary). Any DNS zone should have at least one secondary master name server (although multiple secondaries may exist), as well as the (mandatory) primary name server.

- *Caching server.* **Caching servers** store recently accessed DNS records from other domains to avoid incurring the performance overhead involved in making a remote query each time a resource outside the local domain is accessed. The best way to understand how caching works is to examine the distinction between your refrigerator and the grocery store. Just as your refrigerator determines what you can eat right now, what's in your cache defines what names outside the local domain can be resolved immediately. Likewise, the grocery store defines a big set of all the things you might eat, and the global DNS database defines a big set of all the names and addresses you might try to resolve.

While either primary or secondary DNS servers can provide caching functions, it's also possible to set up and configure separate **caching-only servers** within a specific domain. The goal of a caching-only server is to speed access to specific domain names by storing a copy of the lookup data locally, while providing neither primary nor secondary DNS server functions. Size and Internet access volume are the factors that determine if an organization implements separate caching-only servers. Only large organizations and service providers typically need to specialize their DNS services to this extent; for smaller organizations, combining primary or secondary responses for inbound lookups can occur alongside cache lookups for outbound traffic, without significantly affecting performance.

Secondary, or slave, DNS servers are important because they provide a back-up copy of the domain database for a specific zone. Thus, secondary DNS servers can continue to handle name service requests for their zones even if the primary name server goes out of service. In addition, secondary servers can help distribute the load for DNS lookups when they are available. Often, DNS servers that are authoritative, or primary, for specific zones also function as slave, or secondary, DNS servers for other nearby zones. This permits hosts in one zone to gain easy access to DNS data from those other zones.

The Client Side of DNS

Ultimately, requests for address translations and other DNS services originate from a network client. The piece of software that accesses DNS name servers is called a **name resolver**, or just a **resolver**. Resolvers issue requests for service, called **name queries** or **address requests**, to domain name servers. (A name query seeks to resolve an address to a domain name, also known as an **inverse DNS query** or reverse DNS lookup, and an address request seeks to resolve a domain name to a corresponding numeric IP address.)

Resolvers also interpret responses from the name servers that they query, regardless of whether those responses contain resource record data or error messages. Such errors may stem from any of the following causes, among others:

- Invalid domain name
- Invalid IP address
- Inability to locate an IP address that corresponds to the requested domain name
- Inability to reach an authoritative name server for the requested domain

Based on whether the response to a query is an IP address, a domain name, other RR data, or an error message, a resolver sends appropriate information to the application that requested access to a resource through a domain name. In most cases, the resolver is built right into the TCP/IP stack for whatever operating system is in use, as is the case with modern versions of Windows, including Windows 2000.

How Domain Name Servers Work

When a TCP/IP client uses a resolver to send a name query to a DNS server, that client obtains the address for the DNS server it queries from its TCP/IP configuration data. Servers are queried in the order in which they appear in TCP/IP configuration files (or related Registry entries, which is how this works in modern versions of Windows), starting from the top down. This explains why you want to vary the order in which DNS servers are listed when manually configuring clients to balance the load across multiple DNS servers. (Note that supplying one or more DNS server addresses is yet another service that DHCP performs automatically for its clients.)

The process by which the queried domain name server replies works as follows:

- DNS servers retrieve name data from the general domain namespace.

- Any given DNS server can always provide data about zones for which that server is authoritative.

- Any given DNS server can search its cached domain name data and answer queries for which that server is not authoritative, unless that query originates from a root server (which requires the authoritative DNS server for the zone in question to respond).

- When a local server does not have the information available in its database or its name cache, it may turn to a caching-only server or to other known name servers in the "neighborhood." (Here, the term *neighborhood* refers to the collection of domains for which any given server may be either a primary or a secondary master name server, or for which the addresses of caching-only servers are known.)

- If none of these searches produces a result, the name server sends a request for name resolution to a root server, which directs the query to the **authoritative server** for the database segment in question by contacting the root server for the domain, then following NS pointers until it gets to the right authoritative server. This process always produces some kind of answer (usually, it's the IP address that goes with the name that's to be resolved, but sometimes it can be an error message instead).

This process is known as **domain name resolution**, or **name resolution**. It is interesting that while resolvers issue queries, DNS servers actually handle the real name resolution part of the activity that occurs to resolve such requests.

DNS Root-level Servers

The saying among DNS aficionados is that "all name queries end at the root." That's because the root is the top of the DNS hierarchy, and it knows how to get to any subdomain in the entire hierarchy. This saying also recognizes that any name resolution requests that can't be handled locally, or in the neighborhood, must go to a root server to obtain further resolution.

7

The real process is actually a bit more complex, so first we will explain some related terminology:

- *Recursive query*: Most DNS resolvers issue what is called a **recursive query** from the client side. This means that they delegate the first DNS server that they contact to go out and find the necessary address translation (or error message) on their behalf. In computer science terms, a recursive query is a query that keeps working until an answer of some kind is forthcoming. Thus, if the first DNS server contacted can't resolve a domain name, it next asks the "closest known" name servers in its neighborhood for assistance. When other name servers respond to the first name server's queries, they either provide an answer from their own databases or caches, or provide pointers to other name servers judged to be "closer" to the domain name being sought.

The first DNS server keeps asking for information until it is found because the query is recursive. It issues iterative queries by following pointers to other name servers, which may be at higher levels within the **domain name hierarchy**, or within different subtrees of the DNS name hierarchy altogether. (For example, if a referred server recently visited the domain namespace near where the requested name resides, that server can short-circuit the process of navigating the domain namespace up the requesting server's hierarchy, through the root, and down another part of the hierarchy.) This process repeats until a definitive answer is received, a root server is contacted, or the search terminates in an error condition of some kind. (More about what happens when the search hits a root server later in this section.)

- *Iterative or non-recursive queries*: When one DNS server receives a recursive request, that DNS server issues what are called **iterative queries**, or **non-recursive queries**, to the name servers in its hierarchy, or to servers provided as pointers in reply to earlier iterative requests, until an answer is received. Iterative queries do not cause other queries to be issued, so the first DNS server can be thought of as driving the iterative query process. It navigates the name hierarchy heading for the DNS server that's authoritative for the domain in which the requested name resides, or until it gets to a server that can provide a non-authoritative reply to its query.

In other words, if a DNS server receives a recursive query, it issues iterative queries until one of two things happens: a server that it queries answers the query, or an error message, such as "unknown domain," "unknown domain name," or "invalid domain name," is returned.

From another viewpoint, the difference between a recursive query and an iterative query is that a name server that's presented with a recursive query must produce an answer of some kind, whereas a name server that's presented with an iterative query can simply reply with a pointer to another name server that may (or may not) be able to provide the information requested. You'd think that a name server handling a recursive query could issue its own recursive queries to pass responsibility for resolving the name request to another server. But in practice, only one server fields a recursive query and keeps issuing iterative queries until it gets a definitive answer of one kind (the IP address that matches the domain name) or another (an error message that explains why an IP address can't be supplied).

The reason why some recursive name queries involve a root server is not because the root servers keep all names in the entire DNS namespace close at hand. Rather, it is because a root server always knows how to find whatever DNS server is authoritative for the domain (or subdomain) where the actual data resides. Thus, if all else fails, the root can definitely help get the query resolved.

In fact, when a query arrives that the root server cannot handle from its cache, that root server launches a recursive query of its own. This query climbs down the domain namespace until it reaches the server that is authoritative for the domain requested—or the root server receives a reply that indicates that the request cannot be resolved, for whatever reason. Notice that this kind of query cannot be satisfied with a non-authoritative answer; it must make contact with the name server that's authoritative for the domain being queried. Then, the root server uses the reply to its recursive query to reply to the originating DNS server's iterative query (which, in turn, satisfies the resolver's original recursive query), and the name resolution process ends at long last.

Because the root has access to all elements in the namespace, it can get to an authoritative name server for any domain or domain segment. It does so by following the NS records in the zone databases that it traverses on its way to the DNS server that possesses the proper SOA record. In fact, that's the real explanation for the saying that all name queries end at the root.

THE IMPORTANCE OF DNS CACHING

As we mentioned, most DNS servers can store the results of previous name queries using a form of local data storage called caching. Only if the server needs to resolve a name or address that's not in the cache does it actually need to issue any further queries for name or address resolution.

Thus, the first DNS server to receive a recursive query for information outside the zones in its database first checks its cache to see if the information needed to resolve that request is already present. If it is, it grabs that data from the cache, and there's no need to launch any iterative queries to locate the requested information. Also, as iterative queries navigate the name hierarchy seeking resolution, the other name servers contacted check if they can answer the query from their caches, in addition to their zone databases. This produces a **non-authoritative response** to a name query, but can significantly speed the resolution process. However, root server requests always go to the name server that's authoritative for the domain that contains the requested name or address to make completely sure data is obtained directly from the source. That's why such a reply is called an **authoritative response**.

The value of data in a DNS cache is much like the food in your refrigerator in that such data goes stale over time. However, all data in a DNS cache has an expiration value, after which it is automatically deleted. In fact, DNS data values include all kinds of timing information, which you'll see when we examine the innards of an SOA record later in this chapter.

DNS servers cache not only name and address pairs for addresses they resolved, but they also keep information about name requests that result in error messages. This kind of information is called **negative caching**, but it achieves the same result as positive caching. That is, a negative cache value allows an error message to be accessed locally, instead of requiring that a query be issued, followed by waiting for an error message to come back on its own. Obtaining error messages from IP services often means waiting for numerous timeout intervals to expire, so this can save users lots of time!

In fact, you already know that there is a special kind of DNS server called a caching-only server. Although such special-purpose servers are not available for all DNS implementations, they are an option when configuring Windows servers for DNS. It's important to understand that the sole function of a caching-only server is to look up data outside the local zone and store those results in its cache. Over time, the value of this cache is increasingly evident because users don't have to wait for information from other servers outside the local zone to obtain results for many of their name queries.

DNS CONFIGURATION FILES AND RESOURCE RECORD FORMATS

Thinking back to the origins of DNS, it's easy to describe the contents of the database files that organize DNS data as a way of translating HOSTS file data into equivalent DNS data, then adding necessary information that DNS itself uses. This includes things such as marking sources of authority, handling mail exchange records, and providing information about well-known services.

The files that map host names to addresses are usually named *domain.dns*, in which *domain* is the local domain name or subdomain name for the zone that the DNS server covers. For example, the DNS server for *lanw.com* is named *lanw.com.dns*.

Files that map addresses to domain names for reverse lookups are usually called *addr.in-addr.arpa.dns*, in which *addr* is the network number for the domain in reverse order, without the trailing zeroes. For *lanw.com*, whose network number is 206.224.65.0, that file is named *65.224.206.in-addr.arpa.dns*. Sometimes, such files are also called *in-addr.arpa* files after the label that appears at the end of each reversed address in the files' PTR records. Note that other implementations of DNS (primarily BIND) use a different naming convention for these files, but all DNS implementations require these files to operate no matter how they're named. Essentially, these files contain a snapshot of the DNS database in static form as stored when the database is copied to disk, or before the DNS server is brought down.

Every DNS zone file must contain SOA and NS records, plus records about host names or addresses in that zone. A (address) records provide name-to-address mapping data, while PTR (pointer) records provide address-to-name mapping data. The canonical name (CNAME) records allow you to define aliases for hosts in your zone, mostly as a convenience to make entering such data inside zone files more efficient. Thus, you could define *h54.clearlake.ibm.com* as an alias for *houns54.clearlake.ibm.com*, which means typing 21 keystrokes instead of 25.

Next, you'll take a look at the data you find in the nine common DNS RR types.

Start of Authority (SOA) Record

The first entry in any DNS ....*dns* file—which means both *domain.dns* and *addr.in-addr.arpa.dns* files—must be an SOA record. The SOA record identifies the current name server (or another name server in the same domain or subdomain) as the best source of information for data in its zone. It's important to understand that even though secondary name servers obtain their data from the primary name server in a domain, both secondary and primary name servers can designate themselves as authoritative in their own SOA records. This functionality is, in fact, what allows load balancing across a primary and one or more secondary DNS servers in a domain.

Here's a sample SOA record with complete contents:

```
tree.com. IN SOA apple.tree.com. sue.pear.tree.com (
    1          ; Serial
    10800      ; Refresh after 3 hours
    3600       ; Retry after 1 hour
    604800     ; Expire after 1 week
    86400 )    ; Minimum TTL of 1 day
```

Here's a line-by-line breakdown of this record (note that each semicolon character identifies an in-line comment, which is simply documentation to help explain code to human readers):

- *tree.com. IN SOA apple.tree.com.* All DNS records follow the basic format of this line, in which *tree.com.* is the name of the domain to which the zone file applies; *IN* indicates that this record belongs to the Internet class of record types; *SOA* indicates that the type of record is a Start of Authority record; *apple.tree.com.* is the FQDN for the primary name server for the domain; and *sue.pear.tree.com* is a way of expressing the e-mail address *sue@pear.tree.com* for the administrator who's responsible for that server. Everything else that appears between the opening and closing parentheses supplies specific attributes for this particular SOA record, as noted in the next five list entries.

- *Serial*: An unsigned 32-bit number for the original value (this is what secondary name servers use to compare with the primary's value to see whether or not they need to update their records). This number is incremented each time the value is updated on the primary name server (and will therefore be copied to the secondary name servers each time they check to see if their records need to be updated).

- *Refresh*: The number of seconds that can elapse until the zone database needs to be refreshed (10,800 seconds equals three hours, hence the comment field). This guarantees that no secondary servers will ever be more than three hours out of sync with the primary master.

- *Retry:* The number of seconds that should be allowed to elapse before a failed refresh is attempted again (3600 seconds equals one hour).

- *Expire:* This specifies the number of seconds that should be allowed to elapse before the zone database is no longer authoritative. This reflects the value of a counter that allows the DNS server to calculate how long it has been since the last update occurred.

- *Minimum TTL:* This specifies how long any resource record should be allowed to persist in another non-authoritative DNS server's cache. In other words, this is the value that sets how long a cached entry can persist on DNS servers outside the zone from when the record originates (86,400 seconds is 24 hours, or one day).

This concludes our coverage of the SOA record. Next, you'll explore the A and CNAME records.

Address and Alias Records

In the example that follows, we show how A and CNAME records are used, typically in the *domain.dns* file (for example, *tree.com.dns* for *tree.com*). Then, as before, we explain examples of each record type in detail, and show how to use comments to annotate a DNS configuration file:

```
; Host addresses
localhost.tree.com.     IN A 127.0.0.1
pear.tree.com.          IN A 172.16.1.2
apple.tree.com.         IN A 172.16.1.3
peach.tree.com.         IN A 172.16.1.4
; Multi-homed host
hedge.tree.com.         IN A 172.16.1.1
hedge.tree.com.         IN A 172.16.2.1
; Aliases
pr.tree.com          IN CNAME pear.tree.com
h.tree.com           IN CNAME hedge.tree.com
a.tree.com           IN CNAME apple.tree.com
h1.tree.com          IN CNAME 172.16.1.1
h2.tree.com          IN CNAME 172.16.2.1
```

Given the foregoing text, consider the following explanations and discussion:

- *localhost.tree.com. IN A 127.0.0.1*

This sets the address for the FQDN for the domain name "localhost," which translates into *localhost.tree.com.*, equal to the loopback address. This value is required to allow users to reference the name "localhost" or "loopback" in IP commands and queries.

- *pear.tree.com. IN A 172.16.1.2*

This sets the address for the FQDN *pear.tree.com.*, equal to the IP address 172.16.1.2.

- *h1.tree.com   IN CNAME 172.16.1.1*

  h2.tree.com   IN CNAME 172.17.1.1

This technique is important because it allows individual network interfaces to be accessed by name on a router, or any other IP host that's attached to multiple subnets through multiple network interfaces. (Such devices are called **multi-homed** because they are attached to multiple subnetworks.) This can be important when querying SNMP statistics, or pinging individual interface addresses. DNS, by default, accesses only the first IP address for a host when multiple entries for a single domain name are defined (as must be the case for multi-homed devices). This technique lets you associate a name with each specific interface, rather than having to remember its individual numeric IP address.

Note also that the CNAME record lists the alias first and the true domain name second, and neither domain name ends in a period (and thus is not a true FQDN; those exist in the A and PTR records).

Mapping Addresses to Names

The records in the *db.addr* file are provided to support reverse DNS lookups (in which you begin with an IP address and want to know the domain name that goes with it). For this reason, the order of the octets in the address portions for individual names in the record is reversed. In other words, just as you start with the name that's lowest in the domain name hierarchy when stipulating a domain name, you start at the "back" of the IP address (the fourth octet) and work your way up to the "front" of the address (the first octet). Thus, the hierarchical organization of domain names is matched by a corresponding hierarchical organization for IP addresses, starting from the host portion and working into the network portion, in reverse order.

Reverse address lookups are used primarily to determine if the IP address that a user presents matches the domain name from which the user claims to originate. (When those fail to match, this can be a sign of an impersonation attempt, sometimes called **IP spoofing**—a packet claims to originate on some network other than its true address.) This functionality is built into many UNIX applications, such as rlogin, and several OS vendors actually include a reverse lookup in their resolvers.

Here's a sample of a file named *16.172.in-addr.arpa.dns*. (Notice how they match the addresses from the earlier *tree.com.dns* file, in reverse order. Note also how each reversed address ends with the string *.in-addr-arpa.*, including a period on the end. That's because all these addresses are in the IP address space defined for the Internet, originally known as the ARPANET):

```
1.1.16.172.in-addr-arpa. IN PTR hedge.tree.com
2.1.16.172.in-addr-arpa. IN PTR pear.tree.com
3.1.16.172.in-addr.arpa. IN PTR apple.tree.com
4.1.16.172 in-addr.arpa. IN PTR peach.tree.com
```

There's a direct correspondence between the addresses on the left side and the domain names on the right side. If you want to specify the other interface for *hedge* (the 172.17.1.1 address mentioned in the earlier file), you must do that in the file named *17.172.in-addr.arpa.dns*, not here. Each subnet gets its own such file.

There is one more caveat when dealing with reverse DNS lookups, and that is that the file structure above is classful. DNS can become quite confused if your network is not organized neatly in /8, /16, or /24 subnets. If you need to configure reverse lookups for a classless network, you should read the proposed solution in RFC 2317.

Handling the Loopback Address

You must create a separate *db.127.0.0* file to handle the reserved IP loopback address for individual machines that allows them to point to themselves for purely local IP stack testing. Here's what the whole thing must look like:

```
0.0.127.in-addr-arpa.    IN SOA apple.tree.com.
   sue.pear.tree.com (
   1        ; Serial
   10800    ; Refresh after 3 hours
   3600     ; Retry after 1 hour
   604800   ; Expire after 1 week
   86400 )  ; Minimum TTL of 1 day
0.0.127.in-addr-arpa.    IN NS apple.tree.com
0.0.127.in-addr-arpa.    IN NS hedge.tree.com
1.0.0.127.in-addr-arpa.  IN PTR localhost
```

This file begins with the required SOA record, which indicates that *apple.tree.com* is authoritative for network 127.0.0. It then provides NS records that indicate that both the *apple.tree.com* machine and the *hedge.tree.com* machine can provide NS lookups for the loopback address. It concludes with a PTR record that indicates that the default loopback host address—namely 127.0.0.1—corresponds to the current value of *localhost* on whatever machine might be in use. This is what allows users to make use of either the loopback address (127.0.0.1) or the symbolic name (*localhost*) when testing their local machines. Thus, the loopback file, *0.0.127.in-addr.arpa.dns,* is short and sweet, and easy to present in its entirety. Even better, Windows DNS implementation creates this file for you as part of its automatically created zones facility.

Obtaining and Storing Root Server Data

By now, it should be obvious that knowing how to access the DNS root servers is important for any name server. That's why DNS implementations make it possible to pre-load the name-and-address information for these all-important records into the cache on just about any DNS server. To obtain this file, visit the InterNIC's FTP server at *ftp.rs.internic.net* and look in the /domain subdirectory for a file called *named.root*.

On a Windows server running DNS, you must copy this file to a directory named %SystemRoot%\System32\DNS directory.

Next, you must rename the file to *cache.dns*. Note that %SystemRoot% is a pre-defined environment variable that points to the system directory where Windows stores system files. By default, this is C:\WINNT\ on most systems. Because this part of the directory specification can vary, a symbol is used to produce the required results no matter how a system is configured during setup.

Let's take a look at the header and a couple of records from this file (the <SNIP> comment indicates where we removed certain lines from the file that are not germane to this discussion):

```
;     This file contains root name server info needed to
;     initialize the cache on Internet name servers
;     <SNIP>
;
;     last update:    Aug 22, 1997
;     related version of root zone:   1997082200
;
;
; formerly NS.INTERNIC.NET
;
.                         3600000 IN NS  A.ROOT-SERVERS.NET.
A.ROOT-SERVERS.NET.       3600000    A   198.41.0.4
;
; formerly NS1.ISI.EDU
;
.                         3600000    NS  B.ROOT-SERVERS.NET.
B.ROOT-SERVERS.NET.       3600000    A   128.9.0.107
;
; formerly C.PSI.NET
;<SNIP>
```

Notice that there's no domain name on the far left side. The period there indicates that this is a root server, in the context of an NS record that identifies a DNS name server. The domain name for each server takes the form *.ROOT-SERVERS.NET., in which * is a letter from A through M. Each NS record is followed by an A record that gives the IP address that corresponds to the server just named, so that *A.ROOT-SERVERS.NET.* corresponds to IP address 198.41.0.4.

There's a good reason for caching multiple root server addresses on any DNS server. If any particular root server is unavailable, the next entry in the list is used once the root server's lookup times out. Because you can't do without occasional access to a root server, access to multiple root servers is a good thing (and it provides load-balancing capabilities too).

THE **NSLOOKUP** COMMAND

Both Windows and UNIX, among other operating systems, include support for this versatile command-line tool, which offers general name server lookup capabilities. (The NS in NSLOOKUP comes from the abbreviation for name server information in any NS record in a DNS database.) By default, **NSLOOKUP** queries the default name server specified in the current machine's TCP/IP configuration. (The configuration is located in the Internet Protocol (TCP/IP) Properties window from within the TCP/IP entry on the Local Connection Properties window, available through Start, Settings, Network and Dial-up Connections).

The NSLOOKUP command provides access to all kinds of DNS information, either from the current default server, or from a server whose name or IP address you provide as an argument to this command. It is an essential tool for testing when configuring or troubleshooting a DNS server.

The syntax for NSLOOKUP takes the form:

```
nslookup domain-name [name-server]
```

in which *domain-name* is the domain name to be looked up, and [*name-server*] is the name server on which to look it up. Here, the use of square brackets indicates that the *name-server* argument is optional because NSLOOKUP uses the default name server if no alternate server is specified. Two examples appear in Figure 7-2; the first uses the default, and the second uses an authoritative name server for the domain specified. (Note the differences in output.)

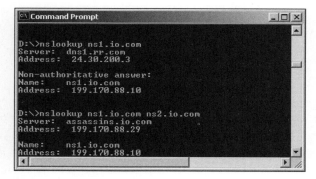

Figure 7-2 Two examples of NSLOOKUP (non-authoritative [default] and authoritative name servers)

Note that the default name server in the first command is identified as *dns1.rr.com,* and provides a "Non-authoritative answer" label before showing a name and address for *ns1.io.com.* In the second command, another name server, *ns2.io.com* at the *io.com* domain, is referenced and shows the name and address without the "Non-authoritative answer" label.

This slight difference is the only way you can tell when a name server is authoritative for a particular domain name (and it depends on what it *doesn't* tell you). Note also that in each response, the name and IP address of the name server where the lookup occurred appear first, and the results of the lookup appear second.

NSLOOKUP Details

To display the help screen for NSLOOKUP, type NSLOOKUP on the command line in the Command Prompt window with no arguments. (To open this window, select Start, Programs, Accessories, Command Prompt). This puts the NSLOOKUP utility in charge of the command line, as signaled by the > prompt that appears instead of the more usual D:\> prompt on the preceding line. At that point, you can enter the string *help*, and the screen shown in Figure 7-3 appears.

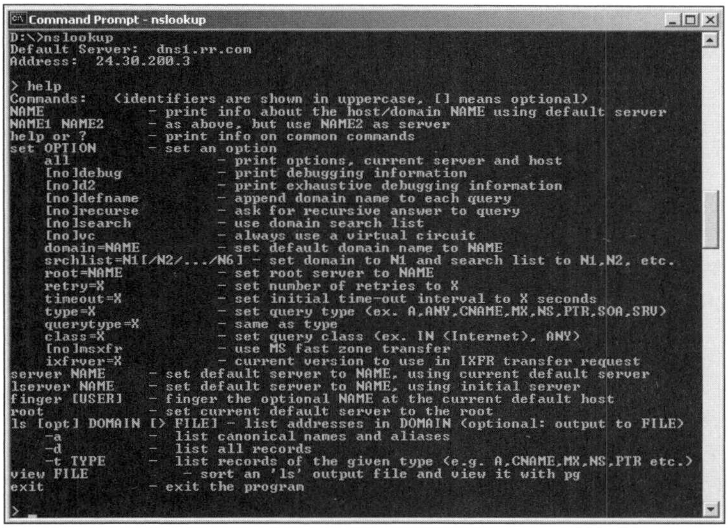
```
Command Prompt - nslookup
D:\>nslookup
Default Server:  dns1.rr.com
Address:  24.30.200.3

> help
Commands:   (identifiers are shown in uppercase, [] means optional)
NAME            - print info about the host/domain NAME using default server
NAME1 NAME2     - as above, but use NAME2 as server
help or ?       - print info on common commands
set OPTION      - set an option
    all                 - print options, current server and host
    [no]debug           - print debugging information
    [no]d2              - print exhaustive debugging information
    [no]defname         - append domain name to each query
    [no]recurse         - ask for recursive answer to query
    [no]search          - use domain search list
    [no]vc              - always use a virtual circuit
    domain=NAME         - set default domain name to NAME
    srchlist=N1[/N2/.../N6] - set domain to N1 and search list to N1,N2, etc.
    root=NAME           - set root server to NAME
    retry=X             - set number of retries to X
    timeout=X           - set initial time-out interval to X seconds
    type=X              - set query type (ex. A,ANY,CNAME,MX,NS,PTR,SOA,SRV)
    querytype=X         - same as type
    class=X             - set query class (ex. IN (Internet), ANY)
    [no]msxfr           - use MS fast zone transfer
    ixfrver=X           - current version to use in IXFR transfer request
server NAME     - set default server to NAME, using current default server
lserver NAME    - set default server to NAME, using initial server
finger [USER]   - finger the optional NAME at the current default host
root            - set current default server to the root
ls [opt] DOMAIN [> FILE] - list addresses in DOMAIN (optional: output to FILE)
    -a          -  list canonical names and aliases
    -d          -  list all records
    -t TYPE     -  list records of the given type (e.g. A,CNAME,MX,NS,PTR etc.)
view FILE           - sort an 'ls' output file and view it with pg
exit            - exit the program

>
```

Figure 7-3 NSLOOKUP help screen explains this command's many subcommands and options

As you can see, there are many things you can do with the NSLOOKUP command. In the section that follows, we explore a few of the more common uses for the NSLOOKUP command.

Using NSLOOKUP

You already know how to identify your default domain name server. (Simply enter the NSLOOKUP command with no arguments, as indicated at the top of the Command Prompt window shown in Figure 7-3.) Once you enter NSLOOKUP's command mode (symbolized by the > prompt), you can use the set OPTION command to examine specific types of resource records. In Figure 7-4, we show what happens when you set the type of record reported to NS (name server)—it shows all NS records in the DNS database for that domain.

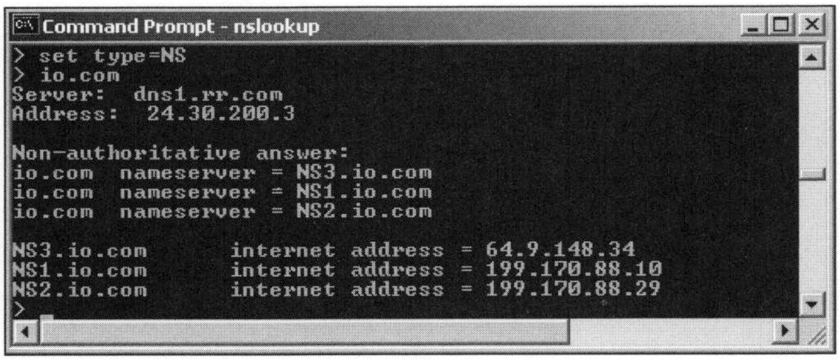

Figure 7-4 Examining *io.com's* NS records using the NSLOOKUP command

Notice that the lookup still uses the default name server (*dns1.rr.com*) to look up this information. That's because we didn't specify a different name server as a second argument on the *io.com* command line. To learn how to fully use NSLOOKUP, please try the various record types and perform lookups yourself.

You might be tempted to extract information from certain well-known name servers. In particular, you might try running the *ls -a* (list canonical names and aliases) or *ls -d* (list all records) commands. Although you may get the occasional name server to cooperate, in most cases you should see output that looks like the information shown in Figure 7-5.

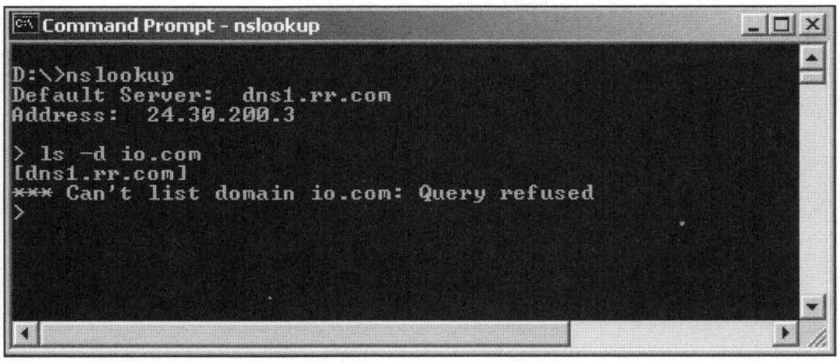

Figure 7-5 When permission is lacking, you get error messages, not answers

If you think about the notion of managing IP security as in part protecting your addresses and resources, you should understand that there's a very good reason why most name servers don't provide this kind of information to anyone except a privileged few administrators. That's because showing this kind of data to random outsiders gives them a perfect map of the IP addresses and domain names used within the DNS zone, for which the server contains the database segment. That's just what hackers need to mount an informed attack on a network, and that's why you won't be able to access that information on any

DNS servers except those you administer yourself. In fact, most sites refuse such requests and any DNS update records from all requesters (deny by default), except for a select group of IP addresses for "trusted hosts" or "trusted users" (allow by exception).

Should you ever be required to manage a DNS server, make sure you thoroughly explore the NSLOOKUP command. Properly used, NSLOOKUP can be an invaluable troubleshooting tool. In the next sections of this chapter, we examine typical packet traces for DNS traffic on the network. This gives you the chance to see how some of the mechanisms we explained in this chapter actually work.

DNS QUERY/RESPONSE PACKET FORMATS

DNS queries use the packet structure shown in Figure 7-6.

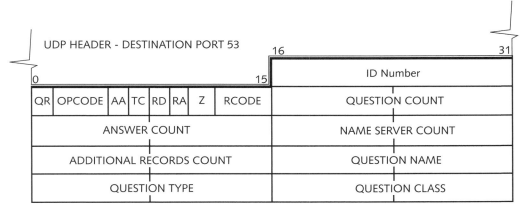

Figure 7-6   Standard DNS query format

DNS response packets include the original question as well as the reply. There are four sections in the DNS response packets:

- *Question section*: This section includes the name that is being resolved.

- *Answer section*: This section includes RRs that answer the question.

- *Authority section*: This section includes RRs that point to an authority.

- *Additional section*: This section includes RRs with additional information relating to the question.

The answer, authority, and additional sections follow the question section, and use the same structure (highlighted in Figure 7-7).

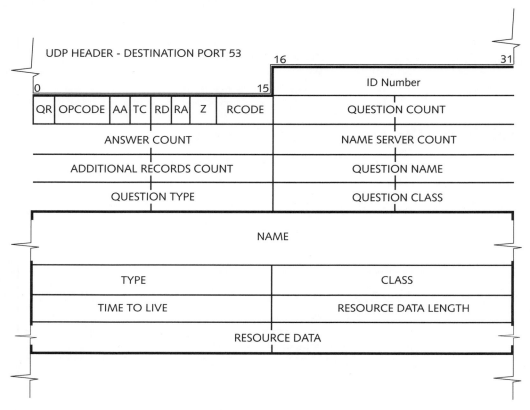

Figure 7-7   DNS responses include the question in the reply

In the next section, we look at each field in a DNS query packet.

ID Number Field

The 2-byte ID Number field is used to associate DNS queries with their responses.

QR (Query/Response) Field

This 1-bit field indicates whether this is a DNS query (set to zero) or a DNS response (set to one).

Opcode (Operation Code) Field

This 4-bit field defines the type of query that is contained in this message. Table 7-1 lists the values that are supported in this field.

Table 7-1 Opcode Field Values

Opcode	Definition	Reference
0	Standard DNS query	
1	Inverse DNS query	
2	Server status request	
3	Reserved	IANA
4	Notify	RFC 1996
5	Update	RFC 2136
6–15	Available for assignment	

For the latest list of assigned Opcode values, refer to *http://www.iana.org*.

AA (Authoritative Answer) Field

This bit is only valid in responses. If set, this bit indicates that the responding name server is the authority for the domain name that is defined in the Question Name field.

TC (Truncation) Field

This is typically seen only in responses. This bit indicates that the response was truncated because it was too large to fit in the data portion of the packet. For example, if a response contains numerous name servers, the packet may exceed the allowable MTU. In this case, the packet will be truncated and the TC field bit is set to one.

RD (Recursion Desired) Field

This bit indicates that the client requests a recursive query if the target name server does not contain the information requested.

RA (Recursion Available) Field

This bit is valid in the response, and indicates whether the responding name server supports recursive queries.

Z (Reserved) Field

Although RFC 1035 defines this field as "reserved" and states that the field should be set to all zeroes, some DNS advancements extended the Rcode field into the Reserved field area. In effect, this removes the Reserved field and extends the Rcode field to seven bits in length.

Rcode (Response Code) Field

This 4-bit field is used in DNS responses to indicate if any errors occurred. Table 7-2 indicates the values that are supported in this field.

Table 7-2   Response Code Field Values

RCODE	Description	Reference
0	No error	RFC 1035
1	Format error	RFC 1035
2	Server failure	RFC 1035
3	Non-existent domain	RFC 1035
4	Not implemented	RFC 1035
5	Query refused	RFC 1035
6	Name exists when it should not	RFC 2136
7	RR set exists when it should not	RFC 2136
8	RR set that should exist does not	RFC 2136
9	Server not authoritative for zone	RFC 2136
10	Name not contained in zone	RFC 2136
11–15	Available for assignment	
16	Bad OPT version or TSIG signature failure	RFC 2671, RFC 2845
17	Key not recognized	RFC 2845
18	Signature out of time window	RFC 2845
19	Bad TKEY mode	RFC 2930
20	Duplicate key name	RFC 2930
21	Algorithm not supported	RFC 2930
22–3840	Available for assignment	
3841–4095	Private use	

For the latest list of assigned Rcode values, refer to *http://www.iana.org*.

Question Count Field

This field indicates the number of entries contained in the question section.

Answer Count Field

This field indicates the number of RRs contained in the answer section.

Name Server Count Field

This field indicates the number of name server RRs in the authority records section.

Additional Records Field

This field indicates the number of other RRs contained in the additional records section.

Question Name Field

This variable-length field consists of a series of length fields followed by some octets of data. For example, Figure 7–8 shows how the URL *http://www.iana.org* would be defined in the Question Name field.

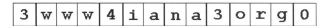

| 3 | w | w | w | 4 | i | a | n | a | 3 | o | r | g | 0 |

Figure 7-8   Numerical delimiters indicate the number of alphanumeric bytes

Question Type Field

This 2–byte field indicates the type of the query. The values possible are defined in Table 7–3.

Table 7-3   Question Type Values

Type	Value	Description	Reference
A	1	Host address	RFC 1035
NS	2	Authoritative name server	RFC 1035
MD	3	Mail destination (obsolete—use MX)	RFC 1035
MF	4	A mail forwarder (obsolete—use MX)	RFC 1035
CNAME	5	Canonical name for an alias	RFC 1035
SOA	6	Marks the start of a zone of authority	RFC 1035
MB	7	Mailbox domain name (EXPERIMENTAL)	RFC 1035
MG	8	Mail group member (EXPERIMENTAL)	RFC 1035
MR	9	Mail rename domain name (EXPERIMENTAL)	RFC 1035
NULL	10	Null RR (EXPERIMENTAL)	RFC 1035
WKS	11	Well-known service description	RFC 1035
PTR	12	Domain name pointer	RFC 1035
HINFO	13	Host information	RFC 1035
MINFO	14	Mailbox or mail list information	RFC 1035
MX	15	Mail exchange	RFC 1035
TXT	16	Text strings	RFC 1035

7

Table 7-3 Question Type Values (continued)

Type	Value	Description	Reference
RP	17	Responsible person	RFC 1183
AFSDB	18	AFS Data base location	RFC 1183
X25	19	X.25 PSDN address	RFC 1183
ISDN	20	ISDN address	RFC 1183
RT	21	Route through	RFC 1183
NSAP	22	NSAP address, NSAP style A record	RFC 1706
NSAP-PTR	23	NSAP pointer RR	
SIG	24	Security signature	RFC 2535
KEY	25	Security key	RFC 2535
PX	26	X.400 mail mapping information	RFC 2163
GPOS	27	Geographical position	RFC 1712
AAAA	28	IP6 address	Thomson
LOC	29	Location information	Vixie
NXT	30	Next domain	RFC 2535
EID	31	Endpoint identifier	Patton
NIMLOC	32	Nimrod locator	Patton
SRV	33	Server selection	RFC 2782
ATMA	34	ATM address	Dobrowski
NAPTR	35	Naming authority pointer	RFC 2168, RFC 2915
KX	36	Key exchanger	RFC 2230
CERT	37	CERT	RFC 2538
A6	38	A6	RFC 2874
DNAME	39	DNAME	RFC 2672
SINK	40	SINK	Eastlake
OPT	41	OPT	RFC 2671
UINFO	100	IANA-Reserved	
UID	101	IANA-Reserved	
GID	102	IANA-Reserved	
UNSPEC	103	IANA-Reserved	
TKEY	249	Transaction key	RFC 2930
TSIG	250	Transaction signature	RFC 2845
IXFR	251	Incremental transfer	RFC 1995
AXFR	252	Transfer of an entire zone	RFC 1035
MAILB	253	Mailbox-related RRs (MB, MG, or MR)	RFC 1035
MAILA	254	Mail agent RRs (obsolete—see MX)	RFC 1035
	255	Request for all records	RFC 1035

As you can see, there are many more types of resource records available to DNS than those we covered earlier in this chapter. But, you're also most likely to encounter those we discussed. Many of the other RR types are seldom used, if ever.

Question Class Field

This 2-byte field indicates the class for the query. The value one indicates Internet class.

Name Field

This field contains the domain name to which this RR belongs. Interestingly, DNS uses a compression technique that eliminates the repetition of a domain name within the DNS response. This field may contain a pointer to another location in the DNS packet that contains the domain name. For example, Figure 7-9 depicts a DNS response with the Name field highlighted.

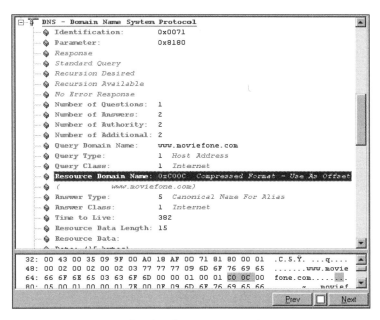

Figure 7-9   To avoid redundancy, DNS replies can contain a pointer to a name rather than repeat it

When compression is used, the leading bits in this field must be 11 (binary). This value is followed by an offset that indicates where the full domain name is located. In Figure 7-9, the value 0xC00C (in binary, that's 11000000-00001100) indicates that this is a pointer to a field that is located at Offset 12 from the start of the DNS portion of the packet. The name *www.moviefone.com* is located at Offset 12.

Type Field

This 2-byte type field is the RR type code for data contained in the Resource Data field of the response. This field can use the same values referred to in Table 7-3.

Class Field

This 2-byte field specifies the class of the data contained in the Resource Data field.

Time to Live Field

This 4-byte field indicates how long the data contained in the Resource Data field should be cached before it is discarded. If this field contains a zero, the resource data can be used once, but should not be cached.

Resource Data Length Field

This 2-byte field indicates the length of the Resource Data field. While this effectively limits the length of the resource data to 65,535 bytes, that's not normally a problem, given that the vast majority of RR data is less than 500 bytes in length.

Resource Data Field

This variable-length field contains the resource information itself, and in some ways may be said to contain the real "payload" of the RR. This is not to say that the other fields aren't important, however.

Now that you've had a chance to inspect the structure and layout of DNS packets, and the resource records they contain, it's easy to see that a relatively simple structure is able to convey powerful and useful information. Also, when zone transfers or other kinds of DNS database updates occur, they take the form of packets that transfer records one at a time. This simple, but elegant, design allows queries and database activity to use the same message types without compromising the integrity of the underlying information.

DNS IMPLEMENTATION

DNS implementations in the real world have two major purposes. One is providing name resolution to your users so they can reach the services provided by the rest of the world, and the other is providing the authoritative hostname-to-IP mapping so that the rest of the world can reach any services you choose to provide, such as a Web server, e-mail server, and perhaps an FTP server. Although these services operate identically from a mechanical perspective, their administration is often quite different.

The primary reason for this is that the commercial tools used to provide DNS resolution to the rest of the world focus on high availability and capacity for a relatively small number of hostname-to-IP mappings. These mappings are typically fairly stable because they use registered Internet addresses, although the products often have features that allow DNS to be used for load balancing both between local servers and geographically distributed servers. DNS servers for internal use usually focus on alleviating administration hassles by leveraging DHCP, WINS, Active Directory, or other LDAP services, to keep track of the highly volatile private IP address space, where users are constantly changing.

Another important difference is the way these systems are named. For ease of manageability, many administrators give workstations names that include the name of the user or department. For instance, the computer name (which is actually the NetBIOS name) on a Windows computer may be *jsmith*, or *jsmith-acct*, for John Smith in the Accounting Department. This information may be automatically given to DNS so that the DNS system creates an A record for *jsmith-acct.ny.mycompany.com*. It is also common practice to descriptively name servers. Obviously, you wouldn't want this information available to everyone on the Internet. For security reasons, consider separating your internal and external DNS servers.

7

THE TROUBLE WITH DNS

Despite DNS' stout capabilities and its many advantages, it does suffer from some short-comings. Chief among these is that DNS database updates normally require that a qualified administrator—one with the proper knowledge and necessary access rights to the zone files—operate directly on the DNS database files, or use special-purpose tools (such as NSUPDATE in the UNIX environment) to make changes. The requirement that DNS databases be edited makes it a chore to manage updates. With the introduction of Windows 2000, Microsoft introduced an implementation of Dynamic DNS (DDNS), but it requires that a Windows DNS implementation be linked to an Active Directory database to work (with DHCP also communicating with Active Directory).

In essence, this requires no changes to DNS itself, beyond the link to Active Directory. Active Directory actually tracks domain name-to-address relationships as they change over time, with the help of DHCP, and submits necessary update requests to the DNS server when such changes occur. In essence, Active Directory is automating what a DNS administrator would have to do manually. This implementation currently works only with Microsoft operating systems. More standard DDNS implementations use a dynamic update facility described in RFC 2136, but are not currently interoperable with the Microsoft DNS implementation included with Windows 2000. Even with these improvements to DNS, direct interaction with DNS zone files is still sometimes required, whether it be through editing zone files in an ASCII editor, using a command-line tool such as NSUPDATE, or by using a GUI interface, as in the Windows implementation.

Another problem to which DNS falls prey might be called "propagation delay," which relates to the amount of time it takes for cached values to catch up with changes to authoritative databases once changes are made to those "master copies" of DNS records. This explains why service providers routinely warn their customers that it might take as long as three days for a name-to-address translation to become completely effective on the Internet, as when transferring a domain name from one provider to another (which invariably means changing the underlying IP address associated with that domain name).

This delay results from the effect of the Time to Live (TTL) value associated with a database entry, which may persist beyond its actual valid life when changes occur. Assume that the prior version of the changed record was read from the database one second before the update occurred. If the standard default TTL remains unchanged at 24 hours, this means the TTL persists for 23 hours, 59 minutes, and 59 seconds past the time when that value changes. Additional copies of that value from another cache can add as much as another 24 hours to that value. Then too, some servers set TTL values for longer periods, and thereby extend the window when an incorrect value appears current following a change. The upshot is that it might conceivably take as long as three days for old values to disappear from caches on the Internet, thereby allowing the new value to operate free of outdated competition, as it were. However, two days is a more typical upper bound for this phenomenon.

Despite issues with DDNS behavior—DNS versions that don't interoperate, and delays before updated values take effect in the global DNS database—the system remains an important and vital component of the Internet infrastructure. Because DNS is such a vast subject, we feel compelled to leave you with some pointers to additional reading should you wish to further investigate this topic:

- Jeffrey Graham, et al.: *Windows 2000 DNS*, New Riders, Indianapolis, IN, copyright 2000, ISBN: 0-7357-0973-4. Good coverage of Windows 2000–based DNS services, with related design, implementation, configuration, and troubleshooting information

- William Wong: *Windows 2000 DNS Server*, Osborne/McGraw-Hill, Berkeley, CA, copyright 2000, ISBN: 0-07-212432-6. Similar topics and coverage as the Graham book

- Cricket Liu, et al.: *DNS and BIND, 3rd Edition*, O'Reilly & Associates, Sebastopol, CA, copyright 1998, ISBN: 1-56592-512-2. Widely regarded as one of the best books on DNS, its focus on BIND helps put the Windows implementation into perspective, and it includes coverage of design principles and inner workings, unavailable elsewhere.

- Craig Hunt: *Linux DNS Server Administration*, Sybex Books, Alameda, CA, copyright 2000, ISBN: 0-7821-2736-3. Hunt has been a noted expert on TCP/IP administration, operation, and troubleshooting for years; this book offers information and advice on how to design and set up Linux DNS servers, as well as great coverage of DNS message layouts and their behavior.

CHAPTER SUMMARY

❑ Because it provides the essential way to get from a symbolic, human-readable domain name for an Internet location to a corresponding numeric, machine-readable IP address, the Domain Name System provides the key address resolution service that makes today's Internet possible. It's almost impossible to overstate the importance of this service to the proper functioning of any large-scale TCP/IP-based internetwork.

❑ The impetus for DNS arose from the difficulty of maintaining static HOSTS files for computers on the ARPANET after the number of hosts climbed into the thousands. DNS was designed to create a flexible, reliable, and robust name and address resolution service that could scale to handle very large address spaces. Its designers succeeded more than they ever could have imagined.

❑ DNS name servers come in multiple varieties. For each zone, a primary name server is mandatory; it contains the master copy of the database for its zone. For each zone, one or more secondary name servers may be created. (At least one secondary is recommended for every zone to ensure improved reliability.) For large or heavily trafficked networks, caching-only name servers offload the task of resolving names and addresses outside the local zones for users, thereby freeing up the primary and secondary name servers for the zone to handle external incoming name resolution requests.

❑ DNS maintains its data on a large collection of name servers around the Internet by carving the domain namespace into a disjoint collection of domain or subdomain databases, also known as database segments, or database zones, each of which belongs to a single authoritative name server for that zone. This permits database segments to be controlled locally, yet available globally. The DNS design also includes provisions for a primary master name server and one or more secondary master name servers for each database zone to help improve reliability (if one DNS server fails, the others continue to function) and availability (proper configuration will balance query loads against all name servers for a zone, not just the primary).

❑ DNS databases consist of a collection of resource records (RRs), in which such databases consist of a collection of zone files that represents a static snapshot of those databases. Every zone file must include a Start of Authority (SOA) record to identify the name server that's primarily responsible for the database segments it manages. Other records in each zone file correspond to its function, and may contain address-to-name mappings for normal domain name resolution, or name-to-address mapping for inverse or reverse DNS lookups.

❑ DNS clients rely on a software component called a resolver to interact with an available DNS server for name resolution services. Resolvers issue recursive queries that go to a designated DNS server, which either answers that query itself, or queries other name servers until an answer is forthcoming. Ordinary DNS servers will accept either authoritative or non-authoritative replies to their queries, but root DNS servers accept only authoritative replies to ensure the validity of the data they supply to DNS servers lower in the domain name hierarchy.

7

❐ DNS packet structures incorporate type information that identifies the kind of RR being carried, and that otherwise describes the record's contents and validity. Understanding DNS Application layer packet structures makes it much easier to appreciate DNS' simplicity and elegance.

KEY TERMS

address (A) record — A DNS resource record that maps domain names to IP addresses.

address request — A DNS service request for an IP address that matches a domain name.

authoritative response — A reply to a query from the name server that's authoritative for the zone in which the requested name or address resides.

authoritative server — The DNS server that's responsible for one or more particular zones in the DNS database environment.

available — The quality of quickly responding to user requests for service. DNS supports use of multiple name servers and caching to increase the accessibility of database data; careful configuration of DNS clients allows them to spread their requests evenly over multiple servers, thereby balancing the processing load. This makes DNS inherently available to its users.

Berkeley Internet Name Domain (BIND) — BIND is the most popular implementation of DNS server software on the Internet today. Originally introduced as part of BSD UNIX 4.3, today there are BIND implementations available for nearly every computing platform, including Windows NT and Windows 2000.

caching — Storing remote information locally once obtained so that if it is needed again it may be accessed much more quickly. Both DNS resolvers (clients) and DNS servers cache DNS data to lower the odds that a remote query will have to be resolved.

caching server — A DNS server that stores valid name and address pairs already looked up, along with invalid names and addresses already detected. Any DNS server can cache data, including primary, secondary, and caching-only DNS servers.

caching-only server — A DNS server that does not have primary or secondary zone database responsibilities, this type of server is used only to cache already-resolved domain names and addresses, and related error information.

canonical name (CNAME) record — The DNS RR used to define database aliases, primarily to make it quicker and easier to edit and manage DNS zone files.

database segment — *See* DNS database segment.

delegation of authority — The principle whereby one name server designates another name server to handle some or all of the zone files for the domain or subdomains under its purview. The DNS NS resource record provides the pointer mechanism that name servers use to delegate authority.

distributed database technology — A database that's managed by multiple database servers, each of which has responsibility for some distinct portion of a global database. As such, DNS is a nonpareil in its effective use of distributed database technology.

DNS database segment — A distinct and autonomous subset of data from the DNS name and address hierarchy. A DNS database segment usually corresponds to a DNS database zone, and is stored in a collection of interrelated zone files. *See also* zone and zone file.

domain name hierarchy — The entire global namespace for the domain names that DNS manages on the Internet. This space includes all registered and active (and therefore, valid and usable) domain names.

domain name resolution — The process whereby DNS translates a domain name into a corresponding numeric IP address.

fully qualified domain name (FQDN) — A special form of a domain name that ends with a period to indicate the root of the domain name hierarchy. You must use FQDNs in DNS A and PTR resource records.

host information (HINFO) record — A DNS resource record that provides information about some specific host, as specified by its domain name.

HOSTS — A special text file that lists known domain names and corresponding IP addresses, thereby defining a static method for domain name resolution. Until DNS was implemented, HOSTS files provided the sole means for name resolution on the precursor to the Internet, the ARPANET.

inverse DNS query — A DNS query that supplies an IP address for conversion to a corresponding domain name. Inverse DNS queries are often used to double-check user identities to make sure that the domain names they present match the IP addresses in their packet headers. *See also* IP spoofing and spoofing.

IP spoofing — A technique whereby a programmer constructs an IP packet that presents domain name credentials that differ from the IP address in the packet header. IP spoofing is often used in illicit network break-in attempts, or to impersonate users or packet origination. *See also* spoofing.

iterative query — A DNS query that targets one specific DNS server, and terminates with whatever response may be forthcoming, whether that response is a definite answer, an error message, a null (no information) reply, or a pointer to another name server.

mail exchange (MX) record — A DNS resource record that's used to identify the domain name for the e-mail server that handles any particular domain or subdomain, or that's used to route e-mail traffic from one e-mail server to another while e-mail is in transit from sender to receiver.

master server — *See* primary DNS server.

multi-homed — Containing multiple network interfaces capable of attaching to multiple subnets.

name query — An inverse DNS query that seeks to obtain a domain name for a corresponding numeric IP address.

name resolution — *See* domain name resolution.

name resolver — A client-side software component, usually part of a TCP/IP stack implementation, that's responsible for issuing DNS queries for applications, and relaying whatever responses come back to those applications.

name server (NS) record — The DNS resource record that identifies name servers that are authoritative for some particular domain or subdomain. Often used as a mechanism to delegate authority for DNS subdomains downward in the domain name hierarchy.

negative caching — A technique for storing error messages in a local cache so that repeating a query that previously produced an error message can be satisfied more quickly than if that query was forwarded to some other DNS name server.

non-authoritative response — Name, address, or RR information from a DNS server that's not authoritative for the DNS zone being queried (such responses originate from caches on such servers).

non-recursive query — *See* iterative query.

NSLOOKUP — A widely implemented command-line program that supports DNS lookup and reporting capabilities. The "ns" in this command name stands for "name server," so it's reasonable to think of this as a general-purpose name server lookup tool.

pointer (PTR) record — The DNS resource record that's used for inverse lookups to map numeric IP addresses to domain names.

primary DNS server — The name server that's authoritative for some particular domain or subdomain, and has primary custody over the DNS database segment (and related zone files) for that domain or subdomain.

primary master — *See* primary DNS server.

recursive query — A type of DNS query that continues until a definitive answer is forthcoming, be it a name-address translation, contents of the requested resource record(s), or an error message of some kind. Clients issue recursive queries to their designated name servers, which issue iterative queries to other name servers until the initial recursive request is resolved.

resolver — *See* name resolver.

resource record (RR) — One of a series of pre-defined record types in a DNS database or a DNS zone file.

reverse DNS lookup — *See* inverse DNS query.

robust — The condition of being ready for use under almost any circumstances; DNS allows multiple name servers to respond to queries about the same database zone to improve the odds that at least one such server will be able to respond to such queries. That's why most DNS experts recommend that there be at least one secondary DNS server for each zone, as well as the primary DNS server that's mandatory for every zone. Access to redundant copies of DNS database data is what makes DNS inherently robust.

root — The highest level in the domain name hierarchy, the root is symbolized by a final period in a fully qualified domain name. Root DNS servers provide the glue that ties together all the disparate parts of the domain name hierarchy, and name resolution for queries that might otherwise go unresolved.

secondary DNS server — A DNS server that contains a copy of a domain or subdomain database, along with copies of the related zone files, but which must synchronize its database and related files with whatever server is primary for that domain or subdomain.

secondary master — *See* secondary DNS server.

slave server — *See* secondary DNS server.

spoofing — Spoofing occurs when incoming IP traffic exhibits addressing mismatches. Address spoofing occurs when an external interface ferries traffic that purports to originate inside a network, or when a user presents an IP address that doesn't match a domain name. Domain name spoofing occurs when a reverse lookup of an IP address does not match the domain where the traffic claims to originate.

Start of Authority (SOA) record — The DNS resource record that's mandatory in every DNS zone file, the SOA record identifies the server or servers that are authoritative for the domain or subdomain to which the zone files or database correspond.

subdomain — A named element within a specific domain name, denoted by adding an additional name and period before the parent domain name. Thus, *clearlake.ibm.com* is a subdomain of the *ibm.com* domain.

text (TXT) record — A DNS resource record that can accommodate arbitrary ASCII text data, often used to describe a DNS database segment, the hosts it contains, and so forth.

tree structure — A type of data structure that's organized, such as a taxonomy or a disk drive listing, in which the entire container acts as the root, and subcontainers may include either other, lower-level subcontainers, or instances of whatever kinds of objects may occur within a container. The domain name hierarchy adheres to an inverted tree structure because the root usually appears at the top of diagrams drawn to represent it.

well-known services (WKS) record — A DNS resource record that describes the well-known IP services available from a host, such as Telnet, FTP, and so forth. WKS records are less available to outsiders than they once were because they identify hosts that could become points of potential attack.

zone — A portion of the domain name hierarchy that corresponds to the database segment managed by some particular name server, or collection of name servers.

zone data file — Any of several specific files used to capture DNS database information for static storage when a DNS server is shut down, or when a secondary DNS server requests synchronization with its primary DNS server's database.

zone file — *See* zone data file.

7

Review Questions

1. What method of name resolution was used on the Internet prior to the introduction of DNS?
   a. dynamic name resolution
   b. static name resolution
   c. active name resolution
   d. passive name resolution

2. What is the name of the file that contains name-to-address mapping information?
   a. LMHOSTS
   b. ZONEINFO
   c. Root.dns
   d. HOSTS

3. What is the name of the most widely used DNS server implementation on the Internet today?
   a. EasyDNS
   b. BIND
   c. WinDNS
   d. JEEVES

4. Which of the following characterizes valid aspects of DNS? (Choose all that apply.)
   a. local control over domain name database segments
   b. designation of optional primary name servers and mandatory secondary name servers
   c. data from all database segments is available everywhere
   d. database information is highly robust and available
   e. requires implementation of a relational database management system, such as Oracle or Sybase

5. In the domain name hierarchy, all domains meet at the root. True or false?
   a. True
   b. False

6. Top-level domain names include two- and three-letter country codes, as well as organizational codes, such as *.com*, *.edu*, and *.org*. True or false?
   a. True
   b. False

7. What is the process whereby a DNS server higher in the domain name hierarchy confers responsibility for portions of the global DNS database to DNS servers lower in its hierarchy?

   a. subordination of authority

   b. database consolidation

   c. delegation of authority

   d. database segmentation

8. Which DNS resource record allows the use of FQDNs for domain names? (Choose all that apply. *Hint*: Check RFC 1035 if in doubt!)

   a. A

   b. SOA

   c. PTR

   d. MX

   e. all of the above

9. Which DNS resource record is used to create aliases for domain names?

   a. A

   b. SOA

   c. PTR

   d. MX

   e. CNAME

10. Which DNS resource record appears at the beginning of every DNS file?

   a. A

   b. SOA

   c. PTR

   d. MX

   e. CNAME

11. Which DNS resource record enables inverse lookups (also known as reverse DNS lookups)?

   a. A

   b. SOA

   c. PTR

   d. MX

   e. CNAME

12. Which DNS resource record maps domain names to IP addresses?

    a. A

    b. SOA

    c. PTR

    d. MX

    e. CNAME

13. Any type of DNS server can also be a caching-only server. True or false?

    a. True

    b. False

14. The primary benefit of caching DNS data is:

    a. faster lookups

    b. reduced remote network traffic

    c. balanced DNS server load

    d. increased server reliability

15. A DNS server that's primary for one DNS database zone can also be secondary for one or more other DNS database zones. True or false?

    a. True

    b. False

16. What is the minimum and maximum number of primary database servers allowed in any single DNS database zone?

    a. 1

    b. 2

    c. 4

    d. 8

    e. 16

17. It is mandatory to have one or more secondary DNS servers for any DNS database zone. True or false?

    a. True

    b. False

18. What size or type of organization is most likely to benefit from a caching-only DNS server? (Choose all that apply.)

    a. small

    b. medium

    c. large

    d. service provider

19. What kind of data is most likely to show up in a response to a DNS query of any kind? (Choose all that apply.)

    a. address forwarding instructions

    b. DNS resource records

    c. address impersonation alerts

    d. error messages

20. Which of the following query sequences represents a typical DNS lookup?

    a. iterative, then recursive

    b. recursive, then iterative

    c. static, then dynamic

    d. dynamic, then static

21. Why do "all DNS queries end at the root?"

    a. The root maintains a copy of the global DNS database.

    b. The root can access any and all authoritative name servers for any database segment.

    c. Any DNS server can access the root at any time.

    d. Multiple root servers prevent the root of domain name hierarchy from becoming bogged down with requests.

22. When using NSLOOKUP, an authoritative response is:

    a. explicitly labeled as such

    b. available only if the authoritative name server is explicitly targeted for lookup

    c. available only by request, using the -a option

    d. implied by the absence of "non-authoritative response" in the reply

23. It is necessary to add resource records for the DNS root servers to the cache of any DNS server during initial configuration and setup. True or false?

    a. True

    b. False

24. One common name for presenting a false IP address or domain name when attempting illicit system entry or communications is:

    a. IP masquerading

    b. IP impersonation

    c. IP spoofing

    d. false IP credentials

25. Because it is a pre-defined domain name and address pair, it is not necessary to create DNS files for the localhost and the loopback addresses 127.0.0.0 and 127.0.0.1. True or false?

 a. True

 b. False

HANDS-ON PROJECTS

Project 7-1

In this project, you learn the basic steps involved in installing the DNS server software that's included as part of all Server versions of Windows 2000. Installing the software is quite easy, as is this project; configuring this software is another matter, however, and that is covered in Project 7-2.

To install the DNS server software:

1. Select **Start**, point to **Settings**, click **Network and Dial-up Connections** to open the Network and Dial-up Connections window, and then select **Optional Networking Components** from the **Advanced** menu. (*Note:* Depending on your system setup, you may have to right-click **Network and Dial-up Connections**, and then click **Open** to open the Network and Dial-up Connections window.)

2. Click the **Networking Services** entry in the Components pane, and then click the **Details** button. The Networking Services window opens.

3. Click the check box to the left of the **Domain Name System (DNS)** entry in the Subcomponents of the Networking Services pane, as shown in Figure 7-10, and then click the **OK** button.

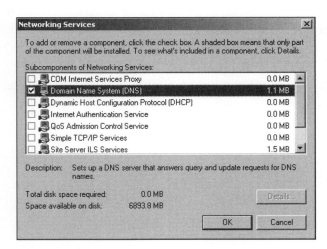

Figure 7-10   Networking Services window with Domain Name System (DNS) highlighted

4. Click the **Next** button. You are prompted to insert the Windows 2000 Server CD. Insert the CD, and the rest of the installation should complete automatically. Close any open windows. Continue to Hands-on Project 7-2.

Project 7-2

In this project, you complete the installation of DNS services for Windows 2000 by configuring a primary master, then a secondary master, for a given DNS database segment.

To configure the first DNS server on a Windows 2000 network:

1. Select **Start**, point to **Programs**, point to **Administrative Tools**, and then click **DNS** to open the DNS management console.

2. Highlight the name of your server, and then select **Configure the server** from the **Action** menu. Click the **Next** button.

3. On the Configure DNS Server Wizard screen, click the **This is the first DNS server on this network** option, and then click **Next**.

4. On the Forward Lookup Zone screen, click the **Yes, create a forward lookup zone** option, as shown in Figure 7-11, and then click the **Next** button.

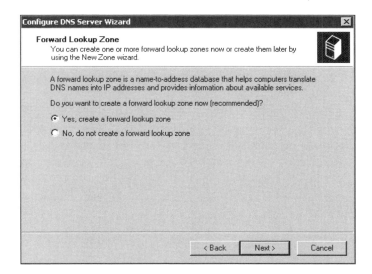

Figure 7-11   Forward Lookup Zone screen

5. On the Zone Type screen, click **Standard Primary**, and then click **Next**.

6. On the Zone Name screen, provide a name for the zone over which this server will have authority (such as mydomain1.com), and then click **Next**.

7. On the Zone File screen (see Figure 7-12), use the filename provided by default, or provide your own, and then click **Next**.

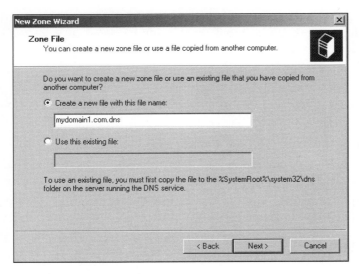

Figure 7-12   Zone File screen

8. On the Reverse Lookup Zone screen, click the **Yes, create a reverse lookup zone** option, and then click **Next**.

9. On the Zone Type screen, select **Standard Primary**, and then click **Next**.

 Indeed, several of the wizard pages have similar titles. Be careful about following exact instructions; when in doubt, consult with your instructor or lab assistant.

10. On the Reverse Lookup Zone screen, provide the Network ID of the addresses that are to be resolved through this reverse lookup. You can opt to provide a pre-defined reverse lookup zone name, but this is not recommended. Click the **Next** button.

11. On the Zone File screen, use the filename provided by default, or provide your own, and then click **Next**.

12. A summary screen displays the settings to be implemented. Click **Finish**.

To create additional zones:

1. Select the **Forward Lookup Zone** folder beneath the DNS server name, and then select **New Zone** from the Action menu.

2. The New Zone Wizard is started. Click the **Next** button.

3. On the Zone Type screen, select **Standard Primary**, and then click **Next**.

4. On the Zone Name screen, provide a name for the zone over which this server will have authority (such as mydomain2.com), and then click **Next**.

5. On the Zone File screen, use the filename provided by default, or provide your own, and then click **Next**.

6. A summary screen displays the settings to be implemented. Click **Finish**.

7. Close any open windows.

Project 7-3

Hands-on Projects 7-3 and 7-4 assume that you are working in a Windows 2000 environment, and that you installed the EtherPeek for Windows demo, as described in Project 1-1.

To examine the DNS packet structure:

1. Start the EtherPeek for Windows demo program. (See Hands-on Project 1-2 for instructions.)

2. Choose **File**, **Open** from the menu.

3. Open the trace file **dns-moviefone.pkt** contained in the **18654-2\Ch7** folder on your hard disk. There are 14 packets in this trace file.

4. The Protocol column indicates that the first two packets are UDP-based, and the subsequent packets are TCP-based. Double-click the first packet in the dns-moviefone.pkt trace file. Answer the following questions about Packet #1:

   a. Is this a DNS request or reply packet?

   b. Does this DNS client desire recursive queries?

   c. What are the query type and class in this DNS packet?

5. Click the **Decode Next** button to view Packet #2. Answer the following questions about Packet #2:

   a. What type of DNS packet is this?

   b. Does this packet contain compressed information? If so, what is the offset of the uncompressed domain name that is being sought?

   c. What is the host IP address associated with moviefone.com?

   d. How many entries are listed in the following fields in this packet?

   Question: _____

   Answer: _____

   Authority: _____

   Additional: _____

6. Close the packet decode window. Close the packet display window. Close the EtherPeek for Windows demo program, unless you proceed immediately to the next project.

7

Project 7-4

To create a DNS filter that captures all DNS traffic:

1. Open the EtherPeek for Windows demo program. (See Hands-on Project 1-2.)

2. Choose **View**, **Filters** from the menu bar. The Filters window appears. There are many filters that are included with the EtherPeek product, and you may see your own IP address filter that you created in an earlier chapter. The DNS filter that appears in the list is a UDP-based DNS filter—it does not capture DNS traffic over TCP, even though DNS traffic can sometimes travel over TCP (especially for zone transfers). In the following steps, you create a DNS filter that looks at the port number, not transfer type, to capture all DNS traffic.

3. Click the **Insert** button. The Edit Filter window appears.

4. Type **DNS by Port** in the filter text book.

5. Click the **Port filter** check box to activate port-based filtering.

6. In the Port 1 box, type **53**. This is the port number used by DNS communications. This value is decimal.

7. Under the Type field, click the directional box and select **Both directions**. This indicates that you are interested in traffic that is coming from or going to the DNS port number.

8. Under the Port 2 field, click the **Any Port** option button. Click **OK** to accept your new filter settings.

9. Double-click the **DNS by Port** filter name. You should see that EtherPeek converted your port number 53 to the word **domain**, indicating that it recognizes that port number as the Domain Services port number. Your filter should look like Figure 7-13.

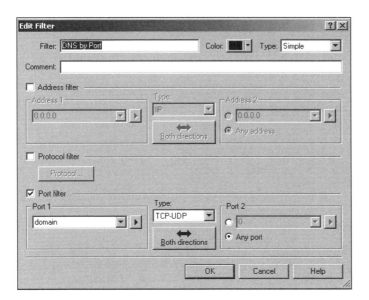

Figure 7-13   Building a DNS filter that is based on port number values, not transport type

Whenever this filter is used, it now captures all DNS traffic, regardless of the transport used.

10. Click the **Cancel** button. Close the Filters window.

To capture and examine your own DNS traffic:

This project assumes you created and saved a filter for your own traffic, as defined in Project 4-2.

1. Click **Capture** on the menu bar, and then click **Start Capture**.

2. Click **OK** to accept the Capture Buffer Options.

3. Click the **Filters** tab. Double-click the filter **My IP Address**. Refer to Project 4-2 if you need to re-create this filter. In the next steps, you edit this filter to look specifically for your own DNS traffic.

4. Click the check box next to **Address filter**, if not selected.

5. Under the Type field in the Address filter area, click the directional box and select **Both directions**. You are interested in traffic to and from your IP address.

6. Click the check box next to **Port filter** to activate port-based filtering.

7. In the Port 1 box, type **53**.

8. Under the Type field, click the directional box and select **Both directions**.

9. Under the Port 2 field, click the **Any Port** option button.

10. Click **OK** to accept your new filter. This filter looks for all traffic to and from your machine that uses port number 53 in the Source or Destination Port Number field. Double-click the **filter**. Your filter should look like Figure 7-14.

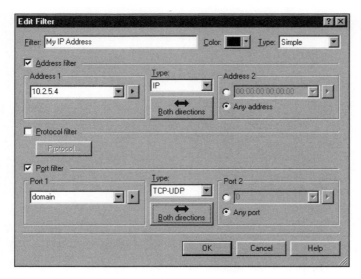

Figure 7-14   Building a DNS filter for your traffic only

11. Click the **Cancel** button to close the Edit Filter window.

12. To test your filter, click the **Packets** tab, and then click the **Start Capture** button.

13. Start your Web browser and quickly access the following Web sites:

- *www.iana.org*

- *www.packet-level.com*

- *www.ietf.org*

- *www.cisco.com*

14. When you finish, press **Alt+Tab** as many times as necessary to return to the EtherPeek window. Click **OK**. Your DNS traffic is listed in the Capture window.

15. Close the EtherPeek for Windows demo program. Close the Web browser.

Project 7-5

In this project, you learn how to configure a caching-only server for Windows 2000. Because a caching-only server has no zone responsibilities, and all Windows DNS servers perform caching, the requirements to set up such a server are so simple as to be trivial, especially by comparison with primary master or secondary master name servers.

To configure a caching-only server:

1. Complete the initial steps to install the DNS server software, as covered in Hands-on Project 7-1.

2. Click **Start**, point to **Programs**, point to **Administrative Tools**, and then click **DNS**.

3. Click to select **DNS**.

4. Click the **Action** menu, and then click **Connect to Computer**. The Select Target Computer window appears.

5. Click the **This Computer** option, and then click **OK**.

6. Click to select the server name.

7. Click the **Action** menu, and then click **Properties**.

8. Click the **Root Hints** tab.

9. Verify that the listed root hints are correct, and then click **OK**.

10. Close any open windows.

7

CASE PROJECTS

1. XYZ Corporation employs 40,000 people, with their own associated IP addresses, and operates over 400 servers, including e-mail (SMTP and POP3), FTP, Web, and DHCP at two locations: one in Muncie, Indiana, the other about 20 miles away in Hartford City. Dual T1 lines, for total aggregate bandwidth of 3.088 Mbps, link the two sites, and each site contains roughly half of the employees and servers. Perforce, each site operates on multiple, separate subnets inside a single Class B address that the company owns. Make a case for setting up a single, separate DNS server at each location, explaining how each might back up the other, and what benefits this might provide for XYZ Corporation users. Explain how the relative speed of the 100BaseT LANs used at each location compares to accessing the WAN link between the two sites.

2. Explain what it is about the communications architecture and flow of TCP/IP traffic that makes caching-only servers useful for ISPs. Please consider the way that IP clients connect to most ISPs and how their TCP/IP stacks are configured when you formulate your answer.

3. Explain why two name servers is the minimum number you would ever want to run in a networked IP environment. Consider the following factors that can influence the total number of name servers present on a typical organization's internetwork:

   ■ If there is a name server available directly on each network or subnet in a local internetwork, routers need not become potential points of failure. Consider also that multi-homed hosts make ideal locations for DNS because they can directly service all the subnets to which they're connected.

   ■ In an environment in which diskless nodes or network computers depend on a server for network and file access, at a minimum, installing a name server on that particular server makes DNS directly available to all such machines.

- Where large time-sharing machines, such as mainframes, terminal servers, or clustered computers, operate, a nearby DNS server can offload name services from the big machine, yet still provide reasonable response time and service.

- Running an additional name server at an off-site location—logically, at the site of the ISP from which your organization obtains an Internet connection—keeps DNS data available even if your Internet link goes down, or local name servers are unavailable. A remote secondary name server provides the ultimate form of backup, and helps to ensure DNS reliability.

Given the foregoing information, and the fact that XYZ Corporation operates three subnets at each of its Indiana locations, plus a large clustered terminal server at each location, explain how XYZ might want to operate as many as nine name servers for its network environment.

CHAPTER

8

THE DYNAMIC HOST CONFIGURATION PROTOCOL (DHCP)

> **After reading this chapter and completing the exercises you will be able to:**
>
> ♦ Understand the basic services DHCP offers to its clients
>
> ♦ Explain DHCP's background, history, and origins
>
> ♦ Describe the basic software components that permit DHCP to function
>
> ♦ Understand the specifics of IP address management using DHCP
>
> ♦ Read and understand basic DHCP message types
>
> ♦ Explain and configure basic settings for DHCP services

If there was any particular TCP/IP Application layer protocol and service that could vie for the designation "a TCP/IP network administrator's best friend," it would have to be DHCP. That's because DHCP eliminates the tedious labor involved in manually managing IP addresses, which requires administrators to configure each typical client machine by hand, and keep track of which machines (or interfaces, on multi-homed machines) are using which IP addresses.

DHCP provides a way for a client computer that lacks an IP address to request one from any listening DHCP server. In addition to providing a usable IP address, DHCP also delivers the necessary configuration information to clients to tell them the addresses of their IP gateways, addresses for one or more DNS servers for domain name resolution, and so forth. DHCP also manages address allocations over time so that a group of machines larger than some particular range of IP addresses can share that address range, and still obtain access to the network and the Internet.

INTRODUCING DHCP

DHCP is a service that permits network administrators to set up servers to allocate and manage collections of IP addresses for workstations, desktop computers, and other client machines that do not require fixed IP addresses. In the absence of Dynamic DNS—which can automatically propagate IP address changes into the DNS hierarchy, rather than requiring manual database updates—and for "important public presences" (such as publicly accessible Web, e-mail, FTP, and other servers and services), most servers require IP addresses that seldom change, and then only under duress. Other, less public hosts—particularly desktop clients—are well served by DHCP.

DHCP can also supply important IP configuration data for clients, including the subnet mask, the local IP gateway (router) address, and even DNS and WINS data, where needed or appropriate. The entire point of DHCP, in fact, is to make it possible to administer client IP address assignments and configuration data from a single, centralized server, rather than requiring administrators to manually configure client machines one at a time. As organizations grow and the number of desktops that must be managed increases, DHCP quickly becomes a necessity rather than a luxury.

Microsoft always had a vested interest in DHCP, viewing it as a key ingredient in managing IP configuration data for numerous desktops. Representatives from Microsoft helped define RFCs 1534, 2131, 2132, and 2241, all of which are important to DHCP's definition and operation. Thus, it should come as no surprise that Microsoft's implementation of DHCP is highly regarded and supports all the RFCs just mentioned.

DHCP servers can manage one or more ranges of IP addresses, each of which may be called an **address pool** (if considered as a range of available addresses from which unused addresses may be allocated), or an **address scope** (if considered as a range of numeric IP addresses that fall under DHCP's control). Within any individual IP address scope (usually represented as a contiguous range of IP addresses), DHCP can exclude individual addresses or address ranges from dynamic allocation to client machines. This permits DHCP to manage existing IP address ranges, from which router and server IP addresses may have already been assigned. DHCP can allocate all remaining unallocated addresses to clients on demand, in which each such allocation is called an address lease (or lease, for short).

Here's a brief rundown of how DHCP works, from a client perspective:

- When TCP/IP is configured on the client computer, the *Obtain an IP address automatically* option button is the only necessary set-up element (see Figure 8-1). Everything is automatic (which explains the terrific appeal that DHCP holds for network administrators and users alike).

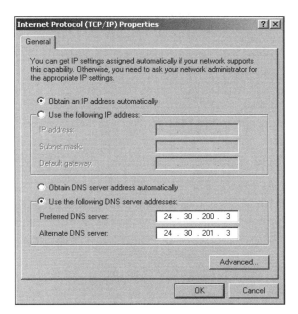

Figure 8-1   Enabling DHCP in the Internet Protocol (TCP/IP) Properties window is almost too easy

- The next time the workstation attempts to access the network (older versions of Windows must be rebooted first), it broadcasts a DHCP address request to the network because it has no IP address, but is now configured as a **DHCP client**. All **DHCP servers** present on the same cable segment or broadcast domain receive this request, and send back a message that indicates a willingness to grant an address lease, if an address is available. If no DHCP server is present on that cable segment or broadcast domain, a special piece of software called a **DHCP relay agent** on Windows machines, or a BOOTP relay agent in more general terms, must be present on any cable segment that is not part of a DHCP broadcast domain, so it can forward that address request to a DHCP server whose address it knows. Such relays may be installed on Windows 2000 Professional or Server machines, or on routers attached to cable segments that are not part of a DHCP broadcast domain. After that, the relay acts as an intermediary between the DHCP server and the client; otherwise, the process works as follows:

1. The client accepts an address lease offer (usually the first one it receives) and sends a packet to the server that extended the offer.

2. In reply, the server proffers an IP address for a specific period of time (which is why it's called a lease) that the client uses thereafter.

3. When half the lease period expires, the client attempts to renew the lease. Usually, the DHCP server that granted the lease will renew it, but if it doesn't respond, the client tries to renew again at other times during the lease period.

Only if the client is unable to renew its lease before expiration must that client repeat the DHCP Request Process, as described in Step 1.

Leases that range from one to three weeks in length are typical on networks where machines seldom move and the workforce is stable. Lease periods of four to eight hours are common on ISP networks, where clients come and go all the time. Lease periods average between one and three days for networks on which lots of temps or roving workers come and go regularly. By default, Windows 2000 sets DHCP leases at eight days, and Windows NT sets DHCP leases at 36 hours. There are numerous DHCP servers for Linux systems, but at least one uses a default DHCP lease of 24 hours. You can use these numbers as guidelines for how you might set your leases on a Windows DHCP server by taking into account the notion that where IP addresses are scarce and activity levels are high, leases will usually be short. Where IP addresses are plentiful, or when activity levels are low, leases can be much longer without causing "address starvation" (when a user is unable to obtain an IP address because all available addresses are in use).

You can view lease information in DHCP packets using an analyzer, such as EtherPeek for Windows. See the section titled "The Standard Address Discovery Process" later in this chapter for details.

DHCP's Origins

Actually, the DHCP protocol is an extension of an earlier IP protocol called BOOTP. BOOTP (which stands for Bootstrap Protocol) was originally developed to permit diskless workstations to bootstrap from a **Programmable Read-Only Memory (PROM)** or **Erasable PROM (EPROM)** on their network interface cards. Once started, that bootstrap code executes a hard-coded routine that allows such machines to immediately access the network so that they can load their operating systems and network configuration data from a server elsewhere on the network.

Although DHCP offers considerably more functionality than its predecessor, BOOTP and DHCP protocol formats remain compatible. Thus, an alternative to using a DHCP relay agent on cable segments on which no DHCP server is physically attached is to configure routers to pass BOOTP requests across cable segments.

DHCP Software Elements

Three pieces of software that work together define a complete DHCP networking environment:

- *DHCP client*: The DHCP client software, or other similar software available for most other modern operating systems, is enabled at a client machine when you select the *Obtain an IP address automatically* button in the Internet Protocol (TCP/IP) Properties window shown in Figure 8-1. This software broadcasts requests for service and lease renewal requests on behalf of its clients, and handles address and configuration data for the client when an address lease is granted. Windows 9x, Windows NT, Windows 2000, Macintosh, Linux, and UNIX machines all include built-in DHCP client software. DHCP is, in fact, a mainstay of modern networking.

- *DHCP server*: DHCP server software listens and responds to client and relay requests for address services. The DHCP server also manages address pools and related configuration data. Most current DHCP servers can manage multiple address pools (UNIX, post-SP4 Windows NT 4.0 and Windows 2000), whereas other implementations can manage only a single address pool (pre-SP4 Windows NT 4.0 and earlier versions of Windows NT).

- *DHCP relay agent*: DHCP clients broadcast address requests to their network segments. Because broadcasts are not normally forwarded through routers, this means software on the same cable segment must respond to a broadcast request for service, or that request is ignored. Thus, the job of the DHCP relay agent software is to intercept address requests on a local cable segment and repackage those requests as a unicast to one or more DHCP servers whose IP addresses are known. The server sends its replies to those requests to the relay agent, which then uses the requester's MAC layer address to forward that reply back to the very client that requested an address. Please note that most other **DHCP requests**—such as lease renewals or surrenders—occur as unicast messages because as soon as a machine obtains an IP address and a default IP gateway address, it is able to communicate directly with the DHCP server and no longer needs an intermediary.

DHCP Lease Types

A DHCP server recognizes three types of address leases:

- *Manual*: With a **manual address lease**, the administrator explicitly assigns all IP addresses manually. Use this type of address lease if you want DHCP to manage all IP addresses, but want to directly control all address assignments. For large networks, this is easier than managing IP addresses on individual machines, but still too labor intensive for most applications.

- *Automatic*: The DHCP server permanently assigns certain IP addresses. When used with a mix of dynamic IP address leases, **automatic address leases** make it possible to manage fixed server and router IP addresses along with dynamic client addresses. In other words, this allows the DHCP server to manage all addresses on a network, including those that normally wouldn't be assigned and reassigned routinely, as well as ordinary client addresses.

- *Dynamic*: The DHCP server assigns addresses for specific periods of time. Use a **dynamic address lease** to assign addresses to clients or other machines when fixed IP addresses are not required. Given the preponderance of clients on most networks, this is the most prevalent type of DHCP address lease.

More About DHCP Leases

Even though clients usually keep their addresses indefinitely, they can cancel their address leases at any time, thereby returning their addresses to the pool of free IP addresses that the DHCP server manages. On Windows computers (Windows 9x, NT, 2000, or newer versions), the ipconfig command supports the /release and /renew switches to permit clients to release or renew their current DHCP leases at will. Clients ordinarily attempt to renew existing releases by default, but you can instruct a DHCP server to deny lease renewals, or even cancel leases, when necessary.

Here's a brief explanation of why dynamic address leasing is the best practice presently used for clients:

- Server addresses (and sometimes their associated services) are advertised using the DNS, which resolves domain names into IP addresses, and vice versa.

- DNS is not a dynamic environment so all address updates must be entered manually (either through a GUI interface on NT or Windows 2000, or by editing text files on UNIX systems).

- Client addresses usually come into play only when e-mail addresses of the form *user@domain.name* must be resolved. E-mail servers can resolve this information when clients connect so dynamic address resolution works perfectly well for clients. Hence, client addresses typically have no impact on DNS, or vice versa, and can change, as needed.

Thus, the inability of older DNS implementations to dynamically update their domain name–to–IP address (A) and IP address–to–domain name (PTR) records explains why DHCP has been used primarily for managing client addresses. As mentioned in Chapter 7 of this book, newer DNS versions (including a so-called Dynamic DNS, or DDNS, that Microsoft includes with Windows 2000) can address this issue by creating ways for DHCP to communicate name-to-address mapping changes to DNS servers. Even so, the problem of the delay inherent in waiting for changes to propagate through the entire global DNS database remains unaltered so public IP addresses (and their mappings) tend to change as little as possible anyway. At present, only clients are not adversely affected by using dynamic IP addresses, which explains why DHCP remains such an important client IP address management tool today.

A typical IP addressing scheme on a network might look like this:

- *Servers* have fixed IP addresses because their DNS entries must stay consistent. This applies to name servers for DNS, e-mail servers, login hosts, file and print servers, database servers, and any server with resources to which users regularly attach.

- *Routers* (or IP gateways, be they routers or other machines) have fixed IP addresses because their addresses are key parts of any subnet's IP configuration. Likewise, any boundary or border routers must be treated the same way because they represent points of entry (and exit) between internal and external networks.

- *Clients* use dynamic IP addresses because e-mail access through POP3, SMTP, and IMAP4 avoids the need for fixed addresses (resolution occurs each time a message transfer is made).

UNDERSTANDING IP ADDRESS MANAGEMENT WITH DHCP

When a DHCP client has no IP address (booting for the first time, or after a lease expires), it must broadcast a request for an IP address to obtain one—this process is called **DHCP Discovery**. DHCP servers that can hear this **discovery broadcast** offer an IP address to a client for a specific amount of time (the **lease time**). The default DHCP lease time varies according to which server is used (eight days for Windows 2000 and 36 hours for Windows NT 4.0, for example).

In the middle of the lease time, the client starts a **renewal process** to determine if it can keep the address past the lease time. If the client cannot renew the address from that DHCP server within the stipulated lease period, that client must begin the more desperate process of renewing the address from another DHCP server (assuming the original DHCP server is no longer available). This is called the **rebinding process**. If rebinding fails, a client must completely **release** its address.

DHCP messages from a client to a server are sent to the DHCP server on port number 67. DHCP messages from a server to a client are sent to the DHCP client on port number 68.

The DHCP Discovery process relies on the initial DHCP broadcast. Naturally, routers do not forward these discovery broadcasts so the entire discovery process is a **local process**. There must be a DHCP server on the local network segment. Because it is impractical to place a DHCP server on every network segment, the DHCP specification includes the **relay agent process** to help route the DHCP discovery broadcasts to another network segment. The details for the relay agent process are covered in detail in the section titled "DHCP Relay Agents" later in this chapter.

THE STANDARD ADDRESS DISCOVERY PROCESS

When a DHCP client boots up, it performs the Standard Address Discovery process before it can communicate on the network. After the process completes successfully, the DHCP client tests the IP address using a duplicate IP address ARP broadcast.

For more information on the duplicate IP address ARP broadcast, refer to the section titled "Hardware Addresses in the IP Environment" in Chapter 3.

The DHCP Discovery process actually uses four packets:

- DHCP Discover packet
- DHCP Offer packet
- DHCP Request packet
- DHCP Acknowledge packet

Figure 8-2 shows the summary packets from the DHCP boot process. Packet #1 is the Discover packet from the DHCP client. Packet #2 is the Offer from the server. Packet #3 is the Request from the client. Packet #4 is the Acknowledgment packet that finishes the process.

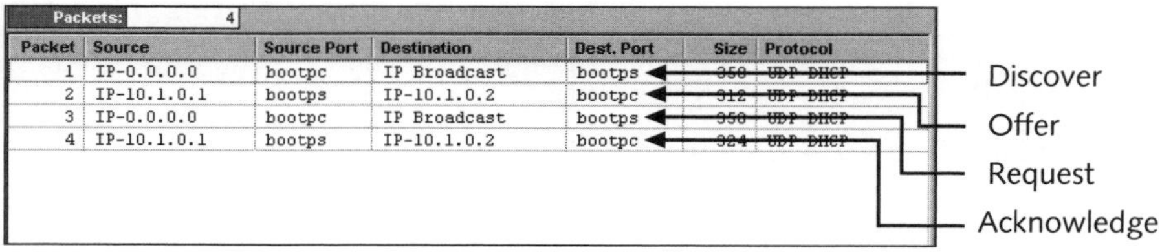

Figure 8-2   Four-packet DHCP boot process

During the DHCP boot sequence, the DHCP client receives an IP address and a lease time. The client determines the renewal and rebind time based on the value of the lease time.

In this next section, we examine each packet in the discovery process and learn how the DHCP client obtains an IP address and lease time.

The Discover Packet

During the DHCP Discovery process, the client broadcasts a Discover packet that identifies the client's hardware address. The Discover packet's IP header contains the source IP address 0.0.0.0 because the client does not yet know its address. The Ethernet header contains the all-nets broadcast destination address 255.255.255.255.

If the DHCP client was on the network before, the client also defines a **preferred address**—typically the client prefers the last address it used.

Figure 8-3 shows a Discover packet that includes a preferred address, 10.0.99.2. In this packet, we compressed the Ethernet header, IP header, and UDP header. The UDP header includes the source port 68 and the destination port 67.

```
◆ Flags:         0x00
◆ Status:        0x00
◆ Packet Length:350
◆ Timestamp:    01:53:51.930270 02/27/2000
⊞ ⦿ Ethernet Header
⊞ ⦿ IP Header - Internet Protocol Datagram
⊞ ⦿ UDP - User Datagram Protocol
⊟ ⦿ BootP - Bootstrap Protocol
    ◆ Operation:               1  [42]  Boot Request
    ◆ Hardware Address Type:    1  [43]  Ethernet (10Mb)
    ◆ Hardware Address Length:  6  [44]  bytes
    ◆ Hops:                     0  [45]
    ◆ Transaction ID:           990067459  [46-49]
    ◆ Seconds Since Boot Start: 0  [50-51]
    ◆ Flags:                    0x0000  [52-53]
    ▨ IP Address Known By Client: 0.0.0.0  [54-57]  IF Address Not Known By Cl
    ▨ Client IP Addr Given By Srvr: 0.0.0.0  [58-61]
    ▨ Server IP Address:        0.0.0.0  [62-65]
    ▨ Gateway IP Address:       0.0.0.0  [66-69]
    ▧ Client Hardware Address:  00:A0:CC:30:C8:DB  [70-75]
    ◆ Unused:                   0x00000000000000000000  [76-85]
    ◆ Server Host Name:
    ◆ Data: (64 bytes)  [86-149]
    ◆ Boot File Name:
    ◆ Data: (128 bytes)  [150-277]
⊟ ⦿ DHCP - Dynamic Host Configuration Protocol
    ◆ DHCP Magic Cookie:           0x63825363  [278-281]
    ◆ Message Type- DHCP Option
    ◆ Option Code:        53  [282]  Message Type
    ◆ Option Length:      1   [283]
    ◆ Message Type:       1   [284]  Discover
    ◆ Client Identifier- DHCP Option
    ◆ Option Code:        61  [285]  Client Identifier
    ◆ Option Length:      7   [286]
    ◆ Hardware Type:      1   [287]
    ▧ Hardware Address:   00:A0:CC:30:C8:DB  [288-293]
    ◆ Requested IP Address- DHCP Option
    ◆ Option Code:        50  [294]  Requested IP Address
    ◆ Option Length:      4   [295]
    ▨ Address:            10.0.99.2  [296-299]
    ◆ Host Name Address- DHCP Option
    ◆ Option Code:        12  [300]  Host Name Address
    ◆ Option Length:      9   [301]
    ◆ String:             UTBPOPKI.  [302-310]
    ◆ Parameter Request List- DHCP Option
    ◆ Option Code:        55  [311]  Parameter Request List
    ◆ Option Length:      8   [312]
    ◆ Requested Option:   1   [313]  Subnet Mask
    ◆ Requested Option:   3   [314]  Routers
    ◆ Requested Option:   6   [315]  Domain Name Servers
    ◆ Requested Option:   15  [316]  Domain Name
    ◆ Requested Option:   44  [317]  NetBIOS (TCF/IP) Name Servers
    ◆ Requested Option:   46  [318]  NetBIOS (TCF/IP) Node Type
    ◆ Requested Option:   47  [319]  NetBIOS (TCF/IP) Scope
    ◆ Requested Option:   57  [320]  Maximum Message Size
    ◆ DHCP Option End
    ◆ Option Code:        255 [321]  End
    ◆ Extra bytes (Padding):
    ◆ Data: (24 bytes)  [322-345]
    ◆ Frame Check Sequence:  0x1CDF4421  [346-349]
```

Figure 8-3   DHCP Discover packet is always sent as a hardware and IP broadcast

Because DHCP is built upon the BOOTP foundation, many analyzer vendors still use the term BOOTP when defining the port numbers and the heading values. EtherPeek uses the term BOOTP for the initial header definition inside its decodes.

In the DHCP Discover packet shown in Figure 8-3, the **Message Type** value is one—this indicates that this packet is a DHCP Discover packet. The Message Type values are listed in the section titled "DHCP Options Fields" later in this chapter.

The **Client Identifier** field value is based on the client's hardware address (0x00–A0–CC–30–C8–DB).

During the IP address request (and even separately, if desired), a DHCP client can ask for other configuration information. Note that in Figure 8-3 the client includes a series of requests at the end of the standard DHCP discover request. These requests are defined as **DHCP options** and are explained in RFC 2132, "DHCP Options and BOOTP Vendor Extensions." These options are listed online at *http://www.iana.org*. The options defined in Figure 8-3 include the following:

- *Option 1:* Client's subnet mask
- *Option 3:* Routers on the client's subnet
- *Option 6:* Domain Name Server
- *Option 15:* Domain name
- *Option 44:* NetBIOS over TCP/IP name server
- *Option 46:* NetBIOS over TCP/IP node type
- *Option 47:* NetBIOS over TCP/IP scope
- *Option 57:* Maximum DHCP message size
- *Option 255:* End of options

The DHCP server may not answer any configuration option requests until the client accepts the IP address. These options are covered in the section titled "DHCP Options Fields" later in this chapter.

The Offer Packet

The DHCP server sends the Offer packet to offer an IP address to the DHCP client. The DHCP server sends this packet by unicast to the DHCP client.

The Offer packet includes the IP address that is offered to the client, and sometimes answers to the requested options in the DHCP Discover packet.

Figure 8-4 shows the DHCP Offer packet decoded by EtherPeek. In this packet, we compressed the Ethernet header, IP header, and UDP header.

```
  ◆ Flags:        0x00
  ◆ Status:       0x00
  ◆ Packet Length:312
  ◆ Timestamp:    01:53:51.931572 02/27/2000
⊞ ❡ Ethernet Header
⊞ ❡ IP Header - Internet Protocol Datagram
⊞ ❡ UDP - User Datagram Protocol
⊟ ❡ BootP - Bootstrap Protocol
  ◆ Operation:                 2  [42]   Boot Reply
  ◆ Hardware Address Type:     1  [43]   Ethernet (10Mb)
  ◆ Hardware Address Length:   6  [44]   bytes
  ◆ Hops:                      0  [45]
  ◆ Transaction ID:            990067459  [46-49]
  ◆ Seconds Since Boot Start:  0  [50-51]
  ◆ Flags:                     0x0000  [52-53]
  ▦ IP Address Known By Client:  0.0.0.0  [54-57]   IP Address Not Known By C
  ▦ Client IP Addr Given By Srvr: 10.1.0.2  [58-61]
  ▦ Server IP Address:         0.0.0.0  [62-65]
  ▦ Gateway IP Address:        0.0.0.0  [66-69]
  ▦ Client Hardware Address:   00:A0:CC:30:C8:DB  [70-75]
  ◆ Unused:                    0x00000000000000000000  [76-85]
  ◆ Server Host Name:
  ◆ Data: (64 bytes)  [86-149]
  ◆ Boot File Name:
  ◆ Data: (128 bytes)  [150-277]
⊟ ❡ DHCP - Dynamic Host Configuration Protocol
  ◆ DHCP Magic Cookie:         0x63825363  [278-281]
  ◆ Message Type- DHCP Option
  ◆ Option Code:        53  [282]   Message Type
  ◆ Option Length:      1   [283]
  ◆ Message Type:       2   [284]   Offer
  ◆ Server Identifier- DHCP Option
  ◆ Option Code:        54  [285]   Server Identifier
  ◆ Option Length:      4   [286]
  ▦ Address:            10.1.0.1  [287-290]
  ◆ IP Address Lease Time- DHCP Option
  ◆ Option Code:        51  [291]   IP Address Lease Time
  ◆ Option Length:      4   [292]
  ◆ Value:              1800  [293-296]
  ◆ Subnet Mask- DHCP Option
  ◆ Option Code:        1   [297]   Subnet Mask
  ◆ Option Length:      4   [298]
  ▦ Address:            255.255.0.0  [299-302]
  ◆ DHCP Option End
  ◆ Option Code:        255  [303]   End
  ◆ Extra bytes (Padding):
  ◆ Data: (4 bytes)  [304-307]
  ◆ Frame Check Sequence:  0x1CDF4421  [308-311]
```

Figure 8-4   DHCP Offer packet includes the suggested IP address for the DHCP client

Note in the IP address field that the DHCP server offers 10.1.0.2 to the client. Apparently, the server could not offer the preferred address. The DHCP Offer packet also includes the IP address of the DHCP server (10.1.0.1), the IP lease time (1800 seconds), and the subnet mask (255.255.0.0).

In the IP header, the DHCP server addresses this packet to the offered IP address, 10.1.0.2, even though at this point the DHCP client does not recognize that address. The data link header addresses this packet directly to the destination hardware address—that's all that is needed to get this packet to the destination. The IP header isn't even referenced to route this packet because it's sent from one device to another on the local subnet only.

The Request Packet

Once the Offer packet is received, the client can either accept the offer by issuing a DHCP Request packet, or reject the offer by sending a DHCP Decline packet. Typically, a client only sends a Decline if it received more than one Offer. For example, if there is more than one DHCP server on the subnet, the client may receive multiple replies. The client would respond with a Request to the first Offer received and send a Decline to the second and subsequent Offers received.

Figure 8-5 shows a DHCP Request packet. In this Request, you can see the client now requests answers to the same parameters listed in the original Discover packet. The client now knows the DHCP server's address and places the Offered address in the Requested IP Address field.

Figure 8-5 DHCP client may list additional configuration parameters in the DHCP Request packet

In the IP header, this packet is sent to the IP broadcast address even though the client knows the IP address of the DHCP server. See the "Broadcast and Unicast in DHCP" section for more information about when a DHCP server uses unicast or broadcast.

Again, the client requests numerous parameters from the DHCP server. If possible, the server should respond with the answers to the client's parameter queries.

The Acknowledgment Packet

The Acknowledgment packet is sent from the server to the client to indicate the completion of the four-packet DHCP Discovery process. This response contains answers to any options to which the DHCP server replies. Figure 8-6 shows the DHCP Acknowledgment (ACK) packet.

Figure 8-6   DHCP server answers as many parameter queries as possible in the DHCP ACK packet

The Acknowledgment packet shown in Figure 8-6 includes some answers to the client's request for information, as listed below:

- The client subnet mask is 255.255.0.0.
- The client's default gateway address is 10.0.0.1.
- The client's DNS server address is 10.0.0.1.

Successful completion of this four-packet process does not mean the client starts using the IP address immediately, however. Most IP hosts perform a duplicate IP address test immediately following the Acknowledgment packet receipt. For example, after the preceding process, the DHCP client sends an ARP packet that lists the IP address 10.1.0.2 as the target IP address and the source IP address.

THE ADDRESS RENEWAL PROCESS

When a DHCP client receives an address from a DHCP server, the client also receives a lease time and notes the time that the address was received. The lease time defines how long the client can keep the address. The DHCP client then computes the renewal time (T1) and rebinding time (T2) based on the lease time.

The Renewal Time (T1)

T1 is defined as the time that the client tries to renew its network address by contacting the DHCP server that sent the original address to the client. The Renewal packet is unicast directly to the DHCP server.

The DHCP specification, RFC 2131, defines the default value for T1 as:

```
0.5 * duration_of_lease
```

This is equal to one-half of the lease time.

If the DHCP client does not receive a reply to the renewal request, it will divide the remaining time between the current time and the T2 time, and then retry the renewal request.

The Rebinding Time (T2)

T2 is defined as the time that the client begins to broadcast a renewal request hoping that another DHCP server can extend the lease time. The DHCP specification, RFC 2131, defines the default value for T2 as:

```
0.875 * duration_of_lease
```

If the DHCP client does not receive a reply to the rebind request, the DHCP client reduces the time remaining between the current rebinding time and the expiration of the lease time and retry. The DHCP client continues to retry the rebinding process until one minute from the **lease expiration time**. If the client is unsuccessful in renewing the lease, it must give up the address at the expiration of the lease time, and **reinitialize** (start the DHCP Discovery process using source IP address 0.0.0.0).

Figure 8-7 shows the relationship between the lease time, T1, T2, and the eventual address expiration.

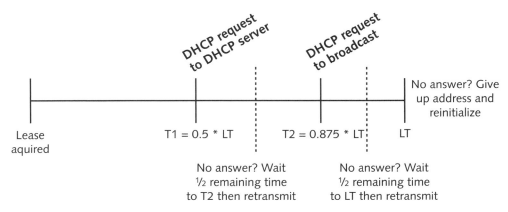

Figure 8-7   DHCP timeline includes the lease time (LT), renewal time (T1), and rebinding time (T2)

On an analyzer, it is easy to spot the renewal and rebinding processes. As you see in Figure 8-8, repeated DHCP communications directly to the DHCP server are an indication that the DHCP client is in the renewal process. When we see the client start to send broadcasts from a valid IP address, we can assume the client is now in the rebinding process. Finally, the client changes its source IP address to 0.0.0.0 when the rebinding process fails, and it must rebroadcast a DHCP Discover packet.

Figure 8-8 shows the summary of a client that performs the renewal and rebinding processes before finally giving up and reinitializing.

Packet	Source	Destination	Dest. Port	Size	Protocol	
1	IP-10.1.0.3	IP-10.1.0.1	bootps	346	UDP DHCP	Renewal attempts
2	IP-10.1.0.3	IP-10.1.0.1	bootps	346	UDP DHCP	
3	IP-10.1.0.3	IP Broadcast	bootps	346	UDP DHCP	
4	IP-10.1.0.3	IP Broadcast	bootps	346	UDP DHCP	Rebind attempts
5	IP-10.1.0.3	IP Broadcast	bootps	346	UDP DHCP	
6	IP-10.1.0.3	IP Broadcast	bootps	346	UDP DHCP	
7	IP-0.0.0.0	IP Broadcast	bootps	346	UDP DHCP	Start over

Packets: 7

Figure 8-8   DHCP client begins advertising an address of 0.0.0.0 when it gives up its IP address

THE DHCP ADDRESS RELEASE PROCESS

Although not required by the specification, the client should release its address by sending a DHCP Release packet to the server (called the release process). The DHCP Release packet is sent over UDP, and the DHCP server does not send any acknowledgment. If the client does not send the DHCP Release packet, the DHCP server automatically releases the address at the lease expiration time.

DHCP PACKET STRUCTURES

In this section, we cover the DHCP packet structures and define the field values and options. Figure 8-9 shows the standard DHCP packet structure.

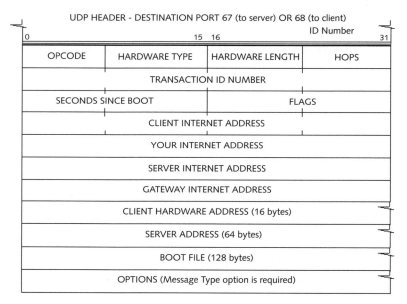

Figure 8-9   DHCP packet structure

Operation Code Field

This 1-byte field indicates whether this packet is a DHCP request (0x01) or **DHCP reply** (0x02). The detail on the type of request or reply is defined inside the DHCP options section as a Message Type. See the section titled "DHCP Options Fields" later in this chapter for more details.

Hardware Type Field

This 1-byte field identifies the hardware address type, and matches the values assigned for ARP hardware type definitions. The hardware type list is defined by IANA and maintained at *http://www.iana.org*. The value one denotes the hardware as 10 MB Ethernet.

Hardware Length Field

This 1-byte field indicates the length of the hardware address. For example, the value six is used for 10 MB Ethernet to indicate a 6-byte hardware address.

Hops Field

This field is set to zero by the client, and may be used by relay agents as they assist a client in obtaining an IP address and/or configuration information. See the section titled "DHCP Relay Agents" later in this chapter.

Transaction ID Number Field

This 4-byte field contains a random number selected by the client, and is used to match requests and responses between the client and server.

Seconds Since Boot Field

This 2-byte field indicates the number of seconds that elapsed since the client began requesting a new address, or renewal of an existing address.

Flags Field

The first bit of the 2-byte Flags field can be toggled to one to indicate that the DHCP client cannot accept unicast MAC layer datagrams before the IP software is completely configured. As explained in the section titled "The Standard Address Discovery Process" earlier in this chapter, the DHCP client broadcasts the initial Discover packet. The DHCP server can respond with either a unicast or broadcast Offer packet. In Figure 8-4, the server responds with a unicast packet.

If a client cannot accept these unicast packets, it toggles the **broadcast bit** in the Flags field to one. If a DHCP server or relay agent sends a unicast packet to the client, it may discard it. The remaining bits in this 2-byte field are set to zero.

Client IP Address Field

The DHCP client fills in this 4-byte field with its IP address after it is assigned and bound to the IP stack. This field is also filled in during the renewal and rebind states. When the DHCP client first boots up, however, this field is padded with 0.0.0.0.

8

Your IP Address Field

This 4-byte field contains the address being offered by the DHCP server. Only the DHCP server can fill in this field.

Server IP Address Field

This 4-byte field contains the IP address of the DHCP server to use in the boot process. The DHCP server puts its address in this field.

Gateway IP Address Field

This 4-byte field contains the address of the DHCP relay agent, if one is used.

Client Hardware Address Field

This 16-byte field contains the hardware address of the client. Upon receipt by the DHCP server, this address is maintained and associated with the IP address assigned to the client. In case this field is deemed to be insufficient, the Client Identifier option (61) can be used to provide unique identification of a machine.

Server Host Name Field

This 64-byte field can contain the server host name, but such information is optional. This field can contain a **null-terminated string** (all zeroes).

Boot File Field

This field contains an optional boot filename or null-terminated string.

The preceding discussion covered the various fields in a DHCP message layout, in their normal order of appearance. In the sections that follow, we change our focus to zero in on the various DHCP options, in which all of the various types of data that DHCP messages can ferry are identified.

DHCP Options Fields

DHCP options are used to expand the data that is included in the DHCP packet. The DHCP options are listed in Table 8-1. As you review this table, you begin to realize the power of DHCP.

Table 8-1   DHCP Options

Tag	Name	Length	Meaning
0	Pad	0	None
1	Subnet Mask	4	Subnet mask value
2	Time Offset	4	Time offset in seconds from UTC
3	Router	N	N/4 router addresses
4	Time Server	N	N/4 time server addresses
5	Name Server	N	N/4 IEN-116 server addresses
6	Domain Server	N	N/4 DNS server addresses
7	Log Server	N	N/4 logging server addresses
8	Quotes Server	N	N/4 quotes server addresses
9	LPR Server	N	N/4 printer server addresses
10	Impress Server	N	N/4 Impress server addresses
11	RLP Server	N	N/4 RLP server addresses
12	Hostname	N	Hostname string
13	Boot File Size	2	Size of boot file in 512-byte chunks
14	Merit Dump File	N	Client to dump and name the file to dump it to
15	Domain Name	N	DNS domain name of the client
16	Swap Server	N	Swap server address
17	Root Path	N	Path name for root disk
18	Extension File	N	Path name for more BOOTP info
19	Forward On/Off	1	Enable/disable IP forwarding
20	SrcRte On/Off	1	Enable/disable source routing
21	Policy Filter	N	Routing policy filters
22	Max DG Assembly	2	Max datagram reassembly size
23	Default IP TTL	1	Default IP Time to Live
24	MTU Timeout	4	Path MTU aging timeout
25	MTU Plateau	N	Path MTU plateau table
26	MTU Interface	2	Interface MTU size
27	MTU Subnet	1	All subnets are local
28	Broadcast Address	4	Broadcast address
29	Mask Discovery	1	Perform mask discovery
30	Mask Supplier	1	Provide mask to others
31	Router Discovery	1	Perform router discovery
32	Router Request	4	Router solicitation address
33	Static Route	N	Static routing table
34	Trailers	1	Trailer encapsulation

8

Table 8-1 DHCP Options (continued)

Tag	Name	Length	Meaning
35	ARP Timeout	4	ARP cache timeout
36	Ethernet	1	Ethernet encapsulation
37	Default TCP TTL	1	Default TCP Time to Live
38	Keepalive Time	4	TCP keep-alive interval
39	Keepalive Data	1	TCP keep-alive garbage
40	NIS Domain	N	NIS domain name
41	NIS Servers	N	NIS server addresses
42	NTP Servers	N	NTP server addresses
43	Vendor Specific	N	Vendor-specific information
44	NETBIOS Name Srv	N	NETBIOS name servers
45	NETBIOS Dist Srv	N	NETBIOS datagram distribution
46	NETBIOS Node Type	1	NETBIOS node type
47	NETBIOS Scope	N	NETBIOS scope
48	X Window Font	N	X Window font server
49	X Window Manager	N	X Window display manager
50	Address Request	4	Requested IP address
51	Address Time	4	IP address lease time
52	Overload	1	Overload "sname" or "file"
53	DHCP Msg Type	1	DHCP message type
54	DHCP Server Id	4	DHCP server identification
55	Parameter List	N	Parameter request list
56	DHCP Message	N	DHCP error message
57	DHCP Max Msg Size	2	DHCP maximum message size
58	Renewal Time	4	DHCP renewal time (T1)
59	Rebinding Time	4	DHCP rebinding time (T2)
60	Vendor Class ID	N	Vendor class Identifier
61	Client ID	N	Client Identifier
62	NetWare/IP Domain	N	NetWare/IP domain name
63	NetWare/IP Option	N	NetWare/IP sub options
64	NIS-Domain-Name	N	NIS+ v3 client domain name
65	NIS-Server-Addr	N	NIS+ v3 server addresses
66	Server-Name	N	TFTP server name
67	Bootfile-Name	N	Boot filename
68	Home-Agent-Addrs	N	Home agent addresses
69	SMTP-Server	N	Simple Mail server addresses

Table 8-1   DHCP Options (continued)

Tag	Name	Length	Meaning
70	POP3-Server	N	Post Office server addresses
71	NNTP-Server	N	Network News server addresses
72	WWW-Server	N	WWW server addresses
73	Finger-Server	N	Finger server addresses
74	IRC-Server	N	Chat server addresses
75	StreetTalk-Server	N	StreetTalk server addresses
76	STDA-Server	N	ST Directory Assistance addresses
77	User-Class	N	User class information
78	Directory Agent	N	Directory agent information
79	Service Scope	N	Service location agent scope
80	Naming Authority	N	Naming authority
81	Client FQDN	N	Fully qualified domain name
82	Agent Circuit ID	N	Agent circuit ID
83	Agent Remote ID	N	Agent remote ID
84	Agent Subnet Mask	N	Agent subnet mask
85	NDS Servers	N	Novell Directory Services
86	NDS Tree Name	N	Novell Directory Services
87	NDS Context	N	Novell Directory Services
88	IEEE 1003.1 POSIX	N	IEEE 1003.1 POSIX time zone
89	FQDN	N	Fully qualified domain name
90	Authentication	N	Authentication
91	Vines TCP/IP	N	Vines TCP/IP server option
92	Server Selection	N	Server selection option
93	Client System	N	Client system architecture
94	Client NDI	N	Client network device interface
95	LDAP	N	Lightweight Directory Access Protocol
96	IPv6 Transitions	N	IPv6 transitions
97	UUID/GUID	N	UUID/GUID-based Client Identifier
98	User-Auth	N	Open Group's user authentication

"N" in length column represents a variable number.

The complete list of DHCP options is contained in RFC 2132. Only one DHCP option is required in all DHCP packets—Option 53: DHCP Message Type. This option is covered next.

DHCP Option 53: Message Type

This required option indicates the general purpose of any DHCP message.

The eight DHCP message types are listed in Table 8-2.

Table 8-2   DHCP Message Types

Number	Message Type	Description
0×01	DHCP Discover	Sent by the DHCP client to locate available servers
0×02	DHCP Offer	Sent by the DHCP server to the DHCP client in response to Message Type 0×01 (this packet includes the offered address)
0×03	DHCP Request	Sent by the DHCP client to the DHCP server requesting offered parameters from one server specifically—as defined in the packet
0×04	DHCP Decline	Sent by the DHCP client to the DHCP server indicating invalid parameters
0×05	DHCP ACK	Sent by the DHCP server to the DHCP client with configuration parameters, including the assigned network address
0×06	DHCP NAK	Sent by the DHCP client to the DHCP server to refuse a request for configuration parameters
0×07	DHCP Release	Sent by the DHCP client to the DHCP server to relinquish a network address and cancel the remaining lease
0×08	DHCP Inform	Sent by a DHCP client to the DHCP server to ask for only configuration parameters (the client already has an IP address)

As you may recall, the DHCP boot sequence uses the following message types:

- *DHCP Message Type 1:* Discover (client to server)
- *DHCP Message Type 2:* Offer (server to client)
- *DHCP Message Type 3:* Request (client to server)
- *DHCP Message Type 5:* ACK (server to client)

This sequence of messages represents the exchanges that occur when a client requests an address for the first time, or whenever it must negotiate a new lease. Because the ipconfig parameters /release, /renew, /showclassid, and /setclassid all involve DHCP, each one is associated with one or more DHCP message types as well (primarily within the context of DHCP Message Type 3, with numerous other options).

BROADCAST AND UNICAST IN DHCP

As you examine DHCP communications, you will note they use a strange mix of broadcast and unicast addressing. DHCP clients must use broadcast until obtaining IP addresses through a successful completion of the Discovery, Offer, Request, and

Acknowledgment processes. Table 8-3 clarifies when a DHCP server uses broadcast and unicast.

Table 8-3   DHCP Broadcast and Unicast Rules

Gateway IP Address Setting	Client IP Address Setting	Address Used
non-zero	N/A	Unicast packets from DHCP server to the relay agent
zero	non-zero	Unicast DHCP Offer and DHCP ACK messages to the client IP address
zero	zero	[Broadcast bit set] DHCP server broadcasts DHCP Offer and DHCP ACK messages to 0xFF.FF.FF.FF
zero	zero	[Broadcast bit not set] DHCP server unicasts DHCP Offer and DHCP ACK messages to the client IP address and the value contained in the Your IP Address field.

8

DHCP RELAY AGENTS

The DHCP boot up process relies heavily on broadcasts, but most routers do not forward broadcasts. This forces the need for one DHCP server on each network segment, or a special functionality defined to get discover broadcasts to remote DHCP servers. The relay agent function addresses this second configuration design.

The relay agent function is typically loaded on a router connected to the segment containing DHCP clients. This relay agent device is configured with the address of the DHCP server, and can communicate unicast directly with that server.

Figure 8-10 shows the general design of a network that supports a DHCP relay agent.

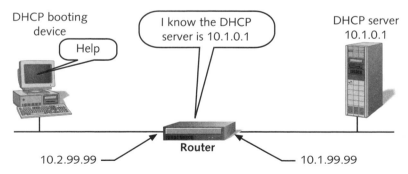

Figure 8-10   A network configuration using DHCP relay agent software on a router

In Figure 8-10, the DHCP client broadcasts a DHCP Discover message on network 10.2.0.0. The router is configured with DHCP relay agent software. This relay agent accepts the DHCP broadcast and sends a unicast packet to the DHCP server at 10.1.0.1 on behalf of the DHCP client. The relay agent includes the hardware address of the DHCP client inside the DHCP Discover packet and interestingly, the relay agent sends this request from its IP address on the network of the DHCP client (10.2.99.99).

The DHCP server notes the source IP address and uses this information to determine what IP network the true requester is on. The DHCP server responds directly to the DHCP relay agent, which, in turn, replies to the DHCP client.

Figure 8-11 shows the communication sequence on a network that supports a DHCP relay agent.

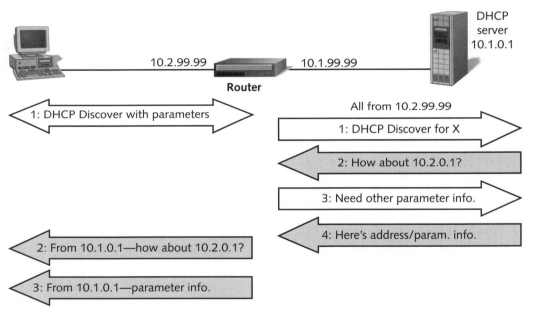

Figure 8-11   DHCP relay communications process

MICROSOFT DHCP SCOPES AND CLASSES

Microsoft uses the term **scope** to define a set of IP addresses that the Windows 2000 DHCP server can assign to clients. Because these DHCP servers do not communicate with each other, it is the responsibility of the DHCP server to ensure that there is no overlapping of scope values between the servers. Likewise Microsoft refers to a collection of multiple individual scopes as a **superscope**. Older versions of DHCP server software (before the release of SP4 for Windows NT 4.0 Server) could handle only a single DHCP scope; since then, the software is able to handle multiple scopes, collectively known as a superscope.

THE FUTURE OF DHCP

As IPv6 development and deployment move forward, DHCP's role changes significantly. One of the great advantages of IPv6 is **autoconfiguration**—IPv6 hosts can create local IP addresses using their hardware addresses and the Neighbor Discovery process. For more information on the Neighbor Discovery process, refer to Chapter 13, "IPv6."

This autoconfiguration capability implies that DHCP is no longer necessary. It may, however, still be used to supply configuration parameters that are not configurable through other means.

TROUBLESHOOTING DHCP

The best way to troubleshoot DHCP is with an analyzer—compare a problematic boot up sequence with the standard four-packet boot up sequence. To determine what address a Windows 2000 device was assigned, run the IPCONFIG utility. This tool, shown in Figure 8-12, displays the current IP address.

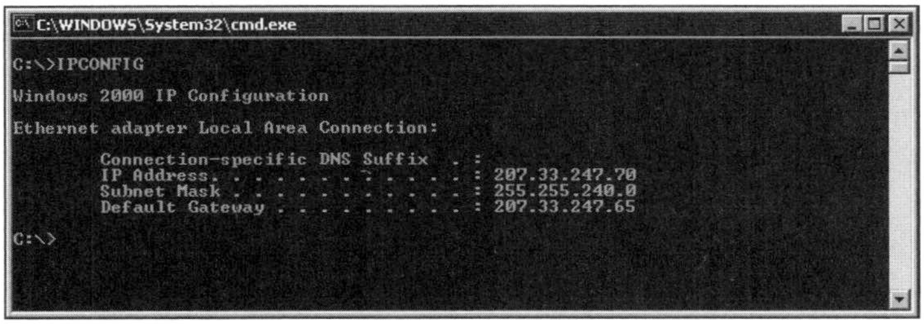

Figure 8-12   IPCONFIG displays IP address information

You can release and/or renew an IP address using the following commands:

- ipconfig /release   Releases the IP address for the specified adapter
- ipconfig /renew   Renews the IP address for the specified adapter

All in all, DHCP remains one of the most useful and usable of the TCP/IP Application layer services available to network administrators. Because it so greatly simplifies and centralizes the management of IP addresses and all kinds of related configuration information, it is a true godsend to those administrators who are responsible for large, complex, and widely distributed TCP/IP networks.

CHAPTER SUMMARY

❑ DHCP provides a way for computers to obtain usable, unique IP addresses and necessary TCP/IP configurations even when no IP addresses were assigned to those machines. As long as a DHCP server or relay is available on the cable segment where an initial DHCP Request message is broadcast, the DHCP service makes it easy and automatic to include computers on a TCP/IP network.

❑ From the administrative side, DHCP makes is easy to define and manage pools of IP addresses, which Microsoft calls a scope in the singular (a single range of IP addresses under DHCP's management), and a superscope (a collection of IP address scopes) in the plural.

❑ DHCP's origins lie in an earlier TCP/IP Application layer protocol, called BOOTP, used to enable diskless workstations to boot remotely across a network. Basic BOOTP and DHCP formats are entirely compatible so that by configuring a router to forward BOOTP, it also forwards DHCP packets.

❑ DHCP supports three types of address allocation: manual, in which administrators directly manage all addresses; automatic, in which relatively static address assignments may be made under DHCP's control; and dynamic, in which addresses are allocated with explicit expiration intervals called leases. Many of DHCP's functions and messages relate to obtaining, renewing, and releasing dynamic address leases, primarily for client machines.

❑ DHCP supports a wide variety of message types and options, but only Message Type 53 (DHCP Message) is mandatory for any given DHCP message. Because DHCP can ferry a surprisingly large range of configuration information (including all kinds of network services, such as e-mail and NetBIOS over TCP/IP), the protocol makes use of several message options.

❑ A protocol analyzer is especially effective when diagnosing DHCP difficulties, particularly those related to the DHCP boot sequence, because it can display the sequence of messages that occurs on a network, which may then be compared to the usual, prescribed sequence.

KEY TERMS

address pool — A contiguous range of numeric IP addresses, defined by a starting IP address and an ending IP address, to be managed by a DHCP server.

address scope — *See* scope.

autoconfiguration — The process of automatically assigning configuration without any manual intervention. In the case of IPv6, as referenced in this chapter, clients can autoconfigure their IP addresses either with or without the use of DHCP. For more information on IPv6, refer to Chapter 13.

automatic address lease — A type of DHCP address lease in which a DHCP server can make a permanent allocation of an address within its address pool; usually applied when allocating addresses to servers, routers, or other devices that require stable IP address assignments.

broadcast bit — A single bit at the start of the Flags field of the DHCP packet that indicates whether this client can receive unicast packets before the four-packet DHCP boot up process completes.

Client Identifier — An identification number that the DHCP server uses to keep track of the client and its IP address, lease time, and other parameters. Typically, the client's hardware address is used as the Client Identifier value.

DHCP client — The software component on a TCP/IP client, usually implemented as part of the protocol stack software, that issues address requests, lease renewals, and other DHCP messages to a DHCP server.

DHCP Discovery — The four-packet process used to obtain an IP address, lease time, and configuration parameters. The four-packet process includes the Discover, Offer, Request, and Acknowledgment packets.

DHCP options — Parameter and configuration information that defines what the DHCP client is looking for. Two special options—0: Pad and 255: End—are used for housekeeping. Pad simply ensures that the DHCP fields end on an acceptable boundary, and End denotes that there are no more options listed in the packet. Refer to Table 8-1 to view a partial list of DHCP options.

DHCP relay agent — A special-purpose piece of software built to recognize and redirect DHCP Discovery packets to known DHCP servers. When any cable segment or broadcast domain has no DHCP server directly attached, but includes DHCP clients that will need address management services and configuration data, it is necessary to install a DHCP relay agent on that cable segment or broadcast domain (or to enable routers to forward BOOTP packets to segments where DHCP servers are indeed available).

DHCP reply — A DHCP message that contains a reply from a server to a client's DHCP request message.

DHCP request — A DHCP message from a client to a server, requesting some kind of service; such messages occur only after a client receives an IP address, and can use unicast packets (not broadcasts) to communicate with a specific DHCP server.

DHCP server — The software component that runs on a network server of some kind, responsible for managing TCP/IP address pools or scopes, and for interacting with clients to provide them with IP addresses and related TCP/IP configuration data on demand.

discovery broadcast — The process of discovering a DHCP server by broadcasting a DHCP Discover packet onto the local network segment. If a DHCP server does not exist on the local segment, a relay agent must forward the request directly to the remote DHCP server. If no local DHCP server or relay agent exists, the client cannot obtain an IP address using DHCP.

8

dynamic address lease — A type of DHCP address lease in which each address allocation comes with an expiration timeout so that address leases must be renewed before expiration occurs, or a new address will have to be allocated instead. Used primarily for client machines that do not require stable IP address assignments.

Erasable PROM (EPROM) — An erasable form of non-volatile computer memory that not only can be programmed with certain key information such as system or operating system boot up parameters, but whose contents can be erased and rewritten, as needed. An EPROM can be recorded and re-recorded while the chip is already socketed on a motherboard or interface card.

lease expiration time — The end of the lease time. If a DHCP client does not renew or rebind its address by the lease expiration time, it must release the address and reinitialize.

lease time — The amount of time that a DHCP client may use an assigned DHCP address.

local process — A process or execution thread that executes on a local host (that does not involve remote execution or behavior).

manual address lease — A type of DHCP address lease wherein the administrator takes full responsibility for managing address assignments, using DHCP only as a repository for such assignment data, and related TCP/IP configuration data.

Message Type — A required option that indicates the purpose of a DHCP packet— the eight message types are Discover, Offer, Request, Decline, Acknowledge, Negative Acknowledge (NAK), Release, and Inform.

null-terminated string — A string of bytes that contains the value zero. When a field is filled with a null-terminated string, it is said to be "zero-padded."

preferred address — An address the DHCP client remembers from the previous network session. Most DHCP client implementations maintain a list of the last IP addresses they used, and indicate a preference for the last-used address. This adds a somewhat static view of the network addressing system, but there is no guarantee the clients can continue to receive the same address each time they boot. In IPv6, the term "preferred address" refers to the one address, among the many that may be associated with the same interface, whose use by higher-layer protocols is unrestricted.

Programmable Read-Only Memory (PROM) — A write-once form of computer memory used to create non-volatile storage for certain key information, such as system or operating system boot up parameters. PROMs are burned (written to) using special data recording methods, such as ultraviolet light, before such chips are installed on a motherboard or interface card.

rebinding process — The process of contacting any DHCP server through the use of a broadcast to obtain renewal of an address.

reinitialize — The process of beginning the standard DHCP Discovery process anew after failure of the renewal and rebinding processes. During the reinitializing phase, the DHCP client has no IP address and uses 0.0.0.0 as its source address.

relay agent process — A process or execution thread that executes on a local host (which may be on a Windows workstation, server, or router) and forwards DHCP broadcasts as unicasts directed to a remote DHCP server for clients operating outside a DHCP broadcast domain.

release — The process of releasing an IP address by formally sending a DHCP Release packet (Message Type 0x07) to the DHCP server. If a client shuts down without sending the Release packet, the DHCP server maintains the lease until expiration.

renewal process — The process of renewing the IP address for continued use. By default, a DHCP client begins the renewal process halfway between the lease grant and the lease expiration time.

scope — Defined by Microsoft as a group of addresses that can be assigned by a Microsoft DHCP server. Other vendors refer to this as an address pool or address range.

superscope — Defined by Microsoft as a collection of IP address scopes, as managed by any single DHCP server. Other vendors refer to this as a collection of address pools or address ranges.

8

REVIEW QUESTIONS

1. DHCP only manages IP addresses. True or false?

   a. True

   b. False

2. Which of the following terms describes a single group of IP addresses managed by DHCP? (Choose all that apply, across multiple operating systems.)

   a. address pool

   b. address group

   c. address scope

   d. address superscope

3. When configuring a modern Windows TCP/IP client with DHCP, only a single configuration setting is required on that machine. True or false?

   a. True

   b. False

4. For dynamic DHCP addresses, at what point in the DHCP lease period does the first lease renewal attempt occur?

   a. one-quarter of the way through the lease period

   b. halfway through the lease period

   c. three-quarters of the way through the lease period

   d. seven-eighths of the way through the lease period

5. Which of the following represents a valid DHCP software component? (Choose all that apply.)

a. DHCP client

b. DHCP resolver

c. DHCP server

d. DHCP primary master

e. DHCP secondary master

f. DHCP relay

6. When a DHCP server is not available on the same cable segment as a DHCP client, which technique permits their initial broadcast requests to be serviced? (Choose all that apply.)

a. None. A DHCP server must be available on any cable segment or broadcast domain where a DHCP client resides.

b. Install a DHCP relay agent on any cable segment or broadcast domain where a DNS server is not directly attached.

c. Install a remote DHCP agent on any cable segment or broadcast domain where a DNS server is not directly attached.

d. Configure internal routers to forward BOOTP from cable segments or broadcast domains where DHCP clients reside to segments where DHCP servers reside.

e. Configure internal routers to forward BOOTP from cable segments or broadcast domains where DHCP servers reside to segments where DHCP clients reside.

7. What's a typical dynamic IP lease period for an office environment where office workers come and go regularly?

a. four to eight hours

b. one to three days

c. one week

d. two to three weeks

8. What's a typical dynamic IP lease period for an ISP network?

a. four to eight hours

b. one to three days

c. one week

d. two to three weeks

9. How does a DHCP relay forward the DHCP server's reply to a client's initial address request?

a. It uses a temporary IP address created for the requester.

b. It uses the IP address offered to the requester.

    c. It uses the MAC layer address for the requester.

    d. It broadcasts a reply, for which the requester listens.

10. When using DHCP to create addresses for servers or routers that DHCP will manage, what type of address lease is most appropriate?

    a. permanent

    b. manual

    c. automatic

    d. dynamic

11. When using DHCP to create addresses for network clients (typical end–user machines), what type of address lease is most appropriate?

    a. permanent

    b. manual

    c. automatic

    d. dynamic

12. Which issue explains why DHCP was not traditionally used to manage server and router addresses?

    a. Routers and servers require static IP address assignments.

    b. DHCP is a client-only solution.

    c. DHCP may only be updated manually so it's not suitable for servers or routers.

    d. Servers and routers often depend on DNS, which must be manually updated when addresses change.

13. Which of the following types of machines has no limitations regarding dynamic IP address assignments?

    a. servers

    b. routers

    c. clients

    d. none of the above

14. Which of the following UDP and TCP port numbers are associated with DHCP?

    a. 57 and 58

    b. 67 and 68

    c. 77 and 78

    d. 116 and 117

8

15. How would you best describe the process of DHCP discovery broadcasts *not* forwarded by routers?

    a. remote process

    b. limited process

    c. local process

    d. client process

16. What type of address does a client define in the Discover packet if it was previously active on the network?

    a. prior address

    b. former address

    c. preferred address

    d. renewal address

17. Which of the following DHCP option types is not related to NetBIOS over TCP/IP? (Choose all that apply.)

    a. 1

    b. 3

    c. 15

    d. 44

    e. 46

    f. 47

18. What type of packet does a DHCP server send to a DHCP client in reply to a Discover packet?

    a. Reply packet

    b. Offer packet

    c. Release packet

    d. Renewal packet

19. How does a DHCP client accept an offer from a DHCP server?

    a. by issuing a DHCP Accept packet

    b. by issuing a DHCP Request packet

    c. by issuing a DHCP Decline packet

    d. by issuing a DHCP Renewal packet

20. What kind of DHCP packet does the server send to the client to denote completion of the DHCP Discovery process?

    a. DHCP Accept packet

    b. DHCP Request packet

    c. DHCP Acknowledgment (ACK) packet

    d. DHCP Renewal packet

21. At what time during the DHCP release renewal period will a DHCP client issue a renewal request if the first renewal request receives no reply?

    a. halfway through the release renewal period

    b. three-quarters of the way through the release renewal period

    c. seven-eighths of the way through the release renewal period

    d. when the renewal period expires

22. At what time during the DHCP release renewal period will a DHCP client enter the rebinding time interval?

    a. 0.5

    b. 0.75

    c. 0.875

    d. 1.0

23. Even though it's not required by the specification, DHCP clients should release their addresses by sending DHCP Release packets to the DHCP server. True or false?

    a. True

    b. False

24. Which of the following fields indicates if a DHCP packet is a DHCP Request or a DHCP Reply?

    a. Operation Code field

    b. Hardware Type field

    c. Transaction ID field

    d. Flags field

25. Which of the following best describes the function of the DHCP Options field in a DHCP message?

    a. provides information about additional payload fields

    b. used to expand the data included in the DHCP packet

    c. provides a bit mask to interpret field values

    d. provides specific addresses for DHCP clients to use, in order of usage attempts

26. DHCP clients use broadcast addressing only when they do not have current, valid IP addresses to use. True or false?

    a. True

    b. False

27. Where is the DHCP relay agent function loaded on a network segment that does not include an active DHCP server?

    a. on every DHCP client machine

    b. on at least one DHCP client machine

    c. on a specially designated DHCP relay machine

    d. on a router connected to the segment containing DHCP clients

28. IPv6 autoconfiguration makes DHCP completely unnecessary. True or false?

    a. True

    b. False

Hands-on Projects

Project 8-1

The following Hands-on Projects assume that you are working in a Windows 2000 environment, and you installed the EtherPeek for Windows demo program, as defined in Project 1-1.

To examine a DHCP boot sequence:

1. Start the EtherPeek for Windows demo program according to the instructions in Hands-on Project 1-2.

2. Click **File**, **Open**, and open the trace file **DHCPboot.pkt** contained in the **18654-2\Ch8** folder on your hard disk. The packet summary window appears.

3. Double-click **Packet #1** to open the decode window. Answer the following questions:

    a. What value is contained in the Client Identifier field?

    b. How can you verify that the Client Identifier value is the same as the client's hardware address?

    c. What is the host name?

    d. Can this client accept unicast replies during the boot up process?

    e. List the option codes used in this DHCP packet:

    _____   _____   _____

    _____   _____   _____

    _____   _____   _____

4. Click the **Decode Next** button until you locate the DHCP Offer, Request, and ACK packets. Examine each DHCP packet. This is a normal DHCP boot sequence.

5. Close the decode window. Close the packet summary window.

Project 8-2

To interpret the process of DHCP renewal, rebind, and reinitialize sequences:

1. Click **File**, **Open**, and open the trace file **DHCPlab.pkt** contained in the **18654–2\Ch8** folder on your hard disk. The packet summary window appears.

2. Double-click **Packet #3** to open the decode window. Answer the following questions about this packet:

   a. Does this DHCP client already have an IP address?

   b. What Message Type is used in this packet?

   c. What is the purpose of this packet?

   d. Does the client receive a reply to this packet?

   e. What DHCP process is the client performing at this time?

3. Click the **Decode Next** button until you see Packet #5. Answer the following questions about this packet:

   a. Does this DHCP client still have an IP address?

   b. What is the Message Type used in this packet?

   c. What is the primary difference between this packet and Packet #3?

   d. Does the client receive a reply to this packet?

   e. What DHCP process is the client performing at this time?

4. Click the **Decode Next** button until you see Packet #10. Answer the following questions about this packet:

   a. Does this DHCP client still have an IP address?

   b. What is the Message Type used in this packet?

   c. Does the client receive a reply to this packet?

   d. What DHCP process is the client performing at this time?

5. Examine the remaining DHCP packets in the trace file. Did the client get the requested IP address?

6. Close the decode window. Close the packet summary window.

Project 8-3

To edit and test a DHCP filter:

1. Click **View**, **Filters** to open the Filter window.

2. Double-click the **DHCP** filter. As you see, this is a Protocol filter.

3. Click the **Protocol** button to view the protocol selected for this filter. You should see the DHCP protocol highlighted.

4. Click **OK** to close the Protocol window.

8

5. This filter captures all DHCP packets that the analyzer sees. You are interested in capturing only DHCP packets that come from the IP address 0.0.0.0, indicating that a new device is booting onto the network, or a DHCP client reinitialized. Click the **Address filter** check box.

6. Click the down arrow in the **Type** field (next to the Address 1 section). Select **IP**.

7. The value 0.0.0.0 is automatically placed in the Address 1 field. This is acceptable. You do not need to change the directional information or add an Address 2 value. Click **OK**. Next, you test your filter by applying it to an existing trace file.

8. Click **File**, **Open**, and open the trace file **DHCPlab.pkt** contained in the **18654-2\Ch8** folder on your hard disk. The packet summary window appears.

9. Select the **Edit** menu, and then choose **Select**.

10. Scroll down in the Selection criteria box until you see the DHCP filter. Click the check box next to the **DHCP** filter.

11. Click the **Select Packets** button. Four packets are highlighted in the summary window.

12. Click the **Hide Unselected** button to view the packets that matched your filter.

13. Click the **Close** button to close the Select window. Double-click each packet to view the full decode window and further examine the packet.

14. Close the EtherPeek for Windows demo program.

CASE PROJECTS

1. You are a network administrator for a large bagel manufacturer that has 32 bakeries located throughout the United States, United Kingdom, and Switzerland. Your company wants to move to a DHCP network design using private IP addresses. Each bakery consists of only three computers, but all the bakeries communicate with the corporate headquarters in Yonkers, New York.

   How can you design a DHCP solution for these locations?

2. You consult for various large networking companies. One of your clients complains that laptop users cannot connect to the network in the evening. They know the network is set up for DHCP addressing—they have, however, configured a static address for the laptop. The address is within the valid range of IP addresses defined for the network. How can you determine the cause of this problem?

3. Your design company installed two Microsoft DHCP servers—one on each of the two floors of your office building in Vienna, Austria. When your clients on the lower floors try to boot onto the network, they get a message that the IP address is in use. How can you determine the cause of the problem and recommend a solution for this network?

9

SECURING TCP/IP ENVIRONMENTS

> **After reading this chapter and completing the exercises you will be able to:**
> ♦ Understand basic concepts and principles for maintaining computer and network security
> ♦ Recognize security issues inherent in TCP/IP architecture
> ♦ Explore well-known potential points for attacks on TCP/IP
> ♦ Understand the form that most TCP/IP attacks usually take
> ♦ Recount the basic routines involved in identifying, addressing, and repairing IP security problems
> ♦ Explore the resources and tools available to help maintain effective, strong IP security on your systems and networks

TCP/IP was originally designed in an age when networking was a marvel of technology, and when network access was available only to a privileged few. The basic protocols that support the environment were generally devoid of security features or functions. In fact, it's possible to describe TCP/IP's inherent security model as "optimistic" in the sense that even obvious exposure of potentially valuable information—such as accounts and passwords—was not considered unsafe or unsound until the Internet was around for quite some time.

If it seems that security in a TCP/IP environment is an afterthought, that's because security features and functions represent improvements and enhancements layered on top of original implementations. Much of what you'll learn in this chapter revolves around addressing potential **holes** or points of exposure left open in the original implementations of many IP-based protocols and services. Securing TCP/IP, therefore, requires that you recognize and understand such potential exposures, comprehend how they may be addressed, learn how to assess potential security threats or vulnerabilities, and act accordingly. Thus, TCP/IP security is a matter of routine observance, regular assessment, and keeping up with the current state of possible attacks, threats, and vulnerabilities.

UNDERSTANDING COMPUTER AND NETWORK SECURITY

When people think of computer or network security, they tend to think immediately about hackers or **crackers** in more or less the same thought. And although protecting a system or network does indeed mean closing the door against outside attack, it also means protecting your systems, data, and applications from any sources of damage or harm (inadvertent or intentional), whether they originate inside or outside your organization's boundaries. Thus, planning for disaster recovery, making regular back ups, using anti-virus software, and maintaining **physical security** over computing resources can be every bit as important to security as locking out unwanted intrusions.

In fact, the International Computer Security Association (ICSA) estimates that over 90% of the time, cost, and effort involved in dealing with loss of data or services from a network originates from banal causes such as viruses, power outages, and "inside jobs." This same group estimates that 70% of all network or system break-ins originate with employees who are already inside whatever security barrier guards the network's external boundaries in most organizations.

Therefore, there's more to network security than simply barring the door to ill-intentioned outsiders. The same is true for TCP/IP-related security matters. Fundamentally, all forms of network security in any organization focus on three major areas of potential (and great) concern, as you will learn in the section that follows:

- Physical security (controlling physical access)
- Personnel security (managing human access)
- Software security (managing software behavior and vulnerabilities)

The Three Legs of Network Security

Before we jump into the important details related specifically to TCP/IP security issues, we feel obligated to provide a little background on the three most important elements involved in creating secure systems and networks. Some of this information may seem like common sense or common knowledge—that's exactly what it is. But, we like to say that although most information technologists are 98% technology and 2% common sense, computer and network security is more like 2% technology and 98% common sense. So forgive us if we belabor the obvious, but you'd be surprised how many people try to solve personnel- or situation-related security problems with technology, rather than attacking such problems more directly.

It's best to think of computer and network security as a tripod that rests equally on all three of these metaphorical legs:

- *Physical security*: Unless you take steps to prevent unauthorized users from taking physical possession of your servers, routers, firewalls, and other network gear, you cannot prevent them from breaking into your systems at their leisure. Physical security is synonymous with "controlling physical access" and should be carefully monitored for any equipment that is important to your computer or network security, or that could compromise that security. This means locking up such gear in equipment rooms or wiring closets (and being sure that ventilation and power supplies are adequate) to prevent the unauthorized from gaining access. It might also mean checking visitors, using ID badges, or even using special card-key locks to permit only certain authorized users to access equipment.

- *Personnel security*: The best passwords and access controls in the world are worthless unless you also train staff how to maintain **personnel security**. When passwords are too hard to remember and there's no **security policy** to forbid such behavior, it's typical for people to tack notes on their terminals with their passwords for all to see (and use). It's important to formulate a security policy for your organization, make sure employees follow that policy, and avoid forms of laziness and "cheating" that undo the best physical and **software security** measures.

- *System and network security*: This includes analyzing the current software environment, identifying and eliminating potential points of exposure, closing well-known **back doors**, and preventing documented exploits. Although the other two legs of the tripod are equally important, because this is a book on TCP/IP, we concentrate on system and network security throughout this chapter.

Understanding Typical IP Attacks, Exploits, and Break-ins

Let's start with a little network and computer security terminology to help you understand the most immediate items of concern for TCP/IP:

- An **attack** represents some kind of unauthorized user's attempt to obtain access to information, to damage or destroy such information, or to otherwise compromise system security, preferably without detection until the deed is done. The most extreme case, of course, is when outsiders obtain administrative access to a system and can then do whatever they want with it.

- An **exploit** documents any successful attack, usually in the context of a recipe, or by including software tools used to mount an attack. Fortunately, when exploits are published, the good guys find out about them as quickly as the bad guys, and can start working out ways to defeat, nullify, or prevent that exploit from being repeated. This explains why it's so important to keep up with current events in network and system security—new exploits (and related patches and fixes) are constantly reported. By subscribing to any of several excellent security-focused mailing lists (*http://www.ntsecurity.net*, *http://www.cert.org*, *http://www.microsoft.com/security/*, and so forth), you can receive this kind of information via e-mail as soon as it's available.

- A **break-in** refers to a successful attempt to compromise a system's security. This can be something as innocuous as gaining access to directories, in which unauthorized users are not allowed, to taking over complete control of systems. These tend to fall in the realm of unfortunate events, in the "bad to worse" category. Most security experts acknowledge that the bulk of system break-ins are not reported publicly because organizations do not wish to advertise their security problems to the world!

As you already learned, each IP-based service can be associated with one or more well-known port addresses, on which they listen for service requests. These addresses represent TCP or UDP ports, and are designed to respond to attempted connections to begin the process of responding to legitimate requests for service. Unfortunately, the same ports that handle perfectly valid requests for service can also become points of attack—well-advertised points of attack, in fact—so the same door you open for your intended users sometimes opens for malefactors as well.

Equally unfortunate, TCP/IP was originally designed around an **optimistic security model**. TCP/IP's original designers didn't consider that the mechanisms they created to handle service requests could also expose servers to hijack attempts, compromise, or mangling of their data and services.

There's an entire catalog of ways in which TCP/IP can be attacked. For example, bad guys can do any or all of the following:

- They can attempt to impersonate valid users by attacking well-known accounts (such as a root on a UNIX host, or Administrator on Windows NT or Windows 2000), and repeatedly trying to guess their associated passwords. Successfully stealing a valid account and password permits straightforward **user impersonation**. Trying every likely or possible password for an account is called a **brute force password attack**.

- They can attempt to take over existing communications sessions by inserting manufactured IP packets that shift control to them and their machines. This is called **session hijacking**.

- They can attempt to snoop inside traffic moving across the Internet to look for unprotected account and password information (which could lead to user impersonation), or to obtain other sensitive information while it's in transit. This is called **packet sniffing** or **packet snooping**.

- They can create so much traffic aimed at a particular protocol or service that the underlying server is overwhelmed, or create pathologically incomplete or incorrect packets that cause a server to wait forever for additional data that never arrives. Because this results in blocking legitimate users from accessing a service, it's called a Denial of Service (DoS) attack.

Throughout this chapter, you may notice a common theme: There is an inverse relationship between flexibility and security. Put another way, the more flexible a system is, the less secure it is. This is important because the designers of TCP/IP and most protocols try to make the protocols as flexible as possible. The fact that TCP/IP is suitable for military and civilian use, and that the protocol has survived so many years while the applications and equipment surrounding it evolve rapidly, shows just how flexible this suite is. A great deal of this flexibility comes from peripheral protocols, such as Internet Control Message Protocol (ICMP), Simple Network Management Protocol (SNMP), Address Resolution Protocol (ARP), and various routing protocols. Ironically, the interaction between these protocols and IP is what is compromised most often. Therefore, much of modern security practice is nothing more than disabling the features these protocols provide. For example, on a normal network, the proxy ARP function can be very useful because it allows hosts to communicate across a routed network without having their default gateways manually configured (it adds flexibility). However, an **attacker** could either deny service to a host, or redirect traffic from a host to its own machine by sending illegitimate proxy ARPs. You can prevent this by disabling proxy ARP, or manually configuring MAC addresses and disabling ARP altogether. The question then becomes, if you are responsible for a network of 1000 PCs, is the security of your data worth the effort to prevent this attack? Answering this question is one reason corporations expend so much effort on security assessments.

Like the protocols that surround it, IP also features a great deal of flexibility, such as the ability to broadcast to all hosts without manually specifying each address, and the ability to support multiple Layer 2 topologies by fragmenting large frames into smaller ones. Unfortunately, disabling these core features would render the entire protocol useless, so alternate solutions must be found to prevent these features from being used for wrongdoing. These solutions typically involve products that are external to the protocol, such as proxy servers and firewalls, rather than a reconfiguration of the protocol itself.

As you'll learn later in this chapter, much of the routine IP security work that a network administrator must perform consists of monitoring recent exploits, and taking preventive measures to avoid falling victim to those same exploits. It also means being aware of potential points of exposure, and taking preemptive measures to prevent such potential danger.

Common Types of IP-related Attacks

Although the details of the individual attacks to which IP protocols and services are prey differ considerably from one case to another, these attacks tend to fall into four general categories:

- *DoS attacks*: In a DoS attack, a service is inundated with service requests, or malformed service requests cause a server to hang. In either case, legitimate users are denied access to the server's services because it is kept busy or becomes unavailable. Although DoS attacks don't involve any destruction of data or outright compromises of system or network security, they do deny users access to any services that might otherwise be available on the server under attack. Unfortunately, DoS attacks are easy to mount and difficult to stop, and certain IP services are unusually vulnerable to such attacks. Thus, whereas DoS attacks pose more of a nuisance than a security threat, they are no less vexing when they occur.

- *IP service attacks*: Numerous IP services are subject to attack **(IP service attacks)**, often through their well-known ports (but sometimes through other ports as well) in ways that can expose the underlying systems to inspection or manipulation, particularly when the underlying file system is accessible. For example, services, such as FTP and HTTP (Web), that permit anonymous logins are notoriously prone to file system penetration when access roots for anonymous users coincide with file system roots for drives or logical disk volumes.

- *IP service implementation vulnerabilities*: Sometimes hackers discover bugs in specific implementations of IP services on particular platforms that can be exploited to permit normally illegal operations to occur on machines where those services are available. Windows NT, for instance, was subject to several debugger-based attacks when developers left debugging switches active in code, which were then exploited through a TCP/IP-based network session to assert system-level access for anonymous or null user sessions (which normally can't do much of anything on a well-secured system).

- *Insecure IP protocols and services*: Some protocols, such as FTP and Telnet, can require user account names and passwords to permit access to their services. But these protocols do not encrypt that data; if malefactors sniff IP packets between senders and receivers while this information is visible, they can obtain valid account name and password pairs to use to break into a system. There isn't much you can do about this, except to restrict public access to systems in which compromise won't be a problem. Otherwise, you must require users to switch to more secure implementations of such services, when they're available (as is the case with Secure Telnet, or Stelnet, for instance). Alternately, you can force users to use Virtual Private Network (VPN) connections (which encrypt all traffic between senders and receivers) when insecure protocols or services are employed.

What IP Services Are Most Vulnerable?

One kind of IP service that's vulnerable to attack is a so-called **remote logon service**. This includes the well-known Telnet remote terminal emulation service, as well as the so-called Berkeley remote utilities, a.k.a. **r–utils**, which include a variety of commands to execute remote commands **(rexec)**, launch a remote UNIX shell **(rsh)**, print remotely **(rpr)**, and so forth. The inclusion of these r-utils in the Berkeley Software Distribution (BSD) version of UNIX in the 1980s is what gave these utilities their names, but it is their ability to execute remote commands or sessions on other machines elsewhere on the network that makes them a potential security threat.

Along the same lines, remote control programs, such as pcAnywhere, Carbon Copy, Timbuktu, ReachOut, and so on, can also become security threats. For instance, older versions of the Symantec program pcAnywhere made themselves open to other pcAnywhere clients elsewhere on a network, by default, without requiring a password for access. Your authors learned quickly that when we attached a Windows system to our local cable modem infrastructure, requiring (and encrypting) an account name and a password to access pcAnywhere are essential to keep other users from obtaining access to that machine. Although we were prepared to deal with this situation, we noticed at least half a dozen other Windows users on our local cable segment who had left themselves open to system penetration from anyone who had access to the right software.

Other services that can be vulnerable to attack are those that permit **anonymous access**—this makes anonymous Web and FTP conspicuous targets, for instance. That's one reason why we strongly recommend that any such services and data you offer to the Internet be duplicated elsewhere, preferably somewhere safe that's not publicly accessible. It also explains why many organizations choose to situate their public Web servers at an ISP, or use commercial Web-hosting services. In that situation, an attack on a publicly accessible system cannot simultaneously turn into an attack on an in-house network. Most organizations also maintain one or two back up copies of any public server on other private networks that are not publicly accessible. They can use a private copy to re-create a public one on short notice, should the public one become compromised or damaged by a successful attack.

Sadly, it's the case that almost any IP service can become a potential point of attack. The more sensitive the information that a service is known to carry, or the greater the range of access that a service may be granted (such as SNMP, which sets and collects system configuration and management data on servers, routers, hubs, switches, and other network devices), the more likely it is to provide a potential point of illicit entry into a system or network. Ultimately, nothing in the broad world of IP services is entirely exempt from compromise!

Of Holes, Back Doors, and Other Illicit Points of Entry

This terminology applies both to the operating systems and the IP services that run on them, where either (or both) may become points of attack:

- *Hole*: A weak spot or known place of attack on any common operating system, application, or service. In the UNIX world, outsiders employ numerous techniques to hijack the superuser account and gain root-level access to a machine. Likewise, Windows NT and Windows 2000 are subject to some well-crafted exploits that can crack the Administrator account and give outsiders unlimited access to a system.

- *Back door*: An undocumented and illicit point of entry into an operating system or application added by a system's programmers to bypass normal security. Although neither UNIX nor Windows NT nor 2000 offers such things, there are plenty of ways in which obtaining physical access to a machine delivers the same results, or where access to encrypted password files can occur through guile or ignorance. Thus, for example, Windows NT 4.0 was prone to an attack called GetAdmin, wherein the presence of a debugging flag inadvertently left turned on in the operating system kernel made it possible for any user account except Guest to be added to the local Administrators group. Although this is not precisely a back door in the strictest of terms, because it led any user to Administrator-level access, it had to be taken seriously and was quickly repaired. (See MS Knowledge Base article Q146965 for more information on this topic.)

- *Vulnerability*: A **vulnerability** is a protocol, service, or system facility that is known to be susceptible to attack. Some such attacks are fiendishly clever and require deep knowledge or programming skills from their creators. Once documented, however, anyone with access to the details of a particular vulnerability can exploit it, much to the vexation of system and network administrators.

Although preventing unauthorized remote access to your systems is a legitimate and important concern, especially when systems are Internet-accessible, we also feel compelled to restate the importance of maintaining physical security over such systems as well. This is because, even though physical security isn't unique to TCP/IP, any knowledgeable systems professional with the right tool kit can break into just about any system in 15 minutes or less, if allowed unsupervised and unrestricted access to the computer on which such a system resides! Thus, no matter how well you secure your IP environment, if you don't think holistically and include all aspects of your systems in your security plan, your IP security efforts may be for naught.

The need for physical protection applies equally to important data assets—such as emergency repair disks, copies of the Registry, back-up tapes, and so forth. That's because such files contain hashed versions of all passwords. **Password hashing** algorithms are all too often well known, so anybody who obtains any of these items can attempt to crack those passwords at their leisure. By using a brute force password attack, hackers can try hashing all possible combinations of letters, numbers, and symbols until they find a hash that equals the hash in the password file (or Registry, emergency repair disk, or back-up tape). If the passwords are long enough, and contain an appropriate mix of letters, numbers, and symbols, this attack can take a very long time to run and is less likely to be successful. That's why it's important to change passwords regularly.

However, there is a shortcut for hackers, called a **dictionary attack**, which consists of creating hashed values for all words in a specialized dictionary of terms, then comparing those values to the hashed values in password files. Because the uninformed user will often choose a password that can be found in an English dictionary, he or she inadvertently reduces the time required to crack the password from weeks to seconds. When a match is eventually found, the software reports the relevant account and the clear text version of the password is ready for illicit use. For those in the know, this grim possibility also explains why strong passwords (those that contain a combination of letters, numbers, and symbols, and a required minimum length) are a must for most Windows and UNIX systems.

Principles of IP Security

Given the many potential points of attack and the many ways in which the unscrupulous can try to take advantage of those uninformed about IP security, the following is a list of specific recommendations that we strongly suggest you apply to your systems:

- *Avoid unnecessary exposure*: Install no unused or unneeded IP-based protocols or services on your servers. Each point of entry is also a point of potential attack. Why expose something that you don't need or use?

- *Block all unused ports*: A relatively simple software program called a **port scanner** can attempt to communicate with any IP-based system while cycling through all valid TCP and UDP port addresses. Use a port scanner on your firewalls and servers (rest assured that hackers will whenever they can). Close all unused ports—each point of entry could invite an attack.

- *Prevent internal address "spoofing"*: When someone wants to break into a network, he or she often sends packets from outside the network, which masquerade as internal communications from an internal subnet. This technique relies on formulating packets that appear to be legitimate to casual inspection, but that could never legally take the form in which they appear (hence the term **spoofing**). There's no way that a packet that claims to originate inside your network should ever show up at a router or firewall interface where external traffic enters your network. Make sure you check for, and specifically block, spoofing attempts.

- *Filter out unwanted addresses*: By subscribing to Internet and e-mail monitoring services, such as *mail.com,* and obtaining lists of undesirable or questionable Internet addresses, you can preempt potential points of attack (or spam) by rejecting packets from certain domain names and IP addresses. Obviously, whenever actual attacks occur, you might also want to block the addresses from which they originate.

- *Exclude access by default, include access by exception*: This is what we call a **pessimistic security model**—exclude users from access to resources, by default, then add whatever users need access to such resources as exceptions to the general exclusionary rule. This keeps permissive defaults (like those that the Windows NTFS file system uses) from permitting users access to resources you don't want them to see.

- *Restrict outside access to "compromisable" hosts*: Any time you expose information, resources, or services to the public, you should expect attacks and be able to recover from compromises without undue loss of services or data. That's why only hosts that can be compromised without causing harm to your organization should be exposed, and why maintaining safe, private copies of public data is important.

9

- *Do unto yourself before others do unto you*: Perform regular attacks on your own systems and networks to be sure you've closed all obvious points of attack, addressed all existing exploits, and covered all security bases. Make this kind of activity part of your regular maintenance routine and monitor security-related mailing lists and newsgroups for late-breaking news and information. Consider hiring an outside security firm to attack your systems and networks if you really want to be sure your security is sufficiently tight.

In general, if you're prepared to deal with predictable security threats and have taken reasonable precautions, you may not be break-in proof, but you will be better off than most sites. Remember that you don't have to create a site that's impossible to compromise, just one that's hard enough to compromise that a run-of-the-mill hacker or cracker realizes you know what you're doing, and therefore will look for other, less-well-run sites to attack.

Common IP Points of Attack

As you've learned, TCP/IP is by its very nature a trusting protocol stack. Over the years, designers, implementers, and product developers tried to secure the protocol and, in essence, plug known holes or vulnerabilities whenever possible. The following sections provide more details about common attacks, about which all knowledgeable IP professionals must be concerned.

Viruses, Worms, and Trojan Horse Programs

There are several types of **malicious code** that can disrupt operations or corrupt data. **Viruses**, **worms** (often referred to as **mobile code**), and **trojan horses** are three such types of malicious code. The ILOVEYOU worm that was unleashed in May 2000 is an example of such code. This worm offered the first major attack that included a method of hiding the **file extension** to make an attachment appear innocent. This process of hiding the file extension is called **file extension obfuscation**.

The ILOVEYOU worm contains an e-mail attachment named LOVE-LETTER-FOR-YOU.TXT.vbs. When this worm executes, it tries to send copies of itself, using Microsoft Outlook, to all entries in all e-mail **address books** known to Outlook. This spreads the infection via e-mail.

At one time, it was assumed that only files that end in .exe, .com, and .bat could contain virus code. Now, however, we know that other types of files, such as Visual Basic Script (VBS) files, for example, can carry viruses as well.

According to the Computer Emergency Response Team (CERT) at Carnegie-Mellon University, the ILOVEYOU mail has the following characteristics and possible destructive tendencies:

- The message contains an attachment named LOVE-LETTER-FOR-YOU.TXT.VBS.

- The message contains the subject "ILOVEYOU."

- The body of the message reads, "kindly check the attached LOVELETTER coming from me."

When the worm executes, it searches for certain types of files and makes changes to those files depending on the file type. For files on fixed or network drives, it takes the following actions:

- For files with .vbs or .vbe extensions, the worm replaces the files with a copy of itself.

- For files with .js, .jse, .css, .wsh, .sct, or .hta extensions, the worm replaces the files with a copy of itself and changes the extension to .vbs. For example, a file named x.css is replaced with a file named x.vbs containing a copy of the worm.

- For files with .jpg or .jpeg extensions, the worm replaces the files with a copy of itself and adds a .vbs extension. For example, a file named x.jpg is replaced by a file named x.jpg.vbs containing a copy of the worm.

- For files with .mp2 or .mp3 extensions, the worm creates a copy of itself in a file named with a .vbs extension in the same manner as for a .jpg file. The original file is preserved, but its attributes are changed to Hidden.

 For more information on the ILOVEYOU virus, see *http://www.cert.org/advisories/CA-2000-04.html*.

The first step to protecting yourself from these malicious and mobile codes is to implement a virus protection software package that checks all e-mail attachments, regardless of their extensions.

You can use a **hex reader** to look inside suspect files without launching them. In Figure 9-1, we used Hex Workshop (by Breakpoint Software) to look inside an e-mail attachment. We can easily see the text contained in the executable code (Vbs.OnTheFly Created By OnTheFly.Infect execute as vbs). This appears to indicate that the file contains some malicious code.

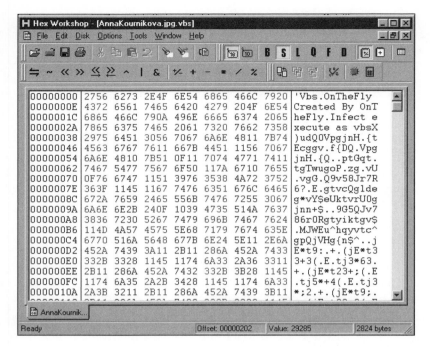

Figure 9-1 Opening attachments with Hex Workshop can identify malicious code

Trojan horse programs must be installed on a computer system in order to run. Typically, users are tricked into installing these programs. **Back Orifice** is an example of a trojan horse program. It is often disguised as a remote administration tool and consists of client and server software portions. The intruder uses the Back Orifice server program to control the Back Orifice client with all the privileges of the user who installed the client program. Back Orifice packets use UDP packets sent to port 31337.

Denial of Service (DoS) Attacks

Denial of Service attacks are designed to interrupt or completely disrupt operations of a network device or network communications. By overloading a network device, or confusing it in some way, an attacker can make a device deny service to other users or hosts on the network. The name "denial of service" is based on the idea that an overloaded **victim** cannot provide services to its valid clients.

The standard DoS attack consists of an attacker and a victim. One example of a DoS attack is shown in Figure 9-2. In this example, an attacker is sending an **incomplete fragment set** to the victim. As we tap into the network, we see a stream of fragments sent to 10.0.0.1 from 10.0.99.2 (this number may be spoofed). As you learned in Chapter 3, the fragment recipient holds onto the fragments for the length of the TTL value of the first fragment received. In this attack, the TTL value is set very high (256 seconds) and thousands of fragments are transmitted to the recipient. The last fragment of the set, however, is intentionally left out of the set. The recipient must hold onto the fragments in an attempt to reassemble them before the TTL value expires.

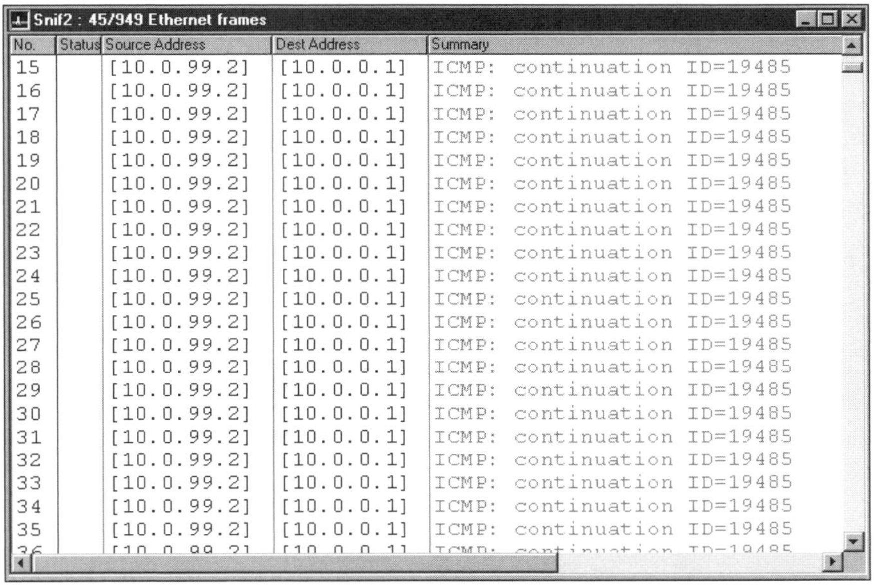

No.	Status	Source Address	Dest Address	Summary
15		[10.0.99.2]	[10.0.0.1]	ICMP: continuation ID=19485
16		[10.0.99.2]	[10.0.0.1]	ICMP: continuation ID=19485
17		[10.0.99.2]	[10.0.0.1]	ICMP: continuation ID=19485
18		[10.0.99.2]	[10.0.0.1]	ICMP: continuation ID=19485
19		[10.0.99.2]	[10.0.0.1]	ICMP: continuation ID=19485
20		[10.0.99.2]	[10.0.0.1]	ICMP: continuation ID=19485
21		[10.0.99.2]	[10.0.0.1]	ICMP: continuation ID=19485
22		[10.0.99.2]	[10.0.0.1]	ICMP: continuation ID=19485
23		[10.0.99.2]	[10.0.0.1]	ICMP: continuation ID=19485
24		[10.0.99.2]	[10.0.0.1]	ICMP: continuation ID=19485
25		[10.0.99.2]	[10.0.0.1]	ICMP: continuation ID=19485
26		[10.0.99.2]	[10.0.0.1]	ICMP: continuation ID=19485
27		[10.0.99.2]	[10.0.0.1]	ICMP: continuation ID=19485
28		[10.0.99.2]	[10.0.0.1]	ICMP: continuation ID=19485
29		[10.0.99.2]	[10.0.0.1]	ICMP: continuation ID=19485
30		[10.0.99.2]	[10.0.0.1]	ICMP: continuation ID=19485
31		[10.0.99.2]	[10.0.0.1]	ICMP: continuation ID=19485
32		[10.0.99.2]	[10.0.0.1]	ICMP: continuation ID=19485
33		[10.0.99.2]	[10.0.0.1]	ICMP: continuation ID=19485
34		[10.0.99.2]	[10.0.0.1]	ICMP: continuation ID=19485
35		[10.0.99.2]	[10.0.0.1]	ICMP: continuation ID=19485
36		[10.0.99.2]	[10.0.0.1]	ICMP: continuation ID=19485

Figure 9-2 Continuous fragments may indicate an attack

Other DoS attacks include the SYN Flood, Smurf, and WinNuke. All three of these attacks exist because the protocols rely on the software implementation to conform to and enforce the rules, rather than implementing a function to regulate usage in the protocol itself. As you can see from the following descriptions, these attacks are less complicated than other attacks such as session hijacking because their only goal is to break the communications, rather than divert stolen data or gain access to a computer.

- A **SYN Flood attack** uses the three-way TCP handshake process (covered in Chapters 5 and 6) to overload a device on a network. In this attack, the source sends multiple SYN packets to the victim with no intent to complete the handshake. The purpose of this attack is to create enough half-open connections on the victim to overwhelm it and cause it to refuse any additional, valid TCP connection requests.

- In a **Smurf attack**, a malicious host crafts and sends ICMP Echo Requests to a broadcast address. The attacker places the victim's IP address in the Source IP Address field. The replies send a hailstorm of ICMP Echo Replies to the victim.

- In a **WinNuke attack**, a NetBIOS packet is sent with the Urgent flag bit set. This particular packet format can cause older versions of Windows to go to the blue screen.

Protecting your network against DoS attacks is extremely difficult because there are so many components of a modern TCP/IP network that are vulnerable. From using all available TCP connections via the SYN Flood, to simply filling up your bandwidth to the Internet with gigantic PING packets, the possibilities are almost endless.

Distributed Denial of Service Attacks (DDoS)

Distributed Denial of Service (DDoS) attacks are basically denial of service attacks that are launched from numerous devices. In February 2000, DDoS attacks brought down such e-giants as Yahoo! and eBay.

DDoS attacks consist of four main elements:

- Attacker
- Handler
- Agent
- Victim

The attacker is the person who sets up the attack sequence, as shown in Figure 9–3.

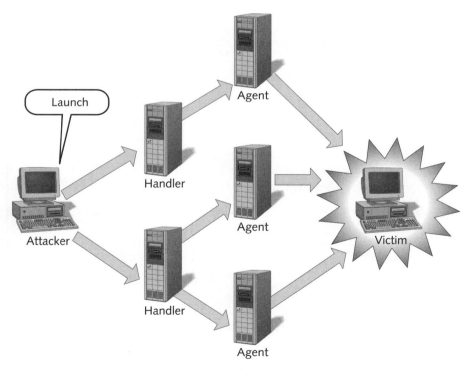

Figure 9-3   In a Distributed Denial of Service attack, agents launch the attack on the victim

Often, the attacker is nowhere to be found when the attack is actually launched. They set up the attack to transpire many minutes, hours, days, or even months after they have covered their tracks and left the scene of the future attack. The attacker first locates a host that it can compromise. This **compromised host** becomes the **handler**, or manager, for the DDoS.

The handler locates and recruits other unsecure hosts to act as **agents**, or subordinate devices. It is interesting to note that there can be more than one handler in a sophisticated DDoS attack. There can also be more than one agent per handler. Some communications must occur between the handler and agent in order to manage their relationship. Oftentimes, a file on the handler lists the IP addresses or names of known agents. Likewise, the agents may keep information about their handlers.

The agents actually launch the attack on the victim. At a time determined by the attacker, a handler sends the agents a "go-ahead" message to begin the attack.

The victim is the target of the agent's attack sequence. Where is the actual attacker? Long gone by now.

Buffer Overflows

Buffer overflows are common attacks, but strictly speaking, they are not related to TCP/IP. Instead, they exploit a weakness in many programs that expect to receive a fixed length of input. By sending more data than is expected, the attacker can "overrun" the program's input buffer. In some cases, the extra data can be used to execute commands on the computer with the same privileges as the program. This is why it is important to run processes such as IIS under an account other than the system account. As an example, consider the Microsoft Internet Explorer v4.0 MK Buffer Overrun exploit (known as the "MK Overrun" issue).

CERT identifies the problem: "Internet Explorer can crash when a malicious Web site contains a certain kind of URL (that begins with "mk://") with more characters than the browser supports. The extra characters could form a malicious executable that could then run on your computer." The only solution for this kind of a problem is to obtain and apply a patch or fix from the vendor that is designed to remove the source of vulnerability. Also, when such conditions occur—and they do crop up on a distressingly regular basis—the rogue code that may be introduced by a buffer overrun executes at the same level of rights and privileges as the process under attack. It's a bad idea to run any public IP-based services at System, Administrator, or Domain Administrator account levels, because compromise of the service could then permit its compromiser to take over an entire system or domain!

Spoofing

Spoofing is a process of borrowing identity information, such as an IP address, domain name, NetBIOS name, or TCP or UDP port numbers to hide or deflect interest in attack activities. Several attacks are based on this spoofing technology. For example, there are some NetBIOS attacks in which an attacker sends spoofed "NetBIOS Name Release" or "NetBIOS Name Conflict" messages to a victim machine. This can force a victim to remove its own valid name from its name table, and not respond to other valid NetBIOS requests. Now the victim cannot communicate with other NetBIOS hosts. To protect a network against this type of attack, you can block incoming NetBIOS communications at the boundary of the network. These NetBIOS communications include:

- NetBIOS Name Service, UDP/TCP port 137
- NetBIOS Datagram Service, UDP/TCP port 138
- NetBIOS Session Service, UDP/TCP port 139

Data Link layer frames can also be spoofed with bogus source MAC addresses, but the most common spoofing is, of course, forging the source IP address. Although IP spoofing prevents any useful return traffic, it is an effective way to prevent detection because there are very few ways to find the source of a packet besides the actual Source Address field in the IP header. Most commonly, the spoofed source address is from the RFC 1918 "private" address space, such as 10.0.0.0/8 or 192.168.0.0/16. This is done to make the packet appear to be from the local network. Occasionally, an attacker will put the valid IP address of another host in the Source Address field, as in the Smurf attack. This is done to direct any consequences to the other host. It also can send investigators on a wild goose chase, making the owner of the spoofed IP address appear to be the attacker.

The best method to avoid being the victim of a spoof attack is to use ingress and egress filtering. **Ingress filtering** is the process of applying restrictions to traffic coming into a network, and **egress filtering** is the process of applying restrictions to traffic leaving a network. For example, if your internal network uses 10.0.0.0 addresses to prevent spoofing, your egress rule says "allow traffic from 10.0.0.0 to leave, and deny all other outbound traffic," and your ingress rule says "do not allow traffic from 10.0.0.0 to enter, and allow all other inbound traffic." That way, if a packet tries to enter your network with a source address from your network, that packet is denied entry and the log tells you that the packet is either spoofed, or that you have some very serious routing issues. Obviously, this is a very basic example, used only to illustrate the concept. In the real world, you want to be much more specific about what traffic you allow into and out of your network.

TCP Session Hijacking

TCP session hijacking is a much more complex and difficult attack. The purpose of this attack is not to deny service, but to pretend to be an authorized user in order to gain access to a system. Therefore, the attacker can't just deny service by disabling the network because then the attacker wouldn't be able to access the system either. Instead, the attacker must successfully communicate with the server and client, and at the same time, prevent them from communicating with each other. In theory, this is difficult because the attacker must sniff the connection between the victim and server, and then wait until a TCP session is established, such as a Telnet session. Once established, the attacker must predict the TCP sequence number and spoof the source address on packets to the client and server so that it appears to the client that the attacker is actually the server, and vice versa.

 Recall that the TCP protocol uses the sequence number to acknowledge data received from its peer, and to let the peer know how much data it is sending.

Once the session is hijacked, the attacker can send packets to the server to execute commands, change passwords, or worse. For a detailed description of a variant of this attack, visit *http://www.insecure.org/stf/iphijack.txt.*

The important thing to realize about TCP session hijacking is that typical security mechanisms, such as user names and passwords, and even strong authentication, such as RADIUS with SecureID tokens, are completely bypassed because the attacker waits until *after* the session is established and the victim is authenticated to hijack the connection. Also, whereas the details of this attack are complicated, there are several programs, such as Juggernaut and Hunt, which allow anyone with physical access to a network to perform these attacks, so detailed knowledge of the TCP protocol is no longer necessary.

9

The Anatomy of IP Attacks

IP attacks typically follow a set pattern led by a reconnaissance or **discovery process** to learn about active systems or processes on the network. Next, the attacker focuses on the attack itself—whether the attack consists of planting malicious software on a compromised host, or disrupting host operations through a DoS attack. Finally, a **stealthy attacker** may cover its tracks by deleting log files, or terminating any active direct connections.

Reconnaissance and Discovery Processes

There are several types of reconnaissance probes and discovery processes that can be used to identify active hosts or processes. For example, a simple **PING sweep** can be used to identify the active hosts on an IP network. A PING sweep sends ICMP Echo Request packets to a range of IP addresses to determine which hosts are active.

A port probe is another reconnaissance process used to detect the UDP- and TCP-based services running on a host. Figures 9-4 and 9-5 show the traces of a TCP port probe process. As you can see in these figures, the host 10.1.0.2 sends TCP handshake packets (SYN) to 10.1.0.1, incrementing the destination port number in each subsequent packet.

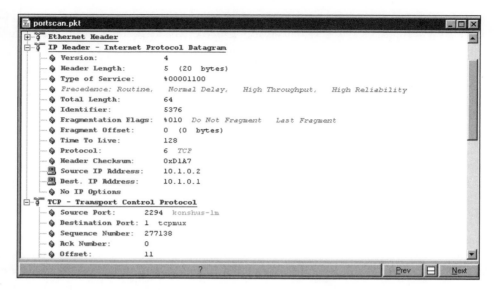

Figure 9-4 Initial TCP port probe

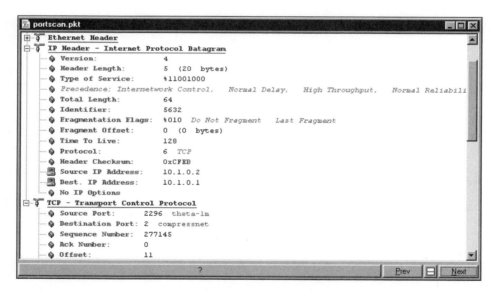

Figure 9-5 Port probe increments the destination port number by one in each attempt

Figures 9-4 and 9-5 show a very simplistic TCP port probe. In order to escape detection, an attacker typically varies the destination port number and interpacket time.

The purpose of the reconnaissance is to find out what you have and what is vulnerable. Tools such as **nmap** are very effective in discretely identifying hosts, including their IP addresses, operating system types, and versions.

The Attack

Once the attacker determines vulnerabilities, he or she can attempt to exploit them. The attack itself may encompass a **brute force attack** process that overwhelms a victim, or a simple, elegant, minimal-packet process that confuses and disrupts operations on the victim. SYN Flood, Smurf, and WinNuke are three attack type examples (described in the "Denial of Service (DoS) Attacks" section earlier in this chapter).

The Cover Up

In an effort to escape detection, many attackers delete log files that may indicate an attack occurred. **Computer forensics** (an examination of any traces of the attack) may be necessary to identify traces that an attacker has been winding its way through a system.

Network Sniffing

One method of passive network attack is based on network "sniffing," or eavesdropping, on network communications using a protocol analyzer or other sniffing software.

What can a network analyzer see? Plenty. Figures 9-6 and 9-7 show how an analyzer can display unencrypted login names and passwords, respectively, from a standard FTP session.

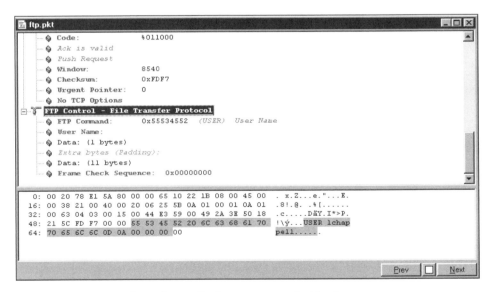

Figure 9-6   Network analyzer displays unencrypted login name

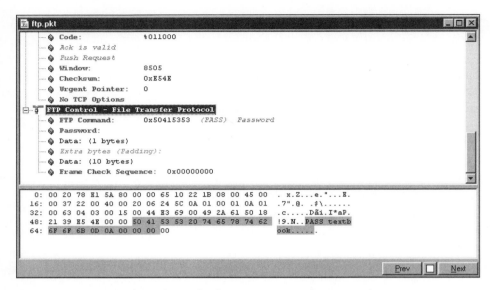

Figure 9-7   Network analyzer displays unencrypted password

There are numerous network analyzers available for eavesdropping on networks. Some of these include tcpdump (UNIX), Ethereal (Linux/Windows), Network Monitor (Windows), AiroPeek Wireless (Windows), as well as EtherPeek for Windows.

There are also some antisniff software packages available to detect and alert you to packet sniffers on the network. AntiSniff by Security Software Technologies (formerly the L0pht group) is the most popular online antisniffer available. These packages are actually something of a hack themselves in that they too bend the rules of networking—what these packages actually do is detect NICs running in promiscuous mode.

Promiscuous mode means that a NIC will pass every frame it receives up to the next layer for processing, whereas a normal NIC will process only frames that have its MAC address in the Ethernet Destination Address field (as well as broadcasts and multicasts for which the NIC registers). In order to see all the traffic on the network, a protocol analyzer's NIC must be in promiscuous mode, otherwise it will be able to sniff only traffic from itself or destined to itself, which is not very useful.

Basically, antisniff software sends an ICMP Echo packet to the IP broadcast address 255.255.255.255. Normally, this packet would be sent in an Ethernet broadcast as well, where the Destination Address field is FF:FF:FF:FF:FF:FF. However, the antisniff software sends the IP broadcast address, but uses a bogus unicast MAC address. The result is that every host on the network sees that the Ethernet frame is not addressed to them and drops the packet. However, any hosts running in promiscuous mode pass the packet up to the IP layer to be processed. The IP layer will then respond to the ICMP Echo with a Reply message. Thus, if the antisniff software receives any ICMP Echo Replies, then it knows someone is eavesdropping and can detect the intruder's IP address.

A final note about antisniff software is that it won't detect network analyzers on "mirrored" or "span" ports, or analyzers using passive taps, because these ports can only receive—they cannot transmit data, including the ICMP Echo Reply, onto the network. This is important because most intrusion detection systems operate in promiscuous mode as well. It is feasible for a sophisticated attacker to use an antisniff package to detect your intrusion detection system. Knowledge of an IDS allows the attacker to take extra precautions to avoid detection.

FIXING IP SECURITY PROBLEMS

As we mention repeatedly in this chapter, security is as much a matter of routine vigilance and regular maintenance as it is a matter of developing and applying security policies, practices, and procedures. In the sections that follow, we cover some of the elements that must be included as part of routine security maintenance. Thus, if we mention patches and fixes, we don't mean you should get the set that's current when you install software, and then forget about them. Instead, you should check for and apply patches and fixes as part of your regular security routine to help maintain a proper level of security on your systems and networks.

The same thing is true for monitoring security information, securing your networks and systems, performing regular security audits, attacking your own networks and systems, and deploying new security protocols, services, tools, and technologies. Regular effort and activity are the keys to maintaining good security in general, and good IP security in particular.

Most well-run organizations schedule software maintenance and updates on at least a monthly basis. What better time to check and recheck security than after you change the systems and software you're trying to protect? Most well-run organizations also conduct internal security audits either semi-annually or quarterly, and submit to external security audits at least once a year. You might consider making such activities part of your routine maintenance as well.

The Importance of Patches and Fixes

Many attacks take advantage of operating system faults and security holes. For example, in November 2000, Microsoft admitted that Windows NT 4.0; Windows 95, 98, 98 Second Edition; and Windows Me systems were vulnerable to a DoS attack. By sending a flood of specially malformed TCP/IP packets to a victim, an attacker could temporarily disrupt networking services or hang the victim's machine. This vulnerability was fixed in the "Incomplete TCP/IP Packet or Vulnerability" patch covered in Microsoft Security Bulletin MS00-091.

Frequently asked questions regarding this vulnerability and the patch may be accessed at *http://support.microsoft.com/default.aspx?scid=KB;en-us;275567&*.

In general, Microsoft security bulletins may be accessed or searched through the Bulletins menu entry at *http://www.microsoft.com/security/*. Likewise, other system and software vendors typically maintain their own lists of security issues and concerns. They also make such information available through mailing lists so you needn't miss any important notifications that may occur. You should make regular visits to their sites, or sign up for their mailing lists, as your needs and preferences dictate.

Knowing Which Ports to Block

Many exploits and attacks are based on common vulnerabilities. Table 9-1 indicates ports that should be blocked, if possible, to minimize the chances of attacks. If you implement our recommended pessimistic security approach, you'll block all these ports as a matter of course, and allow only specific exceptions (for example, an upstream DNS server at a trusted ISP or service provider, from which you obtain DNS updates and share your DNS zone files to improve external access to your name-and-address mapping data).

Table 9-1   Recommended Ports to Block

Port	Service
TCP port 53	DNS zone transfers
UDP port 69	tftpd
TCP port 87	Link port
UDP and TCP ports 111 and 2049	SunRPC and NFS
UDP and TCP ports 135 through 139, inclusive	NetBIOS related ports
TCP ports 512, 513, and 514 (TCP)	BSD UNIX "r" cmds
TCP port 515	lpd
TCP port 540	uucpd
TCP and UDP port 2000	openwindows
UDP and TCP port 6000+	X Windows

For more information on which ports to block, refer to *http://www.cert.org/tech_tips/packet_filtering.html*.

Recognizing Attack Signatures

Most attacks have some sort of identifying communication pattern or **attack signature** by which they may be recognized or identified. These signatures may be used to implement

intrusion detection system (IDS) devices, and can be configured as network analyzer filters as well.

Table 9-2 shows a partial list of trojan horse port numbers that may be used to attack a system. These values are maintained and defined by von Braun Consultants and Simovits Consulting (*http://www.simovits.com* [choose the News archive link, and then the List of Trojan Horses... link]):

Table 9-2   Trojan Horse Port Numbers

Port Number	Trojan Horse Name
1 (UDP)	Sockets des Troie
2	Death
20	Senna Spy FTP server
21	Back Construction, Blade Runner, Cattivik FTP Server, CC Invader, Dark FTP, Doly Trojan, Fore, Invisible FTP, Juggernaut 42, Larva, Motlv FTP, Net Administrator, Ramen, Senna Spy FTP server, The Flu, Traitor 21, WebEx, WinCrash
22	Shaft
23	Fire HacKer, Tiny Telnet Server - TTS, Truva Atl
25	Ajan, Antigen, Barok, Email Password Sender - EPS, EPS II, Gip, Gris, Happy99, Hpteam mail, Hybris, I love you, Kuang2, Magic Horse, MBT (Mail Bombing Trojan), Moscow Email trojan, Naebi, NewApt worm, ProMail trojan, Shtirlitz, Stealth, Tapiras, Terminator, WinPC, WinSpy
30	Agent 40421
31	Agent 31, Hackers Paradise, Masters Paradise
41	Deep Throat, Foreplay
48, 50	DRAT
58, 59	DMSetup
79	CDK, Firehotcker
80	711 trojan (Seven Eleven), AckCmd, Back End, Back Orifice 2000 Plug-Ins, Cafeini, CGI Backdoor, Executor, God Message, God Message Creator, Hooker, IISworm, MTX, NCX, Reverse WWW Tunnel Backdoor, RingZero, Seeker, WAN Remote, Web Server CT, WebDownloader
81	RemoConChubo
99	Hidden Port, NCX
110	ProMail trojan
113	Invisible Identd Deamon, Kazimas
119	Happy99
121	Attack Bot, God Message, JammerKillah
123	Net Controller
133	Farnaz

9

Table 9-2 Trojan Horse Port Numbers (continued)

Port Number	Trojan Horse Name
137	Chode
137 (UDP)	Msinit
138	Chode
139	Chode, God Message worm, Msinit, Netlog, Network, Qaz
142	NetTaxi
146	Infector
146 (UDP)	Infector
170	A-trojan
334, 411	Backage
420	Breach, Incognito
421	TCP Wrappers trojan
455	Fatal Connections
456	Hackers Paradise
513	Grlogin
514	RPC Backdoor
531	Net666, Rasmin
555	711 trojan (Seven Eleven), Ini-Killer, Net Administrator, Phase Zero, Phase-0, Stealth Spy
605	Secret Service
666	Attack FTP, Back Construction, BLA trojan, Cain & Abel, NokNok, Satans Back, Door - SBD, ServU, Shadow Phyre, th3r1pp3rz (= Therippers)
667	SniperNet
669	DP trojan
692	GayOL
777	AimSpy, Undetected
808	WinHole
911	Dark Shadow
999	Deep Throat, Foreplay, WinSatan
1000	Der Späher / Der Spaeher, Direct Connection
1001	Der Späher / Der Spaeher, Le Guardien, Silencer, WebEx
1010, 1011, 1012, 1015, 1016	Doly Trojan
1020	Vampire
1024	Jade, Latinus, NetSpy

This is not a complete list of all trojan horse programs that use these port numbers, but it is reasonably complete as we write this chapter. You can keep up-to-date on this subject by following the CERT announcements online at *http://www.cert.org*, or by subscribing to the mailing list at the same URL for more direct notification.

IP Security

The IP Security Protocol Working Group (IPSEC) defined **IP Security (IPSec)** to provide cryptographic security services to support explicit and strong authentication, integrity and access controls, and confidentiality of IP datagrams.

The IPSec standards define an IP Authentication Header (AH) and IP Encapsulating Security Payload (ESP) method to enable host-to-host security to encrypt data and protect information from network sniffers. In practice, the ESP method is the most widely used; the AH method is seldom used.

About Firewalls, Proxy Servers, and Other Boundary Devices

Many modern organizations make use of key devices or services to help maintain a safe boundary between their networks and systems and the outside world. In this section, you will encounter mention of devices called firewalls, proxy servers, bastion hosts, demilitarized zones, intrusion detection systems, and boundary routers or border routers.

We explain these concepts and how they apply to network security, adding a few other terms that you're likely to encounter when securing IP-based networks. Remember, managing and securing network boundaries is an entire field of network specialization unto itself; we can scratch only the surface of this fascinating area and point you to additional sources for more details.

The following are some important devices and services that you can use to help protect the perimeter of your networks:

- *Bastion host*: In medieval terms, a bastion is a fort designed to repel the attacks of enemies and prevent their advances into the inner keep of a castle. In network security terms, a **bastion host** is a hardened computer specifically designed to resist and oppose illicit or unwanted attempts at entry, whose job is to guard the boundary between internal and external networks. Thus, firewall services, proxy servers, and intrusion detection systems are usually situated on some type of bastion host. Normally, bastion hosts run only software related to their boundary management functions; it's not a good idea to use bastion hosts for more routine network services (such as database, file and print, e-mail, and so forth) not only because that exposes them to direct attack, but also because you want bastion hosts to concentrate entirely on their primary functions of protecting your network boundaries.

- *Boundary (or border) router*: A **boundary router** or **border router** sits on the boundary between networks (usually between private networks under the purview of some organization and public networks where "anything goes"). Because such routers often block access on the basis of IP addresses, domain names, or socket addresses, these devices are sometimes called screening routers. On the best-protected networks, outside attackers must first penetrate a screening router before they can even begin to attack a firewall. Often on such networks, a kind of DMZ is defined between the screening router and firewall, where externally accessible resources (those "compromisable hosts" we talked about earlier) might also reside.

- *Demilitarized zone (DMZ)*: A sort of virtual "no-man's land" that sits between an internal network and the outside world, a **demilitarized zone (DMZ)** is an area that's accessible to both outsiders and insiders, but which establishes a buffer area between what's completely inside and outside a network boundary. Many organizations that host their own Internet servers or services situate them in a DMZ (with private copies of the same information safely ensconced somewhere on the inside network) as a way of making them public, without completely exposing them to the outside world. It's common for a screening router, or a screening router and a firewall, to be installed between the DMZ and the outside world. Likewise, it's common for a firewall, or a firewall and a screening router, to be installed between the DMZ and the inside world.

- *Firewall*: A **firewall** is a specially "hardened" software service, or a software/hardware product, that erects a barrier to inspect and control traffic flow between networks (usually between networks that are inside and outside a boundary). Firewalls operate at the Internet (Layer 3), Transport (Layer 4), and Application (Layers 5 through 7) layers of the TCP/IP network model (layer numbers mentioned refer to corresponding ISO/OSI network reference model layers). Thus, firewalls can inspect the payloads of IP packets and follow sequences of such packets to determine if higher-level attacks are underway as well as inspect domain names, IP and port addresses, and other Layer 3 information. Firewalls often include proxy server software and intrusion detection systems as part of their overall configurations so that all boundary-checking facilities are on a single hardened device.

- *Network address translation*: Network Address Translation (NAT) software permits internal network addresses to be "translated" into public network addresses when packets leave inside networks so that only public IP addresses are exposed on the public Internet. This prevents would-be hackers from learning much about the addressing scheme inside a private network, which goes a long way to foiling break-in attempts. NAT is often used in tandem with private IP addresses, as defined in RFC 1918, for extra security. (Remember, private IP addresses can't be routed on the public Internet, making it nearly impossible to spoof such addresses in an external attack.)

- *Proxy server*: A special set of software services that interposes itself between users and servers so that users connect with a proxy service that then connects to a target service, instead of permitting users to connect directly with services without intermediation. This gives proxy software a chance to block unwanted types of access or connections, and inspect user behavior for suspicious activities. Proxy server software often runs on firewalls because they define the boundary between "inside" and "outside" on most networks.

- *Screening host*: When users from outside the network attach to a service inside the network, they actually attach to the firewall, which establishes a proxy session into the private side of the network from there. Thus, the firewall appears to be the **screening host** upon which all externally accessible services reside, even though this is not usually the case.

- *Screening router*: Also a boundary or border router; the term **screening router** refers to the ways in which such devices can be used to filter inbound and/or outbound traffic on the basis of IP and port addresses, domain names, and protocols or services requested.

So much for defining specialized security devices and related software. Next, we'll examine what makes them special, and what they can do for your network and system security needs.

More About Firewalls

In a house or a car, a firewall is a barrier that's built into the structure to prevent the spread of fire from one part of the structure to another. On a network, a firewall is a barrier that acts to control traffic flow and access between networks. In particular, firewalls are designed to inspect incoming traffic and block or filter traffic based on a variety of criteria, including the originating domain name or IP address, the IP service or port address requested, and so forth.

You normally find firewalls astride the boundary between a public network, such as the Internet, and private networks inside an organization. However, we know of some organizations that place firewalls at organizational boundaries, such as the network links between divisions or departments. Some organizations even use firewalls as an extra form of protection for access to sensitive data assets. For example, placing a firewall between all users and one or more servers where an organization's patents, trade secrets, personnel records, and other confidential data are kept adds an extra layer of security and access control around those key information assets.

Even though you can buy firewall software to turn an ordinary PC running Windows or some flavor of UNIX into a firewall that may host other services, firewalls usually reside in a separate, isolated physical device. That's because the job they do is so important that you don't want them burdened with other server responsibilities, such as e-mail, database, and so forth.

Firewalls are also isolated because they are obvious, exposed points of attack. What's the use of trying to protect the network boundary if the firewall compromises other services as well? Thus, firewalls tend to focus on implementing security functions, including address filtering, packet filtering, proxy services, and network address translation, and leave other functions to other servers.

Useful Firewall Specifics

Should you find yourself considering a firewall, be aware that firewalls usually incorporate four major elements:

1. *Screening router functions* permit the firewall to block or filter traffic according to numerous values or criteria (including domain name, IP address, port address, and message type).

2. *Proxy service functions* permit the firewall to interpose itself in all communications between networks to protect address privacy, perform NAT services, and monitor for suspicious activities.

3. *"Stateful inspection" of packet sequences and services* means that the firewall makes decisions to permit or deny a packet based on other packets. Unlike the screening firewall, where all traffic to a given port is blocked regardless of any other packet, a stateful firewall is more sophisticated. For instance, it does not allow a TCP packet with the SYN-ACK flag to pass unless it previously saw a TCP packet between the same source and destination with the SYN flag set. Likewise, it does not allow an ICMP Echo Reply to pass unless it previously saw an ICMP Echo Request. This allows it to prevent the kinds of attacks that only reveal themselves over time, based on ongoing patterns of behavior. (For example, denial of service attacks and dictionary password attacks both involve highly repetitive network traffic patterns.) By watching for such patterns to occur, and blocking them as they're noticed, stateful inspection permits a firewall to keep operating even when attacks are underway. This is also a function associated with IDSs.

4. *Virtual Private Network services* deal with systems and services that do not themselves encrypt any traffic. Earlier, we mentioned that one way to accommodate inherently unsecure services that send account names and passwords in the clear is to embed them within VPN connections, which normally also encrypt all traffic. (Strictly speaking, VPNs use tunneling protocols and need not encrypt tunneled traffic; practically speaking, virtually all such traffic is encrypted to provide an extra layer of privacy and protection.) Thus, it should come as no surprise that this kind of functionality is becoming increasingly important on firewalls.

We hope it's clear that any firewall is like a router in that it must have at least two network interfaces (and IP addresses) to do its job: one for the outside side of the connection, and the other for the inside side of the connection where the firewall forms the boundary between the two. It's also not unusual for firewalls to offer what are called reverse proxy services. This facility makes it possible for the firewall to act as a screening host, and present the external appearance that all internal services are situated on the firewall itself.

In general, firewalls also support a special interface called SOCKS. **SOCKS** is a protocol that defines how proxy mechanisms work to control traffic between networks. A SOCKS server sits between the inside and outside interfaces on the firewall, and allows internal users to access the external network, while blocking external users from accessing the internal network. A key element of SOCKS is its ability to create a proxied connection that acts as if an internal client is talking directly to an external server, where the client actually talks to the SOCKS server, and the SOCKS server in turn talks to the target external server. Key aspects of SOCKS version 5 are defined in RFC 1928 and include authentication features to check user identities as well as the ability to define specific packet filtering and security policies as part of the firewall's behavior.

Commercial Firewall Features

In addition to the features and functions mentioned in the preceding sections, which are nearly ubiquitous in all firewalls, there are additional features and functions that you may find in some, but not necessarily all, firewalls. Sometimes, such features can make a big difference, depending on your security needs. That's why we present and explain them here.

- *Address translation/privacy services*: These services mask internal network addresses from the public side, and permit use of RFC 1918 private IP addresses, where appropriate. Note that public IP addresses cost money these days; by using private IP addressing inside your network along with NAT, you can save money on IP address charges without materially affecting capability or performance. *But beware*: Some secure protocols, such as IPSec, occasionally require end-to-end communications, which means that private IP addresses may not work unless your proxy server specifically supports the protocol or service in use.

- *Specific filtering mechanisms*: Although most firewalls let you screen on IP addresses, you will want to check their abilities where domain names, port addresses, and packet types are concerned. Some firewalls have more flexible address-matching characteristics than others. (You can use wildcards to filter entire families of addresses with a single entry only on some firewalls.)

- *Alarms and alerts*: Most firewalls record information when thresholds are exceeded or specific events occur (alarms and **alerts**), but some are more flexible in their notification methods and in how they report such things.

- *Logs and reports*: **Logs** and **reports** are where event information and traffic statistics are recorded. If you require specific capabilities from these subsystems, be aware that firewalls vary greatly in their logging and reporting capabilities.

- *Transparency*: **Transparency** translates to users not noticing there's a firewall in the way when it's highly transparent, but as it becomes increasingly opaque, it becomes more noticeable. Whereas most firewalls are transparent to users, they are less so for administrators who must configure and maintain them. Be sure to investigate how this attribute affects both communities when considering any specific firewall.

- *Intrusion detection systems (IDSs)*: Some firewalls include rudimentary intrusion detection subsystems, while others interact readily with full-blown IDSs. The importance of this feature is directly proportional to the general importance of security on your network. Over time, we expect most firewalls to interact with intrusion detection systems as a matter of course. (Because most intrusions occur through the firewall, it's a natural place to situate such a service.) One of the primary advantages of adding an IDS is that such systems can dynamically configure a firewall to block offending or suspect packets, thereby saving an administrator from having to respond to a 3 a.m. page and perform the same action manually. Because automated systems can respond much more quickly than humans to emerging patterns suggestive of attack, they can also automatically preempt most break-in attempts.

- *Management controls*: Routers and firewalls can be reconfigured through ICMP redirect, and routing topology data is also influenced through DNS updates. Therefore, neither routers nor firewalls should accept ICMP redirects or DNS updates from any source except the servers in their upstream hierarchies, which means such information should come only from your ISP, or a known server IP address that you trust. Otherwise, unscrupulous outsiders could reconfigure your routing topology to insert their own networks between your network and other external networks. This would allow them to inspect all traffic leaving and entering your network; this is known as creating a **man-in-the-middle attack** (where the attacker inserts a device or network between source and destination networks).

More About Proxy Servers

Although proxying services for users inside a network to access servers and services outside the boundary gets most of the attention when proxy servers are explained, it's important to remember that proxy servers can work in the other direction too. That is, proxy servers can perform what is sometimes called "reverse proxying" to expose a service inside a network to outside users, as if it resides on the proxy server itself.

Thus, the proxy server gets between both outgoing and incoming service requests, which explains how a proxy server can screen addresses on the public Internet, as well as prevent external users from direct access to internal resources. This is how many companies block employees from accessing sites with questionable content, based on domain name or IP address filters. In fact, a proxy server can operate at the Application layer and block specific newsgroups in a newsreader as well.

Another important proxy behavior is called caching. When users request remote resources (such as particular Web pages, for example), a proxy server can store those pages locally for some time after the requests. If those pages are requested again before they time out of the cache, the request can be satisfied locally, rather than requiring another

HTTP "get" operation to re-read those same pages from the original server. On sites where users are active and multiple users access identical materials, caching can improve performance for users, as well as lower bandwidth consumption on the public Internet. That's what we call a "win–win" situation!

However, a cache is also a potentially valuable location for a system attack (because it makes pages previously viewed accessible to other users). For this reason, network administrators should be on the lookout for cache-related exploits, and apply all relevant patches and fixes to cache collection and management software.

Implementing Firewalls and Proxy Servers

It's important to remember that when implementing boundary controls, you make an implicit decision to link your network and its users to the Internet. Although it's possible to just link an internal network to the Internet without managing the boundary between them, it's increasingly irresponsible to do so. Only a network with no information assets worth protecting should consider taking such a chance, which equates to a policy of "no security." On the other hand, it's worth noting that the most secure networks allow no connections to the Internet at all, and usually operate a separate unclassified network if their users require such access. They even go to extreme lengths to make sure that users can't transfer files from the secure network to the unsecured network (including disabling or removing floppy drives and other removable media from the secured network's computers).

Because most security policies operate somewhere between the two extremes of "anything goes" and "no connection," you will find the following set of steps useful when planning and implementing firewalls and proxy servers on your networks:

- *Plan*: Before you actually acquire a firewall, you must understand them in general, and research your needs in particular. The planning phase consists of reviewing what's available, selecting the most likely candidates, obtaining information, and analyzing what you learn.

- *Establish requirements*: Before you can use a firewall, you must know what you want it to do, and how you will use it. To establish requirements, you must document the characteristics of your network environment, decide what traffic you want to permit and what traffic you want to disallow, and apply your security policy to your decisions to make sure all the pieces fit together properly.

- *Install*: Having obtained a firewall (and proxy server and/or IDS, where relevant), you must install the related hardware and software to put it into operation. Start out by placing it off the beaten track—in other words, when you bring up the firewall for the first time, it shouldn't be in the production role of managing the boundary right away. Run it in a controlled environment, out of public view, until it's ready to go into place in the "Implement" step later in this list.

- *Configure*: Once the physical elements and the software that goes with them are installed, the real fun begins. You must research and analyze the firewall's default configuration and learn how to alter it to meet your specific requirements. Try to make as few assumptions as possible, and confirm every possible aspect of explicit behavior. Also, contact the vendor and make sure you have the most current version of software, and any relevant patches and fixes, ensuring that the product is as up-to-date as possible. Products sometimes sit on shelves for months before passing into buyers' hands, and this kind of technology sits still for no one. This will protect you from potential exploits when you implement your firewall.

- *Test*: If you did your homework, this should be a pro forma step, but it's often quite revealing about the extent to which we are all willing to make assumptions. What you want to do is to inspect the configuration settings you made for the firewall (and other related software) to see how they compare to your requirements. If you're as human as we are, you will find the occasional mistake that needs cleaning up, and the occasional assumption that runs contrary to your requirements. Likewise, you may discover unexpected side effects from factory defaults that require change or correction.

- *Attack*: During this phase you should run a port scanner, a security monitor or analyzer, and any other possible attacks on your own network. The idea is to bang on your configuration to see how it looks and behaves from the outside. Obviously, you want to exercise as much of your firewall's capabilities as you can to see how it behaves when under attack.

- *Tune*: In response to what you learn in the test and attack phases, refine your configuration and do your best to meet your security policy's requirements to the extent that the hardware and software allow. Repeat the **test-attack-tune cycle** as many times as necessary, until you get to the point where no changes are needed from one iteration to the next.

- *Implement*: Now that you've fixed the defaults, rooted out faulty assumptions, and closed the door on potential points of attack, you're ready to put the firewall (and related software) into a production role. At this point, you've checked everything that you can to make sure you've created as secure an implementation as possible, so you should be able to proceed with confidence.

- *Monitor and maintain*: Post implementation is when the real work begins. You must monitor event logs, traffic statistics, and error messages from the firewall, but you should also monitor security newsgroups and mailing lists for new exploits (particularly those that might involve your environment). That way, you'll be ready to make the necessary adjustments.

Repeat the test-attack-tune cycle, as needed, to compensate for new exploits and attacks as you learn about them. While you're at it, remember that 90% of the costs of running a system are related to maintenance (not acquisition and training), so maintenance and upkeep are the most important parts of managing a firewall!

Planning, Installing, and Configuring

During the initial phases of your firewall's deployment, you must bring your knowledge completely up-to-date for whatever firewall you choose. This applies not only to understanding general firewall capabilities and limitations, but also the specifics of the firewall that you choose to deploy on your network. Check with the vendor for known exploits, software updates, patches, fixes, and other enhancements to the product since it first shipped. You may not have the most current version of that product in your hands right now, so your job is to bring it up-to-date.

You should also visit related mailing lists or newsgroups to look for late-breaking reports on attacks, exploits, or known software problems or deficiencies. Although the vendor is a good source for such information, it's important to check user information sources, security advisory groups, and other more neutral sources of information to make sure you're getting the whole story.

Sometimes, a vendor is not as willing as other users or security advisory groups to share the bad news with you. You can also ask this community of users, experts, and industry groups for advice during the planning, requirements analysis, installation, and configuration phases. Vendor tech support staff are not always as knowledgeable as the people who work on the front lines of the network security battle.

If a vendor offers training or consulting services to help you through these phases, investigate the offerings. You might also want to ask the vendor, as well as the community, for a consulting referral to make sure you can get expert help if and when you need it.

Our last word on this subject is this: Don't ever work straight out of the box with a firewall or proxy server without checking for additional changes, updates, patches, fixes, and workarounds. The state of the art has probably advanced since that product went into the box, so it's your job to catch up!

More About the Test-Attack-Tune Cycle

When you get into this part of a firewall's deployment, it's critical that you keep records. First, document your configuration as completely as possible and store the records in a secure place. Next, you'll want to use a port mapper, or some related attack software (such as nmap or **Legion**), to find out which TCP and UDP ports remain open on your firewall. Be sure to document any unexpected open ports that you find along the way, and check the applications and services you need to use to make sure you haven't disabled functionality that your users expect to find working properly.

If you find unexpected open ports, you must analyze them for risk. We repeat that the safest course of action is to close all ports that you are not actively using because this limits points of potential attack. Be wary, in fact, of creating exceptions to port and service policies (which we believe should be disabled, by default, and enabled only by exception). It may be convenient to open your firewall to remote control, but it's important to understand the kinds of exposure and potential points of attack that then might be opened.

Finally, you want to create a battery of **attack tools** with which to assault your firewall. We recommend the following tools for this job, among numerous available options:

- Network Associates CyberCop ASaP (*http://www.mcafeeb2b.com/services/cybercop-asap.asp*)
- GNU NetTools (*http://cs.wheatonma.edu/nbuggia/NetTools/*)
- A port mapper such as Legion ((*http://www.slacker.org*, search for "legion") or nmap (*http://www.insecure.org/nmap/*)
- Internet Security System's various security scanners (*http://www.iss.net*)

You can also use other commercial, shareware, and freeware utilities. Your authors also maintain a list of security resources online at *http://www.lanw.com/training/interop/securityurls.htm*—a great place to start prospecting for other potential candidates for your toolbox. You'll find numerous vendor listings for firewall and proxy server products here as well, along with listings for general information resources on these subjects.

We find the following general resources to be particularly useful:

- "Internet Firewalls: Frequently Asked Questions" (*http://www.interhack.net/pubs/fwfaq/*)
- Firewall Product Overview (*http://www.thegild.com/firewall/*)

You can also simply search on "firewalls" at Yahoo!, or use your favorite Internet search engine, to find a variety of useful references.

More About Intrusion Detection Systems (IDSs)

Intrusion detection systems make it much easier to automate the process of recognizing and responding to potential attacks and other suspicious forms of network traffic. Unlike systems that require human monitoring and pattern recognition skills to be applied to network traffic and usage patterns, IDSs actively recognize and respond to intrusion attempts in real time. Most of them disconnect a user who's exhibiting suspicious behavior, and run a reverse DNS lookup to identify the user's real IP address and location (as far as possible). Some IDSs can even send e-mail to intermediate ISPs and let them know that their sites are being used to stage attacks. Most IDSs automatically gather records of suspicious behavior to create a "paper trail" for prosecution later.

The problem with old-fashioned manual systems is that any hope of catching the bad guys requires network administrators to notice whenever an attack gets underway. Also, IDSs are much more capable of performing ongoing statistical analyses of traffic and individual account characteristics. Thus, they can detect "slow break-in attempts" (where repeated password guesses may be deliberately spaced out over time to avoid detection) and unusual usage patterns on user accounts, stifle DoS attacks, and deal with lots of problems that humans might not see until it's too late.

Increasingly, firewalls include hooks to allow them to interact with IDSs, or include their own built-in IDS software. We believe that automating this function will become increasingly prevalent and affordable as Internet access and related security concerns become even more ubiquitous.

Windows 2000: Another Generation of Network Security

As we write this chapter, Windows 2000 has been on the market for a little over a year. This new version of Microsoft's flagship server and workstation operating system includes numerous security enhancements and improvements that make it more immune to compromise than earlier versions of Windows 9x and Windows NT.

Unfortunately, the continuing presence of these older systems for the foreseeable future means that Windows 2000 supports older security models and software to maintain backwards compatibility. Thus, many of the security enhancements we're about to mention won't really take full effect until these older operating systems are retired.

Nevertheless, Windows 2000 offers the following improvements that should help maintain tighter security than Windows NT could ever deliver:

- *Kerberos version 5*: This software adds greatly to the ability of Windows to authenticate users and servers, and manage session-level security and encryption; it is much stronger than anything Windows NT offers. This is an explicitly IP-based service.

- *Public Key Infrastructure (PKI)*: This permits two parties to securely exchange sensitive information by using digital certificates to prove identities for both parties, and it relies on one or more trusted third parties (called certificate authorities, or CAs) to verify the validity of the certificates involved. In addition, use of public and private keys provides non-repudiation for messages (a message that originated from a specific user can be read only if it indeed originated from that user; if that happens, that user cannot deny responsibility for the message, and thus, cannot repudiate it). They also provide for secure exchange of information (because a message encrypted with a user's public key can be decrypted only by the party that holds that same user's private key). This is an explicitly IP-based service.

- *Directory Service Account Management*: The Windows 2000 Active Directory provides more granular assignment of management responsibility than ever before so that access to resources is not the "all or nothing" grant it was for domains in the Windows NT environment. This too is an explicitly IP-based service.

- *CryptoAPI Version 2*: This programming interface provides access to strong encryption services for applications and data exchanges of all kinds. It's a Windows development tool, however, and not explicitly IP-based.

9

- *NTFS encryption*: With Windows 2000, NTFS gains an encryption attribute that allows entire volumes, directories, or individual files to be stored in a strong encrypted form. This is a Windows file system enhancement, and is not explicitly IP-based.

- *Secure Channel Security protocols (SSL 3.0/PCT)*: New implementations of Secure Sockets Layer and **Private Communication Technology (PCT)** make it easier for two parties to exchange information across the Internet or other public networks without risking exposure or compromise. As its explanation should indicate, this is an explicitly IP-based service.

- *Transport Layer Security (TLS) protocol*: **Transport Layer Security (TLS)** IP implementations make it possible to encrypt and protect segments at the Transport layer, thereby protecting the contents of all communications across the Internet at the Transport layer.

- *Internet Security Framework*: Support for IPSec, plus support for new tunneling protocols for VPN connections (such as the Layer 2 Tunneling Protocol, or L2TP, and an improved implementation of the Point-to-Point Tunneling Protocol, or PPTP) make it easier to securely exchange information across the Internet and other public networks.

Of course, these improvements still promise more to Windows 2000 users than they are able to deliver as we write this material. As we all get to know Windows 2000 better, we will patch holes, prevent exploits, and deal with system foibles, just as we did with Windows NT and other Windows implementations. However, Windows 2000 has a lot more tools in its security arsenal than Windows NT so we hope that its potential can be fully actualized in improvements and enhancements made to this operating system going forward!

Updating Anti-Virus Engines and Virus Lists

Because of the frequency of introduction of new viruses, worms, and trojans, it is essential to update anti-virus engine software and virus definitions on a regular basis. Most capable anti-virus packages—such as Norton AntiVirus, Trend Micro's PC-cillin, Network Associates' VirusScan, and so forth—include automatic update facilities to make this kind of activity as easy and painless as possible. For large networking environments where you may not want end users managing their own downloads and updates, such products also support staging servers (where updates can be rolled out from a local copy, and a network administrator can manage update contents and frequencies).

It's important to recognize anti-virus protection as a key ingredient in any security policy, and to make sure that all points through which data may enter a network be subject to inspection, detection, and filters, or quarantines, to prevent viruses from leaving the wild and entering your systems and networks. Here again, most capable anti-virus packages will transparently and automatically check e-mail attachments, inbound file transfers, floppy disks, and other media, and other potential sources of infection, and screen out suspect materials without requiring user input or interaction.

Testing Your Network

A security policy is a document that reflects an organization's understanding of what information assets and other resources need protection, how they are to be protected, and how they must be maintained under normal operating circumstances, or restored in the face of compromise or loss. The following is a sample security policy recommended by CERT:

A. Prepare
  1. If you have a security policy, consult it.
  2. If you do not have a security policy:
       i.   consult with management
       ii. consult with your legal counsel
       iii. consider contacting law enforcement agencies
       iv. notify others within your organization
  3. Document all of your recovery steps.

B. Regain control
  1. Disconnect the compromised system(s) from the network.
  2. Make a complete copy of the compromised system(s).

C. Analyze the intrusion
  1. Look for modifications made to system software and configuration files.
  2. Look for modifications to data.
  3. Look for tools and data left behind by the intruder.
  4. Review log files.
  5. Look for signs of a network sniffer.
  6. Check other systems on your network.
  7. Check for systems involved or affected at remote sites.

D. Contact the CERT/CC and other sites involved
  1. Follow the guidelines outlined in
     http://www.cert.org/tech_tips/incident_reporting.html.
  2. Contact the CERT Coordination Center.
  3. Obtain contact information for other sites involved and contact them.

E. Recover from the intrusion
  1. Reinstall your operating system from distribution media.
  2. Disable unnecessary services.
  3. Install all vendor security patches. See *http://www.microsoft.com/security/*.
  4. Consult CERT advisories, summaries, and vendor-initiated bulletins.
  5. Use caution when restoring data from back ups because they may contain data already altered by the intruder.
  6. Change passwords.

F. Improve the security of your system and network using the lessons learned

G. Educate your users about the dangers of executing unknown programs or e-mail attachments

H. Reconnect to the Internet

      I. Update your security policy
         1. Document lessons learned from being compromised.
         2. Calculate the cost of this incident.
         3. Incorporate necessary changes (if any) in your security policy.

In general, a security policy defines the kinds of security practices and procedures to follow to avoid compromise or loss of data and systems. But it must also address what actions to take if compromise or loss occurs. Thus, it makes your security routine explicit and concrete, but also explains how to recover in the event that something unexpected or untoward affects your networks or systems. Remember also that a good security policy addresses all three legs of the security tripod we introduced earlier in this chapter—physical security, personnel security, and software security. Think of this document as a summary of your security practices and procedures, and you'll not only be motivated to build a good security policy, you'll also immediately understand that this document must be updated and maintained the same way that you must update and maintain the policies, practices, and procedures on which it rests.

For additional information about security policies, and some excellent examples of security policy documents, visit any or all of the following Web sites:

- The System and Administration, Networking, and Security (SANS) Institute offers some of the best security training and certification programs around. Thus, it should come as no surprise that its "Model Security Policies" training materials are second to none. Documents and templates can be downloaded from *http://www.sans.org/newlook/resources/policies/policies.htm*.

- The Department of Defense funds the Software Engineering Institute (SEI) at Carnegie-Mellon University. This group's efforts include an emphasis on system and network security, and it offers the technical report "Operationally Critical Threat, Asset, and Vulnerability Evaluation (OCTAVE)," which makes a great template for a security policy. To learn more, please visit *http://www.sei.cmu.edu/publications/documents/99.reports/99tr017/99tr017abstract.html*.

- Murdoch University's Office of Information Technology Services offers an online document titled "Information Technology Security Policy" that includes a detailed section on how to create a formal security policy document. For those seriously interested in formulating their own such documents, this is a must-read. View it at *http://wwwits2.murdoch.edu.au/security/policy.html*.

CHAPTER SUMMARY

❏ To create a strong foundation for system and network security, it's necessary to formulate a policy that incorporates processes, procedures, and rules regarding physical and personnel security issues, as well as addressing system and software security issues. Likewise, system and software security should address any potential causes of loss or harm to information systems and assets, including back-ups, disaster recovery, and internal safeguards as well as guarding the network perimeter or boundary.

❑ In security terms, an attack represents an attempt to break into or otherwise compromise the privacy and integrity of an organization's information assets. An exploit documents a successful attack, whereas a break in is usually the result of a successful attack.

❑ In its original form, TCP/IP implemented an optimistic security model, wherein little or no protection was built into its protocols and services. Recent improvements, enhancements, and updates to TCP/IP include many ways in which this model is mitigated with a more pessimistic security model. Unfortunately, TCP/IP remains prey to many kinds of attacks and vulnerabilities, including denials of service (which may be from a single source or distributed across numerous sources), service attacks, service and implementation vulnerabilities, man-in-the-middle attacks, and more.

❑ Basic principles of IP security include avoiding unnecessary exposure by blocking all unused ports and installing only necessary services. They also include judicious use of address filtering to block known malefactors and stymie address spoofing. We advocate adoption of a pessimistic security policy, wherein access is denied, by default, and allowed only with considered exceptions. Finally, it's a good idea to monitor the Internet for security-related news and events—especially exploits—and to regularly attack your own systems and networks to learn how to block or defeat attacks documented in such exploits.

❑ It's necessary to protect systems and networks from malicious code such as viruses, worms, and trojan horses. Such protection means using modern anti-virus software, which should be part of any well-built security policy.

❑ Would-be attackers usually engage in a well-understood sequence of activities called reconnaissance and discovery as the attempt to footprint systems and networks, looking for points of attack. Judicious monitoring of network activity, especially through an intrusion detection system, can help block such attacks (and may even be able to identify their sources, if not their perpetrators).

❑ Establishing system and network security means formulating a security policy, then doing what's necessary to enforce that policy. But maintaining system and network security also involves constant activity that must include keeping up with security news and information; applying necessary patches, fixes, and software updates; regular security audits; and self attacks to maintain the required level of security.

❑ Maintaining a secure network boundary remains a key ingredient for good system and network security. This usually involves the use of screening routers, firewalls, and proxy servers, which may be on separate devices, or integrated into a single device that straddles the network boundary. Some network architectures also make use of a demilitarized zone (DMZ) between the internal and external networks, where services can more safely be exposed to the outside world, and where inside users can access proxy, caching, and other key services for external network access.

❑ When establishing a secure network perimeter, it's essential to repeat the test-attack-tune cycle while you're preparing to deploy security devices until no further

9

tuning changes are necessitated by the test and attacks that precede them. This is the only method of ensuring that your network boundary is as secure as possible; it's also necessary to repeat this process as relevant new exploits or vulnerabilities become known.

◻ Windows 2000 includes notable security improvements and enhancements as compared to other Windows versions. Especially noteworthy are Kerberos authentication and session security controls; PKI for secure, private exchange of sensitive data; and various new protocols and services, such as IP Security, NTFS encryption, SSL, PCT, and TLS, all of which help to protect and secure IP-based client-server network traffic.

KEY TERMS

address book — A database of e-mail addresses. Local address books are often exploited in worm and mobile code attacks.

agent — The device that actually inflicts the painful attack on the victim in a Distributed Denial of Service attack.

alert — An automatic notification from a software program (in the context of IP security, this means a router, firewall, proxy server, or IDS) that indicates an unusual error or condition, an exceeded monitoring threshold, or an executed trigger.

anonymous access — A type of IP service access, wherein users need not provide explicit account and password information; this applies to FTP and Web services, among others.

attack — An attempt to break into or compromise a system or network, or deny access to that system or network.

attack signature — A recognizable communication pattern or packet used in an attack. A signature may be the port number used in an attack, or a string of characters embedded in the data portion of the packet.

attack tools — Any of a set of software tools that malefactors might use to try to launch an attack against a system or a network. Network or system administrators should consider obtaining and using such tools themselves to make sure they won't work in unsupervised circumstances for unauthorized users.

attacker — The actual source of an attack sequence. Clever attackers in a DDoS attack often hide behind a handler and agent.

back door — An undocumented and illicit point of entry into a system or a network, often built into software or a system by its original engineers.

Back Orifice — A remote control trojan horse attack developed by a group called the "Cult of the Dead Cow" (CDC).

bastion host — A specially hardened computer designed to straddle the boundary between internal and external networks, where firewalls, proxy servers, IDSs, and border routing functions normally operate.

border router — A network device that straddles the boundary between internal and external networks, and manages the inbound traffic permitted to reach the inside networks, and the outbound traffic allowed to proceed beyond the boundary.

boundary router — *See* border router.

break-in — An attempt to impersonate a valid user on a system, or otherwise gain entry to a system or network, to obtain illicit access to the resources and information it contains.

brute force attack — An attack that typically consists of numerous requests for service. This type of attack focuses on overloading the resources of the victim, including CPU, disk access, or other local resources.

brute force password attack — A systematic attempt to guess all possible password strings as a way of trying to break into a system. Such an attack literally attempts all conceivable character combinations that might represent a valid password. These attacks can take a long time, and can usually be detected and prevented by IDSs.

compromised host — A host that was broken into and gave up Administrator or root access.

computer forensics — The process of examining the "footprints" that an attacker leaves behind. Some areas of interest include the temp files—deleted files that remain in the Recycle Bin or in a recoverable state—and local system memory.

cracker — A person who attempts to break into a system by impersonating valid users, or using other methods of penetration that do not necessarily involve deep system skills or knowledge.

demilitarized zone (DMZ) — An intermediate network that sits between the boundary of an organization's internal networks and one or more external networks, such as the Internet. A DMZ is usually separated from external networks by a screening router, and from internal networks by a screening router and a firewall.

dictionary attack — A type of brute force password attack in which hashed values for all words in a specialized dictionary of terms are compared to hashed values in password files. This type of attack usually takes only seconds to process.

discovery process — The process of learning which computers or processes are running on a network.

Distributed Denial of Service (DDoS) attack — An attack that uses a managed group approach to set up a compromised host as a handler, and recruits agents that perform the actual attack on the victim.

egress filtering — The process of applying restrictions to traffic leaving a network.

exploit — A documented system break-in technique that's published for potential reuse by others.

file extension — The ending of a filename that indicates the type of the file. Viruses are often contained in .exe, .com, and .vbs file formats.

file extension obfuscation — The process of hiding a filename extension by placing a false extension before the actual extension. For example, the ILOVEYOU e-mail message contained an attachment named "LOVE-LETTER-FOR-YOU.TXT.vbs."

9

For systems that hide the extension, this file appears as a .txt file and is assumed to be harmless.

firewall — A special type of bastion host that performs traffic inspection and screening to prevent unauthorized external access to internal networks and manage internal access to external networks.

handler — A manager system in a DDoS attack. The handler is a compromised host on which an attacker has placed DDoS code. The handlers locate agents to perform the actual attack on a victim system.

hex reader — A software package that allows you to open an executable file to examine the contents of the code in hexadecimal format without launching the file.

hole — A system or software vulnerability that defeats, bypasses, or ignores system or software security settings and restrictions.

incomplete fragment set — A fragmentation attack that consists of numerous fragments directed toward a victim, but does not contain the final fragment of the set. The victim attempts to cache all the fragment pieces while trying to reassemble the fragment sets after all fragments are received.

ingress filtering — The process of applying restrictions to traffic coming into a network.

intrusion detection system (IDS) — A special-purpose software system that inspects ongoing patterns of network traffic, looking for signs of impending or active attack. Most IDSs can foil break-in attempts and also attempt to establish the identity of the attacker or attackers. Best of all, IDSs work automatically and require no immediate human attention to handle most attacks.

IP Security (IPSec or **IP Sec)** — A security specification supporting various forms of encryption and authentication, along with key management and related supporting functions. Optional in IPv4, IPSec is a required part of IPv6.

IP service attack — A system attack that concentrates on known characteristics and vulnerabilities of one or more specific IP services, or that uses well-known port addresses associated with such services for its own nefarious ends.

Legion — A NetBIOS file share scanner with brute force password attack capabilities that should be part of any Windows IP administrator's attack tool kit.

log — A file-based record of system activities and events that relate to some specific software system, such as a server, firewall, and so forth. Postmortem examination of logs is sometimes required to develop attack signatures and determine the extent of system compromise when successful attacks occur.

malicious code — A program that is written with the intent of harming or disrupting host operations.

man-in-the-middle attack — A type of system or network attack where an attacking system interposes itself between the target network and the next normal link on that network's usual routing chain.

mobile code — Also referred to as a worm, mobile code moves from machine to machine without user intervention. The ILOVEYOU e-mails contained mobile code that accessed the local address book and mailed itself to all addresses listed.

nmap — An infamous port scanner that is primarily UNIX or Linux based, nmap should be part of any IP administrator's attack tool kit.

optimistic security model — The original basis for TCP/IP security, this model assumes that it is safe to enforce little or no security on normal network communications. (This explains why services such as Telnet and FTP routinely pass account and password information in clear text across networks.)

packet sniffing — A technique that involves using a protocol analyzer to decode and examine the contents of IP packets to attempt to identify sensitive information, including accounts and passwords for subsequent break-in attempts or other nefarious purposes.

packet snooping — *See* packet sniffing.

password hashing — A method for storing passwords in encrypted form for authentication purposes. Modern operating systems, such as Windows NT and Windows 2000, UNIX, and Linux, hash passwords to improve security on stored forms. Unfortunately, when hackers or crackers gain access to the files in which hashed passwords live, if the hashing algorithm is known, they can use dictionary-based brute force password attacks to identify most or all passwords in such files.

personnel security — The aspect of security that concentrates on informing users about security matters, and training them on proper application of security policies, procedures, and practices.

pessimistic security model — A model of system and network security that assumes it is always necessary to enforce strong security measures so that access to all resources should be denied to all users, by default, and allowed only to those with a legitimate need to access such resources, on a case-by-case basis.

physical security — That aspect of security that concerns itself with limiting physical access to system and network components to prevent unauthorized users from attempting direct attacks on such components. Because lax physical security can easily lead to compromise, strong physical security is always a good idea.

PING sweep — An ICMP Echo-based operation used to locate active devices on a network. The term "sweep" refers to the process of testing an entire range of IP addresses for active devices.

port scanner — A special purpose software tool that cycles through either well-known TCP and UDP ports with easy vulnerabilities (Legion), or all possible TCP and UDP port addresses, looking for open ports that can then be probed for access or exploited for vulnerabilities.

Private Communication Technology (PCT) — An IP-based Application layer protocol documented in RFC 2246 that's used to create a secure channel to prevent anyone from eavesdropping on client-server and server-client communications across the Web.

remote logon service — Any type of network service that permits users elsewhere on a network to use the network to log onto a system as if they were attached locally, while operating remotely. Such services are favorite attack points because they're designed to give outsiders access to systems and services.

9

report — A document prepared by a system or service that documents traffic volume and characteristics for that system or service, usually to represent routine usage or activity, but also to report on observed events or conditions that may have security implications.

rexec — An abbreviation for *remote execution*, this is one of the BSD UNIX remote utilities (r–utils) that permits network users to execute single commands on a remote host.

rpr — An abbreviation for *remote print*, this is one of the BSD UNIX remote utilities (r–utils) that permits network users to print a file on a remote host.

rsh — An abbreviation for *remote shell*, this is one of the BSD UNIX remote utilities (r–utils) that permits network users to launch and operate a login session on a remote host.

r–utils — An abbreviation for *remote utilities*, this is a collection of software programs originally included as part of BSD UNIX v4.2, designed to provide remote access and login services for users. Hence, they are a common point of attack.

screening host — The role that a firewall or proxy server plays when presenting an internal network service for external consumption.

screening router — A boundary router that's been configured to monitor and filter inbound traffic on the basis of IP or port addresses, domain names, or spoofing attempts.

security policy — A document that represents the concrete manifestation of an organization's requirements for security practices, rules, and procedures, and which identifies all assets worth protecting, and lays out disaster or business recovery processes should system loss or compromise occur.

session hijacking — An IP attack technique whereby an imposter takes over an ongoing communications session between a client and server, thereby assuming whatever rights and permissions the hijacked session may enjoy. This is a difficult technique to pull off, and recent changes to TCP sequence numbers make this harder to accomplish today than it was prior to their implementation.

Smurf attack — An ICMP-based attack in which the attacker sends a PING packet to the broadcast address using the victim's IP address as the source of the PING.

SOCKS — An IETF standards track protocol that defines how proxy mechanisms work to control traffic between networks.

software security — The aspect of security that focuses on monitoring and maintaining systems and software to prevent and oppose as many potential sources of attack as possible. From this perspective, software security is both a mindset and a regular routine, rather than a "set it and forget it" kind of activity.

spoofing — Using another address or name as the source of the packet to hide the true source of the communication.

stealthy attacker — An attacker that hides its tracks. Stealthy attackers may ensure no log entries implicate their actions and no live connections remain after they launch their attack.

SYN Flood attack — An attack that sends multiple handshake establishment request packets (SYN) in an attempt to fill the connection queue and force the victim to refuse future valid requests.

test-attack-tune cycle — The most important part of deploying security systems or components, this set of activities should be repeated until test and attack operations produce no further changes to system or component configuration or tuning. This set of activities provides the best and most reasonable guarantee that systems and components are as resistant to attack as possible.

transparency — An important characteristic for any system or service that interposes itself between end users and the services or resources they seek to access, more transparency means that users notice intermediaries less, and less transparency means they notice them more. The ideal state is absolute transparency, where users do not notice that intermediaries are at work.

Transport Layer Security (TLS) — A special Transport layer protocol that works with TCP so that client/server applications can communicate in a way designed to prevent eavesdropping, tampering, or message forgery.

trojan horse — A program that appears innocent, but contains malicious code. The ILOVEYOU e-mail attack is a perfect example of a trojan horse. The .vbs file contained mobile code that e-mailed itself to all entries in a victim's address book.

user impersonation — A system or network attack technique whereby an unauthorized user presents valid credentials that rightfully belong to an authorized user to gain entry, and exploits whatever rights and privileges that the impersonated user's identity allows. (This explains why impersonating users with administrative rights and privileges is the ultimate goal of an impersonation attack.)

victim — The focus of an attack. Interestingly, in the case of mobile code and worms, the victims often become the attackers by allowing the code to infect other computers because they are not identified or eradicated.

virus — A code that can spread through a machine to alter or destroy files.

vulnerability — Any aspect of a system that is open to attack, especially any well-known protocol, service, subsystem, or hole that is documented and relatively easy to exploit.

WinNuke attack — An attack that is based on an illogical packet structure—a NetBIOS packet that has the Urgent bit set to one.

worm — A malicious mobile code that can move from one computer to another until it is eradicated.

REVIEW QUESTIONS

1. More than 70% of all network or system break-ins originate outside an organization's network boundary. True or false?

   a. True

   b. False

2. Which of the following does *not* account for the vast majority of losses of data or services from systems and networks?

   a. viruses

   b. power outages

   c. internal security breaches

   d. external security breaches

3. Which of the following statements best explains why physical security for network and system components and devices is so important?

   a. Physical access to components and devices is necessary for successful penetration of hardened systems.

   b. Any good security policy must address physical security concerns.

   c. Physical access to components and devices makes it possible for a knowledgeable intruder to break into such systems.

   d. None of the above; physical security is not an important concern.

4. Which of the following correctly lists the three legs of network security?

   a. network, boundary, software

   b. physical, personnel, system and network security

   c. physical, personnel, component

   d. physical, network, software

5. Which of the following document types is an attacker most likely to use when attempting to break into a system or network?

   a. attack profile

   b. exploit

   c. security policy

   d. password hash

6. TCP/IP implements a pessimistic security policy. True or false?

   a. True

   b. False

7. When an attacker systematically tries all conceivable passwords for an account, what is this attack called?

   a. brute force attack

   b. session hijacking

   c. packet sniffing

   d. brute force password attack

8. Which of the following types of attack is the least likely to result in damage or loss of data?

   a. IP service attack

   b. man-in-the-middle attack

   c. DoS or DDoS attack

   d. virus

   e. buffer overflow

9. By default, which of the following IP services sends accounts and passwords in clear text when authenticating users? (Choose all that apply.)

   a. FTP

   b. Telnet

   c. Stelnet

   d. Web access using SSL

10. Which one of the following common characteristics makes both FTP and HTTP (Web) vulnerable IP services?

   a. TCP transport

   b. long timeout variables

   c. anonymous login

   d. automatic retry algorithms

11. Which of the following definitions best describes a back door?

   a. a weak spot or known point of attack on any common operating system

   b. an undocumented and illicit point of entry into a system or application

   c. any protocol, service, or system facility known to be susceptible to attack

   d. an alternate, but legitimate, means of entry into a system or application

12. Which of the following best describes a vulnerability?

   a. a weak spot or known point of attack on any common operating system

   b. an undocumented and illicit point of entry into a system or application

   c. any protocol, service, or system facility known to be susceptible to attack

   d. an alternate, but legitimate, means of entry into a system or application

13. Which of the following is NOT a recognized principle of IP security?

   a. Avoid unnecessary exposure.

   b. Block all unused ports.

   c. Prevent address spoofing.

   d. Enable access by default, deny access by exception.

   e. Do unto yourself before others do unto you.

14. What kind of malicious software does ILOVEYOU use?

    a. virus

    b. worm

    c. trojan horse

    d. ActiveX control

15. What TCP value setting helps attackers perpetrate the incomplete fragments DoS attack?

    a. TCP window size

    b. TCP buffer size

    c. TCP TTL

    d. TCP MTU

16. Which of the four main elements in a DDoS attack is least likely to be actively engaged when an attack occurs?

    a. attacker

    b. handler

    c. agent

    d. victim

17. Which two of the four main elements in a DDoS attack coordinate and execute the actual attack?

    a. attacker

    b. handler

    c. agent

    d. victim

18. What technique might an attacker use to hide or deflect interest in attack behaviors or activities?

    a. user impersonation

    b. spoofing

    c. man–in–the–middle attack

    d. reconnaissance

19. Which of the following attacks uses the NetBIOS Urgent flag bit set?

    a. PING of death

    b. SYN Flood

    c. Smurf

    d. WinNuke

20. What is the most common step that attackers take to attempt to escape detection after a successful break-in?

 a. Reconfigure the system to give themselves administrative privileges.

 b. Delete log files to remove all traces of the attack.

 c. Reformat all hard drives to destroy any potential evidence.

 d. Copy all password files for other systems.

21. Which of the following statements best explains the importance of applying system and application patches and fixes?

 a. As vulnerabilities or exploits are exposed, system and application vendors provide patches and fixes to repair, defeat, or mitigate potential attacks. Thus, it's usually a good idea to apply them.

 b. Applying patches and fixes is an important part of general system and application maintenance.

 c. It's necessary to apply only patches and fixes that are relevant to actual, ongoing security problems.

 d. It's a good idea to wait until a patch or fix has been around for a while to see if it works appropriately.

22. Which of the following UDP/TCP port number ranges corresponds to the Berkeley r-utils?

 a. 111 and 2049

 b. 135 through 139

 c. 512 through 514

 d. 1001 and 1002

23. Which of the following trojan horses might use port 25 for an attack? (Choose all that apply.)

 a. Magic Horse

 b. Back Orifice 2000

 c. ProMail trojan

 d. MBT

 e. Doly trojan

24. What type of computer should be used to house firewall and/or proxy server software?

 a. secure host

 b. bastion host

 c. screening host

 d. screening router

25. Which of the following tools is a candidate for an attack tool kit? (Choose all that apply.)

    a. EtherPeek

    b. nmap

    c. Legion

    d. GNU NetTools

HANDS-ON PROJECTS

Project 9-1

The following Hands-on Projects assume that you are working in a Windows 2000 environment, and you installed the EtherPeek for Windows demo program, as defined in Project 1-1.

As you work through the Hands-on Projects, if the global statistics dialog box opens, click OK and continue with the project.

To examine a local scan:

1. Launch the EtherPeek for Windows demo program (see Hands-on Project 1-2 for instructions).

2. Click **File**, **Open**, select the trace file **arpscan.pkt** (located in the **18654-2\Ch9** folder on your hard disk), and click the **Open** button. The packet summary window appears. This file contains a reconnaissance probe using ARP broadcasts to find active hosts.

3. Double-click **Packet #1** in the trace file. The packet decode window appears. You see the Ethernet header addressed to broadcast (0xFF–FF–FF–FF–FF–FF).

4. Click the **Decode Next** and **Decode Prev** buttons to scroll through the packet, and answer the following questions:

    a. What is the IP address of the device sending out the ARP broadcasts?

    b. What hosts were discovered?

    c. How could this type of scan be used on a small routed network?

5. Close the packet decode window, close the arpscan.pkt trace file, and proceed immediately to Hands-on Project 9-2.

Project 9-2

To examine a port scan:

1. Click **File**, **Open**, select the trace file **portscan.pkt** (located in the **18654–2\Ch9** folder on your hard disk), and click the **Open** button. The packet summary window appears. This file contains a TCP reconnaissance probe process.

2. Double-click **Packet #1** to view the full decode of the packet. The first packet was sent to destination port number 1. What TCP flag is set in this packet?

3. Click the **Decode Next** button. Examine the flags in the response packet. What flags are set in this packet?

4. Click through the remaining packets in the trace file and answer these questions:

   a. How obvious is this port probe?

   b. If this probe continues through all the ports, will it detect the DHCP service process?

   c. Based on this set of probes, what ports are active on the destination device?

5. Close the EtherPeek for Windows demo program.

Project 9-3

Your firewall is configured to block all TCP handshake packets sent to the Echo port. In this project, you build a filter to check for any packets sent to the Echo port, and test this filter on the portscan.pkt trace file to ensure it works properly.

To create a filter to catch port scans to blocked ports:

1. Launch the EtherPeek for Windows demo program.

2. Click **View**, **Filters** to open the Filters window. Click the **Insert** button.

3. Enter the name **Echo filter** in the Filter text box.

4. Click the **Port filter** check box. Enter **7** (the Echo port number) in the Port 1 text box.

5. In the Type area between the Port 1 and Port 2 boxes, click the **Port 1 to 2** button and select **Both directions**.

6. Click **OK**. This filter will locate packets from port 7.

7. Close the Filters window. Next, test the filter to see if it can catch the Echo packets in the portscan.pkt file.

8. Click **File**, **Open**, select **portscan.pkt** (located in the **18654–2\Ch9** folder on your hard disk), and click the **Open** button. The packet summary window appears.

9. Click **Edit**, **Select** to open the Select window.

9

10. In the Selection criteria section, scroll down to locate **Echo filter**, and click the check box to the left. Click the **Select Packets** button. The filter is applied to the packets.

11. The Selection Results window appears and defines how many packets matched the selection criteria. Click the **Hide Unselected** button.

12. Click the **Close** button in the Select window.

13. Did your filter work? Do you see packets to and from the Echo port? This filter can be used to catch packets addressed to or from the Echo port. For example, if you set up a firewall to block all traffic to and from the Echo port, you can test the firewall by setting up this filter inside the firewall.

14. Close the EtherPeek for Windows demo program.

Project 9-4

In this project, you set up a Boolean filter to locate all traffic to and from the following suspect port numbers:

◻ 31337 Back Orifice

◻ 31335 Trinoo agent to handler communications

◻ 27444 Trinoo handler to agent communications

To set up a filter to catch traffic associated with Back Orifice and Trinoo communications:

1. Launch the EtherPeek for Windows demo program.

2. Click **View**, **Filters** to open the Filters window. Click the **Insert** button [image].

3. Enter the name **BO–Trinoo** in the Filter text box.

4. Click the down arrow in the **Type** list box and select **Advanced**.

5. Click the **And** button and select **Port**. The Port Filter window appears.

6. Type **31337** in the Port 1 text box.

7. Be sure the directional button between the **Port 1 and 2** sections is labeled "Both directions". Click **OK**. The first filter criterion is placed in the Edit Filter window.

8. Because you are interested in packets that match 31337, 31335, or 27444, use the OR operand. Click the **Or** button and select **Port**. The Port Filter window appears.

9. Type **31335** in the Port 1 field.

10. Be sure the directional button is labeled "Both directions". Click **OK**. The second filter criterion is placed in the Edit Filter window.

11. Click the **Or** button and select **Port**. The Port Filter window appears.

12. Type **27444** in the Port 1 field.

13. Be sure the directional button is labeled "Both directions". Click **OK**. The third and final filter criterion is placed in the Edit Filter window.

14. Click **OK** to close the Edit Filter window.

15. Close the EtherPeek for Windows demo program.

By running this filter on a network, you can capture traffic that is on the way to or coming from these suspect ports.

CASE PROJECTS

1. You are a newly hired network administrator for a small school. Each of the 12 classrooms has at least one computer. These computers are connected using a hub. A DSL router connects this network to the Internet. What steps can be taken to protect this network from hacks coming in from the Internet?

2. You are the network security technician for a large shoe manufacturer based in Detroit, MI. Your internetwork connects six buildings through fiber links. You have experienced numerous attacks on your corporate Web server. The company CEO decides to pay for a firewall. Describe the filters you will implement in your firewall, and note how you will test your firewall.

3. After class ends today, you note a message on the employment board listing a network administrator job opening. Wow! You jump at the chance to take this job and, lucky for you, you're hired. Your first assignment is to design a security policy for the entire school campus. This security policy will be posted for all students, instructors, and school visitors to follow. Create a detailed security policy using information cited in this book and from new sources you find on the Internet.

9

CHAPTER

10

ROUTING IN THE **IP** ENVIRONMENT

After reading this chapter and completing the exercises you will be able to:

♦ Understand how basic routing works, and how routing tables help control this behavior

♦ Explain the various types of routing protocols, including distance vector and link-state protocols

♦ Describe the various techniques used to ensure rapid convergence of routing table updates, and why such techniques are necessary

♦ Understand the difference between routing within the confines of a company or organization using an interior routing protocol, and between or among organizations using an exterior routing protocol

♦ Describe router connections on internal and external networks, including the Internet

♦ Explain basic router diagnostic troubleshooting concepts, tools, and techniques

You should recall from previous chapters that when a computer wants to send a packet to a destination that is not on its local subnetwork, it sends that packet to its default gateway (which is usually a router, or a server configured to act like a router). Then, that default gateway forwards the packet to its true destination, or to another router that knows how to reach that destination.

This process, known as packet forwarding, certainly sounds simple enough. But you should ask, "How does any router know where to send a packet?" In this chapter, we explain in detail the processes and protocols that routers use to make forwarding decisions and speed packets on their way to their intended destinations, whenever possible, and how they handle routing and delivery problems or failures.

UNDERSTANDING ROUTING

We start our discussion by explaining the routing table. This table is a database that lives in the memory of the router. Entries in this database are known as "routes" and consist of a network address, a "next hop" (routing jargon for the IP address of the next router in the path to the destination), various metrics, and vendor-specific information. A routing table is a compilation of all the networks that the router can reach. On small networks, this might be only a few entries. Most large enterprise networks have several hundred entries in their routing tables. The biggest, of course, is the Internet. As of this writing, the routing tables of the Internet's backbone routers contain well over 100,000 entries. Figure 10-1 shows an example of a small routing table from a Cisco router. In it, you can see that the network destination is shown as an IP address followed by a slash (/) for clarity, and a number that denotes the length of the subnet mask. So 137.20.30.0/24 means the mask is 24 bits long, or 255.255.255.0. This entry has a next hop of 137.20.25.2, out its Serial0 interface. Also notice the "O IA" in front of the route entry. This indicates that the route was learned via OSPF. We'll discuss that in more detail later in the chapter.

The routing table is used as follows: When a packet is received on a network interface, the first thing the router must do is find out where the packet wants to go, so the router reads the first field in the IP header, which is the Destination Address, and then looks in the Network field of its routing table for a match. If it finds a match, then it sends the packet to the corresponding next hop, which is usually another router on a directly connected network.

 It is important to understand that the details of the process mentioned above may vary by manufacturer and are not standardized by any protocol. The methods used inside a router to forward packets are completely proprietary.

Now that you have a basic understanding of the routing table, we can begin to answer the question, "How does the router know where to send packets?" Or, more specifically, "How are entries placed in the routing table?"

A route entry can be placed in a routing table in three basic ways. The first way is through direct connection. For example, a router that is connected to networks 10.1.0.0/16 and 10.2.0.0/16 knows about both networks because it is configured with the IP addresses for those networks.

Codes: C - connected, S - static, I - IGRP, R - RIP, M - mobile, B - BGP
        D - EIGRP, EX - EIGRP external, O - OSPF, IA - OSPF inter area
        N1 - OSPF NSSA external type 1, N2 - OSPF NSSA external type 2
        E1 - OSPF external type 1, E2 - OSPF external type 2, E - EGP
        i - IS-IS, L1 - IS-IS level-1, L2 - IS-IS level-2, * - candidate default
        U - per-user static route, o - ODR

Gateway of last resort is 137.20.25.2 to network 0.0.0.0

```
        172.168.0.0/24 is subnetted, 2 subnets
B           172.168.70.0 [20/170] via 137.20.10.70, 1:11:35
O E2        172.168.80.0 [110/20] via 137.20.25.2, 01:11:26, Serial0
        200.200.100.0/32 is subnetted, 1 subnets
O IA        200.200.100.1 [100/115] via 137.20.25.2, 01:12:06, Serial0
        137.20.0.0/16 is variably subnetted, 16 subnets, 4 masks
O E1        137.20.200.16/28 [110/164] via 137.20.25.2, 01:12:06, Serial0
O IA        137.20.240.1/32 [110/65] via 137.20.25.2, 01:12:06, Serial0
O IA        137.20.224.0/20 [110/1626] via 137.20.25.2, 01:12:06, Serial0
O IA        137.20.30.0/24 [110/120] via 137.20.25.2, 01:11:51, Serial0
C           137.20.25.0/24 is directly connected, Serial0
C           137.20.10.0/24 is directly connected, Ethernet0
O IA        137.20.60.1/32 [110/75] via 137.20.25.2, 01:12:07, Serial0
O E1        137.20.40.16/28 [110/164] via 137.20.25.2, 01:11:30, Serial0
O IA        137.20.33.0/24 [110/115] via 137.20.25.2, 01:11:33, Serial0
O E2        137.20.86.0/24 [110/20] via 137.20.25.2, 01:12:08, Serial0
B           137.20.81.0/24 [200/0] via 137.20.86.1, 01:11:59
B           137.20.82.0/24 [200/0] via 137.20.86.1, 01:11:59
O IA        137.20.100.33/32 [110/114] via 137.20.25.2, 01:12:08, Serial0
O IA        137.20.100.35/32 [110/114] via 137.20.25.2, 01:11:53, Serial0
O IA        137.20.64.0/20 [110/74] via 137.20.25.2, 01:12:09, Serial0
        170.10.0.0/24 is subnetted, 1 subnets
B           170.10.10.0 [20/170] via 137.20.10.70, 01:11:37
        160.10.0.0/24 is subnetted, 1 subnets
B           160.10.10.0 [20/170] via 137.20.10.70, 01:11:37
        161.10.0.0/24 is subnetted, 1 subnets
B           161.10.10.0 [20/170] via 137.20.10.70, 01:11:37
C           200.200.200.0/24 is directly connected, Loopback0
O*E1    0.0.0.0/0 [110/167] via 137.20.25.2, 01:12:09, Serial0
B           160.0.0.0/4 [20/170] via 137.20.10.70, 01:11:37
```

10

Figure 10-1   Routing table from Cisco router

The second is that it can be manually configured. To do this, you log on to the router and use the menus or command line to define the network it can reach, the next hop, and any metrics. You repeat this process for every network you want to reach. This method has several advantages and disadvantages. The primary advantage is control. With static routes, you specify the exact configuration and it doesn't change. Other significant advantages are that it is very simple, secure, and the router immediately knows how to get to a network. The disadvantages are that on a large network, you really don't want to type several hundred entries into each router, and worse, any time a network changes, you must remember to go back to every single router on your network and make the appropriate change. As you can see in Figure 10-1, these tables can sometimes be confusing; it is easy to make mistakes, and often extremely difficult to find them.

The third way that an entry can be placed in a routing table is dynamically, by using a **routing protocol**. Routers use routing protocols to share information about the various networks on an internetwork. Thus, you simply configure the protocol on each router, and the routers will convey **Network Layer Reachability Information (NLRI)** to each other. The advantages and disadvantages of routing protocols are the opposite of the manual ones: They're much easier to maintain in a large environment, but they represent a point of failure that attackers can easily exploit; it can take a long time for a router on one side of an internetwork to learn about a network on the other side of an internetwork, and more advanced routing protocols can be incredibly complex. Also, there is an inherent lack of control. For instance, if there are multiple paths to get to a network, the routing protocol will decide which one to take. You can, of course, tweak the metrics to make one path preferred, but you should completely understand the consequences of changes before you make them.

At this point, we want to clarify a potential point of confusion: There are two types of protocols that cross an internetwork—routing protocols and routed protocols. Rout*ing* protocols are used to exchange routing information. Routing Information Protocol (RIP) and Open Shortest Path First (OSPF) are routing protocols. (Recall that in our discussion of the route entry in Figure 10-1, the route was learned via OSPF.)

Routed protocols are Layer 3 protocols that are used to get packets through an internetwork. IP is the routed protocol for the TCP/IP protocol suite. Upon receipt of a TCP/IP packet, routers strip off the data link header and examine the IP header to determine how to route the packet. Internetwork Packet Exchange (IPX) is the routed protocol for the IPX/SPX protocol suite.

Layer-3 switches are devices that can perform switching based on MAC address and, when necessary, examine the Network layer header to make routing decisions. In essence, layer-3 switches are a cross between a switch and a router.

There are two primary ways to group routing protocols. The first is by the method they use to communicate. The two primary "flavors" employed by routing protocols are **distance vector** and **link–state**.

The second grouping is an administrative one. When organizations began to connect to the Internet, they quickly realized that because the designs and philosophies of one company were often incompatible with another, they needed a way to extract this information. The solution was to create routing domains, or Autonomous Systems, which we'll define later. Thus, each organization can have complete control over its own routing domain, allowing it to set appropriate security and performance-tuning policies without impacting other organizations. The routing protocols used inside a routing domain are called **Interior Gateway Protocols (IGPs)**, and the routing protocols used to connect these routing domains are known as **Exterior Gateway Protocols (EGPs)**.

The remainder of this section is devoted to the various types of routing protocols and their behavior. We start with a discussion of distance vector and link-state routing protocols, followed by interior and exterior protocols.

Distance Vector Routing Protocols

There are several **distance vector routing protocols** in use today. The most popular by a wide margin is Routing Information Protocol (RIP), followed by a Cisco proprietary protocol called Interior Gateway Routing Protocol (IGRP). These protocols have several things in common that distinguish them from link-state protocols.

The primary distinction is that they periodically broadcast their entire routing tables to all neighbors. This is done in conjunction with timers so when a router receives a list of networks from a neighbor, it installs them in its routing table and sets a timer. If the timer expires before it receives another broadcast update, it removes the routes from its routing table. This means that the time it takes for a network to **converge**—where all routers on the network have an accurate, stable routing table—is a function of this timer. For instance, if a router advertises a network to a neighbor, then a change occurs where the network is no longer available, the neighbor still forwards packets to this defunct network until the timer expires. If there are several routers between these two, the convergence time can quickly turn into several minutes.

The second major distinction is that they "route by rumor." If you have three routers, where Router A is connected to Router B, and Router B is connected to Router C, Router A will send a message to Router B that says, "I have a route to Network 1." When Router B receives that message, it sends a message to Router C that says, "I have a route to Network 1" instead of "Router A has a route to Network 1, and I have a route to Router A." This sounds harmless enough until you realize that Router C doesn't know that Router A exists. It only knows that Router B can get to Network 1. This lack of complete information can cause several problems, which we'll discuss in detail later.

Also, a distance vector routing protocol shares information about how far away all networks are to the destination. Routing decisions are based on how far away networks are in distance—not the amount of time it takes to get to the destination. And, they are considered quite "chatty" and inefficient.

In Figure 10-2, the following steps are taken to set up the routing tables on these three routers (A, B, and C).

1. Each router boots up and defines its own distance vector as zero.

2. Each router calculates a cost for its distance to each connected link. In this example, we assume that the cost is calculated as one for each hop.

3. Each router announces its distance vector information, which defines network reachability, on all directly connected links. For example, Router A states that it is zero hops to Networks 1 and 2. Router B states that it is zero hops from Networks 2 and 3. Router C states that it is zero hops from Networks 3 and 4.

4. Upon receipt of this information from other routers, each router updates its routing table to reflect the new distance vector information. For example, in Figure 10-2, Router B learns of Network 1 from Router A's broadcast. Router B realizes it is one hop away from Network 1. Likewise, Router C realizes that it is two hops away from Network 1. If a device on Network 4 wants to communicate with a device on Network 1, it must cross three routers—the device itself is three hops away from Network 1.

5. Upon receipt of new route information, the routers send routing update information to other directly connected networks. This is called a **triggered update**. For example, Router B sends new route information to Network 2 after it receives new route information from Router C. After receiving information from Router A, Router B sends new route information to Network 3.

6. Distance vector routers periodically broadcast or multicast their route information on directly connected links. This is called a **periodic update**.

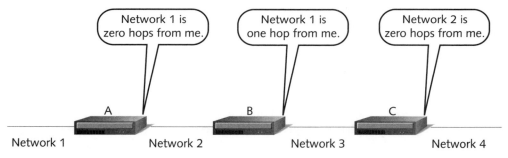

Figure 10-2   On distance vector networks, each router tracks the distance to other networks

Routing Loops

One of the most difficult challenges in automating the routing process is preventing **routing loops**. There are many different kinds of routing loops, but the simplest example of a routing loop occurs when one router believes the best path to a network is via a second router, and at the same time, the second router believes the best path to that network is through the first router. These two routers will pass a packet destined for the network in question back and forth until the Time to Live (TTL) on the packet expires.

For example, on the network depicted in Figure 10-2, consider what happens when Router C goes down—the route to Network 4 is gone. Router B (which is one hop away from Network 4) does not assume that the path to Network 4 is gone—it realizes that Router A still has a path to Network 4 (although it is two hops away). Router B recalculates its distance vector information and adds a metric of one to the distance to Network 4. Router B now believes that Network 4 is three hops away going through Router A. Upon receipt of this information, Router A recalculates its distance to Network 4—Router A now believes it is four hops away from Network 4. Upon hearing this new calculation, Router B recalculates its routing table again. This process continues to **infinity**—well, not really.

The method distance vector protocols use to prevent packets from endlessly circulating around a routing loop is called **counting to infinity**. By defining "infinity" as a certain number of hops away (for example, 16 for RIP), the protocol is essentially saying, "any route with a hop count of 16 is unreachable" so packets to that network will be dropped instead of forwarded. Although this doesn't prevent routing loops, it does limit damage when they occur. The downside is that an artificial limit is placed on the size of your network. The network **diameter** cannot be more than 15 hops.

Another loop-avoidance scheme in distance vector routing protocols is **split horizon**. Split horizon simply prevents a router from advertising a network on the same interface from which it learned that network. Another feature often coupled with split horizon is called **poison reverse**. Poison reverse is a method of "poisoning a route" to indicate that you cannot get there. We cover split horizon and poison reverse in more detail in the "Routing Characteristics" section later in this chapter.

Link-State Routing Protocols

Link-state routing protocols differ from distance vector routing protocols in two primary ways. The first is that they do not route by rumor. Each router generates information about only its directly connected links, and these are passed around the entire network so that every router in the area has an identical view of the network topology. Then the routers individually run an algorithm known as the **Dijkstra algorithm** to determine the optimal path through the internetwork.

The second major difference is that they do not periodically broadcast their entire tables. Link-state protocols build adjacencies with neighboring routers, and after an initial full exchange of information, they send only an update when a link state changes (for example, goes "up" or "down"). This update occurs almost immediately after the change occurs, so unlike a distance vector protocol, the link-state protocol does not have to wait until a timer expires. Thus, the convergence time for link-state protocols is relatively short. This not only saves significant time, but bandwidth as well because neighbors only send tiny Hello packets at a short interval to make sure the neighbor is still reachable, rather than their full routing tables.

Link-state routing uses the following processes:

1. Link-state routers meet their **neighbor routers** through a process called the **Hello process**.

10

2. Each router builds and transmits a **link-state advertisement (LSA)** that contains the list of its neighbors and the cost to cross the network to each of those neighbors. Costs are typically based on fixed values that are calculated based on link bandwidth.

3. As these LSAs are propagated through the network and received by other routers, each router builds a picture of the network.

4. Link-state routers convert that picture into a **forwarding table**. They sort this table according to the lowest cost route. This table is used to determine how packets should be forwarded through the router.

5. Link-state routers periodically multicast summaries of their link-state databases on directly connected links.

6. If a receiving router does not have certain route information, or detects that its information is out of date, that router can request updated information.

In Figure 10-3, we examine a link-state network. In this configuration, Routers A, B, and C send Hello packets to Network 1. As they hear each other's Hello packets, each router builds an **adjacencies database**. This database contains information about local networks and neighbor routers only. For example, Router C's adjacencies database includes Networks 1 and 4 and Routers A, B, and C. Router C does not know anything about Networks 2 and 3 because no LSA was sent advertising them.

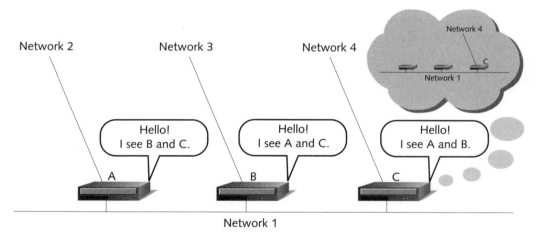

Figure 10-3   On a link-state network, the adjacencies database is simply a picture of the local network

Each of these routers sends an LSA that includes information about its neighbors and the cost to get to each of those neighbors.

Upon receipt of this LSA, Router B copies the route information and floods the LSA on to Network 3. Likewise, Router A forwards this LSA to Network 2. Upon receipt of the LSAs, which provide details on Networks 2 and 3, Router C's network picture grows into a link-state diagram.

This LSA continues to flood through the network so all routers can obtain a common view of the network. This distribution of firsthand information ensures that more timely and accurate routing data is exchanged.

The process of convergence is much more efficient in link-state routing than distance vector routing. The loop problem is resolved because link-state routers identify and resolve loops as they build their pictures of the network. Link-state routers can also forward LSAs before recalculating costs, unlike distance vector routers. Because OSPF is a link-state routing protocol, it displays all of the characteristics mentioned in this section.

ROUTING CHARACTERISTICS

When designing or operating a routing hierarchy, it's important to understand the characteristics of the networks involved and how they are interconnected. It's also important to understand the requirements and limitations of the various routing protocols that may be in use on an internetwork. You will learn more about these issues throughout this chapter, but those topics receive particular emphasis in the sections that follow next.

10

Route Convergence

As mentioned earlier in this chapter, convergence is the process of disseminating new routing information through an internetwork. Ideally, a network should be in a **converged state**, where all routers know the current networks available and their associated costs.

In each of the routing designs shown earlier, if Network 3 suddenly becomes unavailable, each router must learn about this so that they stop forwarding any packets that are destined to Network 3. The distance vector network converges more slowly than the link-state network.

Split Horizon

Split horizon is one of the methods devised to speed up the process of convergence and resolve the counting-to-infinity problem, in most cases. The basic rule of split horizon is to never advertise a path back out the way you learned about it. Figure 10-4 provides an example. In this figure, Router A learned about Network 3 from Router B, which advertised it as one hop away if you must go through Router B to get there. Router A adds its own cost of one hop and now updates its routing table to reflect that Network 3 is two hops away. Router A advertises this information on to Network 1. According to the rules of split horizon, Router A is not permitted to advertise a path to Network 3 back the same way it learned about it.

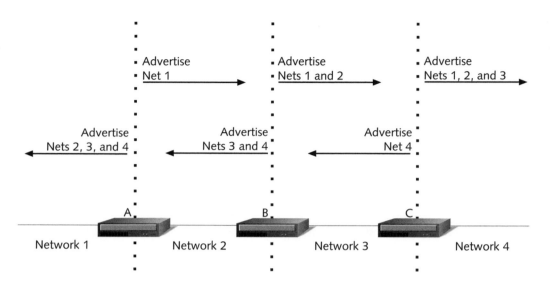

Figure 10-4   The rule of split horizon states that route information cannot be sent back the direction from which it came

Poison Reverse

Poison reverse is a technique for assigning costs to routes designed to prevent routing loops. When one router learns about a route or a set of routes from another router, it assigns those routes an infinite cost value so that it will never end up advertising routes back to their sources. Because the routes A–B–C and C–B–A–B–C both define ways to get from A to C, C has no business advertising that longer route to B because B already has a direct link to A. The poison reverse technique prevents this kind of thing from happening (and also prevents further recursion of such loops because repeating already-visited links only makes the loop longer, yet still topologically equivalent).

Time to Live (TTL)

To ensure that packets cannot loop endlessly through a network, each packet has a **lifetime value**—Time to Live—defined in the Network layer header. As packets travel through an internetwork, routers examine the TTL value to determine whether the packet has enough life remaining to be forwarded. For example, when a packet arrives at a router with a TTL value of eight, the router decrements this TTL value to seven before forwarding it. If, however, a packet arrives with a TTL value of one, the router cannot forward it because the Time to Live field cannot be decremented to zero and forwarded.

As you learned in Chapter 4, routers transmit ICMP Time Exceeded messages in response to expired packets.

Multicast Versus Broadcast Update Behavior

Some routing protocols can only use broadcasts to distribute their routing updates. Others can use either broadcasts or multicasts for their periodic updates. Broadcasts, of course, cannot traverse routers. Routers can be configured to forward multicasts, however.

There are two versions of RIP. Version 1 sends broadcast updates. Version 2, which supports non-default subnet masks (see Chapter 2 for variable-length subnet mask [VLSM] information), can send multicast updates. OSPF can also send multicasts.

ICMP Router Advertisements

As mentioned in Chapter 4, some routers can be configured to send periodic ICMP Router Advertisement packets. These periodic ICMP Router Advertisements do not mean that ICMP is a routing protocol. They simply allow hosts to passively learn about available routes.

These unsolicited ICMP Router Advertisements are sent periodically to the all-hosts multicast address 224.0.0.1. The advertisements typically include the IP address of the router that sent the ICMP Router Advertisement packet. The router also includes a life-time value to indicate how long the receiving host should keep the route entry.

For more information on ICMP Router Advertisements, refer to Chapter 4 and RFC 1256, "ICMP Router Discovery Messages."

Black Holes

A **black hole** occurs on a network when a router discards packets without any notification of the problem. Because the sender doesn't receive notification indicating its packets were discarded, it continues to retransmit until it times out—the actions are dependent on the upper layers. For example, if the communication is TCP-based, the TCP layer retransmits the packet and awaits an ACK response. Black holes are created when ICMP is turned off on a router.

There are many types of black hole routers. One specific example of a black hole router is shown in Figure 10-5. In this example, Router B is a **Path Maximum Transmission Unit black hole router** (referred to as a PMTU black hole router). The 4352 PMTU packet arrives at the router, but this router does not support PMTU discovery—it does not send an ICMP reply indicating the supported PMTU for the next hop. It just discards the packets.

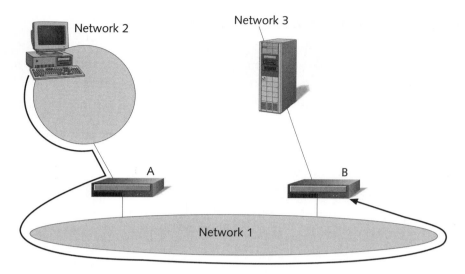

Figure 10-5 A PMTU black hole router silently discards oversized packets

Areas, Autonomous Systems, and Border Routers

To reduce the number of entries in the link-state database, OSPF utilizes **areas**. Contiguous groups of physical networks can be gathered into areas. The OSPF specification defines the need for a **backbone area**, Area 0. All other areas must be connected directly to this area (although there is some allowance for special tunneled connections). The routers that connect these areas are called **Area Border Routers** (ABRs). These ABRs can summarize routing information before sending link-state packets to other networks. Figure 10-6 depicts a network that uses multiple areas.

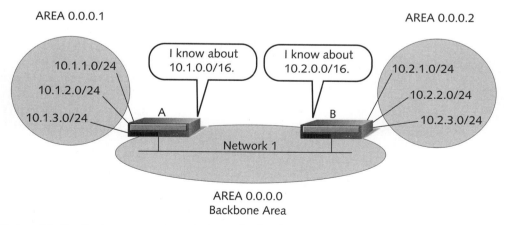

Figure 10-6 Each area must connect to the backbone area 0.0.0.0

In this example, Area 1 consists of three variable-length subnets. Instead of advertising all three subnets, Router A summarizes these three networks into a single entry—10.1.0.0/16. Router B only needs a single route entry that summarizes all three networks. Likewise, Area 2 consists of three networks that can be summarized as 10.2.0.0/16.

Extremely large networks can be broken down into regions called **Autonomous Systems (ASs)**. These Autonomous Systems are under the same administrative control. For example, if one company takes over another company, the parent company may contain their networks under one AS. The subsidiary, however, may support a separate AS.

All routers inside an AS use one or more Interior Gateway Protocols (IGPs) to support internal routing. RIP and OSPF are examples of Interior Gateway Protocols.

To connect between Autonomous Systems, routers use Exterior Gateway Protocols (EGPs). Border Gateway Protocol (BGP) is an example of an Exterior Gateway Protocol.

Figure 10-7 depicts the relationship between ASs, IGPs, and EGPs.

10

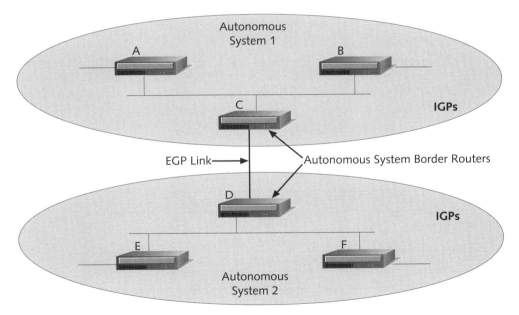

Figure 10-7   An Exterior Gateway Protocol is used to connect two Autonomous Systems

The routers that connect Autonomous Systems are called **Autonomous System Border Routers (ASBRs)**.

INTERIOR GATEWAY PROTOCOLS (IGPS)

Interior Gateway Protocols are used to exchange routing information within an AS. These protocols are also referred to as **intra-domain routing protocols**. The most commonly used IGPs are RIP (versions 1 and 2) and OSPF.

RIP

RIP is a basic distance vector routing protocol. There are two versions of RIP—version 1 (defined in RFC 1058) and version 2 (defined in RFC 2453). RIP version 2 adds support for variable-length subnets.

RIP communications are UDP-based. RIP-based routers send and receive datagrams on UDP port number 520.

In this next section, we examine the packet structures and functionality of RIPv1 and RIPv2.

RIPv1

When RIPv1 routers first come up, they send a RIP announcement about their directly connected links. Next, the router sends a RIP request to identify other networks. These two steps are used to build the routing table.

RIPv1 routers broadcast RIP network announcements every 30 seconds. Each RIP packet can contain information for up to 25 networks. Because RIPv1 does not support non-default subnet masks, the routers make assumptions on the network portion of the addresses based on whether the address is a Class A, B, or C.

Figure 10-8 shows the format of a RIPv1 packet.

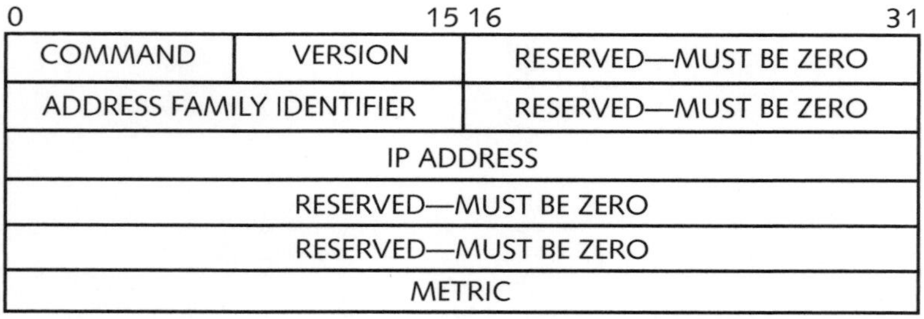

0	15 16	31
COMMAND	VERSION	RESERVED—MUST BE ZERO
ADDRESS FAMILY IDENTIFIER		RESERVED—MUST BE ZERO
IP ADDRESS		
RESERVED—MUST BE ZERO		
RESERVED—MUST BE ZERO		
METRIC		

Figure 10-8   The RIPv1 packet format

The fields of the RIP packet are defined below.

Command   This 1-byte field indicates whether this packet is a RIP request (1) or a response (2).

Version This 1-byte field indicates whether this is a RIPv1 (1) packet or RIPv2 (2) packet.

Reserved These 2-byte fields are reserved and set to all zeroes.

Address Family Identifier This 2-byte field is used to define the protocol that is using RIP. The value two indicates that IP is using RIP.

IP Address This 4-byte field contains the IP address.

Metric This 4-byte field contains the distance metric for the address listed above.

Figure 10-9 depicts a RIPv1 packet.

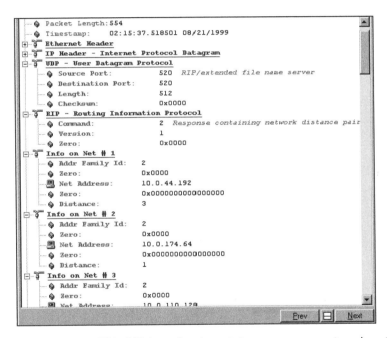

Figure 10-9   This RIP broadcast contains numerous network entries

RIPv1 does an adequate job of providing routing information. It has two major faults, however—it does not support non-default subnet masks and it takes too long to converge. Updating to RIPv2 solves the first problem. Replacing RIP-based routing with OSPF solves the second problem.

RIPv2

The primary differences between RIPv1 and RIPv2 are the support of variable-length subnet masks, some very basic authentication, and support for multicast routing updates. The RIPv2 IP multicast address is 224.0.0.9.

Figure 10–10 shows the format of a RIPv2 packet.

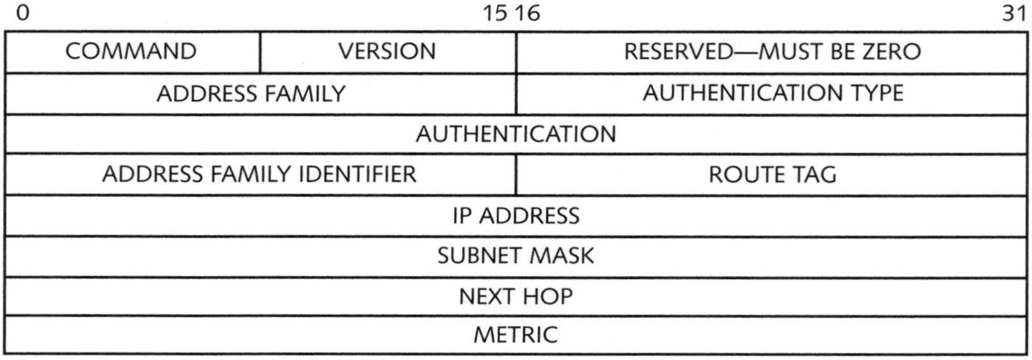

| 0 | | 15 16 | | 31 |

COMMAND	VERSION	RESERVED—MUST BE ZERO
ADDRESS FAMILY		AUTHENTICATION TYPE
AUTHENTICATION		
ADDRESS FAMILY IDENTIFIER		ROUTE TAG
IP ADDRESS		
SUBNET MASK		
NEXT HOP		
METRIC		

Figure 10-10   The RIPv2 packet format

As you see in Figure 10–10, there are some new fields and new field uses in a RIPv2 packet.

Command   This 1-byte field indicates whether this packet is a RIP request (1) or a response (2).

Version   The value two in this 1-byte field is used to indicate that this packet is a RIPv2 packet.

Reserved   This 2-byte field is reserved and set to all zeroes.

Address Family   This 2-byte field is used to define the protocol that is using RIP. The value two indicates that IP is using RIP. The value 0xFFFF indicates that the remainder of the message contains authentication. That leaves space for only 24 entries in the rest of the RIP packet.

Authentication Type   There is only one authentication type currently defined—type 2.

Authentication Information   This 16-byte field contains a **plain text password**. If the password is shorter than 16 bytes, it is left-justified and padded with 0x00s on the right.

Address Family Identifier   When this field contains the value 0x02, the next 20 bytes contain a route entry.

Route Tag   This 2-byte field can be used to indicate whether the route information that follows is an **internal route entry** (received from within this routing area), or an **external route entry** (learned through another IGP or EGP outside this routing area).

IP Address This 4-byte field contains the IP address being advertised.

Subnet Mask This 4-byte field contains the subnet mask associated with the IP address being advertised.

Next Hop or Another Router Typically, in RIP, routers only advertise for networks to which they can route packets. In RIPv2, however, the 4-byte Next Hop field can be used to associate another router with a route entry. The value 0.0.0.0 in this field indicates that this router is advertising networks to which it can route packets.

Metric The 4-byte Metric field indicates the distance, in hops, to the advertised network. This field is not used in request packets.

RIPv2 takes advantage of numerous improvements over its predecessor, RIPv1, and is still widely used on smaller, less complex networks to this day. Because RIPv2 is relatively easy to set up, configure, and manage, it should remain prevalent for the foreseeable future. For more complex enterprise-level networks, however, the OSPF protocol fits much better, as you will learn in the following section.

Open Shortest Path First (OSPF)

OSPF, defined in RFC 2328, is the premier link-state routing protocol used on TCP/IP networks. (The word "Open" in Open Shortest Path First refers to the non–proprietary nature of this protocol.) OSPF routing is based on configurable values (metrics) that may be based on network bandwidth, delay, or monetary cost. By default, the metric used for route determination is based on network bandwidth.

The basic architectural definition of OSPF is shown in Figure 10-11. First, OSPF devices multicast Hello packets to the directly connected links to learn about their neighbors. As the OSPF routers hear each other's Hello packets, they begin to include their neighbors' addresses in their next Hello packets. Depending on the configuration and type of media, the OSPF routers establish adjacencies with some of these neighbors. Once an adjacency is established, they share copies of all the LSAs (assuming they're in the same area). After the LSAs are shared, they continue sending Hello packets every 10 seconds (by default) as a keep-alive mechanism to ensure that the other router is still present and responding, thus building a small picture of their local worlds.

10

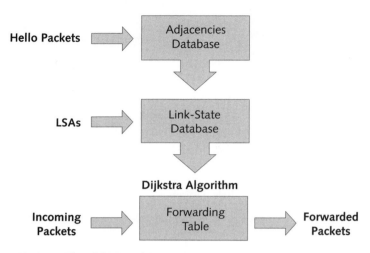

Figure 10-11   The OSPF architecture

On a broadcast-based network, on which there can be more than two routers connected to a given segment, a full mesh is required for each router to establish an adjacency with every other router. Because of the processing and memory demands, this is not a scalable architecture. To alleviate some of this overhead, OSPF uses the concept of a **designated router (DR)**. Each broadcast segment has one DR, which is elected based on the router's priority (a number from zero to 255, where higher numbers are preferred, and zero indicates the router is incapable of becoming the DR). The router with the second highest priority becomes the **backup designated router (BDR)**. Both of these routers establish adjacencies with all other OSPF-speaking routers on the subnet, but all other routers will establish only two adjacencies: one to the DR and one to the BDR. The DR's responsibility is to inform all other routers of LSAs. The aptly named BDR's purpose is to allow service to be restored very quickly in the event of an outage affecting the DR.

All other routers multicast a LSA to the DR multicast address (224.0.0.6). This LSA represents the router and the costs associated with accessing the network.

There are five basic types of LSAs:

- *Type 1 (Router Links Advertisement)*: This packet is flooded within an area and contains information about the router's neighbors. All routers send this type of LSA.

- *Type 2 (Network Links Advertisement)*: This packet is generated by the DR on behalf of the LAN. It lists all the routers on the LAN. Only DRs send this type of LSA.

- *Type 3 (Network Summary Link Advertisement)*: This packet is generated by an ABR to define the networks that are reachable outside an area. ABRs send this type of LSA.

- *Type 4 (AS Boundary Router Summary Link Advertisement)*: This packet describes the cost of the path from the sending router to an AS boundary router. ABRs send this type of LSA.

- *Type 5 (AS External Link Advertisement)*: This packet is flooded to all the routers throughout an entire AS to describe the cost from the sending AS boundary router to destinations outside the AS. ASBRs send this type of LSA.

When routers advertise themselves, they transmit the Type 1 packets to the Shortest Path First (SPF) router's multicast address (224.0.0.5).

The DR transmits a Type 2 LSA on behalf of the network. This unique packet lists all the routers connected to the LAN.

On each local network, OSPF uses the router IDs to establish one **master router**. All other OSPF routers are defined as **slave routers**. Periodically, the master router transmits a Database Description (DD) packet that describes the contents of the link–state database. Other routers send acknowledgments indicating successful receipt of the DD packets.

If the master does not receive an ACK from one of the slave routers, it sends a copy of the LSA directly to that SPF router.

Figure 10-12 shows the general sequence of communications used in OSPF.

10

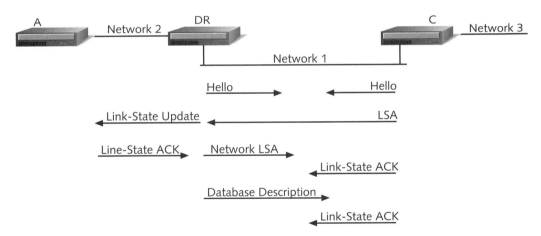

Figure 10-12 The OSPF Hello, link-state advertisement, and link-state update processes

Upon receipt of these LSAs, the OSPF routers build a link–state database, or a picture of the entire network—networks connected by routers with costs associated for all links.

This database cannot be used to route packets efficiently, however. The Dijkstra algorithm is run on the contents of the database to prioritize paths when multiple paths to a network exist. The result is the forwarding database. This table is referenced when the OSPF router wants to forward packets.

OSPF supports variable-length subnet masks and route summarization to reduce the number of routing entries maintained in the OSPF table.

Figure 10-13 shows the format of an OSPF packet header.

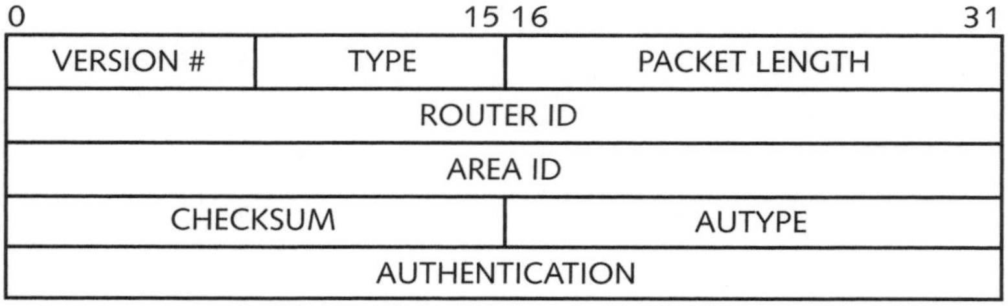

```
0                        15 16                          31
┌──────────────┬──────────────┬──────────────────────────┐
│  VERSION #   │    TYPE      │      PACKET LENGTH        │
├──────────────┴──────────────┴──────────────────────────┤
│                      ROUTER ID                          │
├────────────────────────────────────────────────────────┤
│                       AREA ID                           │
├───────────────────────────┬────────────────────────────┤
│         CHECKSUM          │          AUTYPE            │
├───────────────────────────┴────────────────────────────┤
│                   AUTHENTICATION                        │
└────────────────────────────────────────────────────────┘
```

Figure 10-13   The standard OSPF header structure

The following section details these header fields.

Version Number

This 1-byte field contains the OSPF version number. The current widely implemented version of OSPF is version 2.

Type

The 1-byte Type field defines the purpose of the OSPF packet. The Typefield values are described in Table 10-1.

Table 10-1   Type Field Values

Type Number	Type	Description
1	Hello Packet	Used to locate neighboring routers
2	Database Description	Used to transmit database summary information
3	Link-State Request	Used to request link-state database information
4	Link-State Update	Used to flood LSAs to other networks
5	Link-State Acknowledgment	Used to ACK receipt of link-state information

Packet Length

This 2-byte field indicates the length of this OSPF packet. The Length field includes the OSPF header and any valid data that follows. It does not include any packet padding, if used.

Router ID

This 4-byte field contains the ID of the transmitting router.

Area ID

This 4-byte field contains the number of the area to which the transmitting router belongs. The field value can be expressed in decimal or dotted decimal notation. Often, as a way of managing large networks, designers assign the Area ID the same value as a network that resides inside it, and display the Area ID in dotted decimal notation (for example, Area 10.32.0.0). Other times, it is simpler to use non-technical numbers to represent areas, such as a business unit, customer code, or zip code. These can be written as decimal numbers (for example, Area 95129).

Checksum

This 2-byte field contains the result of a checksum calculation run on the contents of the OSPF packet. The Authentication field is not included in this calculation.

AuType

This 2-byte field defines the authentication type that is used in this packet. Refer to Appendix D of RFC 2328 for more details on authentication types.

Authentication

The authentication process uses this 4-byte field.

After the OSPF header, the format of the packet varies depending on the type of LSA packet.

Figure 10-14 depicts an OSPF Hello packet. As you can see, this router indicates that 10.2.99.99 is the DR.

10

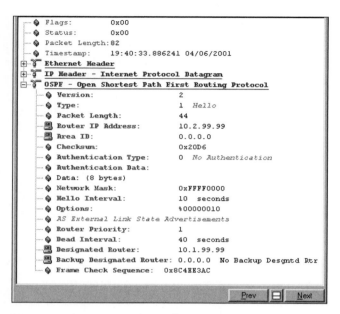

```
--◆ Flags:        0x00
--◆ Status:       0x00
--◆ Packet Length:82
--◆ Timestamp:    19:40:33.886241 04/06/2001
+-🗝 Ethernet Header
+-🗝 IP Header - Internet Protocol Datagram
-🗝 OSPF - Open Shortest Path First Routing Protocol
  --◆ Version:              2
  --◆ Type:                 1  Hello
  --◆ Packet Length:        44
  --🖳 Router IP Address:    10.2.99.99
  --🖳 Area ID:             0.0.0.0
  --◆ Checksum:             0x20D6
  --◆ Authentication Type:  0  No Authentication
  --◆ Authentication Data:
  --◆ Data: (8 bytes)
  --◆ Network Mask:         0xFFFF0000
  --◆ Hello Interval:       10  seconds
  --◆ Options:              %00000010
  --◆ AS External Link State Advertisements
  --◆ Router Priority:      1
  --◆ Dead Interval:        40  seconds
  --🖳 Designated Router:    10.1.99.99
  --🖳 Backup Designated Router: 0.0.0.0  No Backup Desgntd Rtr
  --◆ Frame Check Sequence: 0x8C4EE3AC
```
```
                              [ Prev  ][ □ ][ Next ]
```

Figure 10-14　An OSPF Hello packet

Enhanced Interior Gateway Routing Protocol (EIGRP)

IGRP was developed in the 1980s by Cisco Systems in an effort to provide a more efficient interior gateway protocol. IGRP was updated in the early 1990s—the updated version is called Enhanced Interior Gateway Routing Protocol (EIGRP).

EIGRP offers a strange mixture of routing technologies. It integrates the capabilities of
link-state routing into a distance vector routing protocol. For more information on
EIGRP, refer to *http://www.cisco.com*.

EXTERIOR GATEWAY PROTOCOLS (EGPS)

Exterior Gateway Protocols are used to exchange routing information between
Autonomous Systems. These protocols are also referred to as **inter-domain routing
protocols**. Interestingly, the name Exterior Gateway Protocol was assigned to the first
implementation of this type of routing. EGP is defined in RFC 904. Currently, Border
Gateway Protocol (BGP) replaces EGP routing.

Border Gateway Protocol (BGP)

BGP is a distance vector protocol and is the replacement for EGP. The current version of BGP is version 4, which is defined in RFC 1771. BGP offers three types of routing operations:

- Inter-autonomous system routing
- Intra-autonomous system routing
- Pass-through autonomous system routing

Figure 10-15 illustrates how BGP is used for **inter-autonomous system routing**. In this configuration, BGP routers that reside in different ASs are configured as peers and exchange information about the internetwork topology of each AS.

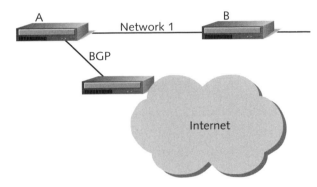

Figure 10-15   Typical BGP design

When BGP is configured for **intra-autonomous system routing**, the BGP routers are located within the same AS. **Pass-through autonomous system routing** enables BGP peer routers to exchange routing information across an AS that does not support BGP.

MANAGING ROUTING ON AN IN-HOUSE INTERNETWORK

Simply configuring an IGP on an in-house network will likely establish connectivity between each subnet; however, there is much more to managing routing than simply establishing connectivity.

The first thing an administrator must consider is policy. IP routing protocols have a shortcoming in that they don't discriminate between users, types of traffic, and so on. They only know how to get to a network. Policy-based routing addresses this shortcoming. Let's suppose you have a network with two paths between point A and point B. One path is a 128-Kbps ISDN link that directly connects the two networks, and the other is a T1 that passes through three other networks between A and B. If you're running RIP, it will attempt to send all traffic over the ISDN link because of the shorter hop count. If you are running OSPF, which has a metric based on bandwidth, it may prefer the much-higher-speed T1. The point is that neither of these reflects what you really want to do. For instance, you might want to configure your network so that a certain type of traffic, such as VoIP, will prefer to use the first connection with a low latency, while other traffic, such as HTTP and FTP, is sent via a second link that is larger, but has more latency. This configuration is called "policy routing." Policies can be based on anything, from the type of protocol, as in the example above, to the source or destination address, where your policy could say, "I want all traffic from Host xyz to use Link 1, and other traffic to use Link 2."

 Configuring policies makes your network more efficient, but it also makes it harder to troubleshoot.

Another item for consideration is that most IGPs allow a certain number of simultaneous links to be configured. These are typically managed on a "flow" basis, as opposed to a per-packet load balancing. This means that all traffic between Hosts A and X will take one link, while traffic between B and Y will take another. Per-packet load balancing means the first packet takes Link 1, the second packet takes Link 2, the third packet takes Link 1, and so on. Per-packet load balancing breaks a lot of protocols because packets often arrive out of sequence.

The routing services on your network also require routine maintenance, especially on large networks. You should monitor memory utilization (each type of route takes a certain amount of memory) to make sure that your routers are capable of handling any additions, and employ a management tool that sends alerts when routing problems occur. Also, most routing tables will show the age of a route. In a link-state routing protocol, a young age is a sign of an unstable route. It changed recently, and you should find out why. For instance, if you observe a route in your table that has an age of 23 minutes, but you haven't made any changes to your network in six weeks, you could have a problem.

Finally, an administrator should maintain a map of the network, indicating the network addresses and routing protocols in use. This map should serve as the network design blueprint, and assist in spotting possible routing loops or configuration concerns.

For more information on management processes, refer to Chapter 11, "Monitoring and Managing IP Networks."

HYBRID NETWORKS

Just when you think you're getting a handle on these routing protocols, reality rears its ugly head. Your network grows. You want to migrate to a different protocol. You merge with another company and need to simultaneously support two protocols. If you thought the protocols were complicated individually, wait until you try **redistributing** routes from one to another.

The practice of redistribution is fraught with danger. What happens when you redistribute a network from a classless protocol to a class-oriented protocol, which only understands the major network and not the VLSM you're using? And how can you convert the bandwidth, delay, load, reliability, and MTU size of EIGRP and IGRP into the simple hop counts that RIP uses? Because the solutions to these particular problems are largely vendor specific, they're beyond the scope of this book. But you should recognize that these are just a few of the challenges involved with supporting multiple routing protocols. Carefully consider your design and thoroughly test your plans before implementing them. And, always have a back-out plan to reverse the changes if things go wrong.

ROUTING ON AND OFF A WIDE AREA NETWORK

You must consider many factors when choosing a routing protocol for your enterprise. In this section, we discuss some various network models and appropriate routing protocols. In most cases, your only choices are RIP or OSPF, and in almost all cases, OSPF is preferable. However, the following situations deserve more thought.

Several Small Offices

If the network in question is relatively small—perhaps a dozen locations or less, where each has its own subnet plus an Internet connection or two—you should strongly consider using no routing protocol. RIP and OSPF are certainly options, but you should avoid RIP for all but the smallest, least complex internetworks, and OSPF probably isn't worth the configuration effort necessary to set it up and manage it properly. Whenever possible, the simplest solution is best. As of this writing, RIP should be considered only in the following special circumstances:

- When connecting to a server that supports routing so that the server can dynamically choose the best path. (If the server supports OSPF, by all means, use that instead.)

- When routers that do not support any other protocols are employed. (These are common in the Internet Access Device [IAD] market for Small-Office/Home-Office [SOHO] firewall/NAT/broadband devices.)

Hub and Spoke

Many corporations have a central office with many satellites or branches. Usually, all branch offices connect directly to the hub where enterprise systems like ERP packages, a mainframe, and most servers reside. The distinguishing feature on this network is that the router in the hub needs to know how to get to many sites, but the routers at the branch offices only have a single connection out of the office.

If there is only one connection, what sense does it make to use precious bandwidth (not to mention router processor and memory resources) advertising all routes to each spoke? For routers on the ends of the spokes, all you need is a single default route that points to the hub. In this situation, an **On-Demand Routing (ODR)** protocol is a good choice.

If the hub-and-spoke environment uses frame relay, be wary of implementing any distance vector protocols. Frame relay and ATM use virtual circuits so that one physical interface can actually be logically partitioned into several logical interfaces. Commonly, all these are terminated at a hub, so to get from Router A to Router C, you must go in and back out the same interface on Router B. So, when Router A advertises its networks to Router B, Router B receives and installs them in its routing table, but it won't send them back out the same interface, so Router C never receives the routing updates. Why? Split horizon means that it doesn't advertise to avoid what appears to be an apparent routing loop (but isn't).

Multiprotocol

If your company also uses Novell's IPX protocol, you may have to run one routing protocol for IP and another routing protocol for IPX. Cisco's EIGRP, however, can support both at the same time. This can conserve a lot of resources in some cases. Of course, it does require that you use only Cisco equipment.

Mobile Users

One of the most difficult types of networks to implement and manage is one where the users are always moving around. From laptop and PDA users to telecommuters and companies that frequently rearrange workspaces to accommodate changes in personnel, it is clear that trends are emerging in the new millennium that yesterday's TCP/IP wasn't built to handle.

Fortunately, the last few years witnessed a remarkable maturation of technologies to support a highly mobile workforce. This includes data-enabled cellular devices, 802.11b wireless technologies, and lots of dial-up and broadband for home-based connections. But how does IP work with this? Primarily via DHCP. Unfortunately, there are many applications, such as voice and security, that need hosts to maintain a stable IP address, regardless of where they are currently located or connected.

In turn, this raises an interesting question: How can you route packets if your host uses an IP address that isn't part of the local subnet? While this is actually a workable scenario, it's by no means obvious. The following sections offer two possible solutions to the problem of "mismatched addresses."

Mobile IP

Mobile IP is defined by the IETF in RFCs 2002 through 2006. Mobile IP allows an IP host to travel anywhere there is a Mobile IP **agent** (a router configured with the protocol), and still maintain its home IP address. At a high level, it works like this: The host uses the ICMP Router Discovery Protocol to determine whether or not it's on its home network or a foreign network. If it is on a foreign network, it registers with a Foreign Agent. The Foreign Agent then routes packets to the Home Agent. The Home Agent establishes a tunnel back to the Foreign Agent, which then delivers the packets to the host.

An application for this technology might be carrying an IP phone from one office to another on your company's network. This technology has many applications in the military because military units are highly mobile, yet need to retain a static IP address for security reasons.

Local Area Mobility (LAM)

This technology is a Cisco proprietary feature that is similar to Mobile IP, but operates by using the routing table, and is much simpler, with very little impact on the network. When a router is configured with LAM, it watches for traffic on its LAN that does not match its own IP address. When it finds this traffic, it installs an ARP entry in its cache and a **host route** (a route entry with a 32-bit subnet mask) in its routing table. Then LAM is redistributed into the primary routing protocol. Soon, all the other routers learn of the host route and forward the appropriate traffic. Hosts on the home subnet are still able to communicate with the estranged node because the router on the home subnet proxies ARP (RFC 826) for it, and then routes the packets to the next hop listed in its routing table.

One of the keys to this technology's operation is the host route. This works because when routers look up an address in the routing table, they always take the longest match. For instance, if the routing table has an entry for 192.168.1.0/24 and the mobile host is 192.168.1.57, then a 192.168.1.57/32 route is propagated through the network. And each router has both routes in its table. If a router has a packet destined for 192.168.1.42, it doesn't match the 192.168.1.57/32 entry (obviously), but it does match the 192.168.1.0/24 entry. Conversely, when a packet arrives destined for 192.168.1.57, it matches *both* entries, but it prefers the longer one (/32) because it is more specific.

10

ROUTING TO AND FROM THE INTERNET

As of this writing, BGPv4 is the exterior routing protocol in use on the Internet. Although BGP probably doesn't deserve its arcane reputation, it certainly requires a major hardware investment if it is to be deployed properly. Fortunately, only a few companies have networks complex enough to require BGP. As a general rule, only networks that connect to multiple Internet providers should use BGP. Even so, no discussion of routing would be complete without covering this essential networking protocol because it is part and parcel of the Internet backbone (as far as such an entity really exists).

Although BGP is a distance vector protocol, it tracks hops between pairs of Autonomous Systems, rather than tracking hop counts of actual routers. As an example, let's say AS100 advertises a route to network 67.24.20.0/22 into AS200 and AS2000. When a route is advertised out of an AS, the BGP include an AS number. So AS200 and AS2000 receive 67.24.20.0/22 100. Then AS200 advertises it to AS300, and prepends its AS number so AS300 receives a route 67.24.20.0/22 200 100. At the same time, AS2000 and AS300 advertise that route to AS3000 and prepend their AS numbers. So AS3000 receives two routes:

- 67.24.20.0/22 2000 100

- 67.24.20.0/22 300 200 100

All other metrics being equal (and BGP has a *lot* of other metrics), AS3000 prefers the shorter AS path through AS2000 and AS100. It is important to note that even if the path through AS2000 has 20 router hops and the path through AS300 has three, AS3000 still prefers the shorter AS path because it has no way of knowing the actual distances involved. Remember that this protocol is largely administrative, and in the real world, these decisions are often made based on dollars and agreements between NSPs, rather than the actual best physical path.

Even for corporate networks that use two or more ISPs, it is generally preferable to advertise only a default route from each ISP, and configure the BGP and IGP redistribution to determine which default route it should take. It was common to redistribute an IGP into a BGP, but because many networks now use private RFC 1918 addresses, such as 10.0.0.0 and Network Address Translation, redistribution into BGP is pointless.

SECURING ROUTERS AND ROUTING BEHAVIOR

The two aspects of routing services that must be secured are the routers and the routing protocols. Routers contain network addressing information and a doorway between networks. These doorways should be guarded closely to ensure no malicious packets cross them. Securing routers is similar to securing most host systems. Turn off unnecessary services, shut down unnecessary listening ports, configure strong access security to prevent tampering, and, of course, secure physical access to the boxes. Consider assigning secure passwords to the routers and using an encrypted communications technology to access them. Too often, network administrators use standard Telnet to access and configure the routers. Telnet sends unencrypted login names and passwords across the network, which are susceptible to eavesdropping by network analyzers.

Securing routing protocols is somewhat more challenging. It's necessary to prevent prying eyes from seeing the information disclosed by the routing protocols because they contain information that makes internal systems much easier to attack. It's also important to prevent Denial of Service (DoS) attacks when unauthorized users forge bogus routing packets and attempt to make your routers create loops or black holes, or worse, forward the traffic to the attacker, at which point it might be able to capture the transported data.

Unfortunately, securing routing protocols requires the cooperation of the protocols. For instance, OSPF, as seen in the packet headers, supports several forms of authentication, including MD5. Configuring this authentication means that a router will not form an adjacency with another router unless it knows the password. RIPv1, on the other hand, has no security, while RIPv2 has a password, but this is of little value because it is sent in plain text.

For more information on TCP/IP security issues and options, refer to Chapter 9.

TROUBLESHOOTING IP ROUTING

Most IP routing problems deal with a lack of connectivity across routers. There are numerous utilities and tools available to test route connectivity. The following four tools are included with Windows 2000:

- *ROUTE*: Used to view the host's local routing table, and add and remove route entries
- *PING*: Used to send ICMP Echo messages and test connectivity
- *TRACERT*: Sends ICMP echoes with incrementally increasing TTL values to identify the path to a destination
- *PATHPING*: Another utility used to discover the path from a host to a destination

For more information on ROUTE, PING, TRACERT, and PATHPING, refer to Chapter 4, "Internet Control Message Protocol." For command syntax, refer to Appendix C.

CHAPTER SUMMARY

- ❐ Routing protocols and routers provide a mechanism that can forward traffic from a sender's subnet to an intended receiver's subnet. Generally, routers depend on access to tables of information that describe known routes and default routers so that traffic can be directed properly within any given internetworked environment, or forwarded outside that environment for delivery elsewhere.

- ❐ Routers depend on various routing protocols to manage the packet forwarding process. Interior routing protocols are designed for use within autonomous routing domains, like those that fall under the purview and control of a single company or organization. Exterior routing protocols provide a means whereby routers belonging to multiple companies or organizations can safely and securely forward data and manage routing information amongst the parties involved in a common connection.

❏ Distance vector routing protocols such as RIP represent the oldest and simplest type of routing protocols, in which the number of router transitions (called hops) provides a crude metric of routing cost, and where no routing loops should occur as part of the routing topology. Link-state routing protocols like OSPF provide more sophisticated routing metrics and controls, and can not only deal with multiple routes between a sender and receiver, but can also use more powerful route metrics to balance loads across such links, or failover from less expensive to more expensive routes, as needed.

❏ The OSPF protocol supports much more sophisticated routing structures that break up a network into routing areas to help optimize routing tables and behavior. In addition, OSPF recognizes special categories of routing areas, such as a backbone area (where all individual areas interconnect) and Autonomous Systems, which represent individual routing regions that fall under specific administrative and management control. In such cases, Area Border Routers may connect separate routing areas to the backbone, or to other routing areas.

❏ Managing routing on a complex network means understanding how and when to use exterior and interior routing protocols, and how to establish the right kinds of connections between multiple routing domains. Private WAN links, Internet connections, and Mobile IP users all require special handling where routing is concerned to make sure that systems and services behave as required. It's especially important to understand how and when interior routing protocols, such as OSPF, must interoperate with exterior routing protocols, such as BGP.

❏ Because router tables define the topology and behavior of IP networks, it's essential to manage router security and updates as safely as possible. For those reasons, using strong passwords and secure links to access and update routers and their configurations is absolutely essential.

❏ Key troubleshooting tools for inspecting and diagnosing routing problems through a Windows 2000 IP host include ROUTE, TRACERT, PING, and PATHPING. To become as proficient in managing routes and routers as possible, make yourself completely familiar with these command-line utilities.

KEY TERMS

adjacencies database — A database of the local network segment and its attached routers. Designated routers share the adjacencies database view across link-state networks.

agent — In general, an agent is a piece of software that performs services on behalf of another process or user. In the case of Mobile IP, the agent in question is a special piece of router software that tunnels from a remote subnet to a user's home subnet to set up connections for a specific static IP address.

Area Border Router — A router used to connect separate areas.

areas — Groups of contiguous networks. Areas are used in link-state routing to provide route table summarization on larger networks.

Autonomous System (AS) — A group of routers that is under a single administrative authority.

Autonomous System Border Router (ASBR) — A router that connects an independent routing area, or AS, to another AS or the Internet.

backbone area — A required area to which all other routers should be attached directly or through a tunnel.

backup designated router (BDR) — The router with the second highest priority on a broadcast segment of a link-state network. The BDR allows service to be restored quickly in the event of an outage affecting the DR. *See also* designated router.

black hole — A point on the network where packets are silently discarded.

converge — The process of ensuring all routers on a network have up-to-date information about available networks and their costs.

converged state — A network state in which all routers are synchronized to share a complete view of the network.

counting to infinity — A network routing problem caused by a routing loop. Packets circulate continuously until they expire.

designated router (DR) — The router with the highest priority on a segment of a link-state network. A DR advertises LSAs to all other routers on the segment.

diameter — The number of hops that a network routing protocol can span; RIP has a network diameter of 15; most other routing protocols (such as OSPF and BGP) have an unlimited network diameter.

Dijkstra algorithm — An algorithm used to compute the best route on a link-state network.

distance vector — The source point or location for determining distance to another network.

distance vector routing protocol — A routing protocol that uses information about the distances between networks, rather than the amount of time it takes for traffic to make its way from the source network to the destination network. RIP is a distance vector routing protocol.

Exterior Gateway Protocol (EGP) — The original exterior gateway protocol defined for use on the Internet, EGP has now been supplanted by the more modern and efficient Border Gateway Protocol, or BGP.

external route entry — A route entry received from a different area.

forwarding table — The actual table referenced to make forwarding decisions on a link-state network.

Hello process — A process link-state routers use to discover neighbor routers.

host route — A routing table entry with a 32-bit subnet mask designed to reach a specific network host.

infinity — In the case of routing, infinity is the maximum number of hops that a packet can cross before being discarded. In an IP packet, the Time to Live field is used to define the remaining lifetime of a packet.

inter-autonomous system routing — A term used in BGP, this refers to the ability to provide routing between Autonomous Systems.

10

inter-domain routing protocols — Routing protocols used to exchange information between Autonomous Systems.

interior Gateway Protocols (IGPs) — Routing protocols used within an Autonomous System.

internal route entry — A route entry learned from within the same area as the computing device.

intra-autonomous system routing — A term used in BGP that refers to the ability to provide routing within an Autonomous System.

intra-domain routing protocols — Routing protocols used to exchange routing information between separate Autonomous Systems.

lifetime value — The time that a packet can remain on the network. Routers discard packets when their lifetimes expire.

link-state — A type of routing protocol that uses and shares information only about adjacent neighbors, and that uses transit time to assess link costs, rather than hop counts or routing distances.

link-state advertisement (LSA) — A packet that includes information about a router, its neighbors, and the attached network.

link-state routing protocol — A routing protocol based on a common link-state picture of the network topology. Link-state routers can identify the best path based on bandwidth, delay, or other path characteristics associated with one or more links available to them. OSPF is a link-state routing protocol.

master router — In link-state routing, a router that distributes its view of the link-state database to slave routers.

neighbor routers — On a link-state network, neighbor routers are connected to the same network segment.

Network Layer Reachability Information (NLRI) — The information about available networks, and the routes whereby they may be reached, which routing protocols collect, manage, and distribute to the routers or other devices that use such routing protocols.

On-Demand Routing (ODR) — A low-overhead feature that provides IP routing for sites on a hub-and-spoke network. Each router maintains and updates entries in its routing table only for hosts whose data passes through the router, thus reducing storage requirements and bandwidth.

pass-through autonomous system routing — A term used in BGP routing, this routing technique is used to share BGP routing information across a non-BGP network.

Path Maximum Transmission Unit black hole router — A router that silently discards packets that are too large to be forwarded and have the Don't Fragment bit set.

periodic update — In general, an update to data values that occurs at a regular interval or time period. In the case of routing protocols, most distance vector protocols include periodic updates to help maintain router table currency.

plain text password — A password that is transferred across the cable in plain ASCII text.

poison reverse — A process used to make a router undesirable for a specific routing path. This process is one of the methods used to eliminate routing loops.

redistributing — The method whereby information collected and managed by one routing protocol is exchanged with similar (but usually not identical) information managed by another routing protocol.

routing loops — A network configuration that enables packets to circle the network. Split horizon and poison reverse are used to resolve routing loops on distance vector networks. OSPF networks automatically resolve loops by defining best paths through an internetwork.

routing protocol — A Layer 3 protocol designed to permit routers to exchange information about networks that are reachable, the routes by which they may be reached, and the costs associated with such routes.

slave router — On an OSPF network, this type of router receives and acknowledges link-state database summary packets from a master router.

split horizon — A rule used to eliminate the counting-to-infinity problem. The split horizon rule states that information cannot be sent back the same direction from which it was received.

triggered update — An update that occurs in response to some specific event in a network environment, usually associated with a router entering or leaving that environment, or some change in cost assessments or configurations for network links.

10

REVIEW QUESTIONS

1. Which of the following phrases represents the best synonym for routing?

   a. packet delivery

   b. packet handling

   c. packet forwarding

   d. packet tracking

2. Where is routing information stored in most routers and other similar devices?

   a. routing database

   b. routing table

   c. routing directory

   d. route lookup cache

3. Which field in the IP header must a router read to decide where to direct an incoming packet?

   a. Source Address

   b. Destination Address

   c. Flags

   d. TTL value

4. Which of the following statements best represents the primary advantage of a static route (which must be entered and updated manually in a routing table)?

   a. control

   b. flexibility

   c. ease of management

   d. manual entry

5. What is the primary advantage of using a routing protocol?

   a. It permits routers to share information about network topology.

   b. It supports dynamic update of routing tables.

   c. It represents a single point of failure or attack.

   d. its inherent lack of control

6. Routed protocols are used to exchange routing information. True or false?

   a. True

   b. False

7. Which two of the following are ways to group routing protocols?

   a. communications methods: distance vector and link-state

   b. static configuration versus dynamic update

   c. Interior versus Exterior Gateway Protocols

   d. size of networks that particular routing protocols can accommodate

8. Which of the following routing protocols is also a distance vector protocol? (Choose all that apply.)

   a. OSPF

   b. IGRP

   c. BGP

   d. RIP

9. Which of the following routing protocols is a link-state protocol?

   a. OSPF

   b. IGRP

   c. BGP

   d. RIP

10. Which of the following characteristics is true of distance vector routing protocols? (Choose all that apply.)

   a. They periodically broadcast their entire routing tables to all neighbors.

   b. Convergence is a function of the update timer.

   c. The network diameter (maximum number of hops between any two routers) is essentially unlimited.

   d. The path cost is based on time, not on distance (number of hops).

11. Which of the following definitions best explains split horizon?

   a. All routes that originate elsewhere are set to infinite distance.

   b. It prevents a router from advertising a network to the interface that provides the original network information.

   c. It avoids routing loops.

   d. It creates routing loops.

12. Which of the following characteristics is true of link-state routing protocols? (Choose all that apply.)

   a. Routers build adjacencies tables to send updates only when link states change.

   b. The protocol is not dependent on timer values, so convergence time is short.

   c. The protocol uses Hello packet to make sure neighbors are reachable.

   d. Network diameter is limited to 15 hops maximum.

13. Which of the following definitions best describes a network that is in a converged state?

   a. Routers are waiting for table updates to finish propagating.

   b. All routers know current available networks and their associated costs.

   c. All routers use static routing tables.

   d. All routers use link-state routing protocols.

14. Which header field value is used to discard packets that might otherwise loop endlessly through a network?

   a. Source Address

   b. Destination Address

   c. Flags

   d. TTL value

15. Which version of RIP uses multicast packets for updates, rather than broadcasts?

   a. RIPv1

   b. RIPv2

   c. RIPv3

   d. OSPF

10

16. Which definition best describes a black hole on a network?

    a. A router discards packets and provides notification that a problem exists.

    b. A router silently discards packets without notification of a problem.

    c. A network route disappears without notification of a state change.

    d. A router does not support PMTU discovery.

17. Which phenomenon causes a black hole to occur?

    a. One or more routers become unavailable.

    b. Link–states change without notification.

    c. ICMP is disabled on a router.

    d. ICMP is enabled on a router.

18. What is the name of the OSPF area to which all other areas must be connected?

    a. backbone area

    b. Autonomous Systems

    c. stub areas

    d. interconnect area

19. To interconnect Autonomous Systems, routers use Exterior Gateway Protocols, such as BGP. True or false?

    a. True

    b. False

20. At which field does the RIPv2 header begin to differ from the RIPv1 header?

    a. Address Family

    b. Authentication Type

    c. Authentication

    d. Address Family Identifier

21. Which of the following router designations helps make OSPF more efficient than RIP when it comes to managing local routing behavior?

    a. default gateway setting

    b. designated router setting

    c. Router Links Advertisement

    d. Network Links Advertisement

22. Which OSPF packet type number is associated with the Hello packets used to verify reachability?

   a. 1

   b. 2

   c. 3

   d. 4

   e. 5

23. Which of the following scenarios justifies use of static routing configurations?

   a. up to a dozen locations, each with a single subnet, and one or two Internet connections

   b. from a dozen to a hundred locations, each with multiple subnets, and two or more Internet connections

   c. more than a hundred locations, each with multiple subnets, and two or more Internet connections

   d. None of the above; static routing is not recommended under any circumstances.

24. In a hub-and-spoke routing configuration how many routes do the routers at the ends of the spokes (away from the hub) need to know?

   a. one

   b. two

   c. many

   d. all

25. What is the critical ingredient needed to support Mobile IP on a modern network?

   a. a mobile router that follows the user around

   b. a router configured as a Mobile IP agent

   c. a properly configured client

   d. Mobile IP is not possible on modern networks.

HANDS-ON PROJECTS

The following Hands-on Projects assume that you are working in a Windows 2000 environment, and that you installed the EtherPeek for Windows demo software (included on the accompanying CD).

Project 10-1

To build an advanced filter for RIP and OSPF routing traffic:

1. Launch the EtherPeek for Windows demo program.

2. Click **View** on the menu bar, and then click **Filters**. The Filters window appears.

3. Click the **Insert** button . The Edit Filter window appears.

4. Type **RIP-OSPF** in the Filter text box.

5. Click the arrow next to the Type text box, and select **Advanced**. The Edit Filter window changes to show an Advanced box.

6. Click the **And** button, and select **Protocol**.

7. Click the boxed plus sign in front of the frame type used on your network. (Most TCP/IP networks use the Ethernet Type 2 frame type.) The pre-defined protocol filter list appears.

8. Click the boxed plus sign in front of **IP**. Scroll down to OSPF. Click the boxed plus sign to the left of the **OSPF**, and notice that EtherPeek has pre-defined filters for the five types of OSPF packets. Click the **OSPF** entry to ensure you capture all OSPF traffic.

9. Click the **OK** button. The value *Protocol OSPF* is shown in the Advanced box in the Edit Filter window.

10. Because you are interested in packets that are either OSPF or RIP, click the **Or** button, and select **Protocol**. Click the boxed plus sign in front of the frame type used on your network again.

11. Click the boxed plus sign in front of **IP**. Scroll down to UDP. Click the boxed plus sign in front of **UDP**. Scroll down and click **RIP**. The UDP processes are sorted based on port numbers. Because RIP uses port number 520, it is far down on the list.

12. Click the **OK** button. The value *Protocol RIP* is shown in the Advanced box in the Edit Filter window. Click the **OK** button to exit the Edit Filter window.

13. Click **Capture** on the menu bar, and then click **Start Capture** (or press **Ctrl+Y**). Click the **OK** button to accept the capture buffer settings. The Capture window opens.

14. Click the **Filters** tab and click the check box next to the **RIP-OSPF** filter you just created.

15. Click the **Start Capture** button. Click the **Packets** tab to view the traffic being saved to the buffer.

16. After you capture some traffic in the trace buffer, click the **Stop Capture** button, and then examine the contents and determine which routing protocol is used in your classroom.

17. Close the packet summary window. Close the EtherPeek demo unless you plan to proceed immediately to Hands-on Project 10-2.

Project 10-2

To read and interpret OSPF packets:

1. Open the EtherPeek for Windows demo program if it is not already running.

2. Click **File** on the menu bar, and then click **Open**.

3. Open the file **ospf1.pkt** from the **18654-2\Ch10** folder on your hard disk. Scroll through the packets in this trace file and answer the following questions.

   a. What is the IP address of the device that is sending these packets?

   b. What is the destination IP address of these packets?

   c. What is that address used for?

   d. What is the designated router on this network?

   e. What type of packet is Packet #1?

4. Draw a diagram of this network based on these packets.

5. Close the EtherPeek for Windows demo program.

CASE PROJECTS

1. You are installing a new network for a film studio based in Cannes, France. Design an OSPF network that has the following characteristics:

   ◻ Four areas (number the areas)

   ◻ Three networks in each area

   ◻ Route summarization at the area borders

   ◻ One Autonomous System

2. Your stock brokerage company, which consists of three RIP-based networks, recently acquired a small electronics trading company. The trading company's network is OSPF-based. Because your company plans to allow the trading company to continue operations just as it did before the takeover, you must devise a plan for transparently connecting the two networks.

   Write a "network integration plan" that details the options for integrating the networks, and how you suggest this task be accomplished.

11

MONITORING AND MANAGING IP NETWORKS

After reading this chapter and completing the exercises you will be able to:

♦ Understand the basic principles and practices involved in managing modern networks

♦ Explain the role that the Simple Network Management Protocol can play on an IP-based network

♦ Distinguish between in-band and out-of-band network management tools and techniques

♦ Understand the basic structure and function of SNMP management data, including Management Information Bases, Abstract Syntax Notation, and related SNMP management objects

♦ Explain the function of the standard remote monitoring SNMP Management Information Base known as RMON

♦ Understand how to install, configure, and use SNMP consoles, tools, and utilities

♦ Explain the issues involved in integrating SNMP-based network management tools with other network management environments

As networks grow and become more complex, organizational needs to inspect, manage, and control the resulting networks grow increasingly important. In fact, an entire discipline devoted to understanding the requirements for and activities involved in managing networks has developed in response to such needs.

In this chapter, you'll learn enough about the basic terminology, tools, and concepts involved in general network management to put managing IP-based networks into proper perspective. You'll learn about the key IP-based network management protocol, known as Simple Network Management Protocol (SNMP). You'll also learn about the typical tools and technologies whereby SNMP is used to help manage networks, and how to use these tools and technologies to perform basic network monitoring and management.

UNDERSTANDING NETWORK MANAGEMENT PRACTICES AND PRINCIPLES

The tasks involved in managing a network depend on the ability to collect data about a network and detect network-related occurrences, usually called events. This means being able to monitor and control all of the devices that go into a modern network, from hubs and routers, to servers, switches, and gateways of various kinds. Protocols and services designed to collect data over time from these devices, and recognize and communicate about specific events that may occur within such devices, or on the networks that interconnect them, make it possible for modern network management tools to function.

To some extent, network management is a term that's open to multiple interpretations. It can mean anything from the activities that a part-time administrator on a small-scale network might perform only occasionally, to the kinds of network operations centers that large-scale communications providers, companies, and organizations staff around the clock, 365 days a year. For that reason, it's important to understand and distinguish between theories that purport to drive network management, and the practices that represent network management.

Throughout the remainder of this chapter, you'll gain a more detailed understanding about what kinds of data must be collected, how it is aggregated and inspected to check the health of a network, and how it may be analyzed to observe trends or detect problems on such networks. Likewise, you'll become aware of how event-reporting mechanisms can explicitly flag potential or actual network problems, and why handling such events is a critical component of any network management environment.

In the sections that follow, you'll learn about an official open standard devoted to the science of network management, and how it relates to practical network management issues and concerns. You'll also learn how careful, comprehensive network management requires ways for network management data and events to be reported even when the network itself may be out of commission.

Network Management Architectures

As with so many other specialized, highly technical fields of endeavor, network management has a definite view of the systems and networks under its purview, and a distinct set of terms and concepts by which it recognizes and names the components of a managed network environment. End stations are usually known as **managed devices**, and may be any kind of system—a desktop computer, server, router, hub, switch, PBX, or some other kind of equipment involved in networking—where management-related software is installed and running.

This special software is what makes a managed device live up to that name because the software is what recognizes events as they occur, and enables managed devices to send alerts. The same software also permits collection of ongoing data that characterizes or describes the managed devices upon which that software runs, and also permits inspection and collection of data about the network link or links that connect such devices to a network.

On the data collection end, two kinds of activities occur within a management utility or facility, called a **management entity**, whose job is to provide access to management data, controls, and behaviors:

1. When alerts are received, appropriate responses must be generated. Such responses can include operator notification, event logging, system shutdown and possibly even restart, and various kinds of automated attempts to repair affected systems or services.

2. Regular polling or sampling of management data occurs, whereby the management entity requests updates from managed devices to reflect recent data intervals related to traffic characterization and error and utilization levels, and reports on application- or service-specific activity.

It's helpful to think of the management entity as a service that handles management functions, instigates polling and data collection, and acts as a repository for data collected over time. Likewise, the management entity also responds to events as they occur, but can log and characterize such network behaviors and activities as well.

At each managed device, a special piece of software called a **management agent** responds to polls for collected data, where the management agent itself has custody of a **management database (MDB)** of information that it collects and maintains over time. Management entities usually function within the context of a **network management system (NMS)**, in which agents and entities use specific **network management protocols** to communicate and exchange data. Each NMS relies on the protocols that support it and the management databases it knows how to accommodate and analyze to provide the kinds of management functions it can deliver. For TCP/IP, the name of the management protocol is SNMP.

Most typical NMS environments support one or more management entities within the context of the NMS, where each such entity typically interacts with many managed devices in the course of obtaining management data, and reacting to network and device events. As is common in many large-scale environments, there may be entire hierarchies of management entities. In that case, **management proxies** at a lower level in the hierarchy communicate with higher-level management entities to deliver status and event information. This permits large-scale, end-to-end management systems to cover many kinds of devices and locations, but also means that the details of device management may be two or even three layers below the enterprise level. This relationship is depicted in Figure 11-1.

11

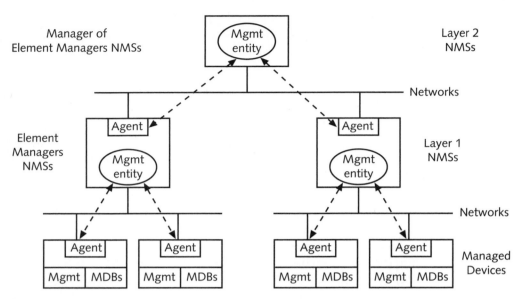

Figure 11-1   On an enterprise network, multiple layers of NMSs permit a single view of an entire multisite and multiplatform network

In the following section, you will learn about an open standard model for network management that was designed to incorporate all the different kinds of activities and concerns that an NMS must address.

OSI Network Management Model

Just as the ISO/OSI network reference model defines a common frame of reference for networking protocols and services, the ISO/OSI network management model (OSI network management model for short) defines a common frame of reference for network management, and provides an excellent framework for understanding the major functions that NMSs perform. The OSI network management model incorporates the following five layers:

- *Accounting management*: **Accounting management** focuses on measuring network and service utilization parameters so that individual users or groups can be controlled or regulated. While it may sometimes even be used to assign usage charges back to organizational units (usually called chargebacks), accounting management permits network access to be controlled in a way designed to be fair to all users, or to reflect organizational priorities that may favor some classes of users over others.

- *Configuration management*: **Configuration management** focuses on documenting network and system configuration data, and monitoring the effects of the use of various versions of hardware and software on network behavior, reliability, and performance. Thus, every network device has a variety of associated configuration data that may include information about the operating system or firmware, network interface(s), protocols and related settings, services and related settings, and so forth. By providing centralized access to and control over such information, NMSs can add tremendous value and flexibility to a network.

- *Fault management*: **Fault management** focuses on detecting, logging, and repairing network and system problems (whenever possible) to keep a network operating properly. Within the general range of NMSs, support for fault management is nearly universal, whereas other components of the OSI network management model may not be as fully supported.

- *Performance management*: **Performance management** focuses on measuring and monitoring network traffic levels, utilization, and other statistical metrics for network and system behavior to help maintain network and system performance at acceptable levels. Important metrics include network utilization and throughput, user and service response times, error rates, and traffic characterization. Proper performance management depends on building network performance baselines (snapshots of average network behavior and characteristics) so that abnormal performance may be distinguished from normal performance. Most management entities measure performance continuously, and use threshold values to trigger alerts and take appropriate actions.

- *Security management*: **Security management** focuses on controlling access to network resources to avoid denials of service and unwanted access or incursions into network resources, and restrict access to resources solely on the basis of proper authentication and authorization. Security management subsystems identify and flag sensitive network resources, and determine access control lists to limit their exposure to authorized users. Such systems also monitor network access points and employ intrusion detection schemes, packet and address filters, service filters, and other forms of access control to ensure that unwanted forms of access or use are explicitly denied whenever possible. Much of what was covered in Chapter 9 of this book might fall under the purview of the security management system in an NMS but in reality, this kind of functionality tends to be spread across multiple systems on most ordinary networks.

11

Practical Network Management

When it comes to performing the tasks associated with managing a network, and the devices and resources which it comprises, the OSI network management model does an excellent job of categorizing and cataloging the tasks and activities involved. But alas, the frequency of appearance of full-fledged NMSs on most modern networks falls somewhere between "seldom" and "never."

Although vendors, such as Tivoli Systems (with its Tivoli Management Environment product family) and Computer Associates (with its CA Unicenter product family), among others, will happily sell their network management systems to organizations, managing a modern network seldom occurs within the confines of any single NMS. Certain device or software vendors may sometimes fail to provide a management agent that's compatible with some particular NMS, some new application or service won't yet be able to report to or interact with some NMSs, and so on. The net effect is that complete, end-to-end management within any particular NMS is desirable, but seldom 100% achievable. Thus, system or network administrators must invariably learn and use multiple tools—sometimes, a great many of them—to do their jobs!

Much of modern network management consists of using the OSI network management model as an ideal against which to manage one's networks and devices, with whatever management tools are available. The important thing is to make systematic network management a priority, and obtain the right mix of software components and tools that can be used as part of a program of regular, scheduled network maintenance and care. As with the subdiscipline of network and system security, network management itself is as much a matter of what one does by rote and routine, as it is a matter of buying and using the right software tools.

In-band Versus Out-of-band Management

When planning a **distributed management solution**, consider the path that the management data must take. For example, perhaps you have a management device on your desk that receives alerts from various routers on the network. What path do the alert packets travel?

There are two path options for network management information—in-band and out-of-band. **In-band management** traffic travels along the network data path. **Out-of-band management** traffic alerts travel on a separate non-data path.

Figure 11-2 shows a network that can support only in-band management traffic. If a management alert is triggered on Router 2, there is only one path to the manager station. The management alert must travel along the data path. No additional or special network cabling is required to support in-band management communications. If Router 2 detects a problem, the alert travels through Router 1 to the manager.

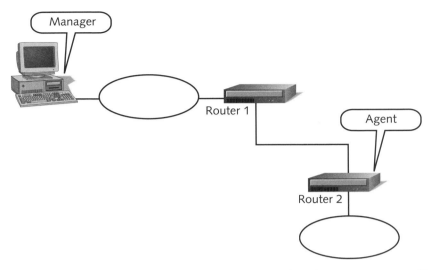

Figure 11-2   Network that can support only in-band management traffic

Although everything appears to work properly in this scenario, consider what would happen if Router 2 detected that the Ethernet network between the two routers failed. The alert cannot make it across the network to the manager because it cannot be forwarded across the Ethernet network.

An out-of-band management solution supports communications between management agents and the manager device, regardless of the status of the data network. For example, Figure 11-3 shows a network that contains an out-of-band link between Router 2 and the manager station. If an agent detects a fault, the agent sends an alert to the manager using the out-of-band connection.

The importance of out-of-band management is impossible to overstate—basically, it can give the management entity a way to access managed devices through an alternate connection even when the network it's supposed to manage may be unavailable. Although this will not suffice to handle any and all possible failure scenarios (for example, when the failure of a key router results in the loss of a routing area's Internet connection and is not amenable to out-of-band access), an out-of-band link provides a much-appreciated way to access and control devices when networks fail, permitting quick and efficient restoration of network services.

In the next section, we examine the premier management protocol used in all types of TCP/IP-based networks—SNMP.

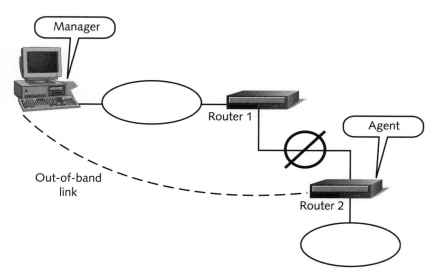

Figure 11-3 Network that contains an out-of band link

UNDERSTANDING SNMP

SNMP is a request/response-based protocol used to transport management messages between an **SNMP agent** (the client process) and an **SNMP manager** (the server process). There are several versions of SNMP currently defined:

- *SNMP version 1 (SNMPv1):* This is the original version of SNMP, which does not incorporate much in the way of security features. Rather, it uses plain text passwords, called community names, or strings, passed between the SNMP client and manager to validate the authenticity of the data and/or the requestor of the data. Community names are discussed in more detail in the section titled "SNMP Security" later in this chapter.

- *SNMP version 2 (SNMPv2):* This version includes two improvements: protocol enhancements and security enhancements. Very few vendors could agree on how to implement the security enhancements, so they were primarily overlooked, but the protocol enhancements were implemented. Some of these protocol enhancements include enhanced object identifiers, support for macros, bulk data transfers, and support for multiple protocols.

- *SNMP version 3 (SNMPv3):* This, the most recent SNMP version, primarily addresses the security shortcomings of the other two versions in four areas: authentication (to ensure the validity of the user), privacy (to maintain confidentiality), authorization (to restrict access), and remote configuration and administration capabilities.

This section focuses on SNMPv1 because it is still the most widely implemented version of SNMP.

SNMPv1 consists of the following basic elements:

- Management Information Base (MIB) objects
- SNMP agents
- SNMP managers
- SNMP messages

Let's examine each of these elements in detail.

Management Information Base (MIB) Objects

A **Management Information Base (MIB)** is a database of **manageable objects** for a device. For example, a manageable router supports MIBs filled with router-type objects, such as interfaces, forwarded packets, filtered packets, and so forth. The following lists some of the MIBs implemented on SNMP-managed networks:

- MIB-2 (RFC 1213)
- ATM MIB (RFC 2515)
- Printer MIB (RFC 1759)
- IPv6 MIB (RFC 2465)

Within any given MIB, a formal specification, known as the **Structure of Management Information (SMI)**, defines the format for all **objects** maintained in that MIB. In fact, SMI defines object formats in any MIB using a particular form of notation called **Abstract Syntax Notation One (ASN.1)**.

ASN.1 is a language used to describe a type of object and the **object identifier** (OID). In SNMP, the object identifier is used to reference a single MIB object. The object identifier is a sequence of non-negative integers that traverses an **object tree**. The tree starts with the root, as shown in Figure 11-4. The "branches" of the object tree are referred to as **subordinates**. In SNMP, objects are identified by writing the path used to get to a specific device identifier on an object tree.

11

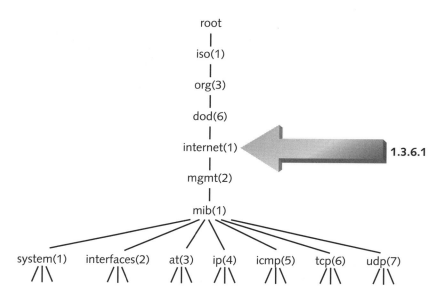

Figure 11-4   ASN.1 representation uses a structured object identifier

Using Object Identifiers

The network management object identifiers are under the iso(1), org(3), dod(6), internet(1), or 1.3.6.1 branch of the name space. The major branches are listed in Table 11-1.

Table 11-1   SMI Tree Branches

Branch	Branch Name
1	iso
1.3	org
1.3.6	dod
1.3.6.1	internet
1.3.6.1.1	directory
1.3.6.1.2	mgmt
1.3.6.1.2.1	mib-2
1.3.6.1.2.1.2.2.1.3	ifType
1.3.6.1.2.1.10	transmission
1.3.6.1.2.1.10.23	transmissionppp
1.3.6.1.2.1.27	application
1.3.6.1.2.1.28	mta
1.3.6.1.3	experimental
1.3.6.1.4	private
1.3.6.1.4.1	enterprise

Table 11-1 SMI Tree Branches (continued)

Branch	Branch Name
1.3.6.1.5	security
1.3.6.1.6	SNMPv2
1.3.6.1.6.1	snmpDomains
1.3.6.1.6.2	snmpProxys
1.3.6.1.6.3	snmpModules
1.3.6.1.7	mail
1.3.6.1.8	features

Currently, MIB-2 is the popular general MIB supported by most SNMP-managed devices. MIB-2 contains subordinates to further define the area of management. Table 11-2 lists some of the key subordinates that reside under the MIB-2 branch.

Table 11-2 MIB-2 Subordinates

Subordinate	Description	Reference
1	System	RFC 1213
2	Interfaces	RFC 1213
3	Address Translation	RFC 1213
4	Internet Protocol	RFC 1213
5	Internet Control Message Protocol	RFC 1213
6	Transmission Control Protocol	RFC 1213
7	User Datagram Protocol	RFC 1213
8	Exterior Gateway Protocol	RFC 1213
13	AppleTalk	RFC 1742
14	Open Shortest Path First	RFC 1253
15	Border Gateway Protocol	RFC 1657
16	Remote Network Monitoring	RFC 1271
23	Routing Information Protocol version 2	RFC 1389
42	Token Ring Station Source Route	RFC 1748
43	Printer MIB	RFC 1759

Refer to *http://www.iana.org* for a complete list of MIB subordinates and SMI definitions.

In some instances, vendors may implement a **private MIB** that focuses specifically on a particular product's manageable elements. For example, an Internet server manufacturer may want to manage disk I/O and caching functionality. Private objects are maintained under the number 1.3.6.1.4.

Loading MIBs

Most hardware vendors provide MIB agent information in their software or operating systems, and most network management platforms provide MIB information for the more popular hardware platforms. However, many vendors support additional features not defined in the SNMP protocol RFCs that make them proprietary. If your management station is unable to get requested information from a managed device, the MIB that has that particular piece of information might be missing. Generally, if the management station cannot retrieve a particular MIB variable, either the station does not recognize the MIB variable, or the agent does not support that particular MIB variable, in which case you must load the MIB into the management station, usually with a MIB compiler.

It is important to pay attention to the order in which MIBs are loaded into the management station because many MIBs use definitions that are defined in other MIBs. For example, if MIB X imports a definition from MIB Y, some MIB compilers require you to load MIB X prior to loading MIB Y. If you load the MIBs in the wrong order, the MIB compiler might generate an error about what was imported claiming it as *undefined*. If this happens, look at the loading order of the MIB definitions from the IMPORTS section of the MIB module, and make sure that you loaded all the preceding MIBs first.

Remote Monitoring (RMON)

The RMON MIB is used to monitor and administer remote segments of a distributed network. There are some unique challenges in managing a distributed environment. First, a distributed environment is usually fairly large with many devices to manage. Second, distributed networks usually evolve over time and become **heterogeneous environments** (contain dissimilar equipment running different versions of software). Finally, in a distributed environment, you generally do not have personnel at each facility, who can assist in managing and troubleshooting, so you must find a cost-effective solution. RMON was developed to address all of the challenges pertaining to managing a distributed environment.

RMON places agents, called **network probes**, at various locations on the distributed network. Probes are standalone devices that contain a NIC, a processor, memory, and software; the probes are attached to the network like any other physical device. A probe can also be a software feature on an internetworking device, such as a router or switch, and is configured like any other software feature. The probes communicate with the network management station in-band and report whatever information the network management station requested. An advantage to using probes is that they can collect and store data offline. This is helpful in certain circumstances, such as a remote location that does not need to be in constant communication with the central location (to save WAN costs), or if communications to the network management console were disrupted (such as a circuit failure).

The first version of RMON, as outlined in RFC 1757, was Ethernet-based. Its OID is (1.3.6.1.2.1.16) and it has nine distinct groups of objects. The implementation of any or all of these groups is not mandatory. If a remote monitoring device uses a group, then it must use all objects in the same group. For example, a managed agent that uses the host group must use the hostControlTable, the hostTable, and the hostTimeTable. The following lists some of the commonly used groups:

- *Ethernet statistics*: This group contains statistics captured by the network probe for every Ethernet interface being monitored on this device.

- *History control*: This group records and stores intermittent statistics from an Ethernet network.

- *Alarm*: This group intermittently performs statistical sampling on variables in the network probe, which are compared to previously determined limits. If the monitored variable crosses a limit, an event is generated.

- *Host*: This group contains statistics about each host found on the network.

- *HostTopN*: This group creates reports describing the hosts that head a list arranged by one of its statistics.

- *Matrix*: This group stores statistics for communications between sets of two addresses.

- *Filter*: This group allows packet filtering.

- *Packet capture*: This group allows packet capturing, after the packets flow through a channel.

- *Event*: This group controls event initiation and notification from the monitored device.

If a group has a dependency, when you use the group, you must use the corresponding dependent group. For instance, using the packet capture group requires using the filter group. Many groups in the RMON MIB have one or more tables that include control parameters, and one or more data tables that contain the results of the operation. Control tables can usually be modified, whereas data tables are usually read-only.

The next version of RMON, defined in RFC 1513, is called RMON token ring. It added support for token ring networks by creating a tenth group, called the token ring group, which functions much like the Ethernet statistics group, but uses information relevant to token ring. The token ring group contains four subgroups: ring station, ring station order, ring station configuration, and source routing.

11

These first two implementations of RMON (Ethernet and token ring) are primarily concerned with physical and data link information, and do not take into consideration the remaining five layers of the seven-layer OSI model. RMON2, defined in RFC 2021, extends the capabilities of RMON by adding 10 object groups, identified as groups 11 through 20, which provide a means to manage and report issues in the upper layers. This allows upper-layer protocols, such as EGP and even SNMP, to be monitored in the same manner as lower-layer protocols, such as IP, ICMP, TCP, and UDP.

SNMP Agents

SNMP agent software is placed on devices that can be managed by SNMP managers. The agent software contains the MIB for the device being managed. For example, an SNMP agent on a router will contain a MIB that provides specific information regarding that router's manageable objects. (Many router and switch manufacturers include an SNMP agent in their products.)

SNMP agents answer to the SNMP manager's queries for information about the objects in the agent's MIB. These SNMP agents also send alerts to the SNMP managers when a specific event occurs or a defined threshold is reached.

SNMP Managers

SNMP managers query SNMP agents for the information maintained about MIB objects. SNMP managers also set thresholds on the SNMP agents.

SNMP Messages

SNMP managers and agents communicate over UDP with a specific set of commands. These commands are as follows:

- GET-REQUEST
- GET-RESPONSE
- GET-NEXT
- SET
- TRAP

These five commands are the core of SNMP communications. The GET-REQUEST, GET-RESPONSE, GET-NEXT, and SET commands use UDP port 161. The TRAP command uses port 162, as shown in Figure 11-5.

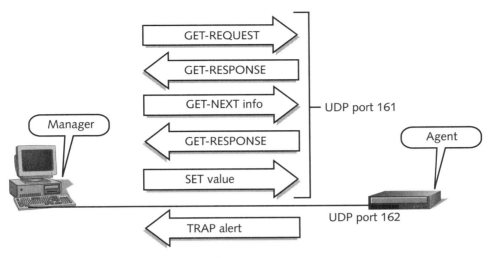

Figure 11-5   Core SNMP commands

GET Commands (GET-REQUEST/GET-RESPONSE)

The GET-REQUEST command is used to read a single entry within a MIB. The SNMP manager transmits the GET-REQUEST command and indicates the MIB entry of interest using its ASN.1 representation. GET-REQUESTS are the most commonly seen SNMP communications. The GET-RESPONSE command is sent in reply.

GET-NEXT

When an SNMP manager wants to read a series of entries in a MIB table, it uses the GET-NEXT command. The MIB objects desired follow the GET-NEXT command. Upon receipt of this packet, the SNMP agent responds with the GET-RESPONSE command.

SET

The SET command is used to set thresholds on SNMP agents. These thresholds can be referred to generically as **event thresholds**, not alarm thresholds, because they signify only that an event occurred. That event might not be an error condition or cause for alarm. The SET command may also be used to perform other functions, including managing device configurations, timeouts, locking devices to accept SET commands from only a single management station, and even enabling or disabling SNMP itself. In fact, it's entirely appropriate to regard the SET command as the "active controller" for SNMP capabilities and reporting on managed devices.

TRAP

TRAP messages are unique among SNMP commands. These messages are sent unsolicited by the SNMP agent to the SNMP manager when an event setting is exceeded. Unlike the other SNMP message types, TRAP messages use port 162 in the Source and Destination Port fields of the UDP header. Figure 11-6 shows a TRAP message.

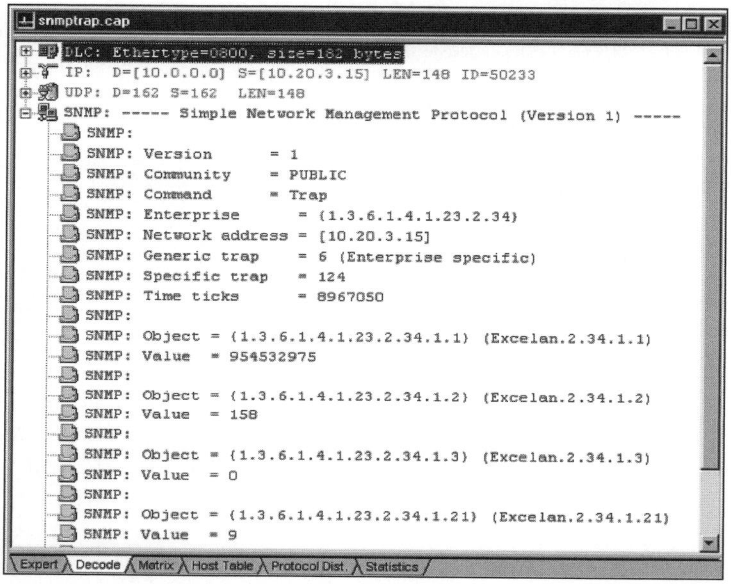

```
snmptrap.cap                                                    _ □ ×
DLC: Ethertype=0800, size=182 bytes
IP:  D=[10.0.0.0] S=[10.20.3.15] LEN=148 ID=50233
UDP: D=162 S=162  LEN=148
SNMP: ----- Simple Network Management Protocol (Version 1) -----
SNMP:
SNMP: Version      = 1
SNMP: Community    = PUBLIC
SNMP: Command      = Trap
SNMP: Enterprise        = {1.3.6.1.4.1.23.2.34}
SNMP: Network address = [10.20.3.15]
SNMP: Generic trap      = 6 (Enterprise specific)
SNMP: Specific trap     = 124
SNMP: Time ticks        = 8967050
SNMP:
SNMP: Object = {1.3.6.1.4.1.23.2.34.1.1} (Excelan.2.34.1.1)
SNMP: Value  = 954532975
SNMP:
SNMP: Object = {1.3.6.1.4.1.23.2.34.1.2} (Excelan.2.34.1.2)
SNMP: Value  = 158
SNMP:
SNMP: Object = {1.3.6.1.4.1.23.2.34.1.3} (Excelan.2.34.1.3)
SNMP: Value  = 0
SNMP:
SNMP: Object = {1.3.6.1.4.1.23.2.34.1.21} (Excelan.2.34.1.21)
SNMP: Value  = 9
Expert ∧ Decode ∧ Matrix ∧ Host Table ∧ Protocol Dist. ∧ Statistics
```

Figure 11-6   SNMP TRAP message

SNMP Security

Because SNMP exchanges information about current operating status and statistics, and provides a means to modify device configurations, you may expect a very robust security system. Unfortunately, SNMPv1 offers a very simple password system, which should not be considered secure. SNMP requests include a **community name**, which is a type of password. There are three basic community names:

- Read–Only (or Monitor) community name
- Read/Write (or Control) community name
- Alert (or Trap) community name

The Read–Only community name is used to access the MIB and read the object values. The Read/Write community name is used to change the contents of the MIB. For example, to add entries to a route table, you must have Read/Write community access. You can also modify several configuration parameters on SNMP-managed devices, such as Layer 3 addressing, routing protocols, and access lists. Finally, the Alert community name is used to access the trap settings on an SNMP manager. The trap settings indicate the devices permitted to receive traps that signal whenever a particular event occurs.

Each community name typically has a different word associated with it. The access level provided depends on which community name is included in the SNMP message. For example, perhaps you assigned the following community names for your network:

- Read-Only community name: Admin1
- Read/Write community name: Admin2
- Alert community name: Admin3

If you plan to add entries to a router's MIB, you must set the manager to use the name Admin2.

In SNMPv1 and SNMPv2, these community names cross the network in plain text, making them even more insecure. Most vendors also use the default Read-Only community name PUBLIC, and the default Read/Write community name PRIVATE, making it even easier to break into an SNMP system. Please note that the Read-Only community allows individuals only to view SNMP data (which can be bad enough), while the Read/Write community allows them to change such data (which can be even worse). Refer back to Figure 11-6; you can easily read the community name PUBLIC in this file. A good hacker can gain enough access with SNMP community names to do serious damage to your network directly, or gain permissions on the systems to do more damage indirectly. This is especially dangerous in the case of Windows 2000, in which the SNMP service runs under the System account, and thus has administrative privileges.

11

INSTALLING AND CONFIGURING SNMP AGENTS AND CONSOLES

There are almost as many SNMP agents as there are network devices because SNMP agents act as an interface between a particular piece of hardware or software and the SNMP protocol. Thus, they are all specific not only to a vendor, but also to the individual products. Because agents monitor a diversity of products, such as routers, Enterprise Resource Planning (ERP) packages, PCs and servers, and even power supplies and air conditioners, the actual installation of agents varies a great deal, but they all share some common ground. This section covers some of that common ground and some high-level configuration.

Installation of most agents is already done for you because they are commonly included in the software that runs the device or application. For example, the SNMP agents for Cisco and Nortel routers are included in the Cisco IOS and Nortel RS software that comes installed on the routers from the factory. To use an agent, you need only enter a command to enable it, and then configure some simple options. The SNMP agent for Microsoft Windows 2000 Server runs as a service. It is also included in the operating system, but is not installed by default. To install it, select Add/Remove Programs from Control Panel. Under Windows Components, highlight Management and Monitoring Tools and click the Details button. Click the check box that appears next to Simple Network Management Protocol.

Most of these agents include the open MIB: MIB-2 (RFC 1213) and the relevant parts of the vendor's private MIB. The vendor's private MIB should contain all of the objects specific to this device or program. Occasionally, you may have to update this when a new MIB is released, but generally, this is accomplished via normal version upgrades for the product. For example, in Windows, the MIB upgrade is applied via service packs released for the whole operating system, rather than manually updating just the MDB.

Once the agent is installed, you should see the device listening on UDP port 161. For instance, if you type *netstat -a* from a command prompt in Windows 2000, you should see the following:

```
Proto Local Address    Foreign Address
UDP   servername:snmp   *:*
```

Note that for well-known services, Microsoft replaces the port number after the colon with the name of the service. Otherwise, it would say *servername*:161.

Agent Configuration

Most agent configuration is very simple. The three most common tasks when configuring an agent are:

1. Filling in system information, such as Contact and Location. These are simple text fields that are not required. They can be helpful when troubleshooting, but too much information can also be a security risk.

2. Specifying a Read-Only community string. The default is typically the word PUBLIC.

3. Specifying a Read/Write community string. The default is typically the word PRIVATE.

Either a Read-Only or Read/Write community string must be set before a management console can retrieve data from the agent. A Read/Write community string must be set before a management console can modify the configuration of the device through the SNMP agent.

To deal with security issues surrounding community names and weak, plain text passwords, newer SNMP specifications support more stringent authentication. Many vendors also implement access control, such that the agent will only respond to requests from a specific IP address. You should definitely take advantage of all these features.

Another significant piece of configuration on the agent is support for SNMP traps. When you configure the SNMP Trap service, you must supply an IP address for the management console. This is the destination to which traps will be sent. Because there are several changes to a system that can be trapped, but only a small fraction of these are important to you at any given time, most vendors also allow you to specify by groups or by specific traps, which should be sent, and at what time. An agent is often configured so that a trap is sent when a threshold is passed, such as 20% free disk space left. Other times, a trap is sent any time an error is detected. Configuring traps can be time consuming, but it is not overly complex. Keys to success are quality documentation and maintaining consistency across many similar devices.

Console Installation

Network management console installation is considerably more complex. Like SNMP agents, there are many proprietary consoles that differ greatly; we discuss only installation concerns common to all consoles.

Before installing your console, you should understand that it will be a focal point for all of your network management. To be effective, it must be able to view and modify myriad configuration details for nearly every device on your network. Therefore, physical and network security for this server are primary concerns.

The installation of the network console typically involves a software installation from a CD-ROM, which varies by vendor and hardware platform. Because these consoles often track a significant amount of data, you usually must configure a SQL Server or Oracle database as well. Once installed, you add the vendor-specific MIBs for all the products you want to manage to the console's MDB. This way, the console will understand the messages it receives from the agents. This architecture is also important because you won't have to replace your console every time you upgrade network devices or managed software to a new version. You can simply add the new MIB to your console.

In practice, most SNMP consoles are part of a software package commonly called a "framework." Products such as HP's OpenView, Computer Associates' Unicenter TNG, and IBM's Tivoli are called frameworks because they provide the basic SNMP service to other packages, so that vendor- and product-specific management programs (plug-ins such as Cisco's CiscoWorks2000 and Nortel's Optivity) can be added to a single console and managed together, rather than requiring dozens of separate management consoles. They also provide standard features that all these programs can share, such as automated discovery of network devices; the ability to send alerts by e-mail, pager, or other means; as well as more advanced features, such as correlating and intelligently interpreting alarms. An example of this last feature is when a WAN link goes down, your network management station may discover that it cannot reach the WAN link or the servers and applications on the other side of that link. Hopefully, it will realize that the only real problem is the WAN link, and thus, send an alert only to the WAN team, not to the application and server teams.

11

Console Configuration

Configuration of network management consoles is a very complex and prolonged task. For many packages, the initial configuration may take six months or longer! But the configuration is never truly finished. To effectively use most of the features these products offer, they typically require dedicated resources and constant maintenance.

The configuration begins with a discovery process. The console must find out what devices it is managing. This can be a manual process, in which you manually enter information about the systems, or an automated process, in which the console sends SNMP queries to every IP address in a range, and then adds them to its database. Using public MIBs, the console can generally determine the make, model, and version of most devices, but you will almost certainly want to add information about each managed node.

Once the managed nodes are discovered and defined, you can configure graphs and charts to view statistics about the general health of the network. Simpler versions of these, such as a light that turns red or green, indicate that a service is available or unavailable, and are often distributed remotely to executives' desktops, or operations centers and help desks. More advanced statistics are often displayed on the desktops of specialists, such as the network or database team. These graphs and other statistics are useful for troubleshooting, trending, documentation, and many other applications.

Another useful feature that requires considerable configuration is called an alert. These are often configured on the agents, as previously discussed, so that SNMP traps are sent to the console whenever a threshold is passed. Then, on the console, you must specify what the system should do when it receives a trap. Most consoles have very powerful scripting capabilities. These scripts can be configured to send an e-mail with an error code and IP address, or a text pager message with some description of the problem. They can also take action. For example, if a server logs an event that indicates a service stopped responding, the console's script can stop and restart the service.

All of these features make frameworks a very powerful tool, but one that requires much effort. Keep in mind that the real utility they offer is scalability. Although this may not seem obvious at first, the goal of a network management system is to automate the tasks of the network administrators so that a network can grow without requiring more administrators.

SNMP CONSOLES, TOOLS, UTILITIES, AND KEY FILES

This section describes some of the types of tools and utilities you must deploy and maintain in an SNMP network management system. To start, you should have a console. Although there are many of these available, the lion's share of the market belongs to three products (described in the "Console Installation" section earlier in this chapter):

- HP OpenView's Network Node Manager (NNM)

  http://managementsoftware.hp.com/products/nnm/

- IBM's Tivoli NetView

   http://www.tivoli.com/products/index/netview/

- Computer Associates' Unicenter TNG

   http://www.cai.com/unicenter/

There are also many smaller utilities that are helpful when supporting a management system. A popular utility, known as a MIB browser, is used for viewing the MIBs themselves. Advent's SNMP Utilities Release 3.0 includes a standard and an HTML MIB browser. You can find more information at *http://www.adventnet.com/products/snmputilities/faq.html*.

Solar Winds offers a very popular suite of SNMP utilities that includes MIB browsers and sweepers. Sweepers are used to "sweep" a subnet. They send SNMP queries to every device in the subnet, quickly displaying a list of all the information available. For example, using the Network Browser utility on a Windows NT Server, Sweepers return a list of all shares (including hidden and administrative shares), all user accounts (including hidden accounts), complete information about all network interfaces, and more. All this is retrieved via SNMP GET commands. After using this product, you will certainly gain an appreciation of the security concerns regarding SNMP. More information on Solar Winds can be found at *http://www.solarwinds.net/*.

Logisoft AR offers another suite of SNMP utilities. These tools allow you to manually create GET commands and send them to other devices. For more information, visit the Web site at *http://www.logisoftar.com/SnmpUtils.htm*.

One last suite of tools worth mentioning is CMU's SNMP Utils. You can find more information at *http://www.gaertner.de/snmp/welcome-3.7last.html*.

11

INTEGRATING **SNMP** WITH OTHER MANAGEMENT ENVIRONMENTS

Some of the more widely used network management environments, such as HP OpenView and Tivoli Unicenter TNG, use SNMP in conjunction with other software modules to provide a more comprehensive network management environment. These modules take the data provided by the SNMP devices and use it to compile a database of events. Some of the more common modules include: PING, which ensures connectivity to managed devices (even if the device does not support any other management feature, such as SNMP); database change control modules to track changes in device configuration files; dynamic topological maps that present a graphic representation of how the network looks; inventory modules that track current inventory, and provide specific information regarding software and firmware version levels; and service-level tracking to report on how the network is performing in agreement with predefined service-level agreements.

Finally, to effectively use the data gathered via SNMP, other managed environments usually have reporting capabilities, which can take data in its raw form from SNMP devices, and present it in a way that makes it more meaningful. Most of the network management platforms contain a device, called a poller, that periodically sends out requests to devices on the network to gather information (such as bandwidth utilization, CPU utilization, disk usage, network errors, and so on), and stores it in a database for later retrieval. This database can then be accessed by a report-generation tool to compile vital network statistics that give the network manager an idea of how the network is performing, much in the way a doctor can use our vital signs to determine our overall health.

TROUBLESHOOTING SNMP

Implementations of SNMPv1 are fairly straightforward and usually easy to troubleshoot, although there are certain things to consider when problems arise. Because of the popularity of SNMP, many vendors incorporated SNMP agent functionality in their products. This has led to some problem areas when the vendors use enhanced OIDs, or private OIDs, not specifically defined in the RFCs. For example, an NMS can request a certain SNMP object from a device that is in the private object space (1.3.6.1.4), but not defined in the same way on both the SNMP agent and the network management server. The NMS receives either a "no such object" error, or worse, erroneous information. The best way to identify and correct this type of problem is to use a protocol analyzer and examine the packets going between the devices. It should become clear where the disconnect occurred, and what corrective action must take place. It is not uncommon for vendors to periodically update their MIBs and make them available to their customers.

Another common error occurs in the use of community names. Community names must match on both the SNMP agent and the network management station. These community names are case sensitive—*PUBLIC* is different than *public*. Also, remember there are three levels of community strings: Read-Only (Monitor), Read/Write (Control), and Alert (Trap). Make sure the password matches the level you attempt to use on the agent, as well as the network management station. Again, if you do not have access to the agent or the management station, a protocol analyzer can assist you in troubleshooting this type of error.

CHAPTER SUMMARY

❏ Network management involves placing specific software components, called management agents, into managed devices that can report or respond to polls from a management entity in a network management system (NMS) somewhere on a network.

❏ Although much network management activity occurs over the network being managed (called in-band management), most NMSs provide various methods for out-of-band management so that managed devices can be accessed for management purposes even when the network itself is unavailable.

❏ Network management systems rely on two kinds of activities to perform management tasks: the ability of managed devices to issue alerts when specific events occur, and the ability of management entities to poll managed devices regularly to collect and aggregate data about managed devices, and the networks that interconnect them.

❏ The discipline of network management is described in the OSI network management model, which recognizes the five following layers of activity: accounting management, which links users and groups to utilization of the network; configuration management, which collects and controls configuration data for managed devices; fault management, which gathers, reports, and attempts to repair network and related system faults as they occur; performance management, which characterizes and reports on network behavior and throughput; and security management, which sets access controls on network resources, and monitors network access for illicit attempts at entry.

❏ For IP-based networks, the Simple Network Management Protocol (SNMP) carries management-related messages and data among network management agents and network management entities. Although three versions of SNMP were defined and codified, SNMPv1 remains the most common version in use today.

❏ SNMP's management data resides in a database of manageable objects called a Management Information Base, or MIB, on a per-device basis. Common MIBs that appear on IP-based networks include the standard MIB-2 device MIB, a standard ATM MIB, a standard printer MIB, and an IPv6 MIB. The Structure of Management Information for MIBs adheres to Abstract Syntax Notation One (ASN.1), a language used to describe the types of identifiers for objects in a MIB. At present, MIB-2 is the most popular MIB supported by SNMP-managed network devices.

❏ When loading MIBs into a management station, order is important, owing to dependencies between individual MIBs. It's essential to load MIBs referenced in other MIBs first to satisfy cross-MIB references.

❏ The Remote Monitoring (RMON) MIB is used to monitor and manage remote segments on a distributed network. RMON uses probes to collect and report on network status and activity, and provide a reasonably comprehensive view of network traffic, errors, and behavior.

❏ SNMP messages use UDP for transport and IP for network access. The five SNMP commands used to coordinate communications between managers and agents are: GET-REQUEST, GET-RESPONSE, GET-NEXT, SET, and TRAP.

❏ Unfortunately, because SNMPv1 is the most frequently used version of SNMP but supports little or no security, ensuring SNMP security requires changing default community names, and managing the transit of SNMP messages across organizational network boundaries.

❏ Troubleshooting SNMP requires a good working knowledge of local network conditions, community names, security precautions in place, and enhanced object identifiers (OIDs) in use.

11

KEY TERMS

Abstract Syntax Notation One (ASN.1) — A language used to describe a type of object and the object identifier.

accounting management — One of the five layers in the OSI network management model, accounting management focuses on measuring network and service utilization so that individual users or groups can be controlled or regulated.

community name — A word used as a password to obtain Read-Only (Monitor community), Read/Write (Control community), or Alert (Trap community) information. Also called a string.

configuration management — One of the five layers in the OSI network management model, configuration management focuses on documenting and controlling network and system configuration data.

distributed management solution — A management design that offers management information about devices that are distributed throughout a network. Distributed management systems can have one or more managers.

event threshold — A defined point that generates an SNMP TRAP message. Although an event threshold may indicate that a problem occurred, it may also simply indicate that a non-alarm event occurred.

fault management — One of the five layers in the OSI network management model, fault management focuses on detecting and logging network and system problems, and repairing such problems whenever possible.

heterogeneous environment — A networking environment composed of dissimilar equipment, often from a variety of vendors.

in-band management — A management design that uses the data path as the main path for all management data. The primary problem associated with in-band management designs is that data cannot reach the manager when the data path is not functioning.

manageable objects — The elements or characteristics of a device that can be queried by SNMP managers for their settings or status. The MIB maintains the list of manageable objects.

managed device — Any kind of system or device where management agent software is installed and running, ready to issue alerts, or respond to a polling request for management data.

management agent — The software component on a managed device that gathers management data into a local management database, can respond to polls for such data from a management entity, or issue an alert to a management entity when some specific event occurs, or a threshold is exceeded.

management database (MDB) — The collection of data about a single managed device, which a management agent gathers for delivery to a management entity; also, the aggregated collection of data from all managed devices gathered in an NMS, which describes a network's status and condition.

management entity — A software process that polls for and collects management data from managed devices, and can respond to alerts from managed devices under its control.

Management Information Base (MIB) — A database of objects or characteristics that can be managed for a device.

management proxy — A special component of network management software that permits multiple NMSs to be managed at a lower level by a single higher-level NMS. Basically, the management proxy handles reporting and polling requirements for higher-level systems by translating between the message formats and data used in lower-layer and higher-layer systems, and vice versa.

network management protocol — Any of several Application layer protocols and services used to convey network management messages, including commands, polling requests and responses, and alerts. For TCP/IP networks, SNMP is the standard management protocol that's most widely used.

network management system (NMS) — The software and hardware platform within which management entities function, and where network management functions may be installed, configured, managed, and controlled.

network probe — A standalone self-contained device that monitors and manages remote segments of a network.

object — An item that may be managed by an SNMP agent.

object identifier (OID) — A sequence of non-negative integers used to reference a single MIB object.

object tree — A tree-like structure that is used to define and organize the managed objects in a MIB.

out-of-band management — A management design that uses a path separate from the data path for the exchange of SNMP management data. Because it is using a separate path, out-of-band management data can still reach the manager when the primary data path becomes unavailable.

performance management — One of the five layers of the OSI network management model, performance management focuses on measuring and monitoring network traffic levels, utilization, and other statistical metrics for network and system behavior.

private MIB — A proprietary MIB that defines the manageable objects of a vendor's device.

security management — One of the five layers of the OSI network management model, security management focuses on controlling access to network resources to avoid denials of service and unwanted access or incursions into network resources, and restrict access to resources solely on the basis of proper authentication and authorization.

SNMP agent — A piece of software that resides in a manageable object and communicates via SNMP commands to SNMP managers. The SNMP agent software maintains the MIB.

11

SNMP manager — The software used to send SNMP commands to an SNMP agent.

Structure of Management Information (SMI) — A defined structure for objects contained in a MIB. The structure is tree-like in appearance, organized much like a hierarchy of files and directories on a hard disk.

subordinates — Branches in the tree-structured design of a MIB.

REVIEW QUESTIONS

1. Which two of the following activities are key to performing network management functions?

   a. the ability to gather management data by polling managed devices

   b. the ability to remotely control managed devices

   c. the ability to interact with management databases

   d. the ability of managed devices to issue alerts in response to specific events

   e. the ability for multiple levels of NMSs to be integrated and controlled

2. A managed device can be any kind of system in which a management agent is at work, ready to respond to polls, or react to local operating conditions. True or false?

   a. True

   b. False

3. Which software component runs on a managed device to handle management functions and collect management data?

   a. management agent

   b. management entity

   c. management console

   d. NMS

   e. management proxy

4. Which software component runs on an NMS to coordinate management activities and aggregate collected management data?

   a. management agent

   b. management entity

   c. management console

   d. NMS

   e. management proxy

5. Which software component allows multiple levels of NMSs to be managed as a group?

   a. management agent

   b. management entity

   c. management console

   d. NMS

   e. management proxy

6. Which layer in the OSI network management model is responsible for monitoring user and group access to the network to ensure that fair access is delivered, or organizational access priorities are met?

   a. accounting management

   b. configuration management

   c. fault management

   d. performance management

   e. security management

7. Which layer in the OSI network management model is responsible for detecting and logging errors, and attempting to correct such errors whenever possible?

   a. accounting management

   b. configuration management

   c. fault management

   d. performance management

   e. security management

8. Real-world NMSs that completely implement the OSI network management model are seldom if ever found in the workplace. True or false?

   a. True

   b. False

9. Which of the following statements best summarizes out-of-band network management?

   a. It is a technique whereby alternate communications frequencies are used on a broadband network.

   b. It is a technique whereby an alternate communications link or technology is used to access a managed device.

   c. It is a technique whereby network access to a managed device may be turned on or off.

   d. It is a technique whereby the network link to a managed device is used for management functions, as well as ordinary network communications and access.

10. The name of the network management protocol associated with TCP/IP is:

   a. Simple Mail Transfer Protocol (SMTP)

   b. Network News Transport Protocol (NNTP)

   c. Common Management Information Protocol (CMIP)

11

    d. Network Management Transport Protocol (NMTP)

    e. Simple Network Management Protocol (SNMP)

11. Which of the following components is associated with version 1 of the standard TCP/IP network management protocol? (Choose all that apply.)

    a. MIB objects

    b. agents

    c. managers

    d. consoles

    e. messages

12. What kind of MIB object would an IP-managed router support? (Choose all that apply.)

    a. network interfaces

    b. application statistics

    c. packet statistics

    d. none of the above

13. Which of the following MIB-2 subordinates corresponds to the OSPF routing protocol?

    a. 1

    b. 2

    c. 7

    d. 14

    e. 23

14. What term designates a proprietary or special-purpose MIB that a device vendor might create to augment a standard management MIB like MIB-2?

    a. proprietary MIB

    b. special-purpose MIB

    c. private MIB

    d. public MIB

    e. non-standard MIB

15. Which explanation best documents why it is imperative to load MIBs in the proper order?

    a. Network management won't work unless proper MIB order is preserved.

    b. If one MIB uses objects defined in another MIB, it won't be able to resolve their definitions if the defining MIB is not loaded first.

    c. Any MIB that references objects in another MIB must be loaded before the referenced MIB can be referenced.

    d. Undefined objects cannot be resolved.

16. An RMON agent is called a proxy. True or false?

    a. True

    b. False

17. If a remote monitoring device implements any particular RMON object group, it must implement all objects in that group. True or false?

    a. True

    b. False

18. Which of the following statements best explains the relationship between managers and agents for SNMP?

    a. Agents query managers for MIB data.

    b. Managers query agents for MIB data.

    c. Managed devices contain agents.

    d. NMSs contain managers.

19. Which of the following SNMP message types is the only type that is sent unsolicited by an SNMP agent to an SNMP manager?

    a. GET commands

    b. SET

    c. TRAP

    d. TRIGGER

20. SNMP community names fall into which three of the following categories?

    a. Default community name

    b. Host community name

    c. Read-Only community name

    d. Read/Write community name

    e. Alert community name

21. For SNMP, the default community name is always DEFAULT. True or false?

    a. True

    b. False

22. Which TCP or UDP port address does an SNMP management agent listen on?

    a. 139

    b. 161

    c. 179

    d. 500

23. The software tool used to inspect the contents of an SNMP MIB is commonly called a:

    a. MIB reader

    b. MIB inspector

    c. MIB browser

    d. MIB editor

24. To properly present SNMP management data to observe trends or analyze statistics, a report generator may be applied to the management database. True or false?

    a. True

    b. False

25. What side effect is most likely to occur when vendors use enhanced OIDs, or private OIDs, for MIB objects not specifically defined in management-related RFCs, and agents and managers do not share common OID definitions? (Choose all that apply.)

    a. The agent may fail, and cease to operate.

    b. The agent may return a "no such object" error message.

    c. The NMS may fail, and cease to operate.

    d. The agent may report about an object other than the one requested.

    e. The manager will update the agent with the correct OID.

26. In all versions, SNMP offers strong authentication to protect the community names used to access management data and controls. True or false?

    a. True

    b. False

HANDS-ON PROJECTS

Project 11-1

The following Hands-on Projects assume that you are working in a Windows 2000 environment, and you installed the EtherPeek for Windows demo software (included on the CD-ROM that accompanies this book). Internet access is also required for some of these projects.

To build a basic filter for SNMP GET-REQUEST, GET-RESPONSE, and GET-NEXT traffic using a pre-defined protocol definition:

1. If EtherPeek is not already running, start the program. See Hands-on Project 1-2 for instructions.

2. Click **View** on the menu bar, and then click **Filters**. The Filters window appears.

3. Click the **Insert** button 🔳. The Edit Filter window appears.

4. Type **SNMP** in the Filter text box.

5. Click the **Protocol filter** check box.

6. Click the **Protocol** button.

7. Click the boxed plus sign to expand the menu item for the frame type you are using on the classroom network. If you do not know what frame type you are using, consider capturing some packets on the network and examining the headers.

8. Click the boxed plus sign next to **IP** to expand the IP-based protocol list.

9. Click the boxed plus sign next to **UDP** to expand the UDP-based protocol list.

10. Click **SNMP**. This filter captures all packets addressed to or from port 11. SNMP TRAP messages will not be captured using this filter. You will create a more complex SNMP filter in Project 11-2.

11. Click **OK** to return to the Edit Filter window.

12. Click **OK** to accept your filter.

13. Proceed immediately to Hands-on Project 11-2.

Project 11-2

To build an advanced filter based on SNMP GET-REQUEST, GET-RESPONSE, GET-NEXT, and TRAP traffic:

1. In the Filters window in EtherPeek, click the **Insert** button 🔳. The Edit Filter window appears.

2. Type **SNMP-All** in the Filter text box to name your filter.

3. Click the down arrow next to the **Type** field, and then click **Advanced**. The Edit Filter window appears.

4. Click the **And** button, and then click **Protocol**.

5. Click the boxed plus sign next to the frame type used on your network. The predefined protocol filter list appears.

6. Click the boxed plus sign next to **IP**. Click the boxed plus sign next to **UDP**. Click **SNMP**.

7. Click **OK**. The value *Protocol SNMP* is shown in the Edit Filter window.

8. Because you are interested in packets that are either SNMP GET (or GET-REQUEST, GET-RESPONSE, or GET-NEXT) or SNMP TRAP messages, click the **Or** button, click **Protocol**, and again click the boxed plus sign next to the frame type used on your network.

9. Click the boxed plus sign next to **IP**. Click the boxed plus sign next to **UDP**. Scroll down and click **SNMP-Trap**.

10. Click the **OK** button to return to the Edit Filter window. Click **OK** to return to the Filters window.

11. Proceed immediately to Hands-on Project 11-3.

Project 11-3

To build an advanced filter based on SNMP GET-REQUEST, GET-RESPONSE, and GET-NEXT traffic from unauthorized sources:

1. In the Filters window in EtherPeek, click the **Insert** button 📇. The Edit Filter window appears.

2. Type **SNMP-Unauthorized** in the Filter text box to name your filter. In this project, we assume that your network has one SNMP manager that uses the IP address 10.23.3.4. You will build a filter for all SNMP traffic that comes from devices other than 10.23.3.4. You'll also use the port definition method for building your SNMP filter.

3. Click the arrow next to the **Type** field. Select **Advanced**. The Edit Filter window appears.

4. Click the **And** button. Select **Port**.

5. Enter the value **161** in the Port 1 field. Leave Port 2 as *Any port*.

6. Click **OK** to return to the Edit Filter window.

7. Click the **And** button. Click **Address**.

8. Verify that **IP** is listed in the **Type** field. Click **IP**.

9. Enter the address **10.23.3.4** in the Address field. Leave Address 2 as any address.

10. Click **OK**. The Edit Filter window appears. Currently, the filter is looking for all SNMP GET-REQUEST, GET-RESPONSE, and GET-NEXT traffic from 10.23.3.4. However, you are looking for the SNMP traffic from unauthorized systems.

11. Click the box that shows the Address filter that you just created. Click the **Not** button. You have now defined a filter for all SNMP traffic using port 161 from any device except 10.23.3.4. Click **OK**.

12. Close the EtherPeek for Windows demo program.

CASE PROJECTS

1. Your company recently decided to install a network management system. Currently, the WAN has seven networks separated by routers. The networks support 12 servers and 145 clients. Write a short plan for setting up a management solution for your network.

2. You are hired to write a MIB for the routers that your company manufactures. Currently, your company makes only 100-Mbps routers that connect Ethernet and token ring networks. Write a structured tree design for a MIB that could be used to manage your company's router devices. Feel free to research other router product MIBs that currently exist in the industry.

3. You have been analyzing your network's SNMP traffic for one week. You defined a series of SNMP communications crossing the network from a non-authorized system. When you examine the SNMP traffic, you find that the ASN.1 object identifiers are not decoded. The object identifiers all start with 1.3.6.1.4.1.111. Specifically, a management device on the network continuously sends queries for the object 1.3.6.1.4.1.111.4.1.1.3. You want to determine what the SNMP traffic is reporting. Do some research on the Internet to identify the element being reported, and classify the SNMP management traffic.

11

12

TCP/IP, NETBIOS, AND WINS

> **After reading this chapter and completing the exercises you will be able to:**
>
> ◆ Decide where and when to use NetBIOS on your network
>
> ◆ Explore the various ways of resolving NetBIOS names
>
> ◆ Understand how to resolve NetBIOS names on your network in the most efficient manner
>
> ◆ Set up a WINS server for your network, and integrate WINS services with DNS

This chapter introduces the Network Basic Input/Output System (NetBIOS), an older networking technology that was once the foundation for Windows networking, and file and printer sharing. You'll learn what NetBIOS is, how it works, and how it was updated to be useful in a TCP/IP networking environment. This chapter also examines the **Windows Internet Name Service (WINS)** as a means of resolving NetBIOS resource names, and how to integrate WINS with the DNS servers typically used on modern TCP/IP networks.

WHAT IS NETBIOS (AND WHY DO I CARE)?

For most Windows clients now in service, NetBIOS is the native method used to access network resources and share their own resources with others. In theory, a network that has nothing but Windows 2000 clients and servers on it doesn't require NetBIOS. In practice, however, there are few networks that do not use NetBIOS to share resources with clients.

NetBIOS has two serious drawbacks. The most serious is that it does not have a network component to its name space. NetBIOS names are only names, not addresses. Because of this limitation, NetBIOS requires TCP/IP, or some other network-aware protocol, to be useful across network boundaries. The second drawback is less serious, but seems even more intractable. NetBIOS is a very chatty protocol, constantly sending short messages for a wide variety of purposes. This characteristic, which was trivial on the 20- to 40-machine networks of the 1980s, can become a real weakness on networks with hundreds of clients, particularly when WAN connections are used for name resolution.

Despite these limitations, and significant improvements in Windows networking over the past several years, NetBIOS is still a nearly indispensable part of any Windows network.

Historic Limitations of NetBIOS

NetBIOS was developed by Sytek in 1985, and later adopted by IBM and Microsoft as a means of naming network resources on small peer-to-peer networks. Initially, NetBIOS was a method of naming computers (assumed to be identical to users), then users, and then other resources on a local area network. Later, the concepts of **workgroups** and domains were added to Windows networking, also represented as NetBIOS names. The original NetBIOS was not a protocol, but an **Application Programming Interface (API)** used to call network resources. The NetBIOS Enhanced User Interface (NetBEUI) was an extension of NetBIOS that provided an actual transmission protocol, spanning Layers 2 through 5 of the ISO/OSI network reference model (OSI reference model).

NetBIOS and NetBEUI were the default Windows networking methods until the introduction of Windows NT 3.51. All versions of Windows, including Windows 2000, support NetBIOS and NetBEUI for backward compatibility. Even the most recent Windows networking approaches, such as **Common Internet File System (CIFS)** and **Server Message Block (SMB)**, accommodate NetBIOS at their cores.

Each NetBIOS resource has a unique 15-character name, followed by a one-character (2-byte) code indicating the type of resource. No provision was ever made for sharing NetBIOS resources outside the local network. The flat structure of the NetBIOS name space left no way to distinguish between "John at IBM Almaden" and "John at IBM Armonk," except to give each of them a unique NetBIOS name. Despite the addition of NetBIOS group names for Windows domains and workgroups, there is no real hierarchy to the NetBIOS name space. From a NetBIOS perspective, there is only one network—*this* network. With no network component, such as that in IP addresses, NetBIOS and NetBEUI are fundamentally unroutable. In fact, most routers are pre-configured *not* to route NetBEUI packets. Considering that a resource with a NetBIOS name of "John" on one network might be entirely different than—and yet indistinguishable from—a resource called "John" on some other network, this is just as well!

In the early 1990s, Novell realized it could route NetBIOS traffic by encapsulating it inside its IPX protocol. This allowed NetWare networks to use IPX's representation of network hierarchy to overcome the limitations of NetBIOS. Microsoft followed suit shortly thereafter, creating a way to encapsulate NetBIOS traffic in User Datagram Protocol (UDP) or TCP packets running over IP. Starting with NT 3.51, NetBIOS over TCP/IP (called NetBT or NBT) has been the default Windows networking scheme.

Routing NetBIOS traffic to a different network implies some way to identify the computer offering those resources—to resolve the NetBIOS name to a particular process running on a particular machine. In 1987, Microsoft proposed using NetBIOS Name Servers (NBNSs). This was finally implemented in the WINS server, first in Windows NT Server, and now in Windows 2000 Server.

NetBIOS in Windows 2000

NetBIOS, along with its extensions and derivatives, has been the foundation of Windows peer-to-peer networking from the beginning. Although Microsoft made efforts to overcome the early limitations of NetBIOS, the desire to maintain backward compatibility meant it could never completely abandon NetBIOS and NetBEUI. Even recent additions to Windows networking suc has CIFS and SMB are actually built on a core of NetBIOS.

Windows 2000 is the first Microsoft operating system to use DNS, rather than some derivative of NetBIOS, as its preferred method of resolving names and addresses. Even so, Windows 2000 DNS services can be integrated with WINS services to ensure interoperability with older Windows systems.

Windows 2000 can be configured in different ways to accommodate different networking environments. On a pure Windows 2000 network, you can rely solely on Active Directory (AD) and DNS over TCP/IP for network name and address resolution. AD uses Microsoft's implementation of the Lightweight Directory Access Protocol (LDAP). To share resources with machines running older versions of Windows operating systems, however, you must enable NetBIOS name resolution. Depending on the age of the operating systems and the types of interactions you want to maintain with them, you may also need to install and configure NetBEUI—now called **NetBIOS Frame (NBF)** protocol—for backward compatibility.

12

NetBIOS has been updated, encapsulated, modified, and enhanced for more than 15 years. In the process, it gradually gained functionality, added like layers of an onion. The following section peels back the layers to the core, and gradually rebuilds Windows networking and its use of NetBIOS so you can understand how this fundamental component does its job.

NetBIOS in Perspective

NetBIOS exists at several levels in the Windows 2000 networking scheme. Windows 2000 is a transitional operating system in that it attempts to move away from the dependence on NetBIOS and NetBEUI found in older Windows operating systems. A Windows 2000 network can be configured to find and resolve the names of network resources in many different ways. The three ways that are important for present purposes are: to completely ignore NetBIOS and instead rely solely on DNS, to completely separate NetBIOS and TCP/IP, or to combine NetBIOS and TCP/IP.

The preferred form of networking in an all-Windows 2000 environment is direct hosting of the (SMB) protocol, with Active Directory as the domain controller, and DNS for name resolution. If a computer is set up for direct hosting of SMB, then SMB makes calls through the Windows Sockets (Winsock) API instead of the NetBIOS API. This arrangement works only on networks that have no Windows operating systems older than Windows 2000, however. If you have Windows 2000 systems in combination with Linux or other UNIX systems, this might be your best solution. Remember that neither older clients nor older applications (such as the network browser functions in Windows Explorer) can identify or access network resources unless NetBIOS is enabled.

At the other extreme are networks in which you have older clients, and some reason for wanting all browsing of network resources to be confined to the local network segment. To achieve full backward compatibility, Windows 2000 can use NBF as a network transport protocol. To deliberately restrict resource sharing to the local network segment, bind Windows File and Print Sharing to NBF, but not to TCP/IP.

Several intermediate solutions are possible, in which NetBIOS traffic is carried over TCP/IP, or over both TCP/IP and NBF. NetBIOS over TCP/IP is called NetBT or NBT. NetBIOS names can be resolved by any of several combinations of methods, from network broadcasts and **LMHOSTS** files, to WINS servers integrated with DNS. The bulk of this chapter is devoted to these intermediate solutions utilizing NetBT. NetBT is both the most common and useful approach to sharing network resources in a Windows environment.

The default configuration for Windows 2000 machines is to have both NetBT and NBF enabled. When a resource is called by an application, both NetBT and NBF send a network request for that resource. Windows 2000 uses the protocol that responds first. For resources shared on the same local network, NBF typically responds more quickly than NetBT. Because NBF is not routable, only NetBT can return requests for NetBIOS resources off the local network.

Figure 12-1 shows the relationship among key pieces of the Windows 2000 operating system and protocol stacks for the methods of using network resource names just described. It also shows the relationship of these pieces to the OSI reference model.

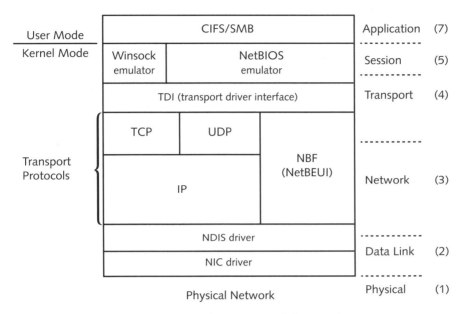

Figure 12-1   Relationship among key pieces of the Windows 2000 operating system and protocol stacks, and the OSI reference model

At the top of the figure is a typical application that uses network resources. In this example, the application is the CIFS service, using SMB. Other Application layer functions include the Network Browser function in Windows Explorer, which uses the NetBIOS API, and such TCP/IP applications as HTTP or SMTP, which use the Winsock API.

The presentation function, Layer 6 of the OSI reference model, is not represented. In fact, the Presentation layer is seldom implemented in any Windows networking protocol.

The Windows 2000 operating system uses a NetBIOS emulator to permit applications, such as SMB and Lotus Notes, to make NetBIOS calls and translate those calls into commands sent to the Windows 2000 **Transport Driver Interface (TDI)**. The TDI is a reference standard governing the way in which the upper layers of all network transport protocols are written. Conforming to the TDI means applications can interact with any of the network transport protocols in a common fashion. Winsock calls also have their emulator in the **kernel**. The TDI and these various API emulators are all executed in the kernel and handle the session control functions—Layer 5 of the OSI reference model.

Note that TCP/IP and NBF are both considered transport protocols, and that they span Layers 3 and 4 of the OSI reference model. Normally, CIFS and SMB make calls to the

NetBIOS API using a **dynamic link library (DLL)** at the application level. These calls are executed on the NetBIOS emulator running in the kernel. If SMB is configured for direct hosting, its calls are made to the Winsock API instead, and executed on the Winsock emulator. This provides SMB the equivalent of a direct connection to TCP/IP.

The **Network Driver Interface Specification (NDIS)** driver(s) presents the transport protocols with a common set of entry points for the network adapter(s) installed on the computer. Note that NDIS drivers straddle Layers 2 and 3 of the OSI reference model. The NIC drivers are vendor-supplied drivers specific to their particular NICs.

Everything from Layer 2 up through Layer 5 of the OSI reference model is handled in the I/O module of the kernel in Windows 2000. Because these functions are handled in the kernel, they run faster and in a more protected way than in earlier Windows operating systems.

The Physical layer is handled outside the kernel, and is at Layer 1 of the OSI reference model.

What is NetBIOS Used For?

NetBIOS is a naming convention, a network API, and a set of protocols used for sharing network resources. NetBIOS names can identify a computer, a user, a process, or any of several kinds of groups. Applications call these resources by their NetBIOS names through a NetBIOS provider function running as a DLL in the Windows 2000 operating system. Examples of applications that use NetBIOS include the Network Browser function in Windows Explorer, Windows File and Print Sharing (when bound to NetBIOS, as it is by default), Lotus Notes, Microsoft Exchange, and various network protocols, such as LAN Manager.

How Does NetBIOS Work?

Broadly speaking, NetBIOS operates by maintaining a list of unique names assigned to network resources; providing the services to establish, defend, and resolve these names; and carrying the necessary communications between applications that make use of these network resources; Named resources include files, services (processes), users, computers, and Windows workgroups and domains. NetBIOS ensures that names are accurate, current, and unique, and provides the APIs with access to these resources. An application makes a call to the NetBIOS API to access a named resource, or discover the names of available resources. Depending on the precise configurations of NetBIOS on the particular machine, NetBIOS may take a variety of steps to resolve the name to an address. It can then send messages to query the named resource, or open and maintain a session.

NetBIOS traffic consists of NetBIOS frames of one of two types: datagrams or session frames. Datagrams are used for connectionless "announcement" type traffic, or for request and response traffic that does not require the establishment and maintenance of a reliable connection between two hosts. The NetBIOS name services and **datagram services** are carried in datagrams. NetBIOS sessions are used in situations that require a reliable connection, such as interactions with a process running on another host.

NetBIOS may also provide the actual protocol (in the form of NBF or NetBEUI) used to transport NetBIOS messages. When NetBIOS messages are carried over NBF or NetBEUI protocols, the messages are encapsulated directly within the IEEE 802.2 LLC portion of the network data frame. FDDI and all of the IEEE 802 series network protocols support the 802.2 Logical Link Control (LLC) standard. The IEEE 802 series network protocols include 802.11 (wireless LANs), 802.3 (Ethernet), and 802.5 (token ring).

When NetBIOS is run over TCP/IP as NetBT, datagrams are carried in UDP packets and session frames are carried in TCP packets. UDP is a connectionless protocol, whereas TCP creates and maintains a reliable connection more consistent with NetBIOS session needs.

Registering and Defending NetBIOS Names

The process of asserting that a name exists and belongs to a particular computer, user, process, or group is called name registration. When a computer (called an "end node" in Microsoft NetBIOS documentation) or a user logs onto a NetBIOS network, or when a process with a NetBIOS name starts up, it attempts to register its name by sending a Name Registration Request packet. Depending on the way in which that node and network are configured, it may send the packet as a broadcast, as a unicast to the WINS server, or both. If another node on that network already claimed the requested name, the WINS server, or the existing name holder, challenges the use of the name by the new node by sending it a negative Name Registration Reply.

NetBIOS Name Resolution

NetBIOS names can be resolved by several different methods, depending on client configuration, and the types of services available. These alternative configurations and services are discussed in detail in the section titled "NetBIOS Name Registration and Resolution" later in this chapter.

Name resolution methods fall into three basic categories:

- Look up in a list on the local machine
- Broadcast queries on the local subnet
- Direct queries to name servers

Local lists include the NetBIOS name cache, LMHOSTS file, and the HOSTS file. Broadcast Name Queries are answered by the host being sought, or by a WINS proxy. WINS is the typical name server for NetBIOS, but Microsoft DNS servers can be configured to use WINS to resolve NetBIOS names as well.

Other NetBIOS Services

Name services are the most important NetBIOS services, but some applications may use NetBIOS for other services as well (see Figure 12-2). Applications such as the Network

12

Browser, LAN Manager, Exchange, or Lotus Notes may use NetBIOS datagram and **session services**, as well as name services. Although these services are not discussed in this chapter in any detail, you should be aware of these potential user requirements when deciding whether to enable NetBIOS on your network.

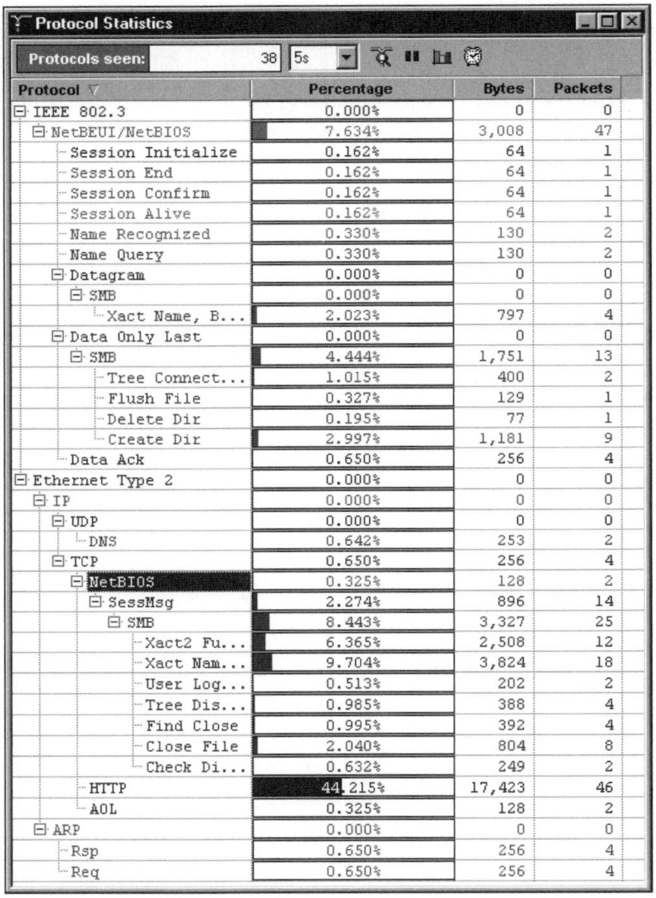

Protocol Statistics

Protocols seen: 38   5s

Protocol	Percentage	Bytes	Packets
IEEE 802.3	0.000%	0	0
NetBEUI/NetBIOS	7.634%	3,008	47
Session Initialize	0.162%	64	1
Session End	0.162%	64	1
Session Confirm	0.162%	64	1
Session Alive	0.162%	64	1
Name Recognized	0.330%	130	2
Name Query	0.330%	130	2
Datagram	0.000%	0	0
SMB	0.000%	0	0
Xact Name, B...	2.023%	797	4
Data Only Last	0.000%	0	0
SMB	4.444%	1,751	13
Tree Connect...	1.015%	400	2
Flush File	0.327%	129	1
Delete Dir	0.195%	77	1
Create Dir	2.997%	1,181	9
Data Ack	0.650%	256	4
Ethernet Type 2	0.000%	0	0
IP	0.000%	0	0
UDP	0.000%	0	0
DNS	0.642%	253	2
TCP	0.650%	256	4
NetBIOS	0.325%	128	2
SessMsg	2.274%	896	14
SMB	8.443%	3,327	25
Xact2 Fu...	6.365%	2,508	12
Xact Nam...	9.704%	3,824	18
User Log...	0.513%	202	2
Tree Dis...	0.985%	388	4
Find Close	0.995%	392	4
Close File	2.040%	804	8
Check Di...	0.632%	249	2
HTTP	44.215%	17,423	46
AOL	0.325%	128	2
ARP	0.000%	0	0
Rsp	0.650%	256	4
Req	0.650%	256	4

Figure 12-2   NetBIOS is often used under both TCP/IP and NBF on one network

NetBIOS Names

NetBIOS names are based on the user name during logon, and the information configured for the specific computer in the Network applet in Control Panel. This configuration information can be entered manually, either in dialog boxes or by directly editing the Registry, or supplied by a Microsoft DHCP server during system start-up. The user name, computer name, and Windows domain name, or Windows workgroup name, form the basis of NetBIOS names defining the user name of the person making a resource request, and the services available on a particular machine, membership in a particular workgroup, and so forth.

Structure of NetBIOS Names

NetBIOS names are of two general types—unique names and group names. Unique names resolve to a single address. Examples include computer names and user names. Group names may resolve to multiple addresses. Examples of group names are the Windows domain name and workgroup names.

NetBIOS names are 16 characters long, divided into two parts. The first 15 characters are the name itself. The last character is a code describing the class of resource to which the name belongs. NetBIOS names that are less than 15 characters long are padded to the right with blanks to make up the full 15 characters. For example, the NetBIOS name for the messenger service on a computer called "Frank" would be "FRANK   0x03", where the five characters that make up the name "Frank" are followed by 10 "blank" characters (0x20). The name ends with a hexadecimal number (03 in this example) indicating the kind of resource this name represents. NetBIOS names are not case sensitive, but it is customary for Microsoft and other vendors to represent them as all uppercase.

Classes of resources are discussed in the next section.

Hexadecimal numbers are numbers in base 16, which are extremely handy in computing because four bits (half of a byte, sometimes also called a "nibble") can represent exactly 16 different values from zero to 15. Whereas common decimal numbers count from zero to nine and then increment the next place to one, hexadecimal numbers count from zero to 15 and then increment the next place to one. Because Arabic numerals don't have symbols to represent a single numeral larger than nine, the first six letters of the Roman alphabet are pressed into service to stand for the numbers 10 (A), 11 (B), 12 (C), 13 (D), 14 (E), and 15 (F). In base 16, if you add one to "F," you get 16, represented as "10." Because the numerical representation of the value 16 in base 16 looks exactly like the numerical representation of the value 10 in base 10, we need some way to tell which type of number we are trying to represent. One common way to distinguish the two, and the method used here, is to preface all hexadecimal numbers with the string "0x"; for example, 0x1F.

12

NetBIOS Name Types and Suffixes

As stated previously, NetBIOS names end with a one-character (2-byte) suffix. This is a code indicating the service or function called by that name. Suffixes are represented as hexadecimal numbers in the range from 00 to FF. Table 12-1 shows examples of NetBIOS suffixes for different types of NetBIOS names. The examples in Table 12-1 are all from Windows networking, but other applications, such as Lotus Notes and Microsoft Exchange, also make use of NetBIOS names.

Table 12-1   NetBIOS Suffixes and Meanings

Name	Name Type	NetBIOS Suffix (hex)	Meaning
computername	Unique name	00	Workstation service
computername	Unique name	01	Messenger service
computername	Unique name	03	Messenger service
computername	Unique name	06	Remote Access Server (RAS)
computername	Unique name	1F	NetDDE service
computername	Unique name	20	Server service
computername	Unique name	21	RAS Client service
computername	Unique name	BE	Network Monitor Agent service
computername	Unique name	BF	Network Monitor Application service
domainname	Group name	00	Registers the computer as a member of the Windows domain or workgroup
domainname	Group name	1B	Registers the computer as the Domain Master Browser
domainname	Group name	1C	Domain controllers
domainname	Group name	1E	Used to facilitate browser elections
username	Unique name	03	Messenger service

NetBIOS Scope Identifier

NetBIOS also provides the NetBIOS scope identifier, which is a backdoor to add further differentiation to resource names. The scope identifier adds a character string to the end of the name, separated from the rest of the name by a period (.) character. It is used in much the same way as the domain name in IP.

Unfortunately, the NetBIOS scope cannot be assigned directly to a network resource. Instead, the scope is assigned to the computer through DHCP, or through directly changing parameters in the Windows Registry. A scope set manually in the Registry overrides any scope that a DHCP server may attempt to assign. Once the scope is assigned, NetBIOS communications can only take place between nodes with the identical scope. In other words, the scope identifier supersedes any other methods for sharing resources across network boundaries. Microsoft recommends that this capability not be used because it can be difficult to maintain and troubleshoot, and it interferes with other more advanced methods of sharing resources across network boundaries.

The NetBIOS scope parameter was originally intended to help larger organizations subnet their NetBIOS networks. In practice, it may be more useful to very small networks as a means of limiting exposure to intrusion. By assigning an unexpected scope identifier to all nodes on the local network, a small network can add one more layer of difficulty for intruders attempting to mimic legitimate users.

Beware, however, because the scope parameter is not set directly in any dialog box, it can be difficult to maintain for more than a few users. Also, the use of the scope identifier makes any other means of sharing NetBIOS resources across network boundaries unusable.

NetBIOS Name Registration and Resolution

NetBIOS names are registered and resolved using a variety of methods. The methods include:

- NetBIOS name cache
- Broadcasts on the local network or IP subnet
- NetBIOS Name Servers (NBNSs) such as WINS
- LMHOSTS file
- HOSTS file
- DNS

The primary methods are broadcast and WINS. Either can be used exclusively, or the two methods can be mixed; other methods can also be added. Depending on how NetBIOS and these supporting functions are configured on a particular machine and its network, processes will attempt different resolution methods, and attempt them in a different order. Each of these methods is discussed in the following sections.

Although the precise mix of name registration and resolution techniques for each client is determined by its configuration, all clients have certain techniques in common.

When a name is to be resolved, the node first checks to see if the name is its own name.

When a node has TCP/IP configured, names presented by a process for resolution are checked to see if they are in fact NetBIOS names. If the name is more than 15 characters long, or contains a period character, the name is resolved using DNS by a call to Winsock, rather than to NetBIOS.

Most name registration and resolution regimes allow the node to check the NetBIOS name cache before attempting to register or resolve a name by other methods.

12

Name Resolution Regimes by Node Type

In NetBIOS, the name registration and name resolution methods used by a computer (end node) are nominally associated with the node type. The node type is set either by DHCP (by using the network's Properties dialog box), or by setting parameters directly in the Registry. There are four basic types of NetBIOS nodes: b-node, p-node, m-node, and h-node. In addition, Microsoft made certain enhancements to the b-node for clients in some of its operating systems. Each of these is described in the sections that follow.

B-Node (Broadcast Node)

A b-node registers and resolves names by using only broadcasts. The b-node approach is good for very small networks; however, the broadcast activity on networks over 15 to 20 nodes can cause significant amounts of network bandwidth to be consumed by NetBIOS broadcasts. Also note that ordinary b-nodes cannot make use of WINS. This is the default node type for Windows 2000 clients if WINS is not enabled.

To register a name, a b-node broadcasts a Name Registration packet onto the local network or IP subnet. If no other node responds with a negative Name Registration Reply packet, the b-node assumes it owns the name and begins defending it against any subsequent attempts to register that name. When the b-node computer or process shuts down, it simply stops defending the NetBIOS name of that resource, thus releasing the name.

To resolve a name, the b-node broadcasts a Name Request packet. Then, the host or node owning that name responds with a Name Request Reply packet. If no reply is received within the specified timeout, the name is considered unresolvable and NetBIOS returns an error.

P-Node (Peer Node)

A p-node attempts to register and resolve names using the local WINS server. This eliminates broadcast traffic from NetBIOS name service tasks, but introduces a single point of failure if only one WINS server is configured.

To register a name, the p-node sends a Name Registration Request packet as a unicast to the configured WINS server. If the name is not yet registered to another resource, the WINS server sends a positive Name Registration Reply packet and adds the new name and address pair to its records. If the name is already registered to another node, the WINS server sends a message to the registered name owner to check if the name is still in use. If the name is in use, the WINS server sends a negative Name Registration Reply packet to the p-node.

When a p-node computer or process shuts down gracefully, it sends a Name Release Request packet to the WINS server to indicate that it is no longer using the name, thus releasing the name. Names held in the WINS server have a Time to Live (TTL), which can be set in the server configuration to any value between one minute and 365 days. The default TTL for WINS name records is six days. When its TTL expires, the name is released. When the WINS server sends a positive Name Registration Reply message, it includes the name's TTL. The p-node attempts to renew this name at half the TTL.

To resolve a name, a p-node sends a Name Query packet to the WINS server. If the WINS server is able to resolve the name, it sends the information back to the p-node in a positive Name Query Response packet. If it is unable to resolve the name, the WINS server sends a negative Name Query Response packet. If more than one WINS server is configured for the p-node, it will attempt to query these servers in order until it receives a reply, either positive or negative. Windows 2000 and Windows 98 can be configured to use up to 12 WINS servers. Earlier versions of Windows clients can use only two WINS servers. P-nodes do not use broadcasts to resolve names.

M-Node (Mixed Node)

The m-node is a mixture of two other node types. It first tries the b-node style registration and resolution using broadcasts on the local network, then it tries p-node style, attempting to contact the configured WINS server. P-node methods are used only when broadcast methods fail. This approach has advantages where the WINS server is remote and most traffic is bound for the local network, rather than for nodes served by the WINS server. It also permits local names to be resolved without the WINS server.

H-Node (Hybrid Node)

The h-node is a hybrid that uses the p-node method as its first choice, and only uses broadcast methods of the b-node type when the p-node attempts fail. This keeps broadcast traffic on the local subnet to a minimum, but permits it as a backup in case the WINS server fails. This is the default node type for Windows 2000 clients with WINS enabled.

Enhanced B-Node

To overcome some of the limitations of b-node name resolution, Microsoft added two alternative methods to create a modified or enhanced b-node. The enhanced b-node first uses the NetBIOS name cache, then the LMHOSTS file, and only then tries resolution in the normal b-node fashion. WFW 3.11, Microsoft LAN Manager, and Windows 2000 use this enhanced b-node. In Windows 2000 clients, the use of the LMHOSTS file can be disabled in the TCP/IP Properties dialog box.

NetBIOS Name Cache and LMHOSTS File

The NetBIOS name cache is a temporary file that resides in memory, pairing NetBIOS names and IP addresses. Names are added to the NetBIOS name cache as they are discovered during name resolution and computer start-up, which is when the name cache is initialized by reading the LMHOSTS file. By default, names in the NetBIOS name cache time out after 10 minutes. You can set this timeout parameter in the Registry.

The LMHOSTS file is a plain text file that resides in the *<windows root>*\system32\ drivers\etc directory. It lists NetBIOS names and their associated IP addresses. LMHOSTS is patterned on the HOSTS file specified for IP in BSD UNIX. It follows the same basic structure, usage, and syntax, but adds features unique to NetBIOS. Characters that were not supported in the original DNS specification, for example, can be represented in the LMHOSTS file by enclosing the name in quotation marks, and representing the non-DNS character with its hex value ("FRANK   \0x14").

In the LMHOSTS file, you can choose which names are to be pre-loaded into the NetBIOS name cache, include additional and/or alternative LMHOSTS files by reference, and include domain designations, as well as the names of unique resources. Each of these features is supported by a syntax including keywords. See the sample LMHOSTS file installed on Windows 2000 computers for details.

You can create and edit the LMHOSTS file with any plain text editor, such as Notepad. You should not use word processors, such as Microsoft Word or WordPad, to edit plain text files, as these programs will introduce extraneous characters used for formatting and page layout. Also note that the entire LMHOSTS file, including comment lines, is parsed each time it is used for a lookup. Keeping the file short can improve performance.

The LMHOSTS file is a static list. As such, it is a useful tool for small networks with stable NetBIOS names and IP addresses. Keeping the LMHOSTS file current on a larger or more dynamic network can be difficult or impossible.

WINS Name Registration and Resolution

WINS servers are discussed in more detail in the "WINS Servers" section later in this chapter. This section deals particularly with name registration and resolution using WINS servers.

WINS servers are NetBIOS Name Servers that set up and maintain a dynamic database of NetBIOS names and their associated IP addresses. WINS servers do not participate in broadcast or b-node name registration and resolution. Instead, they rely on direct communications (unicasts) between themselves and the clients (end nodes) attempting to register and resolve NetBIOS names. WINS clients configured as p-nodes, m-nodes, or h-nodes may attempt to register or resolve NetBIOS names by contacting the WINS server(s) configured for their use. See the section titled "Name Resolution Regimes by Node Type" earlier in this chapter for the differences in name registration and resolution behavior among these three types. When interacting with the WINS server, all three node types behave the same way.

WINS-enabled clients can be configured to use more than one WINS server. Older WINS clients could only be configured to use one primary and one secondary WINS server. Clients in Windows 98 and Windows 2000 can be configured with up to 11 secondary WINS servers. The client attempts to use the primary WINS server first. (This is the first in the list, if you are configuring the client from the TCP/IP Properties dialog box.) If the primary WINS server does not respond, the client uses any secondary WINS server(s) configured for it, using them in the order listed in the TCP/IP Properties dialog box.

When a node, user, or process with a NetBIOS name signs onto the network or starts up, it attempts to register its name. If it is configured to use WINS, it sends a Name Registration Request packet to the WINS server. If the name is in the proper form for NetBIOS names, and no record for that name already exists in the WINS server's database, the WINS server sends a positive Name Registration Reply packet to the node and enters the name in its database. The WINS server's response includes the TTL (six days by default) for the name. The node attempts to renew this name at half the TTL value—three days time if it received the default TTL. If a name is not renewed within the TTL, the name is released, and made available for use by the next entity attempting to register it.

If the name already exists in the database, the WINS server sends a **Wait Acknowledgement (WACK)** to the node attempting to register. This message acknowledges the receipt of the Name Registration Request packet without either granting or denying it, but asks the node to wait. At the same time, the WINS server attempts to contact the registered owner of the name to see if the name is still in use. If the owner responds, then the WINS server sends a negative Name Registration Reply packet to the node attempting to register the name. If the registered owner does not respond, then the WINS server grants the name to the node attempting to register, sending it a positive Name Registration Reply packet. (In earlier versions of WINS, the server responded to an apparent name conflict by asking the registering node itself to send a challenge to the name holder.)

In some circumstances, the WINS server may issue either a Name Conflict Demand packet or a Name Release Demand packet to a name holder or a node attempting to register a name in conflict. These so-called "demand" packets are requests that have no response associated with them. They are treated as imperatives, and a node must comply. The Name Conflict Demand packet tells a node that its name is in conflict. The node notifies the user of this situation, and the node eventually releases the name. The Name Release Demand packet tells the receiving node to immediately remove the name from its name table. Typically, these types of packets are only sent when, for example, you are reconfiguring your network, and names and addresses are being assigned and reassigned in rapid succession.

WINS servers support a special name registration regime called burst mode. When a large network first comes to life at the start of the workday, for example, many hundreds or thousands of Name Registration Requests may pour in within a few seconds of one another. To prevent the WINS server from being overwhelmed by a sudden spike in utilization, WINS servers can go into burst mode. In burst mode, the server responds to every Name Registration Request packet with a positive Name Registration Reply, without attempting to resolve any conflicts. The trick is this: It includes in each positive response a small TTL, and gives a slightly different TTL to each node. Because the nodes will attempt to renew their names in half the TTL, name conflict resolutions can be deferred until the spike passes. In this way, the server itself can fan out the queue, spreading the workload over a longer time period. You can change the queue size that triggers burst mode handling (it's set to 500 registrations by default) in the WINS Server Console.

Linux and UNIX machines can also access NetBIOS resources using the **Samba** suite of applications for those operating systems. Samba uses SMB and NetBT for resource sharing on IP networks. When properly configured, Samba hosts can access resources through any WINS server, and Windows clients can access resources through the Samba server, all using a core of NetBT. Samba, like Linux, is Open Source software (it can be altered and redistributed without fees or restrictions).

DNS and the HOSTS File

The preferred configuration for Windows 2000 clients is to use DNS for name resolution. If TCP/IP is enabled, even clients not configured to use DNS as their primary name resolution method can attempt to resolve names by querying DNS, particularly if the name appears to follow DNS naming conventions and violates NetBIOS naming conventions. Some applications or clients may also attempt to resolve names by consulting the HOSTS file.

The HOSTS file is a static list of IP name and address pairs, located in the *<windows root>*\system32\driver\etc directory, the same location as the LMHOSTS file. Some windows implementations of UNIX programs, such as Telnet and FTP, may consult the HOSTS file as a matter of course, even before querying DNS. Most Windows applications do not use the HOSTS file. Like the LMHOSTS file, the format and syntax of the HOSTS file are taken from the BSD version of UNIX. The HOSTS file does not use the special syntax and keywords to support NetBIOS names found in the LMHOSTS file, however.

In UNIX and Linux systems, the ordinary order in which name resolution methods are attempted is:

- Local host
- HOSTS file
- DNS
- NetBIOS

Microsoft is also attempting to move DNS closer to the top of the search order for its native clients. To better integrate older Windows clients into the Internet world, Microsoft created its own version of DNS **(Microsoft DNS**, or **MS DNS)** that queries WINS servers to resolve NetBIOS names. This functionality is discussed in detail in the section titled "WINS Servers" later in this chapter.

NetBIOS Over TCP/IP

NetBIOS using TCP/IP as its transport protocol is known as NetBT or NBT. NetBT allows NetBIOS to use TCP/IP's network addressability to make resources available across network and IP subnet boundaries.

NetBEUI and NetBIOS were literally made for each other, but TCP/IP and NetBIOS come from very different worlds. To coexist with TCP/IP, NetBIOS had to accommodate TCP/IP's conventions.

There were some similarities, and some features were modified or added to NetBIOS to make it more like TCP/IP. The NetBIOS name was somewhat like the TCP/IP host name. A NetBIOS scope identifier was added as a sort of analog of the TCP/IP domain. Where TCP/IP applications, such as Telnet and FTP, were associated with a well-known port, services (an equivalent term in many ways) in NetBIOS were identified by a hexadecimal code, the last character of the NetBIOS name.

Naming conventions between the two were also different. The original DNS standards for characters that could be used to express a host name were more restrictive than those for NetBIOS names. At the same time, a NetBIOS name was not really separable from the NetBIOS suffix. Both parts were required to define a particular service.

These problems were solved by making slight adjustments to NetBIOS, and creating a set of steps to make NetBIOS names and commands transportable—and translatable—over a TCP/IP connection. The solutions arrived and were published in 1987 in RFCs 1001 and 1002.

UDP was a good analog to NetBEUI datagram traffic. Both are connectionless request/response-oriented protocols. For NetBEUI sessions, TCP provided a good replacement, offering reliable connections between hosts. The Internet Assigned Numbers Authority (IANA) and its predecessors attempted to keep the services offered on the lower-numbered ports of both UDP and TCP identical, offering different qualities of service for the same applications on one or the other protocol. Therefore, for both TCP and UDP protocols, NetBIOS and NetBT are assigned the ports listed in Table 12-2.

12

Table 12-2   TCP/UDP Ports for NetBIOS Services

TCP/UDP Port	NetBIOS Services
137	Name services
138	Datagram services
139	Session services

NetBIOS Names and IP Names

To convert a NetBIOS name into a name that is recognizable and routable by DNS, two things had to happen: the NetBIOS name had to become a usable host name, and a domain portion of the name had to be added.

The NetBIOS name had to be restated in a way that replaced any characters not recognizable by DNS. DNS names must be printable, but some of the most commonly used service identifiers in NetBIOS names (that last or 16th character) are hexadecimal values below 0x20 (the "space" or "blank" character). In the ASCII code set, none of these characters is printable. To solve this and related incompatibilities between the two sets of permissible characters, a scheme was devised to encode NetBIOS names in such a way that any 16-character NetBIOS name would be represented as a 32-character ASCII string composed of the capital letters "A" through "P." This created a usable equivalent of a host name. See Figure 12-3.

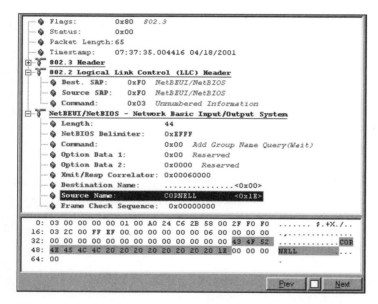

Figure 12-3   Under NetBEUI or NBF, NetBIOS names are transmitted in ASCII

The encoding scheme is simple enough. It is presented here only because one day you may use a network analyzer that doesn't translate NetBIOS names back into their native format when decoding packets. The NetBIOS name, along with its service identifier, contains important information for network diagnostics. If you understand the encoding scheme, you will not be at a loss when presented with a string of 32 capital letters, instead of the NetBIOS name of the service you were trying to diagnose.

Here's how it's done. Imagine the NetBIOS name expressed as a string of 2-byte hexadecimal numbers in the range 0x00 through 0xFF. One 2-byte hexadecimal number equals one name character. The printable NetBIOS name characters take their hexadecimal values from the ASCII character set. Remember that NetBIOS names shorter than 15 characters are padded with blanks (0x20) to the right to make up the total of 15. The last character is the service identifier.

Now here's the trick. Break each hexadecimal number into two parts, and treat each digit as if it is a separate value. The largest hexadecimal character, 0xFF, thus becomes 0xF and 0xF. (In decimal numbers, that's 15 and 15.) Add to each of these hexadecimal digits the value of the ASCII capital letter "A" character (0x41), and you come up with 0x50 and 0x50. This translates to the ASCII characters P and P. In fact, using this encoding method, you can't arrive at any letter higher than P or lower than A. Using the same method for the space character (0x20), you have 0x2 + 0x41 = 0x43 (ASCII letter "C"), and 0x0 + 0x41 = 0x41 (ASCII letter "A"). You find a lot of "CACACACA" strings in encoded NetBIOS names. The same trick works in reverse, subtracting 0x41 from each encoded character, then recombining the results, as higher-, then lower-order digits of a hexadecimal number (beginning from the left), to restore the NetBIOS name as it was originally represented (including its padding, of course). Figure 12-4 depicts an encoded NetBIOS name.

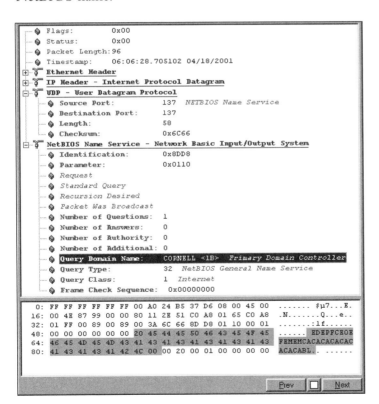

Figure 12-4   Under NetBT, NetBIOS names are encoded for DNS compatibility

To convert the (translated) NetBIOS name into a fully qualified domain name (FQDN), a domain portion of the name had to be added as well. Initially, the NetBIOS scope identifier was put forward as a way to create a "NetBIOS domain name." The problem with this approach is obvious today in the context of the Internet, but it was not so obvious when it was first proposed. The problem is a NetBIOS scope identifier is a user-configurable string, and it adds, in any case, only one level of hierarchy. Internet domain names, on the other hand, are regulated and restricted, and they conform to a deeper and more rigorously enforced hierarchy. For computers connected to the Internet, the NetBIOS scope identifier should be a legitimate Internet domain name, if it is used at all. Using some other sort of scope identifier leads to problems with reverse lookup, misrouting, and several other problems for Internet-connected hosts.

WINS SERVERS

In essence, WINS is Microsoft's imitation of DNS, repurposed for the NetBIOS name space. When Microsoft began to experiment with sharing NetBIOS resources across network boundaries, it became clear that some type of NBNS was required. This service was modeled on the successful DNS servers used for TCP/IP networks, and was described in a functional way in RFCs 1001 and 1002. Name servers for NetBIOS over TCP/IP must still conform to these RFCs. Microsoft's latest version of an NBNS is WINS.

Microsoft continued to improve the functionality of the WINS server and integrate it into the rest of the Windows networking scheme, including integration with AD and Microsoft's implementation of DNS.

The rest of this section explains how WINS operates, and describes thevarious WINS configurations on Microsoft networks under Windows 2000.

How WINS Works

WINS is a server service, running under Windows NT Server or Windows 2000 Server. A WINS server registers NetBIOS names and IP addresses, and can be configured to return the IP address associated with a resource name or (for reverse WINS or WINS-R) the NetBIOS names associated with an IP address.

A WINS server keeps these name and address pairs in a database. Each resource record (RR) in the database contains a NetBIOS name and its associated IP address, as well as the TTL and version number for that record. The version number is used to facilitate replication of the database onto other WINS servers.

WINS servers do not participate in b-node or broadcast name registration or resolution. Instead, WINS servers exchange unicast name registration and resolution messages directly with p-node, h-node, and m-node WINS clients. WINS servers can also communicate with one another, WINS proxies, and Microsoft DHCP and DNS servers.

Different WINS Configurations

WINS servers can be deployed in several different ways to meet the needs of different networks. The same physical machine can be the WINS server, the DNS server, and the AD domain controller, or these functions can be enabled on different physical machines. A single WINS server can serve multiple subnets, but reliance on one server introduces a single point of failure. In addition, having the WINS server off the local subnet introduces extra WAN traffic. If possible, you should have at least one secondary WINS server to avoid the single point of failure problem. If your subnets are large enough to justify it, you may want to have a separate WINS server for each. The replication capability of the WINS server design makes it easy to keep records current in a distributed environment, and the local availability of WINS servers can cut down on WAN traffic. This section describes four different WINS topologies: a single WINS server, WINS server with WINS proxy, distributed WINS services, and the integration of WINS with Microsoft DNS.

WINS Server

You can set up and configure a WINS server on any Windows NT server or Windows 2000 server in the initial configuration dialog box, by using the WINS console (under Administrative Tools), or by directly editing the Registry. In Windows 2000, you can also use command-line tools to configure WINS servers. Use the command *netsh> wins* to enter the WINS context. Enter *?* to display the online Help for that context.

Administrator-level access to the WINS server allows you to:

- Check server statistics
- Check the database and version numbers for consistency
- Mark records for eventual deletion (called "tombstoning" the records)
- Remove old records (scavenge the database)
- Search for active registrants
- Back up and restore the database
- Create or delete static records
- Delete dynamic records (Windows 2000 only)
- Export the database as a csv text file (Windows 2000 only)
- Set replication parameters

12

In Windows 2000, you can grant membership in the WINS Users group to give members read-only access to the WINS Console.

The only absolute location requirement for a WINS server is that it be accessible to its clients over a TCP/IP connection. As a practical matter, you want to configure your WINS topology to optimize security, server availability, and network traffic. For a network on a single segment, this is easy. For networks that span multiple network segments, you can use any combination of WINS proxies, WINS server replication, and WINS-enabled Microsoft DNS.

Because Microsoft DHCP servers can update the WINS database directly upon assigning a lease (if the lease includes WINS information), the WINS server and the DHCP server are often configured on the same machine to eliminate some traffic.

WINS Proxy

WINS clients are available for recent versions of DOS, OS/2, and all versions of Windows. In addition, WINS clients are available for Linux and UNIX machines running Samba. Nevertheless, particularly with older NetBIOS clients, you may wish to configure some machines as b-nodes. To integrate b-node clients with a WINS-enabled network, you can install a WINS proxy on any Windows NT or Windows 2000 server or workstation. The WINS proxy is a WINS client that attempts to resolve any b-node Name Query broadcasts it hears on its own network segment by querying the WINS server(s) configured for it. If the WINS proxy can resolve the name using WINS, or its own local NetBIOS name cache, it sends a positive Name Query Response packet to the sender of the broadcast Name Query. The WINS proxy will not attempt to register names (other than its own) with the WINS server. The presence of a WINS proxy allows b-node clients to access resources off the local network, despite their inability to use WINS directly.

You can configure any Windows NT or 2000 computer to be a WINS proxy by setting the EnableProxy parameter in the Registry to one. The default is zero (see Table 12-3).

Table 12-3   EnableProxy Registry Setting

Registry Information	Details
Location	HKEY_LOCAL_MACHINE\SYSTEM\CurrentControlSet\Services\NetBT\Parameters
Data type	REG_DWORD
Valid range	0–1
Default value	0
Present by default	No

Alternately, you can bind the proxy to a specific adapter by using the same parameter and value for the adapter's Registry key, which is:

```
HKEY_LOCAL_MACHINE\SYSTEM\CurrentControlSet\Services\NetBT\
Parameters\Adapters\Interfaces\<NIC>
```

In the example just given, the term *<NIC>* is the designation of the particular adapter.

Note that in Windows 2000, the EnableProxy parameter is not present in the Registry by default. In the absence of this parameter, the operating system assumes the default behavior, which is not to act as a WINS proxy.

WINS Replication

If your network depends on WINS, you should seriously consider installing more than one WINS server, even if one server could handle normal traffic. On networks including multiple segments, multiple WINS servers are also advisable, if not absolutely required.

WINS servers can share the information in their databases by using replication, in which a server pulls down records from its partner. There are two basic types of relationships between WINS servers—push replication and pull replication—corresponding to the type of event that triggers an exchange of data between them. A WINS server configured as a push partner notifies the other server that there are records to be pulled, either when the push partner starts up, or when a certain number of its records have been updated since its partner's last pull. A server configured as a pull partner, on the other hand, pulls the database from its replication partner at a specified time interval. To optimize system performance, you can change the push/pull relationship between servers, and set the time interval and number of updated records triggering replication for each.

When an RR in the WINS database is registered or renewed, that RR's version number is incremented. The highest version number is always the most recent information for that RR. WINS servers use the version number to decide whether a record has been or needs to be updated.

Integrating WINS and DNS

This section assumes you read and understood the basics of the chapter on DNS. If parts of this discussion of integrating WINS and DNS seem cryptic to you, consult Chapter 7 for more information.

The Microsoft DNS server implementation (MS DNS) can be configured to use WINS to resolve NetBIOS names in the primary or zone root domain. MS DNS cannot resolve NetBIOS names that are not direct children of the zone root or primary DNS domain. The name *frank.example.com* is a direct child of the *example.com* domain; therefore, the DNS server serving that primary domain can safely use WINS to resolve the name. The name *frank.accounting.example.com* is not a direct child of the *example.com* domain; therefore, it cannot be resolved as a NetBIOS name by the DNS servers serving the *example.com* primary domain. This limitation is a legacy of the original design of NetBIOS. Because a NetBIOS name has no network component, it is only a name, not an address.

If you have subdomains on your network, you have two choices for integrating WINS with MS DNS. If the subdomains are large enough, you may want to delegate those

12

domains so that each has its own Start of Authority (SOA) with its own zone root DNS (see Figure 12-5). MS DNS servers in each of these can then resolve NetBIOS names by means of WINS because they will be serving a primary domain.

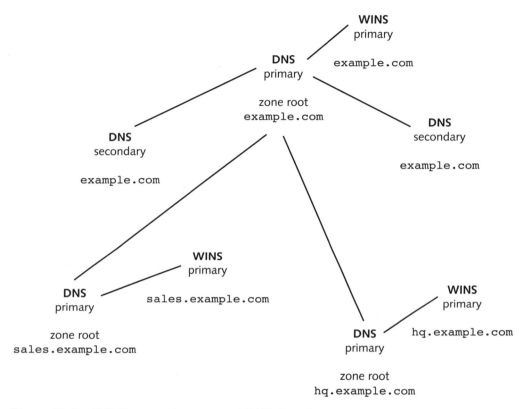

Figure 12-5 WINS servers in zone root DNS domains

Alternately, you can create a special domain just for NetBIOS clients (see Figure 12-6). Remember that a DNS domain is a logical, not physical, entity. If all the NetBIOS clients belong to the *netbios.example.com* domain, you can make that a primary domain. This second solution may integrate more easily with a network that has a mix of Linux, UNIX, and Microsoft DNS servers. If you choose to create a special domain just for NetBIOS names, you must add that domain name to each client's DNS suffix search list. If the special NetBIOS domain is listed in its DNS suffix search list, a client uses that domain to search for NetBIOS resources. You can manually add an entry to a client's DNS suffix search list (in TCP/IP Properties), or through DHCP.

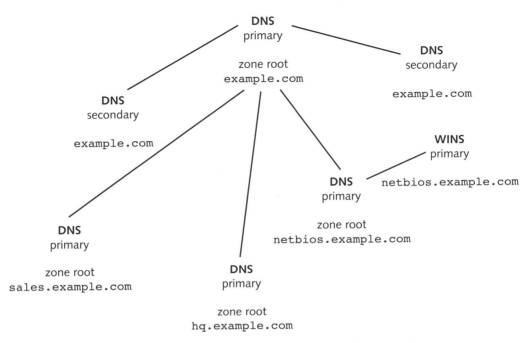

Figure 12-6   This network uses a special domain just for WINS resolution

How does DNS know that *frank.example.com* is a NetBIOS name and not an IP name? This is a good question, the short answer to which is: "it doesn't." Because the form is correct for IP, a MS DNS server for the *example.com* domain first checks the A records in its own database. Only when it fails to find the correct records there does it search its cache of NetBIOS names for that domain or, failing that, contact the configured WINS server(s). If the WINS server responds, the MS DNS server caches the response and passes the information on to the process that made the original Name Resolution Request.

When you configure a MS DNS server, you can point it to one or more WINS servers to use for NetBIOS name resolution. You can do this in the initial configuration, by using the DNS Console, or by directly editing the Registry. The name of the WINS server is entered as an RR in the MS DNS server's database. The schematic view of the WINS RR looks like this:

```
owner class WINS [LOCAL] [L<value>] [C<value>]
<wins_address>
```

Terms in lowercase are tokens; terms in uppercase are literals. Terms in angle brackets are values; terms in square brackets are optional. No brackets are used in the actual database

12

entry. Terms are separated by spaces, and no term can contain a space. Each term is described as follows:

- *Owner*: The "owner" term denotes the domain that owns this record. This term should always be set to @ to indicate that this domain is the zone of origin for this record.

- *Class*: The "class" term is always set to *IN* because MS DNS servers only understand the Internet class of addresses (not CHAOS or any of the other possible, but rarely used, values for this term).

- *WINS*: The "WINS" term denotes that this is the WINS record, and should appear exactly as shown in the preceding example. The owner, class, and WINS terms are created automatically when you check the *Use WINS lookup* check box on the WINS tab of the Server Properties dialog box for a given server.

- *LOCAL*: The "LOCAL" term is optional. When present, it tells the DNS server not to include this RR in data transfers to other DNS servers. If the server is communicating with non-Microsoft DNS servers, including the WINS RR in the transfer could result in errors or in failed zone transfers. The only time you should omit this term is when the server is communicating only with other MS DNS servers. You can use the *Do not replicate this record* check box to include (checked) or omit (unchecked) this term from the WINS RR on the WINS tab of the Server Properties dialog box.

- *L<value>*: The "L<value>" term is optional and is the look-up timeout value. Note that there are no spaces (or quotes or brackets) in the term. The value immediately follows the capital L. The default time to wait before the DNS server considers the WINS server to be unresponsive is two seconds. You can set this timeout value on the WINS tab of the Server Properties dialog box by using the Advanced button to open the Advanced dialog box.

- *C<value>*: The "C<value>" term is optional and specifies the WINS cache timeout value. Note that there are no spaces (or quotes or brackets) in the term. The value immediately follows the capital C. The default time to wait before considering cached WINS responses to be out-of-date is 15 minutes. Note that WINS responses do not follow the normal DNS practice of using the minimum TTL set in the SOA record for the zone as their default. Instead, they use this WINS cache timeout value. You can set the timeout value on the WINS tab of the Server Properties dialog box by using the Advanced button to open the Advanced dialog box.

- *Wins_address*: The "wins_address" term is the IP address of the WINS server. When multiple WINS servers are configured for a DNS server, their addresses are listed in search order from left to right, separated from one another by a single space. You can add the addresses of the WINS servers to use, and in what order, on the WINS tab of the Server Properties dialog box.

MS DNS servers in the *in-addr.arpa* domain provide reverse lookup, returning the name(s) associated with a particular IP address. MS DNS servers in the reverse look-up zone root can be configured to use WINS-R to find the NetBIOS resources associated with a particular IP address. The WINS server uses a NetBIOS Adapter Status Query to find the name(s) associated with a given IP address, and returns this information to the MS DNS server. You can configure WINS-R for MS DNS servers in the reverse look-up zone root in the same ways that you configure WINS for servers in the forward look-up domain. Servers in the reverse look-up domain keep the WINS-R information in a resource record that has the following form:

```
owner class WINS-R [LOCAL] [L<value>] [C<value>]
<domain_to_append>
```

The terms in their form, meaning, and usage are the same as in the example previously given for forward WINS resolution, with two exceptions.

The "WINS-R" term denotes that this is the reverse look-up version of WINS, and should appear as shown. If you use the DNS Console to open the Properties dialog box for a server in the reverse look-up domain, you will see a WINS-R tab instead of a WINS tab. The check box to enable this feature is labeled *Use WINS-R lookup.*

The "domain_to_append" term is the domain name that should be appended to all NetBIOS names found by the WINS server when they are returned by the DNS server in response to queries. Enter the string to use in the *Domain to append to returned name* text entry box on the WINS-R tab of the Server Properties dialog box.

In addition, the reverse look-up features of MS DNS allow you to have the MS DNS server parse the host portion of the name as a NetBIOS name, parse the domain name portion as a NetBIOS scope identifier, and present it to the WINS server for resolution. If you want to use this feature, click the Advanced button on the WINS-R tab of the Properties dialog box for that server, and check the *Submit DNS domain as NetBIOS scope* check box to enable the feature. The Advanced dialog box also allows you to set the Lookup and Cache timeouts for WINS-R.

12

TROUBLESHOOTING WINS AND NETBIOS

Errors in Windows name resolution, like most network errors, fall into two broad categories: outright failure and degradation of service. In some ways, total failure is easier to troubleshoot. The fact that there is a problem is never open to debate. Also, the causes themselves tend to be starker: misconfiguration of a client, user error in logging onto the network, and the ever popular (but not to be underestimated) loose connection of a network cable, adapter card, or power cord. The accumulation of several of sub-optimizations seldom leads to outright failure of a service. On the other hand, that is the most common cause (or constellation of causes) for poor performance.

When the network itself is in good shape, the failure of NetBIOS services are most often due to misconfiguration of end nodes or to server failure. Poor performance, on the other hand, is more likely to be the cumulative result of minor configuration errors in the server, or in some significant number of end nodes. Server topology also has a large impact on overall performance. Setting up WINS services for a network with many subnets requires not only considerations of security and availability, but also of load optimizing across WAN links. Push-type replication partners, in true NetBIOS fashion, can be very chatty. You have to trade off the frequency of WINS server updates against the frequency of incorrect positive Name Query responses. Incorrect name resolutions can also generate significant traffic and generally degrade performance.

This section lists a few useful tools for diagnosing NetBIOS and WINS problems, and offers a brief list of the types of problems you may encounter with WINS and NetBIOS.

Tools for Troubleshooting NetBIOS and WINS Problems

The tools that are useful for diagnosing and troubleshooting TCP/IP networks in general are also useful in maintaining NetBIOS and WINS services. PING is an excellent way to test connectivity, for example. TRACEROUTE and NETSTAT are also useful diagnostic tools. These are all dealt with in more detail elsewhere, however. This section looks more closely at three tools that are useful in troubleshooting name resolution problems.

NBTSTAT

NBTSTAT is a command-line program that returns statistics on NetBIOS, using NetBT if TCP/IP is installed on the machine from which it is run. NBTSTAT is available on all Windows NT and Windows 2000 servers and workstations. This is a simple tool that can give you instant feedback on the state of particular NetBIOS clients, and on NetBIOS name resolution in general. The -n argument returns a list of all the local NetBIOS names in a tabular form similar to Table 12-1. The -r argument returns a list of names resolved by broadcast and by WINS, and includes a summary count of name resolutions and registrations by each method. The -s argument returns the NetBIOS sessions table, showing open sessions with their destination IP address. The -S (uppercase "S") argument shows the same thing, but attempts to resolve the remote host name using the HOSTS file.

For a full list of the arguments and their syntaxes, type NBTSTAT with no argument at a command prompt.

NBTSTAT is a fast way to check the status of a particular NetBIOS host, or get a quick snapshot of NetBIOS name resolution activity on the local network segment. If, for example, a node appears to have trouble communicating with the WINS server, a quick check with NBTSTAT may show it is actually attempting to use broadcast name resolution.

WINS and DNS Consoles

The WINS Server Console and the DNS Server Console each offer some diagnostic tools for NetBIOS name resolution and registration problems. In the WINS Console, you can search for active registrants by name or by owner. Figure 12-7 shows how each was registered.

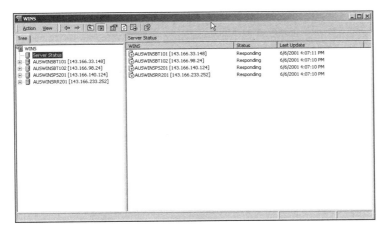

Figure 12-7   WINS servers view of the Windows 2000 Microsoft Management Console

The DNS Console in Windows 2000 is actually more geared to monitoring and system diagnostics than the WINS server. If you integrated WINS and DNS, you can use the DNS Performance Monitor to get a view of DNS statistics, including a fair set of WINS-specific traffic volume and utilization statistics. Remember that these are all reported in terms of the particular DNS server, not in terms of the WINS server itself. Unexpected values for any of these statistics, such as a high number of WINS lookups received and a low number of WINS responses sent, may indicate a problem, either with the servers, or with the configuration of some clients.

SNMP for WINS

WINS operating parameters, including details about server replication behavior and server performance, are stored in a Management Information Base (MIB). You can use a Simple Network Management Protocol (SNMP) manager to access this data for troubleshooting and performance monitoring.

Packet Analyzers

Programs like NetMon that capture network traffic and decode the packets are extremely useful network troubleshooting devices. More sophisticated versions, such as EtherPeek and Sniffer Pro, are even better because they can display statistics in a variety of ways, use filters, and even send user-configured test packets onto the network and monitor the results.

These programs allow you to check the packets themselves to see if they are properly formed. You can look inside the packets to see what information is being provided to each end of a request/response pair. You can even set triggers and alarms to capture traffic of a particular kind, at a particular time, or when a particular network event occurs. These are powerful and flexible tools. Packet analysis would be a very difficult and elusive problem without a first-rate packet analyzer like EtherPeek.

Typical Errors in NetBIOS and WINS

As just one example of the kinds of problems that are easy to solve with a packet analyzer, but quite troublesome without one, consider the following case:

An end node can correctly register its computer name, user names, and domain, but an application running on that end node that uses NetBIOS cannot seem to access network resources. The user is logged on correctly, and the resources the application is trying to access are shared to that user. Capturing several packets from that end node while it attempts to use the suspect application quickly clears up the mystery. The application program is attempting to access resources using the computer name instead of the current user name. The application is at fault (probably due to a slip by the programmer in not keeping variables straight—all too easy to do!).

Other typical errors in NetBIOS and WINS include:

- Misconfiguration of end nodes due to user error
- Incorrect network logon due to user error
- Wrong node type due to user error or misconfigured DHCP
- Timeouts set too low to allow for network latency
- Unwanted traffic due to misconfiguration of end nodes and/or servers, or client/server topology
- Malicious errors (intrusion, node masquerading, forced name releases)
- Unusual numbers of forced name releases due to incorrect end node shutdown
- Bogged-down servers due to incorrect configuration or topology

 Remember that most parameters set in the Registry will override DHCP.

Chapter Summary

- NetBIOS was the native Windows approach to networking, and is still woven deep into the Windows approach to sharing network resources. Whatever the theory or hope for the future, NetBIOS is still virtually indispensable in the Windows environment.

- NetBIOS and NetBEUI (NBF) are inherently non-routable. NetBIOS must be bound to a routable network protocol such as TCP/IP (as NetBT or NBT) to be used across network boundaries.

- A NetBIOS name can be resolved in three ways: look it up in a locally held list, ask the server (WINS, DNS, or Samba), or ask the whole local network segment (using a broadcast). For a small network with static addresses and stable names, a list works well. For larger networks or dynamic networks of any size, lists are impractical. Again, for smaller networks with all end nodes on a single segment or subnet, broadcast name resolution may work well. On larger networks, or networks requiring sharing across network boundaries, broadcasts do not work. That leaves resolution through a name server as the only viable choice for larger networks, or for networks spread across multiple subnets. The primary NetBIOS Name Server is WINS, but Microsoft's version of DNS can also use WINS to resolve NetBIOS names.

- Windows networking clients or end nodes can be configured to use one of four basic regimes of name registration and resolution. These are referred to as the "node type" for the end node. Very schematically, the choices are:

  - b-node uses broadcast only (default for Window 2000 clients without WINS enabled)

  - p-node uses (WINS) name servers only

  - m-node uses broadcast with (WINS) servers as a backup or auxiliary

  - h-node uses (WINS) servers with broadcast as a backup (default for Windows 2000 clients when WINS is enabled)

- WINS servers are like DNS servers designed to serve only the NetBIOS name space. When Microsoft's own DNS servers are configured to query WINS to resolve NetBIOS names, they begin to combine the best of both worlds. Remember, however, that MS DNS can only resolve NetBIOS names for the zone root. NetBIOS names only understand one network—this network.

12

Key Terms

Application Programming Interface (API) — A collection of tools, protocols, and programming code used in developing software applications that are consistent and compatible with the operating system.

Common Internet File System (CIFS) —A Microsoft proposal for a standard file access method for the Internet, based on NetBIOS and related native Microsoft operating system protocols and APIs. The actual method used is a protocol called SMB that makes use of NetBIOS.

datagram service — In NetBIOS, NetBEUI, or NBF, datagram service is a connectionless protocol used to send messages and responses. When these protocols run over TCP/IP (as NetBT), datagram services and name services use UDP (on UDP ports 138 and 137, respectively). When a more reliable connection is required, these protocols use TCP to provide session services.

dynamic link library (DLL) — A piece of executable code (or data) used by other Windows applications to perform a particular function or set of functions.

kernel — The central element of a computer operating system. When the operating system starts, the kernel begins running in main memory. It handles the most critical tasks.

LMHOSTS — A plain text file that lists NetBIOS names and their associated IP addresses. A LMHOSTS file is similar to a HOSTS file but includes features unique to NetBIOS.

Microsoft DNS (MS DNS) — Microsoft's implementation of the DNS standard that contains extensions that enable MS DNS servers to query WINS to resolve NetBIOS names. For reverse lookup in the *in.addr.arpa* domain, MS DNS servers can use WINS-R to return the NetBIOS names associated with an IP address.

NetBIOS Frame (NBF) — The successor to NetBEUI as the native NetBIOS transport protocol in Windows 2000.

Network Driver Interface Specification (NDIS) — Pieces of software (compliant with this specification) that make it possible for Transport layer processes to interact with NICs in a common way, despite differences in specific card design or NIC driver implementation.

Samba — A suite of Open Source applications that provides file and print sharing using SMB/CIFS (over NetBT) for a variety of operating systems, notably Linux and UNIX.

Server Message Block (SMB) —Both the name of a client/server file-sharing protocol developed by 3Com, IBM, and Microsoft, and the messages it uses. SMB protocol is an Application layer protocol that uses NBT in a Windows 2000 environment, or NetBEUI in an environment that includes older Windows operating systems. It can also run over IPX/SPX.

session service — In NetBIOS, NetBEUI, and NBF, a network resource may be a process running on a network-connected computer. To interact with these processes, these protocols use the session service for reliable connection-oriented network communications. In Windows 2000, when NBF is run over TCP/IP (as NetBT), TCP is used for establishing and maintaining session services.

Transport Driver Interface (TDI) — A Microsoft specification that governs how the upper layers of all network transport protocols are written. The Windows redirector and server bypass NetBIOS and use TDI directly, thus avoiding NetBIOS restrictions.

Wait Acknowledgment (WACK) — A response packet sent by WINS servers to acknowledge the receipt of a request without granting or denying it, but asking the client to wait. This prevents communications with a busy WINS server from timing out unnecessarily.

Windows Internet Name Service (WINS) — A server service in Windows NT Server and Windows 2000 Server that resolves NetBIOS names and addresses in much the same way that a DNS server does for IP host names.

workgroup — In Windows, a group of peers able to share files over the network. A workgroup is a less highly integrated grouping than a domain, and implies fewer centralized monitoring and control capabilities.

REVIEW QUESTIONS

1. Which feature was most important to the original developer of NetBIOS? (Choose all that apply.)

   a. robust internetworking architecture

   b. reliable delivery mechanisms

   c. permitting dissimilar systems to exchange data

   d. support for long-haul connections

   e. high performance

2. What is the name of the native NetBIOS transport protocol that ships with Windows 2000?

   a. NetBT

   b. NBF

   c. NetBOY

   d. NBT

3. Over which network operating system can NetBIOS data be transported? (Choose all that apply.)

   a. IEEE 802.3 (Ethernet)

   b. IPX/SPX

   c. TCP/IP

   d. IEEE 802.5 (token ring)

4. Which of the following organizations develops and maintains RFCs?

   a. ISO

   b. IANA

   c. IETF

   d. OSI

12

5. What does it mean when a document is published as an RFC?

   a. The RFC is a Standard.

   b. The RFC is an Open Source software document.

   c. Developers must follow the RFC's guidelines.

   d. Government contractors must follow the RFC's guidelines.

   e. The document is in the public domain.

   f. none of the above

6. NBT and NBF protocols can both be routed. True or false?

   a. True

   b. False

7. List in ascending order the layers of the OSI reference model that are served by NetBEUI.

   a. Application

   b. Data Link

   c. Network

   d. Physical

   e. Presentation

   f. Session

   g. Transport

8. Which term represents a type of NetBIOS traffic? (Choose all that apply.)

   a. datagram

   b. payload

   c. session

   d. nomination

9. Which protocol provides session services? (Choose all that apply.)

   a. UDP

   b. NetBT

   c. TCP

   d. NetBEUI

10. Which TCP port is assigned by the IANA for the use of NetBIOS? (Choose all that apply.)

   a. 135

   b. 136

   c. 137

   d. 138

   e. 139

11. How many characters are in a NetBIOS name?

    a. 8

    b. 16

    c. 32

    d. 64

12. When a NetBIOS name is encoded in a form that can be parsed by DNS, how many characters are used to create the resulting host name?

    a. 8

    b. 16

    c. 32

    d. 64

13. On any Windows operating system, NetBIOS is enabled by default. True or false?

    a. True

    b. False

14. What kind of NetBT packets are increased when a significant number of WINS clients on a network simply power down rather than shut down "gracefully" (with the Shut Down command)?

    a. Name Resolution Demands

    b. Negative Symbolic Name Responses

    c. Name Release Demands

    d. Shut-down Warning Demands

15. By default, what is the number of Name Registration Requests in the queue that triggers burst mode in a WINS server?

    a. 50

    b. 800

    c. 500

    d. 8000

16. When NetBT is enabled for an end node, that end node must be assigned a NetBIOS scope identifier, either in DHCP, or by directly editing the Registry. True or false?

    a. True

    b. False

17. The zone root DNS server for *frank.com* can use WINS to resolve which of the following addresses? (Choose all that apply.)

    a. frankofred.frank.com

    b. funk.frank.com

    c. frank.frank.frank.com

    d. frank.funk.frank.com

18. Reverse WINS lookup makes use of NBTSTAT commands. For what DNS domain is reverse WINS (WINS-R) enabled?

    a. any secondary child of the zone root

    b. in-addr.arpa

    c. in-ardor.napa

    d. frank.funk.frank.com

19. What networking scheme do RFCs 1001 and 1002 describe?

    a. NetBT

    b. NBF

    c. SNMP

    d. CIFS

20. WINS cannot be reliably queried over the Internet for NetBIOS name resolution. True or false?

    a. True

    b. False

21. Which NetBIOS node type does not use broadcasts for name resolution?

    a. h-node

    b. p-node

    c. b-node

    d. m-node

22. Which tool would you use to check a NetBIOS client on the local network, assuming TCP/IP is enabled on both your machine and the other? (Choose all that apply.)

    a. NSLOOKUP

    b. SNMP

    c. PING

    d. NBTSTAT

23. WINS proxies are used to register NetBIOS names for b-node clients. True or false?

   a. True

   b. False

24. For which operating system is WINS clients available? (Choose all that apply.)

   a. UNIX

   b. OS/2

   c. DOS

   d. Linux

25. How many bytes long is a NetBIOS suffix denoting the type of service?

   a. 1

   b. 2

   c. 4

   d. 16

HANDS-ON PROJECTS

The following Hands-on Projects assume that you are working in a Windows 2000 environment.

Project 12-1

To use NBTSTAT from the command prompt to query NetBT resources:

1. Click **Start**, point to **Programs**, point to **Accessories**, and then click **Command Prompt**. The Command Prompt window appears.

2. Type **nbtstat** on the command line, and press **Enter**. The NBTSTAT help screen scrolls by.

3. Use the scroll bar at the right of the Command Prompt window to scroll to the top of the NBTSTAT text. NBTSTAT lists a definition of its function, a schematic view of its syntax (showing the order in which arguments are to be included if more than one is included in a single instance), and the meaning and usage of each argument. Notice that these arguments are case sensitive—"-a" and "-A" are not the same argument and will produce different responses.

4. Scroll back down the Command Prompt window to the command prompt.

5. Type **nbtstat –c** on the command line, and press **Enter**. NBTSTAT displays a list of NetBIOS names and addresses found in the cache for this (the local) machine (see Figure 12-8).

12

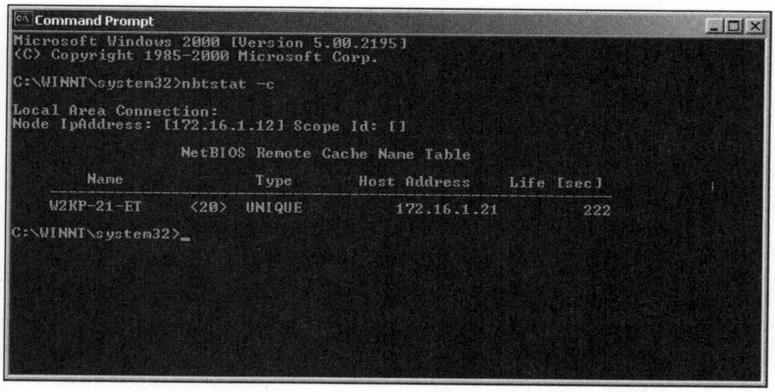

Figure 12-8 NBTSTAT -c command

6. Scroll through the NBTSTAT information and identify a name from the list of NetBIOS names presented to use in the next step. Scroll, if necessary, to bring the command prompt back into view.

7. On the command line, type **nbtstat -a** *remotename* (substituting the NetBIOS name you identified from the cache display a moment ago for *remotename*), and press **Enter** (see Figure 12-9). NBTSTAT displays a list of Net BIOS names returned by the *remotename* computer.

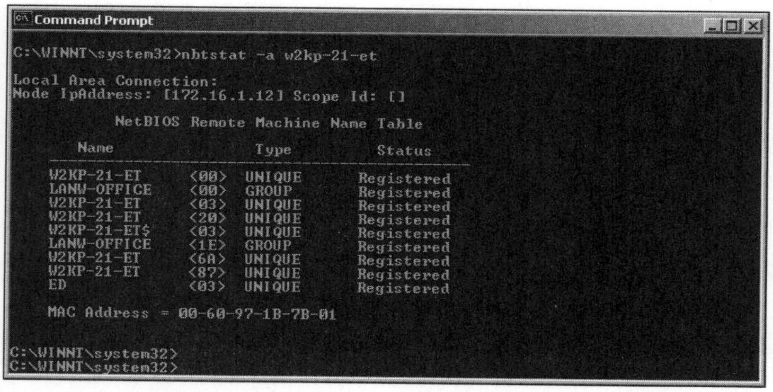

Figure 12-9 NBTSTAT -a command

8. Scroll, if necessary, to view all of the information presented in response to your last command. Scroll back down, if necessary, to bring the command prompt into view.

9. Close the Command Prompt window.

Project 12-2

To find the default location for the HOSTS and LMHOSTS files, and to read the information in the LMHOSTS.SAM sample file:

1. Click **Start**, point to **Programs**, point to **Accessories**, click **Windows Explorer**, and then double-click the drive on which the Windows 2000 operating system software is installed.

2. Navigate to the directory *<windows root>***system32\drivers\etc**.

3. In this subdirectory, you should find several files. Open the file named **HOSTS** by double-clicking it.

4. If a dialog box opens asking you which program to use to open this type of file, choose **Notepad** or any plain text editor. (Do not use WordPad or Microsoft Word.) Note that only the local host or loopback address 127.0.0.1 is active or uncommented in the Windows 2000 HOSTS file, by default.

5. When you are done reading the brief HOSTS file header, close the HOSTS file without saving any changes.

6. Open the **LMHOSTS.SAM** sample file, if it is present, or open the **LMHOSTS** file, if the sample file is not in this folder.

7. Read the introduction on the first page of the LMHOSTS file, taking note of the additional terms used to enable special LMHOSTS functions for NetBIOS, such as the #PRE keyword, used to load NetBIOS names into the NetBIOS name cache on system start-up.

8. When you finish browsing the LMHOSTS file or the sample file, close the file without saving any changes.

9. Close the text editor if it doesn't close automatically.

Project 12-3

To capture NetBT or NBF (NetBEUI) packets and examine their packet structures:

1. Follow the steps in Project 1-2 to launch the EtherPeek for Windows demo program.

2. Click the **Capture** menu, and click **Start Capture**.

3. The Capture Options window appears. Click **OK** to accept the defaults. The Capture window appears.

4. Click the **Start Capture** button in the Capture window. *Remember:* The Capture window is active only for 30 seconds in the demo. If you do not capture the traffic you want within 30 seconds, either open a new Capture window, or exit the EtherPeek for Windows demo and restart the program. The demo allows five capture windows to be started per program launch.

12

5. To generate traffic, double-click the **My Network Places** icon on the desktop, and double-click any network printer to generate session traffic. (There is no need to actually print—merely attempting to "browse" the printer will be enough to generate many packets.)

6. Press **Alt+Tab** to return to the EtherPeek demo.

7. The demo automatically stops capturing after 30 seconds. If the demo is still capturing, click the **Stop Capture** button to stop the capture process. Otherwise, click **OK** in the capture stopped notification dialog box.

8. Select the **Protocols** tab at the bottom of the Capture window.

9. Find the NetBIOS protocol in the hierarchical listing of protocols shown under "IEEE 802.3."

10. Click the boxed plus and minus signs to the left to expand or collapse the hierarchical view until you can select the entire NetBIOS protocol family, without including any neighboring protocols.

11. Right-click **NetBIOS**, choose **Select Related Packets**, and then choose **By Protocol**.

12. A dialog box opens stating how many individual packets were included in the selection. Click **Hide Unselected**. The Capture window immediately takes you to Packets view.

13. You should see only packets that EtherPeek interprets as belonging to the NetBIOS family of protocols.

14. Click any individual packet to remove the highlighting from the rest of the list.

15. Double-click any NetBIOS or related packet in Packets view to open the selected packet in the packet decode window. The larger, upper pane of the window contains the full decode of the packet contents, including an interpretation of many of the specific NetBIOS commands (encoded in the Flags sections of the packets), as well as those of SMB and related protocols. This decoding is done item by item, in order, from the front of the packet (the top of the pane) to the frame check sequence at the end (the bottom of the pane). The smaller window at the bottom contains two versions of the packet data—the hexadecimal contents of the packet on the left, and the raw ASCII interpretation of these hexadecimal values on the right.

16. Click the **Decode Prev** and **Decode Next** buttons to view other packets. Notice the level of detail in the contents of NetBIOS packets. NetBIOS and its related protocols attempt to keep track of many more parameters than does UDP, for example. Close the packet decode window (click the Close button in the upper-right corner of the current window) to return to Packets view.

17. Right-click one of the NetBIOS packets in Packets view, and click **Protocol Info**. An informational dialog box about the protocol identified in the selected packet appears.

18. Read the contents of the informational dialog box. NetBIOS has an extraordinarily large number of specific frame types, each dedicated to one particular function.

Over the years, many of these have been reused for newer functions. Others are there only for backward compatibility. The Protocol Info dialog box is particularly useful in analyzing NetBIOS traffic. When you finish reading the information, click **Close**.

19. When you finish examining the packet, leave the EtherPeek for Windows demo open and proceed immediately to the next project.

Project 12-4

This Hands-on Project assumes that you already have the EtherPeek for Windows demo program open, and that you captured some NetBT session traffic. You can repeat the steps outlined in Hands-on Project 12-3, if necessary.

To use EtherPeek to view NetBT session traffic:

1. If you hid some packets, unhide them now by clicking the **Edit** menu, and then clicking **Unhide All Packets**.

2. Open the Filters window (click the **Filters** tab).

3. Click the **Insert** button 🖼 to open the Edit Filter window.

4. Check the **Port filter** check box. This sets a filter that looks for a specific port number in all packets.

5. Enter **139** in the Port 1 text box, as this is the default port for NetBT session traffic.

6. In the Type field, select **TCP-UDP**, if necessary.

7. Click the **Port 1 to 2** button and choose **Both directions** to have this filter check for the specified port in either the source or the destination.

8. In the Filter text box, type **NetBIOS Sessions** to name this filter.

9. Click **OK** to create the filter and add it to all filter lists.

10. Click the **Packets** tab and make sure all packets are visible (not hidden).

11. Click the **Edit** menu, and then click **Select** to open the Select dialog box.

12. In the Selection Criteria section, click the **Matches one or more filters** option, if necessary.

13. Use the scroll bars at the right of this window to find the filter you just created, **NetBIOS Sessions**, and click the check box next to that entry.

14. In the *Select packets that* section, click **Match**, if necessary. In the *Current selection* section, choose **Replace**, if necessary.

15. Click the **Select Packets** button to select all packets in the current Capture window that are addressed to or from port 139, under either the UDP or the TCP protocol.

16. The Selection Results dialog box opens, showing you how many packets were selected. Click the **Hide Unselected** button. *Note*: If the Selection Results dialog

12

box says you have no packets selected, that means there were no visible packets in the active (front-most) Capture window that contained a reference to port 139. Check your work to make sure you are working in the correct Capture window (if you have more than one open), and that all packets are visible. If all is correct, repeat the steps in Hands-on Project 12-3 to capture packets containing NetBT session traffic. Click **Close** to close the Select dialog box.

17. In the Packets view of the Capture window, double-click the first packet to open it in a packet decode window.

18. Notice that the Ethernet header shows the MAC addresses of the source and destination, and the IP header shows their IP addresses. These can be important in looking at session traffic, but for present purposes, you can use the boxed plus and minus icons at the left to collapse these two headers, leaving the remaining headers fully expanded.

19. Notice the TCP header begins with the source and destination TCP ports. Port 139 is there (of course), identified by EtherPeek as "netbios-ssn" (for NetBIOS Session). The other port, however, may be any of a variety of unused ports. This can be confusing because EtherPeek (and other sources) associates these ports with names most people find totally unfamiliar, such as "iad2."

Many ports in the range above 1023 were formerly unassigned. Some protocols, notably NetBIOS, use these ports for temporary connections, such as NetBIOS or TCP sessions. Some of these ports are, in fact, assigned. EtherPeek, like most protocol analyzers, makes its port assignment identifications based on the lists published by (IANA). The ports may once have been assigned to a group working on advanced routing protocols, for example. Today, the port might not be used for that original purpose, but the port assignment still stands. The port assignment shown in EtherPeek packet decodes, or in RFCs, or even in the IANA's most recent publications, may have little to do with the actual traffic moving on that port inside your Windows network.

20. Notice the NetBIOS header section. This further identifies the contents as a NetBIOS session, but you are most likely to see that the actual contents of the session are some form of SMB transaction or message. SMB is closely related to NetBIOS in its origins. Claims to the contrary notwithstanding, the two are intimately intertwined.

21. Scroll to the bottom of the window and look for the payload of the packet, if present. This can be found in the Data sections, usually the last Data section in the packet.

22. Notice that the decode pane of the packet decode window lists these data items simply as "Data: (*some number of* bytes)."

23. Click this **Data** item. Look at the raw hex and ASCII sections at the bottom of the packet decode window. Scroll (if necessary) until you see the portion of each of these two additional views that is highlighted. This part of the packet is the "data." The highlights match in both panes.

24. Use the **Decode Next** and **Decode Prev** buttons at the bottom of the packet decode window to step through the unhidden packets, looking at the ASCII version of each payload data section.

25. Notice that although most of the raw decode is indecipherable, some key items are in plain text. You may see the names of NetBIOS resources, such as user or machine names, names of various services, or share names of disks or print services. These bits of information offer clues as to what resources NetBIOS and SMB are attempting to share, and how they are attempting to share them.

26. Keep in mind that an ordinary text editor capable (as most are) of displaying a binary file and its ASCII equivalent could read this part of the packet data just as well as EtherPeek or any other packet analyzer. This is another good reason to keep your local NetBIOS traffic safely behind a firewall on your local network, rather than sending it promiscuously across the public Internet. Sessions set up across a Virtual Private Network (VPN) are more secure than ordinary browsing or file accesses over NetBT alone.

27. When you finish examining the packets, leave the EtherPeek for Windows demo program open and proceed immediately to the next project.

Project 12-5

This project assumes that the EtherPeek for Windows demo program is open, and you automatically collected global statistics for the allowed five minutes from a network that has both NetBT and NBF enabled (the default configuration for Windows 2000 clients with WINS and TCP/IP enabled).

12

To use EtherPeek to view the range of NetBIOS packet types:

1. Open the Protocol Statistics window by clicking **Statistics** on the menu bar, and then clicking **Protocols**.

2. If you're capturing NetBIOS traffic in a Capture window, you can also look at the Protocols view of that Capture window (by clicking the **Protocols** tab at the bottom of the Capture window). Because the Capture sample is limited to 30 seconds or 250 packets, however, the global statistics should show more information.

3. Notice that there are two sets of protocols, ranged hierarchically under two headings: "IEEE 802.3" and "Ethernet Type 2." These are alternate implementations of Ethernet. If the hierarchies are not already fully expanded, select each top-level heading, in turn, and hold down the **Ctrl** key while clicking the right arrow to completely expand each hierarchy.

4. Notice that NetBIOS appears in two different places—once under each of these top-level headings. Under "IEEE 802.3," it appears as "NetBEUI/NetBIOS." Under "Ethernet Type 2," it appears under TCP (or UDP) within the IP protocol family as "NetBIOS." Where it appears under IEEE 802.3, it is what we referred to in this chapter as "NBF." The NetBIOS that appears under TCP/IP is what we referred to in this chapter as "NetBT."

The reason for the dual hierarchy in EtherPeek is that the protocol analyzer reads the packet data in sequence from the beginning to the end of each packet, and makes its protocol designations based directly on what it finds there. Older "Type 2" Ethernet implementations have a slightly different header format than the newer IEEE 802.3 version of Ethernet. Most Ethernet implementations of the TCP/IP protocol stack conform to the Type 2 Ethernet standard. In addition, the Type 2 Ethernet packets do not support the IEEE 802.2 LLC header, but 802.3 does. Recall that NBF, the NetBIOS native transport protocol, is encapsulated directly under the 802.2 LLC header.

5. Look at the variety of packet sub-types arranged under each of these versions of NetBIOS. Recall that this represents only five minutes of traffic.

6. Use the Protocol Statistics window to help you calculate how many NetBIOS packets of both types are present in the five-minute sample. Collapse each NetBIOS protocol display so that only the top level ("NetBEUI/NetBIOS" or "NetBIOS") is visible. The statistics for all sub-protocols are rolled up into this top-level heading when the view is collapsed in this way. (When the view is expanded so that all the sub-protocols are displayed, the Bytes and Packets values for a top-level heading represent only those packets that could not be assigned to any underlying sub-protocols.)

7. Open the Node Statistics window by clicking **Statistics** on the menu bar, and then clicking **Nodes** to find the number of active nodes, but be careful—this window counts each MAC address found in network traffic as a node. This can include broadcast addresses and multiple addresses for multi-homed machines, plus firewalls and routers.

8. Make a rough calculation of the number of packets per second per active NetBIOS end node on the local network segment.

9. Multiply the result by 100 active nodes. This is why people say NetBIOS is a "chatty" protocol. Five minutes may not have been enough to show it in its full operation, but NetBIOS has a strong built-in bias that "more information, more often, is always better." Imagine that level of activity going over your dial-up WAN connection. This is why network administrators are careful to set up their networks to limit, or even completely suppress, NetBIOS traffic outside the local network segment.

10. Close the EtherPeek for Windows demo.

CASE PROJECTS

1. Your company's main office is in Denver, with a branch office in San Leandro, CA. The California branch was only a three-person outpost for almost a year. You just added another 20 employees and workstations, which are now served by a

local WINS server, with a WINS server in Denver as the secondary. All the users, both in Denver and San Leandro, are in the same domain. The San Leandro server is configured as a pull partner to the server in Denver. There is little need to share dynamic resources between the two offices so you set the pull interval high (30 minutes). The two offices communicate over TCP/IP Internet connections through their local ISPs. While you wait for the DSL upgrade, the San Leandro office still connects over the same ISDN line used by the previous (much smaller) staff. When the June bill for ISDN arrives, you realize something is terribly wrong—the bill skyrocketed. You expected it to be much higher than before, but the ISDN line must be up nearly 24 hours a day. There are seldom more than one or two people in the office between 8:00 p.m. and 6:00 a.m. You check the logs, and it's not HTTP or FTP traffic (at least not the bulk of it). What do you check next? What do you think the problem might be? How do you check?

2. You hit the big time and sold your 60-person operation to Gigundo Corp. for a tidy sum. While you idle about waiting to collect, your new partners come to you with the mildly shocking news that they sold your domain name (for a third-round draft pick and an unspecified number of AOL CDs). They want to fold your small operation into their network, but they want to do it along Gigundo departmental lines. They have only 14 subdomains on their network, corresponding to their somewhat old-fashioned and very hierarchical internal organization. They are an all-UNIX shop, except for the Sales Department, which is composed mostly of older Windows clients. Your shop is a mix of Windows NT 4.0, Windows 98, and Windows 2000, all on Windows 2000 DNS servers configured to use your WINS servers for NetBIOS resolution. As you ask yourself philosophically, "Well, who else would have paid that much for us?" you search for the right way to tell them their idea is not really the best approach. Why do you think that? What is a better approach? Your old domain name is gone, and you must integrate more closely with the rest of Gigundo. Politics aside, what are the best alternate ways to proceed to integrate your shop with theirs? What are the operational advantages and pitfalls of the alternatives?

3. When the six-person field sales force moved back under the same roof with Engineering, you simply reconfigured their workstations for DHCP, and set them up to be automatically added to the WINS server (running in the same physical box as the DHCP server). When Sales complained that they weren't able to reach network resources, you captured some traffic from their machines and found they were all misconfigured, as if DHCP had handed out the wrong configuration information to every one of them. You checked the DHCP server and confirmed that the configuration is sound. Then you realized what it must be—the Sales employees brought their machines with them from the temporary offices they occupied for the last three months. You had to go to each machine to quickly resolve the problem. What was it? How did you solve it?

12

4. Your friend has a small design shop with all Windows NT 4.0 and Windows 2000 workstations. He has one older Windows NT computer acting as a file server, and a Linux computer running as a firewall on the DSL line. Previous to the Windows NT/2000 network, your friend's shop used what he assumed was the default Windows networking scheme—NetBIOS over NetBEUI. Now a new client wants your friend's shop to log onto its WINS server so they can share resources more directly. With security in mind, what do you tell your friend to do? Why? What are his (and his client's) alternatives?

13

INTERNET PROTOCOL VERSION 6 (IPv6)

After reading this chapter and completing the exercises you will be able to:

♦ Understand the limitations of IPv4 and how IPv6 can overcome them

♦ Understand the structure and capabilities of the new IPv6 address space, and how it is used

♦ Understand the coexistence of IPv6 and IPv4, and how to use both versions simultaneously during the long transition from IPv4 to IPv6

♦ Plan an effective introduction of IPv6 on your networks

This chapter introduces the new version of IP, sometimes called **Internet Protocol next generation (IPng)**, or more commonly, Internet Protocol version 6 (IPv6). This chapter describes what prompted the introduction of a new Internet protocol and the new IPv6 address space, as well as the new IPv6 features for routing, Quality of Service (QoS), autoconfiguration, mobile users, and security. The chapter ends with a brief discussion of alternate strategies for the gradual introduction of IPv6.

Note that IPv6 is still very much a work in progress. While you may consider many of the basic frameworks, such as addressing and the use of the address space, stable, many other features, such as support for security, autoconfiguration, QoS, and mobile users, are still under discussion. This chapter presents the best information available at the time of writing, but considers only RFCs published before May 2001. This effort to present IPv6 gives you an excellent opportunity to observe the RFC process at work, especially if you investigate the current state of the RFCs we mention in this chapter, and take the time to identify new IPv6-related RFCs as well.

WHY CREATE A NEW VERSION OF IP?

IPv4 is clearly one of the most successful network protocols ever designed. Because IP packet-switched networking is robust, scalable, and relatively simple, it has rapidly become the standard of choice for computer networking. In terms of connected devices, only the largest national telephone networks and the global telephone network as a whole are larger than the Internet. So why change something that obviously works very well? Good question!

You could say that IPv4 is a victim of its own success. The IPv4 address space, at 32 bits, allows the creation of some four billion unique IP addresses. At the time IPv4 was created, that amounted to nearly two addresses for every human on the planet.

Because of the classful, or hierarchical, way in which IP addresses were originally allocated and structured, the **usable address space**—the number of hosts that could actually be connected to the Internet—was much smaller than the theoretical maximum. Without some form of hierarchy, however, routing would become impossible. Each new connection would require looking up the one address you wanted among four billion possible addresses. With a hierarchical namespace, only a relatively small part of any address is relevant to the routing decision that is made at any particular hop in a path between a sender and a receiver.

The shortage of IP addresses has eased somewhat due to Classless Inter-Domain Routing (CIDR) notation and the resulting changes in address allocation. Network Address Translation (NAT), combined with the blocks of addresses set aside for "private" IP addresses in RFC 1918 (addresses which are not to be routed over the Internet itself), has also helped. Dynamic Host Configuration Protocol (DHCP), which allows a block of addresses to be shared among a (potentially larger) group of hosts, has also helped ease the shortage of IP addresses. Although each of these adaptations contributed to resolving the problem, not all of them combined could stem the tide forever.

The Internet engineering community recognized these and related problems in the early 1990s and began developing solutions. The result of their combined efforts over many years of experiment and discussion is IPv6. Although the address shortage is and always has been the driving consideration in the upgrade from IPv4 to IPv6, many other problems and opportunities were tackled at the same time. IPv6 includes important changes in the way IP handles security, autoconfiguration, and QoS, and it improves the efficiency of routing and the handling of mobile users. After all, if you intend to revise a communications environment as complex and important as IP, you might as well make it an across-the-board improvement!

Much of this chapter describes the basic shape of IPv6 in three key areas: address space, routing considerations, and the new IPv6 packet structure. It then describes new or enhanced features of IPv6 in the areas of autoconfiguration of hosts, security, QoS, and support for mobile users. The chapter ends with a brief look at the techniques required to smoothly introduce IPv6 in a world still dominated by, and dependent on, IPv4.

THE IPv6 ADDRESS SPACE

By far, the most critical shortcoming of IPv4 is its lack of universally valid IP addresses. Users at fixed sites in North America and, to a lesser extent, in Western Europe can use any number of work-arounds to maintain connectivity. However, the address shortage severely constrains continued rapid growth throughout the rest of the world, as well as the addition of mobile users and the proliferation of truly Internet-connected local networks in homes and small offices. The address crunch is literally choking further development of the Internet and a vast number of technologies poised to take advantage of the promise of universal connectivity.

IPv6 solves this problem by creating an address space that's more than 20 orders of magnitude larger than IPv4's address space. Routing in such a large space would be impossible without some notion of hierarchy. The IPv6 address space provides hierarchy in a flexible and well-articulated fashion with plenty of room for future growth.

Address Format and Allocations

IPv6 addresses are 128 bits long. An IPv6 address may be viewed as a string that uniquely identifies one single network interface on the global Internet. Alternately, that string of 128 bits can be understood as an address with a network portion and a host portion. How much of the address belongs to either portion depends on who's looking at it, and where they are located in relation to the host with that address. If an entity is on the same subnet as the host, it shares a large part of the address with it, and only the last part of the address must be evaluated to uniquely identify a particular host. If the entity doing the evaluation is near a backbone, and the address is for a host near the edge of the Internet, only a small part at the beginning of the address is needed to send a packet on its way toward the host.

Address Format and Notation

Addresses in both versions of IP are actually binary numbers. That is, they are strings of ones and zeroes representing bits turned on or off. IPv6 addresses are 128 bits long and IPv4 addresses are 32 bits long. When they are written down, IPv6 addresses are expressed using hexadecimal notation (00-FF), unlike IPv4 addresses, which are usually expressed using decimal notation (0-255). Because IPv6 addresses are much longer than IPv4 addresses, they are broken up differently. Instead of four 8-bit numbers expressed as decimals and separated by dots or periods, IPv6 uses eight 16-bit numbers separated by the colon character (:). Both of the following strings represent valid IPv6 network addresses:

```
FEDC:BA45:1234:3245:E54E:A101:1234:ABCD
1018:FD0C:0:9:90:900:10BB:A
```

Because of the way in which IPv6 addresses are structured and allocated, there are often many zeroes in such an address, but, just as in IPv4, there is no need to show leading zeroes. IPv6 allows a special notation that means "fill out this portion of the address with enough 16-bit sets of zeroes to make the whole address 128 bits long." Use this notation where several contiguous 16-bit sections of an address are all zeroes. For example, you could express the following IPv6 address:

```
1090:0000:0000:0000:0009:0900:210D:325F
```

as

```
1090::9:900:210D:325F
```

The adjacent pair of colon characters (**::**) stands for the number of contiguous 16-bit groups of zeroes needed to make this address a proper 128-bit IPv6 address. You can use this kind of notation only once in any address; otherwise, it would be impossible to determine how many sets of ":0000:" you should add where!

Network and Host Address Portions

To represent a network prefix in IPv6, you may also use a type of notation familiar from CIDR, as used in IPv4. You can use "/decimal number" after an address, where the decimal number after the slash shows how many of the leftmost contiguous bits of the address are a part of the network prefix. For example:

```
1090::9:900:210D:325F / 60
1018:FD0C:0:9:90:900:10BB:A / 24
```

The following describes just the subnet portion of the above addresses:

```
1090:: / 60
1018:FD00 / 24
```

Trailing zeroes from the representation of a single 16-bit group cannot be omitted. If there are less than four (hexadecimal) digits in a 16-bit group, the missing digits are assumed to be leading zeroes. In IPv6 address notation ":A:", for example, always expands to ":000A:", never to something like ":00A0:" or ":A000:".

Scope Identifier

Multicast addresses in IPv6 use a 4-bit **scope identifier** to define the portion of the Internet over which the multicast group is valid. This is discussed in detail in the section titled "Multicast Addresses" later in this chapter.

Interface Identifiers

With one important exception, IPv6 requires that every network interface have its own unique identifier. Thus, whether the node itself is a workstation, a laptop, a cell phone, a car, or a toaster, each single interface within each device must have its own unique

interface identifier. The caveat is that in the restricted case, where a host with multiple interfaces can perform dynamic load balancing across all those interfaces, all such interfaces may share a single identifier.

IPv6 further specifies that these interface identifiers follow the IEEE **EUI-64 format**. For Ethernet networks, the IPv6 interface identifier is based directly on the MAC address of the NIC. The MAC address of an Ethernet NIC is a 48-bit number expressly designed to be globally unique. The first 24 bits represent the name of the card's manufacturer, and within that name, perhaps the individual production run. The second 24 bits are chosen by the manufacturer to ensure uniqueness among its own cards. All that is required to create a unique interface identifier in this case is padding the number. The IEEE EUI-64 format adds the 16 bits (0xFFFE) between the two halves of the MAC address to achieve a unique 64-bit number.

Not all interfaces have this kind of globally unique identifier built in. Serial connections, or the ends of IP tunnels, for example, also must be identified uniquely within their contexts. These interfaces may have their identifiers configured by random number generation, may be configured by hand, or may use some other method.

To prepare for a day when globally unique identifiers (as opposed to locally unique ones) may have special importance, IPv6 requires that bits five and six of the first octet of the EUI-64 format interface identifier be set as outlined in Table 13-1.

Table 13-1   Global/Local and Individual/Group Bits in the IPv6 Interface ID

Bit 5	Bit 6	Meaning
0	0	Locally unique, individual
0	1	Locally unique, group
1	0	Globally unique, individual
1	1	Globally unique, group

13

Not coincidentally, this allows administrators to create locally unique individual interface identifiers in the following form:

```
::3
::D4
```

The precise techniques used to create unique interface identifiers are specified for each type of network: Ethernet, token ring, FDDI, and so forth.

In April 2001, Sony announced that all of its products would henceforth be manufactured with "built-in IP addresses." Presumably, this means Sony intends to embed a serial number of some sort that could be used to generate a unique interface identifier for every individual device it manufactures. With some 18 billion billion possible combinations, a 64-bit identifier allows plenty of room to grow.

To meet concerns about privacy and long-term security, RFC 3041 proposes methods for changing an interface's unique identifier over time, particularly when it is derived from the MAC address of the interface card. This is proposed as an optional approach to generating a unique interface identifier for those concerned with the security implications of having their identity defined with certainty, presumably through unauthorized traffic analysis.

IPv6 Addresses That Contain IPv4 Addresses

To ease the introduction of IPv6 and allow both versions of IP to coexist, the IETF defined two types of IPv6 addresses that contain IPv4 addresses within them. These are known as the **IPv4–compatible address** and the **IPv4–mapped address**. The first 80 bits of both types are set to all zeros. The last 32 bits of each contain the IPv4 address, which can be expressed in the ordinary way for IPv4 addresses (four dotted decimal numbers). The 16 bits immediately preceding the IPv4 address are set differently to distinguish between the two types of IPv6 addresses. In an IPv4-compatible IPv6 address, these 16 bits are set to all zeroes (0x0000). In an IPv4-mapped IPv6 address, the 16 bits immediately preceding the IPv4 address are set to all ones (0xFFFF).

Nodes that need to tunnel IPv6 packets through IPv4 routers use the IPv4-compatible addresses. These are called dual stack nodes. That is, they understand both IPv4 and IPv6. IPv6 nodes that need to communicate with IPv4 nodes that do not understand IPv6 at all use the IPv4-mapped addresses.

A Proposal for Native IPv6 Addresses in URLs

A recent IETF draft proposed a method for expressing IPv6 addresses in a form compatible with HTTP URLs. Because the colon character (:) is used by most browsers to set off a port number from an IPv4 address, native IPv6 addresses in their ordinary notation would cause problems. The proposal is to use another pair of reserved characters, the square brackets ([and]), to enclose the IPv6 address. The draft suggests that these square bracket characters be reserved in URLs exclusively for expressing IPv6 addresses.

Address Types

IPv6 allows only a few address types, and it sets up those types to allow maximum throughput of ordinary traffic on the now much larger Internet. In a sense, the old IPv4 classful address structure was designed as much for ease of human understanding as it was for machine usability. The new IPv6 address types take advantage of years of experience with routing across large hierarchical domains to streamline the whole operation. The IPv6 address space is optimized for routing.

Special Addresses

A few individual addresses are reserved for special use. These are the so-called unspecified address and the loopback address. The **unspecified address** is all zeroes and can be represented as two colon characters (::) in normal notation. This is essentially the address that is no address. It cannot be used as a destination address. Thus far, the only proposed use for the unspecified address is for nodes that do not yet know their own addresses, but must send a message upon machine start-up. Such a node might, for example, send a message asking attached routers on the local link to announce their addresses, thereby allowing the new node to understand where it is.

The loopback address is all zeroes except for the very last bit, which is set to one. It can be represented as two colon characters and a one (::1) in ordinary notation. The loopback address is simply a diagnostic tool, and cannot be routed or used as either a source or destination address for packets sent onto the local network. When a packet is sent with the loopback address as its destination, it means the IPv6 stack on the sending host simply sent the message to itself, down through the stack and then back up without ever going out to the local link. Such behavior is important to make sure that a device's IP stack was properly installed and configured. (Think of it this way: A device that can't "talk to itself" surely can't talk to other devices either.)

In IPv4, an entire Class A network, 127.x.x.x, was dedicated to the loopback function, removing millions of addresses from the available pool. This is a small but clear example of the way in which actual use guided the design improvements built into IPv6.

No More Broadcasts

Another result of actual use experience is the abandonment of the broadcast address in IPv6. Broadcasts are extremely expensive in terms of bandwidth and routing resources. In IPv6, any functions once handled by a broadcast in IPv4 can be replicated with a multicast. The key distinction between the two versions is that nodes must subscribe to multicasts. In addition, multicasts are easier to control and route effectively in IPv6, in part due to the new Scope field and other address and routing features, as described below.

Multicast Addresses

Multicast addresses in IPv6 are used to send an identical message to multiple hosts. On a local Ethernet, hosts can listen for traffic addressed to multicasts to which they subscribe. On other types of networks, multicast traffic must be handled in a different way, sometimes by a dedicated server that forwards multicasts to each individual subscriber.

The whole point of multicast is that it is subscription based. Nodes must announce that they wish to receive multicast traffic bound for a particular multicast address. For multicast traffic originating off the local link, the connecting router(s) must subscribe to the same multicast traffic on behalf of connected nodes.

13

Multicast addresses follow the format shown in Figure 13-1. The first byte is set to all ones (0xFF), indicating a multicast address. The second byte is divided into two fields. The Flags field is four bits long and is followed by a Scope field, which is also four bits long. The remaining 112 bits define the identifier for the multicast group.

8	4	4	112 bits
11111111	FLAGS	SCOPE	GROUP ID

Figure 13-1   IPv6 multicast address format

The Flags field is treated as a set of individual 1-bit flags. No meaning has yet been assigned to the first three (leftmost) flags. They are reserved for future use and must all be set to zero. The last (rightmost) flag is set to one when the multicast address is a temporary or transient address. If the address is a well-known multicast address, this flag is set to zero.

As you can imagine, the entire Internet could easily be brought to its knees without some way to limit the range over which multicast traffic is forwarded. The Scope field of the multicast address limits the range of addresses over which the multicast subscriber group is valid. Possible values for the Scope field are shown in Table 13-2.

Table 13-2   IPv6 Multicast Address Scope Field Values

Hex	Decimal	Scope Assignment
0	0	Reserved
1	1	Interface-local scope
2	2	Link-local scope
3	3	Draft reserves for subnet-local
4	4	Draft proposes admin-local
5	5	Site-local scope
6	6	Unassigned
7	7	Unassigned
8	8	Organization-local scope
9	9	Unassigned
A	10	Unassigned
B	11	Unassigned
C	12	Unassigned
D	13	Unassigned
E	14	Global scope
F	15	Reserved

Transient or temporary multicast addresses are established for some particular temporary purpose, and then abandoned. This is analogous to the way in which TCP might use an unassigned port for a temporary session. The Group ID of a temporary multicast address is meaningless outside its own scope. That is, two groups with identical Group IDs, but different scopes, are completely unrelated when the "T" flag is set to one. In contrast, well-known Group IDs (where the T bit is set to zero) are assigned to such entities as all routers or all DHCP servers. In combination with the Scope field, this allows a multicast address to define all routers on the local link or all DHCP servers on the global internet.

Although the last 112 bits of the multicast address are assigned to the Group ID, the first 80 bits are set to all zeroes for all multicast addresses currently defined or planned for the future. The remaining (rightmost) 32 bits of address space must contain the whole non-zero part of the Group ID. With over four billion possible Group IDs, this should be sufficient for all foreseeable purposes.

A special type of multicast address called the solicited node address is used to support Neighbor Solicitation (NS). The structure of this address and the method used to create it are described later in this chapter.

Anycast Addresses

IPv6 introduces a new type of address called an anycast address. Packets addressed to an anycast address go to the nearest single instance of that address. "Near" in this case is defined in terms of a router's view of network distance. The anycast address is used to address functions that are commonly deployed on the Internet at multiple network locations. Examples include routers, DHCP servers, and the like. Rather than using a multicast address to send a packet to all NTP servers on the local link, a node can send a packet to the anycast address for all NTP servers and be assured that the packet will be delivered to the nearest server with that anycast address.

An anycast address takes the same format as a unicast address, and is indistinguishable from a unicast address. Each server or node wishing to receive anycast traffic must be configured to listen for traffic sent to that address.

RFC 2373 requires all subnets to support the subnet router anycast address. Likewise, all routers on a given subnet must support the subnet router anycast address. The format of the subnet router anycast address is the subnet prefix followed by all zeroes. In other words, the subnet prefix takes as many bytes or bits as are required to precisely identify the subnet that the routers serve. Their anycast address is that subnet prefix padded to the right with enough zeroes to make up 128 bits. The subnet router anycast address is intended for use, for example, by mobile users seeking to communicate with any router on their home networks.

RFC 2526 proposes that the highest 128 interface ID values in each subnet be reserved for assignment to subnet anycast addresses. This means the 64-bit interface ID portion of these addresses would be all ones, except for the Global/Local bit, which must be set to zero (local), and the last seven binary digits, which form the anycast ID. The only particular anycast assignment suggested in this RFC is for the Mobile IPv6 home agent servers, which are to be assigned an anycast ID of 126 (decimal) or 0xFE. All other anycast IDs are reserved.

Unicast Addresses

The unicast address, as its name implies, is sent to one network interface. It can be thought of as the basic or ordinary address in the IPv6 address space. The format follows the one described earlier, a 64-bit interface ID in the least significant bits, and a 64-bit network portion of the address in the most significant bits. (If *n* is a symbol for a 16-bit number in the networking portion, and *h* is a symbol for a 16-bit number in the host portion, such an IPv6 address takes the general form *n:n:n:n:h:h:h:h*).

Aggregatable Global Unicast Addresses

To aid in routing and the administration of addresses, IPv6 creates a particular kind of unicast address called the **aggregatable global unicast address**. The layout of such addresses breaks the leftmost 64 bits of the address (the network portion) into explicit fields to allow for easier routing. Specifically, it allows routes to these addresses to be "aggregated," that is, combined into a single entry in the router table. The format of an aggregatable global unicast address is shown in Figure 13-2.

3	13	8	24	16	64 bits
FP	TLA ID	RES	NLA ID	SLA ID	INTERFACE ID

Figure 13-2   Aggregatable global unicast address format

The FP or Format Prefix field is a 3-bit identifier used to show to which part of the IPv6 address space this address belongs. At this writing, all aggregatable addresses must have 001 (binary) in this field.

The TLA ID or Top-level Aggregation ID field is 13 bits long and allows 2^{13} top-level routes, or some 8000 highest-level groups of addresses.

The next field, marked "RES," is eight bits long and is reserved for future use.

The NLA ID or Next-level Aggregation ID field is 24 bits long. This field allows the entities controlling any one of the TLAs to divide their address blocks into whatever size blocks they wish. These entities are likely to be large ISPs, or other very large Internet entities. They can share some of this address space with others. They might reserve only half of these bits for themselves, for example, allowing smaller ISPs to allocate very large blocks of addresses. The smaller ISPs could then subdivide these blocks further, if there were enough space in the NLA field to permit them to do so.

The SLA ID or Site-level Aggregation ID field is 16 bits long and permits the creation of 65,535 addresses as a flat address space. Alternately, users could set it up hierarchically and use this portion of the address to create 255 subnets with 255 addresses each. As the name implies, it is anticipated that individual sites will be allocated an address block of this size.

The Interface ID field is the same EUI-64 format interface identifier described in the earlier section.

Link-Local and Site-Local Addresses

Another example of the ways in which IPv6 builds on the experience of IPv4 is the creation of link-local and site-local addresses. Similar to the 10.x.x.x or 192.68.x.x addresses of IPv4, these private addresses are not to be routed outside their own areas, but use the same general 128-bit address length and the same interface ID format as any other unicast address. The formats for each of these address types are shown in Figure 13-3.

IPv6 Link-Local Address Format

10 bits	54 bits	64 bits
1111111010	0	INTERFACE ID

IPv6 Site-Local Address Format

10 bits	38 bits	16 bits	64 bits
1111111011	0	SUBNET ID	INTERFACE ID

Figure 13-3   IPv6 link-local and site-local address formats

The **link-local address** has its first 10 (leftmost) bits set to 1111111010 (all ones except for the last three digits, which are set to 010 [binary]). The next 54 bits are set to all zeroes. The final (rightmost) 64 bits of the link-local address represent a normal interface ID. When a router sees a link-local address prefix in a packet, it knows it can safely ignore it, as that packet is intended only for the local network segment.

The **site-local address** has its first 10 (leftmost) bits set to 1111111011 (all ones except for the last three digits, which are set to 011 [binary]). The next 38 bits are set to all zeroes, and the next 16 bits after that contain the subnet ID that defines the "site" to which this address is local. As in other unicast type addresses, the final (rightmost) 64 bits represent a standard interface ID. Site-local addresses allow packets to be forwarded internally within a site, but prevent such packets from being visible across the global Internet.

Site-local and link-local addresses are each assigned 1/1024 part of the IPv6 address space (according to RFC 2373), as shown in Table 13-3.

Table 13-3   IPv6 Address Space Allocations

Allocation	Prefix (binary)	Fraction of Address Space
Reserved	0000 0000	1/256
Unassigned	0000 0001	1/256
Reserved for NSAP Allocation	0000 001	1/128
Reserved for IPX Allocation (draft proposes returning to unassigned)	0000 010	1/128
Unassigned	0000 011	1/128
Unassigned	0000 1	1/32
Unassigned	0001	1/16
Aggregatable Global Unicast Addresses	001	1/8
Unassigned	010	1/8
Unassigned	011	1/8
Unassigned	100	1/8
Unassigned	101	1/8
Unassigned	110	1/8
Unassigned	1110	1/16
Unassigned	1111 0	1/32
Unassigned	1111 10	1/64
Unassigned	1111 110	1/128
Unassigned	1111 1110 0	1/512
Link-Local Unicast Addresses	1111 1110 10	1/1024
Site-Local Unicast Addresses	1111 1110 11	1/1024
Multicast Addresses	1111 1111	1/256

Address Allocations

The raw address space available in a 128-bit numbering scheme is truly vast, on the order of 3.4×10^{38} unique values. Even with careful adherence to hierarchical addressing, reservations for special purpose addresses, and additional reservations mentioned further in this section, IPv6 still pre-allocates only about 15% of the available addresses. That leaves at least 2.89×10^{38} addresses available for other uses!

Special addresses, such as the loopback address, the unspecified address, and IPv6 addresses that contain IPv4 addresses, are all taken from the Reserved category shown in Table 13-3, the group of addresses beginning with "0000 0000" (binary).

Multicast Allocations

Multicast is allocated all the IPv6 addresses beginning with 0xFF, as shown in Table 13-3. This constitutes 1/256 of the available address space. The maximum possible number of multicast addresses is further constrained by the requirement that the Group ID be contained in the last (rightmost) 32 bits of the address. This still leaves room for over four billion well-known multicast addresses, as well as a far larger number of usable transient multicast addresses.

Unicast and Anycast Allocations

As the name implies, the routes to addresses taken from the aggregatable global unicast address blocks can easily be aggregated together. Various schemes have been advanced for allocating IPv6 addresses. The current scheme is to assign address blocks to "exchanges," which then make further distributions. This sidesteps the issue rather than actually resolving the objections raised to earlier proposals for separate blocks to be assigned by "Providers" and on a geographic basis (physical location of the hosts involved).

RFC 2373 notes that all addresses beginning with 001 through 111 (except the multicast addresses, which begin with 1111 1111, binary) must have a 64-bit interface identifier as the least significant (rightmost) portion. This entire section of addresses, though mostly still unallocated, is clearly intended to serve individual devices.

NSAP Allocation

As shown in Table 13-3, 1/128 of all the IPv6 address space was set aside for addresses using **Network Service Access Point (NSAP)** type addressing. These networks (such as ATM, X.25, and so forth) typically set up point-to-point links between hosts. This is a very different paradigm from the one built into IP. For this reason, it is still unclear whether such networks will want to map IPv6 addresses to their own addressing schemes, map their own quite different addresses into IPv6, or follow some other approach to integrating IP. In any case, a large block of addresses is assigned for such uses.

IPX Allocation

The Novell IPX network addressing scheme was also allocated a significant block of addresses in RFC 2373, as shown in Table 13-3. At that time (July 1998), the draft definition of the addresses in this block was still under study. The latest version of the Novell Netware product available at this writing, Netware 5, uses IP rather than IPX as its default network protocol. Although no formal standard has yet been adopted, the most recent drafts call for eliminating the explicit allocation for IPX, and returning this block of addresses to the Unassigned category.

ROUTING CONSIDERATIONS

How will routers change under IPv6? The short answer is, not much. This seems surprising until you realize that IPv6 was designed in very large part to solve the routing problems encountered during the most explosive growth of the IPv4 Internet. IPv6 was designed from the ground up with routing efficiency and throughput in mind.

The structure of aggregatable global unicast addresses virtually builds the advantages of CIDR into the protocol's native address space. The IPv6 header, the option headers, and the way in which they all fit together to form an IPv6 packet are all designed to optimize router performance.

Many of the same routing approaches familiar to IPv4, such as RIP, BGP-4, and OSPF, make the transition to IPv6 with only minor changes. In many ways, the most important upgrades to these protocols are new provisions for the much longer IPv6 addresses.

From top to bottom and side to side, IPv6 is designed to reduce the workload of Internet routers. Experience with IPv4 has shown that there are significant advantages for routing when the address space matches the actual network topology. The allocation schemes for IPv6 addresses attempted to build in as much of this aggregatability as possible without unduly "tyrannizing" users. As the debate stands today, it seems that occasional network renumbering may be the price to pay for efficient routing, particularly over the vast new address space provided by IPv6. IPv6 support for autoconfiguration takes some of the sting out of this requirement. Another effort to reduce network administration costs is the way in which nodes "discover" their own environments, as discussed in the following section.

Neighbor Discovery and Router Advertisement

IPv6 **Neighbor Discovery (ND)** protocol, specified in RFC 2461, provides mechanisms for nodes to find out on what link they are located, what the subnet prefix is, where the link's working routers are, who their neighbors are, which of them are active, and for all of these cases, to associate the link layer address (such as an Ethernet MAC address) with the IPv6 address. ND also provides information about how nodes should configure themselves on start-up.

To accomplish these and related goals, ND uses five new ICMP message types:

- *Router Solicitation (RS):* When an interface becomes active, a node may send a **Router Solicitation (RS)**, asking any routers connected to the local link to identify themselves by sending their Router Advertisements immediately (rather than waiting for the next scheduled advertisement).

- *Router Advertisement (RA)*: Routers periodically, or on request, send out messages that contain at least one and possibly more of their own link layer addresses, the network prefix of the local subnet, the Maximum Transmission Unit (MTU) for the local link, suggested hop limit values, and other parameters useful for nodes on the local link. **Router Advertisements (RAs)** can also contain flagged parameters indicating what type of autoconfiguration new nodes should use.

- *Neighbor Solicitation (NS)*: A node can send a **Neighbor Solicitation (NS)** to find (or verify) the link layer address of a local node, see if that node is still available, or check that its own address is not in use by another node.

- *Neighbor Advertisement (NA)*: When requested, or when its own link layer address changes, a node sends a **Neighbor Advertisement (NA)** including its IPv6 address and its link layer address.

- *Redirect*: When a router knows a better first hop for a particular address (better than itself), it sends a Redirect message to the sender. One typical case might be when a node attempts to contact a node on the same segment by first sending the packet to the router. In its Redirect, the router identifies the destination as existing on the same network segment as the sender. A router might also use Redirects to load balance traffic across multiple interfaces.

At first glance, ND may seem a bit like NetBIOS. The difference is in the relative simplicity of the goals of ND, and in the nearly 15 years of additional experience with networks available to its designers. ND makes only sparing use of messages. Although a Neighbor Solicitation is made to a special multicast address, the Neighbor Advertisement sent in response is sent as a unicast directly to the soliciting node. Also, nodes do not advertise their existence every few minutes, as routers do.

ND takes over the functions handled in the IPv4 environment by ARP and Reverse ARP. It also performs many of the functions handled by ICMP Router Discovery and ICMP Redirect in IPv4.

ND makes use of multicast addresses, such as the "all routers" address with link-local scope (FF02::2), the "all nodes" address with link-local scope (FF02::1), and a special address called the solicited node address.

The **solicited node address** is a multicast address with link-local scope that helps reduce the number of multicast groups to which nodes must subscribe to make themselves available for solicitation by other nodes on their local links. A single node may have multiple unicast addresses and multiple anycast addresses. The higher-order (toward the left) bits of these addresses may be different. A node may have addresses from more than one access provider, for example. In order to effectively mask these differences (which are unimportant in terms of Neighbor Solicitation in any case), every node is required to compute and join the solicited node address for each unicast and anycast address assigned to it. The solicited node address is FF02:0:0:0:0:1:FF*xx.xxxx* (where *xx.xxxx* stands for the lowest-order [rightmost] 24 bits of the unicast or anycast address associated with that interface).

Path MTU Discovery and Changes in Fragmentation

Under IPv4, routers could fragment packets to make sure no packet was transmitted onto a link that was larger than the MTU, or maximum packet size allowed on that link. IPv6 changes that. Senders are required to check the Path MTU (PMTU) between themselves and the destination before they send, and size their packets accordingly. (This is discussed further in the section titled "Fragment Extension Header" later in this chapter.) The sending node handles all fragmentation before the packet is sent. If a router discovers an IPv6 packet larger than the MTU of the next hop, it discards the packet. If that packet comes from a unicast address, the router sends an ICMPv6 packet too large message to the sender. Presumably, this causes the sender to repeat its transmission with the correct fragment size.

Note that IPv6 also mandates a new minimum MTU of 1280 bytes for Internet links.

Every network segment or link has its own MTU. This is the size of the largest packet that can be transmitted on that link. For ordinary Ethernet, the MTU is 1500 bytes, for example. Under IPv4, if a packet of 2500 bytes is routed onto such an Ethernet segment, the router doing the forwarding fragments the packet. It breaks that packet into as many pieces or fragments as required to ensure that each fragment (along with its new header and information required to correctly reassemble the pieces) can fit within the MTU for the next segment. The great variety of network types supported by the Internet and its precursors made packet fragmentation at network boundaries absolutely essential. The Internet still contains many network types, but IETF, building on the experience with IPv4, changed the way fragmentation is handled. The sending host is now responsible for setting the correct packet size for the MTU of the chosen path. IETF made the changes to reduce router workload and improve overall throughput.

IPv6 PACKET FORMATS

IPv6 packets consist of a fixed, constant format 40-byte header, optional extension headers, and the payload (data) all encapsulated within a Data Link layer frame. The Ether Type value assigned to IPv6 is 0x86DD, as shown in Figure 13-4.

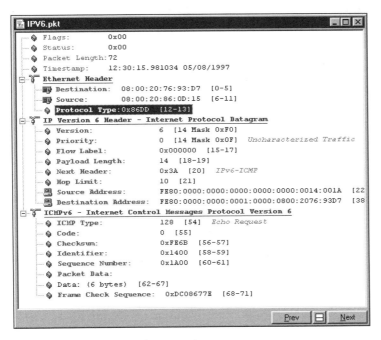

Figure 13-4   IPv6 packet structure

Basic IPv6 Header Format

The IPv6 header was designed to reduce processing time at the destination, and on intervening routers. The IPv6 header format differs from the IPv4 packet structure in the following basic ways:

- Six IPv4 header fields were removed: Internet Header Length, Type of Service (and Precedence), Identification, Flags, Fragment Offset, and Header Checksum.

- Three IPv4 fields were renamed or altered: Total Length, Protocol, and Time to Live.

- Two new fields were added: Class and Flow Label.

Figure 13-5 shows the new IPv6 basic header format.

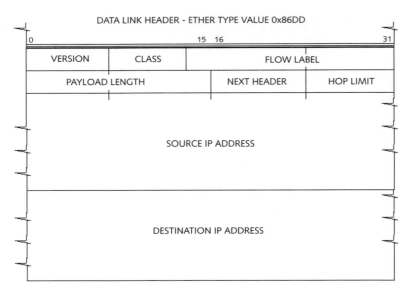

Figure 13-5   IPv6 header format

The IPv6 header is not variable length—it is always 40 bytes long. Options are handled through extension headers placed after the main IPv6 header.

Options are required to break on 64-bit boundaries, using padding, as necessary, to maintain this structure. This speeds parsing of the extension headers and the packet as a whole. For networks that may run 100 Mbps, 1 Gbps, or faster, such techniques greatly enhance throughput because they make it much easier to encode parsing logic in hardware or firmware.

There is no longer a need for an Internet Header Length field, nor the calculations it required to establish the boundaries between parts of a packet. The new Payload Length field gives the length of everything following the IPv6 header itself. This means payload length also includes the length of any option or extension headers present.

IPv6 no longer allows packets to be fragmented en route. If a packet is too large for the PMTU of the next hop, the packet is discarded. The original sender must check the PMTU to the destination and fragment the data to match before sending a packet. A fragmentation header takes over the remaining supported functions that were handled by the fragmentation fields in the IPv4 header.

A quick examination of the IPv6 header fields shows the new, streamlined operation of this Network layer header.

Version Field

The Version field simply indicates that this header is an IPv6 header, with the value six in this 4-bit field.

Class Field

The new Class field is used to support prioritization of traffic. Originally named the Priority field, this 8-bit field structure is depicted in Figure 13-6.

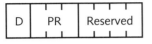

D = Delay Sensitive
PR = Precedence
Reserved = Set to 0000

Figure 13-6   The Class field structure

The first bit of the Class field indicates whether this traffic is delay sensitive. If this bit is set to one, the traffic is considered time sensitive. For example, interactive data exchanges, as well as voice and video communications, require low–delay connections. Thus, packets carrying those types of payloads will normally set the first bit of the Class field to one.

The Precedence field is similar to the IPv4 header Precedence field and allows an application to differentiate traffic types based on their priorities. Accordingly, routers can reference the Precedence bits to determine how to prioritize traffic through the router processing and queuing system.

The last three bits of the Class field are reserved at this time. For more information on the definition of Class values, refer to the **Differentiated Services (diffserv)** working group information at *http://www.ietf.org*.

Flow Label Field

A **flow** is a set of packets for which a source requires special handling by the intervening routers.

The IPv6 specification is intentionally vague about the use of flow labels. In fact, the use of flow labels is not required at all. If the Flow Label field is not used, it is padded with 20 zero bits.

13

Payload Length Field

In IPv4, the Total Length field indicated the length of the payload, including the IP header and any fragmented data that followed. To determine how much data followed the IPv4 header, the receiving device had to calculate the IPv4 Internet Header Length value and subtract it from the IPv4 Total Length field value.

In IPv6, the Payload Length field indicates the amount of data following, but not including, the IPv6 header. This is an example of the header streamlining process that reduces the number of calculations to be performed on an IP header. The Payload Length field is two bytes long.

Next Header Field

In IPv4, the Protocol field defined the upcoming header structure, such as UDP (17) and TCP (6). In IPv6, the Next Header field (one byte) indicates the upcoming extension header, transport protocol, or other protocol, as listed in Table 13-4. To determine the transport protocol carried in an IPv6 packet, a node must check through each of the headers until it comes to a Next Header field value that indicates a transport protocol. In order to speed the process, the extension and options headers are laid out so that the Next Header field is the first field in the header.

Table 13-4   Next Header Values

Next Header Value	Header Type	Next Header Value	Header Type
0	Reserved (IPv4)	44	Fragmentation Header (IPv6)
0	Hop-by-Hop Options (IPv6)	45	Inter-Domain Routing Protocol (IDRP)
1	ICMP (IPv4)	51	Authentication Header
2	IGMP (IPv4)	52	Encrypted Security Payload
3	Gateway-to-Gateway Protocol	58	ICMPv6
4	IP in IP (IPv4 encapsulation)	59	No Next Header (IPv6)
5	Stream	60	Destination Options Header (IPv6)
6	TCP	80	ISO CLNP
17	UDP	88	IGRP
29	ISO TP4	89	OSPF
43	Routing Header (IPv6)	255	Reserved

Many of these values are common to the IPv4 Protocol field and the IPv6 Next Header field.

In IPv6, any extension header must be inserted between the IP header and any higher-layer protocol headers. Currently, the IPv6 specification supports the following six extension headers:

- Hop-by-Hop Options
- Routing
- Fragmentation
- Authentication
- Encrypted Security Payload
- Destination Options

IPv6 supports chaining headers together after the basic IPv6 header. For more information on extension headers, refer to the "Extension Headers" section later in this chapter.

Hop Limit Field

The 1-byte IPv4 Time to Live field has been renamed the Hop Limit field in IPv6. This matches its actual use, in either version of IP.

Source Address Field

The Source Address field indicates the 16-byte IP address of the sending host.

Destination Address Field

This Destination Address field indicates the 16-byte address of the destination IP host.

Extension Headers

The IPv6 header can be followed by the UDP, TCP, other protocol, or by one or more extension headers. The currently defined extension headers are "chained" after the basic IPv6 header through the use of the Next Header field in the basic IPv6 header and the extension headers themselves. For example, Figure 13-7 illustrates the structure of a packet that contains several extension headers after the basic IPv6 header.

13

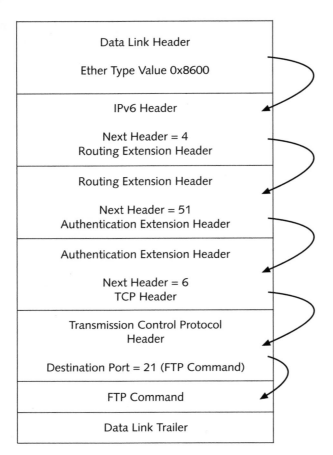

Figure 13-7 IPv6 header chains on an Ethernet network

The IPv6 specification defines a recommended order for the extension headers as follows:

1. IPv6

2. Hop-by-Hop Options

3. Destination Options

4. Routing

5. Fragment

6. Authentication

7. Encapsulated Security Payload (ESP)

8. Destination Options

9. Upper-layer header (such as UDP, TCP, and ICMP)

The Destination Options header is the only header that may appear in more than one location. It may appear in either or both (or none) of the locations shown. When it appears earlier in the packet, it is for use at an intervening destination. When it appears after the ESP header, it can only be examined at the final destination. The next section examines the various extension headers defined by the specification.

Hop-by-Hop Options Extension Header

As shown in Figure 13-8, the Hop-by-Hop Options extension header structure allows maximum flexibility in header definition and functionality. The only two fields defined for this header are the Next Header field and the Extended Header Length field. The Next Header field references the Next Header value as defined in Table 13-4. The Header Length field indicates the length of the Hop-by-Hop Options extension header, excluding the minimum eight bytes required of all extension and options headers. Apart from this requirement, the header is not a set length.

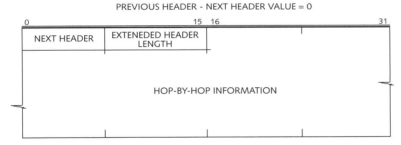

Figure 13-8   Hop-by-Hop Options extension header

The Hop-by-Hop Options extension header is designed to carry information that affects routers along a path. For example, if a multicast transmission is required to provide some special routing instructions on an internetwork, the instructions can be carried in the Hop-by-Hop Options extension header. Intervening routers along a path can examine this header as defined. Two proposed uses of the Hop-by-Hop Options extension header include the router alert and the jumbogram large payload options, described in the "Quality of Service" section later in this chapter.

Routing Extension Header

The Routing extension header supports strict or loose source routing for IPv6. This header includes fields for the intermediary addresses through which the IPv6 packet should be forwarded. The format of the Routing extension header is shown in Figure 13-9.

13

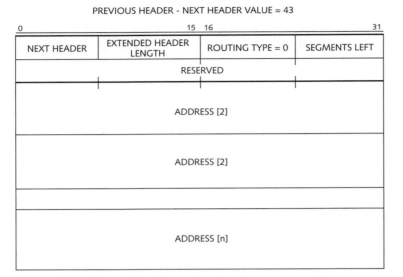

Figure 13-9   Routing extension header

The first 1–byte field of this header indicates the next header that follows the Routing extension header. The Extended Header Length field defines the length of this header, excluding the minimum eight bytes required of all extension and options headers. Apart from this requirement, the header is not a set length.

Although designed to make it useful in a range of situations, only one option has been defined for the Routing extension header: the Type 0 routing option. This option uses the Routing header like a routing slip in an office. The sender calculates the path among all the routers it wishes this packet to visit. It places their addresses in an ordered list in the Options header, with the final destination router at the end of the list. It places the address of the first router to be visited in the Destination Address field of the IPv6 header. Intervening routers forward the packet normally without having to examine the contents of any headers. When the packet arrives at the first destination (the first router), the router examines the packet and finds this header. If all is correct, the router places the address of the next router in the list in the Destination Address field, and places its own address at the bottom of the list. This process continues until the packet reaches its final destination. Up to 255 routers may be included in such a list.

Fragment Extension Header

As mentioned earlier in this chapter, IPv6 does not support fragmentation at forwarding routers. All packets are treated as if an implicit Do Not Fragment bit was set. The PMTU Discovery process is used to provide source stations with the maximum fragment size supported by a path.

PMTU Discovery procedures are similar in IPv6 and IPv4. For more information on PMTU Discovery, refer to Chapter 4.

If a transmitting device needs to send packets that are larger than the PMTU, the IPv6 Fragment extension header is used. The Fragment extension header format is shown in Figure 13-10.

PREVIOUS HEADER - NEXT HEADER VALUE = 44

0		15 16		31
NEXT HEADER	RESERVED	FRAGMENT OFFSET	RES	M
IDENTIFICATION				

Figure 13-10   Fragment extension header

The fields of the Fragment extension header are almost identical to the IPv4 fragment fields except for the use of the Flags field. IPv6 has one Flags field, More Fragments. The Flags field is set to one in all fragment packets except the last one.

Authentication Extension Header

The Authentication extension header is designed to specify the true origin of a packet by preventing address spoofing and connection theft. The Authentication header also provides an integrity check on those parts of the packet that do not change in transit. (Authentication would not be calculated over the Routing header, for example.) In addition, the Authentication header can provide a limited defense against replay attacks. End devices may, if configured to do so, reject packets that are not properly authenticated.

13

The Authentication extension header format is shown in Figure 13-11.

PREVIOUS HEADER - NEXT HEADER VALUE = 51

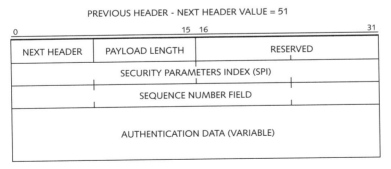

0		15 16	31
NEXT HEADER	PAYLOAD LENGTH	RESERVED	
SECURITY PARAMETERS INDEX (SPI)			
SEQUENCE NUMBER FIELD			
AUTHENTICATION DATA (VARIABLE)			

Figure 13-11   Authentication extension header

The Authentication extension header starts with a 1-byte Next Header field that indicates the next header in the chain.

The 1-byte Payload Length field indicates the number of 4-byte words following the **Security Parameters Index (SPI)** field. The bits in the reserved field should be set to all zeroes.

The SPI field contains values that may point to an index or table of security parameters, or a Security Association (SA), at the receiver. The SPI is always a pointer to security details on its partner.

The Sequence Number field is used to ensure receivers recognize old packets on the network.

The Authentication Data field contents are based on a computation of a cryptographic checksum on the payload data, some fields in the basic IPv6 and extension headers, and a secret shared by the authenticated devices.

Encapsulating Security Payload Extension Header

The authentication process defined by the Authentication extension header does not encrypt or protect data from sniffing attacks. Data is still in its native transmission format. The **Encapsulating Security Payload (ESP)** extension header should be used to encrypt data. This header must always be the last header of the IP header chain. The Encapsulating Security Payload extension header indicates the start of encrypted data.

The format of the Encapsulating Security Payload extension header is shown in Figure 13-12.

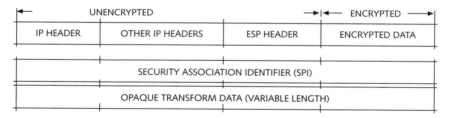

Figure 13-12   Encapsulating Security Payload extension header

The ESP extension header is followed by an authentication checksum to protect against attackers that corrupt or truncate encrypted data. The exact format of the encrypted parameters is based on the particular encryption algorithm in use.

Destination Options Extension Header

The Destination Options extension header provides a method for extending the IPv6 header to support options for packet handling and preferences. This extension header allows for future proprietary or standards-based communications. Option type numbers must be registered with IANA and documented in a specific RFC.

The Destination Options extension header is the only header that may appear in more than one location. In may appear either immediately before the Routing extension header, and/or as the last header before the actual higher-layer protocol data (that is, after any ESP or Authentication headers). When it appears earlier in the packet, it is intended for use at an intermediate destination. The only such use defined so far is in conjunction with the Routing header. When it appears after the ESP header, it can only be examined at the final destination.

As shown in Figure 13-13, the Destination Options extension header uses the same format as the Hop-by-Hop Options extension header.

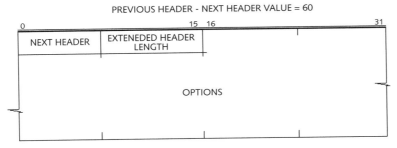

Figure 13-13   Destination Options extension header

New and Enhanced IPv6 Features

IPv6 contains several new and improved features to support autoconfiguration of hosts, enhance security, provide selectable levels of service, and support the special needs of mobile users. Each of these areas is discussed in the following sections.

13

Autoconfiguration

Autoconfiguration allows a host to find the information it needs to set up its own IP networking parameters by querying other nodes. BOOTP was an early attempt at this kind of capability. DHCP is a common autoconfiguration tool deployed across many parts of the Internet today. Three things combine to make autoconfiguration particularly important for the Internet. The first is the sheer number of nodes to be configured. Network administrators would be kept very busy indeed if they had to configure each node by hand. The second is the rate of change and the frequency of renumbering. Changing ISPs can mean renumbering many network hosts. Without renumbering to match actual network topology, routing performance suffers. The better the autoconfiguration tools, the easier it is for network administrators to accept renumbering gracefully. The third, and perhaps most compelling, reason for autoconfiguration is user mobility. Mobile nodes that may roam from one part of the network to another include not only laptops, but also cellular phones, PDAs, and other personal devices. The potential advantages of a system that allows these devices to connect seamlessly to the Internet from any location are great.

There are two basic approaches to autoconfiguration: stateful methods, such as DHCP, and stateless methods. DHCP is considered "stateful" because the DHCP server must maintain awareness of the status or state of its pool of available addresses, the presence or absence on the network of permitted clients, and a variety of other parameters. Stateless autoconfiguration, on the other hand, simply presents the required configuration information to all comers. Each method has its advantages and disadvantages, as described in the following sections.

Stateless Autoconfiguration

For segments and nodes that support multicasting, RFC 2462 proposes several tools to support stateless autoconfiguration of attached nodes. The ND protocol allows routers to be configured to present the minimum information a host needs when joining a network link. This information includes the network prefix of the segment and the router's own address, and it may include the segment MTU and preferred number of "maximum hops" for various routes. The router can also use flagged addresses to direct a node using stateless autoconfiguration to a DHCP server to find the rest of the information it needs to complete its configuration.

When an interface initializes on an IPv6 network segment or link (usually on node start-up), it first attempts to calculate its own link-local address. This means calculating its own EUI-64 interface ID, and forming a generic link-local address by adding that interface ID to the well-known link-local network prefix.

To verify that this "tentative" address is actually unique on the local link, the node sends out an NS with this address as its destination. If another node responds, the host knows it must recompute the link-local address. This should be done manually for both interfaces generating the duplicate address. If no duplicates are found, the node actually assigns the address to the interface and treats it as a "preferred," that is, fully functioning, address.

Addresses are leased for a "valid lifetime." When that valid lifetime expires, the address becomes invalid. Invalid addresses cannot be used as either the source or destination address. At a configurable length of time before an address becomes invalid, it moves from "preferred," or fully valid, to "deprecated." A deprecated address allows nodes to continue to function while they renew the lease on their addresses. Deprecated addresses may be used as normal, but should not be used for anything other than the completion of sessions initiated before the address became deprecated.

To forestall spoofing attacks, nodes use a default value of two hours for the valid lifetime when encountering any RA that attempts to set the valid lifetime to a value less than two hours. The one exception to this rule occurs when RAs use IPv6 Authentication headers. When an RA is authenticated, nodes update the valid lifetime of their addresses as directed.

While performing the duplicate address check, the node can also send an RS to prompt any attached routers to send their RAs. IPv6 hosts know that there may be more than one response to such solicitations, and they are prepared to cache and update results from multiple attached routers. If no routers are present on a local link, the node should use a stateful autoconfiguration method, such as **Dynamic Host Configuration Protocol version 6 (DHCPv6)**.

Stateless autoconfiguration can be used alone or in conjunction with a stateful auto-configuration method, such as DHCPv6. Routers on the local link can be configured to provide pointers to DHCPv6 servers, for example. Although autoconfiguration is primarily for hosts rather than routers, all interfaces on a link, including all interfaces in any attached routers, must at least perform a duplicate address check upon initializing.

DHCPv6

In its basic tasks and broad outlines, DHCPv6 is much like DHCPv4 under IPv4. Both are stateful methods for configuring hosts. Both rely on dedicated servers to hold databases of information about hosts and their IP and other configuration parameters. Hosts connect to the DHCP server as clients and download the information they need to set themselves up for IP, and possibly for other protocols as well, such as Microsoft NetBT or NetBIOS.

Apart from obvious differences in the length and format of the addresses themselves, DHCPv6 has some significant differences from earlier versions. Perhaps the most far reaching is that nodes under IPv6 can gain at least a locally functioning address without any help from DHCP. In effect, this means that all DHCPv6 clients are fully functioning hosts and able to actively search for the server using multicast solicitations. DHCPv6 clients can, for example, discover whether their DHCPv6 servers are on the local link. In addition, they can use a relay server on the local segment to receive configuration information from an off-link server.

13

DHCPv6 also shares certain primary features with stateless autoconfiguration under IPv6. All autoconfigured addresses are leased and use the same "dual lifetimes" paradigm for name lease renewal. All interfaces under IPv6 inherently support multiple addresses. To support dynamic renumbering, IPv6 nodes using autoconfiguration of either type must listen for updates to their addresses. For nodes using stateless autoconfiguration, this means listening to RAs. For nodes configured with DHCPv6, this means they must listen on their UDP port for new reconfiguration messages.

Because all IPv6 nodes must support authentication (using the IPv6 Authentication header), both DHCPv6 servers and routers can be configured to send their advertisements in an authenticated form. This allows nodes to have greater confidence in the validity of reconfiguration messages.

DHCPv6 can be set up to dynamically update DNS records. This is a key part of maintaining efficient routing. Networks can renumber, and that renumbering will be reflected quickly in DNS, thereby removing (or at least mitigating) one of the strongest objections to the whole idea of renumbering—the threat of extended periods of traffic disruption.

DHCPv6 uses special multicast addresses. There are also changes in the structure and specific content of DHCP messages. For these and other details from the latest draft proposal for DHCPv6, see the IETF Web site at *http://www.ietf.org.*

Security

Security covers a broad range of related concerns. It may mean the ability to detect alterations made to a communication after some particular point in time. It may also mean the ability to check the credentials of a user to keep or share a secret, or to prove and maintain the integrity of any of these.

Like any defense, security is only as strong as the weakest link in the chain, which is human error in most security systems. Security designers cannot change humans, but they can eliminate opportunities for error wherever possible. Therefore, security designers must make sure all parts of their systems match, and that a weakness in one small part does not undermine the effectiveness of the whole. Precision and a rigorous adherence to procedures are typical of computer security systems design.

This helps explain why the IETF proposed not one or two tools for Internet security, but a whole architecture embracing a suite of protocols called Internet Protocol Security (IPSec). This architecture attempts to do two important things. First, it provides an integrated and balanced framework in which others can create, test, and distribute tools to protect the security of traffic at the IP level. Second, it provides default implementations of a suite of such tools, ready to use today in both IPv4 and IPv6.

The biggest change from IPv4 to IPv6 is that security, in the form of IPSec, is now a required part of IPv6. Support for this basic security architecture is built into the architecture of the protocol suite, rather than implemented as an add-on. Additional or alternate security methods are expected and encouraged, but every compliant implementation of IPv6 must support at least the minimum standard set of IPSec protocols and procedures.

Terms of Encryption

This section introduces some basic concepts and terminology related to security, authentication, error checking, and data compression.

Computer security takes advantage of the fact that computer information is basically just numbers. It is based on sets of mathematical manipulations called **transformations**. By performing one or more transformations on a set of starting values and then sending the result, designers can achieve a variety of goals.

For example, designers can make the original document (called the **plain text**) unreadable. This is called **encryption** and its purpose is to keep communications secret or private. The now-scrambled document is called the **ciphertext**. The secret sharer is told what manipulations to perform on the ciphertext to change it back to the plaintext. This reverse process is called **decryption**. The original sender may have used some information not contained in the original message in order to do the encryption. For example, the sender might have added the value 13 to every character. The encryption algorithm would be p + k = c, where p is the plain text value, k is some value (13, in this particular case), and c is the resulting ciphertext. In this example, the term k is a **key** whose value must be shared (along with the algorithm itself) in order to decrypt the message.

Transformations can also serve other purposes. If a calculation is made using the contents of a packet, and the result of that calculation is sent along with the packet, a receiver who knows how the calculations were performed can make those same calculations on the contents of the packet received, and compare the results with the values obtained by the sender. If there is a difference, the contents changed in transit. This approach is used in authentication and error checking.

A third use of transformations is compression. Compression attempts to find patterns in the plain text and express those patterns in fewer characters. Compression must use some regular algorithm, just like encryption, so the process can be performed in reverse to restore the text.

In theory, perfect compression and perfect encryption yield identical results. That is, the resulting ciphertext appears completely random, with absolutely no pattern, and is reduced to such an extent that it has the maximum possible density of information. In practice, of course, the algorithms are different because the goals are different. Even so, if compression and encryption are used on the same information, compression must be applied first in order to be effective. Once the data is encrypted, the near-randomness of the ciphertext prevents compression from finding any usable pattern.

Security Architecture

13

IPSec specifies an integrated set of security tools, and the relationships among them. This section briefly describes the tools and shows how they fit together to form the security architecture. The following sections discuss in detail some of the key tools in action.

IPSec provides various kinds of security at the IP layer (and/or at higher layers). Specifically, RFC 2401 says the goals of IPSec are to provide the kinds of security listed below:

- *Access control:* **Access control** means restricting who may view or use certain resources, including access to bandwidth or a computer, as well as access to information. Authentication is critical for access control. IPSec provides various forms of authentication. In addition, the standards mandate particular forms of access control for particular parts of the security system itself.

- *Connectionless integrity*: **Connectionless integrity** is defined in two parts. *Integrity* means a communication is not changed. *Connectionless* means that this integrity check does not extend to the connection itself (by detecting packets arriving out of sequence, for example). Instead, a function that provides connectionless integrity checks the integrity of each packet individually. IPSec's authentication capabilities support this goal.

- *Data origin authentication*: **Data origin authentication** is the ability to verify that the data received did in fact come from the named source. IPSec's authentication capabilities support this goal.

- *Protection against replays*: Replay attacks capture legitimate traffic, such as a sequence of packets from a user logon, and send the traffic again, masquerading as a trusted communications partner. Countermeasures against replays (**protection against replays**) may include placing a unique and frequently changing token in each communication, such that seeing a previously used token in an allegedly new communication would prove it a replay and thereby invalidate it. IPSec provides a form of partial sequence integrity.

- *Confidentiality*: **Confidentiality** prevents unauthorized people from viewing communications. IPSec supports the use of a variety of encryption tools to provide confidentiality.

- *Limited traffic flow confidentiality*: By supporting certain types of tunneling, IPSec can, to some extent, hide the true path between two communications partners, referred to as **limited traffic flow confidentiality**. This prevents an adversary from knowing who is talking to whom, or when.

To achieve the security goals listed above, IPSec relies on a whole suite of applications and security protocols. The most important of these are the Authentication header (AH) and the ESP header. In addition, IPSec relies on a variety of protocols to handle the generation and distribution of keys, and the exchange of other security data required to coordinate secure communications among partners. These include the Internet Key Exchange (IKE) protocol, the Internet Security Association and Key Management Protocol (ISAKMP), and tools specified in other drafts and RFCs, including those covering the IP security Domain of Interpretation (DOI) for ISAKMP. Individual algorithms, such as Triple-DES encryption (3DES), are covered in their own RFCs or drafts. Compression, though not strictly a part of IPSec, must be used in a way that is compatible with encryption and authentication. RFC 2393 specifies the IP Compression (IPComp) standards. Various parts of IPSec support negotiation of compression techniques.

IPSec Implementation and Basic Operation

IPSec is implemented in the IP layer, either in an individual host or in a dedicated computer used as a **security gateway**. When implemented in a host, IPSec may be an integral part of the IP stack, or it may be implemented "underneath" an existing IP stack, operating between the previously installed IP layer and the local link network drivers. When implemented in this way, a security system is sometimes called a **bump-in-the-stack (BITS)** implementation. Freestanding cryptographic devices through which a host's communications are processed are sometimes called a **bump-in-the-wire (BITW)** implementation.

IPSec must scan every packet inbound or outbound on the system on which it operates. IPSec checks each packet, scanning the IP and upper-layer headers, looking for user-defined "selectors," which are then matched against entries in the user-defined **Security Policy Database (SPD)**. Typically, there is a separate SPD for inbound and outbound traffic, and such a pair for each interface sending or receiving IPSec traffic. The SPD tells IPSec how to handle each packet. Typically, the choices are to let it pass unchanged, apply the specified security processing, or discard the packet. You can use wildcards and value ranges, as well as unique values, to define selectors in the SPD.

IPSec uses a set of behaviors matched with destination addresses to define the type of processing to be done on packets. These are called **Security Associations (SAs)**. An SA is the three-part combination of a destination address, an SPI, and a security protocol (either AH or ESP). The SPI is a pointer or identifier derived from the protocol type and associated with the SA at the time of its creation. It can be an alternate identifier for the SA. In addition, SAs come in two modes, tunnel mode and traffic mode, as described in the next section.

Multiple SAs can be combined in a single SPD entry called an **SA bundle**. For example, this allows a user to specify that communications bound for destination "A" should use ESP (from one SA), and then apply AH (from the second SA in this bundle). Each SA can specify only one of these protocols. If more than one protocol is needed, more than one SA must be bundled.

SAs are typically created by the entity that wishes to receive secure communications. When a new SA is created, the creator can add its own SPI to help with inbound processing. (This value must be larger than 255). Key management protocols (ISAKMP) are used to exchange information about SAs between prospective partners.

SAs are indexed in the **Security Association Database (SAD)**. SPD entries (with lists of SAs associated with a given policy) point to the SAs they reference in this SAD. When an outbound packet matches selectors that say it should be processed by IPSec, the SPD applies the SAs shown for that policy. If the selectors say the packet should be processed, but no appropriate SA seems to exist, IPSec tries to create one, and then lists it in the SAD.

For inbound traffic, processing is a bit different. IPSec looks at the packet and attempts to match the packet's inbound destination address, the SPI, and the IPSec protocol (AH or ESP) with an SA shown in the SAD. If there is no such SA, IPSec discards the packet. Many of the headers of incoming packets are already encrypted. This means an SA used for inbound processing often sets some parameters to OPAQUE because the headers are indecipherable until the appropriate SA is applied, perhaps by another SA later in the same bundle. IPSec keeps trying various SAs until a match is found. If no match is found, the packet is discarded. IPSec keeps track of the SAs successfully applied to the incoming packet, and can store the sequence as a chunk of useful management information. It also attempts to match the successful sequence of SAs with an existing security policy in the SPD.

13

Traffic Mode and Tunnel Mode

IPSec SAs can operate in one of two modes: **traffic mode** or **tunnel mode**. Traffic mode is used only between two hosts. When a security gateway is accepting packets addressed to itself (rather than packets to be forwarded), it acts as a host and can use traffic mode. Tunnel mode must be used when a security gateway is involved, even if only one end of the communication is a gateway. Hosts can also use tunnel mode to tunnel to another host.

In traffic mode, the security protocols are applied to the packets themselves in the normal manner. In the case of ESP, that means they are applied to the packet payload (the PDU) and to any Destination Option header located after the ESP header. ESP does not process the parts of the packet located before the ESP header. For AH, normal processing means applying authentication to everything after the AH, and to any headers before the AH that can be expected to remain the same during transmission.

In tunnel mode, the security protocol can be applied to the whole packet, which is then encapsulated in another IP packet for tunneling. Additional processing may be done on this outer packet as well.

As mentioned previously, SAs can be applied in sequence to form an SA bundle. In traffic mode, there is little point in applying more than two SAs (one for ESP and one for AH) to any outbound packet. In tunneling mode, however, multiple SAs can be applied to send packets within packets, routing the innermost packet to its final destination using a variety of intervening hops. Such approaches may be applied to defeat traffic analysis, or to simply reach a host behind a gateway with a different SA than the ultimate destination.

Keys and Coordination

IPSec can use IKE or ISAKMP for key management services. ISAKMP has a broader range of capabilities and is designed expressly to support the negotiation of SAs and other parameters between potential communications partners. IPSec also supports the use of other proprietary key management protocols, as well as manual configuration of keys and all other parameters.

The actual encryption techniques used for AH and ESP can be negotiated separately, or be configured by hand.

Quality of Service (QoS)

QoS is handled by the diffserv working group at the IETF. Differentiated services are what QoS is all about. The concept is quite simple: it should be possible to choose (and pay for) something other than the default level of service. This might be assured delivery, expedited delivery, temporary assignment of unusually large bandwidth, low latency, lowest delivered cost (perhaps at the expense of quick delivery), or any of several parameters of particular value to certain users at certain times and places. The **Resource Reservation Protocol (RSVP)** was one early attempt to promote a more formal approach to dynamic resource allocation on the Internet.

The latest drafts from the diffserv working group propose two basic approaches to QoS: **per-hop behaviors (PHBs)** and **per-domain behaviors (PDBs)**. Per-hop behaviors, as their name implies, are applicable along any path traced through routers supporting the required level of service, and are able to understand the signaling of packets requesting it. Per-domain behaviors are available across all hops within a given domain. Decisions about QoS are made at the edge of such domains. Traffic traversing the domain is handled with a certain QoS. The "domains" referred to in PDB may not be actual IP subnets, but rather a group of routers offering a certain unified approach to QoS.

QoS was implemented in one form or another in IPv4 for many years; however, it was never widely used. There may be many reasons for this, not the least of which is the explosive growth in demand for plain old "default" quality Internet service. Put another way, as a social matter, differentiation tends to be an aspect of plenty, not of scarcity. Until Internet connectivity and bandwidth are truly plentiful, the widespread adoption of differentiated QoS is unlikely.

Router Alerts and Hop-by-Hop Options

IPv6 recognizes and responds to the current low demand for differentiated QoS, yet still makes provisions for its gradual adoption in a graceful way. The IPv6 header eliminates all the fields relating to QoS, which were carried in the IPv4 header. In their stead, IPv6 allows options headers, such as the Hop-by-Hop Options extension header, the Routing extension header, and the Destination Options extension header, to be used in flexible ways to implement current and future QoS schemes. By eliminating fields in the basic IPv6 header, which would have to be examined by every router, IPv6 speeds up the processing of "default quality" service on the Internet. By creating headers that can be examined by all or by selected hops on a path through the Internet, IPv6 creates tools that can be used by QoS protocols to gain precise control of both per-hop and per-domain behaviors.

RFC 2711 defines the router alert option in the Hop-by-Hop Options extension header. The router alert option tells intervening routers to examine the packet more closely for important information. If this option is not present, routers can assume that any packet not addressed directly to them contains nothing of interest and should be forwarded normally. IPv6 packets containing RSVP instructions must use the router alert option in the Hop-by-Hop Options extension header. The router alert option is shown in Figure 13-14.

13

0 0 0	0 0 1 0 1	0 0 0 0 0 0 1 0	VALUE (2 octets)

Length -2

Figure 13-14 Router alert option in Hop-by-Hop Options extension header

The first byte of the option is the Option Type field. Note that the first three bits of the Option Type field are set to all zeroes. The first two zeroes mean, "If you don't understand this option, ignore it, and continue processing the rest of the header." The last of these three zeroes means, "The data in this option cannot change enroute." The remaining five bytes of the Option Type field equal five, identifying the option as the Hop-by-Hop option.

The second byte of the option is the Option Data Length field. The "payload" of the router alert option is only two bytes long, so this field is set to two.

Only three possible values for the router alert option are defined in RFC 2711. All the rest are reserved for assignment by the Internet Assigned Numbers Authority (IANA). The possible values are shown in Table 13-5.

Table 13-5 IPv6 Router Alert Option Values

Value	Meaning
0x0	Datagram contains a Multicast Listener Discovery message
0x1	Datagram contains RSVP message
0x2	Datagram contains an Active Networks message
0x3-FFFF	Reserved by IANA for future use

Jumbograms

RFC 2675 proposes one other type of special service for IPv6 packets: a very large packet called a **jumbogram**. The standard IPv6 packet header Payload Length field, at two bytes long, allows packets to carry up to 64K bytes of data. Jumbograms use the Hop-by-Hop Options extension header to add an alternate Packet Length field of 32 bytes. This allows the packet to carry a single chunk of data larger than 64K bytes, anywhere up to over four billion bytes. For an ordinary Internet link, this size packet is a plain absurdity. On the backbone and other high-capacity network links, however, there are significant operational advantages to carrying fewer very large packets. The jumbogram allows these links to carry such large packets without straining the fabric of IPv6.

Mobile Users

Two related kinds of mobility need support in IPv6: ordinary mobility, and what some Internet drafts refer to as **micro-mobility**. Micro-mobility is generally dealt with at the link layer, below IP, as it maintains connectivity to a local link over a wireless connection. Examples include the hand-off of cellular phones as they pass from one radio cell to another, and maintaining the identity of a laptop computer as it moves between access points in a wireless LAN. The solutions and standards to support a more robust micro-mobility are still under development.

The other kind of mobility takes place on a slightly larger scale, such as logging onto a network in Copenhagen and conducting business with a client in Paris, as if you were still at home in Singapore, without having to send all your messages halfway around the world.

There is some commonality between the approaches taken in IPv4 and IPv6 for support of mobile users. This is not surprising, as many of the techniques used in Mobile IPv4 came directly from work done on that same problem in IPv6.

IPv6 has capabilities that IPv4 lacks, and Mobile IPv6 takes advantage of them. However, the standards for Mobile IPv6 are still far from settled. This section offers a quick overview of proposed approaches. As with many other aspects of IPv6, you should check the IETF site for the most recent developments.

The Mobile Problem

As in IPv4, mobile users in IPv6 require the help of a router located on their home networks, called a **home agent (HA)**. Unlike Mobile IPv4, Mobile IPv6 does not require a **foreign agent (FA)** on the visited network. Instead, the mobile user registers its current location as a **Care-of Address (COA)** with its home agent. The HA takes care of housekeeping tasks on the home network, such as making sure that renumbering does not wipe out the mobile user's home address while he's away, storing and forwarding messages directed to his home address, and so forth. The mobile user at the COA can send and receive messages directly without sending everything through the home agent. When the mobile user moves to a new foreign location, Mobile IPv6 allows messages that were aimed at that first COA to be forwarded to the new COA without having to retrace steps, or be sent by way of the user's home address.

Described in this cursory way, Mobile IP may seem fairly straightforward. The user roams and the HA takes care of details at the home address. The two stay in touch, making sure no communications are dropped. Apart from the housekeeping details back on the home network, Mobile IPv6 really comes down to two major problems: routing and identity. When all nodes stay in a fixed location, the questions "who?" and "where?" have the same answer. Mobility splits those two concepts, allowing the same entity (the mobile user) to exist virtually in two (or more) places on the Internet at the same time. IPv6 allows multiple addresses for the same interface, so being in two places (network addresses) at once is perfectly legal. The problems include determining which is the "real" place to send messages for this mobile node, and determining if either (or any) of these entities is the "real," or authentic, mobile user.

The following section addresses the issue of routing for Mobile IPv6, or how to determine the real place to send messages for a mobile node. To determine if an entity is an authentic mobile user, Mobile IPv6 uses Authentication headers, although they are imperfect. Running authentication over the messages sent by the mobile user (or to the mobile user from its HA) allows all parties to be sure they are, in fact, dealing with

13

the real mobile user, and the mobile user can be sure the home agent is really the home agent. The reason strong and reliable authentication is so critical for Mobile IPv6 is that without it ordinary mobile operations present a perfect opportunity for duplicity. They are open to man-in-the-middle attacks, in which a third party gets between two communications partners and masquerades to both of them, compromising their privacy and security. In addition, mobile users are, by definition, transient. They are here one minute and gone the next. This eliminates some possible countermeasures.

Unfortunately, the mechanisms for key exchange in support of strong authentication are still somewhat cumbersome. This puts them at odds with the hoped-for seamless ease of use of Mobile IPv6. It is still not clear where the balance between ease of use and secure authentication for Mobile IPv6 will be found.

Binding and Routing for Mobile IPv6

Mobile IPv6 starts when a node establishes itself on a foreign network. A **foreign network** is one that has a different network prefix than the user's own home address. The standard doesn't specify how the mobile node is to gain this connection, which is a separate issue. Mobile IPv6 only requires that the mobile node have an address on a foreign network. To form its new unique address on the foreign network, the mobile node uses the same interface identifier it used on its home network.

Using this foreign address as the source address, the mobile node sends an ICMPv6 Home Agent Address Discovery message to find a router on its home network that is willing and able to act as a home agent. Routers advertise this ability by setting the H bit in their RAs. Any HA on the home network should be able to respond to these ICMPv6 messages with a reply giving a list of all the HAs on the home network.

When the mobile node identifies an HA on its home network, it attempts to tell the HA its new location, the Care-of Address, or COA, as discussed previously. The mobile node sends a message called a **binding update** (using the Routing header and the Destination Option header), asking the HA to add this new COA to its **binding table**. The HA's binding table binds the mobile user's COA and home address, much like a routing table, and allows it to reroute traffic addressed to the user's home address to the user's new COA.

If requested (and it typically will be in all initial binding updates), the HA responds with a **binding acknowledgement**. If the binding update is successful, the acknowledgement contains the lifetime for the binding and the length of time (in seconds) that the HA is prepared to continue to perform HA services. The binding must be updated before it expires. Whether the maximum possible lifetime of a binding should be infinite or limited to 30 days is still under discussion.

If the binding update is rejected, the binding acknowledgement can show several reasons for this, including the HA's own overload, or any of several errors in the request, including a failure of the duplicate address check, which the HA must perform before updating the home registration binding.

When a duplicate address check is required, the HA uses the interface ID contained in the Home Address portion of the binding update to form the link-local and site-local addresses for that interface, and checks that they are not in use on the home network.

The IPSec AH must cover both the binding update and any acknowledgement, regardless of whether encryption (ESP) is applied or not. The contents of the Destination Options header (which contains the binding options) must not change enroute.

Once the binding is established, the HA can intercept mail sent to the mobile user's home address and tunnel it (by encapsulating it) to the user's primary COA. The user can establish a reverse tunnel to the HA as well.

The mobile user can communicate directly with other nodes on the Internet using its COA as the source address in IPv6 headers. Correspondents (nodes with which the mobile user is in communication) can send a **binding request** to the mobile user, asking the user to tell them its current COA and home address. This is like asking "Where are you now, and who are you when you're at home?" In this way, interrupted conversations can be smoothly resumed, even when the mobile node is changing locations.

When the mobile node moves from one COA (call it COA1) to another (call it COA2), it may ask a home agent on COA1 to forward mail to its new primary COA at COA2. A mobile node may have more than one COA at the same time, but only one can be the primary COA at any one time. By setting short lifetimes on the bindings for such alternate COAs, nodes can transition smoothly, without leaving a flurry of bounced packets in their wake.

The ultimate goal of Mobile IPv6 is to let users move across the network address space in a way that is as transparent to upper-layer protocols as possible. Although it will take more experience of actual implementations to work out all the issues, Mobile IPv6 still promises to be one of the main forces driving the adoption of IPv6 as a whole, as millions of cell phones and PDAs are waiting to log on.

13

TRANSITION: COEXISTENCE OF IPv4 AND IPv6

IPv6 and IPv4 will probably exist side by side for many years, possibly forever (or whatever that works out to be in "Internet years"). There will be no "flag day," or moment of throwing the switch to light up the new Internet and shut down the old one. Instead, just like the introduction of many other improved technologies, the two must find some way to coexist during what may prove to be a long transition.

The designers of IPv6 anticipated this, and created a set of techniques to allow IPv6 to function adequately in a world dominated by IPv4. The designers also built in tools to allow IPv6 to support the last legacy installations of IPv4. The next three sections deal with the main thrust of these techniques.

Dual Stack Approach

The obvious solution to an Internet running two versions of IP is to have it populated by hosts and routers that also run two versions of IP. With trivial exceptions, the wires, airwaves, and glass fibers don't care which protocol they're carrying. The same network will support both versions, if only the hosts and, more importantly, the routers can support both sets of protocols.

IPv6 has enjoyed wide support among leading manufacturers almost from the beginning. These manufacturers still support it today, and are moving to bring products to market, implementing different parts of the full IPv6 suite in a phased way from 2001 through 2005. Experimental versions of the IPv6 stack are available on several host platforms, with variations in terms of what parts of the full suite of protocols they implement, as well as how they implement them.

Dual stack implementations for individuals or small offices may work as experiments, but will be limited by the availability of dual stack routers at ISPs at the edge of the Internet for the near term. The most important dual stack machines will be the routers themselves. A dual stack router can provide a connection between the IPv4 Internet and an office (or a set of ISP customers) that already made the switch to IPv6. As discussed in the next section, these early adopters will communicate with one another via tunneling through the IPv4 cloud.

Tunneling Through the IPv4 Cloud

The Internet will probably move to IPv6 "from the edges in." That is, IPv6 will be adopted first by smaller organizations with greater flexibility and a higher tolerance for the difficulties of pioneering. From the points of view of route aggregation and bandwidth usage, these smaller organizations are at the edges, and the **6bone** and high-capacity networks are at the center. How are these islands of IPv6 adrift in a vast ocean of IPv4 routers and hosts to communicate with one another? Through tunnels.

To send a packet to a distant IPv6 network through intervening IPv4 routers, the IPv6 packet is formed normally and sent to a router capable of encapsulating it in an IPv4 packet. The routers on both ends of the tunnels must be dual stack routers, capable of understanding both IPv4 and IPv6. When the interim IPv4 packet reaches the distant IPv6 dual stack router, that router strips off the IPv4 packet and routes the packet on its local IPv6 network normally. There are several variations of this theme to accommodate particular scenarios and particular device capabilities. IPv4-compatible IPv6 addresses were designed expressly for this kind of situation, where IPv6 routers need to understand IPv4.

An alternate scheme is also currently being tested. For IPv4 nodes or networks with public IPv4 addresses, the alternate scheme proposes forming a legitimate IPv6 address by adding the 32 bits of the IPv4 address to the network prefix 2002/16. This creates an address of the form: 2002:IPv4address:SLA:Interface ID. The interface ID would be the normal 48 bits, the site-level address would be the normal 16 bits, and the combination of the 2002/16 prefix plus the 32 bits of the IPv4 address would make up the first 48 bits of the new address.

Longer term, this scheme would simply inflict many of the problems of IPv4 routing on the IPv6 routers. In the short term, however, when IPv6 addresses are very few, it may provide a way to get connectivity between widely dispersed IPv6 islands, without the need for configured tunnels.

Native IPv6

We may not fully realize how much of the apparent congestion of the Internet is due to the headaches of routing and sharing scarce IPv4 addresses until IPv6 begins to come into its own. At some point in the next three years, the switch over will begin in earnest, as improved performance combined with greater availability and ease of use of IPv6 are recognized.

IPv6 Rate of Adoption

The address crunch is not going away, but neither are the addresses already granted under IPv4. The biggest push for the adoption of IPv6 is coming from those who were not a part of the initial Internet "land rush" of the 1990s (that is, the developing world, particularly East Asia). It also means whole classes of technologies not even considered by the first designers of the Internet.

These new technologies, such as cellular phones, PDAs, and the like, have two reasons to embrace IPv6. First, they want the address space, as communications technologies, in particular, need vast numbers of connected users to achieve network effects. To understand network effects, consider the relative usefulness of having a telephone in New York City in 2001, versus having one of the three telephones in Dodge City, Kansas, in 1902. Sometimes a lot more users make something a lot more useful. Second, communications technologies need the improved functionality of the IPv6 protocol suite.

In 2001, IPv6 is still experimental. By 2003, it will begin to be widely implemented. You may have the opportunity to experiment with IPv6 at some sites even before that. For all of us, the upcoming adoption of IPv6 promises to be an interesting experience!

13

CHAPTER SUMMARY

☐ The new version of the Internet Protocol, IPv6, must be adopted to solve the IP address shortage. IPv6 supports more than 10^{27} times the number of addresses that IPv4 currently supports.

❑ Solving the address shortage is a prerequisite for solving any other problems of the Internet, and for pursuing the many outstanding opportunities that the Internet presents, both for new devices and for new users.

❑ IPv6 builds on lessons learned in IPv4 to streamline headers, allocate and aggregate addresses, and generally improve routing behavior. Thus, even though the IPv6 address space is enormously larger than the IPv4 address space, most experts believe it will enjoy faster routing behavior (and therefore, better perceived performance) than current IPv4 environments can support.

❑ IPv6 addresses are 128 bits long, but typically include a 48-bit interface ID that, for many nodes, will be globally unique in its own right.

❑ IPv6 introduces a Neighbor Discovery protocol that helps support stateless autoconfiguration, and provides improved support for mobile users.

❑ IPv6 makes it relatively painless to renumber networks. When network numbering schemes match actual network topologies, routing becomes much more efficient.

❑ IPv6 supports a robust, built-in security architecture with modular components included in IPv6's required core implementation.

❑ IPv6 incorporates incremental updates to most core IP-related protocols, including IP and TCP. At the same time, IPv6 remains broadly compatible with IPv4, and the two will exist side by side for many years.

❑ Migration to IPv6 will be driven by the desire for globally routable addresses (not private or NAT addresses), and the need for new functionality.

❑ If the Internet does not accommodate mobile users, they will find other means to establish and maintain connectivity. IPv6 remains their best bet.

KEY TERMS

:: — In IPv6 addresses, the pair of colon characters stands for several contiguous 16-bit groups, each of which is all zeroes. This notation can be used only once in any address.

6bone — The experimental backbone of the IPv6 Internet. This is a collection of routers, hosts, and network connections over a variety of media, used to test the emerging standards of the next generation Internet Protocol.

access control — In IPSec, or other security, the ability to prevent unauthorized use of resources. It provides the ability to prevent intrusion into reserved spaces, real or theoretical.

aggregatable global unicast address — The layout of these IPv6 addresses breaks the leftmost 64 bits of the address into explicit fields to allow for easier routing. Specifically, it allows routes to these addresses to be "aggregated," that is, combined into a single entry in the router table.

binding acknowledgement — The response sent in reply to a binding update. It is optional in some cases.

binding request — In Mobile IP, a message sent (typically from a correspondent) to the mobile user, asking for both its current COA and home address.

binding table — The home agent's binding table binds the mobile user's COA and home address, much like a routing table, and allows the home agent to reroute traffic addressed to the user's home address out to the new COA.

binding update — In Mobile IP, a message sent from the mobile user either to a home agent or to another node, which keeps a binding cache for mobile users, asking them to change this binding. The binding update may take several specific forms.

bump-in-the-stack (BITS) — A method of implementing IPSec and other security tools such that they appear to operate "between" the network protocol stack (such as IP) and the Data Link layer drivers.

bump-in-the-wire (BITW) — A method of implementing IPSec and other security tools as a freestanding processor on the trusted network, but before the public network. Often a simple integrated device literally plugged into the host computer on one side and the local link on the other.

Care-of Address (COA) — In Mobile IP, the remote or foreign address through which a mobile node may be reached.

ciphertext — The result of performing encryption on plain text. The encrypted or enciphered data is called ciphertext.

confidentiality — The ability to restrict access to some resource by any but authorized users. The typical approach is encryption, rendering the data unusable without the keys and algorithm needed to decrypt it.

connectionless integrity — In IPSec or similar security regimes, the ability to provide integrity, but without the ability to ensure the connection itself.

data origin authentication — In IPSec or similar security areas, the ability to verify the source of received information, or to check that the source possesses some trusted token.

decryption — The process of "unlocking" or making encrypted data readable.

Differentiated Services (diffserv) — The name of the IETF working group studying that area of interest.

dual stack — Two different implementations of similar protocols, such as IPv4 and IPv6. The transition from IPv4 to IPv6 will require several routers and hosts to operate in dual stack mode during the transition, allowing them to communicate on both networks.

Dynamic Host Configuration Protocol version 6 (DHCPv6) — The updated version of this protocol for IPv6. DHCPv6 defines the behavior of servers and clients in the stateful assignment of parameters for configuration of the clients' network (and other) settings. DHCPv6 can interoperate with stateless autoconfiguration.

Encapsulating Security Payload (ESP) — A header in an IPv6 packet and/or the security protocol that uses that extension header. ESP provides encryption services under IPSec.

13

encryption — The process of rendering data unintelligible in a way that is reversible by applying a secret key.

EUI-64 format — An IEEE transformation, permitting the burned-in MAC addresses of NICs to be padded in particular ways to create globally unique 48-bit interface identifiers for each interface.

flow — A set of packets for which a source requires special handling by intervening routers.

foreign agent (FA) — An entity in the Mobile IPv4 scheme no longer used in IPv6.

foreign network — A network that has a different network prefix than the mobile user's own home address.

home agent (HA) — In Mobile IP, a router on the mobile user's home network, willing and able to store and forward messages on behalf of the mobile agent while it is roaming.

interface identifier — In IPv6 addressing, unicast and anycast addresses have the lower-order bits of their addresses reserved for a bit string that uniquely identifies a particular interface, either globally or (at a minimum) locally.

Internet Protocol next generation (IPng) — An older name for the most recent version of IP. It is more often called IPv6.

IPv4-compatible address — IPv4-compatible addresses are used by nodes that need to tunnel IPv6 packets through IPv4 routers. These are dual stack nodes, as they understand both IPv4 and IPv6.

IPv4-mapped address — IPv4-mapped addresses are used by IPv6 nodes, which need to communicate with IPv4 nodes that do not understand IPv6 at all.

jumbograms — A proposal for allowing very large (beyond 4-gigabyte) packets to be transported using IPv6. Used only in special circumstances, such as on large backbone routes.

key — In cryptography, a secret piece of information used in encoding or encrypting the information to be hidden. Keys are used in conjunction with a transformation.

limited traffic flow confidentiality — In IPSec, the ability to defeat traffic analysis by hiding the path, frequency, source, destination, and volume of traffic between correspondents.

link-local address — The link-local address has the first 10 (leftmost) bits set to 1111111010 (all ones except for the last three digits, which are set to 010 [binary]). The next 54 bits are set to all zeroes. The last (rightmost) 64 bits of the link-local address are the normal interface ID. When a router sees the link-local address prefix in a packet, it knows it can safely ignore it, as the packet is intended only for the local network segment.

micro-mobility — Generally dealt with at the link layer, below IP. It has to do with maintaining connectivity to a local link over a wireless connection. Examples of micro-mobility include the hand-off of cellular phones as they pass from one radio cell to another, and maintaining identity of a laptop computer as it moves between access points in a wireless LAN.

Neighbor Advertisement (NA) — When requested, or when its own link layer address changes, a node sends a Neighbor Advertisement including its IPv6 address and its link layer address.

Neighbor Discovery (ND) — A protocol in IPv6 that permits nodes and routers on a local link to keep one another updated about any recent changes in their network connectivity or status.

Neighbor Solicitation (NS) — A node can send a Neighbor Solicitation to find (or verify) the link layer address of a local node, see if that node is still available, or check that its own address is not in use by another.

Network Service Access Point (NSAP) — These networks (such as ATM, X.25, and so forth) typically set up point-to-point links between hosts. This is a very different paradigm from the one built into IP.

per-domain behavior (PDB) — In differentiated service, a class of descriptors of available service levels, or a way of describing the entities offering such differentiated service levels—in this case, a "domain." Services are provided as specified throughout the domain, and change at the edge of the domain. Per-domain behaviors are available across all hops within a given domain.

per-hop behavior (PHB) — In differentiated service, a class of descriptors of available service levels. One way of describing the entities offering such differentiated service levels—in this case, individual routers, or a path traced through individual routers.

plaintext — The data to be encrypted when still in its original (readable or usable) form.

protection against replays — The ability to distinguish between "live" traffic from a trusted source and copies of such traffic masquerading as authentic communications. Protection against replays are typically based on packet sequence numbering and checking.

Resource Reservation Protocol (RSVP) — A protocol aimed at regularizing and formalizing the practice of securing particular levels of service for traffic flows over the Internet.

Router Advertisement (RA) — A message, or advertisement, sent out by a router, periodically or on request, that contains its own link layer address, the network prefix of the local subnet, the MTU for the local link, suggested hop limit values, and other parameters useful for nodes on the local link. RAs can also contain flagged parameters indicating the type of autoconfiguration new nodes should use.

Router Solicitation (RS) — Asking any routers connected to the local link to identify themselves by immediately sending their RAs rather than waiting for the next scheduled advertisement.

SA bundle — An ordered set of Security Associations that should be applied to match a certain security policy.

scope identifier — In IPv6, a 4-bit field limiting the valid range for a multicast address. In IPv6 multicast addresses, not all values are defined, but among those defined are the site-local and the link-local scope. Multicast addresses are not valid outside their configured scope, and will not be forwarded beyond it.

13

Security Association (SA) — In IPSec, the three-part combination of a destination address, an SPI, and a security protocol such as Authentication or ESP. The SA defines a set of processes or transformations to be performed on traffic bound for the named destination.

Security Association Database (SAD) — In IPSec, a notional or conceptual store of Security Associations that maps their particular characteristics onto a general description of an abstract SA.

security gateway — In IPSec, a router using secured communications that provides secured and authenticated routing for other IPSec traffic.

Security Parameters Index (SPI) — In IPSec, a value that, along with the security protocol and the destination address, uniquely defines a Security Association.

Security Policy Database (SPD) — In IPSec, a mapping of security selectors (selection criteria) with policies, or sets of procedures, to be followed in the selected situation.

site-local address — The site-local address has the first 10 (leftmost) bits set to 1111111011 (all ones except for the last three digits, which are set to 011 [binary]). The next 38 bits are set to all zeroes, and the next 16 bits after that contain the subnet ID that defines the "site" to which this address is local. As in other unicast type addressees, the last (rightmost) 64 bits are the standard interface ID. Site-local addresses allow packets to be forwarded internally to the site, but prevent the packets from being shared across the global Internet.

solicited node address — A multicast address with link-local scope, which helps reduce the number of multicast groups to which nodes must subscribe in order to make themselves available for solicitation by other nodes on their local link. The solicited node address is FF02:0:0:0:0:1:FF*xx.xxxx*, where "*xx.xxxx*" stands for the lowest-order (rightmost) 24 bits of the unicast or anycast address associated with that interface.

traffic mode — In IPSec, a method of applying Security Associations to traffic bound from one host to another. Encryption or authentication may be applied on a per-packet basis, with ESP encrypting only the higher-level protocol payload, and AH authenticating only that same portion, plus any headers that will not change in transit.

transformations — In cryptography, a set of mathematical manipulations.

tunnel mode — In IPSec, a method of applying Security Associations, possibly in an extended nested sequence, to packets that are encapsulated and tunneled from or to at least one security gateway.

unspecified address — In IPv6, the unspecified address is all zeroes, and can be represented as "::" in normal notation. This is essentially the address that is no address. It cannot be used as a destination address.

usable address space — The number of hosts that can actually be connected to the Internet.

REVIEW QUESTIONS

1. Which of the following new or enhanced features is included as part of IPv6? (Choose all that apply.)

   a. increased IP address space

   b. improved routing characteristics

   c. enhanced Quality of Service (QoS) options

   d. improved support for mobile users

   e. built-in security features and functions

2. How many bits wide is an IPv6 address?

   a. 32

   b. 64

   c. 128

   d. 256

3. What is the correct interpretation of the symbol :: in an IPv6 address?

   a. Substitute as many zeroes as are needed to construct a complete address.

   b. Substitute eight zeroes.

   c. Substitute 16 zeroes.

   d. Substitute 32 zeroes.

4. The special IP address symbol :: can occur more than once in an IPv6 address. True or false?

   a. True

   b. False

5. The basic numerical notation used to convey IPv6 addresses in writing is:

   a. binary

   b. decimal

   c. hexadecimal

   d. none of the above

6. What does the "slash-decimal" notation (for example, 1090:9:900:210D:100:100:227:325F / 60) that can follow an IPv6 address denote?

   a. number of bits in the network portion of the address

   b. number of bits in the subnet mask portion of the address

   c. number of bits in the host portion of the address

   d. number of bits in the multicast scope identifier

13

7. How can you convert a 48-bit MAC Ethernet address into the IEEE EUI-64 format?

   a. Pad the beginning of the string with hexadecimal 0x0000.

   b. Pad the end of the string with hexadecimal 0xFFFF.

   c. Separate the manufacturer ID (first 24 bits) from the NIC sequence number (last 24 bits) with hexadecimal 0xFFFE.

   d. Separate the manufacturer ID (first 24 bits) from the NIC sequence number (last 24 bits) with hexadecimal 0xFFFF.

8. Each type of network, such as Ethernet, token ring, FDDI, SONET, and so forth, has its own precise techniques to create unique IPv6 interface identifiers. True or false?

   a. True

   b. False

9. What type of IPv6 address can contain an IPv4 address? (Choose all that apply.)

   a. IPv4-superset

   b. IPv4-container

   c. IPv4-compatible

   d. IPv4-mapped

10. Both types of IPv6 addresses that can contain IPv4 addresses exist to permit (a) IPv6 peers to tunnel IPv6 traffic through IPv4 links and (b) IPv6 nodes to communicate with IPv4-only nodes (and hence, they do not understand IPv6 addresses or protocols). True or false?

    a. True

    b. False

11. Which of the following special IPv6 addresses may not be used as a destination address?

    a. multicast address

    b. anycast address

    c. ::1 (loopback address)

    d. :: (all zeroes address)

12. Which technique replaces use of broadcasts in IPv6? (Choose all that apply.)

    a. multicast

    b. anycast

    c. unicast

    d. none of the above

13. What information does the second byte of a multicast address convey?

    a. first the Scope field, then the Flags field

    b. first the Flags field, then the Scope field

    c. interface, site, organization, and global scope settings

    d. transient address versus well-known address

14. Which type of device defines the "nearest" instance of an anycast address?

    a. client

    b. anycast server

    c. local router

    d. edge or border router

15. What single anycast address must be supported on all subnets?

    a. DHCP

    b. NFS

    c. NTP

    d. subnet router

16. How many levels of aggregation do IPv6 unicast addresses support?

    a. one

    b. two

    c. three

    d. four

17. Which two kinds of IPv6 addresses correspond to the private IPv4 addresses defined in RFC 1918?

    a. subnet-local

    b. link-local

    c. interface-local

    d. site-local

18. From which category of IPv6 addresses do special addresses come, such as the loopback address and addresses that contain IPv4 addresses?

    a. reserved with 0:0 prefix

    b. unassigned with 0:1 prefix

    c. aggregatable global unicast addresses

    d. link-local unicast addresses

    e. multicast addresses

13

19. What kinds of networks does the block of IPv6 addresses known as Network Service Access Point serve?

    a. conventional LANs

    b. mobile radio networks

    c. networks that use NSAP addresses, such as ATM and X.25

    d. IPX networks

20. What is the name of the IPv6 protocol defined in RFC 2461 that defines mechanisms for nodes to determine their link addresses, subnet prefixes, working routers, and so forth?

    a. Routing Information Protocol (RIP)

    b. Border Gateway Protocol (BGP)

    c. Autoconfiguration Protocol (ACP)

    d. Neighbor Discovery (ND) protocol

21. Which ICMP message type does the protocol described in RFC 2461 use? (Choose all that apply.)

    a. Router Solicitation

    b. Interface Advertisement

    c. Neighbor Solicitation

    d. Echo Request

    e. Neighbor Advertisement

22. IPv6 does not permit routers to fragment packets; instead, senders are required to check the PMTU and size their packets accordingly. True or false?

    a. True

    b. False

23. The IPv6 packet header is always a fixed length of 24 bytes. True or false?

    a. True

    b. False

24. Which of the following best describes the function of the Hop-by-Hop extension header for IPv6?

    a. It provides the destination address for the next router in the route path.

    b. It defines Authentication Header data.

    c. It defines the upper-layer protocol in the payload.

    d. It carries information that affects routers along a path, such as the router alert of the jumbogram large payload option.

25. Which of the following best describes the function of the Routing extension header for IPv6?

    a. It specifies intermediary router addresses through which the IPv6 packet should be forwarded.

    b. It controls the presence or absence of source routing for IPv6.

    c. It provides for strict routing controls for IPv6 packets.

    d. It specifies the ultimate destination address for a packet.

26. Which function is the Authentication extension header for IPv6 designed to support? (Choose all that apply.)

    a. It provides encryption information for the packet payload.

    b. By providing proof of identity, it prevents spoofing and connection theft.

    c. It can perform encryption or compression services, but not both at the same time.

    d. It provides a limited defense against replay attacks.

    e. It provides an integrity check on those parts of the packet that remain constant while it's in transit.

27. The Neighbor Discovery protocol in IPv6 supports stateless autoconfiguration of attached nodes. True or false?

    a. True

    b. False

28. Which activity occurs during the process of IPv6 autoconfiguration? (Choose all that apply.)

    a. The node checks its calculated link-local address with a Neighbor Solicitation to make sure that address is not already in use.

    b. The node makes a Router Solicitation to obtain Router Advertisements from attached routers.

    c. The node attempts to calculate a link-local address by prefixing its EUI–64 interface ID with the well-known link-local prefix.

    d. Once a DHCP server is identified, it always provides all necessary information to complete the autoconfiguration process.

    e. all of the above

29. Which of the following represents a valid enhancement found in DHCPv6, or a valid related enhancement that is part of the basic IPv6 environment? (Choose all that apply.)

    a. IPv6 interfaces support multiple addresses in DHCPv6.

    b. IPv6 nodes must listen for address updates to support automatic renumbering.

    c. Nodes under IPv6 can obtain locally functioning addresses without any interaction with DHCP at all.

13

     d. DCHPv6 servers and routers can be configured to send advertisements in authenticated form.

     e. DHCPv6 can be set up to dynamically update DNS records.

30. Which method represents valid implementations of IPSec? (Choose all that apply.)

     a. in a dedicated computer called a security gateway

     b. as an integral part of the IP stack on a host

     c. as a configuration option to the IP protocol

     d. as a fill-in layer between the previously installed IP layer and the local link network drivers (also known as a "bump-in-the-stack" or BITS implementation)

     e. in a free-standing cryptographic device (also known as a "bump-in the-wire" or BITW implementation)

HANDS-ON PROJECTS

This project assumes that you have access to the Internet, and that you installed the EtherPeek for Windows demo program.

Project 13-1

To identify sources of IPv6 product updates:

1. Start Internet Explorer (click **Start**, point to **Programs**, and click **Internet Explorer**).

2. In the Address text box, type **http://www.ipv6.org**, and then press **Enter** to access the IPv6 Web site.

3. Browse the site to locate information on installing and configuring IPv6 on various operating systems.

4. Compose a list of sites that maintain IPv6 update information for your classroom equipment.

5. In the Address text box, type **http://www.visc.vt.edu/ipv6/**, and then press **Enter**.

6. Browse this site and identify update information.

Both of these sites are excellent links for IPv6 information.

Project 13-2

To examine IPv6 communications:

1. Start the EtherPeek for Windows demo program.

2. Click **File**, **Open**.

3. Insert the CD that accompanies this book into your CD-ROM drive. Open the **18654-2\Ch13** folder on your hard disk.

4. Select the trace file **ipv6dump.pkt**. Click **Open**. The packet summary window appears.

5. Click and drag the summary window columns to increase their size, making the IPv6 source and destination addresses viewable.

6. Scroll down to **Packet #28**, and double-click this packet. The decode window appears and displays the IPv6 packet structure.

7. Answer the following questions about this packet:

   a. What is the purpose of this packet?

   b. What is the hop count limit on this packet?

   c. Compare the Ethernet header source/destination addresses to the IPv6 header source/destination addresses. How do they compare?

8. Click the **Decode Next** button to view Packet #29. What is the purpose of this packet?

9. Close the decode window. Close the packet summary window and proceed immediately to the next project.

Project 13-3

To build an IPv6 filter:

1. In the EtherPeek demo, click **View**, **Filters** to open the Filters window. Click the **Insert** button 📖 . The Edit Filter window appears.

2. Enter the name **IPv6** in the Filter text box.

3. Click the **Protocol filter** check box.

4. Click the **Protocol** button.

5. Click the boxed plus sign to the left of the frame type used on your network.

6. Click to highlight **IPv6**, and then click **OK**.

7. Click **OK** to close the Edit Filter window, and click the **Close** button in the upper-right corner to close the Filter window.

8. What do you think this filter is based on?

9. To test your filter, open the **ipv6dump.pkt** file (in the **18654-2\Ch13** folder on your hard disk).

10. Click **Edit**, **Select**.

11. In the Selection criteria area, scroll down to locate and then click the check box next to the **IPv6** filter.

12. Click the **Select Packets** button. The Selection Results dialog box appears, stating that 242 packets are selected.

13. In the Selection Results dialog box, click the **Hide Unselected** button. Click the **Close** button in the Select window. The packet summary window should show 242 packets highlighted out of the entire 250-packet trace file.

13

CASE PROJECTS

1. Because of the ongoing need that routers will no doubt experience to support both IPv4 and IPv6 (particularly away from the network edges, where wholesale IPv6 upgrades will at first be most likely), such machines will need to support both protocol stacks simultaneously. Explain what kinds of connections a dual stack router can support, and why such connections are necessary. Do you think that the overhead involved in handling dual stacks will increase or lower the protocol processing load that such devices must handle?

2. Discuss the pros and cons of constructing IPv6 addresses directly from IPv4 addresses by adding the 32 bits of the IPv4 address to the network prefix 2002/16, along with an IPv6 site-level address and the interface ID, so that the resulting IPv6 address takes the form 2002:IPv4address:SLA:Interface ID/16. Here, the interface ID remains set at the 48 bits normal for IPv4 MAC layer addresses, and the site-level address remains set at its normal 16-bit level for IPv6. What does this do from the perspective of ease of implementation? What does it do to IPv6 routing behavior?

3. Analyze the following methods of implementing IP Security on an existing network:

   ◘ Install a security gateway between the router and the single external interface to the Internet.

   ◘ Install the IPSec protocols as part of the IP stack on every network host.

   ◘ Use the BITS technique to place IPSec between the IP stack and the link layer drivers on each network host.

   ◘ Use the BITW technique to impose IPSec on all outbound traffic leaving through the single external interface to the Internet.

For each of these approaches, answer the following questions:

1. How many machines require software changes to implement this method?

2. Where do potential performance bottlenecks occur?

3. Can this method support completely secure communications all the way from the originating host to the destination host?

4. What kinds of restrictions from the Security Policy Database are users most likely to notice after IPSec is installed?

A

IMPORTANT RFCs

This appendix lists the RFCs mentioned in this book. They can be found at the following Web sites, or via the Network Analysis Survival Kit (WildPackets, Inc.) included on the CD accompanying this book:

- *http://www.cis.ohio-state.edu/hypertext/information/rfc.html*
- *http://www.ietf.org*

RFC Number	Title	Guide to TCP/IP Chapter
768	User Datagram Protocol	5
791	Internet Protocol	3
792	Internet Control Message Protocol	4
793	Transmission Control Protocol	5
812	NICNAME/WHOIS	6
821	Simple Mail Transfer Protocol	6
826	An Ethernet Address Resolution Protocol	3, 10
854	Telnet Protocol Specification	6
855	Telnet Option Specifications	6
857	Telnet Echo Option	6
862	Echo Protocol	6
864	Character Generator Protocol	6
865	Quote of the Day Protocol	6
882	Domain Names—Concepts and Facilities	7
883	Domain Names—Implementation and Specification	7
894	A Standard for the Transmission of IP Datagrams over Ethernet Networks	3
896	Congestion Control in IP/TCP Internetworks	5
903	A Reverse Address Resolution Protocol	3
904	Exterior Gateway Protocol Formal Specification	10
950	Internet Standard Subnetting Procedure	4
959	File Transfer Protocol (FTP)	6

RFC Number	Title	Guide to TCP/IP Chapter
1001	Protocol Standard for a NetBIOS Service on a TCP/UDP Transport: Concepts and Methods	6, 12
1002	Protocol Standard for a NetBIOS Service on a TCP/UDP Transport: Detailed Specifications	6, 12
1035	Domain Names—Implementation and Specification	7
1042	A Standard for the Transmission of IP Datagrams over IEEE 802 Networks	3
1055	A Nonstandard for Transmission of IP Datagrams over Serial Lines: SLIP	1, 3
1058	Routing Information Protocol	10
1122	Requirements for Internet Hosts—Communication Layers	5
1144	Compressing TCP/IP Headers for Low-Speed Serial Links	3
1163	A Border Gateway Protocol (BGP)	3
1191	Path MTU Discovery	4
1213	Management Information Base for Network Management of TCP/IP-based Internets: MIB-II	11
1256	ICMP Router Discovery Messages	4, 10
1050	RPC: Remote Procedure Call Protocol Specification	6
1288	The Finger User Information Protocol	6
1305	Network Time Protocol (Version 3) Specification, Implementation and Analysis	4
1332	The PPP Internet Protocol Control Protocol (IPCP)	3
1349	Type of Service in the Internet Protocol Suite	3
1350	The TFTP Protocol (Revision 2)	6
1356	Multiprotocol Interconnect on X.25 and ISDN in the Packet Mode	3
1393	Traceroute Using an IP Option	4
1442	Structure of Management Information for Version 2 of the Simple Network Management Protocol (SNMPv2)	6
1443	Textual Conventions for Version 2 of the Simple Network Management Protocol (SNMPv2)	6
1444	Conformance Statements for Version 2 of the Simple Network Management Protocol (SNMPv2)	6
1445	Administrative Model for Version 2 of the Simple Network Management Protocol (SNMPv2)	6
1446	Security Protocols for Version 2 of the Simple Network Management Protocol (SNMPv2)	6
1447	Party MIB for Version 2 of the Simple Network Management Protocol (SNMPv2)	6

A

RFC Number	Title	Guide to TCP/IP Chapter
1448	Protocol Operations for Version 2 of the Simple Network Management Protocol (SNMPv2)	6
1449	Transport Mappings for Version 2 of the Simple Network Management Protocol (SNMPv2)	6
1450	Management Information Base for Version 2 of the Simple Network Management Protocol (SNMPv2)	6
1513	Token Ring Extensions to the Remote Network Monitoring MIB	11
1519	Classless Inter-Domain Routing (CIDR): An Address Assignment and Aggregation Strategy	2
1534	Interoperation Between DHCP and BOOTP	8
1626	Default IP MTU for Use Over ATM AAL5	3
1661	The Point-to-Point Protocol (PPP)	1, 3
1662	PPP in HDLC-like Framing	3
1757	Remote Network Monitoring Management Information Base	11
1759	Printer MIB	11
1771	A Border Gateway Protocol 4 (BGP-4)	10
1812	Requirements for IP Version 4 Routers	4
1869	SMTP Service Extensions	6
1877	PPP Internet Protocol Control Protocol Extensions for Name Server Addresses	3
1878	Variable Length Subnet Table for IPv4	2
1903	Textual Conventions for Version 2 of the Simple Network Management Protocol (SNMPv2)	6
1904	Conformance Statements for Version 2 of the Simple Network Management Protocol (SNMPv2)	6
1905	Protocol Operations for Version 2 of the Simple Network Management Protocol (SNMPv2)	6
1906	Transport Mappings for Version 2 of the Simple Network Management Protocol (SNMPv2)	6
1907	Management Information Base for Version 2 of the Simple Network Management Protocol (SNMPv2)	6
1908	Coexistence between Version 1 and Version 2 of the Internet-standard Network Management Framework	6
1909	An Administrative Infrastructure for SNMPv2	6
1910	User-based Security Model for SNMPv2	6
1918	Address Allocation for Private Internets	2, 9, 10, 13

RFC Number	Title	Guide to TCP/IP Chapter
1928	SOCKS Protocol Version 5	9
1945	Hypertext Transfer Protocol—HTTP/1.0	6
2002	IP Mobility Support	10
2003	IP Encapsulation within IP	10
2004	Minimal Encapsulation within IP	10
2005	Applicability Statement for IP Mobility Support	10
2006	The Definitions of Managed Objects for IP Mobility Support Using SMIv2	10
2018	TCP Selective Acknowledgement Options	5
2021	Remote Network Monitoring Management Information Base Version 2 Using SMIv2	11
2026	The Internet Standards Process—Revision 3	1
2131	Dynamic Host Configuration Protocol	8
2132	DHCP Options and BOOTP Vendor Extensions	8
2136	Dynamic Updates in the Domain Name System (DNS UPDATE)	7
2141	URN Syntax	6
2241	DHCP Options for Novell Directory Services	8
2246	The TLS Protocol Version 1.0	9
2317	Classless IN-ADDR.ARPA Delegation	7
2328	OSPF Version 2	10
2427	Multiprotocol Interconnect over Frame Relay	3
2453	RIP Version 2	10
2465	Management Information Base for IP Version 6: Textual Conventions and General Group	11
2474	Definition of Differentiated Service Field (DS Field) in the IPv4 and IPv6 Headers	3
2515	Definitions of Managed Objects for ATM Management	11
2581	TCP Congestion Control	5
2700	Internet Official Protocol Standards	1

B

KEY IP RESOURCES ONLINE

All of the Web page addresses (URLs) listed in this appendix, as in the entire book, are listed on the "Guide to TCP/IP" Web page at *http://www.lanw.com/books/gd2tcpip.htm*. The links are reviewed and updated regularly.

GENERAL IP/INTERNET OVERVIEWS

Brent Baccala, Editor, "Connected: An Internet Encyclopedia," *http://www.freesoft.org/CIE/index.htm*. A complete Internet encyclopedia, with in-depth coverage of TCP/IP, including full text of all RFCs.

Raj Jain, "Computer Networking and Internet Protocols: A Comprehensive Introduction," *http://www.cis.ohio-state.edu/~jain/bnr/index.html*. Excellent, in-depth coverage of TCP/IP basics and numerous protocols and services, including high-speed options not included in this text.

Gary C. Kessler, "An Overview of TCP/IP Protocols and the Internet," *http://www.hill.com/library/publications/tcpip.shtml*. Outstanding overview of TCP/IP development, history, and basic structure.

IP/INTERNET HISTORIES

"History of the Internet: Internet Histories," *http://www.isoc.org/internet/history/*. A compendium of Internet histories, including the development of TCP/IP, assembled by the Internet Society (ISOC). The first entry on this page, "A Brief History of the Internet," recounts Internet history as told by those who made it happen, followed by a narrative on the same subject by Vint Cert—both are worth reading!

GENERAL POINTERS TO INTERNET AND NETWORKING TOPICS

Connected: An Internet Encyclopedia of Surf Sites: *http://www.freesoft.org/CIE/Project/surfsite.htm*

RFC Resources

- List of general RFC sites:
  http://dir.yahoo.com/Computers_and_Internet/Standards/RFCs/

- Ohio States's RFCs archive: *http://www.cis.ohio-state.edu/Services/rfc/index.html*

- RFCs indexed by Glimpse: *http://www.pasteur.fr/infosci/RFC/*

- Internet RFC Archives: *http://www.faqs.org/rfcs/*

IP Addressing, Subnetting, and Supernetting

Chuck Semeria, "Understanding IP Addressing: Everything You Ever Wanted To Know," *http://www.3com.com/solutions/en_US/ncs/501302.html*. One of the most comprehensive and readable pieces on all aspects of IP addressing available anywhere (65 pages).

Joe Rudich, *Windows NT Systems* magazine, June 1999: "Practical Subnet Design," *http://www.ntsystems.com/db_area/archive/1999/9906/306fe1.shtml*. Brief but cogent coverage of the ins and outs of IP subnetting.

Binary Arithmetic Overviews

"Binary Arithmetic" (from the Connected: An Internet Encyclopedia site), *http://www.freesoft.org/CIE/Topics/19.htm*. More profusely illustrated version of the same information covered in the text; recommended for "visual thinkers."

Randall Hyde, "The Art of Assembly Language Programming," Chapter 1: Data Representation, *http://webster.cs.ucr.edu/Page_asm/ArtofAssembly/CH01/CH01-1.html*. The best coverage of binary numbering and arithmetic available anywhere.

Guy C. Yost, "Establishing an Internet Presence: Part II—Obtaining an IP Address," *http://www.naspa.com/PDF/96/T9604013.pdf*. Great overview of what's involved in obtaining an IP address, including cost and ownership considerations.

General IP Protocol Information

Protocol Directory: *http://www.protocols.com/pbook/toc.htm*

Protocols.com is a great resource for information on all kinds of networking protocols, including all notable members of the TCP/IP protocol suite. Visit *http://www.protocols.com/pbook/tcpip.htm* to go straight to the TCP/IP Suite information. This site is definitely worth adding to your Bookmarks or Favorites lists.

DNS Information

DNS Resources Directory: *http://www.dns.net/dnsrd/*

The be-all and end-all of DNS-related Web sites, this one has pointers to everything DNS-related known to man.

DHCP Information

DHCP Resources: *http://www.nts.com/library/tldhcp.html*

Efficient Networks has put together an outstanding compendium of DHCP resources, including white papers, tutorials, hot lists, FAQs, and more. Its own local "DHCP Overview" is an excellent supplement to this text. Also, be sure to visit the "Resources for DHCP" site at *http://www.dhcp.org* for more information about the standard and its evolution.

IP Security

- Computer Security FAQs: *http://www.faqs.org/faqs/computer-security/*
- One of the ultimate resources for security-related information of all kinds, this list includes lots of IP-related security coverage.
- Windows Security pointers: *http://www.lanw.com/training/interop/securityurls.htm*
- Ed Tittel and James Michael Stewart teach classes at least three times a year on this topic, and maintain a comprehensive list of Windows security resources, many of which address IP security matters.
- SecurityFocus: *http://www.securityfocus.com/*
- One of the best all-around computer and network security sites.
- System, Administration, Networking, and Security (SANS) Institute: *http://www.sans.org*
- One of the best purveyors of security training and certification, with a decided emphasis on TCP/IP.
- SearchSecurity.com: *http://searchsecurity.techtarget.com/*
- A great general computer and network security site, with excellent coverage of IP security topics and technologies.
- SecurityPortal.com: *http://www.securityportal.com/*

Another great general computer and network security site, with great coverage of IP security topics, protocols, and technologies.

IP ROUTING

- Kentrox Pacesetter: *http://www.kentrox.com/support/tn/pacesetter/iproute.htm*

  Although this discussion is particular to the Kentrox Pacesetter router, it's general enough to be worth reviewing anyway. Check it out.

- TechEncyclopedia: *http://www.techweb.com/encyclopedia/defineterm?term=routing*

  A visit to the CMP TechWeb TechEncyclopedia with "routing" selected as the search term turns up a plethora of pointers to useful information and resources.

- TechFest: *http://www.techfest.com/networking/prot.htm*

  This location at TechFest covers protocols in general, but has a peachy section on routing that is well worth further investigation.

SNMP

- SNMP Resources: *http://www.pmoyer.org/web/snmp.html*

  A great, if somewhat eccentric, collection of resources about SNMP.

- CobraNet SNMP Resources: *http://www.peakaudio.com/CobraNet/Developer/ SNMP_Resources.html*

  SimpleWeb is a well-known source for SNMP standards news and information. Aimed at would-be MIB developers, this collection of resources is more mainstream.

- SNMP Resources: *http://members.tripod.lycos.nl/engelander/SNMP.html*

  A European site for SNMP tutorials, pointers, standards, and other information.

- SNMPWorld.com: *http://silver.he.net/~rrg/SNMP_NEWS.htm*

  The title for this site says it all—great pointers to a wide range of SNMP resources.

NETBIOS OVER TCP/IP

- Globetrotting.com: *http://www.globetrotting.com/tcp/tcpip_msnetworking.htm*

  A useful, if somewhat rambling, tutorial on the relationships between NetBIOS and TCP/IP in the Windows environment.

- Microsoft Developer Network Search: *http://search.microsoft.com/us/dev/default.asp*

  A quick visit to the MSDN search engine, with the search term "NetBIOS over TCP/IP" will turn up a lot of useful resources.

- Chaminade.org: *http://www.chaminade.org/MIS/Tutorials/TCPIP.htm#NetBIOS*

  This is part of a general tutorial on Windows TCP/IP that's quite good, and includes a great overview of NBT, WINS, and related topics.

IPv6

- Nokia: *http://www-nrc.nokia.com/ipv6/ipv6/*

  Nokia, the Finnish telecom giant, offers a good pictorial IPv6 tutorial. Worth visiting.

- IPv6 Forum: *http://www.ipv6forum.com/*

  The IPv6 Forum is an industry group devoted to furthering the development and deployment of IPv6. Its home page includes numerous pointers to articles, Web sites, and more through an IPv6 Resources menu entry.

- RIPE: *http://www.viagenie.qc.ca/en/ipv6/tutorial-ipv6-ripe33/html-800x600/*

  RIPE stands for Reseaux Internet Protocol Europeans, the European Internet Protocol Research group. They presented a tutorial on IPv6 in May 1999 that's still worth reading for more information.

- Raj Jain, "IP Next Generation," *http://www.cis.ohio-state.edu/~jain/bnr/f18_ip6.htm.*

  The ubiquitous Raj Jain has a complete IPv6 presentation available online from a 1998 presentation. A bit dated, but still worth a visit.

- About.com: *http://compnetworking.about.com/compute/compnetworking/cs/ipv6/*

  About.com has some great articles, tutorials, and overviews of IPv6 available. Check it out.

TCP/IP NEWSGROUPS

- *comp.protocols.tcp-ip.domains*
- *comp.protocols.tcp-ip.ibmpc*
- *comp.protocols.tcp-ip*

C

COMMAND-LINE IP UTILITIES

This appendix lists the Windows 2000 command-line utilities that can be used to obtain TCP/IP configuration information and test IP connectivity. The command parameters and uses are listed for the following utilities:

- ARP
- IPCONFIG
- NETSTAT
- PATHPING
- PING
- ROUTE
- TRACERT

ARP

The ARP utility reads and manipulates local ARP tables (data link address-to-IP address tables).

Syntax:

arp –s *ip_address datalink_address* [*interface_address*]
arp –d *ip_address* [*interface_address*]
arp –a [*ip_address*]
arp –N [*interface_address*]

Parameter	Description
-a *or* -g	Displays current entries in the ARP cache. If ip_address is specified, the IP and data link address of the specified computer appear. If more than one network interface uses ARP, entries for each ARP table appear.
ip_address	Specifies an Internet address
-N *interface_address*	Displays the ARP entries for the network interface specified by interface_address
-d	Deletes the host specified by interface_address
-s	Adds the host and associates the Internet address ip_address with the data link address datalink_address. The physical address is given as six hexadecimal bytes separated by hyphens. The entry is permanent.
datalink_address	Specifies a physical address
interface_address	If present, this specifies the Internet address of the interface whose address translation table should be modified. If not present, the first applicable interface will be used.

IPCONFIG

The IPCONFIG utility displays and modifies IP address configuration information.

Syntax:

ipconfig /? | /all | /release [*adapter*] | /renew [*adapter*]
            | /flushdns | /registerdns
            | /showclassid *adapter*
            | /setclassid *adapter* [classidtoset]

Parameter	Description
adapter	Used to indicate the full name of an adapter, or match a pattern with * (any character) and ? (one character)
/?	Displays the help message
/all	Displays complete configuration information
/release	Uses DHCP to release the IP address for the specified adapter
/renew	Uses DHCP to renew the IP address for the specified adapter
/flushdns	Purges the DNS cache
/registerdns	Uses DHCP to refresh all DHCP leases and re-registers DNS names
/displaydns	Displays the contents of the DNS cache
/showclassid	Displays all the DHCP class IDs allowed for the adapter
/setclassid	Modifies the DHCP class ID

By default, this command displays only the IP address, subnet mask, and default gateway for each adapter bound to TCP/IP.

NETSTAT

This utility displays protocol statistics and details about the current TCP/IP network connections.

Syntax:
netstat [–a] [–e] [–n] [–s] [–p *protocol*] [–r] [*interval_seconds*]

Parameter	Description
-a	Lists all current connections and open, listening ports on the local system
-e	Displays Data Link layer statistics (can also be used with the -s parameter)
-n	Displays addresses and port numbers in numerical form
p *protocol*	Shows the connections for the specified protocol. The protocol defined may be UDP or TCP. When used with the -s parameter, the protocol definition IP may also be used.
-r	Displays the routing table (also see the ROUTE command)
-s	Displays statistics organized based on the protocols, such as IP, UDP, and TCP by default (can also be used with the -p parameter to define a subset of the default)
interval_seconds	Redisplays the statistics on a regular basis using the interval_seconds value between displays. Press Ctrl+C to stop displaying the statistics. If this parameter is not included, the statistics appear only once.

PATHPING

This utility is used to test router and link latency along a path to a host. PATHPING uses a combination of TRACERT and PING to first determine the path to a specified host, and then test the round trip to the host to identify packet loss to the destination and each router along the path. PATHPING uses ICMP Echo packets.

Syntax:
pathping [–n] [–h *maximum_hops*] [–g *host_list*] [–p *period*]
         [–q *number_of_queries*] [–w *timeout*] [–t] [–r] *target_name*

Parameter	Description
-n	Determines that addresses should not be resolved to host names
-h *maximum_hops*	Defines the maximum number of hops to search for target
-g *host_list*	Defines that a loose source route should be used along the path defined by the host_list
- p *period*	Defines the waiting period between pings in milliseconds
- q *number_of_queries*	Defines the number of queries per hop
- w *timeout*	Defines the timeout for each reply in milliseconds

PING

The PING utility executes an end–to–end connectivity test to other devices and obtains the round–trip time between source and destination device. PING uses the ICMP Echo and Echo Reply packets to test connectivity.

Excessive usage may appear to be a Denial of Service attack.

Syntax:
ping [-t] [-a] [-n *count*] [-l *size*] [-f] [-i *TTL*] [-v *TOS*]
     [-r *count*] [-s *count*] [[-j *host-list*] | [-k *host-list*]]
     [-w *timeout*] *destination-list*

Parameter	Description
-t	Pings the specified host until interrupted (press Ctrl+C to stop sending)
-a	Resolves addresses to hostnames
-n *count*	Indicates the number of Echo Requests to send
-l *size*	Sends a specific size of data. If this size is greater than the local network can handle, the sender will generate fragmented packets directly on the network.
-f	Sets the Don't Fragment flag in the packet
-i *TTL*	Sets the Time to Live value in the packet
-vTOS	Sets the type of service in the packet
-r *count*	Indicates that the PING process should record the route for the number of count hops specified.
-s *count*	Indicates that the PING process should maintain Timestamp information for the number of count hops specified
-j *host_list*	Indicates that the PING process should follow a loose source route path along the host_list path
-k *host_list*	Indicates that the PING process should follow a strict source route along the host_list path
-w *timeout*	Indicates the number of milliseconds the host should wait for each reply

C

ROUTE

The ROUTE utility reads and manipulates IP routing tables on a local device and identifies the current default gateway setting.

Syntax:
route [–f] [–p] [*command*] [*destination*] [MASK *network_mask*] [*gateway*] [METRIC *metric*]
    [IF *interface*]

Parameter	Description
-f	Clears the routing tables of all gateway entries. If this is used with one of the commands listed below, the tables are cleared prior to running the command.
-p	When combined with the ADD command, creates a route that is persistent across system boots (not supported in Windows 95)
command	Specifies one of four commands: PRINT Prints/views a route ADD Adds a route DELETE Deletes a route CHANGE Modifies an existing route
destination	Specifies the host to send command
MASK	If the mask keyword is present, the next parameter is interpreted as the network_mask parameter, which specifies a subnet mask value to be associated with a route entry. If not specified, it defaults to 255.255.255.255.
gateway	Specifies a gateway
interface	Specifies the interface number for the route
METRIC	Calculates the cost, or metric, for the destination

TRACERT

The TRACERT utility traces the routers along a path and obtains round-trip times from source to path routers, and from the source to the destination host.

Syntax:
tracert [-d] [-h *maximum_hops*] [-j *host_list*] [-w *timeout*] *target_name*

Parameter	Description
-d	Tells the system not to resolve addresses to hostnames
-h *maximum_hops*	Specifies the maximum number of hops to search for target
-j *host_list*	Loose source route along host list
-w *timeout*	Number of milliseconds to wait for each reply

Consider using a more robust trace route utility, such as NeoTrace Pro from NeoWorx. The demonstration version of NeoTrace Pro is on the CD accompanying this book.

This appendix is a compilation of the Windows 2000 Registry settings listed in tables throughout this book.

Table D-1 ArpUseEtherSNAP Registry Setting

Registry Information	Details
Location	HKEY_LOCAL_MACHINE\SYSTEM\CurrentControlSet\ Services\Tcpip\Parameters
Data type	REG_DWORD
Valid range	0–1
Default value	0
Present by default	No

The Registry entry ArpUseEtherSNAP must be set to one to enable use of the Ethernet 802.2 SNAP frame format for IP and ARP traffic over Ethernet. See Chapter 3 for more information.

Table D-2 ArpCacheLife Registry Setting

Registry Information	Details
Location	HKEY_LOCAL_MACHINE\SYSTEM\CurrentControlSet\ Services\Tcpip\Parameters
Data type	REG_DWORD
Valid range	0–0xFFFFFFFF
Default value	120
Present by default	No

You can change the ARP cache lifetime default value of the ArpCacheLife Registry setting. See Chapter 3 for more information.

Table D-3   DefaultTTL Registry Setting

Registry Information	Details
Location	HKEY_LOCAL_MACHINE\SYSTEM\CurrentControlSet\ Services\Tcpip\Parameters
Data type	REG_DWORD
Valid range	1–255
Default value	128
Present by default	No

You can set the default TTL for a host using the DefaultTTL Registry setting. See Chapter 3 for more information.

Table D-4   DefaultTOS Registry Setting

Registry Information	Details
Location	HKEY_LOCAL_MACHINE\SYSTEM\CurrentControlSet\ Services\Tcpip\Parameters
Data type	REG_DWORD
Valid range	0–255
Default value	0
Present by default	No

You can set the default TTL for a host using the DefaultTOS Registry setting. The Registry entry is set in decimal for the entire TOS field. See Chapter 3 for more information.

Table D-5   EnablePMTUDiscovery Registry Setting

Registry Information	Details
Location	HKEY_LOCAL_MACHINE\SYSTEM\CurrentControlSet\ Services\Tcpip\Parameters
Data type	REG_DWORD
Valid range	0 or 1
Default value	1
Present by default	No

You can disable PMTU Discovery by setting the EnablePMTUDiscovery Registry setting to zero. See Chapter 4 for more information.

Table D-6 EnablePMTUBHDetect Registry Setting

Registry Information	Details
Location	HKEY_LOCAL_MACHINE\SYSTEM\CurrentControlSet\Services\Tcpip\Parameters
Data type	REG_DWORD
Valid range	0–1
Default value	0
Present by default	No

To enable a Windows 2000 host to detect black hole routers, set the EnablePMTUBHDetect Registry setting to one. See Chapter 4 for more information.

Table D-7 PerformRouterDiscovery Registry Setting

Registry Information	Details
Location	HKEY_LOCAL_MACHINE\SYSTEM\CurrentControlSet\Services\Tcpip\Parameters\Interfaces\<*interface*>
Data type	REG_DWORD
Valid range	0–1
Default value	1
Present by default	Yes

Changing the PerformRouterDiscovery Registry setting to zero disables the ICMP Router Discovery process. See Chapter 4 for more information.

Table D-8 SolicitationAddressBCast Registry Setting

Registry Information	Details
Location	HKEY_LOCAL_MACHINE\SYSTEM\CurrentControlSet\Services\Tcpip\Parameters\Interfaces\<*interface*>
Data type	REG_DWORD
Valid range	0–1
Default value	0
Present by default	No

Changing the SolicitationAddressBCast Registry setting to one enables a Windows 2000 host to use the IP subnet broadcast to perform ICMP Router Solicitation. See Chapter 4 for more information.

Table D-9 MaxUser Port Registry Setting

Registry Information	Details
Location	HKEY_LOCAL_MACHINE\SYSTEM\CurrentControlSet\ Services\Tcpip\Parameters
Data type	REG_DWORD
Valid range	5000–65534
Default value	5000
Present by default	No

You can increase the supported maximum user port number by adding the MaxUserPort Registry entry. See Chapter 5 for more information.

Table D-10 TcpMaxConnectRetransmissions Registry Setting

Registry Information	Details
Location	HKEY_LOCAL_MACHINE\SYSTEM\CurrentControlSet\ Services\Tcpip\Parameters
Data type	REG_DWORD
Valid range	0–255
Default value	2
Present by default	No

The TcpMaxConnectRetransmissions Registry setting defines the number of SYN retries sent when attempting to establish a TCP connection. See Chapter 5 for more information.

Table D-11 TcpNumConnections Registry Settings

Registry Information	Details
Location	HKEY_LOCAL_MACHINE\SYSTEM\CurrentControlSet\ Services\Tcpip\Parameters
Data type	REG_DWORD
Valid range	0–0xFFFFFE
Default value	0xFFFFFE (16,777,214) connections
Present by default	No

The TcpNumConnections setting defines the number of TCP connections that can be open at one time. See Chapter 5 for more information.

Table D-12   KeepAliveTime Registry Setting

Registry Information	Details
Location	HKEY_LOCAL_MACHINE\SYSTEM\CurrentControlSet\Services\Tcpip\Parameters
Data type	REG_DWORD
Valid range	0–0xFFFFFFFF
Default value	0x6DDD00 (7,200,000) milliseconds
Present by default	No

The KeepAliveTime Registry setting defines how long to wait before sending the first TCP keep-alive packet. See Chapter 5 for more information.

Table D-13   KeepAliveInterval Registry Setting

Registry Information	Details
Location	HKEY_LOCAL_MACHINE\SYSTEM\CurrentControlSet\Services\Tcpip\Parameters
Data type	REG_DWORD
Valid range	0–0xFFFFFFFF
Default value	0x3E8 (1000) milliseconds
Present by default	No

The KeepAliveInterval setting defines the delay between keep-alive retransmissions when no acknowledgments are received. See Chapter 5 for more information.

Table D-14   TcpTimeWaitDelay Registry Setting

Registry Information	Details
Location	HKEY_LOCAL_MACHINE\SYSTEM\CurrentControlSet\Services\Tcpip\Parameters
Data type	REG_DWORD
Valid range	30–300
Default value	0xF0 (240)
Present by default	No

You can control the TimeWait delay by changing the TcpTimedWaitDelay Registry setting. See Chapter 5 for more information.

Table D-15   TcpMaxDataRetransmissions Registry Setting

Registry Information	Details
Location	HKEY_LOCAL_MACHINE\SYSTEM\CurrentControlSet\ Services\Tcpip\Parameters
Data type	REG_DWORD
Valid range	0–0xFFFFFFFF
Default value	5
Present by default	No

The maximum retransmission count is set in the TcpMaxDataRetransmissions Registry setting. See Chapter 5 for more information.

Table D-16   TcpInitialRTT Registry Setting

Registry Information	Details
Location	HKEY_LOCAL_MACHINE\SYSTEM\CurrentControlSet\ Services\Tcpip\Parameters
Data type	REG_DWORD
Valid range	0–0xFFFF (seconds)
Default value	3 (seconds)
Present by default	No

The TcpInitialRTT Registry setting defines the initial retransmission timeout (RTO). See Chapter 5 for more information.

Table D-17   GlobalMaxTcpWindowSize Registry Setting

Registry Information	Details
Location	HKEY_LOCAL_MACHINE\SYSTEM\CurrentControlSet\ Services\Tcpip\Parameters
Data type	REG_DWORD
Valid range	0–0x3FFFFFFF (bytes)
Default value	0x4000 (16,384 bytes)
Present by default	No

The maximum receive window size can be set using the GlobalMaxTcpWindowSize Registry setting. See Chapter 5 for more information.

Table D-18 TcpWindowSize Registry Setting

Registry Information	Details
Location	HKEY_LOCAL_MACHINE\SYSTEM\CurrentControlSet\ Services\Tcpip\Parameters\Interface*Interfacename*
Data type	REG_DWORD
Valid range	0–0x3FFFFFFF (bytes)
Default value	0xFFFF (the lesser of 17,520 for Ethernet, 65,535 bytes for other networks, or GlobalMaxTcpWindowSize; see the regentry.chm file for other exceptions)
Present by default	No

The maximum receive window size for an interface can be set using the TcpWindowSize setting. This setting, if existent, overrides the GlobalMaxTcpWindowSize Registry setting for the interface on which it is configured. See Chapter 5 for more information.

Table D-19 TcpUseRFC1122UrgentPointer Registry Setting

Registry Information	Details
Location	HKEY_LOCAL_MACHINE\SYSTEM\CurrentControlSet\ Services\Tcpip\Parameters
Data type	REG_DWORD
Valid range	0–1
Default value	0
Present by default	No

Windows 2000 can be configured to interpret the Urgent Pointer field according to RFC 1122, if desired. See Chapter 5 for more information.

Table D-20 EnableProxy Registry Setting

Registry Information	Details
Location	HKEY_LOCAL_MACHINE\SYSTEM\CurrentControlSet\ Services\NetBT\Parameters
Data type	REG_DWORD
Valid range	0–1
Default value	0
Present by default	No

The Registry entry EnableProxy must be set to one to configure any Windows NT or 2000 workstation or server to be a WINS proxy. See Chapter 12 for more information.

D

E

CONTENTS OF THE CD

The CD that accompanies this book includes the trace files that are referenced in this book. The CD also includes many of the utilities recommended by the authors for TCP/IP analysis and understanding.

TOOLS

The following tools are included on the CD:

- EtherPeek for Windows Demo (WildPackets, Inc.)

- IP Subnet Calculator (WildPackets, Inc.)

- NetScanTools Standard Edition (Northwest Performance Software)

- Network Analysis Survival Kit (WildPackets, Inc.)

- NeoTrace Pro Demo (NeoWorx)

- PacketScrubber (WildPackets, Inc.)

- ProConvert (WildPackets, Inc.)

These tools are listed and defined in the next section.

EtherPeek for Windows Demo

EtherPeek, developed by WildPackets, Inc., is the analyzer used throughout this book. EtherPeek is based on Windows and offers network trending, alarms and alerts, visual representation of network traffic, and packet capture and display capabilities.

IP Subnet Calculator

IP Subnet Calculator is a Windows-based calculator used to determine IP address configurations using class-based and classless IP network addresses. Originally developed by Scott Haugdahl, this tool is distributed by WildPackets, Inc. There is a Palm Pilot version of the subnetwork calculator available as well. To download the Subnet Calculator, visit *http://www.wildpackets.com/products/ipsubnetcalculator*.

NetScanTools Standard Edition

NetScanTools is a multifunctional utility for troubleshooting and testing TCP/IP devices. The Standard Edition is the limited version of the product—NetScanTools Professional Edition offers much more capability and is highly recommended by the authors. The Standard Edition can be used to perform basic tests. Use the Help Wizard to determine what information can be learned using the Standard Edition of NetScanTools. For the complete version of NetScanTools Standard Edition or to get the full NetScanTools Pro Edition, visit *http://www.nwpsw.com.*

Network Analysis Survival Kit

Originally developed by Scott Haugdahl, the Network Analysis Survival Kit (NASK) provides a searchable database of the RFCs and relevant IETF working group papers. This tool also contains many rare documents, such as a very complete OUI listing and details of NetBIOS operations. For more information, visit *http://www.wildpackets.com.*

NeoTrace Pro Demo

The NeoTrace Pro Demo is an advanced trace route utility that includes name resolution and path testing capabilities. After you set up your home location, the NeoTrace Pro utility will depict the path to the destination device on a global map. To obtain the complete version of the NeoTrace Pro utility, visit *http://www.neoworx.com.*

PacketScrubber

PacketScrubber is used to sanitize trace files by converting their confidential information to generic information, as defined. You can choose to sanitize just the IP addresses in the packets, or other information, such as the DNS address information exchanged. For the complete version of PacketScrubber, visit *http://www.wildpackets.com/products/packetscrubber/.*

ProConvert

ProConvert is used to convert trace files between formats. If you have another analyzer available, consider converting between the EtherPeek trace file format (.pkt format) and your analyzer's format to compare the decodes. For the complete version of ProConvert, visit *http://www.wildpackets.com/products/proconvert/.*

Trace Files

The CD contains numerous trace files that are used for the exercises and examples in this book. These trace files are in the EtherPeek .pkt format. To view these files on another analyzer, use the ProConvert tool and convert the trace files to the desired format.

The following table lists the trace files contained on the CD.

arp.pkt	Contains three types of ARP packets—a standard ARP request, a standard ARP reply, and a duplicate ARP test
arpscan.pkt	Shows an ARP-based reconnaissance probe process. This ARP scan is probably generated by a program—the ARP queries are not generated manually.
DHCPboot.pkt	Shows the basic DHCP boot sequence including the DHCP Discover, Offer, Request, and Acknowledgement. Notice that ARP is used to test two addresses before assigning one, and the DHCP client uses ARP to test the assigned address before using it.
DHCPlab.pkt	Contains some DHCP reconnect sequences. Note the ICMP Echo packets used to test addresses.
dns-moviefone.pkt	Shows a TCP-based connection to an HTTP server (moviefone). The process starts with a standard DNS query for the IP address of movie-fone.com.
fragments.pkt	Shows a fragmented communication between two devices on Ethernet networks. The fragmented communication starts as an oversized PING packet. It is broken down into several smaller packets that can fit on the Ethernet network.
ftp.pkt	Shows a connection to an FTP server and the basic command set needed to log on with a valid password and view the directory contents
icmplab.pkt	Shows a simple request to communicate on RPC port number 111 on a device that does not support that service. The response is in the form of an ICMP Destination Unreachable packet.
ipv6dump.pkt	Contains IPv6 traffic
ospf1.pkt	Shows several OSPF Hello packets sent from the designated router. Activating the Timestamp column in the EtherPeek summary decode window enables you to view the 10-second interval between ICMP Hello packets.
ping.pkt	Shows a simple PING request and reply. Look inside the hex decode of the packet to see the data with which the packet is padded.
portscan.pkt	Contains a TCP reconnaissance probe process
problem1.pkt	Illustrates a communication problem as referenced in Chapter 3
transfer.pkt	Shows an FTP connection sequence in which a file is transferred from one host to another. By following the packet sequences, you can identify the directory viewed and the file transferred.

E

TCP/UDP PORT NUMBERS

The ultimate resource for TCP/UDP port addresses is the Internet Assigned Numbers Authority (IANA), which is now part of the Internet Corporation for Assigned Names and Numbers (ICANN). Feel free to visit either of these Web sites:

- *http://www.iana.org*
- *http://www.icann.org*

The master list of port addresses was updated on June 14, 2001 (as of this writing), and is updated regularly. Visit the master list at *http://www.iana.org/assignments/port-numbers*. If you frequent any of the security sites we recommend in Appendix B, "Key IP Resources Online," they will basically provide security updates that mention when UDP or TCP ports become the focus of new exploits or vulnerabilities. It may take IANA as long as 60 days to add this information to its list so be aware that the information listed at this URL is not always completely current. But a judicious combination of current events analysis and use of the master IANA port numbers list should help you determine which TCP and UDP ports correspond to specific services, and which ones correspond to potential exploits or vulnerabilities.

Remember, if you can close unneeded ports and protocols, and uninstall unneeded services, your networks will be more secure than if you leave such potential points of attack open to outsiders. Remember also, however, that dynamic ports must be available for routine TCP and UDP connections to occur between clients and servers. Judicious combination of such necessary access and a firewall, proxy server, or screen router (preferably a service that can determine if the port addresses are being used for beneficial or malign ends) should help prevent unnecessary exposure.

G

DHCP OPTIONS

For a succinct definition of DHCP, plus access to RFC 1531, visit *http://www.protocols.com/pbook/tcpip1.htm#DHCP*. For complete information on the DHCP options, visit RFC 1531 (for instance, at *http://www.cis.ohio-state.edu/cgi-bin/rfc/rfc1531.html*). We recommend special attention to the following elements in that document:

- Figure 1, which shows the layout and format of a DHCP message, along with discussion of the Options field (and relevant sub-fields, as covered on pages 9–12 of the document)

- Table 3, which covers basic DHCP fields and options, as covered on page 25 of the document

The complete collection of "DHCP Options and BOOTP Vendor Extensions" appears in RFC 1533 (for instance, at *http://www.cis.ohio-state.edu/cgi-bin/rfc/rfc1533.html*). As with RFC 1531, we recommend special attention to Section 9 of RFC 1533, which covers DHCP extensions in great detail, on pages 23–27.

Glossary

4.2BSD — The version of the Berkeley Software Distribution (BSD) of UNIX that was the first to include a TCP/IP implementation.

6bone — The experimental backbone of the IPv6 Internet. This is a collection of routers, hosts, and network connections over a variety of media, used to test the emerging standards of the next generation Internet Protocol.

:: — In IPv6 addresses, the pair of colon characters stands for several contiguous 16-bit groups, each of which is all zeroes. This notation can be used only once in any address.

Abstract Syntax Notation One (ASN.1) — A language used to describe a type of object and the object identifier.

Acceptable Use Policy (AUP) — A formal policy document that dictates what kinds of online behavior or system use is acceptable to the overall user community.

access control — In IPSec, or other security, the ability to prevent unauthorized use of resources. It provides the ability to prevent intrusion into reserved spaces, real or theoretical.

accounting management — One of the five layers in the OSI network management model, accounting management focuses on measuring network and service utilization so that individual users or groups can be controlled or regulated.

acknowledgement — Notification of successful receipt of data. The ACK flag is set in acknowledgement packets.

address (A) record — A DNS resource record that maps domain names to IP addresses.

address book — A database of e-mail addresses. Local address books are often exploited in worm and mobile code attacks.

address pool — A contiguous range of numeric IP addresses, defined by a starting IP address and an ending IP address, to be managed by a DHCP server.

address request — A DNS service request for an IP address that matches a domain name.

Address Resolution Protocol (ARP) — This Network layer protocol translates numeric IP addresses into the equivalent MAC layer addresses necessary to transfer frames from one machine to another on the same cable segment or subnet.

address scope — *See* scope.

addressing — A method of assigning a unique symbolic name or numerical identifier to an individual network interface on a network segment, to make every such interface uniquely identifiable (and addressable).

adjacencies database — A database of the local network segment and its attached routers. Designated routers share the adjacencies database view across link-state networks.

Advanced Research Projects Agency (ARPA) — An agency within the U.S. Department of Defense that funded forward-thinking research in computing technology.

advertised window — The amount of data that a receiver states it can handle in its TCP buffer space. The actual window size is based on the lower value of the number of bytes that the network can handle and the advertised window. An advertised window of zero indicates that the receiver has no available TCP buffer space. To avoid Silly Window Syndrome, the sender must not send any more data until the receiver advertises a window size of at least the size of the MSS.

advertising rate — The rate at which a service (typically a routing service) is announced on a network. An example of an advertising rate is the 10-minute advertising rate for ICMP Router Advertisement packets.

agent — 1. In general, an agent is a piece of software that performs services on behalf of another process or user. In the case of Mobile IP, the agent in question is a special piece of router software that tunnels from a remote subnet to a user's home subnet to set up connections for a specific static IP address. 2. The device that actually inflicts the painful attack on the victim in a Distributed Denial of Service attack.

aggregatable global unicast address — The layout of these IPv6 addresses breaks the leftmost 64 bits of the address into explicit fields to allow for easier routing. Specifically, it allows routes to these addresses to be "aggregated," that is, combined into a single entry in the router table.

alarm — Notification of events or errors on the network. In the context of IP security, an alarm might indicate that some kind of attack is underway.

alert — An automatic notification from a software program (in the context of IP security, this means a router, firewall, proxy server, or IDS) that indicates an unusual error or condition, an exceeded monitoring threshold, or an executed trigger.

allowable data size — The amount of data that can be transferred across a link; the MTU.

American Standard Code for Information Interchange (ASCII) — The most widely used method for encoding character (keyboard) data into a collection of 8-bit digital patterns for input, storage, and display on a computer.

analog phone lines — Conventional voice-grade phone lines may be used with standard telephone modems (modulator/demodulator devices) that convert digital data into analog signals for transmission over such lines, and reconvert analog signals back into digital data on the receiving end of a point-to-point connection.

anonymous access — A type of IP service access, wherein users need not provide explicit account and password information; this applies to FTP and Web services, among others.

anycast address — A new type of address in IPv6, an anycast address is an ordinary address that can be assigned to more than one host or interface. Packets pointed to an anycast address are delivered to the holder of that address nearest to the sender in terms of routing distance. An anycast address does not apply to IPv4.

AppleTalk — The native protocol suite for Apple Macintosh computers.

Application layer — The uppermost layer of the ISO/OSI network reference model (and the TCP/IP model) where the interface between the protocol suite and actual applications resides.

application process — A system process that represents a specific type of network application or service.

Application Programming Interface (API) — A collection of tools, protocols, and programming code used in developing software applications that are consistent and compatible with the operating system.

Application Specific Integrated Circuit (ASIC) — A special-purpose form of integrated circuit. An ASIC provides a way to implement specific programming logic directly into chip form, thereby also providing the fastest possible execution of such programming logic when processing data. ASICs are what make it possible for high-speed, high-volume routers to perform complex address recognition and management functions that can keep up with data volumes and time-sensitive processing needs.

Archie — A TCP/IP-based archive protocol based on databases of anonymous FTP directories around the Internet, where users can search for content based on filenames and associated titles.

Area Border Router — A router used to connect separate areas.

areas — Groups of contiguous networks. Areas are used in link-state routing to provide route table summarization on larger networks.

ARP cache — A temporary table in memory that consists of recent ARP entries. Entries in the ARP cache are discarded after two minutes on Windows 2000 systems.

ARPANET — An experimental network, funded by ARPA, designed to test the feasibility of a platform-neutral, long-distance, robust and reliable internetwork that provided the foundation for what we know today as the Internet.

Asynchronous Transfer Mode (ATM) — A variable-speed, long-haul broadband networking technology that supports extreme bandwidth in its fastest versions. ATM lets virtual circuits be established between communication peers, and relies on higher-layer protocols (for example, TCP) to provide reliable communications. ATM segments all traffic into 48-byte sequences with a 5-byte header to create a 53-byte ATM frame called a cell. ATM's use of fixed-length transmission units permits it to run at extremely high speeds with maximum efficiency.

attack — An attempt to break into or compromise a system or network, or deny access to that system or network.

attack signature — A recognizable communication pattern or packet used in an attack. A signature may be the port number used in an attack, or a string of characters embedded in the data portion of the packet.

attack tools — Any of a set of software tools that malefactors might use to try to launch an attack against a system or a network. Network or system administrators should consider obtaining and using such tools themselves to make sure they won't work in unsupervised circumstances for unauthorized users.

attacker — The actual source of an attack sequence. Clever attackers in a DDoS attack often hide behind a handler and agent.

authoritative response — A reply to a query from the name server that's authoritative for the zone in which the requested name or address resides.

authoritative server — The DNS server that's responsible for one or more particular zones in the DNS database environment.

auto-reconfiguration — The process of automatically changing the configuration of a device. For example, when a PMTU host receives an ICMP Destination Unreachable: Fragmentation Needed and Don't Fragment was Set ICMP packet, that host can reconfigure the outgoing MTU size to match the size dictated by the restricting link.

auto-recovery — The process of automatically recovering from a fault. For example, the process of black hole detection enables a host to auto-recover from a communication failure caused by a router that does not forward packets and does not send any messages indicating that an error occurred.

autoconfiguration — The process of automatically assigning configuration without any manual intervention. In the case of IPv6, as referenced in Chapter 13, clients can autoconfigure their IP addresses either with or without the use of DHCP.

automatic address lease — A type of DHCP address lease in which a DHCP server can make a permanent allocation of an address within its address pool; usually applied when allocating addresses to servers, routers, or other devices that require stable IP address assignments.

Autonomous System (AS) — A group of routers that is under a single administrative authority.

Autonomous System Border Router (ASBR) — A router that connects an independent routing area, or AS, to another AS or the Internet.

available — The quality of quickly responding to user requests for service. DNS supports use of multiple name servers and caching to increase the accessibility of database data; careful configuration of DNS clients allows them to spread their requests evenly over multiple servers, thereby balancing the processing load. This makes DNS inherently available to its users.

available routes — The known functional routes on an internetwork. Available routes are not necessarily the optimal routes. On IP networks, routers periodically advertise available routes.

average response time — The median time required to reply to a query. The history of network average response times is used to provide a measurement for comparison of current network responses.

back door — An undocumented and illicit point of entry into a system or a network, often built into software or a system by its original engineers.

Back Orifice — A remote control trojan horse attack developed by a group called the "Cult of the Dead Cow" (CDC).

backbone area — A required area to which all other routers should be attached directly or through a tunnel.

backup designated router (BDR) — The router with the second highest priority on a broadcast segment of a link-state network. The BDR allows service to be restored quickly in the event of an outage affecting the DR. *See also* designated router.

backwards compatibility — A feature that enables a device, process, or protocol to operate with earlier versions of software or hardware that do not support all the latest, up-to-date or advanced features. For example, a PMTU host can automatically and incrementally reduce the MTU size it uses until it learns the supported PMTU size.

bandwidth — A measurement of the amount of information that can cross a network. For example, Ethernet has 10-Mbps bandwidth available.

bastion host — A specially hardened computer designed to straddle the boundary between internal and external networks, where firewalls, proxy servers, IDSs, and border routing functions normally operate.

Berkeley Internet Name Domain (BIND) — BIND is the most popular implementation of DNS server software on the Internet today. Originally introduced as part of BSD UNIX 4.3, today there are BIND implementations available for nearly every computing platform, including Windows NT and Windows 2000.

Best Current Practice (BCP) — A specific type of Internet RFC document that outlines the best ways to design, implement, or maintain TCP/IP-based networks.

best-effort delivery — A simple network transport mechanism that relies on the underlying Network, Data Link, and Physical layer facilities available to handle delivery of PDUs from sender to receiver, without adding additional robustness or reliability features; UDP uses best-effort delivery.

bidirectional — Two-way. Traffic that is bidirectional goes both ways. In the case of HTTP communications, data flows from the server to the client, and requests flow from the client to the server.

binding acknowledgement — The response sent in reply to a binding update. It is optional in some cases.

binding request — In Mobile IP, a message sent (typically from a correspondent) to the mobile user, asking for both its current COA and home address.

binding table — The home agent's binding table binds the mobile user's COA and home address, much like a routing table, and allows the home agent to reroute traffic addressed to the user's home address out to the new COA.

binding update — In Mobile IP, a message sent from the mobile user either to a home agent or to another node, which keeps a binding cache for mobile users, asking them to change this binding. The binding update may take several specific forms.

bit-level integrity check — A special mathematical calculation performed on the payload of a packet (a datagram at the Data Link layer) before the datagram is transmitted, whose value may be stored in a datagram's trailer. The calculation is performed again on the receiving end and compared to the transmitted value; if the two values agree, the reception is assumed to be error-free; if the two values disagree, the datagram is usually silently discarded (no error message).

black hole — A point on the network where packets are silently discarded.

black hole router — A router that cannot forward packets for some reason (such as an unsupported PMTU size), and does not inform the source of the communication fault. IP hosts typically require additional capabilities to detect and recover from communications that fail due to black hole routers.

Bootstrap Protocol (BOOTP) — A Layer 3 or TCP/IP Internet layer protocol designed to permit diskless workstations to obtain network access and an operating system image across the network as they begin booting.

Border Gateway Protocol (BGP) — A widely used routing protocol that connects to common Internet backbones (for example, Internet Service Providers), or other routing domains within the Internet where multiple parties jointly share responsibility for managing traffic. BGP replaces Exterior Gateway Protocol (EGP) and is defined in RFC 1163. BGP exchanges reachability information with other BGP routers.

border router — A network device that straddles the boundary between internal and external networks, and manages the inbound traffic permitted to reach the inside networks, and the outbound traffic allowed to proceed beyond the boundary.

boundary router — *See* border router.

break-in — An attempt to impersonate a valid user on a system, or otherwise gain entry to a system or network, to obtain illicit access to the resources and information it contains.

broadcast — A specific type of network transmission (and address) that is meant to be noticed and read by all recipients on any cable segment where that transmission appears; a way of reaching all addresses on any network.

broadcast address — The all-ones address for a network or subnet, this address provides a way to send the same information to all interfaces on a network.

broadcast bit — A single bit at the start of the Flags field of the DHCP packet that indicates whether this client can receive unicast packets before the four-packet DHCP boot up process completes.

broadcast packet — A type of network transmission intended for delivery to all devices on the network. The Ethernet broadcast address is 0xFF-FF-FF-FF-FF-FF.

brute force attack — An attack that typically consists of numerous requests for service. This type of attack focuses on overloading the resources of the victim, including CPU, disk access, or other local resources.

brute force password attack — A systematic attempt to guess all possible password strings as a way of trying to break into a system. Such an attack literally attempts all conceivable character combinations that might represent a valid password. These attacks can take a long time, and can usually be detected and prevented by IDSs.

bump-in-the-stack (BITS) — A method of implementing IPSec and other security tools such that they appear to operate "between" the network protocol stack (such as IP) and the Data Link layer drivers.

bump-in-the-wire (BITW) — A method of implementing IPSec and other security tools as a freestanding processor on the trusted network, but before the public network. Often a simple integrated device literally plugged into the host computer on one side and the local link on the other.

byte stream — A continuous stream of data that contains no boundaries.

cable modem — A communication device designed to send and receive networking signals, mainly for Internet access, over two data channels on a broadband CATV network. Although cable TV lines can support bandwidth up to 27 Mbps, the more common rate for cable modem users is 1.5 Mbps (the local provider's data rate).

cable segment — Any single collection of network media and attached devices that fits on a single piece of network cable, or within a single network device, such as a hub, or in a virtual equivalent, such as a local area network emulation environment on a switch.

caching — Storing remote information locally once obtained so that if it is needed again it may be accessed much more quickly. Both DNS resolvers (clients) and DNS servers cache DNS data to lower the odds that a remote query will have to be resolved.

caching server — A DNS server that stores valid name and address pairs already looked up, along with invalid names and addresses already detected. Any DNS server can cache data, including primary, secondary, and caching-only DNS servers.

caching-only server — A DNS server that does not have primary or secondary zone database responsibilities, this type of server is used only to cache already-resolved domain names and addresses, and related error information.

canonical name (CNAME) record — The DNS RR used to define database aliases, primarily to make it quicker and easier to edit and manage DNS zone files.

capture filter — A method used to identify specific packets that should be captured into a trace buffer based on some packet characteristic, such as source or destination address.

Care-of Address (COA) — In Mobile IP, the remote or foreign address through which a mobile node may be reached.

Carrier Sense Multiple Access with Collision Detection (CSMA/CD) — The formal name for the contention management approach that Ethernet uses, CSMA basically means "listen before attempting to send" (to make sure no later message tramples on an earlier one), and "listen while sending" (to make sure that messages sent at roughly the same time don't collide with one another).

Centre European Researche Nucleaire (CERN) — The European Organization for Nuclear Research, where Tim Berners-Lee invented the protocols and services that defined the World Wide Web between 1989 and 1991.

Character Generator (Chargen) — A basic TCP/IP service that uses TCP and UDP port 19. In response to any request message, a Chargen server generates an arbitrary stream of characters to test reply-handling capabilities.

checkpoint — A point in time at which all system state and information is captured and saved so that subsequent failure in systems or communications can resume at that point in time, with no further loss of data or information.

checksum — A special mathematical value that represents the contents of a message so precisely that any change in the contents will cause a change in the checksum; calculated before and after network transmission of data, then compared—if transmitted and calculated checksums agree, the assumption is that the data arrived unaltered.

ciphertext — The result of performing encryption on plain text. The encrypted or enciphered data is called ciphertext.

circuit switching — A method of communications wherein a temporary or permanent connection between a sender and a receiver, called a circuit, is created within a communications carrier's switching systems. Because temporary circuits come and go constantly, circuits are switched around all the time, hence the term.

Classless Inter-Domain Routing (CIDR) — A form of subnet masking that does away with placing network and host address portions precisely on octet boundaries, but instead uses the /n prefix notation, in which n indicates the number of bits in the network portion of whatever address is presented.

Client Identifier — An identification number that the DHCP server uses to keep track of the client and its IP address, lease time, and other parameters. Typically, the client's hardware address is used as the Client Identifier value.

client/server — A type of relationship between two computer hosts in which one host takes on the role of requesting services (the client) and the other the role of responding to service requests (the server)—these roles are seldom, if ever, reversed.

command connection — A connection that carries only commands and their associated replies. No data crosses a command connection.

command-line parameter — Options added to a command issued at a prompt (not in a windowed environment). For example, in the command *arp -a*, the *-a* is the parameter for the command *arp*.

Commercial Internet Exchange (CIX) — An early consortium of commercial Internet users that pioneered the extension of Internet use to e-commerce and business communications.

Common Internet File System (CIFS) — A Microsoft proposal for a standard file access method for the Internet, based on NetBIOS and related native Microsoft operating system protocols and APIs. The actual method used is a protocol called SMB that makes use of NetBIOS.

community name — A word used as a password to obtain Read-Only (Monitor community), Read/Write (Control community), or Alert (Trap community) information. Also called a string.

compressed SLIP (C-SLIP) — A special form of SLIP that does away with source and destination address information as data is transmitted across the link. (This information is negotiated between point-to-point communication peers as the link is established, and need not be sent with every frame; omitting this data improves communication efficiency.)

compromised host — A host that was broken into and gave up Administrator or root access.

computer forensics — The process of examining the "footprints" that an attacker leaves behind. Some areas of interest include the temp files—deleted files that remain in the Recycle Bin or in a recoverable state—and local system memory.

confidentiality — The ability to restrict access to some resource by any but authorized users. The typical approach is encryption, rendering the data unusable without the keys and algorithm needed to decrypt it.

configuration management — One of the five layers in the OSI network management model, configuration management focuses on documenting and controlling network and system configuration data.

congestion — A condition of overload on a network or at a receiver. When the network is congested, senders cannot continue to send TCP packets. To avoid congesting a receiver, the receiver advertises a window size of zero.

Congestion Avoidance algorithm — A defined method to avoid overloading a network. This mechanism is used to slowly and incrementally increase the window size of communications.

congestion control — A TCP mechanism, also available from other protocols, that permits network hosts to exchange information about their ability to handle traffic volumes, and thereby cause senders to decrease or increase the frequency and size of their upcoming communications.

connection-oriented — A type of networking protocol that relies on explicit communications and negotiations between sender and receiver to manage delivery of data between the two parties.

connectionless — A type of networking protocol that makes no attempt to cause network senders and receivers to exchange information about their availability or ability to communicate with one another; also known as "best-effort delivery."

connectionless integrity — In IPSec or similar security regimes, the ability to provide integrity, but without the ability to ensure the connection itself.

connectionless protocol — A protocol that simply sends datagrams without establishing, managing, or otherwise handling a connection between sender and receiver; UDP is a connectionless transport protocol.

connectivity tests — Tests to determine the reachability of a device. IP PING and TRACEROUTE are two utilities that can be used for connectivity testing.

constant-length subnet masking (CLSM) — An IP subnetting scheme in which all subnets use the same size subnet mask, which therefore divides the subnetted address space into a fixed number of equal-size subnets.

converge — The process of ensuring all routers on a network have up-to-date information about available networks and their costs.

converged state — A network state in which all routers are synchronized to share a complete view of the network.

core services — Primary and key services used in TCP/IP networking. FTP, DNS, and DHCP are considered core services. These services are assigned the well-known port numbers between 0 and 1023.

counting to infinity — A network routing problem caused by a routing loop. Packets circulate continuously until they expire.

cracker — A person who attempts to break into a system by impersonating valid users, or using other methods of penetration that do not necessarily involve deep system skills or knowledge.

current window — The actual window size being used at the time. A sender determines the current window size by using the receiver's advertised window and the network congestion window (what the network can handle).

Cyclical Redundancy Check (CRC) — A special 16- or 32-bit equation performed on the contents of a packet. The result of the CRC equation is placed in the Frame Check Sequence field at the end of a frame. A CRC is performed by NICs on all outgoing and incoming packets.

daemon — Taken from Clerk Maxwell's famous physics idea, a daemon is a computer process whose job is to "listen" for connection attempts for one or more specific network services, and to hand off all valid attempts to temporary connections known as sockets attempts.

data encapsulation — The technique whereby higher-level protocol data is enclosed within the payload of a lower-layer protocol unit, and labeled with a header (and possibly, a trailer) so that the

protocol data unit may be safely transmitted from a sender to a receiver. At the Data Link layer, this means providing necessary delimitation, addressing, bit-level integrity check, and protocol identification services in the header and trailer.

data frame — The basic PDU at the Data Link layer, a frame represents what will be transmitted or received as a pattern of bits on a network interface.

data link address — The address of the local machine based on the hardware address. The data link address is also referred to as the MAC address.

data link driver — The software that enables the NIC to communicate with a local operating system. The data link driver places the frame (except the CRC) around the IP datagram and ensures packets are of proper length before handing the frame to the NIC. On incoming frames, the data link driver examines the protocol identification field and passes the packet to the appropriate protocol stack.

Data Link layer — Layer 2 of the ISO/OSI network reference model, the Data Link layer is responsible for enabling reliable transmission of data through the Physical layer at the sending end, and for checking such reliability upon reception at the receiving end.

data offset value — A numerical count that indicates the number of bits or bytes within a field, or the payload in which specific information of interest begins; works as a "start indicator" for specific data items or elements in packets.

data origin authentication — In IPSec or similar security areas, the ability to verify the source of received information, or to check that the source possesses some trusted token.

data segment — The basic PDU for TCP at the Transport layer. *See also* segment.

data transfer connection — A connection that carries only data. This type of connection is typically established after a command connection is set up. The data connection does not carry commands.

database segment — *See* DNS database segment.

datagram — The basic protocol data unit at the TCP/IP Network Access layer. Used by connectionless protocols at the Transport layer, a datagram simply adds a header to the PDU, supplied from whatever Application layer protocol or service uses a connectionless protocol, such as UDP; hence, UDP is also known as a datagram service.

datagram service — In NetBIOS, NetBEUI, or NBF, datagram service is a connectionless protocol used to send messages and responses. When these protocols run over TCP/IP (as NetBT), datagram services and name services use UDP (on UDP ports 138 and 137, respectively). When a more reliable connection is required, these protocols use TCP to provide session services.

Daytime — A basic TCP/IP service that responds to any service request with the date and time as known to the host that handles the incoming service request.

de facto standard — A standard that is adopted by the majority, but not by a governing body, such as the IEEE.

decode — The interpreted value of a PDU, or a field within a PDU, performed by a protocol analyzer or similar software package.

decoding — The process of interpreting the fields and contents of a packet, and presenting the packet in a readable format.

decryption — The process of "unlocking" or making encrypted data readable.

default gateway — The name given to the router IP address through which a machine attached to a local network must pass outbound traffic to reach beyond the local network, thereby making that address the "gateway" to the world of IP addresses outside the local subnet. Also, a gateway of last resort, where packets are sent when no host route entry or network entry exists in the local host's route table.

Defense Information Systems Agency (DISA) — The agency within the DoD that took over operation of the Internet when ARPA surrendered its control in 1983.

delegation of authority — The principle whereby one name server designates another name server to handle some or all of the zone files for the domain or subdomains under its purview. The DNS NS resource record provides the pointer mechanism that name servers use to delegate authority.

delimitation — The use of special marker bit strings or characters, called delimiters, that distinguish the payload of a PDU from its header and trailer.

delimiter — A special bit string or character that marks some boundary in a PDU, be it at the beginning or end of a PDU, or at the boundary between the header and the payload, or the payload and the trailer.

demilitarized zone (DMZ) — An intermediate network that sits between the boundary of an organization's internal networks and one or more external networks, such as the Internet. A DMZ is usually separated from external networks by a screening router, and from internal networks by a screening router and a firewall.

demultiplexing — The process of breaking up a single stream of incoming packets on a computer, and directing its components to the various active TCP/IP processes based on socket addresses in the TCP or UDP headers.

Denial of Service (DoS) — An attack that causes a system to refuse services because it is busy handling attack requests. For example, repeated two-way handshakes may be caused by a TCP SYN attack.

designated router (DR) — The router with the highest priority on a segment of a link-state network. A DR advertises LSAs to all other routers on the segment.

destination port number — The port address for an incoming TCP/IP communication that identifies the target application or service process involved.

Destination Unreachable packets — ICMP packets that indicate a failure to reach a destination due to a fragmentation problem, parameter problem, or other problem.

DHCP client — The software component on a TCP/IP client, usually implemented as part of the protocol stack software, that issues address requests, lease renewals, and other DHCP messages to a DHCP server.

DHCP Discovery — The four-packet process used to obtain an IP address, lease time, and configuration parameters. The four-packet process includes the Discover, Offer, Request, and Acknowledgment packets.

DHCP options — Parameter and configuration information that defines what the DHCP client is looking for. Two special options—0: Pad and 255: End—are used for housekeeping. Pad simply ensures that the DHCP fields end on an acceptable boundary, and End denotes that there are no more options listed in the packet.

DHCP relay agent — A special-purpose piece of software built to recognize and redirect DHCP Discovery packets to known DHCP servers. When any cable segment or broadcast domain has no DHCP server directly attached, but includes DHCP clients that will need address management services and configuration data, it is necessary to install a DHCP relay agent on that cable segment or broadcast domain (or to enable routers to forward BOOTP packets to segments where DHCP servers are indeed available).

DHCP reply — A DHCP message that contains a reply from a server to a client's DHCP request message.

DHCP request — A DHCP message from a client to a server, requesting some kind of service; such messages occur only after a client receives an IP address, and can use unicast packets (not broadcasts) to communicate with a specific DHCP server.

DHCP server — The software component that runs on a network server of some kind, responsible for managing TCP/IP address pools or scopes, and for interacting with clients to provide them with IP addresses and related TCP/IP configuration data on demand.

diameter — The number of hops that a network routing protocol can span: RIP has a network

diameter of 15; most other routing protocols (such as OSPF and BGP) have an unlimited network diameter.

dictionary attack — A type of brute force password attack in which hashed values for all words in a specialized dictionary of terms are compared to hashed values in password files. This type of attack usually takes only seconds to process.

Differentiated Services (diffserv) — The name of the IETF working group studying that area of interest.

Digital Subscriber Line (DSL) — The generic name for a family of always-on digital lines normally provided by local telephone companies or exchange carriers to link homes or businesses to communications carriers, normally for Internet access. DSL is subject to distance limitations of 17,500 feet from the interface equipment where the DSL line connects to a (usually optical) carrier link and the customer premises.

Dijkstra algorithm — An algorithm used to compute the best route on a link-state network.

Discard — A basic TCP/IP service that silently discards all incoming traffic; generally used to test a requester's ability to emit outgoing communications.

discovery broadcast — The process of discovering a DHCP server by broadcasting a DHCP Discover packet onto the local network segment. If a DHCP server does not exist on the local segment, a relay agent must forward the request directly to the remote DHCP server. If no local DHCP server or relay agent exists, the client cannot obtain an IP address using DHCP.

discovery process — The process of learning which computers or processes are running on a network.

diskless workstation — A workstation that does not contain a hard drive or floppy disk drive from which to boot or read host configuration information.

display filters — Filters that are applied to the packets that reside in a trace buffer for the purpose of viewing only the packets of interest.

distance vector — The source point or location for determining distance to another network.

distance vector routing protocol — A routing protocol that uses information about the distances between networks, rather than the amount of time it takes for traffic to make its way from the source network to the destination network. RIP is a distance vector routing protocol.

distributed database technology — A database that's managed by multiple database servers, each of which has responsibility for some distinct portion of a global database. As such, DNS is a nonpareil in its effective use of distributed database technology.

Distributed Denial of Service (DDoS) attack — An attack that uses a managed group approach to set up a compromised host as a handler, and recruits agents that perform the actual attack on the victim.

distributed management solution — A management design that offers management information about devices that are distributed throughout a network. Distributed management systems can have one or more managers.

divide and conquer — A computer design approach that consists of decomposing a big, hairy problem into a series of smaller, less-complex and interrelated problems, each of which can be solved more or less independently of the others.

DNS database segment — A distinct and autonomous subset of data from the DNS name and address hierarchy. A DNS database segment usually corresponds to a DNS database zone, and is stored in a collection of interrelated zone files. *See also* zone and zone file.

domain — 1. On the Internet, a domain is any of a group of hierarchically organized groups of hosts, usually, but not necessarily, having contiguous IP addresses. Examples include the *.com* and *.net* domains and the country domains *.fr* (France) and *.uk* (United Kingdom). 2. In Windows NT and Windows 2000 networking, a domain is a user-defined group that can include multiple computers and workgroups.

domain name — A symbolic name for a TCP/IP network resource; the Domain Name System (DNS) translates such names into numeric IP addresses so that outbound traffic may be addressed properly. Domain names are administered by several private and public agencies throughout the world.

domain name hierarchy — The entire global namespace for the domain names that DNS manages on the Internet. This space includes all registered and active (and therefore, valid and usable) domain names.

domain name resolution — The process whereby DNS translates a domain name into a corresponding numeric IP address.

Domain Name System (DNS) — The TCP/IP Application layer protocol and service that manages an Internet-wide distributed database of symbolic domain names and numeric IP addresses so that users can ask for resources by name, and get those names translated into the correct numeric IP addresses.

dotted decimal notation — The name for the format used to denote numeric IP addresses, such as 172.16.1.7, wherein four numbers are separated by periods (dots).

Draft Standard — A Standard RFC that has gone through the draft process, been approved, and for which two reference implementations must be shown to work together before it can move on to Internet Standard status.

dual stack — Two different implementations of similar protocols, such as IPv4 and IPv6. The transition from IPv4 to IPv6 will require several routers and hosts to operate in dual stack mode during the transition, allowing them to communicate on both networks.

duplicate ACKs — A set of identical acknowledgements that is sent back-to-back to a TCP sender to indicate that out-of-order packets were received. Upon receipt of these duplicate ACKs, the sender retransmits the data without waiting for the retransmission timer to expire.

duplicate IP address — An IP address that is already assigned to another IP host. IP hosts must perform a duplicate IP address test upon boot up to ensure the address is not already assigned to another IP host. If the address is already in use, the local host's IP stack cannot be initialized.

dynamic address lease — A type of DHCP address lease in which each address allocation comes with an expiration timeout so that address leases must be renewed before expiration occurs, or a new address will have to be allocated instead. Used primarily for client machines that do not require stable IP address assignments.

Dynamic Host Configuration Protocol (DHCP) — A TCP/IP-based network service and Application layer protocol that supports leasing and delivery of TCP/IP addresses and related configuration information to clients that would otherwise require static assignment of such information. For that reason, DHCP is a profound convenience for network users and administrators both.

Dynamic Host Configuration Protocol version 6 (DHCPv6) — The updated version of this protocol for IPv6. DHCPv6 defines the behavior of servers and clients in the stateful assignment of parameters for configuration of the clients' network (and other) settings. DHCPv6 can interoperate with stateless autoconfiguration.

dynamic link library (DLL) — A piece of executable code (or data) used by other Windows applications to perform a particular function or set of functions.

dynamic port number — A temporary port number used just for one communication process. These port numbers are cleared after the connection is closed and a four-minute wait time.

dynamically assigned port address — A temporary TCP or UDP port number allocated to permit a client and server to exchange data with each other only as long as their connection remains active. Also called a dynamic port number.

E1 — A standard European digital communications service used to carry thirty 64-Kbps digital voice or data channels, along with two 64-Kbps control channels, for a total bandwidth of 2.048 Mbps of service. E1 is widely used outside North America as a replacement for T1 service.

E3 — A standard European digital communications service used to carry 16 E1 channels for a total bandwidth of 34.368 Mbps of service. E3 is widely used outside North America as a replacement for T3 service.

Echo — A UDP- or TCP-based connection-testing protocol. These Echo communications simply send packets to the Echo socket to receive an Echo Reply. This type of Echo process is used as an alternative to the ICMP Echo process.

egress filtering — The process of applying restrictions to traffic leaving a network.

Encapsulating Security Payload (ESP) — A header in an IPv6 packet and/or the security protocol that uses that extension header. ESP provides encryption services under IPSec.

encapsulation — The enclosure of data from an upper-layer protocol between a header and an (optional) trailer for the current layer, to identify sender and receiver, and possibly, to include data integrity check information.

encryption — The process of rendering data unintelligible in a way that is reversible by applying a secret key.

end-to-end connection — A network connection in which the original sending and receiving IP addresses may not be altered, and where a communications connection extends all the way from sender to receiver while that connection remains active.

end-to-end minimum MTU size — The smallest data size that can be sent from one host to another host on an internetwork. Packets may be fragmented to reach the end-to-end minimum MTU size, or the PMTU process can be used to determine the minimum size.

end-to-end reliability — A characteristic offered by connection-oriented services to guarantee that data arrives successfully at the desired destination.

ephemeral port — *See* temporary port.

Erasable PROM (EPROM) — An erasable form of non-volatile computer memory that not only can be programmed with certain key information such as system or operating system boot up parameters, but whose contents can be erased and rewritten, as needed. An EPROM can be recorded and re-recorded while the chip is already socketed on a motherboard or interface card.

error recovery — The procedure for retransmitting missing or damaged data. Two examples of error recovery are the immediate drop in the current window size, and immediate retransmission of data—before the retransmission timer expires.

error-detection mechanism — A method for detecting corrupted packets. The CRC process is an error-detection mechanism. The IP header checksum is another method of error detection.

Ethernet — A network access protocol based on carrier sense, multiple access, and collision detection.

Ethernet collision fragments — The garbled traffic on a network produced when two packets transmitted at about the same time collide, resulting in a hodgepodge of signals.

Ethernet II frame type — The de facto standard frame type for TCP/IP communications.

EUI-64 format — An IEEE transformation, permitting the burned-in MAC addresses of NICs to be padded in particular ways to create globally unique 48-bit interface identifiers for each interface.

event threshold — A defined point that generates an SNMP TRAP message. Although an event threshold may indicate that a problem occurred, it may also simply indicate that a non-alarm event occurred.

expired route entry — A route entry that is considered "too old" and won't be used to forward data through an internetwork. Expired route entries may be held in a routing table for a short time in anticipation that the route will become valid again as another device advertises it.

exploit — A documented system break-in technique that's published for potential reuse by others.

Extended Binary Coded Decimal Interchange Code (EBCDIC) — Developed by IBM back in the punch card days, EBCDIC is an 8-bit character set. Today, EBCDIC may still be used to access some IBM mainframes; however, ASCII is a more popular character set.

extended network prefix — The portion of an IP address that represents the sum of the network portion of the address, plus the number of bits used for subnetting that network address. A Class B address with a 3-bit subnetting scheme would have an extended network prefix of /19, 16 bits for the default network portion, plus three bits for the subnetting portion of that address, with a corresponding subnet mask of 255.255.224.0.

Exterior Gateway Protocol (EGP) — The original exterior gateway protocol defined for use on the Internet, EGP has now been supplanted by the more modern and efficient Border Gateway Protocol, or BGP.

external route entry — A route entry received from a different area.

fault management — One of the five layers in the OSI network management model, fault management focuses on detecting and logging network and system problems, and repairing such problems whenever possible.

file extension — The ending of a filename that indicates the type of the file. Viruses are often contained in .exe, .com, and .vbs file formats.

file extension obfuscation — The process of hiding a filename extension by placing a false extension before the actual extension. For example, the ILOVEYOU e-mail message contained an attachment named "LOVE-LETTER-FOR-YOU.TXT.vbs." For systems that hide the extension, this file appears as a .txt file and is assumed to be harmless.

File Transfer Protocol (FTP) — A TCP/IP Application layer service and protocol designed to facilitate transfer of files between a client and a server across a network.

Finger — Short for Finger User Information Protocol, Finger provides information about individual users or hosts on the Internet; a once-popular service, Finger traffic is seldom permitted from outside a host's local area network because of past security exploits using Finger.

firewall — A network boundary device that sits between the public and private sides of a network, and provides a variety of screening and inspection services to ensure that only safe, authorized traffic flows from outside to inside (used in the sense of a barrier designed specifically to block the spread of fire in houses or cars).

flow — A set of packets for which a source requires special handling by intervening routers.

foreign agent (FA) — An entity in the Mobile IPv4 scheme no longer used in IPv6.

foreign network — A network that has a different network prefix than the mobile user's own home address.

forwarding table — The actual table referenced to make forwarding decisions on a link-state network.

fragment — In terms of IP networking, a fragment is a piece of a larger set of data that must be divided to cross a network that supports a smaller MTU than the original packet size.

Fragment Offset field — The field that defines where a fragment should be placed when the entire data set is reassembled.

fragment retransmission process — The process of retransmitting the original unfragmented packet due to transmission error, or fragment packet loss.

fragmentable — Able to be fragmented. A packet must have the May Fragment bit set in order to allow an IP packet to be fragmented if necessary.

fragmentation — The process of dividing a packet into multiple smaller packets to cross a link that supports a smaller MTU than the link where the packet originated.

frame — The basic PDU at the Data Link layer of the ISO/OSI reference model.

Frame Check Sequence (FCS) field — The type of bit-level integrity check used in the trailer of PPP datagrams; the specific algorithm for the FCS is documented in RFC 1661. The FCS field contains a CRC value. All Ethernet and token ring frames have an FCS field.

frame relay — A WAN technology that offers transmission rates up to 1.544 Mbps. Frame relay does not correct transmission errors; it simply discards corrupted frames.

fully qualified domain name (FQDN) — A special form of a domain name that ends with a period to indicate the root of the domain name hierarchy. You must use FQDNs in DNS A and PTR resource records.

gateway — In the TCP/IP environment, the term "gateway" is used to refer to a Network layer forwarding device typically known as a router. The default gateway is the router a host sends a packet to when the host has no specific route to a destination.

Gopher — A TCP/IP Application layer protocol and service that provides access to various types of indexed text and other types of data online, which predates the Web, and presents its contents as a hierarchically structured list of files.

Greenwich Mean Time (GMT) — The mean solar time of the meridian of Greenwich used as the prime basis of standard time throughout the world. Greenwich, England, is where east meets west at the Greenwich Meridian (0° Longitude). Also referred to as Universal Time (UT).

hacker — A person who uses computer and communications knowledge to exploit information or functionality of a device.

half-open connections — A TCP connection that is not completed with a final acknowledgement. These half-open connections may be an indication of a TCP SYN attack.

handler — A manager system in a DDoS attack. The handler is a compromised host on which an attacker has placed DDoS code. The handlers locate agents to perform the actual attack on a victim system.

handshake process — The process of setting up a virtual connection between TCP peers. The handshake process consists of three packets used to set up the starting sequence number that each TCP peer will use for communications. The TCP peers also exchange the receiver window size and an MSS value during this process.

hardware address — The address of the NIC. This address is typically used as the data link address.

header — That portion of a PDU that precedes the actual content for the PDU, and usually identifies sender and receiver, protocols in use, and other information necessary to establish context for senders and receivers.

Hello process — A process link-state routers use to discover neighbor routers.

heterogeneous environment — A networking environment composed of dissimilar equipment, often from a variety of vendors.

hex reader — A software package that allows you to open an executable file to examine the contents of the code in hexadecimal format without launching the file.

High-level Data Link Control (HDLC) — A synchronous communication protocol.

Historic Standard — An Internet RFC that was superseded by a newer, more current version.

hole — A system or software vulnerability that defeats, bypasses, or ignores system or software security settings and restrictions.

home agent (HA) — In Mobile IP, a router on the mobile user's home network, willing and able to store and forward messages on behalf of the mobile agent while it is roaming.

hop — A single transfer of data from one network to another, through some kind of networking device. Router-to-router transfers are often called hops. The number of hops often provides a rough metric of the distance between a sender's network and a receiver's network. The number of routers that a packet must cross, or the number of routers that a packet crosses, represents the hop count from the source network to the target network.

host — TCP/IP terminology for any computer that possesses one or more valid TCP/IP addresses (and hence, is reachable on a TCP/IP-based network). A host can also be a computer that offers TCP/IP services to clients.

host information (HINFO) record — A DNS resource record that provides information about some specific host, as specified by its domain name.

host portion — The rightmost bits in an IP address, allocated to identify hosts on a supernetwork, network, or subnetwork.

host probe — A reconnaissance process used to determine which hosts are active on an IP network. Typically, the PING process is used to perform a host probe.

host route — A routing table entry with a 32-bit subnet mask designed to reach a specific network host.

host route entry — A route table entry that matches all four bytes of the desired destination. Network route table entries only match the network bits of the desired address.

HOSTS — A special text file that lists known domain names and corresponding IP addresses, thereby defining a static method for domain name resolution. Until DNS was implemented, HOSTS files provided the sole means for name resolution on the precursor to the Internet, the ARPANET.

hypermedia — An extension to hypertext that includes the ability to link to graphics, sound, and video elements, as well as text elements.

Hypertext Transfer Protocol (HTTP) — The TCP/IP Application layer protocol and service that supports access to the World Wide Web.

ICMP Echo process — An ICMP process whereby a host sends an Echo packet to another host on an internetwork. If the destination host is active and able, it echoes back the data that is contained in the ICMP Echo packet.

ICMP Echo Request packet — A packet that is sent to a device to test connectivity. If the receiving device is functional and can reply, it should echo back the data that is contained in the data portion of the Echo Request packet.

ICMP error messages — Error messages sent using the ICMP protocol. Destination Unreachable, Time Exceeded, and Parameter Problem are examples of ICMP error messages.

ICMP query message — ICMP messages that contain requests for configuration or other information. ICMP Echo, Router Solicitation, and Address Mask Request are examples of ICMP query messages.

ICMP Router Discovery — A process in which hosts send ICMP Router Solicitation messages to the all-router multicast address (224.0.0.2). Local routers that support the ICMP Router Discovery process reply with an ICMP Router Advertisement unicast to the host. The advertisement contains the router's address and a Lifetime value for the router's information.

ICMP Router Solicitation — The process that a host can perform to learn of local routers. ICMP Router Solicitation messages are sent to the all-routers multicast address of 224.0.0.2.

IEEE 802 — A project undertaken by the IEEE in 1980 that covers Physical and Data Link layers for networking technologies in general (802.1 and 802.2), plus specific networking technologies, such as Ethernet (802.3) and token ring (802.5), among others.

IEEE 802.3 — The IEEE-defined standard for a carrier sense, multiple access method with collision detection.

IEEE 802.5 — The IEEE-defined standard for token-passing ring Media Access Control method.

in-band management — A management design that uses the data path as the main path for all management data. The primary problem associated with in-band management designs is that data cannot reach the manager when the data path is not functioning.

incomplete fragment set — A fragmentation attack that consists of numerous fragments directed toward a victim, but does not contain the final fragment of the set. The victim attempts to cache all the fragment pieces while trying to reassemble the fragment sets after all fragments are received.

infinity — In the case of routing, infinity is the maximum number of hops that a packet can cross before being discarded. In an IP packet, the Time to Live field is used to define the remaining lifetime of a packet.

informational/supervisory format — A connection-oriented format that can be used by LLC packets.

ingress filtering — The process of applying restrictions to traffic coming into a network.

Institute for Electrical and Electronic Engineers (IEEE) — An international organization that sets standards for all kinds of electrical and electronic equipment, including network interfaces and communications technologies.

Integrated Services Digital Network (ISDN) — An early dial-up digital link technology developed for use on standard telephone lines in the 1980s. Basic rate (BRI) ISDN offers two 64-Kbps voice or data channels and a 16-Kbps data/control channel to consumers for a total bandwidth of 144 Kbps. Primary rate (PRI) ISDN is a heavier-duty version that offers twenty-three 64-Kbps voice or data channels and a single 64-Kbps control/data channel for an aggregate of 1.544 Mbps (identical to T1's bandwidth). PRI is available to businesses and communications carriers. Because ISDN is at least as expensive as faster technologies such as cable modem and DSL for consumers, its usage in the first world is declining rapidly.

inter-autonomous system routing — A term used in BGP, this refers to the ability to provide routing between Autonomous Systems.

inter-domain routing protocols — Routing protocols used to exchange information between Autonomous Systems.

interface identifier — In IPv6 addressing, unicast and anycast addresses have the lower-order bits of their addresses reserved for a bit string that uniquely identifies a particular interface, either globally or (at a minimum) locally.

Interior Gateway Protocols (IGPs) — Routing protocols used within an Autonomous System.

internal route entry — A route entry learned from within the same area as the computing device.

International Standards Organization (ISO) — An international standards organization based in Geneva, Switzerland that sets standards for information technology and networking equipment, protocols, and communications technologies.

International Standards Organization Open Systems Interconnection — *See* International Standards Organization *and* Open Systems Interconnection.

Internet Architecture Board (IAB) — The organization within the Internet Society that governs the actions of both the IETF and the IRTF, and has final approval authority for Internet Standards.

Internet Assigned Numbers Authority (IANA) — The arm of the ISOC originally responsible for registering domain names and allocating public IP addresses. This job is now the responsibility of ICANN.

Internet Control Message Protocol (ICMP) — A Layer 3 (Internetwork layer) TCP/IP protocol used to exchange information about network traffic conditions, congestion, and reachability of specific network addresses. IP PING and TRACEROUTE utilities use ICMP.

Internet Corporation for Assigned Names and Numbers (ICANN) — The organization within the Internet Society that is responsible for proper assignment of all domain names and numeric IP addresses for the global Internet; works in tandem with private companies called name registrars to manage domain names, and with ISPs to manage assignment of numeric IP addresses.

Internet Engineering Task Force (IETF) — The organization within the Internet Society that's responsible for all currently used Internet standards, protocols, and services; and for managing the development and maintenance of RFCs.

Internet Group Management Protocol (IGMP) — A protocol that supports the formation of multicast groups. Hosts use IGMP to join and leave multicast groups. Routers track IGMP memberships and only forward multicasts on a link that has active members of that multicast group.

Internet Message Access Protocol (IMAP) — A TCP/IP-based messaging protocol that allows users to maintain customized message stores on an e-mail server, yet access and manage their e-mail messages on any workstation.

Internet Network Information Center (InterNIC) — A quasi-governmental agency that was responsible for assigned names and numbers on the Internet (this responsibility now falls on ICANN).

Internet Protocol (IP) — The primary Network layer protocol in the TCP/IP protocol suite, IP manages routing and delivery of most real data on TCP/IP-based networks. *See also* Internet Protocol version 4.

Internet Protocol Control Protocol (IPCP) — A special TCP/IP Network Control Protocol used to establish and manage IP links at the Network layer.

Internet Protocol next generation (IPng) — An older name for the most recent version of IP. It is more often called IPv6.

Internet Protocol version 4 (IPv4) — The current version of IP that's in broadest public use at present. (A new version IPv6 is currently under development and partly specified, but not yet widely deployed.)

Internet Protocol version 6 (Ipv6) — The successor to the IPv4 protocol. IPv6 is currently specified, but not yet in full deployment.

Internet Research Task Force (IRTF) — The forward-looking research and development arm of the Internet Society, the IRTF reports into the IAB for direction and governance.

Internet Service Provider (ISP) — An organization that provides Internet access to individuals or organizations as a primary line of business. Currently, ISPs are the source for public IP addresses for most organizations seeking Internet access.

Internet Societal Task Force (ISTF) — The arm of the Internet Society charged with evaluating the societal impact of Internet access, and with making sure that underprivileged or underserved communities can benefit from Internet access as much as possible.

Internet Society (ISOC) — The parent organization under which the rest of the Internet governing bodies fall, ISOC is a user-oriented, public-access organization that solicits end-user participation and input to help set future Internet policy and direction.

Internet Standard — A RFC document that specifies the rules, structure, and behavior of a current Internet protocol or service.

Internetwork Packet Exchange/Sequenced Packet Exchange (IPX/SPX) — The protocol suite associated with earlier implementations of Novell's NetWare network operating system; TCP/IP has largely supplanted IPX/SPX on most modern networks.

intra-autonomous system routing — A term used in BGP that refers to the ability to provide routing within an Autonomous System.

intra-domain routing protocols — Routing protocols used to exchange routing information between separate Autonomous Systems.

intrusion detection system (IDS) — A special-purpose software system that inspects ongoing patterns of network traffic, looking for signs of impending or active attack. Most IDSs can foil break-in attempts and also attempt to establish the identity of the attacker or attackers. Best of all, IDSs work automatically and require no immediate human attention to handle most attacks.

intuitive interface — An interface that is self-explanatory, requiring little or no training to navigate.

inverse DNS query — A DNS query that supplies an IP address for conversion to a corresponding domain name. Inverse DNS queries are often used to double-check user identities to make sure that the domain names they present match the IP addresses in their packet headers. *See also* IP spoofing and spoofing.

IP gateway — TCP/IP terminology for a router that provides access to resources outside the local subnet network address. (A default gateway is the name given to the TCP/IP configuration entry for clients that identifies the router they must use to send data outside their local subnet areas.)

IP renumbering — The process of replacing one set of numeric IP addresses with another set of numeric IP addresses because of a change in ISPs, or an address reassignment.

IP Security (IPSec or IP Sec) — A security specification supporting various forms of encryption and authentication, along with key management and related supporting functions. Optional in IPv4, IPSec is a required part of IPv6.

IP service attack — A system attack that concentrates on known characteristics and vulnerabilities of one or more specific IP services, or that uses well-known port addresses associated with such services for its own nefarious ends.

IP spoofing — A technique whereby a programmer constructs an IP packet that presents domain name credentials that differ from the IP address in the packet header. IP spoofing is often used in illicit network break-in attempts, or to impersonate users or packet origination. *See also* spoofing.

IPCONFIG — A command-line utility used to identify the local host's data link address and IP address.

IPv4-compatible address — IPv4-compatible addresses are used by nodes that need to tunnel IPv6 packets through IPv4 routers. These are dual stack nodes, as they understand both IPv4 and IPv6.

IPv4-mapped address — IPv4-mapped addresses are used by IPv6 nodes, which need to communicate with IPv4 nodes that do not understand IPv6 at all.

ISO/OSI network reference model — The official name for the seven-layer network reference model often used to describe how networks operate and behave.

iterative query — A DNS query that targets one specific DNS server, and terminates with whatever response may be forthcoming, whether that response is a definite answer, an error message, a null (no information) reply, or a pointer to another name server.

jumbograms — A proposal for allowing very large (beyond 4-gigabyte) packets to be transported using IPv6. Used only in special circumstances, such as on large backbone routes.

keep-alive process — The procedure of maintaining an idle connection. TCP connections can be kept alive through TCP keep-alive packets if configured to do so. If the Application layer protocol offers a keep-alive process, the TCP layer should not perform the keep-alive process.

kernel — The central element of a computer operating system. When the operating system starts, the kernel begins running in main memory. It handles the most critical tasks.

key — In cryptography, a secret piece of information used in encoding or encrypting the information to be hidden. Keys are used in conjunction with a transformation.

layer — A single component or facet in a networking model that handles one particular aspect of network access or communications.

layer-3 switch — A type of networking device that combines hub, router, and network management functions within a single box. Layer-3 switches make it possible to create and manage multiple virtual subnets in a single device, while offering extremely high bandwidth to individual connections between pairs of devices attached to that device.

lease expiration time — The end of the lease time. If a DHCP client does not renew or rebind its address by the lease expiration time, it must release the address and reinitialize.

lease time — The amount of time that a DHCP client may use an assigned DHCP address.

Legion — A NetBIOS file share scanner with brute force password attack capabilities that should be part of any Windows IP administrator's attack tool kit.

lifetime value — The time that a packet can remain on the network. Routers discard packets when their lifetimes expire.

limited traffic flow confidentiality — In IPSec, the ability to defeat traffic analysis by hiding the path, frequency, source, destination, and volume of traffic between correspondents.

Link Control Protocol (LCP) — A special connection negotiation protocol that PPP uses to establish point-to-point links between peers for ongoing communications.

link-local address — The link-local address has the first 10 (leftmost) bits set to 1111111010 (all ones except for the last three digits, which are set to 010 [binary]). The next 54 bits are set to all zeroes. The last (rightmost) 64 bits of the link-local address are the normal interface ID. When a router sees the link-local address prefix in a packet, it knows it can safely ignore it, as the packet is intended only for the local network segment.

link-state — A type of routing protocol that uses and shares information only about adjacent neighbors, and that uses transit time to assess link costs, rather than hop counts or routing distances.

link-state advertisement (LSA) — A packet that includes information about a router, its neighbors, and the attached network.

link-state routing protocol — A routing protocol based on a common link-state picture of the network topology. Link-state routers can identify the best path based on bandwidth, delay, or other path characteristics associated with one or more links available to them. OSPF is a link-state routing protocol.

LMHOSTS — A plain text file that lists NetBIOS names and their associated IP addresses. A LMHOSTS file is similar to a HOSTS file but includes features unique to NetBIOS.

load balancing — A method of distributing the processing load for service requests by directing individual requests for service to multiple machines in a way that causes the numbers of such requests per machine to be as nearly equal (or balanced) as possible.

local area network (LAN) — A single network cable segment, subnet, or logical network community that represents a collection of machines that can communicate with one another more or less directly (using MAC addresses).

local process — A process or execution thread that executes on a local host (that does not involve remote execution or behavior).

log — A file-based record of system activities and events that relate to some specific software system, such as a server, firewall, and so forth. Postmortem examination of logs is sometimes required to develop attack signatures and determine the extent of system compromise when successful attacks occur.

logical connection — A virtual connection between hosts, sometimes referred to as a circuit. The TCP handshake is used to set up a logical connection between TCP peers.

Logical Link Control (LLC) — The data link specification for protocol identification as defined by the IEEE 802.2 specification. The LLC layer resides directly above the Media Access Control layer.

logical ring transmission path — The transmission path used by token ring networks, where packets are repeated back onto a ring and pass in a logical, sequential order from one ring station to the next.

loopback — An address that points directly back to the sender. In IPv4, the Class A domain 127.0.0.0 (or 127.0.0.1 for a specific machine address) is reserved for loopback. In IPv6, there is a single loopback address, written "::1" (all zeroes, except for that last bit, which is one). By passing traffic

down through the ICP/IP stack, then back up again, the loopback address can be used to test a computer's TCP/IP software.

looped internetwork — A sub-optimal condition in an internetwork that results in a packet crossing a network segment more than once. Routing protocols attempt to prevent loops, but when they occur, they forward the packet until its TTL reaches zero.

lost segment — A section of TCP data that does not arrive at the destination. Upon detection of a lost segment, a TCP sender must decrease the congestion window to one-half of the previous window size. Lost segments are assumed to be caused by network congestion.

mail exchange (MX) record — A DNS resource record that's used to identify the domain name for the e-mail server that handles any particular domain or subdomain, or that's used to route e-mail traffic from one e-mail server to another while e-mail is in transit from sender to receiver.

malicious code — A program that is written with the intent of harming or disrupting host operations.

man-in-the-middle attack — A type of system or network attack where an attacking system interposes itself between the target network and the next normal link on that network's usual routing chain.

manageable objects — The elements or characteristics of a device that can be queried by SNMP managers for their settings or status. The MIB maintains the list of manageable objects.

managed device — Any kind of system or device where management agent software is installed and running, ready to issue alerts, or respond to a polling request for management data.

management agent — The software component on a managed device that gathers management data into a local management database, can respond to polls for such data from a management entity, or issue an alert to a management entity when some specific event occurs, or a threshold is exceeded.

management database (MDB) — The collection of data about a single managed device, which a management agent gathers for delivery to a management entity; also, the aggregated collection of data from all managed devices gathered in an NMS, which describes a network's status and condition.

management entity — A software process that polls for and collects management data from managed devices, and can respond to alerts from managed devices under its control.

Management Information Base (MIB) — A database of objects or characteristics that can be managed for a device.

management proxy — A special component of network management software that permits multiple NMSs to be managed at a lower level by a single higher-level NMS. Basically, the management proxy handles reporting and polling requirements for higher-level systems by translating between the message formats and data used in lower-layer and higher-layer systems, and vice versa.

manual address lease — A type of DHCP address lease wherein the administrator takes full responsibility for managing address assignments, using DHCP only as a repository for such assignment data, and related TCP/IP configuration data.

master router — In link-state routing, a router that distributes its view of the link-state database to slave routers.

master server — *See* primary DNS server.

Maximum Segment Size (MSS) — The maximum amount of data that can fit in a TCP packet after the TCP header. Each TCP peer shares the MSS during the handshake process.

maximum transmission unit (MTU) — The biggest single chunk of data that can be transferred across any particular type of network medium (1518 bytes is the MTU for conventional Ethernet, for example).

Media Access Control (MAC) address — A special type of network address, handled by a sublayer of the Data Link layer, that's normally preassigned on a per-interface basis to uniquely identify each such interface on any network cable segment (or virtual facsimile). ICANN controls assignment of vendor IDs and interface numbers to make sure all such addresses are guaranteed to be unique. When IP frames are transferred from one interface to another, the MAC layer addresses for the sender and receiver are used to effect the transfer.

Media Access Control (MAC) layer — A sublayer of the Data Link layer. This layer is part of the Media Access Control definition, in which network access methods, such as Ethernet and token ring, apply.

media flow control — The management of data transmission rates between two devices across a local network medium that guarantees the receiver can accept and process input before it arrives from the sender.

Message Type — A required option that indicates the purpose of a DHCP packet—the eight message types are Discover, Offer, Request, Decline, Acknowledge, Negative Acknowledge (NAK), Release, and Inform.

messages — Data that has distinct boundaries and command information within the packet.

metrics — Measurements that may be based on distance (hop count), time (seconds), or other values.

micro-mobility — Generally dealt with at the link layer, below IP. It has to do with maintaining connectivity to a local link over a wireless connection. Examples of micro-mobility include the hand-off of cellular phones as they pass from one radio cell to another, and maintaining the identity of a laptop computer as it moves between access points in a wireless LAN.

Microsoft DNS (MS DNS) — Microsoft's implementation of the DNS standard that contains extensions that enable MS DNS servers to query WINS to resolve NetBIOS names. For reverse lookup in the *in.addr.arpa* domain, MS DNS servers can use WINS-R to return the NetBIOS names associated with an IP address.

millisecond — One-thousandth of a second.

mobile code — Also referred to as a worm, mobile code moves from machine to machine without user intervention. The ILOVEYOU e-mails contained mobile code that accessed the local address book and mailed itself to all addresses listed.

multi-homed — Containing multiple network interfaces capable of attaching to multiple subnets.

multicast address — One of a block of addresses reserved for use in sending the same message to multiple interfaces or nodes. Members of a community of interest subscribe to a multicast address in order to receive router updates, streaming data (video, audio, teleconferencing), and so on. In IPv4, the Class D block of addresses is reserved for multicast. In IPv6, all multicast addresses begin with 0xFF. ICANN, with the help of IANA, manages all such address adjustments.

multicast packet — A packet sent to a group of devices, such as a group of routers.

multiple paths — More than one path to a destination. Meshed and topologically complex networks, such as the Internet, often contain multiple paths. Multiple paths provide redundancy for fault tolerance, and greater bandwidth use.

multiplexing — The process whereby multiple individual data streams from Application layer processes are joined together for transmission by a specific TCP/IP transport protocol through the IP protocol.

Nagle algorithm — A method stating that when small packets are sent, but not acknowledged, no further packets shall be sent. The Nagle algorithm is relevant on a network that supports numerous small packets due to support of interactive applications, such as Telnet.

name query — An inverse DNS query that seeks to obtain a domain name for a corresponding numeric IP address.

name resolution — *See* domain name resolution.

name resolution process — The process of obtaining an IP address based on a symbolic name. DNS is a name resolution process.

name resolver — A client-side software component, usually part of a TCP/IP stack implementation, that's responsible for issuing DNS queries for applications, and relaying whatever responses come back to those applications.

name server (NS) record — The DNS resource record that identifies name servers that are authoritative for some particular domain or subdomain. Often used as a mechanism to delegate authority for DNS subdomains downward in the domain name hierarchy.

National Center for Supercomputing Applications (NCSA) — An arm of the University of Illinois at Champaign-Urbana, where supercomputer research is undertaken, and where the first graphical Web browser, Mosaic, was developed and released in 1994.

National Science Foundation (NSF) — A U.S. government agency charged with oversight and support for government-funded scientific research and development. *See also* NSFNET.

negative caching — A technique for storing error messages in a local cache so that repeating a query that previously produced an error message can be satisfied more quickly than if that query was forwarded to some other DNS name server.

Neighbor Advertisement (NA) — When requested, or when its own link layer address changes, a node sends a Neighbor Advertisement including its IPv6 address and its link layer address.

Neighbor Discovery (ND) — A protocol in IPv6 that permits nodes and routers on a local link to keep one another updated about any recent changes in their network connectivity or status.

neighbor routers — On a link-state network, neighbor routers are connected to the same network segment.

Neighbor Solicitation (NS) — A node can send a Neighbor Solicitation to find (or verify) the link layer address of a local node, see if that node is still available, or check that its own address is not in use by another.

NetBIOS Enhanced User Interface (NetBEUI) — An implementation of NetBIOS protocols and services undertaken by IBM, 3Com, and Microsoft in the 1980s, still used for basic networking in a variety of Microsoft, IBM, and other operating systems.

NetBIOS Frame (NBF) — The successor to NetBEUI as the native NetBIOS transport protocol in Windows 2000.

NetBIOS over TCP/IP (NetBT or NBT) — A set of request/reply messages defined to enable the Application layer API, known as the Network Basic Input/Output System (NetBIOS), originally developed at Sytek for IBM in the early 1980s to work with TCP/IP transport and network protocols. NBT is required for older versions of Windows (those released prior to Windows 2000) on TCP/IP-only networks to support basic Microsoft network messaging and services.

network address — That portion of an IP address that consists of the network prefix for that address; an extended network prefix also includes any subnetting bits. All bits that belong to the extended network prefix show up as ones in the corresponding subnet mask for that network.

Network Address Translation (NAT) — A special type of networking software that manages network connections on behalf of multiple clients on an internal network, and translates the source address for all outbound traffic from the original source to the address of the outbound network interface. NAT software also manages forwarding replies to all outgoing traffic back to its original sender. NAT software is often used to allow clients using private IP addresses to access the Internet.

network analysis — The same as protocol analysis, but a less intimidating term.

Network Basic Input/Output System (NetBIOS) — A high-level set of network protocols and services, developed by Sytek Corporation for IBM in the mid-1980s, that is still widely used in IBM, Microsoft, and other network operating systems.

network congestion — A condition that occurs when the delivery time for packets (also known as network latency) increases beyond normal limits. Congestion can result from several causes, including problems with network links, overloaded hosts or routers, or unusually heavy network usage levels. Packet loss is identified as a characteristic of network congestion.

Network Control Protocol (NCP) — Any of a family of TCP/IP Network layer protocols used to establish and manage protocol links made at the Network layer (TCP/IP's Internet layer).

Network Driver Interface Specification (NDIS) — Pieces of software (compliant with this specification) that make it possible for Transport layer processes to interact with NICs in a common way, despite differences in specific card design or NIC driver implementation.

Network File System (NFS) — A TCP/IP-based, network-distributed file system that permits users to incorporate files and directories on machines across a network to be treated as an extension of their local desktop file systems.

network interface card (NIC) — A hardware device used to permit a computer to attach to and communicate with a local area network.

Network layer — The Network layer operates at Layer 3 of the ISO/OSI network reference model; it handles the logical addresses associated with individual machines on a network by correlating human-readable names for such machines with unique, machine-readable numeric addresses. It also uses addressing information to determine how to send a PDU from a sender to a receiver when the source and destination do not reside on the same physical network segment.

Network Layer Reachability Information (NLRI) — The information about available networks, and the routes whereby they may be reached, which routing protocols collect, manage, and distribute to the routers or other devices that use such routing protocols.

network management protocol — Any of several Application layer protocols and services used to convey network management messages, including commands, polling requests and responses, and alerts. For TCP/IP networks, SNMP is the standard management protocol that's most widely used.

network management system (NMS) — The software and hardware platform within which management entities function, and where network management functions may be installed, configured, managed, and controlled.

network portion — The leftmost octets or bits in a numeric IP address, the network portion of an IP address identifies the network and subnet portions of that address. The value assigned to the prefix number identifies the number of bits in the network portion of any IP address. (For example, 10.0.0.0/8 indicates that the first eight bits of the address are the network portion for the public Class A IP address.)

network prefix — That portion of an IP address that corresponds to the network portion of the address; for example, the network prefix for a Class B address is /16 (meaning that the first 16 bits represent the network portion of the address, and 255.255.0.0 is the corresponding default subnet mask).

network probe — A standalone self-contained device that monitors and manages remote segments of a network.

network reference model — *See* ISO/OSI network reference model.

network route entry — A route table entry that provides a next-hop router for a specific network.

Network Service Access Point (NSAP) — These networks (such as ATM, X.25, and so forth) typically set up point-to-point links between hosts. This is a very different paradigm from the one built into IP.

network services — A generic TCP/IP term for a protocol/service combination that operates at the Application layer in the TCP/IP network model.

Network Time Protocol (NTP) — A time synchronization protocol defined in RFC 1305. NTP provides the mechanisms to synchronize and coordinate time distribution in a large, diverse Internet operating at varying speeds.

next-hop router — The local router that is used to route a packet to the next network along its path.

nmap — An infamous port scanner that is primarily UNIX or Linux based, nmap should be part of any IP administrator's attack tool kit.

non-authoritative response — Name, address, or RR information from a DNS server that's not authoritative for the DNS zone being queried (such responses originate from caches on such servers).

non-recursive query — *See* iterative query.

NSFNET — A public network operated by the National Science Foundation in the 1980s to support the Internet backbone.

NSLOOKUP — A widely implemented command-line program that supports DNS lookup and reporting capabilities. The "ns" in this command name stands for "name server," so it's reasonable to think of this as a general-purpose name server lookup tool.

null-terminated string — A string of bytes that contains the value zero. When a field is filled with a null-terminated string, it is said to be "zero-padded."

numeric address — *See* numeric IP address.

numeric IP address — An IP address expressed in dotted decimal or binary notation.

object — An item that may be managed by an SNMP agent.

object identifier (OID) — A sequence of non-negative integers used to reference a single MIB object.

object tree — A tree-like structure that is used to define and organize the managed objects in a MIB.

octet — TCP/IP terminology for an 8-bit number; numeric IPv4 addresses consist of four octets.

On-Demand Routing (ODR) — A low-overhead feature that provides IP routing for sites on a hub-and-spoke network. Each router maintains and updates entries in its routing table only for hosts whose data passes through the router, thus reducing storage requirements and bandwidth.

Open Shortest Path First (OSPF) Protocol — A sophisticated Layer 3 or TCP/IP Internet layer routing protocol that uses link-state information to construct routing topologies for local internetworks, and provides load-balancing capabilities.

Open Systems Interconnection (OSI) — The name of an open-standard internetworking initiative undertaken in the 1980s, primarily in Europe, and originally intended to supersede TCP/IP. Technical and political problems prevented this anticipated outcome from materializing, but the ISO/OSI reference model remains an enduring legacy of this effort.

optimal route — The best route possible. Typically, routing protocols are used to exchange routing metric information to determine the best route possible. The optimal route is defined as either the route that is quickest, most reliable, most secure, or considered *best* by some other measurement. When TOS is not used, the optimal route is either the closest (based on hop count) or the highest throughput route.

optimistic security model — The original basis for TCP/IP security, this model assumes that it is safe to enforce little or no security on normal network communications. (This explains why services such as Telnet and FTP routinely pass account and password information in clear, or plain, text across networks.)

organizationally unique identifier (OUI) — A unique identifier assigned by IANA or ICANN that's used as the first three bytes of a NIC's MAC layer address to identify its maker or manufacturer.

out-of-band management — A management design that uses a path separate from the data path for the exchange of SNMP management data. Because it is using a separate path, out-of-band management data can still reach the manager when the primary data path becomes unavailable.

out-of-order packets — Packets that do not arrive in the order defined by the sequence number. When a TCP host receives out-of-order packets, that host sends duplicate ACKs that indicate the packets arrived out of order.

overhead — The non-data bits or bytes required to move data from one location to another. The datalink header is the overhead required to move an IP packet from one device to another across a network. The IP header is additional overhead required to move a packet through an internetwork. Ideally, bandwidth, throughput, and processing power should be devoted to moving high amounts of data bytes—not high amounts of overhead bytes.

oversized packets — Packets that exceed the MTU for the network, and usually point to a problem with a NIC or its driver software.

packet — A generic term for a PDU at just about any layer in a networking model, this term is most properly applied to PDUs at Layer 3, or the TCP/IP Internet layer.

packet filter — A specific collection of inclusion or exclusion rules to be applied to a stream of network packets that determines what is captured (and what is ignored) from the original input stream.

packet header — *See* header.

Packet Internetwork Groper (PING) — A TCP/IP Internet layer protocol that's used to determine reachability of a remote host, and to measure round-trip travel time when sending data from a sender to a receiver.

packet priority — A TOS priority that defines the order in which packets should be processed through a router queue.

packet sniffing — A technique that involves using a protocol analyzer to decode and examine the contents of IP packets to attempt to identify sensitive information, including accounts and passwords for subsequent break-in attempts or other nefarious purposes.

packet snooping — *See* packet sniffing.

packet trailer — *See* trailer.

packet-switched network — A network in which data packets may take any usable path between sender and receiver, where sender and receiver are identified by unique network addresses, and there's no requirement that all packets follow the same path in transit (though they often do).

pad — Bytes placed at the end of the Ethernet Data field to meet the minimum field length requirement of 46 bytes. These bytes have no meaning and are discarded by the incoming data link driver when the packet is processed.

pass-through autonomous system routing — A term used in BGP routing, this routing technique is used to share BGP routing information across a non-BGP network.

password hashing — A method for storing passwords in encrypted form for authentication purposes. Modern operating systems, such as Windows NT and Windows 2000, UNIX, and Linux, hash passwords to improve security on stored forms. Unfortunately, when hackers or crackers gain access to the files in which hashed passwords live, if the hashing algorithm is known, they can use dictionary-based brute force password attacks to identify most or all passwords in such files.

path — The route that a packet can take through an internetwork.

path discovery — The process of learning possible routes through a network.

Path Maximum Transmission Unit black hole router — A router that silently discards packets that are too large to be forwarded and have the Don't Fragment bit set.

Path MTU (PMTU) — The MTU size that is supported through an entire path; the lowest common denominator MTU through a path. The Path MTU is learned through the PMTU Discovery process.

Path MTU Discovery — The process of learning the MTU that is supported through an entire path. ICMP is used for PMTU Discovery.

PATHPING — A Windows 2000 utility used to test router and path latency, as well as connectivity.

payload — That portion of a PDU that contains information intended for delivery to an application or to a higher-layer protocol (depending on where in the stack the PDU is situated).

peer layer — Analogous layers in the protocol stacks on a sender and a receiver, the receiving layer usually reverses whatever operations the sending layer performs (which is what makes those layers peers).

peer-to-peer services — An Application layer service in which the roles of client and server are fluid so that a host that is a client to a server for one request/reply stream could potentially be the server to the other host acting instead as a client for another request/reply stream.

per-domain behavior (PDB) — In differentiated service, a class of descriptors of available service levels, or a way of describing the entities offering such differentiated service levels—in this case, a "domain." Services are provided as specified throughout the domain, and change at the edge of the domain. Per-domain behaviors are available across all hops within a given domain.

per-hop behavior (PHB) — In differentiated service, a class of descriptors of available service levels. One way of describing the entities offering such differentiated service levels—in this case, individual routers, or a path traced through individual routers.

performance management — One of the five layers of the OSI network management model, performance management focuses on measuring and monitoring network traffic levels, utilization, and other statistical metrics for network and system behavior.

periodic update — In general, an update to data values that occurs at a regular interval or time period. In the case of routing protocols, most distance vector protocols include periodic updates to help maintain router table currency.

personnel security — The aspect of security that concentrates on informing users about security matters, and training them on proper application of security policies, procedures, and practices.

pessimistic security model — A model of system and network security that assumes it is always necessary to enforce strong security measures so that access to all resources should be denied to all users, by default, and allowed only to those with a legitimate need to access such resources, on a case-by-case basis.

Physical layer — Layer 1 in the ISO/OSI network reference model, the Physical layer is where connections, communications, and interfaces—hardware and signaling requirements—are handled.

physical numeric address — Another term for MAC layer address (or MAC address).

physical security — That aspect of security that concerns itself with limiting physical access to system and network components to prevent unauthorized users from attempting direct attacks on such components. Because lax physical security can easily lead to compromise, strong physical security is always a good idea.

physical star design — The physical layout of a token ring network, where all devices on the network are connected via cable back to a central device, such as a switch or a hub. Logically, however, token ring is a true ring based on the packet transmission path.

PING sweep — An ICMP Echo-based operation used to locate active devices on a network. The term "sweep" refers to the process of testing an entire range of IP addresses for active devices.

plain text — The data to be encrypted when still in its original (readable or usable) form.

plain text password — A password that is transferred across the cable in plain ASCII text.

point-to-point — A type of Data Link layer connection, in which a link is established between exactly two communications partners so that the link extends from one partner (the sender) to the other (the receiver).

Point-to-Point Protocol (PPP) — A Layer 2 or TCP/IP Network Interface layer protocol that permits a client and a server to establish a

communications link that can accommodate a variety of higher-layer protocols, including IP, AppleTalk, SNA, IPX/SPX, NetBEUI, and many others; today's most widely used serial line protocol for making Internet connections.

point-to-point transmission — A type of network communication where pairs of devices establish a communications link to exchange data with one another; the most common type of connection used when communicating with an Internet Service Provider.

Point-to-Point Tunneling Protocol (PPTP) — A Layer 2 or TCP/IP Network Interface layer protocol that permits a client and a server to establish a secure, encrypted communications link that can accommodate just about any kind of PPP traffic.

pointer (PTR) record — The DNS resource record that's used for inverse lookups to map numeric IP addresses to domain names.

poison reverse — A process used to make a router undesirable for a specific routing path. This process is one of the methods used to eliminate routing loops.

port address — *See* port number.

port number — A 16-bit number that identifies either a well-known application service, or a dynamically assigned port number for a transitory sender-receiver exchange of data through TCP or UDP.

port probe — A reconnaissance process used to learn which processes are active on a host device. Typically, port probes use scripted programs to send out sequential queries to obtain all active port information.

port scanner — A special purpose software tool that cycles through either well-known TCP and UDP ports with easy vulnerabilities (such as Legion), or all possible TCP and UDP port addresses, looking for open ports that can then be probed for access or exploited for vulnerabilities.

positive response — An affirmative acknowledgment that data was received. TCP headers with the ACK flag set indicate that the Acknowledgment Number field is valid, and provide the next-expected sequence number from the TCP peer.

Post Office Protocol version 3 (POP3) — A TCP/IP Application layer protocol that supports client downloads of incoming e-mail addresses from an e-mail server to e-mail client software. When using POP3, clients normally manage e-mail messages on their desktop machines.

pre-filter — A type of data filter applied to a raw input stream in a protocol analyzer that selects only packets that meet its criteria for capture and retention; since this filter is applied before data is captured, it's called a pre-filter.

preamble — The initial sequence of values that precedes all Ethernet packets. Placed on the front of the frame by the outgoing NIC and removed by the incoming NIC, the preamble is used as a timing mechanism that enables receiving IP hosts to properly recognize and interpret bits as ones or zeroes.

precedence — A definition of priority for an IP packet. Routers may process higher-priority packets before lower-priority packets when a router queue is congested.

preferred address — An address the DHCP client remembers from the previous network session. Most DHCP client implementations maintain a list of the last IP addresses they used, and indicate a preference for the last-used address. This adds a somewhat static view of the network addressing system, but there is no guarantee the clients can continue to receive the same address each time they boot. In IPv6, the term "preferred address" refers to the one address, among the many that may be associated with the same interface, whose use by higher-layer protocols is unrestricted.

Presentation layer — Layer 6 of the ISO/OSI reference model, the Presentation layer is where generic network data formats are translated into platform-specific data formats for incoming data, and vice versa for outgoing data. This is also the layer where optional encryption or compression services may be applied (or reversed).

primary DNS server — The name server that's authoritative for some particular domain or subdomain, and has primary custody over the DNS database segment (and related zone files) for that domain or subdomain.

primary master — *See* primary DNS server.

Private Communication Technology (PCT) — An IP-based Application layer protocol documented in RFC 2246 that's used to create a secure channel to prevent anyone from eavesdropping on client-server and server-client communications across the Web.

private IP address — Any of a series of Class A, B, and C IP addresses reserved by IANA for private use, documented in RFC 1918, intended for uncontrolled private use in organizations. Private IP addresses may not be routed across the Internet because there is no guarantee that any such address is unique.

private MIB — A proprietary MIB that defines the manageable objects of a vendor's device.

Process layer — A synonym for the TCP/IP Application layer, where high-level protocols and services, such as FTP and Telnet, operate.

Programmable Read-Only Memory (PROM) — A write-once form of computer memory used to create non-volatile storage for certain key information, such as system or operating system boot up parameters. PROMs are burned (written to) using special data recording methods, such as ultraviolet light, before such chips are installed on a motherboard or interface card.

promiscuous mode operation — Network interface card and driver operation used to capture broadcast packets, multicast packets, packets sent to other devices, as well as error packets.

Proposed Standard — An intermediate level for standards-track RFCs, where a Draft Standard goes through initial review, and has two or more reference implementations built to demonstrate interoperability between implementations.

protection against replays — The ability to distinguish between "live" traffic from a trusted source and copies of such traffic masquerading as authentic communications. Protection against replays are typically based on packet sequence numbering and checking.

protocol — A precise set of standards that governs communications between computers on a network. Many protocols function in one or more layers of the OSI reference model.

protocol analysis — The process of capturing packets off the network for the purpose of gathering communication statistics, observing trends, and examining communication sequences.

protocol data unit (PDU) — At any layer in a networking model, a PDU represents the package for data at that layer, including a header and a payload, and in some cases, a trailer.

protocol identification (PID) — A datagram service necessitated when any single protocol carries multiple protocols across a single connection (as PPP can do at the Data Link layer); PIDs permit individual datagram payloads to be identified by the type of protocol they contain.

protocol identification field — A field that is included in most headers to identify the upcoming protocol. The PID of Ethernet headers is the Type field. The PID of IP headers is the Protocol field.

protocol number — An 8-bit numeric identifier associated with some specific TCP/IP protocol.

protocol stack — A specific implementation of a protocol suite on a computer, including a network interface, necessary drivers, and whatever protocol and service implementations are necessary to enable the computer to use a specific protocol suite to communicate across the network.

protocol suite — A named family of networking protocols, such as TCP/IP, IPX/SPX, or NetBEUI, in which each such family enables computers to communicate across a network.

proxy ARP — The process of replying to ARP requests for IP hosts on another network. A proxy ARP network configuration effectively hides subnetting from the individual IP hosts.

proxy server — A special type of network boundary service that interposes itself between internal network addresses and external network addresses. For internal clients, a proxy server makes a connection to external resources on the client's behalf and provides address masquerading. For external clients, a proxy server presents internal resources to the public Internet as if they are present on the proxy server itself.

pseudo-header — A false header structure used to calculate a checksum. The UDP and TCP checksums are based on the pseudo-header values.

public IP address — Any TCP/IP address allocated for the exclusive use of some particular organization, either by IANA or ICANN, or by an ISP to one of its clients.

pull — A method of replicating server data in which the receiver initiates the transfer, thereby pulling that data from its original source.

push — A method of replicating server data in which the sender initiates the transfer, thereby pushing that data to the receiver.

push-pull — A method for replicating data in which the sender initiates data transfer when server data changes, but where receivers also initiate periodic data transfer to maintain ongoing database consistency.

Quality of Service (QoS) — A specific level of service guarantee associated with Application layer protocols in which time-sensitivity requirements for data (such as voice or video) require that delays be controlled within definite guidelines to deliver viewable or audible data streams.

Quote of the Day (QOD) — A basic TCP/IP service that delivers a short stream of text (usually a joke or an epigram) in response to a request for service.

r-utils — An abbreviation for *remote utilities*, this is a collection of software programs originally included as part of BSD UNIX v4.2, designed to provide remote access and login services for users. Hence, they are a common point of attack.

reachability — The ability to find at least one transmission path between a pair of hosts so that they can exchange datagrams across an internetwork.

reassembly — The process applied at the Transport layer where messages segmented into multiple chunks for transmission across the network are put back together in the proper order for delivery to an application on the receiving end. The IP Fragment Offset field is used to identify the order of the fragments for reassembly.

rebinding process — The process of contacting any DHCP server through the use of a broadcast to obtain renewal of an address.

reconnaissance process — The process of learning various characteristics about a network or host. Typically, reconnaissance probes precede network attacks.

recursive query — A type of DNS query that continues until a definitive answer is forthcoming, be it a name-address translation, contents of the requested resource record(s), or an error message of some kind. Clients issue recursive queries to their designated name servers, which issue iterative queries to other name servers until the initial recursive request is resolved.

redirect — Point out another path. Using ICMP, a router can redirect a host to another, more optimal router. A router might also use redirects to balance traffic loads across multiple interfaces.

redistributing — The method whereby information collected and managed by one routing protocol is exchanged with similar (but usually not identical) information managed by another routing protocol.

registered port — A TCP or UDP port number in the range from 1024 to 65,535 and associated with a specific Application layer protocol or service. IANA maintains a registered port number list at *http://www.iana.org*.

Registry setting — A configuration that controls the way in which Windows devices operate. There are numerous settings that define how Windows 2000 operates in a TCP/IP environment.

reinitialize — The process of beginning the standard DHCP Discovery process anew after failure of the renewal and rebinding processes. During the reinitializing phase, the DHCP client has no IP address and uses 0.0.0.0 as its source address.

relay agent process — A process or execution thread that executes on a local host (which may be on a Windows workstation, server, or router) and forwards DHCP broadcasts as unicasts directed to a remote DHCP server for clients operating outside a DHCP broadcast domain.

release — The process of releasing an IP address by formally sending a DHCP Release packet (Message Type 0x07) to the DHCP server. If a client shuts down without sending the Release packet, the DHCP server maintains the lease until expiration.

remote logon service — Any type of network service that permits users elsewhere on a network to use the network to log onto a system as if they were attached locally, while operating remotely. Such services are favorite attack points because they're designed to give outsiders access to systems and services.

Remote Monitoring (RMON) — A TCP/IP Application layer protocol designed to support remote monitoring and management of networking devices, such as hubs, servers, and routers.

Remote Procedure Call (RPC) — A programming interface developed at Sun Microsystems, later standardized as an RFC, that permits a procedure running within a process on one host to use TCP/IP transport and network protocols to invoke and communicate with another procedure in some other process (on the same host or a remote host). RPC was created to make it easier for application developers to create networked applications, and it is still widely used today.

renewal process — The process of renewing the IP address for continued use. By default, a DHCP client begins the renewal process halfway between the lease grant and the lease expiration time.

repeater — A device that repeats bits regardless of their meaning, and without interpretation. A hub repeats bits received in one port out all other ports. A token ring station repeats bits received on the incoming receive pair out the transmit pair.

replication — A technique for controlled copying of data from one repository to another, usually with the idea of improving that data's robustness (if one server goes down, the other server(s) where a copy resides can continue to function) and availability (if multiple servers can handle the same data, the processing load involved can be distributed, or balanced, across all such servers, thereby improving response time to user requests).

reply message — An Application layer service packet sent from one host to another that responds to the other host's request for service.

report — A document prepared by a system or service that documents traffic volume and characteristics for that system or service, usually to represent routine usage or activity, but also to report on observed events or conditions that may have security implications.

Request for Comment (RFC) — An IETF standards document that specifies or describes best practices, provides information about the Internet, or specifies an Internet protocol or service.

request message — An Application layer service packet sent from one host to another that requests the target host to provide some service.

request/reply message — The collection of messages that an Application layer protocol supports; all such messages define the capabilities of the overall service that the protocol provides.

resolver — *See* name resolver.

resource record (RR) — One of a series of predefined record types in a DNS database or a DNS zone file.

Resource Reservation Protocol (RSVP) — A protocol aimed at regularizing and formalizing the practice of securing particular levels of service for traffic flows over the Internet.

restricting link — A link that does not support forwarding based on the current packet format and configuration. PMTU is used to identify restricting links so hosts can re-send packets using an acceptable MTU size.

Retired Standard — An RFC that has reached Standard designation, but that is no longer current, and has been replaced by a newer RFC.

retransmission timeout (RTO) — The time value that determines when a TCP host retransmits a packet after it was lost. The RTO value is exponentially increased after an apparent connection loss.

retransmission timer — The timer that maintains the RTO value.

retries — The number of times a TCP peer re-sends data when no acknowledgement is received.

retry counter — A counter that tracks the number of retransmissions on the network. The most common retry counter found in TCP/IP networking is the TCP retry counter. If a communication cannot be completed successfully before the retry counter expires, the transmission is considered a failure.

retry mechanism — A method for detecting communication problems and re-sending data across the network.

Reverse Address Resolution Protocol (RARP) — A Layer 2 or TCP/IP Network Access protocol that translates numeric IP addresses into MAC layer addresses (usually to verify that the identity claimed by a sender matches its real identity). This protocol was superceded by DHCP.

reverse DNS lookup — *See* inverse DNS query.

reverse proxying — The technique whereby a proxy server presents an internal network resource (for example, a Web, e-mail, or FTP server) as if it were present on the proxy server itself so that external clients can access internal network resources without seeing internal network IP address structures.

rexec — An abbreviation for *remote execution*, this is one of the BSD UNIX remote utilities (r-utils) that permits network users to execute single commands on a remote host.

robust — The condition of being ready for use under almost any circumstances; DNS allows multiple name servers to respond to queries about the same database zone to improve the odds that at least one such server will be able to respond to such queries. That's why most DNS experts recommend that there be at least one secondary DNS server for each zone, as well as the primary DNS server that's mandatory for every zone. Access to redundant copies of DNS database data is what makes DNS inherently robust.

root — The highest level in the domain name hierarchy, the root is symbolized by a final period in a fully qualified domain name. Root DNS servers provide the glue that ties together all the disparate parts of the domain name hierarchy, and name resolution for queries that might otherwise go unresolved.

round–trip time — The amount of time required to get from one host to another host and back. The round-trip time includes the transmission time from the first point to the second point, the processing time at the second point, and the return transmission time to the first point.

route aggregation — A form of IP address analysis that permits routers to indicate general interest in a particular network prefix that represents the "common portion" of a series of IP network addresses, as a way of reducing the number of individual routing table entries that routers must manage.

route priority — A TOS priority that defines the network to route packets. The router must support and track multiple network types to make the appropriate forwarding decision based on the TOS defined in the IP header.

route resolution process — The process that a host undergoes to determine whether a desired destination is local or remote and, if remote, which next-hop router to use.

route tracing — A technique for documenting which hosts and routers a datagram traverses in its path from the sender to the receiver (the TRACEROUTE or TRACERT commands use PING in a systematic way to provide this information).

Router Advertisement (RA) — A message, or advertisement, sent out by a router, periodically or on request, that contains its own link layer address, the network prefix of the local subnet, the MTU for the local link, suggested hop limit values, and other parameters useful for nodes on the local link. RAs can also contain flagged parameters indicating the type of autoconfiguration new nodes should use.

router queues — A router buffering system used to hold packets when the router is congested.

Router Solicitation (RS) — Asking any routers connected to the local link to identify themselves by immediately sending their RAs rather than waiting for the next scheduled advertisement.

routing — The process whereby a packet makes its way from a sender to a receiver based on known path (or routes) from the sending network to the receiving network.

Routing Information Protocol (RIP) — A simple, vector-based TCP/IP networking protocol used to determine a single pathway between a sender and a receiver on a local internetwork.

routing loops — A network configuration that enables packets to circle the network. Split horizon and poison reverse are used to resolve routing loops on distance vector networks. OSPF networks automatically resolve loops by defining best paths through an internetwork.

routing protocol — A Layer 3 protocol designed to permit routers to exchange information about networks that are reachable, the routes by which they may be reached, and the costs associated with such routes.

routing tables — Local host tables, maintained in memory, that list network addresses and costs associated with traveling to a remote destination. The routing tables are referenced before forwarding packets to remote destinations in order to find the most appropriate next-hop router for the packet.

rpr — An abbreviation for *remote print*, this is one of the BSD UNIX remote utilities (r-utils) that permits network users to print a file on a remote host.

rsh — An abbreviation for *remote shell*, this is one of the BSD UNIX remote utilities (r-utils) that permits network users to launch and operate a login session on a remote host.

runts — *See* undersized packets.

SA bundle — An ordered set of Security Associations that should be applied to match a certain security policy.

Samba — A suite of Open Source applications that provides file and print sharing using SMB/CIFS (over NetBT) for a variety of operating systems, notably Linux and UNIX.

scope — Defined by Microsoft as a group of addresses that can be assigned by a Microsoft DHCP server. Other vendors refer to this as an address pool or address range.

scope identifier — In IPv6, a 4-bit field limiting the valid range for a multicast address. In IPv6 multicast addresses, not all values are defined, but among those defined are the site-local and the link-local scope. Multicast addresses are not valid outside their configured scope, and will not be forwarded beyond it.

screening host — The role that a firewall or proxy server plays when presenting an internal network service for external consumption.

screening router — A boundary router that's been configured to monitor and filter inbound traffic on the basis of IP or port addresses, domain names, or spoofing attempts.

secondary DNS server — A DNS server that contains a copy of a domain or subdomain database, along with copies of the related zone files, but which must synchronize its database and related files with whatever server is primary for that domain or subdomain.

secondary master — *See* secondary DNS server.

Secure Sockets Layer (SSL) — A standard programming interface that encrypts outgoing data before passing it to the Transport layer, and that decrypts incoming data before passing it to the Application layer. SSL provides a handy way to improve the security of networked communications.

Secure Telnet (Stelnet) — A special implementation of Telnet that uses SSL, or a secure shell, to encrypt outgoing traffic, and decrypt incoming traffic, to prevent such traffic from being snooped en route between sender and receiver.

Security Association (SA) — In IPSec, the three-part combination of a destination address, an SPI, and a security protocol such as Authentication or ESP. The SA defines a set of processes or transformations to be performed on traffic bound for the named destination.

Security Association Database (SAD) — In IPSec, a notional or conceptual store of Security Associations that maps their particular characteristics onto a general description of an abstract SA.

security gateway — In IPSec, a router using secured communications that provides secured and authenticated routing for other IPSec traffic.

security management — One of the five layers of the OSI network management model, security management focuses on controlling access to network resources to avoid denials of service and unwanted access or incursions into network resources, and restrict access to resources solely on the basis of proper authentication and authorization.

Security Parameters Index (SPI) — In IPSec, a value that, along with the security protocol and the destination address, uniquely defines a Security Association.

security policy — A document that represents the concrete manifestation of an organization's requirements for security practices, rules, and procedures, and which identifies all assets worth protecting, and lays out disaster or business recovery processes should system loss or compromise occur.

Security Policy Database (SPD) — In IPSec, a mapping of security selectors (selection criteria) with policies, or sets of procedures, to be followed in the selected situation.

segment — The name of the PDU for the TCP protocol in a TCP/IP environment.

segmentation — The process whereby TCP takes a large message that exceeds an underlying network medium's MTU, and breaks it up into a numbered sequence of chunks that are less than or equal to the MTU in size.

Selective Acknowledgment — Also referred to as SACK, this method defines how a TCP peer can identify specific segments that were successfully received. This functionality is defined in RFC 2018.

sequence number tracking — The process of following the current sequence number sent by a TCP peer, and sending an acknowledgement value to indicate the next-expected sequence number.

Serial Line Internet Protocol (SLIP) — An IP-only serial line protocol still used to access some UNIX systems. SLIP was once the primary serial protocol used to connect point-to-point, via a modem or other access device, from a user machine or a local network to another local network, service provider, or user machine. SLIP supports only TCP/IP protocols and offers only basic delimitation services. That's why it's no longer widely used for Internet connections.

Server Message Block (SMB) —Both the name of a client/server file-sharing protocol developed by 3Com, IBM, and Microsoft, and the messages it uses. SMB protocol is an Application layer protocol that uses NBT in a Windows 2000 environment, or NetBEUI in an environment that includes older Windows operating systems. It can also run over IPX/SPX.

server-to-server traffic — Traffic between servers that provide an identical service, usually to replicate and synchronize copies of the same data across multiple servers. For critical services like DNS, this kind of traffic helps ensure data robustness and availability.

Service Access Point (SAP) — A protocol identification field that is defined in the 802.2 LLC header that follows the MAC header.

session — A temporary, but ongoing exchange of messages between a sender and a receiver on a network.

session hijacking — An IP attack technique whereby an imposter takes over an ongoing communications session between a client and server, thereby assuming whatever rights and permissions the hijacked session may enjoy. This is a difficult technique to pull off, and recent changes to TCP sequence numbers make this harder to accomplish today than it was prior to their implementation.

Session layer — Layer 5 in the ISO/OSI reference model, the Session layer handles setup, maintenance, and tear-down of ongoing exchanges of messages between pairs of hosts on a network.

session service — In NetBIOS, NetBEUI, and NBF, a network resource may be a process running on a network-connected computer. To interact with these processes, these protocols use the session service for reliable connection-oriented network communications. In Windows 2000, when NBF is run over TCP/IP (as NetBT), TCP is used for establishing and maintaining session services.

silent discard — The process of discarding a packet without notification to any other device that such a discarding process occurred. For example, a black hole router silently discards packets that it cannot forward.

Silly Window Syndrome (SWS) — A TCP windowing problem caused by an application removing only small amounts of data from a full TCP receive buffer, thereby causing a TCP peer to advertise a very small window. To address this problem, TCP hosts wait until the window size reaches the MSS value.

Simple Mail Transfer Protocol (SMTP) — A TCP/IP Application layer protocol that handles transmission of e-mail messages from clients to servers, and message routing from a source server to a destination server.

Simple Network Management Protocol (SNMP) — A TCP/IP Application layer protocol that provides basic network device registration and management capabilities.

site-local address — The site-local address has the first 10 (leftmost) bits set to 1111111011 (all ones except for the last three digits, which are set to 011 [binary]). The next 38 bits are set to all zeroes, and the next 16 bits after that contain the subnet ID that defines the "site" to which this address is local. As in other unicast type addressees, the last (rightmost) 64 bits are the standard interface ID. Site-local addresses allow packets to be forwarded internally to the site, but prevent the packets from being shared across the global Internet.

slave router — On an OSPF network, this type of router receives and acknowledges link-state database summary packets from a master router.

slave server — *See* secondary DNS server.

sliding window — A set of data that is sent along a sliding timeline. As transmitted data is acknowledged, the window moves over to send more data to the TCP peer.

Slow Start algorithm — A method for sending data in exponentially increasing increments, starting typically at twice the MSS value. The Slow Start algorithm is used to learn the network's maximum window size.

Smurf attack — An ICMP-based attack in which the attacker sends a PING packet to the broadcast address using the victim's IP address as the source of the PING.

SNMP agent — A piece of software that resides in a manageable object and communicates via SNMP commands to SNMP managers. The SNMP agent software maintains the MIB.

SNMP manager — The software used to send SNMP commands to an SNMP agent.

SNMP trap — A way for an SNMP agent running on a remote device or host to signal an alarm (an indicator that some error or other untoward event occurred) or alert (an indicator that some threshold value has been exceeded) to a remote management agent for further processing.

socket — *See* socket address.

socket address — A numeric TCP/IP address that concatenates a network host's numeric IP address (first four bytes) with the port address for some specific process or service on that host (last two bytes) to uniquely identify that process across the entire Internet.

SOCKS — An IETF standards track protocol that defines how proxy mechanisms work to control traffic between networks.

software security — The aspect of security that focuses on monitoring and maintaining systems and software to prevent and oppose as many potential sources of attack as possible. From this perspective, software security is both a mindset and a regular routine, rather than a "set it and forget it" kind of activity.

solicited node address — A multicast address with link-local scope, which helps reduce the number of multicast groups to which nodes must subscribe in order to make themselves available for solicitation by other nodes on their local link. The solicited node address is FF02:0:0:0:0:1:FF*xx.xxxx*, where "*xx.xxxx*" stands for the lowest-order (rightmost) 24 bits of the unicast or anycast address associated with that interface.

source port number — The port address for the sender of a TCP or UDP PDU.

split horizon — A rule used to eliminate the counting-to-infinity problem. The split horizon rule states that information cannot be sent back the same direction from which it was received.

spoofing — Spoofing occurs when incoming IP traffic exhibits addressing mismatches. Address spoofing occurs when an external interface ferries traffic that purports to originate inside a network, or when a user presents an IP address that doesn't match a domain name. Domain name spoofing occurs when a reverse lookup of an IP address does not match the domain where the traffic claims to originate.

Standard — An RFC that is officially approved as a specification for a particular protocol or service is called an Internet Standard, or a Standard RFC.

Start of Authority (SOA) record — The DNS resource record that's mandatory in every DNS zone file, the SOA record identifies the server or servers that are authoritative for the domain or subdomain to which the zone files or database correspond.

statistics — Short- or long-term historical information regarding network communications and performance, as captured by a protocol analyzer or other, similar software.

stealthy attacker — An attacker that hides its tracks. Stealthy attackers may ensure no log entries implicate their actions and no live connections remain after they launch their attack.

store and forward — A technique whereby e-mail messages are delivered to a particular server, messages slated for delivery to local clients are stored, and messages slated for delivery to remote clients are forwarded to another e-mail server for routing to their ultimate destination.

Structure of Management Information (SMI) — A defined structure for objects contained in a MIB. The structure is tree-like in appearance, organized much like a hierarchy of files and directories on a hard disk.

Sub-Network Access Protocol (SNAP) — A variation of the 802.2 LLC layer that uses Ethernet type numbers to identify the upcoming protocol.

subdomain — A named element within a specific domain name, denoted by adding an additional name and period before the parent domain name. Thus, *clearlake.ibm.com* is a subdomain of the *ibm.com* domain.

subnegotiation — A secondary process of negotiation that allows for the exchange of parameter information. Telnet uses subnegotiation when the standard set of options and the DO, DON'T, WILL, WON'T system is inadequate.

subnet mask — A special bit pattern that masks off the network portion of an IP address with all ones.

subnetting — The operation of using bits borrowed from the host portion of an IP address to extend and subdivide the address space that falls beneath the network portion of a range of IP addresses.

subordinates — Branches in the tree-structured design of a MIB.

summary address — A form of specialized IP network address that identifies the "common portion" of a series of IP network addresses used when route aggregation is in effect. This approach speeds routing behavior and decreases the number of entries necessary for routing tables.

supernetting — The technique of stealing bits from the network portion of an IP address and lending those bits to the host part, creating a larger address space for host addresses.

superscope — Defined by Microsoft as a collection of IP address scopes, as managed by any single DHCP server. Other vendors refer to this as a collection of address pools or address ranges.

symbolic name — A human-readable name for an Internet resource, such as *www.course.com* or *msnnews.microsoft.com*. Also, a name used to represent a device instead of an address. For example, the name *serv1* could be a symbolic name for a device that uses the IP address 10.2.10.2.

SYN Flood attack — An attack that sends multiple handshake establishment request packets (SYN) in an attempt to fill the connection queue and force the victim to refuse future valid requests.

Synchronous Data Link Control (SDLC) — A synchronous communication protocol.

Synchronous Optical Network (SONET) — A family of fiber-optic digital transmission services that offers data rates from 51.84 Mbps to 13.27 Gbps. SONET was created specifically to provide the flexibility necessary to transport many different kinds of digital signals together, including voice, video, multimedia, and data traffic, and to permit equipment from different vendors to interoperate. SONET provides the infrastructure for high-rate ATM services that in turn support the Internet backbone, and the backbones for most large-scale communications carriers (such as WorldCom and AT&T).

Systems Network Architecture (SNA) — The name of a protocol suite developed by IBM for use in its proprietary mainframe- and minicomputer-based networking environments.

T-carrier — The generic telephony term for trunk carrier connections that offer digital services to communications customers directly from the communications carrier itself (usually a local or long-distance phone or communications company). It is possible, however, to run trunk lines all the way from one location to another, but such lines will always transit the carrier's premises at one or more points in such a connection.

T1 — A digital signaling link, whose name stands for trunk level 1, used as a standard for digital signaling in North America. T1 links offer aggregate bandwidth of 1.544 Mbps, and can support up to 24 voice-grade digital channels of 64 Kbps each, or may be split between voice and data.

T3 — A digital signaling link, whose name stands for trunk level 3, used as a standard for digital signaling in North America. T3 links offer aggregate bandwidth of 28 T1s, or 44.736 Mbps. T3 runs on coax or fiber-optic cable, or via microwave transmission, and is becoming a standard link for small- and mid-scale ISPs.

TCP buffer area — A queuing area used to hold incoming and outgoing TCP packets. If a TCP packet has the Push flag set, the packet should not be held in either the incoming or outgoing TCP buffer area.

teardown sequence — The process of closing a TCP connection.

Telnet — A TCP/IP Application layer protocol and service that permits a client on one network host to interact with another network host as if the machine were a terminal attached to the other machine.

temporary port — A port that is used for the duration of the connection. The port numbers assigned to temporary ports are also called dynamic port numbers or ephemeral port numbers.

terminal access — An unintelligent terminal in which all the data, storage, program processing, and so forth, is handled by the remote host. Thus, only text to be displayed on the terminal and keyboard responses sent from the terminal cross the network.

test-attack-tune cycle — The most important part of deploying security systems or components, this set of activities should be repeated until test and attack operations produce no further changes to system or component configuration or tuning. This set of activities provides the best and most reasonable guarantee that systems and components are as resistant to attack as possible.

text (TXT) record — A DNS resource record that can accommodate arbitrary ASCII text data, often used to describe a DNS database segment, the hosts it contains, and so forth.

throughput difference — The comparative difference in throughput between two paths. Throughput, is measured in Kbps or Mbps.

time synchronization — The process of obtaining the exact same time on multiple hosts. Network Time Protocol (NTP) is a time synchronization protocol.

Time to Live (TTL) — An indication of the remaining distance that a packet can travel. Although defined in terms of seconds, the TTL value is implemented as a number of hops that a packet can travel before being discarded by a router.

Time Wait delay — An amount of time that a TCP host must not use connection parameters after closing down that connection.

timeout mechanism — A method for determining when to stop re-sending data across packets. The timeout mechanism consists of a retry timer and a maximum number of retries.

token — A special sequence of fields that indicates a token ring device has the right to transmit a frame of data onto the network media.

token ring — A token-passing ring Media Access Control protocol. The IEEE 802.5 specifications define the MAC and functional processes of token ring networking.

Token Ring 802.2 LLC frame — A token ring frame that includes the 802.2 LLC layer, which includes a protocol identification field (the Service Access Point field).

Token Ring SNAP frame — A token ring frame that includes the SNAP header, a variation on the 802.2 LLC header. The Token Ring SNAP frame uses an Ether Type value to identify the upcoming protocol.

trace buffer — An area of memory or hard disk space set aside for the storage of packets captured off the network by a protocol analyzer.

TRACEROUTE — *See* TRACERT.

TRACERT — The name of the Windows command that uses multiple PING commands to establish the identity and round-trip times for all hosts between a sender and a receiver. In the UNIX world, this utility is named TRACEROUTE.

traffic mode — In IPSec, a method of applying Security Associations to traffic bound from one host to another. Encryption or authentication may be applied on a per-packet basis, with ESP encrypting only the higher-level protocol payload, and AH authenticating only that same portion, plus any headers that will not change in transit.

trailer — An optional, concluding portion of a PDU that usually contains some kind of data integrity check information for the preceding content of that PDU.

transformations — In cryptography, a set of mathematical manipulations.

Transmission Control Protocol (TCP) — A robust, reliable, connection-oriented protocol that operates at the Transport layer in both the TCP/IP and ISO/OSI reference models, and that gives TCP/IP part of its name.

Transmission Control Protocol/Internet Protocol (TCP/IP) — The name of the standard protocols and services in use on the Internet, denoted by the names of two of its key constituent protocols: the Transmission Control Protocol, or TCP, and the Internet Protocol, or IP.

transparency — An important characteristic for any system or service that interposes itself between end users and the services or resources they seek to access, more transparency means that users notice intermediaries less, and less transparency means they notice them more. The ideal state is absolute transparency, where users do not notice that intermediaries are at work.

Transport Driver Interface (TDI) — A Microsoft specification that governs how the upper layers of all network transport protocols are written. The Windows redirection and server bypass NetBIOS and use TDI directly, thus avoiding NetBIOS restrictions.

Transport layer — Layer 4 of the ISO/OSI network reference model and the third layer of the TCP/IP network model, the Transport layer handles delivery of data from sender to receiver.

Transport Layer Security (TLS) — A special Transport layer protocol that works with TCP so that client/server applications can communicate in a way designed to prevent eavesdropping, tampering, or message forgery.

tree structure — A type of data structure that's organized, such as a taxonomy or a disk drive listing, in which the entire container acts as the root, and subcontainers may include either other, lower-level subcontainers, or instances of whatever kinds of objects may occur within a container. The domain name hierarchy adheres to an inverted tree structure because the root usually appears at the top of diagrams drawn to represent it.

triggered update — An update that occurs in response to some specific event in a network environment, usually associated with a router entering or leaving that environment, or some change in cost assessments or configurations for network links.

Trivial File Transfer Protocol (TFTP) — A basic TCP/IP Application layer service that supports lightweight file transfer from a local host to a remote host (especially in the context of a local user who's logged on to the remote host).

trojan horse — A program that appears innocent, but contains malicious code. The ILOVEYOU e-mail attack is a perfect example of a trojan horse. The .vbs file contained mobile code that e-mailed itself to all entries in a victim's address book.

tunnel mode — In IPSec, a method of applying Security Associations, possibly in an extended nested sequence, to packets that are encapsulated and tunneled from or to at least one security gateway.

two-way handshake — A two-packet handshake that is not fully completed. This process is indicative of the TCP SYN attack.

Type of Service (TOS) — A process used to define a type of path that a packet should take through the network. TOS options include the greatest throughput, lowest delay, and most reliability.

undersized packets — Packets that are below minimum packet size requirements, and point to potential hardware or driver problems.

unicast packet — A packet sent to a single device on the network.

Uniform Resource Identifier (URI) — A generic term for all types of names and addresses that refer to objects on the Web. An URL is one kind of URI.

Uniform Resource Locator (URL) — Web terminology for the address that specifies the protocol (http://), location (domain name), directory (/directory-name/), and filename (example.html) to request a Web browser to access the resource.

Uniform Resource Name (URN) — A URI with a commitment to persistence and availability. URIs are documented in RFC 2141.

Universal Time (UT) — *See* Greenwich Mean Time (GMT); sometimes also called Universal Coordinating Time (UCT), or Zulu Time.

unnumbered format — A format of 802.2 LLC packet that is connectionless.

unsolicited — Unrequested. Unsolicited replies are typically advertisements that occur on a periodic basis. For example, ICMP Router Advertisements typically occur on a seven- to 10-minute basis.

unspecified address — In IPv6, the unspecified address is all zeroes, and can be represented as "::" in normal notation. This is essentially the address that is no address. It cannot be used as a destination address.

usable address space — The number of hosts that can actually be connected to the Internet.

User Datagram Protocol (UDP) — A connectionless, best-effort transport protocol in the TCP/IP protocol suite, UDP operates as an alternative to TCP.

user impersonation — A system or network attack technique whereby an unauthorized user presents valid credentials that rightfully belong to an authorized user to gain entry, and exploits whatever rights and privileges that the impersonated user's identity allows. (This explains why impersonating users with administrative rights and privileges is the ultimate goal of an impersonation attack.)

valid data — Data that follows the headers, but does not consist of any padding or extraneous data.

variable-length subnet masking (VLSM) — A subnetting scheme for IP addresses that permits containers of various sizes to be defined for a network prefix. The largest subnet defines the maximum container size, and any individual container in that address space may be further subdivided into multiple, smaller sub-containers (sometimes called sub-subnets).

victim — The focus of an attack. Interestingly, in the case of mobile code and worms, the victims often become the attackers by allowing the code to infect other computers because they are not identified or eradicated.

virtual connection — A logical connection between two TCP peers. The virtual connection requires end-to-end connectivity.

Virtual Private Network (VPN) — A network connection (containing one or more packaged protocols) between a specific sender and receiver, in which the information sent is often encrypted. A VPN uses public networks—such as the

Internet—to deliver secure, private information from a sender to a receiver.

virus — A code that can spread through a machine to alter or destroy files.

Voice over IP (VoIP) — A network method that bypasses the traditional public switched telephone system and uses IP (for example, the Internet or an intranet) to support voice communication.

vulnerability — Any aspect of a system that is open to attack, especially any well-known protocol, service, subsystem, or hole that is documented and relatively easy to exploit.

Wait Acknowledgment (WACK) — A response packet sent by WINS servers to acknowledge the receipt of a request without granting or denying it, but asking the client to wait. This prevents communications with a busy WINS server from timing out unnecessarily.

WAN protocol — A type of data link protocol designed to transport data over large distances, typically with features that allow carriers to meter usage and bill subscribers. Examples include analog telephone lines, ISDN, T-carrier links, frame relay, or ATM between pairs of communications partners.

watchdog process — A process used by NetWare servers to determine whether the NetWare clients are still active and maintaining the connection between the two devices.

well-known port address — *See* well-known port number.

well-known port number — A 16-bit number that identifies a preassigned value associated with some well-known Internet protocol or service that operates at the TCP/IP Application layer. Most well-known port numbers fall in the range from 0 to 1024, but IANA also documents registered port numbers above that range that behave likewise.

well-known protocol — An 8-bit number that appears in the header of an IP packet and identifies the protocol in use, as per IANA.

well-known service — A synonym for a recognizable TCP/IP protocol or service, these assignments are documented at the IANA site (*http://www.iana.org*).

well-known services (WKS) record — A DNS resource record that describes the well-known IP services available from a host, such as Telnet, FTP, and so forth. WKS records are less available to outsiders than they once were because they identify hosts that could become points of potential attack.

Whois — A client utility used to access a remote server database of domain or IP address registries. Because many domain names are not registered in the databases that Whois searches, this utility is not very useful.

Wide Area Information Service (WAIS) — A TCP/IP Application layer protocol and service designed to provide search access to a variety of document formats, including text, word-processing, database, and other specific file formats.

windowing — The process of acknowledging multiple packets with a single acknowledgement.

Windows Internet Name Service (WINS) — A server service in Windows NT Server and Windows 2000 Server that resolves NetBIOS names and addresses in much the same way that a DNS server does for IP host names.

WINIPCFG — A Windows-based utility used to identify the local host's data link address and IP address.

WinNuke attack — An attack that is based on an illogical packet structure—a NetBIOS packet that has the Urgent bit set to one.

workgroup — In Windows, a group of peers able to share files over the network. A workgroup is a less highly integrated grouping than a domain, and implies fewer centralized monitoring and control capabilities.

worm — A malicious mobile code that can move from one computer to another until it is eradicated.

X.25 — A standard set of protocols defined in the 1970s by the International Telecommunications Union (ITU), designed to send datagrams across a public packet-switched data network using noisy, narrow-bandwidth, copper telephone lines Remains popular outside North America, where obtaining other forms of end-to-end WAN links can be difficult.

zero-window state — A situation when a TCP peer advertises a window value of zero. A TCP host cannot continue sending to a TCP peer that advertises a window of zero.

zone — A portion of the domain name hierarchy that corresponds to the database segment managed by some particular name server, or collection of name servers.

zone data file — Any of several specific files used to capture DNS database information for static storage when a DNS server is shut down, or when a secondary DNS server requests synchronization with its primary DNS server's database.

zone file — *See* zone data file.

Index